Java™ Network Programming

Other Java™ resources from O'Reilly

**Java Books
Resource Center**

java.oreilly.com is a complete catalog of O'Reilly's books on Java and related technologies, including sample chapters and code examples.

OnJava.com is a one-stop resource for enterprise Java developers, featuring news, code recipes, interviews, weblogs, and more.

Conferences

O'Reilly brings diverse innovators together to nurture the ideas that spark revolutionary industries. We specialize in documenting the latest tools and systems, translating the innovator's knowledge into useful skills for those in the trenches. Visit *conferences.oreilly.com* for our upcoming events.

Safari Bookshelf (*safari.oreilly.com*) is the premier online reference library for programmers and IT professionals. Conduct searches across more than 1,000 books. Subscribers can zero in on answers to time-critical questions in a matter of seconds. Read the books on your Bookshelf from cover to cover or simply flip to the page you need. Try it today with a free trial.

THIRD EDITION

Java™ Network Programming

Elliotte Rusty Harold

Beijing · Cambridge · Farnham · Köln · Paris · Sebastopol · Taipei · Tokyo

Java™ Network Programming, Third Edition
by Elliotte Rusty Harold

Copyright © 2005, 2000, 1997 O'Reilly Media, Inc. All rights reserved.
Printed in the United States of America.

Published by O'Reilly Media, Inc., 1005 Gravenstein Highway North, Sebastopol, CA 95472.

O'Reilly books may be purchased for educational, business, or sales promotional use. Online editions are also available for most titles (*safari.oreilly.com*). For more information, contact our corporate/institutional sales department: (800) 998-9938 or *corporate@oreilly.com*.

Editor:	Mike Loukides
Production Editor:	Colleen Gorman
Cover Designer:	Emma Colby
Interior Designer:	David Futato

Printing History:

February 1997:	First Edition.
August 2000:	Second Edition.
October 2004:	Third Edition.

RepKover™ This book uses RepKover™, a durable and flexible lay-flat binding.

ISBN: 0-596-00721-3

[M]

To Grandmama, a great grandmother.

Table of Contents

Preface

Java's growth over the last 10 years has been nothing short of phenomenal. Given Java's rapid rise to prominence and the even more spectacular growth of the Internet, it's a little surprising that network programming in Java is still so mysterious to so many. It doesn't have to be. In fact, writing network programs in Java is quite simple, as this book will show. Readers with previous experience in network programming in a Unix, Windows, or Macintosh environment should be pleasantly surprised at how much easier it is to write equivalent programs in Java. The Java core API includes well-designed interfaces to most network features. Indeed, there is very little application-layer network software you can write in C or C++ that you can't write more easily in Java. *Java Network Programming, 3rd Edition* endeavors to show you how to take advantage of Java's network class library to quickly and easily write programs that accomplish many common networking tasks. Some of these include:

- Browsing the Web with HTTP
- Parsing and rendering HTML
- Sending email with SMTP
- Receiving email with POP and IMAP
- Writing multithreaded servers
- Installing new protocol and content handlers into browsers
- Encrypting communications for confidentiality, authentication, and guaranteed message integrity
- Designing GUI clients for network services
- Posting data to server-side programs
- Looking up hosts using DNS
- Downloading files with anonymous FTP
- Connecting sockets for low-level network communication
- Distributing applications across multiple systems with Remote Method Invocation

Java is the first language to provide such a powerful cross-platform network library, which handles all these diverse tasks. *Java Network Programming* exposes the power and sophistication of this library. This book's goal is to enable you to start using Java as a platform for serious network programming. To do so, this book provides a general background in network fundamentals, as well as detailed discussions of Java's facilities for writing network programs. You'll learn how to write Java programs that share data across the Internet for games, collaboration, software updates, file transfer, and more. You'll also get a behind-the-scenes look at HTTP, SMTP, TCP/IP, and the other protocols that support the Internet and the Web. When you finish this book, you'll have the knowledge and the tools to create the next generation of software that takes full advantage of the Internet.

About the Third Edition

In 1996, in the first chapter of the first edition of this book, I wrote extensively about the sort of dynamic, distributed network applications I thought Java would make possible. One of the most exciting parts of writing subsequent editions has been seeing virtually all of the applications I foretold come to pass. Programmers are using Java to query database servers, monitor web pages, control telescopes, manage multiplayer games, and more, all by using Java's native ability to access the Internet. Java in general and network programming in Java in particular has moved well beyond the hype stage and into the realm of real, working applications. Not all network software is yet written in Java, but it's not for a lack of trying. Efforts are well under way to subvert the existing infrastructure of C-based network clients and servers with pure Java replacements. Clients for newer protocols like Gnutella and Freenet are preferentially written in Java. It's unlikely that Java will replace C for all network programming in the near future. However, the mere fact that many people are willing to use web browsers, web servers, and more written in Java shows just how far we've come since 1996.

This book has come a long way, too. The third edition has one completely new chapter to describe the most significant development in network programming since readers and writers were introduced in Java 1.1. I refer of course to the new I/O APIs in the java.nio package. The ability to perform asynchronous, non-blocking I/O operations is critical for high-performance network applications, especially servers. It removes one of the last barriers to using Java for network servers. Many other chapters have been updated to take advantage of these new I/O APIs.

There've been lots of other small changes and updates throughout the java.net and supporting packages in Java 1.4 and 1.5, and these are covered here as well. New classes addressed in this edition include CookieHandler, SocketAddress, Proxy, NetworkInterface, and URI. IPv6 has become a reality, and is now covered extensively. Many other methods have been added to existing classes in the last two releases of Java, and these are discussed in the relevant chapters. I've also rewritten large parts of the book to reflect changing fashions in Java programming in general and network programming in particular. Applets and CGI programs are emphasized much less. In their place, you'll find more generic discussion of remote code execution and server-side environments, however implemented.

Of course, the text has been cleaned up, too. There's only one completely new chapter here, but the 18 existing chapters have been extensively rewritten and expanded to bring them up-to-date with new developments as well as to make them clearer and more engaging. I hope you'll find this third edition an even stronger, longer-lived, more accurate, and more enjoyable tutorial and reference to network programming in Java than the last edition.

Organization of the Book

This book begins with three chapters that outline how networks and network programs work. Chapter 1, *Why Networked Java?*, is a gentle introduction to network programming in Java and the applications it makes possible. All readers should find something of interest in this chapter. It explores some of the unique programs that become feasible when networking is combined with Java. Chapter 2, *Basic Network Concepts*, and Chapter 3, *Basic Web Concepts*, explain in detail what a programmer needs to know about how the Internet and the Web work. Chapter 2 describes the protocols that underlie the Internet, such as TCP/IP and UDP/IP. Chapter 3 describes the standards that underlie the Web, such as HTTP, HTML, and REST. If you've done a lot of network programming in other languages on other platforms, you may be able to skip these two chapters.

The next two chapters throw some light on two parts of Java programming that are critical to almost all network programs but are often misunderstood and misused, I/O and threading. Chapter 4, *Streams*, explores Java's classic I/O models which, despite the new I/O APIs, aren't going away any time soon and are still the preferred means of handling input and output in most client applications. Understanding how Java handles I/O in the general case is a prerequisite for understanding the special case of how Java handles network I/O. Chapter 5, *Threads*, explores multithreading and synchronization, with a special emphasis on how they can be used for asynchronous I/O and network servers. Experienced Java programmers may be able to skim or skip these two chapters. However, Chapter 6, *Looking Up Internet Addresses*, is essential reading for everyone. It shows how Java programs interact with the domain name system through the InetAddress class, the one class that's needed by essentially all network programs. Once you've finished this chapter, it's possible to jump around in the book as your interests and needs dictate. There are, however, some interdependencies between specific chapters. Figure P-1 should allow you to map out possible paths through the book.

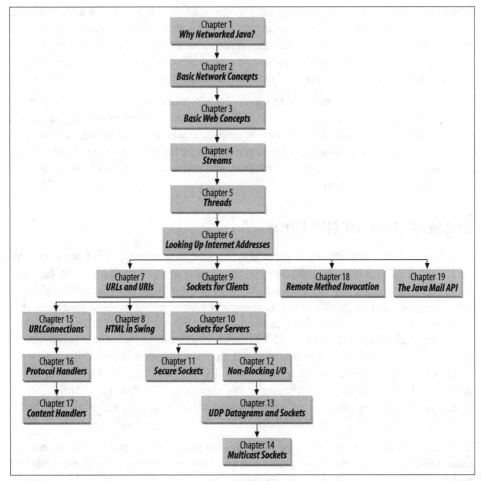

Figure P-1. Chapter prerequisites

Chapter 7, *URLs and URIs*, explores Java's URL class, a powerful abstraction for downloading information and files from network servers of many kinds. The URL class enables you to connect to and download files and documents from a network server without concerning yourself with the details of the protocol the server speaks. It lets you connect to an FTP server using the same code you use to talk to an HTTP server or to read a file on the local hard disk.

Once you've got an HTML file from a server, you're going to want to do something with it. Parsing and rendering HTML is one of the most difficult challenges network programmers can face. Chapter 8, *HTML in Swing*, introduces some little known classes for parsing and rendering HTML documents that take this burden off your shoulders and put it on Sun's.

Chapters 9 through 11 discuss Java's low-level socket classes for network access. Chapter 9, *Sockets for Clients*, introduces the Java sockets API and the Socket class in particular. It shows you how to write network clients that interact with TCP servers of all kinds including whois, finger, and HTTP. Chapter 10, *Sockets for Servers*, shows you how to use the ServerSocket class to write servers for these and other protocols in Java. Chapter 11, *Secure Sockets*, shows you how to protect your client server communications using the Secure Sockets Layer (SSL) and the Java Secure Sockets Extension (JSSE).

Chapter 12, *Non-Blocking I/O*, covers the new I/O APIs introduced in Java 1.4. These APIs were specifically designed for network servers. They enable a program to figure out whether a connection is ready before it tries to read from or write to the socket. This allows a single thread to manage many different connections simultaneously, thereby placing much less load on the virtual machine. The new I/O APIs don't help much for small servers or clients that don't open many simultaneous connections, but they provide huge performance boosts for high volume servers that want to transmit as much data as the network can handle as fast as the network can deliver it.

Chapter 13, *UDP Datagrams and Sockets*, introduces the User Datagram Protocol (UDP) and the associated DatagramPacket and DatagramSocket classes that provide fast, unreliable communication. Finally, Chapter 14, *Multicast Sockets*, shows you how to use UDP to communicate with multiple hosts at the same time. All the other classes that access the network from Java rely on the classes described in these five chapters.

Chapters 15 through 17 look more deeply at the infrastructure supporting the URL class. These chapters introduce protocol and content handlers, concepts unique to Java that make it possible to write dynamically extensible software that automatically understands new protocols and media types. Chapter 15, *URLConnections*, describes the class that serves as the engine for the URL class of Chapter 7. It shows you how to take advantage of this class through its public API. Chapter 16, *Protocol Handlers*, also focuses on the URLConnection class but from a different direction; it shows you how to subclass this class to create handlers for new protocols and URLs. Finally, Chapter 17, *Content Handlers*, explores Java's somewhat moribund mechanism for supporting new media types.

Chapters 18 and 19 introduce two unique higher-level APIs for network programs, Remote Method Invocation (RMI) and the JavaMail API. Chapter 18, *Remote Method Invocation*, introduces this powerful mechanism for writing distributed Java applications that run across multiple heterogeneous systems at the same time while communicating with straightforward method calls just like a nondistributed program. Chapter 19, *The JavaMail API*, acquaints you with this standard extension to Java, which offers an alternative to low-level sockets for talking to SMTP, POP,

IMAP, and other email servers. Both of these APIs provide distributed applications with less cumbersome alternatives to lower-level protocols.

Who You Are

This book assumes you are comfortable with the Java language and programming environment, in addition to object-oriented programming in general. This book does not attempt to be a basic language tutorial. You should be thoroughly familiar with the syntax of Java. You should have written simple applications and applets. You should also be comfortable with basic AWT and Swing programming. When you encounter a topic that requires a deeper understanding for network programming than is customary—for instance, threads and streams—I'll cover that topic as well, at least briefly.

You should also be an accomplished user of the Internet. I will assume you know how to FTP files and visit web sites. You should know what a URL is and how you locate one. You should know how to write simple HTML and be able to publish a home page that includes Java applets, although you do not need to be a super web designer.

However, this book doesn't assume that you have prior experience with network programming. You should find it a complete introduction to networking concepts and network application development. I don't assume that you have a few thousand networking acronyms (TCP, UDP, SMTP, etc.) at the tip of your tongue. You'll learn what you need to know about these here. It's certainly possible that you could use this book as a general introduction to network programming with a socket-like interface, and then go on to learn WSA (the Windows Socket Architecture) and figure out how to write network applications in C++. But it's not clear why you would want to: as I said earlier, Java lets you write very sophisticated applications with ease.

Java Versions

Java's network classes have changed a lot more slowly since Java 1.0 than other parts of the core API. In comparison to the AWT or I/O, there have been almost no changes and only a few additions. Of course, all network programs make extensive use of the I/O classes and many make heavy use of GUIs. This book is written with the assumption that you and your customers are using at least Java 1.1. In general, I use Java 1.1 features like readers and writers and the new event model freely without further explanation.

Java 2 is a bit more of a stretch. Although I wrote almost this entire book using Java 2, and although Java 2 has been available for most platforms for several years, no Java 2 runtime or development environment is yet available for MacOS 9. It is virtually certain that neither Apple nor Sun will ever port any version of Java 2 to MacOS 9.x or earlier, thus effectively locking out 60% of the current Mac-installed base from future developments. This is not a good thing for a language that claims to be "write once, run anywhere." Furthermore, Microsoft's Java virtual machine supports Java 1.1 only and does not seem likely to improve in this respect for the foreseeable future. Thus, while I have not shied away from using Java 2–specific features where they seemed useful or convenient—for instance, the ASCII encoding for the InputStreamReader and the *keytool* program—I have been careful to point out my use of such features. Where 1.1 safe alternatives exist, they are noted. When a particular method or class is new in Java 1.2 or later, it is noted by a comment following its declaration like this:

```
public void setTimeToLive(int ttl) throws IOException // Java 1.2
```

To further muddy the waters, there are multiple versions of Java 2. At the time this book was completed, the current release was the "Java™ 2 SDK, Standard Edition, v 1.4.2_05". At least that's what it was called then. Sun seems to change names at the drop of a marketing consultant. In previous incarnations, this is what was simply known as the JDK. Sun also makes available the "Java™ 2 Platform, Enterprise Edition (J2EE™)" and "Java™ 2 Platform, Micro Edition (J2ME™)". The Enterprise Edition is a superset of the standard edition that adds features like the Java Naming and Directory Interface and the JavaMail API that provide high-level APIs for distributed applications. Most of these additional APIs are also available as extensions to the standard edition, and will be so treated here. The Micro Edition is a subset of the standard edition targeted at cell phones, set-top boxes, and other memory, CPU, and display-challenged devices. It removes a lot of the GUI APIs programmers have learned to associate with Java, although surprisingly it retains many of the basic networking and I/O classes discussed in this book. Finally, when this book was about half complete, Sun released a beta of the "Java™ 2 SDK, Standard Edition, v1.5". This added a few pieces to the networking API, but left most of the existing API untouched. Over the next few months Sun released several more betas of JDK 1.5. The finishing touches were placed on this book and all the code tested with JDK 1.5 beta 2. You shouldn't have any trouble using this book after 1.5 is released. With any luck at all, discrepancies between the final specification and what I discuss here will be quite minor.

To be honest, the most annoying problem with all these different versions and editions was not the rewriting they necessitated. It was figuring out how to identify them in the text. I simply refuse to write *Java™ 2 SDK, Standard Edition, v1.3* or even *Java 2 1.3* every time I want to point out a new feature in the latest release of Java. I normally simply refer to Java 1.1, Java 1.2, Java 1.3, Java 1.4, and Java 1.5. Overall, though, the networking API seems fairly stable. Java 1.1 through Java 1.3 are very similar, and there are a few only major additions in Java 1.4 and 1.5. Very little of the post-1.0 networking API has been deprecated.

About the Examples

Most methods and classes described in this book are illustrated with at least one complete working program, simple though it may be. In my experience, a complete working program is essential to showing the proper use of a method. Without a program, it is too easy to drop into jargon or to gloss over points about which the author may be unclear in his own mind. The Java API documentation itself often suffers from excessively terse descriptions of the method calls. In this book, I have tried to err on the side of providing too much explication rather than too little. If a point is obvious to you, feel free to skip over it. You do not need to type in and run every example in this book, but if a particular method does give you trouble, you are guaranteed to have at least one working example.

Each chapter includes at least one (and often several) more complex programs that demonstrate the classes and methods of that chapter in a more realistic setting. These often rely on Java features not discussed in this book. Indeed, in many of the programs, the networking components are only a small fraction of the source code and often the least difficult parts. Nonetheless, none of these programs could be written as easily in languages that didn't give networking the central position it occupies in Java. The apparent simplicity of the networked sections of the code reflects the extent to which networking has been made a core feature of Java, and not any triviality of the program itself. All example programs presented in this book are available online, often with corrections and additions. You can download the source code from *http://www.cafeaulait.org/books/jnp3/*.

This book assumes you are using Sun's Java Development Kit. I have tested all the examples on Linux and many on Windows and MacOS X. Almost all the examples given here *should* work on other platforms and with other compilers and virtual machines that support Java 1.2 (and most on Java 1.1, as well). The occasional examples that require Java 1.3, 1.4, or 1.5 are clearly noted.

Conventions Used in This Book

Body text is Times Roman, normal, like you're reading now.

A `monospaced typewriter` font is used for:

- Code examples and fragments
- Anything that might appear in a Java program, including keywords, operators, data types, method names, variable names, class names, and interface names
- Program output
- Tags that might appear in an HTML document

A **bold monospaced font** is used for:

- Command lines and options that should be typed verbatim on the screen

An *italicized* font is used for:

- New terms where they are defined
- Pathnames, filenames, and program names (however, if the program name is also the name of a Java class, it is given in a monospaced font, like other class names)
- Host and domain names (*java.oreilly.com*)
- URLs (*http://www.cafeaulait.org/slides/*)
- Titles of other chapters and books (*Java I/O*)

Significant code fragments and complete programs are generally placed into a separate paragraph, like this:

```
Socket s = new Socket("java.oreilly.com", 80);
if (!s.getTcpNoDelay()) s.setTcpNoDelay(true);
```

When code is presented as fragments rather than complete programs, the existence of the appropriate import statements should be inferred. For example, in the above code fragment you may assume that java.net.Socket was imported.

Some examples intermix user input with program output. In these cases, the user input will be displayed in bold, as in this example from Chapter 9:

```
% telnet rama.poly.edu 7
Trying 128.238.10.212...
Connected to rama.poly.edu.
Escape character is '^]'.
This is a test
This is a test
This is another test
This is another test
9876543210
9876543210
^]
telnet> close
Connection closed.
```

The Java programming language is case-sensitive. Java.net.socket is not the same as java.net.Socket. Case-sensitive programming languages do not always allow authors to adhere to standard English grammar. Most of the time, it's possible to rewrite the sentence in such a way that the two do not conflict, and when possible I have endeavored to do so. However, on those rare occasions when there is simply no way around the problem, I have let standard English come up the loser. In keeping with this principle, when I want to refer to a class or an instance of a class in body text, I use the capitalization that you'd see in source code, generally an initial capital with internal capitalization—for example, ServerSocket.

Throughout this book, I use the British convention of placing punctuation inside quotation marks only when punctuation is part of the material quoted. Although I learned grammar under the American rules, the British system has always seemed far more logical to me, even more so than usual when one must quote source code where a missing or added comma, period, or semicolon can make the difference between code that compiles and code that doesn't.

Finally, although many of the examples used here are toy examples unlikely to be reused, a few of the classes I develop have real value. Please feel free to reuse them or any parts of them in your own code. No special permission is required. As far as I am concerned, they are in the public domain (although the same is most definitely not true of the explanatory text!). Such classes are placed somewhere in the `com.macfaq` package, generally mirroring the `java` package hierarchy. For instance, Chapter 4's `SafePrintWriter` class is in the `com.macfaq.io` package. When working with these classes, don't forget that the compiled *.class* files must reside in directories matching their package structure inside your class path, and that you'll have to import them in your own classes before you can use them. The book's web page at *http://www.cafeaulait.org/books/jnp3/* includes a *jar* file containing all these classes that can be installed in your class path.

 Indicates a tip, suggestion, or general note.

 Indicates a warning or caution.

Request for Comments

I enjoy hearing from readers, whether with general comments about this book, specific corrections, other topics you would like to see covered, or just war stories about your own network programming travails. You can reach me by sending email to *elharo@metalab.unc.edu*. Please realize, however, that I receive several hundred pieces of email a day and cannot personally respond to each one. For the best chances of getting a personal response, please identify yourself as a reader of this book. If you have a question about a particular program that isn't working as you expect, try to reduce it to the simplest case that reproduces the bug, preferably a single class, and paste the text of the entire program into the *body* of your email. Unsolicited attachments will be deleted unopened. And please, please send the message from the account you want me to reply to and make sure that your Reply-to address is properly set! There's nothing quite so frustrating as spending an hour or more carefully researching the answer to an interesting question and composing a detailed response, only to have it bounce because my correspondent was sending from a public terminal and neglected to set the browser preferences to include their actual email address.

I also adhere to the old saying "If you like this book, tell your friends. If you don't like it, tell me." I'm especially interested in hearing about mistakes. This is my eighth book. I've yet to publish a perfect one, but I keep trying. As hard as I and the editors at O'Reilly worked on this book, I'm sure there are mistakes and typographical errors that we missed here somewhere. And I'm sure that at least one of them is a really embarrassing whopper of a problem. If you find a mistake or a typo, please let me know so I can correct it. I'll post it on the web page for this book at *http://www.cafeaulait.org/books/jnp3/* and on the O'Reilly web site at *http://www.oreilly.com/catalog/javanetwk/errata/*. Before reporting errors, please check one of those pages to see if I already know about it and have posted a fix. Any errors that are reported will be fixed in future printings.

Comments and Questions

Please address comments and questions concerning this book to the publisher:

> O'Reilly Media, Inc.
> 1005 Gravenstein Highway North
> Sebastopol, CA 95472
> (800) 998-9938 (in the United States or Canada)
> (707) 829-0515 (international or local)
> (707) 829-0104 (fax)

There is a web page for this book, which lists errata, examples, and any additional information. You can access this page at:

> *http://www.oreilly.com/catalog/javanp3/*

To comment on or ask technical questions about this book, send email to:

> *bookquestions@oreilly.com*

For more information about books, conferences, software, Resource Centers, and the O'Reilly Network, see the O'Reilly web site at:

> *http://www.oreilly.com*

The author maintains a web site for the discussion of EJB and related distributed computing technologies at *http://www.jmiddleware.com*. jMiddleware.com provides news about this book as well as code tips, articles, and an extensive list of links to EJB resources.

Acknowledgments

Many people were involved in the production of this book. My editor, Mike Loukides, got this book rolling, and provided many helpful comments along the way that substantially improved the book. Dr. Peter "Peppar" Parnes helped out immensely with the multicast chapter. The technical editors all provided invaluable assistance in hunting down errors and omissions. Simon St. Laurent provided invaluable advice on which topics deserved more coverage. Scott Oaks lent his thread expertise to Chapter 5, proving once again by the many subtle bugs he hunted down that multithreading still requires the attention of an expert. Ron Hitchens shone light into many of the darker areas of the new I/O APIs. Marc Loy and Jim Elliott reviewed some of the most bleeding edge material in the book. Jim Farley and William Grosso provided many helpful comments and assistance on remote method invocation. Timothy F. Rohaly was unswerving in his commitment to making sure I closed all my sockets and caught all possible exceptions, and in general wrote the cleanest, safest, most exemplary code I could write. John Zukowski found numerous errors of omission, all now filled thanks to him. And the eagle-eyed Avner Gelb displayed an astonishing ability to spot mistakes that had somehow managed to go unnoticed by myself, all the other editors, and the tens of thousands of readers of the first edition.

It isn't customary to thank the publisher, but the publisher does set the tone for the rest of the company, authors, editors, and production staff alike; and I think Tim O'Reilly deserves special credit for making O'Reilly Media absolutely one of the best houses an author can write for. If there's one person without whom this book would never have been written, it's him. If you, the reader, find O'Reilly books to be consistently better than most of the drek on the market, the reason really can be traced straight back to Tim.

My agent, David Rogelberg, convinced me it was possible to make a living writing books like this rather than working in an office. The entire crew at *ibiblio.org* over the last several years has really helped me to communicate better with my readers in a variety of ways. Every reader who sent in bouquets and brickbats about the first and second editions has been instrumental in helping me write this much-improved edition. All these people deserve much thanks and credit. Finally, as always, I'd like to offer my largest thanks for my wife, Beth, without whose love and support this book would never have happened.

—Elliotte Rusty Harold
elharo@metalab.unc.edu
September 22, 2004

CHAPTER 1

Why Networked Java?

In the last 10 years, network programming has stopped being the province of a few specialists and become a core part of every developer's toolbox. Today, more programs are network aware than aren't. Besides classic applications like email, web browsers, and Telnet clients, most major applications have some level of networking built in. For example:

- Text editors like BBEdit save and open files directly from FTP servers.
- IDEs like Eclipse and IntelliJ IDEA communicate with CVS repositories.
- Word processors like Microsoft Word open files from URLs.
- Antivirus programs like Norton AntiVirus check for new virus definitions by connecting to the vendor's web site every time the computer is started.
- Music players like Winamp and iTunes upload CD track lengths to CDDB and download the corresponding track titles.
- Gamers playing Quake gleefully frag each other in real time.
- Supermarket cash registers running IBM SurePOS ACE communicate with their store's server in real time with each transaction. The server uploads its daily receipts to the chain's central computers each night.
- Schedule applications like Microsoft Outlook automatically synchronize calendars with other employees in the company.

In the future, the advent of web services and the semantic web is going to entwine the network ever more deeply in all kinds of applications. All of this will take place over the Internet and all of it can be written in Java.

Java was the first programming language designed from the ground up with networking in mind. Java was originally designed for proprietary cable television networks rather than the Internet, but it's always had the network foremost in mind. One of the first two real Java applications was a web browser. As the global Internet continues to grow, Java is uniquely suited to build the next generation of network applications. Java provides solutions to a number of problems—platform independence and security being the most important—that are crucial to Internet applications, yet difficult to address in other languages.

One of the biggest secrets about Java is that it makes writing network programs easy. In fact, it is far easier to write network programs in Java than in almost any other language. This book shows you dozens of complete programs that take advantage of the Internet. Some are simple textbook examples, while others are completely functional applications. One thing you'll notice in the fully functional applications is just how little code is devoted to networking. Even in network intensive programs like web servers and clients, almost all the code handles data manipulation or the user interface. The part of the program that deals with the network is almost always the shortest and simplest.

In brief, it is easy for Java applications to send and receive data across the Internet. It is also possible for applets to communicate across the Internet, though they are limited by security restrictions. In this chapter, you'll learn about a few of the network-centric applications that have been written in Java. In later chapters, you'll develop the tools you need to write your own network programs.

What Can a Network Program Do?

Networking adds a lot of power to simple programs. With networks, a single program can retrieve information stored in millions of computers located anywhere in the world. A single program can communicate with tens of millions of people. A single program can harness the power of many computers to work on one problem.

Network applications generally take one of several forms. The distinction you hear about most is between clients and servers. In the simplest case, clients retrieve data from a server and display it. More complex clients filter and reorganize data, repeatedly retrieve changing data, send data to other people and computers, and interact with peers in real time for chat, multiplayer games, or collaboration. Servers respond to requests for data. Simple servers merely look up some file and return it to the client, but more complex servers often do a lot of processing on the data before answering an involved question. Peer-to-peer applications such as Gnutella connect many computers, each of which acts as both a client and a server. And that's only the beginning. Let's look more closely at the possibilities that open up when you add networking to your programs.

Retrieve Data

At the most basic level, a network client retrieves data from a server. It can format the data for display to a user, store it in a local database, combine it with other data sources both local and remote, analyze it, or all of the above. Network clients written in Java can speak standard protocols like HTTP, FTP, or SMTP to communicate with existing servers written in a variety of languages. However, there are many clients for these protocols already and writing another one isn't so exciting. More importantly, programs can speak custom protocols designed for specific purposes, such as the one used to remotely control the High Resolution Airborne Wideband Camera (HAWC) on the Stratospheric Observatory for Infrared Astronomy (SOFIA). Figure 1-1 shows an early prototype of the HAWC controller.

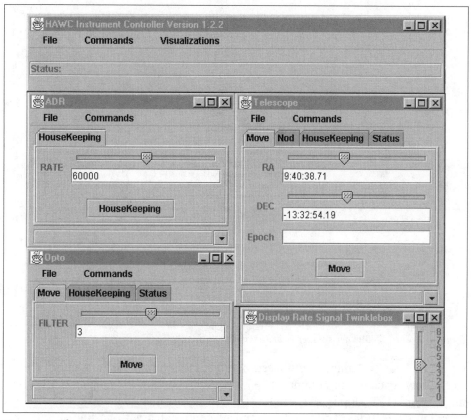

Figure 1-1. The HAWC controller prototype

Also interesting is the use of existing protocols like HTTP to retrieve data that will be manipulated in new and unique ways. A custom network client written in Java can extract and display the exact piece of information the user wants. For example, an indexing program might extract only the actual text of a page while filtering out the HTML tags and navigation links. Of course, not every file downloaded from a web server has to be loaded into a browser window, or even has to be HTML. Custom network clients can process any data format the server sends, whether it's tab-separated text, a special purpose binary format for data acquired from scientific instruments, XML, or something else. Nor is a custom client limited to one server or document at a time. For instance, a summary program can combine data from multiple sites and pages. For example, RSS clients like RSSOwl, shown in Figure 1-2, combine news feeds in several different formats from many different sources and allow the user to browse the combined group. Finally, a Java program can use the full power of a modern graphical user interface to show this data to the user in a way that makes sense for the data: a grid, a document, a graph, or something else. And unlike a web browser, this program can continuously update the data in real time.

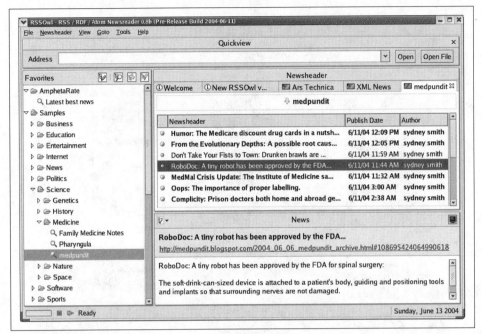

Figure 1-2. The RSSOwl newsreader is written in Java using the SWT API

Of course, not everything transmitted over HTTP is meant for humans. Web services allow machines to communicate with each other by exchanging XML documents over HTTP for purposes ranging from inventory management to stock trading to airline reservations. This can be completely automated with no human intervention, but it does require custom logic written in some programming language.

Java network clients are flexible because Java is a fully general programming language. Java programs see network connections as streams of data that can be interpreted and responded to in any way necessary. Web browsers see only certain kinds of data streams and can interpret them only in certain ways. If a browser sees a data stream that it's not familiar with (for example, a response to an SQL query), its behavior is unpredictable. Web sites can use server-side programs written in Java or other languages to provide some of these capabilities, but they're still limited to HTML for the user interface.

Writing Java programs that talk to Internet servers is easy. Java's core library includes classes for communicating with Internet hosts using the TCP and UDP protocols of the TCP/IP family. You just tell Java what IP address and port you want, and Java handles the low-level details. Java does not support NetWare IPX, Windows NetBEUI, AppleTalk, or other non-IP–based network protocols, but in the first decade of the new millennium, this is a non-issue. TCP/IP has become the *lingua franca* of networked applications and has effectively replaced pretty much all other general-purpose network protocols. A slightly more serious issue is that Java does not provide direct access to the IP layer below TCP and UDP, so it can't be used to write programs like ping or traceroute. However, these are fairly uncommon needs. Java certainly fills well over 90% of most network programmers' needs.

Once a program has connected to a server, the local program must understand the protocol the remote server speaks and properly interpret the data the server sends back. In almost all cases, packaging data to send to a server and unpacking the data received is harder than simply making the connection. Java includes classes that help your programs communicate with certain types of servers, most notably web servers. It also includes classes to process some kinds of data, such as text, GIF images, and JPEG images. However, not all servers are web servers, and not all data is text, GIF, or JPEG. As a result, Java lets you write protocol handlers to communicate with different kinds of servers and content handlers that understand and display different kinds of data. A web browser can automatically download and install the software needed by a web site it visits using Java WebStart and the Java Network Launching Protocol (JNLP). These applications can run under the control of a security manager that prevents them from doing anything potentially harmful without user permission.

Send Data

Web browsers are optimized for retrieving data: they send only limited amounts of data back to the server, mostly through forms. Java programs have no such limitations. Once a connection between two machines is established, Java programs can send data across the connection just as easily as they can receive from it. This opens up many possibilities.

File storage

Applets often need to save data between runs—for example, to store the level a player has reached in a game. Untrusted applets aren't allowed to write files on local disks, but they can store data on a cooperating server. The applet just opens a network connection to the host it came from and sends the data to it. The host may accept the data through HTTP POST, FTP, SOAP, or a custom server or servlet.

Massively parallel computing

There've always been problems that are too big for one computer to solve in a reasonable period of a time. Sometimes the answer to such a problem is buying a faster computer. However, once you reach the top of the line of off-the-shelf systems you can pick up at CompUSA, price begins to increase a lot faster than performance. For instance, one of the fastest personal computers you can buy at the time of this writing, an Apple

PowerMac with two 2.5GHz processors, will set you back about $3,000 and provide speeds in the ballpark of a few gigaflops per second. If you need something a thousand times that fast, you can buy a Cray X1 supercomputer, which will cost you several tens of million dollars, or you can buy a thousand or so PowerMacs for only a few million dollars—roughly an order of magnitude less. The numbers change as the years go by. Doubtless you can buy a faster computer for less money today, but the general rule holds steady. Past a certain point, price goes up faster than performance.

At least since the advent of the cheap microcomputer a quarter of a century ago, programmers have been splitting problems across multiple, cheap systems rather than paying a lot more for the supercomputer of the day. This can be done informally by running little pieces of the problem on multiple systems and combining the output manually, or more formally in a system like Beowulf. There's some overhead involved in synchronizing the data between all the different systems in the grid, so the price still goes up faster than the performance, but not nearly as much faster as it does with a more traditional supercomputer. Indeed, cluster supercomputers normally cost about 10 times less than equally fast non-cluster supercomputers. That's why clusters are rapidly displacing the old style supercomputers. As of June 2004, just under 60% of the world's top 500 publicly acknowledged supercomputers were built from clusters of small, off-the-shelf PCs, including the world's third-fastest. There are probably a few more computers worthy of inclusion in the list hidden inside various government agencies with black budgets, but there's no reason to believe the general breakdown of architectures is different enough to skew the basic shape of the results.

When it comes to grid computing, Java is uniquely suited to the world of massively parallel clusters of small, off-the-shelf machines. Since Java is cross-platform, distributed programs can run on any available machine, rather than just all the Windows boxes, all the Solaris boxes, or all the PowerMacs. Since Java applets are secure, individual users can safely offer the use of their spare CPU cycles to scientific projects that require massively parallel machines. When part of the calculation is complete, the program makes a network connection to the originating host and adds its results to the collected data.

There are numerous ongoing efforts in this area. Among them is David Bucciarelli's work on JCGrid (*http://jcgrid.sourceforge.net/*), an open source virtual filesystem and grid-computing framework that enables projects to be divided among multiple worker machines. Clients submit computation requests to the server, which doles them out to the worker systems. What's unique about JCGrid compared to systems like Beowulf implemented in C is that the workers don't have to trust the server or the client. Java's security manager and byte code verifier can ensure the uploaded computation tasks don't do anything besides compute. This enables grids to be established that allow anyone to borrow the CPU cycles they need. These grids can be campus-wide, company-wide, or even worldwide on the public Internet. There is a lot of unused computing power wasting electricity for no reason at any given time of day on the world's desktops. Java networking enables researchers and other users to take advantage of this power even more cheaply than they could build a cluster of inexpensive machines.

Peer-to-Peer Interaction

The above examples all follow a client/server model. However, Java applications can also talk to each other across the Internet, opening up many new possibilities for group applications. Java applets can also talk to each other, though for security reasons they have to do it via an intermediary proxy program running on the server they were downloaded from. (Again, Java makes writing this proxy program relatively easy.)

Games

Combine the easy ability to include networking in your programs with Java's powerful graphics and you have the recipe for truly awesome multiplayer games. Some that have already been written include Backgammon, Battleship, Othello, Go, Mahjongg, Pong, Charades, Bridge, and even strip poker. Figure 1-3 shows a four-player game of Hearts in progress on Yahoo. Network sockets send the plays back to the central Yahoo server, which copies them out to all the participants.

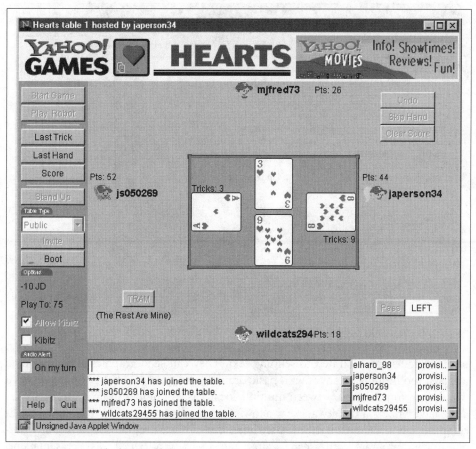

Figure 1-3. A networked game of Hearts using a Java applet from http://games.yahoo.com/

Chat

Real-time chat probably isn't one of the first generation network applications (those would be file transfer, email, and remote login), but it certainly showed up by the second generation. Internet Relay Chat (IRC) is the original Internet chat protocol, and the cause of much caffeine consumption and many late nights in the dorm rooms of highly connected campuses in the 90s. More recently, the focus has shifted from public chat rooms to private instant messaging systems that connect users who already know each other. Network-wise, however, there isn't a huge amount of difference between the two. Perhaps the biggest innovation is the buddy list that allows you to know who among your friends and colleagues is online and ready to chat. Instant messaging systems include AOL Instant Messenger (AIM), Yahoo! Messenger, and Jabber. It isn't hard to find Java clients for any of these. Text typed on one desktop can be echoed to other clients around the world. Figure 1-4 shows the JETI client participating in a Jabber chat room.

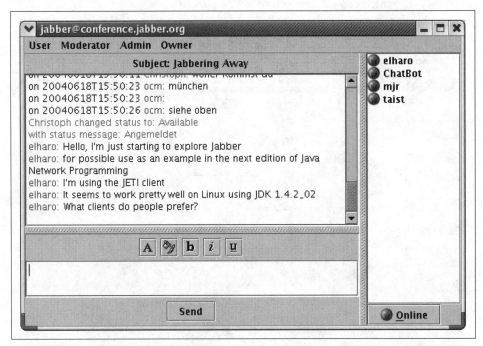

Figure 1-4. Networked text chat using Jabber

Java programs aren't limited to sending text. They can send graphics and other data formats, too. Adding a canvas with basic drawing ability to the chat program allows a whiteboard to be shared between multiple locations. A number of programmers have developed whiteboard software that allows users in diverse locations to draw on their computers. For the most part, the user interfaces of these programs look like any simple drawing program with a canvas area and a variety of pencil, text, eraser, paintbrush, and other tools. However, when networking is added, many different people can collaborate on the same drawing at the same time. The final drawing may not be as polished or as artistic as the Warhol/Basquiat collaborations, but it doesn't require the participants to all be in the same New York loft, either. Figure 1-5 shows several windows in a session of the IBM WebCollab program. WebCollab allows users in diverse locations to display and annotate slides during teleconferences. One participant runs the central WebCollab server that all the peers connect to, while conferees participate using a Java applet loaded into their web browsers.

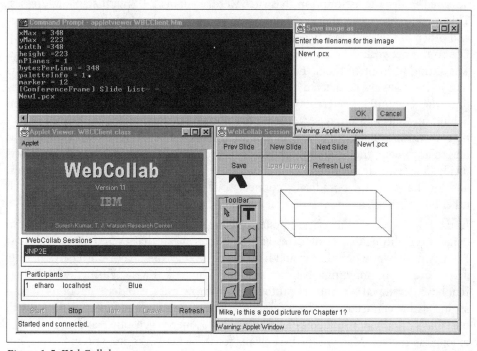

Figure 1-5. WebCollab

Peer-to-peer networked Java programs allow multiple people to collaborate on a document at one time. Imagine a Java word processor that two people, perhaps in different countries, can both pull up and edit simultaneously. More recently, the Java Media Framework 2.0 has added voice to the media that Java can transmit across the network, making collaboration even more convenient. For example, two astronomers could work on a paper while one's in New Mexico and the other in Moscow. The Russian could say, "I think you dropped the superscript in Equation 3.9," and then type the corrected equation so that it appears on both displays simultaneously. Then the astronomer in New Mexico might say, "I see, but doesn't that mean we have to revise Figure 3.2 like this?" and use a drawing tool to make the change immediately. This sort of interaction isn't particularly hard to implement in Java (a word processor with a decent user-interface for equations is probably the hardest part of the problem), but it does need to be built into the word processor from the start. It cannot be retrofitted onto a word processor that did not have networking in mind when it was designed.

File sharing

File transfer is one of the three earliest and most useful network applications (the other two being email and remote login). Traditionally, file transfer required a constantly available server at a stable address. Early Internet protocols such as FTP were designed under the assumption that sites were available 24/7 with stable addresses. This made sense when the Internet was composed mostly of multiuser Unix boxes and other big servers, but it began to fail when people started connecting desktop PCs to the network. These systems were generally only available while a single user was sitting in front of them. Furthermore, they often had slow dialup connections that weren't always connected, and hostnames and IP addresses that changed every time the computer was rebooted or reconnected. Sometimes they were hidden behind firewalls and proxy servers that did not let the outside world initiate connections to these systems at all. While clients could connect from anywhere and send files to anywhere, they couldn't easily talk to each other. In essence, the Internet was divided into two classes of users: high-bandwidth, stable, well-connected server sites, and low-bandwidth, sporadically connected client sites. Clients could talk to each other only through an intermediate server site.

In the last few years, this classist system has begun to break down. High-bandwidth connections through cable modems and DSL lines mean that even a $298 Wal-Mart PC may have bandwidth that would have been the envy of a major university 15 years ago. More importantly, first Napster and now Gnutella, Kazaa, Freenet, and BitTorrent have developed file transfer protocols that throw out the old assumptions of constant, reliable connectivity. These protocols allow sporadically connected clients with unstable IP addresses hidden behind firewalls to query each other and transfer files among themselves. Many of the best clients for these networks are written in Java. For instance, the LimeWire Gnutella client shown in Figure 1-6 is an open source pure Java application that uses a Swing GUI and standard Java networking classes.

The Gnutella protocol LimeWire supports is primarily used for trading music, pornography, and other copyright violations. The more recent BitTorrent protocol is designed for larger files such as Linux distro CD images. BitTorrent is designed to serve files that can be referenced from known keys provided by traditional sources like web sites, rather than allowing users to search for what's currently available. Another unique feature of BitTorrent is that downloaders begin sharing a file while they're still downloading it. This means hosting a large and popular file, such as the latest Fedora core release, doesn't immediately overwhelm a connection because only the first couple of users will get it directly from the original site. Most downloaders will grab much of the file from previous downloaders. Finally, BitTorrent throttles download bandwidth to match upload bandwidth, so leeching is discouraged. One of the best BitTorrent clients, Azureus (*http://azureus.sourceforge.net/*), shown in Figure 1-7, is written in pure Java.

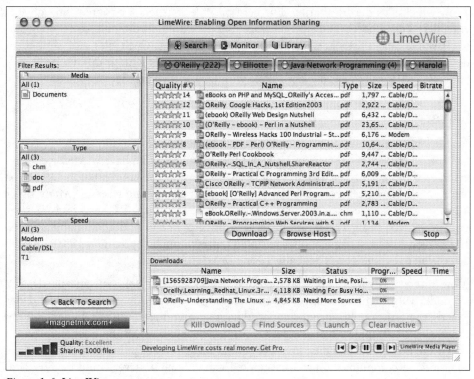

Figure 1-6. LimeWire

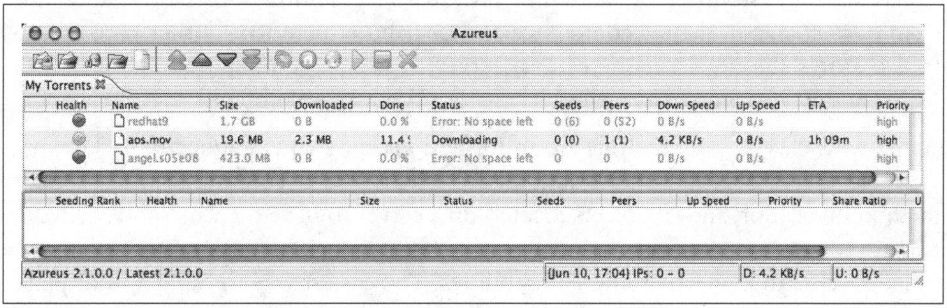

Figure 1-7. Azureus

The free sharing of information between individuals without controllable server inter-
mediaries terrifies all sorts of groups that would like to control the information
whether for profit (the RIAA and the MPAA) or politics (various governments). Many
of these have attempted to use legal and/or technological means to block peer-to-peer
networks. The techies have responded with network protocols that are designed to be
censorship-resistant through encryption and other means. One of the most serious is
Ian Clarke's Freenet (*http://freenet.sourceforge.net/*). In this network protocol,
encrypted files are divided up and duplicated on different computers that do not even

know which files they're sharing. Furthermore, file transfers are routed through several intermediate hosts. These precautions make it extremely difficult for cybervigilantes, lawyers, and the police to find out who is sharing which files and shut them down. Once again, the primary Freenet implementation is written in Java, and most research and development has been done with Java as the language of choice.

Servers

Java applications can listen for network connections and respond to them, so it's possible to implement servers in Java. Both Sun and the W3C have written web servers in Java designed to be as fully functional and fast as servers written in C, such as the Apache HTTP server and Microsoft's Internet Information Server. Many other kinds of servers have been written in Java as well, including IRC servers, NFS servers, file servers, print servers, email servers, directory servers, domain name servers, FTP servers, TFTP servers, and more. In fact, pretty much any standard TCP or UDP server you can think of has probably been ported to Java.

More interestingly you can write custom servers that fill your specific needs. For example, you might write a server that stores state for your game applet and has exactly the functionality needed to let players save and restore their games, and no more. Or, since applets can normally only communicate with the host from which they were downloaded, a custom server could mediate between two or more applets that need to communicate for a networked game. Such a server could be very simple, perhaps just echoing what one applet sent to all other connected applets. Web-Collab uses a custom server written in Java to collect annotations, notes, and slides from participants in the teleconference and distribute them to all other participants. It also stores the notes on the central server. It uses a combination of the normal HTTP and FTP protocols as well as its custom WebCollab protocol.

Along with classical servers that listen for and accept socket connections, Java provides several higher-level abstractions for client-server communication. Remote method invocation allows objects located on a server to have their methods called by clients. Servers that support the Java Servlet API can load extensions written in Java called *servlets* that give them new capabilities. The easiest way to build a multiplayer game server might be to write a servlet rather than an entire server.

Searching the Web

Java programs can wander through the Web, looking for crucial information. Search programs that run on a single client system are called *spiders*. A spider downloads a page at a particular URL, extracts the URLs from the links on that page, downloads the pages referred to by the URLs, and repeats the process for each page it downloads. Generally, a spider does something with each page it sees, from indexing it in a database to performing linguistic analysis to hunting for specific information. This

---

is more or less what services like Google do to build their indices. Building your own spider to search the Internet is a bad idea because Google and similar services have already done the work, and a few million private spiders would soon bring the Net to its knees. However, this doesn't mean you shouldn't write spiders to index your own local Intranet. In a company that uses the Web to store and access internal information, a local index service might be very useful. You can use Java to build a program that indexes all your local servers and interacts with another server program (or acts as its own server) to let users query the index.

The purposes of *agents* are similar to those of spiders (researching a stock, soliciting quotations for a purchase, bidding on similar items at multiple auctions, finding the lowest price for a CD, finding all links to a site, and so on), but whereas spiders run a single host system to which they download pages from remote sites, agents actually move themselves from host to host and execute their code on each system they move to. When they find what they're looking for, they return to the originating system with the information, possibly even a completed contract for goods or services. People have been talking about mobile agents for years, but until now, practical agent technology has been rather boring. It hasn't come close to achieving the possibilities envisioned in various science fiction novels. The primary reason for this is that agents have been restricted to running on a single system—and that's neither useful nor exciting. In fact, through 2003, the only successful agents have been hostile code such as the Morris Internet worm of 1989 and the numerous Microsoft Outlook vectored worms.

These cases demonstrate one reason developers haven't been willing to let agents go beyond a single host: they can be destructive. For instance, after breaking in to a system, the Morris worm proceeded to overload the system, rendering it useless. Letting agents run on a system introduces the possibility that hostile or buggy agents may damage that system, and that's a risk most network managers haven't been willing to take. Java mitigates the security problem by providing a controlled environment for the execution of agents that ensure that, unlike worms, the agents won't do anything nasty. This kind of control makes it safe for systems to open their doors to agents.

The second problem with agents has been portability. Agents aren't very interesting if they can only run on one kind of computer. It's sort of like having a credit card for Nieman-Marcus: a little bit useful and has a certain snob appeal, but it won't help as much as a Visa card if you want to buy something at Sears. Java provides a platform-independent environment in which agents can run; the agent doesn't care if it's visiting a Sun workstation, a Macintosh, a Linux box, or a Windows PC.

An indexing program could be implemented in Java as a mobile agent: instead of downloading pages from servers to the client and building the index there, the agent could travel to each server and build the index locally, sending much less data across the network. Another kind of agent could move through a local network to inventory hardware, check software versions, update software, perform backups, and take care of other necessary tasks. A massively parallel computer could be implemented as a system that assigns small pieces of a problem to individual agents, which then search out idle machines on the network to carry out parts of the computation. The same security features that allow clients to run untrusted programs downloaded from a server lets servers run untrusted programs uploaded from a client.

Electronic Commerce

Shopping sites have proven to be one of the few real ways to make money from consumers on the Web. Although many sites accept credit cards through HTML forms, this method is inconvenient and costly for small payments of a couple of dollars or less. Nobody wants to fill out a form with their name, address, billing address, credit card number, and expiration date every day just to pay $0.50 to read today's *Daily Planet*. A few sites, notably Amazon and Apple's iTunes Music Store, have implemented one-click systems that allow customers to reuse previously entered data. However, this only really helps sites that users shop at regularly. It doesn't work so well for sites that typically only receive a visit or two per customer per year.

But imagine how easy it would be to implement this kind of transaction in Java. The user clicks on a link to some information. The server downloads a small applet that pops up a dialog box saying, "Access to the information at *http://www.greedy.com/* costs $0.50. Do you wish to pay this?" The user can then click buttons that say "Yes" or "No". If the user clicks the No button, then they don't get into the site. Now let's imagine what happens if the user clicks Yes.

The applet contains a small amount of information: the price, the URL, and the seller. If the client agrees to the transaction, then the applet adds the buyer's data to the transaction, perhaps a name and an account number, and signs the order with the buyer's private key. The applet next sends the data back to the server over the network. The server grants the user access to the requested information using the standard HTTP security model. Then it signs the transaction with its private key and forwards the order to a central clearinghouse. Sellers can offer money-back guarantees or delayed purchase plans (No money down! Pay nothing until July!) by agreeing not to forward the transaction to the clearinghouse until a certain amount of time has elapsed.

The clearinghouse verifies each transaction with the buyer and seller's public keys and enters the transaction in its database. The clearinghouse can use credit cards, checks, or electronic fund transfers to move money from the buyer to the seller. Most likely, the clearinghouse won't move the money until the accumulated total for a buyer or seller reaches a certain minimum threshold, keeping the transaction costs low.

Every part of this process can be written in Java. An applet requests the user's permission. The Java Cryptography Extension authenticates and encrypts the transaction. The data moves from the client to the seller using sockets, URLs, servlets, and/ or remote method invocation (RMI). These can also be used for the host to talk to the central clearinghouse. The web server itself can be written in Java, as can the database and billing systems at the central clearinghouse, or JDBC can be used to talk to a traditional database like Informix or Oracle.

The hard part of this is setting up a clearinghouse, and getting users and sites to subscribe. The major credit card companies have a head start, although none of them yet use the scheme described here. In an ideal world, the buyer and the seller should be able to use different banks or clearinghouses. However, this is a social problem, not a technological one, and it is solvable. You can deposit a check from any American bank at any other American bank where you have an account. The two parties to a transaction do not need to bank in the same place.

Ubiquitous Computing

Networked devices don't have to be tied to particular physical locations, subnets, or IP addresses. Jini is a framework that sits on top of Java, easily and instantly connecting all sorts of devices to a network. For example, when a group of coworkers gather for a meeting, they generally bring a random assortment of personal digital assistants, laptops, cell phones, pagers, and other electronic devices with them. The conference room where they meet may have one or two PCs, perhaps a Mac, a digital projector, a printer, a coffee machine, a speaker phone, an Ethernet router, and assorted other useful tools. If these devices include a Java virtual machine and Jini, they form an impromptu network as soon as they're turned on and plugged in. (With wireless connections, they may not even need to be plugged in.) Devices can join or leave the local network at any time without explicit reconfiguration. They can use one of the cell phones, the speaker phone, or the router to connect to hosts outside the room.

Participants can easily share files and trade data. Their computers and other devices can be configured to recognize and trust each other regardless of where in the network one happens to be at any given time. Trust can be restricted; for example, all company employees' laptops in the room are trusted, but those of outside vendors at the meeting aren't. Some devices, such as the printer and the digital projector, may be configured to trust anyone in the room to use their services, but not allow more than one person to use them at once. Most importantly of all, the coffee machine may not trust anyone; but it can notice that it's running out of coffee and email the supply room that it needs to be restocked.

Interactive Television

Before the Web took the world by storm, Java was intended for the cable TV set-top box market. Five years after Java made its public debut, Sun finally got back to its original plans, but this time those plans were even more network-centric. The Java 2 Micro Edition (J2ME) is a stripped-down version of the rather large Java 2 API that's useful for set-top boxes and other devices with restricted memory, CPU power, and user interface, such as Palm Pilots. J2ME does include networking support, though for reasons of size, it uses a completely different set of classes called the Generic Connection Framework rather than the java.net classes from the desktop-targeted J2SE.

The Java TV API sits on top of J2ME to add television-specific features like channel changing and audio and video streaming and synchronization. TV stations can send programs down the data stream that allow channel surfers to interact with the shows. An infomercial for spray-on hair could serve a GUI program that lets the viewer pick a color, enter their credit card number, and send the order through the cable modem and over the Internet using their remote control. A news magazine could conduct a viewer poll in real time and report the responses after the commercial break. Ratings could be collected from every household with a cable modem instead of merely the 5,000 Nielsen families.

Security

Not all network programs need to run code uploaded from remote systems, but those that do (applets, Java WebStart, agent hosts, distributed computers) need strong security protections. A lot of FUD (fear, uncertainty, and doubt) has been spread around about exactly what remotely loaded Java code, applets in particular, can and cannot do. This is not a book about Java security, but I will mention a few things that code loaded from the network is usually prohibited from doing.

- Remotely loaded code cannot access arbitrary addresses in memory. Unlike the other restrictions in the list, which are enforced by a SecurityManager, this restriction is a property of the Java language itself and the byte code verifier.

- Remotely loaded code cannot access the local filesystem. It cannot read from or write to the local filesystem nor can it find out any information about files. Therefore, it cannot find out whether a file exists or what its modification date may be. (Java WebStart applications can actually ask the user for permissions to read or write files on a case-by-case basis.)

- Remotely loaded code cannot print documents. (Java WebStart applications can do this with the user's explicit permission on a case-by-case basis.)

- Remotely loaded code cannot read from or write to the system clipboard. (Java WebStart applications can do this with the user's explicit permission on a case-by-case basis.) It can read from and write to its own clipboard.

- Remotely loaded code cannot launch other programs on the client. In other words, it cannot call System.exec( ) or Runtime.exec( ).

- Remotely loaded code cannot load native libraries or define native method calls.

- Remotely loaded code is not allowed to use System.getProperty( ) in a way that reveals information about the user or the user's machine, such as a username or home directory. It may use System.getProperty( ) to find out what version of Java is in use.

- Remotely loaded code may not define any system properties.

- Remotely loaded code may not create or manipulate any Thread that is not in the same ThreadGroup.

- Remotely loaded code cannot define or use a new instance of ClassLoader, SecurityManager, ContentHandlerFactory, SocketImplFactory, or URLStream-HandlerFactory. It must use the ones already in place.

Finally, and most importantly for this book:

- Remotely loaded code can only open network connections to the host from which the code itself was downloaded.

- Remotely loaded code cannot listen on ports below 1,024.

- Even if a remotely loaded program can listen on a port, it can only accept incoming connections from the host from which the code itself was downloaded.

These restrictions can be relaxed for digitally signed code. Figure 1-8 shows the dialog a Java WebStart application uses to ask the user for additional preferences.

Figure 1-8. Java WebStart requesting the user allow unlimited access for remotely loaded code

Even if you sign the application with a verifiable certificate so the warning is a little less blood-curdling, do not expect the user to allow connections to arbitrary hosts. If a program cannot live with these restrictions, you'll need to ask the user to download and install an application, rather than running your program directly from a web site. Java applications are just like any other sort of application: they aren't restricted as to what they can do. If you are writing an application that downloads and executes classes, carefully consider what restrictions should be put in place and design an appropriate security policy to implement those restrictions.

But Wait! There's More!

Java makes it possible to write many kinds of applications that have been imagined for years, but haven't been practical before. Many of these applications would require too much processing power if they were entirely server-based; Java moves the processing to the client, where it belongs. Other application types require extreme portability and some guarantee that the application can't do anything hostile to its host. While Java's security model has been criticized (and yes, some bugs have been found), it's a quantum leap beyond anything that has been attempted in the past and an absolute necessity for the mobile software we will want to write in the future.

Most of this book describes the fairly low-level APIs needed to write the kinds of programs discussed above. Some of these programs have already been written. Others are still only possibilities. Maybe you'll be the first to write them! This chapter has just scratched the surface of what you can do when you make your Java programs network aware. You're going to come up with ideas others would never think of. For the first time, you're not limited by the capabilities that other companies build into their browsers. You can give your users both the data you want them to see and the code they need to see that data at the same time.

CHAPTER 2

Basic Network Concepts

This chapter covers the background networking concepts you need to understand before writing networked programs in Java (or, for that matter, in any language). Moving from the most general to the most specific, it explains what you need to know about networks in general, IP and TCP/IP-based networks in particular, and the Internet. This chapter doesn't try to teach you how to wire a network or configure a router, but you will learn what you need to know to write applications that communicate across the Internet. Topics covered in this chapter include the definition of network, the TCP/IP layer model, the IP, TCP, and UDP protocols, firewalls and proxy servers, the Internet, and the Internet standardization process. Experienced network gurus may safely skip this chapter.

Networks

A *network* is a collection of computers and other devices that can send data to and receive data from each other, more or less in real time. A network is often connected by wires, and the bits of data are turned into electromagnetic waves that move through the wires. However, wireless networks transmit data through infrared light and microwaves, and many long-distance transmissions are now carried over fiber optic cables that send visible light through glass filaments. There's nothing sacred about any particular physical medium for the transmission of data. Theoretically, data could be transmitted by coal-powered computers that send smoke signals to each other. The response time (and environmental impact) of such a network would be rather poor.

Each machine on a network is called a *node*. Most nodes are computers, but printers, routers, bridges, gateways, dumb terminals, and Coca-Cola™ machines can also be nodes. You might use Java to interface with a Coke machine but otherwise, you'll mostly talk to other computers. Nodes that are fully functional computers are also called *hosts*. We will use the word *node* to refer to any device on the network, and the word *host* to refer to a node that is a general-purpose computer.

Every network node has an *address*, a series of bytes that uniquely identify it. You can think of this group of bytes as a number, but in general the number of bytes in an address or the ordering of those bytes (big endian or little endian) is not guaranteed to match any primitive numeric data type in Java. The more bytes there are in each address, the more addresses there are available and the more devices that can be connected to the network simultaneously.

Addresses are assigned differently on different kinds of networks. AppleTalk addresses are chosen randomly at startup by each host. The host then checks to see if any other machine on the network is using that address. If another machine is using the address, the host randomly chooses another, checks to see if that address is already in use, and so on until it gets one that isn't being used. Ethernet addresses are attached to the physical Ethernet hardware. Manufacturers of Ethernet hardware use pre-assigned manufacturer codes to make sure there are no conflicts between the addresses in their hardware and the addresses of other manufacturer's hardware. Each manufacturer is responsible for making sure it doesn't ship two Ethernet cards with the same address. Internet addresses are normally assigned to a computer by the organization that is responsible for it. However, the addresses that an organization is allowed to choose for its computers are assigned by the organization's Internet Service Provider (ISP). ISPs get their IP addresses from one of four regional Internet Registries (the registry for North America is ARIN, the American Registry for Internet Numbers, at *http:// www.arin.net/*), which are in turn assigned IP addresses by the Internet Corporation for Assigned Names and Numbers (ICANN, at *http://www.icann.org/*).

On some kinds of networks, nodes also have names that help human beings identify them. At a set moment in time, a particular name normally refers to exactly one address. However, names are not locked to addresses. Names can change while addresses stay the same or addresses can change while the names stay the same. It is not uncommon for one address to have several names and it is possible, though somewhat less common, for one name to refer to several different addresses.

All modern computer networks are *packet-switched* networks: data traveling on the network is broken into chunks called *packets* and each packet is handled separately. Each packet contains information about who sent it and where it's going. The most important advantage of breaking data into individually addressed packets is that packets from many ongoing exchanges can travel on one wire, which makes it much cheaper to build a network: many computers can share the same wire without interfering. (In contrast, when you make a local telephone call within the same exchange, you have essentially reserved a wire from your phone to the phone of the person you're calling. When all the wires are in use, as sometimes happens during a major emergency or holiday, not everyone who picks up a phone will get a dial tone. If you stay on the line, you'll eventually get a dial tone when a line becomes free. In some countries with worse phone service than the United States, it's not uncommon to have to wait half an hour or more for a dial tone.) Another advantage of packets is that checksums can be used to detect whether a packet was damaged in transit.

We're still missing one important piece: some notion of what computers need to say to pass data back and forth. A *protocol* is a precise set of rules defining how computers communicate: the format of addresses, how data is split into packets, and so on. There are many different protocols defining different aspects of network communication. For example, the Hypertext Transfer Protocol (HTTP) defines how web browsers and servers communicate; at the other end of the spectrum, the IEEE 802.3 standard defines a protocol for how bits are encoded as electrical signals on a particular type of wire (among other protocols). Open, published protocol standards allow software and equipment from different vendors to communicate with each other: your web browser doesn't care whether any given server is a Unix workstation, a Windows box, or a Macintosh, because the server and the browser speak the same HTTP protocol regardless of platform.

The Layers of a Network

Sending data across a network is a complex operation that must be carefully tuned to the physical characteristics of the network as well as the logical character of the data being sent. Software that sends data across a network must understand how to avoid collisions between packets, convert digital data to analog signals, detect and correct errors, route packets from one host to another, and more. The process becomes even more complicated when the requirement to support multiple operating systems and heterogeneous network cabling is added.

To make this complexity manageable and hide most of it from the application developer and end user, the different aspects of network communication are separated into multiple layers. Each layer represents a different level of abstraction between the physical hardware (e.g., the wires and electricity) and the information being transmitted. Each layer has a strictly limited function. For instance, one layer may be responsible for routing packets, while the layer above it is responsible for detecting and requesting retransmission of corrupted packets. In theory, each layer only talks to the layers immediately above and immediately below it. Separating the network into layers lets you modify or even replace the software in one layer without affecting the others, as long as the interfaces between the layers stay the same.

There are several different layer models, each organized to fit the needs of a particular kind of network. This book uses the standard TCP/IP four-layer model appropriate for the Internet, shown in Figure 2-1. In this model, applications like Internet Explorer and Eudora run in the application layer and talk only to the transport layer. The transport layer talks only to the application layer and the internet layer. The internet layer in turn talks only to the host-to-network layer and the transport layer, never directly to the application layer. The host-to-network layer moves the data across the wires, fiber optic cables, or other medium to the host-to-network layer on the remote system, which then moves the data up the layers to the application on the remote system.

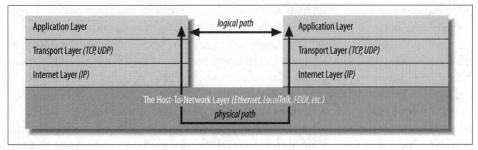

Figure 2-1. The layers of a network

For example, when a web browser sends a request to a web server to retrieve a page, the browser is actually only talking to the transport layer on the local client machine. The transport layer breaks the request up into TCP segments, adds some sequence numbers and checksums to the data, and then passes the request to the local internet layer. The internet layer fragments the segments into IP datagrams of the necessary size for the local network and passes them to the host-to-network layer for transmission onto the wire. The host-to-network layer encodes the digital data as analog signals appropriate for the particular physical medium and sends the request out the wire where it will be read by the host-to-network layer of the remote system to which it's addressed.

The host-to-network layer on the remote system decodes the analog signals into digital data then passes the resulting IP datagrams to the server's internet layer. The internet layer does some simple checks to see that the IP datagrams aren't corrupt, reassembles them if they've been fragmented, and passes them to the server's transport layer. The server's transport layer checks to see that all the data arrived and requests retransmission of any missing or corrupt pieces. (This request actually goes back down through the server's internet layer, through the server's host-to-network layer, and back to the client system, where it bubbles back up to the client's transport layer, which retransmits the missing data back down through the layers. This is all transparent to the application layer.) Once the server's transport layer has received enough contiguous, sequential datagrams, it reassembles them and writes them onto a stream read by the web server running in the server application layer. The server responds to the request and sends its response back down through the layers on the server system for transmission back across the Internet and delivery to the web client.

As you can guess, the real process is much more elaborate. The host-to-network layer is by far the most complex, and a lot has been deliberately hidden. For example, it's entirely possible that data sent across the Internet will pass through several routers and their layers before reaching its final destination. However, 90% of the time your Java code will work in the application layer and only need to talk to the transport layer. The other 10% of the time, you'll be in the transport layer and talking to the application layer or the internet layer. The complexity of the host-to-network layer is hidden from you; that's the point of the layer model.

 If you read the network literature, you're likely to encounter an alternative seven-layer model called the Open Systems Interconnection Reference Model (OSI). For network programs in Java, the OSI model is overkill. The biggest difference between the OSI model and the TCP/IP model used in this book is that the OSI model splits the host-to-network layer into data link and physical layers and inserts presentation and session layers in between the application and transport layers. The OSI model is more general and better suited for non-TCP/IP networks, although most of the time it's still overly complex. In any case, Java's network classes only work on TCP/IP networks and always in the application or transport layers, so for the purposes of this book, absolutely nothing is gained by using the more complicated OSI model.

To the application layer, it seems as if it is talking directly to the application layer on the other system; the network creates a logical path between the two application layers. It's easy to understand the logical path if you think about an IRC chat session. Most participants in an IRC chat would say that they're talking to another person. If you really push them, they might say that they're talking to their computer (really the application layer), which is talking to the other person's computer, which is talking to the other person. Everything more than one layer deep is effectively invisible, and that is exactly the way it should be. Let's consider each layer in more detail.

The Host-to-Network Layer

As a Java programmer, you're fairly high up in the network food chain. A lot happens below your radar. In the standard reference model for IP-based Internets (the only kind of network Java really understands), the hidden parts of the network belong to the *host-to-network layer* (also known as the link layer, data link layer, or network interface layer). The host-to-network layer defines how a particular network interface—such as an Ethernet card or a PPP connection—sends IP datagrams over its physical connection to the local network and the world.

The part of the host-to-network layer made up of the hardware that connects different computers (wires, fiber optic cables, microwave relays, or smoke signals) is sometimes called the physical layer of the network. As a Java programmer, you don't need to worry about this layer unless something goes wrong—the plug falls out of the back of your computer, or someone drops a backhoe through the T-1 line between you and the rest of the world. In other words, Java never sees the physical layer.

For computers to communicate with each other, it isn't sufficient to run wires between them and send electrical signals back and forth. The computers have to agree on certain standards for how those signals are interpreted. The first step is to determine how the packets of electricity or light or smoke map into bits and bytes of data. Since the physical layer is analog, and bits and bytes are digital, this process involves a digital-to-analog conversion on the sending end and an analog-to-digital conversion on the receiving end.

Since all real analog systems have noise, error correction and redundancy need to be built into the way data is translated into electricity. This is done in the data link layer. The most common data link layer is Ethernet. Other popular data link layers include TokenRing, PPP, and Wireless Ethernet (802.11). A specific data link layer requires specialized hardware. Ethernet cards won't communicate on a TokenRing network, for example. Special devices called *gateways* convert information from one type of data link layer, such as Ethernet, to another, such as TokenRing. As a Java programmer, the data link layer does not affect you directly. However, you can sometimes optimize the data you send in the application layer to match the native packet size of a particular data link layer, which can have some affect on performance. This is similar to matching disk reads and writes to the native block size of the disk. Whatever size you choose, the program will still run, but some sizes let the program run more efficiently than others, and which sizes these are can vary from one computer to the next.

The Internet Layer

The next layer of the network, and the first that you need to concern yourself with, is the *internet layer*. In the OSI model, the internet layer goes by the more generic name *network layer*. A network layer protocol defines how bits and bytes of data are organized into the larger groups called packets, and the addressing scheme by which different machines find each other. The Internet Protocol (IP) is the most widely used network layer protocol in the world and the only network layer protocol Java understands. IP is almost exclusively the focus of this book. Other, semi-common network layer protocols include Novell's IPX, and IBM and Microsoft's NetBEUI, although nowadays most installations have replaced these protocols with IP. Each network layer protocol is independent of the lower layers. IP, IPX, NetBEUI, and other protocols can each be used on Ethernet, Token Ring, and other data link layer protocol networks, each of which can themselves run across different kinds of physical layers.

Data is sent across the internet layer in packets called *datagrams*. Each IP datagram contains a header between 20 and 60 bytes long and a payload that contains up to 65,515 bytes of data. (In practice, most IP datagrams are much smaller, ranging from a few dozen bytes to a little more than eight kilobytes.) The header of each IP datagram contains these items, in this order:

4-bit version number
> Always 0100 (decimal 4) for current IP; will be changed to 0110 (decimal 6) for IPv6, but the entire header format will also change in IPv6.

4-bit header length

An unsigned integer between 0 and 15 specifying the number of 4-byte words in the header; since the maximum value of the header length field is 1111 (decimal 15), an IP header can be at most 60 bytes long.

1-byte type of service

A 3-bit precedence field that is no longer used, four type-of-service bits (minimize delay, maximize throughput, maximize reliability, minimize monetary cost) and a zero bit. Not all service types are compatible. Many computers and routers simply ignore these bits.

2-byte datagram length

An unsigned integer specifying the length of the entire datagram, including both header and payload.

2-byte identification number

A unique identifier for each datagram sent by a host; allows duplicate datagrams to be detected and thrown away.

3-bit flags

The first bit is 0; the second bit is 0 if this datagram may be fragmented, 1 if it may not be; and the third bit is 0 if this is the last fragment of the datagram, 1 if there are more fragments.

13-bit fragment offset

In the event that the original IP datagram is fragmented into multiple pieces, this field identifies the position of this fragment in the original datagram.

1-byte time-to-live (TTL)

Number of nodes through which the datagram can pass before being discarded; used to avoid infinite loops.

1-byte protocol

6 for TCP, 17 for UDP, or a different number between 0 and 255 for each of more than 100 different protocols (some quite obscure); see *http://www.iana.org/assignments/protocol-numbers* for the complete current list.

2-byte header checksum

A checksum of the header only (not the entire datagram) calculated using a 16-bit one's complement sum.

4-byte source address

The IP address of the sending node.

4-byte destination address

The IP address of the destination node.

In addition, an IP datagram header may contain between 0 and 40 bytes of optional information, used for security options, routing records, timestamps, and other features Java does not support. Consequently, we will not discuss them here. The interested reader is referred to *TCP/IP Illustrated, Volume 1: The Protocols*, by W. Richard

Stevens (Addison Wesley), for more details on these fields. Figure 2-2 shows how the different quantities are arranged in an IP datagram. All bits and bytes are big-endian; most significant to least significant runs left to right.

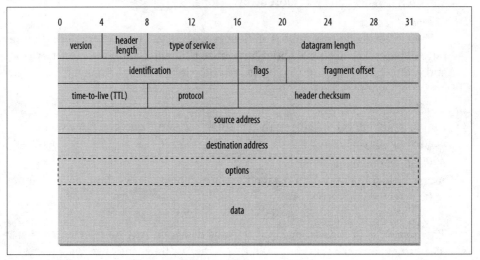

Figure 2-2. The structure of an IPv4 datagram

The Transport Layer

Raw datagrams have some drawbacks. Most notably, there's no guarantee that they will be delivered. Even if they are delivered, they may have been corrupted in transit. The header checksum can only detect corruption in the header, not in the data portion of a datagram. Finally, even if the datagrams arrive uncorrupted, they do not necessarily arrive in the order in which they were sent. Individual datagrams may follow different routes from source to destination. Just because datagram A is sent before datagram B does not mean that datagram A will arrive before datagram B.

The *transport layer* is responsible for ensuring that packets are received in the order they were sent and making sure that no data is lost or corrupted. If a packet is lost, the transport layer can ask the sender to retransmit the packet. IP networks implement this by adding an additional header to each datagram that contains more information. There are two primary protocols at this level. The first, the Transmission Control Protocol (TCP), is a high-overhead protocol that allows for retransmission of lost or corrupted data and delivery of bytes in the order they were sent. The second protocol, the User Datagram Protocol (UDP), allows the receiver to detect corrupted packets but does not guarantee that packets are delivered in the correct order (or at all). However, UDP is often much faster than TCP. TCP is called a *reliable* protocol; UDP is an *unreliable* protocol. Later, we'll see that unreliable protocols are much more useful than they sound.

The Application Layer

The layer that delivers data to the user is called the *application layer*. The three lower layers all work together to define how data is transferred from one computer to another. The application layer decides what to do with the data after it's transferred. For example, an application protocol like HTTP (for the World Wide Web) makes sure that your web browser knows to display a graphic image as a picture, not a long stream of numbers. The application layer is where most of the network parts of your programs spend their time. There is an entire alphabet soup of application layer protocols; in addition to HTTP for the Web, there are SMTP, POP, and IMAP for email; FTP, FSP, and TFTP for file transfer; NFS for file access; NNTP for news transfer; Gnutella, FastTrack, and Freenet for file sharing; and many, many more. In addition, your programs can define their own application layer protocols as necessary.

IP, TCP, and UDP

IP, the Internet protocol, has a number of advantages over competing protocols such as AppleTalk and IPX, most stemming from its history. It was developed with military sponsorship during the Cold War, and ended up with a lot of features that the military was interested in. First, it had to be robust. The entire network couldn't stop functioning if the Soviets nuked a router in Cleveland; all messages still had to get through to their intended destinations (except those going to Cleveland, of course). Therefore IP was designed to allow multiple routes between any two points and to route packets of data around damaged routers.

Second, the military had many different kinds of computers, and all of them had to be able to talk to each other. Therefore the IP had to be open and platform-independent; it wasn't good enough to have one protocol for IBM mainframes and another for PDP-11s. The IBM mainframes needed to talk to the PDP-11s and any other strange computers that might be lying around.

Since there are multiple routes between two points, and since the quickest path between two points may change over time as a function of network traffic and other factors (such as the existence of Cleveland), the packets that make up a particular data stream may not all take the same route. Furthermore, they may not arrive in the order they were sent, if they even arrive at all. To improve on the basic scheme, TCP was layered on top of IP to give each end of a connection the ability to acknowledge receipt of IP packets and request retransmission of lost or corrupted packets. Furthermore, TCP allows the packets to be put back together on the receiving end in the same order they were sent.

TCP, however, carries a fair amount of overhead. Therefore, if the order of the data isn't particularly important and if the loss of individual packets won't completely corrupt the data stream, packets are sometimes sent without the guarantees that TCP provides. This is accomplished through the use of the UDP protocol. UDP is an unreliable protocol that does not guarantee that packets will arrive at their destination or that they will arrive in the same order they were sent. Although this would be a problem for uses such as file transfer, it is perfectly acceptable for applications where the loss of some data would go unnoticed by the end user. For example, losing a few bits from a video or audio signal won't cause much degradation; it would be a bigger problem if you had to wait for a protocol like TCP to request a retransmission of missing data. Furthermore, error-correcting codes can be built into UDP data streams at the application level to account for missing data.

A number of other protocols can run on top of IP. The most commonly requested is ICMP, the Internet Control Message Protocol, which uses raw IP datagrams to relay error messages between hosts. The best-known use of this protocol is in the ping program. Java does not support ICMP nor does it allow the sending of raw IP datagrams (as opposed to TCP segments or UDP datagrams). The only protocols Java supports are TCP and UDP, and application layer protocols built on top of these. All other transport layer, internet layer, and lower layer protocols such as ICMP, IGMP, ARP, RARP, RSVP, and others can only be implemented in Java programs by using native code.

IP Addresses and Domain Names

As a Java programmer, you don't need to worry about the inner workings of IP, but you do need to know about addressing. Every computer on an IPv4 network is identified by a four-byte number. This is normally written in a *dotted quad* format like *199.1. 32.90*, where each of the four numbers is one unsigned byte ranging in value from 0 to 255. Every computer attached to an IPv4 network has a unique four-byte address. When data is transmitted across the network, the packet's header includes the address of the machine for which the packet is intended (the destination address) and the address of the machine that sent the packet (the source address). Routers along the way choose the best route to send the packet along by inspecting the destination address. The source address is included so the recipient will know who to reply to.

There are a little more than four billion possible IP addresses, not even one for every person on the planet, much less for every computer. To make matters worse, the addresses aren't allocated very efficiently. A slow transition is under way to IPv6, which will use 16-byte addresses. This provides enough IP addresses to identify every person, every computer, and indeed every atom on the planet. IPv6 addresses are customarily written in eight blocks of four hexadecimal digits separated by colons, such as *FEDC:BA98:7654:3210:FEDC:BA98:7654:3210*. Leading zeros do not need to be written. A double colon, at most one of which may appear in any address, indicates multiple zero blocks. For example, *FEDC:0000:0000:0000:00DC:0000:7076: 0010* could be written more compactly as *FEDC::DC:0:7076:10*. In mixed networks of IPv6 and IPv4, the last four bytes of the IPv6 address are sometimes written as an IPv4 dotted quad address. For example, *FEDC:BA98:7654:3210:FEDC:BA98:7654: 3210* could be written as *FEDC:BA98:7654:3210:FEDC:BA98:118.84.50.16*. IPv6 is only supported in Java 1.4 and later. Java 1.3 and earlier only support four-byte addresses.

Although computers are very comfortable with numbers, human beings aren't very good at remembering them. Therefore the Domain Name System (DNS) was developed to translate hostnames that humans can remember (like *www.oreilly.com*) into numeric Internet addresses (like *208.201.239.37*). When Java programs access the network, they need to process both these numeric addresses and their corresponding hostnames. Methods for doing this are provided by the `java.net.InetAddress` class, which is discussed in Chapter 6.

Some computers, especially servers, have fixed addresses. Others, especially clients on local area networks and dial-up connections, receive a different address every time they boot up, often provided by a DHCP server or a PPP server. This is not especially relevant to your Java programs. Mostly you just need to remember that IP addresses may change over time, and not write any code that relies on a system having the same IP address. For instance, don't serialize the local IP address when saving application state. Instead, look it up fresh each time your program starts. It's also possible, although less likely, for an IP address to change while the program is running (for instance, if a dialup connection hangs up and then reconnects), so you may want to check the current IP address every time you need it rather than caching it. Otherwise, the difference between a dynamically and manually assigned address is not significant to Java programs.

Ports

Addresses would be all you needed if each computer did no more than one thing at a time. However, modern computers do many different things at once. Email needs to be separated from FTP requests, which need to be separated from web traffic. This is accomplished through *ports*. Each computer with an IP address has several thousand logical ports (65,535 per transport layer protocol, to be precise). These are purely abstractions in the computer's memory and do not represent anything physical, like a serial or parallel port. Each port is identified by a number between 1 and 65,535. Each port can be allocated to a particular service.

For example, HTTP, the underlying protocol of the Web, generally uses port 80. We say that a web server *listens* on port 80 for incoming connections. When data is sent to a web server on a particular machine at a particular IP address, it is also sent to a particular port (usually port 80) on that machine. The receiver checks each packet it sees for the port and sends the data to any programs that are listening to the specified port. This is how different types of traffic are sorted out.

Port numbers between 1 and 1,023 are reserved for well-known services like finger, FTP, HTTP, and IMAP. On Unix systems, including Linux and Mac OS X, only programs running as root can receive data from these ports, but all programs may send data to them. On Windows and Mac OS 9, any program may use these ports without special privileges. Table 2-1 shows the well-known ports for the protocols that are discussed in this book. These assignments are not absolutely guaranteed; in particular, web servers often run on ports other than 80, either because multiple servers need to run on the same machine or because the person who installed the server doesn't have the root privileges needed to run it on port 80. On Unix systems, a fairly complete listing of assigned ports is stored in the file */etc/services*.

Table 2-1. Well-known port assignments

Protocol	Port	Protocol	Purpose
echo	7	TCP/UDP	Echo is a test protocol used to verify that two machines are able to connect by having one echo back the other's input.
discard	9	TCP/UDP	Discard is a less useful test protocol in which all data received by the server is ignored.
daytime	13	TCP/UDP	Provides an ASCII representation of the current time on the server.
FTP data	20	TCP	FTP uses two well-known ports. This port is used to transfer files.
FTP	21	TCP	This port is used to send FTP commands like put and get.
SSH	22	TCP	Used for encrypted, remote logins.
telnet	23	TCP	Used for interactive, remote command-line sessions.
smtp	25	TCP	The Simple Mail Transfer Protocol is used to send email between machines.
time	37	TCP/UDP	A time server returns the number of seconds that have elapsed on the server since midnight, January 1, 1900, as a four-byte, signed, big-endian integer.
whois	43	TCP	A simple directory service for Internet network administrators.
finger	79	TCP	A service that returns information about a user or users on the local system.
HTTP	80	TCP	The underlying protocol of the World Wide Web.
POP3	110	TCP	Post Office Protocol Version 3 is a protocol for the transfer of accumulated email from the host to sporadically connected clients.
NNTP	119	TCP	Usenet news transfer; more formally known as the "Network News Transfer Protocol".
IMAP	143	TCP	Internet Message Access Protocol is a protocol for accessing mailboxes stored on a server.
RMI Registry	1099	TCP	The registry service for Java remote objects. This will be discussed in Chapter 18.

The Internet

The *Internet* is the world's largest IP-based network. It is an amorphous group of computers in many different countries on all seven continents (Antarctica included) that talk to each other using the IP protocol. Each computer on the Internet has at least one unique IP address by which it can be identified. Most of them also have at least one name that maps to that IP address. The Internet is not owned by anyone, although pieces of it are. It is not governed by anyone, which is not to say that some governments don't try. It is simply a very large collection of computers that have agreed to talk to each other in a standard way.

The Internet is not the only IP-based network, but it is the largest one. Other IP networks are called *internets* with a little *i*: for example, a corporate IP network that is not connected to the Internet. *Intranet* is a current buzzword that loosely describes corporate practices of putting lots of data on internal web servers.

Unless you're working in a high security environment that's physically disconnected from the broader network, it's likely that the internet you'll be using is the Internet. To make sure that hosts on different networks on the Internet can communicate with each other, a few rules need to be followed that don't apply to purely internal internets. The most important rules deal with the assignment of addresses to different organizations, companies, and individuals. If everyone picked the Internet addresses they wanted at random, conflicts would arise almost immediately when different computers showed up on the Internet with the same address.

Internet Address Classes

To avoid this problem, blocks of IPv4 addresses are assigned to Internet Service Providers (ISPs) by their regional Internet registry. When a company or an organization wants to set up an IP-based network connected to the Internet, their ISP gives them a block of addresses. Traditionally, these blocks come in three sizes called Class A, Class B, and Class C. A Class C address block specifies the first three bytes of the address; for example, 199.1.32. This allows room for 254 individual addresses from 199.1.32.1 to 199.1.32.254.* A class B address block only specifies the first two bytes of the addresses an organization may use; for instance, 167.1. Thus, a class B address has room for 65,024 different hosts (256 Class C size blocks times 254 hosts per Class C block). A class A address block only specifies the first byte of the address range—for instance, 18—and therefore has room for over 16 million nodes.

---

* Addresses with the last byte either .0 or .255 are reserved and should never actually be assigned to hosts.

There are also Class D and E addresses. Class D addresses are used for IP multicast groups, and will be discussed at length in Chapter 14. Class D addresses all begin with the four bits 1110. Class E addresses begin with the five bits 11110 and are reserved for future extensions to the Internet.

There's no block with a size between a class A and a Class B, or Class B and a Class C. This has become a problem because there are many organizations with more than 254 computers connected to the Internet but less than 65,024. If each of these organizations gets a full Class B block, many addresses are wasted. There's a limited number of IPv4 addresses—about 4.2 billion, to be precise. That sounds like a lot, but it gets crowded quickly when you can easily waste fifty or sixty thousand addresses at a shot.

There are also many networks, such as the author's own personal basement-area network, that have a few to a few dozen computers but not 255. To more efficiently allocate the limited address space, Classless Inter-Domain Routing (CIDR) was invented. CIDR mostly (though not completely) replaces the whole A, B, C, D, E addressing scheme with one based on a specified numbers of prefix bits. These prefixes are generally written as /nn, where nn is a two-digit number specifying the number of bits in the network portion of the address. The number after the / indicates the number of fixed prefix bits. Thus, a /24 fixes the first 24 bits in the address, leaving 8 bits available to distinguish individual nodes. This allows 256 nodes, and is equivalent to an old style Class C. A /19 fixes 19 bits, leaving 13 for individual nodes within the network. It's equivalent to 32 separate Class C networks or an eighth of a Class B. A /28, generally the smallest you're likely to encounter in practice, leaves only four bits for identifying local nodes. It can handle networks with up to 16 nodes. CIDR also carefully specifies which address blocks are associated with which ISPs. This scheme helps keep Internet routing tables smaller and more manageable than they would be under the old system.

Several address blocks and patterns are special. All IPv4 addresses that begin with 10., 172.16. through 172.31., and 192.168. are deliberately unassigned. They can be used on internal networks, but no host using addresses in these blocks is allowed onto the global Internet. These *non-routable* addresses are useful for building private networks that can't be seen from the rest of the Internet or for building a large network when you've only been assigned a class C address block. IPv4 addresses beginning with 127 (most commonly 127.0.0.1) always mean the *local loopback address*. That is, these addresses always point to the local computer, no matter which computer you're running on. The hostname for this address is generally *localhost*. In IPv6 0:0:0:0:0:0:0:1 (a.k.a. ::1) is the loopback address. The address 0.0.0.0 always refers to the originating host, but may only be used as a source address, not a destination. Similarly, any IPv4 address that begins with 0.0 is assumed to refer to a host on the same local network.

Network Address Translation

For reasons of both security and address space conservation, many smaller networks, such as the author's home network, use *network address translation* (NAT). Rather than allotting even a /28, my ISP gives me a single address, *216.254.85.72*. Obviously, that won't work for the dozen or so different computers and other devices running in my apartment at any one time. Instead, I assign each one of them a different address in the non-routable block *192.168.254.xxx*. When they connect to the internet, they have to pass through a router my ISP sold me that translates the internal addresses into the external addresses.

The router watches my outgoing and incoming connections and adjusts the addresses in the IP packets. For an outgoing packet, it changes the source address to the router's external address (*216.254.85.72* on my network). For an incoming packet, it changes the destination address to one of the local addresses, such as *192. 168.254.12*. Exactly how it keeps track of which connections come from and are aimed at which internal computers is not particularly important to a Java programmer. As long as your machines are configured properly, this process is mostly transparent to Java programs. You just need to remember that the external and internal addresses may not be the same. From outside my network, nobody can talk to my system at *192.168.254.12* unless I initiate the connection, or unless I configure my router to forward requests addressed to *216.254.85.72* to *192.168.254.12*. If the router is safe, then the rest of the network is too. On the other hand, if someone does crack the router or one of the servers behind the router that is mapped to *216.254. 85.72*, I'm hosed. This is why I installed a firewall as the next line of defense.

Firewalls

There are some naughty people on the Internet. To keep them out, it's often helpful to set up one point of access to a local network and check all traffic into or out of that access point. The hardware and software that sit between the Internet and the local network, checking all the data that comes in or out to make sure it's kosher, is called a *firewall*. The firewall is often part of the router that connects the local network to the broader Internet and may perform other tasks, such as network address translation. Then again, the firewall may be a separate machine. Modern operating systems like Mac OS X and Red Hat Linux often have built-in personal firewalls that monitor just the traffic sent to that one machine. Either way, the firewall is responsible for inspecting each packet that passes into or out of its network interface and accepting it or rejecting it according to a set of rules.

Filtering is usually based on network addresses and ports. For example, all traffic coming from the Class C network 193.28.25 may be rejected because you had bad experiences with hackers from that network in the past. Outgoing Telnet connections may be allowed, but incoming Telnet connections may not. Incoming connections on port 80 (web) may be allowed, but only to the corporate web server. More intelligent firewalls look at the contents of the packets to determine whether to accept or reject them. The exact configuration of a firewall—which packets of data are and are not allowed to pass through—depends on the security needs of an individual site. Java doesn't have much to do with firewalls—except in so far as they often get in your way.

Proxy Servers

Proxy servers are related to firewalls. If a firewall prevents hosts on a network from making direct connections to the outside world, a proxy server can act as a go-between. Thus, a machine that is prevented from connecting to the external network by a firewall would make a request for a web page from the local proxy server instead of requesting the web page directly from the remote web server. The proxy server would then request the page from the web server and forward the response back to the original requester. Proxies can also be used for FTP services and other connections. One of the security advantages of using a proxy server is that external hosts only find out about the proxy server. They do not learn the names and IP addresses of the internal machines, making it more difficult to hack into internal systems.

While firewalls generally operate at the level of the transport or internet layer, proxy servers normally operate at the application layer. A proxy server has a detailed understanding of some application level protocols, such as HTTP and FTP. (The notable exception are SOCKS proxy servers that operate at the transport layer, and can proxy for all TCP and UDP connections regardless of application layer protocol.) Packets that pass through the proxy server can be examined to ensure that they contain data appropriate for their type. For instance, FTP packets that seem to contain Telnet data can be rejected. Figure 2-3 shows how proxy servers fit into the layer model.

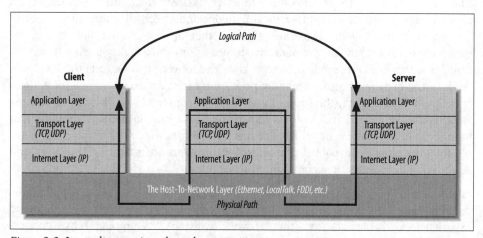

Figure 2-3. Layered connections through a proxy server

As long as all access to the Internet is forwarded through the proxy server, access can be tightly controlled. For instance, a company might choose to block access to *www.playboy.com* but allow access to *www.microsoft.com*. Some companies allow incoming FTP but disallow outgoing FTP so confidential data cannot be as easily smuggled out of the company. Other companies have begun using proxy servers to track their employees' web usage so they can see who's using the Internet to get tech support and who's using it to check out the Playmate of the Month. Such monitoring of employee behavior is controversial and not exactly an indicator of enlightened management techniques.

Proxy servers can also be used to implement local caching. When a file is requested from a web server, the proxy server first checks to see if the file is in its cache. If the file is in the cache, the proxy serves the file from the cache rather than from the Internet. If the file is not in the cache, the proxy server retrieves the file, forwards it to the requester, and stores it in the cache for the next time it is requested. This scheme can significantly reduce load on an Internet connection and greatly improve response time. America Online runs one of the largest farm of proxy servers in the world to speed the transfer of data to its users. If you look at a web server logfile, you'll probably find some hits from clients in the *aol.com* domain, but not as many as you'd expect given the more than twenty million AOL subscribers. That's because AOL proxy servers supply many pages out of their cache rather than re-requesting them for each user. Many other large ISPs do similarly.

The biggest problem with proxy servers is their inability to cope with all but a few protocols. Generally established protocols like HTTP, FTP, and SMTP are allowed to pass through, while newer protocols like Gnutella are not. (Some network administrators would consider this a feature.) In the rapidly changing world of the Internet, this is a significant disadvantage. It's a particular disadvantage for Java programmers because it limits the effectiveness of custom protocols. In Java, it's easy and often useful to create a new protocol that is optimized for your application. However, no proxy server will ever understand these one-of-a-kind protocols. Consequently, some developers have taken to tunneling their protocols through HTTP, most notably with SOAP. However, this has a significant negative impact on security. The firewall is normally there for a reason, not just to annoy Java programmers.

Applets that run in web browsers use the proxy server settings of the web browser itself, generally set in a dialog box (possibly hidden several levels deep in the preferences) like the one in Figure 2-4. Standalone Java applications can indicate the proxy server to use by setting the socksProxyHost and socksProxyPort properties (if you're using a SOCKS proxy server), or http.proxySet, http.proxyHost, http.proxyPort, https.proxySet, https.proxyHost, https.proxyPort, ftpProxySet, ftpProxyHost, ftpProxyPort, gopherProxySet, gopherProxyHost, and gopherProxyPort system properties (if you're using protocol-specific proxies). You can set system properties from the command line using the -D flag, like this:

```
java -DsocksProxyHost=socks.cloud9.net -DsocksProxyPort=1080  MyClass
```

You can use any other convenient means to set these system properties, such as including them in the *appletviewer.properties* file, like this:

```
ftpProxySet=true
ftpProxyHost=ftp.proxy.cloud9.net
ftpProxyPort=1000
gopherProxySet=true
gopherProxyHost=gopher.proxy.cloud9.net
gopherProxyPort=9800
http.proxySet=true
http.proxyHost=web.proxy.cloud9.net
http.proxyPort=8000
https.proxySet=true
https.proxyHost=web.proxy.cloud9.net
https.proxyPort=8001
```

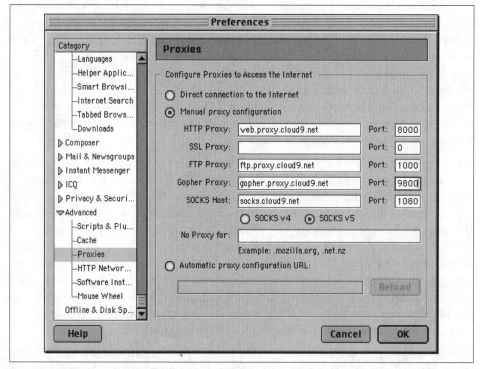

Figure 2-4. Netscape Navigator proxy server settings

The Client/Server Model

Most modern network programming is based on a client/server model. A client/server application typically stores large quantities of data on an expensive, high-powered server while most of the program logic and the user-interface is handled by client software running on relatively cheap personal computers. In most cases, a server primarily sends data while a client primarily receives it, but it is rare for one program to send or receive exclusively. A more reliable distinction is that a client initiates a conversation while a server waits for clients to start conversations with it. Figure 2-5 illustrates both possibilities. In some cases, the same program may be both a client and a server.

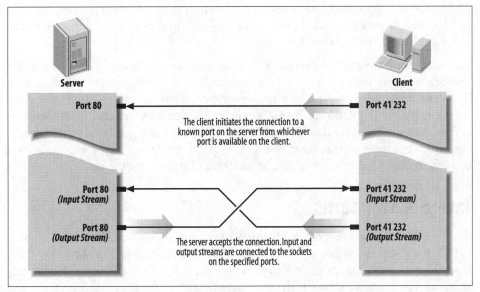

Figure 2-5. A client/server connection

Some servers process and analyze the data before sending the results to the client. Such servers are often referred to as "application servers" to distinguish them from the more common file servers and database servers. A file or database server will retrieve information and send it to a client, but it won't process that information. In contrast, an application server might look at an order entry database and give the clients reports about monthly sales trends. An application server is not a server that serves files that happen to be applications.

You are already familiar with many examples of client/server systems. In 2004, the most popular client/server system on the Internet is the Web. Web servers like Apache respond to requests from web clients like Firefox. Data is stored on the web server and is sent out to the clients that request it. Aside from the initial request for a page, almost all data is transferred from the server to the client, not from the client to the server. Web servers that use CGI programs double as application and file servers. FTP is an older service that fits the client/server model. FTP uses different application protocols and different software, but is still split into FTP servers that send files and FTP clients that receive files. People often use FTP to upload files from the client to the server, so it's harder to say that the data transfer is primarily in one direction, but it is still true that an FTP client initiates the connection and the FTP server responds.

Not all applications fit easily into a client/server model. For instance, in networked games, it seems likely that both players will send data back and forth roughly equally (at least in a fair game). These sorts of connections are called *peer-to-peer*. The telephone system is the classic example of a peer-to-peer network. Each phone can either call another phone or be called by another phone. You don't have to buy one phone to send calls and another to receive them.

Java does not have explicit peer-to-peer communication in its core networking API (though Sun has implemented it in a separate open source project called JXTA). However, applications can easily offer peer-to-peer communications in several ways, most commonly by acting as both a server and a client. Alternately, the peers can communicate with each other through an intermediate server program that forwards data from one peer to the other peers. This is especially useful for applets with a security manager that restricts them from talking directly to each other.

Internet Standards

This book discusses several application-layer Internet protocols, most notably HTTP. However, this is not a book about those protocols and it tries not to say more than the minimum you need to know. If you need detailed information about any protocol, the definitive source is the standards document for the protocol.

While there are many standards organizations in the world, the two that produce most of the standards relevant to network programming and protocols are the Internet Engineering Task Force (IETF) and the World Wide Web Consortium (W3C). The IETF is a relatively informal, democratic body open to participation by any interested party. Its standards are based on "rough consensus and running code" and tend to follow rather than lead implementations. IETF standards include TCP/IP, MIME, and SMTP. The W3C, by contrast, is a vendor organization, controlled by dues-paying member corporations, that explicitly excludes participation by individuals. For the most part, the W3C tries to define standards in advance of implementation. W3C standards include HTTP, HTML, and XML.

IETF RFCs

IETF standards and near-standards are published as Internet drafts and requests for comments (RFCs). RFCs and Internet drafts range from informational documents of general interest to detailed specifications of standard Internet protocols like FTP. RFCs that document a standard or a proposed standard are published only with the approval of the Internet Engineering Steering Group (IESG) of the IETF. All IETF approved standards are RFCs, but not all RFCs are IETF standards. RFCs are available from many locations on the Internet, including *http://www.faqs.org/rfc/* and *http://www.ietf.org/rfc.html*. For the most part RFCs, particularly standards-oriented RFCs, are very technical, turgid, and nearly incomprehensible. Nonetheless, they are often the only complete and reliable source of information about a particular protocol.

Most proposals for a standard begin when a person or group gets an idea and builds a prototype. The prototype is incredibly important. Before something can become an IETF standard, it must actually exist and work. This requirement ensures that IETF standards are at least feasible, unlike the standards promulgated by some other organizations. If the prototype becomes popular outside its original developers and if other organizations begin implementing their own versions of the protocol, a *working group* may be formed under the auspices of the IETF. This working group attempts to document the protocol in an *Internet-Draft*. Internet-Drafts are working documents and change frequently to reflect experience with the protocol. The experimental implementations and the Internet-Draft evolve in rough synchronization, until eventually the working group agrees that the protocol is ready to become a formal standard. At this point, the proposed specification is submitted to the IESG.

The proposal goes through six states or maturity levels as it follows the standardization track:

- Experimental
- Proposed standard
- Draft standard
- Standard
- Informational
- Historic

For some time after the proposal is submitted, it is considered *experimental*. The experimental stage does not imply that the protocol is not solid or that it is not widely used; unfortunately, the standards process usually lags behind *de facto* acceptance of the standard. If the IESG likes the experimental standard or it is in widespread use, the IESG will assign it an RFC number and publish it as an experimental RFC, generally after various changes.

If the experimental standard holds up well in further real world testing, the IESG may advance it to the status of *proposed standard*. A proposed standard is fairly loose, and is based on the experimental work of possibly as little as one organization. Changes may still be made to a protocol in this stage.

Once the bugs appear to have been worked out of a proposed standard and there are at least two independent implementations, the IESG may recommend that a proposed standard be promoted to a *draft standard*. A draft standard will probably not change too much before eventual standardization unless major flaws are found. The primary purpose of a draft standard is to clean up the RFC that documents the protocol and make sure the documentation conforms to actual practice, rather than to change the standard itself.

When a protocol completes this, it becomes an official Internet *standard*. It is assigned an STD number and is published as an STD in addition to an RFC. The absolute minimum time for a standard to be approved as such is 10 months, but in practice, the process almost always takes much longer. The commercial success of the Internet hasn't helped, since standards must now be worked out in the presence of marketers, vulture capitalists, lawyers, NSA spooks, and others with vested interests in seeing particular technologies succeed or fail. Therefore, many of the "standards" that this book references are in either the experimental, proposed, or draft stage. As of publication, there are over 3,800 RFCs. Less than one hundred of these have become STDs, and some of those that have are now obsolete. RFCs relevant to this book are detailed in Table 2-2.

Some RFCs that do not become standards are considered *informational,*. These include RFCs that specify protocols that are widely used but weren't developed within the normal Internet standards track, and haven't been through the formal standardization process. For example, NFS, originally developed by Sun, is described in the informational RFC 1813. Other informational RFCs provide useful information (like users' guides), but don't document a protocol. For example, RFC 1635, *How to Use Anonymous FTP*, is an informational RFC.

Finally, changing technology and increasing experience renders some protocols and their associated RFCs obsolete. These are classified as *historic*. Historic protocols include IMAP3 (replaced by IMAP4), POP2 (replaced by POP3), and Remote Procedure Call Version 1 (replaced by Remote Procedure Call Version 2).

In addition to its maturity level, a protocol has a requirement level. The possible requirement levels are:

Not recommended
    Should not be implemented by anyone.

Limited use
    May have to be implemented in certain unusual situations but won't be needed by most hosts. Mainly these are experimental protocols.

Elective
    Can be implemented by anyone who wants to use the protocol. For example, RFC 2045, *Multipurpose Internet Mail Extensions*, is a Draft Elective Standard.

Recommended
    Should be implemented by Internet hosts that don't have a specific reason not to implement it. Most protocols that you are familiar with (like TCP and UDP, SMTP for email, Telnet for remote login, etc.) are recommended.

Required
    Must be implemented by all Internet hosts. There are very few required protocols. IP itself is one (RFC 791), but even protocols as important as TCP or UDP are only recommended. A standard is only required if it is absolutely essential to the functioning of a host on the Internet.

Table 2-2 lists the RFCs and STDs that provide formal documentation for the protocols discussed in this book.

Table 2-2. Selected Internet RFCs

RFC	Title	Maturity level	Requirement level	Description
RFC 3300 STD 1	Internet Official Protocol Standards	Standard	Required	Describes the standardization process and the current status of the different Internet protocols.
RFC 1122 RFC 1123 STD 3	Host Requirements	Standard	Required	Documents the protocols that must be supported by all Internet hosts at different layers (data link layer, IP layer, transport layer, and application layer).
RFC 791 RFC 919 RFC 922 RFC 950 STD 5	Internet Protocol	Standard	Required	The IP internet layer protocol.
RFC 768 STD 6	User Datagram Protocol	Standard	Recommended	An unreliable, connectionless transport layer protocol.
RFC 792 STD 5	Internet Control Message Protocol (ICMP)	Standard	Required	An internet layer protocol that uses raw IP datagrams but is not supported by Java. Its most familiar use is the *ping* program.
RFC 793 STD 7	Transmission Control Protocol	Standard	Recommended	A reliable, connection-oriented, streaming transport layer protocol.
RFC 2821	Simple Mail Transfer Protocol	Proposed standard	Recommended	The application layer protocol by which one host transfers email to another host. This standard doesn't say anything about email user interfaces; it covers the mechanism for passing email from one computer to another.
RFC 822 STD 11	Format of Electronic Mail Messages	Standard	Recommended	The basic syntax for ASCII text email messages. MIME is designed to extend this to support binary data while ensuring that the messages transferred still conform to this standard.
RFC 854 RFC 855 STD 8	Telnet Protocol	Standard	Recommended	An application-layer remote login service for command-line environments based around an abstract network virtual terminal (NVT) and TCP.
RFC 862 STD 20	Echo Protocol	Standard	Recommended	An application-layer protocol that echoes back all data it receives over both TCP and UDP; useful as a debugging tool.
RFC 863 STD 21	Discard Protocol	Standard	Elective	An application layer protocol that receives packets of data over both TCP and UDP and sends no response to the client; useful as a debugging tool.
RFC 864 STD 22	Character Generator Protocol	Standard	Elective	An application layer protocol that sends an indefinite sequence of ASCII characters to any client that connects over either TCP or UDP; also useful as a debugging tool.

Table 2-2. Selected Internet RFCs (continued)

RFC	Title	Maturity level	Requirement level	Description
RFC 865 STD 23	Quote of the Day	Standard	Elective	An application layer protocol that returns a quotation to any user who connects over either TCP or UDP and then closes the connection.
RFC 867 STD 25	Daytime Protocol	Standard	Elective	An application layer protocol that sends a human-readable ASCII string indicating the current date and time at the server to any client that connects over TCP or UDP. This contrasts with the various NTP and Time Server protocols, which do not return data that can be easily read by humans.
RFC 868 STD 26	Time Protocol	Standard	Elective	An application layer protocol that sends the time in seconds since midnight, January 1, 1900 to a client connecting over TCP or UDP. The time is sent as a machine-readable, 32-bit signed integer. The standard is incomplete in that it does not specify how the integer is encoded in 32 bits, but in practice a two's complement, big-endian integer is used.
RFC 959 STD 9	File Transfer Protocol	Standard	Recommended	An optionally authenticated, two-socket application layer protocol for file transfer that uses TCP.
RFC 977	Network News Transfer Protocol	Proposed standard	Elective	The application layer protocol by which Usenet news is transferred from machine to machine over TCP; used by both news clients talking to news servers and news servers talking to each other.
RFC 1034 RFC 1035 STD 13	Domain Name System	Standard	Recommended	The collection of distributed software by which hostnames that human beings can remember, like *www.oreilly.com*, are translated into numbers that computers can understand, like *198.112.208.11*. This STD defines how domain name servers on different hosts communicate with each other using UDP.
RFC 1112	Host Extensions for IP Multicasting	Standard	Recommended	The internet layer methods by which conforming systems can direct a single packet of data to multiple hosts. This is called multicasting; Java's support for multicasting is discussed in Chapter 14.
RFC 1153	Digest Message Format for Mail	Experimental	Limited use	A format for combining multiple postings to a mailing list into a single message.
RFC 1288	Finger Protocol	Draft standard	Elective	An application layer protocol for requesting information about a user at a remote site. It can be a security risk.
RFC 1305	Network Time Protocol (Version 3)	Draft standard	Elective	A more precise application layer protocol for synchronizing clocks between systems that attempts to account for network latency.
RFC 1738	Uniform Resource Locators	Proposed standard	Elective	Full URLs like *http://www.amnesty.org/* and *ftp://ftp.ibiblio.org/pub/multimedia/chinese-music/Dream_Of_Red_Mansion/HLM04.Handkerchief.au.*

Table 2-2. Selected Internet RFCs (continued)

RFC	Title	Maturity level	Requirement level	Description
RFC 1808	Relative Uniform Resource Locators	Proposed standard	Elective	Partial URLs like */javafaq/books/* and *../examples/07/index.html* used as values of the HREF attribute of an HTML A element.
RFC 1939 STD 53	Post Office Protocol, Version 3	Standard	Elective	An application-layer protocol used by sporadically connected email clients such as Eudora to retrieve mail from a server over TCP.
RFC 1945	Hypertext Transfer Protocol (HTTP 1.0)	Informational	N/A	Version 1.0 of the application layer protocol used by web browsers talking to web servers over TCP; developed by the W3C rather than the IETF.
RFC 2045 RFC 2046 RFC 2047	Multipurpose Internet Mail Extensions	Draft standard	Elective	A means of encoding binary data and non-ASCII text for transmission through Internet email and other ASCII-oriented protocols.
RFC 2068	Hypertext Transfer Protocol (HTTP 1.1)	Proposed standard	Elective	Version 1.1 of the application layer protocol used by web browsers talking to web servers over TCP.
RFC 2141	Uniform Resource Names (URN) Syntax	Proposed standard	Elective	Similar to URLs but intended to refer to actual resources in a persistent fashion rather than the transient location of those resources.
RFC 2373	IP Version 6 Addressing Architecture	Proposed standard	Elective	The format and meaning of IPv6 addresses.
RFC 2396	Uniform Resource Identifiers (URI): Generic Syntax	Proposed standard	Elective	Similar to URLs but cut a broader path. For instance, ISBN numbers may be URIs even if the book cannot be retrieved over the Internet.
RFC 3501	Internet Message Access Protocol Version 4rev1	Proposed standard	Elective	A protocol for remotely accessing a mailbox stored on a server including downloading messages, deleting messages, and moving messages into and out of different folders.

The IETF has traditionally worked behind the scenes, codifying and standardizing existing practice. Although its activities are completely open to the public, it's traditionally been very low-profile. There simply aren't that many people who get excited about the details of network arcana like the Internet Gateway Message Protocol (IGMP). The participants in the process have mostly been engineers and computer scientists, including many from academia as well as the corporate world. Consequently, despite often vociferous debates about ideal implementations, most serious IETF efforts have produced reasonable standards.

Unfortunately, that can't be said of the IETF's efforts to produce web (as opposed to Internet) standards. In particular, the IETF's early effort to standardize HTML was a colossal failure. The refusal of Netscape and other key vendors to participate or even acknowledge the process was a crucial problem. That HTML was simple enough and high-profile enough to attract the attention of assorted market-droids and random flamers didn't help matters either. Thus, in October 1994 the World Wide Web

Consortium was formed as a vendor-controlled body that might be able to avoid the pitfalls that plagued the IETF's efforts to standardize HTML and HTTP.

W3C Recommendations

Although the W3C standardization process is similar to the IETF process (a series of working drafts hashed out on mailing lists resulting in an eventual specification), the W3C is a fundamentally different organization. Whereas the IETF is open to participation by anyone, only corporations and other organizations may become members of the W3C. Individuals are specifically excluded. Furthermore, although nonprofit organizations like the World Wide Web Artists Consortium (WWWAC) may join the W3C, only the employees of these organizations may participate in W3C activities. Their volunteer members are not welcome. Specific individual experts are occasionally invited to participate on a particular working group even though they are not employees of a W3C member company. However, the number of such individuals is quite small relative to the number of interested experts in the broader community. Membership in the W3C costs $50,000 a year ($5,000 a year for nonprofits) with a minimum 3-year commitment. Membership in the IETF costs $0 a year with no commitment beyond a willingness to participate. And although many people participate in developing W3C standards, each standard is ultimately approved or vetoed by one individual, W3C director Tim Berners-Lee. IETF standards are approved by a consensus of the people who worked on the standard. Clearly, the IETF is a much more democratic (some would say anarchic) and open organization than the W3C.

Despite the W3C's strong bias toward the corporate members that pay its bills, it has so far managed to do a better job of navigating the politically tricky waters of Web standardization than the IETF. It has produced several HTML standards, as well as a variety of others such as HTTP, PICS, XML, CSS, MathML, and more. The W3C has had considerably less success in convincing vendors like Netscape and Microsoft to fully and consistently implement its standards.

The W3C has five basic levels of standards:

Note
  A note is generally one of two things: either an unsolicited submission by a W3C member (similar to an IETF Internet draft) or random musings by W3C staff or related parties that do not actually describe a full proposal (similar to an IETF informational RFC). Notes will not necessarily lead to the formation of a working group or a W3C recommendation.

Working drafts
  A working draft is a reflection of the current thinking of some (not necessarily all) members of a working group. It should eventually lead to a proposed recommendation, but by the time it does so it may have changed substantially.

Candidate recommendation

A candidate recommendation indicates that the working draft has reached consensus on all major issues and is ready for third-party comment and implementations. If the implementations do not uncover any obstructions, the spec can be promoted to a proposed recommendation.

Proposed recommendation

A proposed recommendation is mostly complete and unlikely to undergo more than minor editorial changes. The main purpose of a proposed recommendation is to work out bugs in the specification document rather than in the underlying technology being documented.

Recommendation

A recommendation is the highest level of W3C standard. However, the W3C is very careful not to actually call this a "standard" for fear of running afoul of antitrust statutes. The W3C describes a recommendation as a "work that represents consensus within W3C and has the Director's stamp of approval. W3C considers that the ideas or technology specified by a Recommendation are appropriate for widespread deployment and promote W3C's mission."

The W3C has not been around long enough to develop a need for a historical or informational standard status. Another difference the IETF and the W3C is that the W3C process rarely fails to elevate a standard to full recommendation status once work has actively commenced—that is, once a working group has been formed. This contrasts markedly with the IETF, which has more than a thousand proposed and draft standards, but only a few dozen actual standards.

PR Standards

In recent years, companies seeking a little free press or perhaps a temporary boost to their stock price have abused both the W3C and IETF standards processes. The IETF will accept a submission from anyone, and the W3C will accept a submission from any W3C member. The IETF calls these submissions "Internet drafts" and publishes them for six months before deleting them. The W3C refers to such submissions as "acknowledged submissions" and publishes them indefinitely. However, neither organization actually promises to do more than acknowledge receipt of these documents. In particular, they do not promise to form a working group or begin the standardization process. Nonetheless, press releases invariably misrepresent the submission of such a document as a far more significant event than it actually is. PR reps can generally count on suckering at least a few clueless reporters who aren't up to speed on the intimate details of the standardization process. However, you should recognize these ploys for what they are.

CHAPTER 3

Basic Web Concepts

Java can do a lot more than create flashy web pages. Nonetheless, many of your programs will be applets on web pages, servlets running on the server, or web services that need to talk to other web servers and clients. Therefore, it's important to have a solid understanding of the interaction between web servers and web browsers.

The Hypertext Transfer Protocol (HTTP) is a standard that defines how a web client talks to a server and how data is transferred from the server back to the client. The architecture and design of the HTTP protocol is Representational State Transfer (REST). HTTP can be used to transfer data in essentially any format, from TIFF pictures to Microsoft Word documents to DBase files. However, far and away the most common format for data transferred over the Web and in some sense the Web's native format is the Hypertext Markup Language (HTML). HTML is a simple standard for describing the semantic value of textual data. You can say "this is a header", "this is a list item", "this deserves emphasis", and so on, but you can't specify how headers, lists, and other items are formatted: formatting is up to the browser. HTML is a "hypertext markup language" because it includes a way to specify links to other documents identified by URLs. A URL is a way to unambiguously identify the location of a resource on the Internet. To understand network programming, you'll need to understand URLs, HTML, and HTTP in somewhat more detail than the average web page designer.

URIs

A Uniform Resource Identifier (URI) is a string of characters in a particular syntax that identifies a resource. The resource identified may be a file on a server, but it may also be an email address, a news message, a book, a person's name, an Internet host, the current stock price of Sun Microsystems, or something else. An absolute URI is made up of a scheme for the URI and a scheme-specific part, separated by a colon, like this:

```
scheme:scheme-specific-part
```

The syntax of the scheme-specific part depends on the scheme being used. Current schemes include:

data
 Base64-encoded data included directly in a link; see RFC 2397

file
 A file on a local disk

ftp
 An FTP server

http
 A World Wide Web server using the Hypertext Transfer Protocol

gopher
 A Gopher server

mailto
 An email address

news
 A Usenet newsgroup

telnet
 A connection to a Telnet-based service

urn
 A Uniform Resource Name

In addition, Java makes heavy use of nonstandard custom schemes such as *rmi*, *jndi*, and *doc* for various purposes. We'll look at the mechanism behind this in Chapter 16, when we discuss protocol handlers.

There is no specific syntax that applies to the scheme-specific parts of all URIs. However, many have a hierarchical form, like this:

    //authority/path?query

The *authority* part of the URI names the authority responsible for resolving the rest of the URI. For instance, the URI *http://www.ietf.org/rfc/rfc2396.txt* has the scheme *http* and the authority *www.ietf.org*. This means the server at *www.ietf.org* is responsible for mapping the path */rfc/rfc2396.txt* to a resource. This URI does not have a query part. The URI *http://www.powells.com/cgi-bin/biblio?inkey=62-1565928709-0* has the scheme *http*, the authority *www.powells.com*, the path */biblio*, and the query *inkey=62-1565928709-0*. The URI *urn:isbn:156592870* has the scheme *urn* but doesn't follow the hierarchical *//authority/path?query* form for scheme-specific parts.

Although most current examples of URIs use an Internet host as an authority, future schemes may not. However, if the authority is an Internet host, optional usernames and ports may also be provided to make the authority more specific. For example, the URI *ftp://mp3:mp3@ci43198-a.ashvil1.nc.home.com:33/VanHalen-Jump.mp3* has the authority *mp3:mp3@ci43198-a.ashvil1.nc.home.com:33*. This authority has the username *mp3*, the password *mp3*, the host *ci43198-a.ashvil1.nc.home.com*, and the port *33*. It has the scheme *ftp* and the path */VanHalen-Jump.mp3*. (In most cases, including the password in the URI is a big security hole unless, as here, you really do want everyone in the universe to know the password.)

The path (which includes its initial */*) is a string that the authority can use to determine which resource is identified. Different authorities may interpret the same path to refer to different resources. For instance, the path */index.html* means one thing when the authority is *www.landoverbaptist.org* and something very different when the authority is *www.churchofsatan.com*. The path may be hierarchical, in which case the individual parts are separated by forward slashes, and the . and .. operators are used to navigate the hierarchy. These are derived from the pathname syntax on the Unix operating systems where the Web and URLs were invented. They conveniently map to a filesystem stored on a Unix web server. However, there is no guarantee that the components of any particular path actually correspond to files or directories on any particular filesystem. For example, in the URI *http://www.amazon.com/exec/ obidos/ISBN%3D1565924851/cafeaulaitA/002-3777605-3043449*, all the pieces of the hierarchy are just used to pull information out of a database that's never stored in a filesystem. *ISBN%3D1565924851* selects the particular book from the database by its ISBN number, *cafeaulaitA* specifies who gets the referral fee if a purchase is made from this link, and *002-3777605-3043449* is a session key used to track the visitor's path through the site.

Some URIs aren't at all hierarchical, at least in the filesystem sense. For example, *snews://secnews.netscape.com/netscape.devs-java* has a path of */netscape.devs-java*. Although there's some hierarchy to the newsgroup names indicated by the . between *netscape* and *netscape.devs-java*, it's not visible as part of the URI.

The scheme part is composed of lowercase letters, digits, and the plus sign, period, and hyphen. The other three parts of a typical URI (authority, path, and query) should each be composed of the ASCII alphanumeric characters; that is, the letters A–Z, a–z, and the digits 0–9. In addition, the punctuation characters - _ . ! ~ * ' may also be used. All other characters, including non-ASCII alphanumerics such as á and π, should be escaped by a percent sign (%) followed by the hexadecimal code for the character. For instance, á would be encoded as %E1. A URL so transformed is said to have been "x-www-form-urlencoded".

This process assumes that the character set is the Latin 1. The URI and URL specifications don't actually say what character set should be used, which means most software tends to use the local default character set. Thus, URLs containing non-ASCII characters aren't very interoperable across different platforms and languages. With the Web becoming more international and less English daily, this situation has become increasingly problematic. Work is ongoing to define Internationalized Resource Identifiers (IRIs) that can use the full range of Unicode. At the time of this writing, the IRI draft specification indicates that non-ASCII characters should be encoded by first converting them to UTF-8, then percent-escaping each byte of the UTF-8, as specified above. For instance, the Greek letter π is Unicode code point 3C0. In UTF-8, this letter is encoded as the three bytes E0, A7, 80. Thus in a URL it would be encoded as %E0%A7%80.

Punctuation characters such as / and @ must also be encoded with percent escapes if they are used in any role other than what's specified for them in the scheme-specific part of a particular URL. For example, the forward slashes in the URI *http:// www.cafeaulait.org/books/javaio/* do not need to be encoded as %2F because they serve to delimit the hierarchy as specified for the *http* URI scheme. However, if a filename includes a / character—for instance, if the last directory were named *Java I/O* instead of *javaio* to more closely match the name of the book—the URI would have to be written as *http://www.cafeaulait.org/books/Java%20I%2FO/*. This is not as far-fetched as it might sound to Unix or Windows users. Mac filenames frequently include a forward slash. Filenames on many platforms often contain characters that need to be encoded, including @, $, +, =, and many more.

URNs

There are two types of URIs: Uniform Resource Locators (URLs) and Uniform Resource Names (URNs). A URL is a pointer to a particular resource on the Internet at a particular location. For example, *http://www.oreilly.com/catalog/javanp3/* is one of several URLs for the book *Java Network Programming*. A URN is a name for a particular resource but without reference to a particular location. For instance, *urn:isbn: 1565928709* is a URN referring to the same book. As this example shows, URNs, unlike URLs, are not limited to Internet resources.

The goal of URNs is to handle resources that are mirrored in many different locations or that have moved from one site to another; they identify the resource itself, not the place where the resource lives. For instance, when given a URN for a particular piece of software, an FTP program should get the file from the nearest mirror site. Given a URN for a book, a browser might reserve the book at the local library or order a copy from a bookstore.

A URN has the general form:

```
urn:namespace:resource_name
```

The *namespace* is the name of a collection of certain kinds of resources maintained by some authority. The *resource_name* is the name of a resource within that collection. For instance, the URN *urn:ISBN:1565924851* identifies a resource in the *ISBN* namespace with the identifier *1565924851*. Of all the books published, this one selects the first edition of *Java I/O*.

The exact syntax of resource names depends on the namespace. The ISBN namespace expects to see strings composed of 10 or 13 characters, all of which are digits—with the single exception that the last character may be the letter *X* (either upper- or lowercase) instead. Furthermore, ISBNs may contain hyphens that are ignored when comparing. Other namespaces will use very different syntaxes for resource names. The IANA is responsible for handing out namespaces to different organizations, as described in RFC 3406. Basically, you have to submit an Internet draft to the IETF and publish an announcement on the urn-nid mailing list for public comment and discussion before formal standardization.

URLs

A URL identifies the location of a resource on the Internet. It specifies the protocol used to access a server (e.g., FTP, HTTP), the name of the server, and the location of a file on that server. A typical URL looks like *http://www.ibiblio.org/javafaq/ javatutorial.html*. This specifies that there is a file called *javatutorial.html* in a directory called *javafaq* on the server *www.ibiblio.org*, and that this file can be accessed via the HTTP protocol. The syntax of a URL is:

    protocol://username@hostname:port/path/filename?query#fragment

Here the protocol is another word for what was called the scheme of the URI. (*Scheme* is the word used in the URI RFC. *Protocol* is the word used in the Java documentation.) In a URL, the protocol part can be *file*, *ftp*, *http*, *https*, *gopher*, *news*, *telnet*, *wais*, or various other strings (though not *urn*).

The *hostname* part of a URL is the name of the server that provides the resource you want, such as *www.oreilly.com* or *utopia.poly.edu*. It can also be the server's IP address, such as 204.148.40.9 or 128.238.3.21. The *username* is an optional username for the server. The *port* number is also optional. It's not necessary if the service is running on its default port (port 80 for HTTP servers).

The *path* points to a particular directory on the specified server. The path is relative to the document root of the server, not necessarily to the root of the filesystem on the server. As a rule, servers that are open to the public do not show their entire filesystem to clients. Rather, they show only the contents of a specified directory. This directory is called the document root, and all paths and filenames are relative to it. Thus, on a Unix server, all files that are available to the public might be in */var/public/html*, but to somebody connecting from a remote machine, this directory looks like the root of the filesystem.

The filename points to a particular file in the directory specified by the path. It is often omitted—in which case, it is left to the server's discretion what file, if any, to send. Many servers send an index file for that directory, often called *index.html* or *Welcome.html*. Some send a list of the files and folders in the directory, as shown in Figure 3-1. Others may send a 403 Forbidden error message, as shown in Figure 3-2.

The *query* string provides additional arguments for the server. It's commonly used only in *http* URLs, where it contains form data for input to programs running on the server.

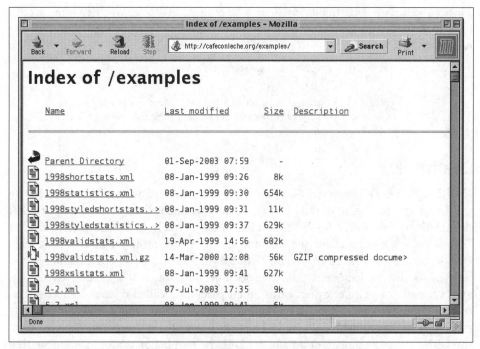

Figure 3-1. A web server configured to send a directory list when no index file exists

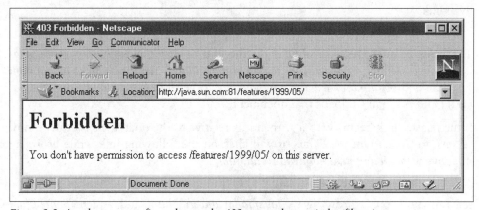

Figure 3-2. A web server configured to send a 403 error when no index file exists

Finally, the *fragment* references a particular part of the remote resource. If the remote resource is HTML, the fragment identifier names an anchor in the HTML document. If the remote resource is XML, the fragment identifier is an XPointer. Some documents refer to the fragment part of the URL as a "section"; Java documents rather unaccountably refer to the fragment identifier as a "Ref". A named anchor is created in an HTML document with a tag, like this:

```
<A NAME="xtocid1902914">Comments</A>
```

This tag identifies a particular point in a document. To refer to this point, a URL includes not only the document's filename but the named anchor separated from the rest of the URL by a #:

```
http://www.cafeaulait.org/javafaq.html#xtocid1902914
```

 Technically, a string that contains a fragment identifier is a URL reference, not a URL. Java, however, does not distinguish between URLs and URL references.

Relative URLs

A URL tells the web browser a lot about a document: the protocol used to retrieve the document, the name of the host where the document lives, and the path to that document on the host. Most of this information is likely to be the same for other URLs that are referenced in the document. Therefore, rather than requiring each URL to be specified in its entirety, a URL may inherit the protocol, hostname, and path of its parent document (i.e., the document in which it appears). URLs that aren't complete but inherit pieces from their parent are called *relative* URLs. In contrast, a completely specified URL is called an *absolute URL*. In a relative URL, any pieces that are missing are assumed to be the same as the corresponding pieces from the URL of the document in which the URL is found. For example, suppose that while browsing *http://www.ibiblio.org/javafaq/javatutorial.html* you click on this hyperlink:

```
<a href="javafaq.html">
```

The browser cuts *javatutorial.html* off the end of *http://www.ibiblio.org/javafaq/javatutorial.html* to get *http://www.ibiblio.org/javafaq/*. Then it attaches *javafaq.html* onto the end of *http://www.ibiblio.org/javafaq/* to get *http://www.ibiblio.org/javafaq/javafaq.html*. Finally, it loads that document.

If the relative link begins with a /, then it is relative to the document root instead of relative to the current file. Thus, if you click on the following link while browsing *http://www.ibiblio.org/javafaq/javatutorial.html*:

```
<a href="/boutell/faq/www_faq.html">
```

the browser would throw away */javafaq/javatutorial.html* and attach */boutell/faq/www_faq.html* to the end of *http://www.ibiblio.org* to get *http://www.ibiblio.org/boutell/faq/www_faq.html*.

Relative URLs have a number of advantages. First—and least important—they save a little typing. More importantly, relative URLs allow a single document tree to be served by multiple protocols: for instance, both FTP and HTTP. The HTTP might be used for direct surfing, while the FTP could be used for mirroring the site. Most importantly of all, relative URLs allow entire trees of documents to be moved or copied from one site to another without breaking all the internal links.

HTML, SGML, and XML

HTML is the primary format used for Web documents. As I said earlier, HTML is a simple standard for describing the semantic content of textual data. The idea of describing a text's semantics rather than its appearance comes from an older standard called the Standard Generalized Markup Language (SGML). Standard HTML is an instance of SGML. SGML was invented in the mid-1970s by Charles Goldfarb, Edward Mosher, and Raymond Lorie at IBM. SGML is now an International Standards Organization (ISO) standard, specifically ISO 8879:1986.

SGML and, by inheritance, HTML are based on the notion of design by meaning rather than design by appearance. You don't say that you want some text printed in 18-point type; you say that it is a top-level heading (<H1> in HTML). Likewise, you don't say that a word should be placed in italics. Rather, you say it should be emphasized (<EM> in HTML). It is left to the browser to determine how to best display headings or emphasized text.

The tags used to mark up the text are case-insensitive. Thus, <STRONG> is the same as <strong> is the same as <Strong> is the same as <StrONg>. Some tags have a matching end-tag to define a region of text. An end-tag is the same as the start-tag, except that the opening angle bracket is followed by a /. For example: <STRONG>this text is strong</STRONG>; <EM>this text is emphasized</EM>. The entire text from the beginning of the start-tag to the end of the end-tag is called an *element*. Thus, <STRONG> this text is strong</STRONG> is a STRONG element.

HTML elements may nest but they should not overlap. The first line in the following example is standard-conforming. The second line is not, though many browsers accept it nonetheless:

```
<STRONG><EM>Jack and Jill went up the hill</EM></STRONG>
<STRONG><EM>to fetch a pail of water</STRONG></EM>
```

Some elements have additional attributes that are encoded as name-value pairs on the start-tag. The <H1> tag and most other paragraph-level tags may have an ALIGN attribute that says whether the header should be centered, left-aligned, or right-aligned. For example:

```
<H1 ALIGN=CENTER> This is a centered H1 heading </H1>
```

The value of an attribute may be enclosed in double or single quotes, like this:

```
<H1 ALIGN="CENTER"> This is a centered H1 heading </H1>
<H2 ALIGN='LEFT'> This is a left-aligned H2 heading </H2>
```

Quotes are required only if the value contains embedded spaces. When processing HTML, you need to be prepared for attribute values that do and don't have quotes.

There have been several versions of HTML over the years. The current standard is HTML 4.0, most of which is supported by current web browsers, with occasional exceptions. Furthermore, several companies, notably Netscape, Microsoft, and Sun, have added nonstandard extensions to HTML. These include blinking text, inline movies, frames, and, most importantly for this book, applets. Some of these extensions—for example, the `<APPLET>` tag—are allowed but deprecated in HTML 4.0. Others, such as Netscape's notorious `<BLINK>`, come out of left field and have no place in a semantically-oriented language like HTML.

HTML 4.0 may be the end of the line, aside from minor fixes. The W3C has decreed that HTML is getting too bulky to layer more features on top of. Instead, new development will focus on XML, a semantic language that allows page authors to create the elements they need rather than relying on a few fixed elements such as P and LI. For example, if you're writing a web page with a price list, you would likely have an SKU element, a PRICE element, a MANUFACTURER element, a PRODUCT element, and so forth. That might look something like this:

```
<PRODUCT MANUFACTURER="IBM">
  <NAME>Lotus Smart Suite</NAME>
  <VERSION>9.8</VERSION>
  <PLATFORM>Windows</PLATFORM>
  <PRICE CURRENCY="US">299.95</PRICE>
  <SKU>DO5WGML</SKU>
</PRODUCT>
```

This looks a lot like HTML, in much the same way that Java looks like C. There are elements and attributes. Tags are set off by < and >. Attributes are enclosed in quotation marks, and so forth. However, instead of being limited to a finite set of tags, you can create all the new and unique tags you need. Since no browser can know in advance all the different elements that may appear, a *stylesheet* is used to describe how each of the items should be displayed.

XML has another advantage over HTML that may not be obvious from this simple example. HTML can be quite sloppy. Elements are opened but not closed. Attribute values may or may not be enclosed in quotes. The quotes may or may not be present. XML tightens all this up. It lays out very strict requirements for the syntax of a well-formed XML document, and it requires that browsers reject all malformed documents. Browsers may not attempt to fix the problem and make a best-faith effort to display what they think the author meant. They must simply report the error. Furthermore, an XML document may have a Document Type Definition (DTD), which can impose additional constraints on valid documents. For example, a DTD may require that every PRODUCT element contain exactly one NAME element. This has a number of advantages, but the key one here is that XML documents are far easier to parse than HTML documents. As a programmer, you will find it much easier to work with XML than HTML.

XML can be used both for pure XML pages and for embedding new kinds of content in HTML and XHTML. For example, the Mathematical Markup Language, MathML, is an XML application for including mathematical equations in web pages. SMIL, the Synchronized Multimedia Integration Language, is an XML application for including timed multimedia such as slide shows and subtitled videos on web pages. More recently, the W3C has released several versions of XHTML. This language uses the familiar HTML vocabulary (p for paragraphs, tr for table rows, img for pictures, and so forth) but requires the document to follow XML's stricter rules: all attribute values must be quoted; every start-tag must have a matching end-tag; elements can nest but cannot overlap; etc. For a lot more information about XML, see *XML in a Nutshell* by Elliotte Rusty Harold and W. Scott Means (O'Reilly).

HTTP

HTTP is the standard protocol for communication between web browsers and web servers. HTTP specifies how a client and server establish a connection, how the client requests data from the server, how the server responds to that request, and finally, how the connection is closed. HTTP connections use the TCP/IP protocol for data transfer. For each request from client to server, there is a sequence of four steps:

Making the connection
> The client establishes a TCP connection to the server on port 80, by default; other ports may be specified in the URL.

Making a request
> The client sends a message to the server requesting the page at a specified URL. The format of this request is typically something like:

```
GET /index.html HTTP/1.0
```

GET specifies the operation being requested. The operation requested here is for the server to return a representation of a resource. /index.html is a relative URL that identifies the resource requested from the server. This resource is assumed to reside on the machine that receives the request, so there is no need to prefix it with http://www.thismachine.com/. HTTP/1.0 is the version of the protocol that the client understands. The request is terminated with two carriage return/linefeed pairs (\r\n\r\n in Java parlance), regardless of how lines are terminated on the client or server platform.

Although the GET line is all that is required, a client request can include other information as well. This takes the following form:

```
Keyword: Value
```

The most common such keyword is Accept, which tells the server what kinds of data the client can handle (though servers often ignore this). For example, the following line says that the client can handle four MIME media types, corresponding to HTML documents, plain text, and JPEG and GIF images:

```
Accept: text/html, text/plain, image/gif, image/jpeg
```

User-Agent is another common keyword that lets the server know what browser is being used, allowing the server to send files optimized for the particular browser type. The line below says that the request comes from Version 2.4 of the Lynx browser:

```
User-Agent: Lynx/2.4 libwww/2.1.4
```

All but the oldest first-generation browsers also include a Host field specifying the server's name, which allows web servers to distinguish between different named hosts served from the same IP address. Here's an example:

```
Host: www.cafeaulait.org
```

Finally, the request is terminated with a blank line—that is, two carriage return/linefeed pairs, \r\n\r\n. A complete request might look like this:

```
GET /index.html HTTP/1.0
Accept: text/html, text/plain, image/gif, image/jpeg
User-Agent: Lynx/2.4 libwww/2.1.4
Host: www.cafeaulait.org
```

In addition to GET, there are several other request types. HEAD retrieves only the header for the file, not the actual data. This is commonly used to check the modification date of a file, to see whether a copy stored in the local cache is still valid. POST sends form data to the server, PUT uploads a resource to the server, and DELETE removes a resource from the server.

The response

The server sends a response to the client. The response begins with a response code, followed by a header full of metadata, a blank line, and the requested document or an error message. Assuming the requested document is found, a typical response looks like this:

```
HTTP/1.1 200 OK
Date: Mon, 15 Sep 2003 21:06:50 GMT
Server: Apache/2.0.40 (Red Hat Linux)
Last-Modified: Tue, 15 Apr 2003 17:28:57 GMT
Connection: close
Content-Type: text/html; charset=ISO-8859-1
Content-length: 107

<html>
<head>
<title>
A Sample HTML file
</title>
</head>
<body>
The rest of the document goes here
</body>
</html>
```

The first line indicates the protocol the server is using (HTTP/1.1), followed by a response code. 200 OK is the most common response code, indicating that the request was successful. Table 3-1 is a complete list of the response codes used by HTTP 1.0; HTTP 1.1 adds many more to this list. The other header lines identify the date the request was made in the server's time frame, the server software (Apache 2.0.40), the date this document was last modified, a promise that the server will close the connection when it's finished sending, the MIME content type, and the length of the document delivered (not counting this header)—in this case, 107 bytes.

Closing the connection

Either the client or the server or both close the connection. Thus, a separate network connection is used for each request. If the client reconnects, the server retains no memory of the previous connection or its results. A protocol that retains no memory of past requests is called *stateless*; in contrast, a *stateful* protocol such as FTP can process many requests before the connection is closed. The lack of state is both a strength and a weakness of HTTP.

Table 3-1. HTTP 1.0 response codes

Response code	Meaning
2xx Successful	Response codes between 200 and 299 indicate that the request was received, understood, and accepted.
200 OK	This is the most common response code. If the request used GET or POST, the requested data is contained in the response along with the usual headers. If the request used HEAD, only the header information is included.
201 Created	The server has created a data file at a URL specified in the body of the response. The web browser should now attempt to load that URL. This is sent only in response to POST requests.
202 Accepted	This rather uncommon response indicates that a request (generally from POST) is being processed, but the processing is not yet complete so no response can be returned. The server should return an HTML page that explains the situation to the user, provides an estimate of when the request is likely to be completed, and, ideally, has a link to a status monitor of some kind.
204 No Content	The server has successfully processed the request but has no information to send back to the client. This is usually the result of a poorly written form-processing program that accepts data but does not return a response to the user indicating that it has finished.
3xx Redirection	Response codes from 300 to 399 indicate that the web browser needs to go to a different page.
300 Multiple Choices	The page requested is available from one or more locations. The body of the response includes a list of locations from which the user or web browser can pick the most appropriate one. If the server prefers one of these locations, the URL of this choice is included in a Location header, which web browsers can use to load the preferred page.
301 Moved Permanently	The page has moved to a new URL. The web browser should automatically load the page at this URL and update any bookmarks that point to the old URL.
302 Moved Temporarily	This unusual response code indicates that a page is temporarily at a new URL but that the document's location will change again in the foreseeable future, so bookmarks should not be updated.
304 Not Modified	The client has performed a GET request but used the If-Modified-Since header to indicate that it wants the document only if it has been recently updated. This status code is returned because the document has not been updated. The web browser will now load the page from a cache.
4xx Client Error	Response codes from 400 to 499 indicate that the client has erred in some fashion, although the error may as easily be the result of an unreliable network connection as of a buggy or nonconforming web browser. The browser should stop sending data to the server as soon as it receives a 4xx response. Unless it is responding to a HEAD request, the server should explain the error status in the body of its response.
400 Bad Request	The client request to the server used improper syntax. This is rather unusual, although it is likely to happen if you're writing and debugging a client.

Table 3-1. HTTP 1.0 response codes (continued)

Response code	Meaning
401 Unauthorized	Authorization, generally username and password controlled, is required to access this page. Either the username and password have not yet been presented or the username and password are invalid.
403 Forbidden	The server understood the request but is deliberately refusing to process it. Authorization will not help. One reason this occurs is that the client asks for a directory listing but the server is not configured to provide it, as shown in Figure 3-1.
404 Not Found	This most common error response indicates that the server cannot find the requested page. It may indicate a bad link, a page that has moved with no forwarding address, a mistyped URL, or something similar.
5xx Server Error	Response codes from 500 to 599 indicate that something has gone wrong with the server, and the server cannot fix the problem.
500 Internal Server Error	An unexpected condition occurred that the server does not know how to handle.
501 Not Implemented	The server does not have the feature that is needed to fulfill this request. A server that cannot handle POST requests might send this response to a client that tried to POST form data to it.
502 Bad Gateway	This response is applicable only to servers that act as proxies or gateways. It indicates that the proxy received an invalid response from a server it was connecting to in an effort to fulfill the request.
503 Service Unavailable	The server is temporarily unable to handle the request, perhaps as a result of overloading or maintenance.

HTTP 1.1 more than doubles the number of responses. However, a response code from 200 to 299 always indicates success, a response code from 300 to 399 always indicates redirection, one from 400 to 499 always indicates a client error, and one from 500 to 599 indicates a server error.

HTTP 1.0 is documented in the informational RFC 1945; it is not an official Internet standard because it was primarily developed outside the IETF by early browser and server vendors. HTTP 1.1 is a proposed standard being developed by the W3C and the HTTP working group of the IETF. It provides for much more flexible and powerful communication between the client and the server. It's also a lot more scalable. It's documented in RFC 2616. HTTP 1.0 is the basic version of the protocol. All current web servers and browsers understand it. HTTP 1.1 adds numerous features to HTTP 1.0, but doesn't change the underlying design or architecture in any significant way. For the purposes of this book, it will usually be sufficient to understand HTTP 1.0.

The primary improvement in HTTP 1.1 is *connection reuse*. HTTP 1.0 opens a new connection for every request. In practice, the time taken to open and close all the connections in a typical web session can outweigh the time taken to transmit the data, especially for sessions with many small documents. HTTP 1.1 allows a browser to send many different requests over a single connection; the connection remains open until it is explicitly closed. The requests and responses are all asynchronous. A browser doesn't need to wait for a response to its first request before sending a second or a third. However, it remains tied to the basic pattern of a client request followed by a server response. Each request and response has the same basic form: a header line, an HTTP header containing metadata, a blank line, and then the data itself.

There are a lot of other, smaller improvements in HTTP 1.1. Requests include a Host header field so that one web server can easily serve different sites at different URLs. Servers and browsers can exchange compressed files and particular byte ranges of a document, both of which decrease network traffic. And HTTP 1.1 is designed to work much better with proxy servers. HTTP 1.1 is a superset of HTTP 1.0, so HTTP 1.1 web servers have no trouble interacting with older browsers that only speak HTTP 1.0, and vice versa.

MIME Media Types

MIME is an open standard for sending multipart, multimedia data through Internet email. The data may be binary, or it may use multiple ASCII and non-ASCII character sets. Although MIME was originally intended just for email, it has become a widely used technique to describe a file's contents so that client software can tell the difference between different kinds of data. For example, a web browser uses MIME to tell whether a file is a GIF image or a printable PostScript file.

 Officially, MIME stands for Multipurpose Internet Mail Extensions, which is the expansion of the acronym used in RFC 2045. However, you will hear other versions—most frequently Multipart Internet Mail Extensions and Multimedia Internet Mail Extensions.

MIME supports more than 100 predefined types of content. Content types are classified at two levels: a type and a subtype. The type shows very generally what kind of data is contained: is it a picture, text, or movie? The subtype identifies the specific type of data: GIF image, JPEG image, TIFF image. For example, HTML's content type is text/html; the type is text, and the subtype is html. The content type for a GIF image is image/gif; the type is image, and the subtype is gif. Table 3-2 lists the more common defined content types. On most systems, a simple text file maintains a mapping between MIME types and the application used to process that type of data; on Unix, this file is called *mime.types*. The most current list of registered MIME types is available from *http://www.iana.org/assignments/media-types/*. For more on MIME, see the *comp.mail.mime* FAQ at *http://www.uni-giessen.de/faq/archiv/mail.mime-faq.part1-9/*.

Web servers use MIME to identify the kind of data they're sending. Web clients use MIME to identify the kind of data they're willing to accept. Most web servers and clients understand at least two MIME text content types, text/html and text/plain, and two image formats, image/gif and image/jpeg. More recent browsers also understand application/xml and several other image formats. Java relies on MIME types to pick the appropriate content handler for a particular stream of data.

Table 3-2. Predefined MIME content types

Type	Subtype	Description
text		The document represents printable text.
	calendar	Calendaring and scheduling information in the iCalendar format; see RFC 2445.
	css	A Cascading Style Sheet used for HTML and XML.
	directory	Address book information such as name, phone number, and email address; used by Netscape vCards; defined in RFCs 2425 and 2426.
	enriched	A very simple HTML-like language for adding basic font and paragraph-level formatting such as bold and italic to email; used by Eudora; defined in RFC 1896.
	html	Hypertext Markup Language as used by web browsers.
	plain	This is supposed to imply raw ASCII text. However, some web servers use `text/plain` as the default MIME type for any file they can't recognize. Therefore, anything and everything, most notably *.class* byte code files, can get identified as a `text/plain` file.
	richtext	An HTML-like markup for encoding formatting into pure ASCII text. It's never really caught on, in large part because of the popularity of HTML.
	rtf	An incompletely defined Microsoft format for word processing files.
	sgml	The Standard Generalized Markup Language; ISO standard 8879:1986.
	tab-separated-values	The interchange format used by many spreadsheets and databases; records are separated by linebreaks and fields by tabs.
	xml	The W3C standard Extensible Markup Language. For various technical reasons, `application/xml` should be used instead, but often isn't.
multipart		Multipart MIME messages encode several different files into one message.
	mixed	Several message parts intended for sequential viewing.
	alternative	The same message in multiple formats so a client may choose the most convenient one.
	digest	A popular format for merging many email messages into a single digest; used by many mailing lists and some FAQ lists.
	parallel	Several parts intended for simultaneous viewing.
	byteranges	Several separately contiguous byte ranges; used in HTTP 1.1.
	encrypted	One part for the body of the message and one part for the information necessary to decode the message.
	signed	One part for the body of the message and one part for the digital signature.
	related	Compound documents formed by aggregating several smaller parts.
	form-data	Form responses.
message		An email message.
	external-body	Just the headers of the email message; the message's body is not included but exists at some other location and is referenced, perhaps by a URL.
	http	An HTTP 1.1 request from a web client to a web server.
	news	A news article.

Table 3-2. Predefined MIME content types (continued)

Type	Subtype	Description
	partial	Part of a longer email message that has been split into multiple parts to allow transmission through email gateways.
	rfc822	A standard email message including headers.
image		Two-dimensional pictures.
	cgm	A Computer Graphics Metafile format image. CGM is ISO standard 8632:1992 for device-independent vector graphics and bitmap images.
	g3fax	The standard for bitmapped fax images.
	gif	A Graphics Interchange Format image.
	jpeg	The Joint Photographic Experts Group file format for bitmapped images with lossy compression.
	png	A Portable Network Graphics Format image. The format was developed at the W3C as a modern replacement for GIF that supports 24-bit color and is not encumbered by patents.
	tiff	The Tagged Image File format from Adobe.
audio		Sound.
	basic	8-bit ISDN μ-law encoded audio with a single channel and a sample rate of eight kilohertz. This is the format used by .au and .snd files and supported by the `java.applet.AudioClip` class.
video		Video.
	mpeg	The Motion Picture Experts Group format for video data with lossy compression.
	quicktime	Apple's proprietary QuickTime movie format. Before being included in a MIME message, QuickTime files must be "flattened".
model		3-D images.
	vrml	A Virtual Reality Modeling Language file, a format for 3-D data on the Web.
	iges	The Initial Graphics Exchange Specification for interchanging documents between different CAD programs.
	mesh	The mesh structures used in finite element and finite difference methods.
application		Binary data specific to some application.
	octet-stream	Unspecified binary data, which is usually saved into a file for the user. This MIME type is sometimes used to serve .class byte code files.
	java	A nonstandard subtype sometimes used to serve .class byte code files.
	postscript	Adobe PostScript.
	dca-rft	IBM's Document Content Architecture-Richly Formatted Text.
	mac-BinHex40	A means of encoding the two forks of a Macintosh document in a single ASCII file.
	pdf	An Adobe Acrobat file.
	zip	A zip compressed file.
	macwriteii	A MacWrite II word-processing document.
	msword	A Microsoft Word document.

Table 3-2. Predefined MIME content types (continued)

Type	Subtype	Description
	xml+xhtml	An XHTML document
	xml	An Extensible Markup Language document.

A MIME-compliant program is not required to understand all these different types of data; it just needs to recognize what it can and cannot handle. Many programs—Netscape Navigator, for example—use various helper programs to display types of content they themselves don't understand.

MIME allows you to define additional nonstandard subtypes by using the prefix x-. For example, the content type `application/x-tex` has the MIME type `application` and the nonstandard subtype x-tex for a TeX document. These x-types are not guaranteed to be understood by any program other than the one that created them. Indeed, two programs may use the same x-type to mean two completely different things, or different programs may use different x-types to mean the same thing. However, many nonstandard types have come into common use; some of the more common ones are listed in Table 3-3.

Table 3-3. X-types

Type	X-subtype	Description
application		Subtypes of an application; the name of the subtype is usually a file format name or an application name.
	x-aiff	SGI's AIFF audio data format.
	x-bitmap	An X Windows bitmap image.
	x-gzip	Data compressed in the GNU gzip format.
	x-dvi	A TeX DVI document.
	x-framemaker	A FrameMaker document.
	x-latex	A LaTeX document.
	x-macBinHex40	Identical to `application/mac-BinHex40`, but older software may use this x-type instead.
	x-mif	A FrameMaker MIF document.
	x-sd	A session directory protocol announcement, used to announce MBONE events.
	x-shar	A shell archive; the Unix equivalent of a Windows or Macintosh self-extracting archive. Software shouldn't be configured to unpack shell archives automatically, because a shell archive can call any program the user who runs it has the rights to call.
	x-tar	A tar archive.
	x-gtar	A GNU tar archive.
	x-tcl	A tool command language (TCL) program. You should never configure your web browser or email program to automatically run programs you download from the web or receive in email messages.

Table 3-3. X-types (continued)

Type	X-subtype	Description
	x-tex	A TeX document.
	x-texinfo	A GNU texinfo document.
	x-troff	A troff document.
	x-troff-man	A troff document written with the *man* macros.
	x-troff-me	A troff document that should be processed using the *me* macros.
	x-troff-ms	A troff document that should be processed using the *ms* macros.
	x-wais-source	A WAIS source.
	x-www-form-urlen-coded	A string that has been encoded like a URL, with + replacing spaces and % escapes replacing non-alphanumeric characters that aren't separators.
audio		
	x-aiff	The same as `application/x-aiff`: an AIFF audio file.
	x-mpeg	The MP3 sound format.
	x-mpeg.mp3	The MP3 sound format.
	x-wav	The Windows WAV sound format.
image		
	x-fits	The FITS image format used primarily by astronomers.
	x-macpict	A Macintosh PICT image.
	x-pict	A Macintosh PICT image.
	x-macpaint	A MacPaint image.
	x-pbm	A portable bitmap image.
	x-portable-bitmap	A portable bitmap image.
	x-pgm	A PGM image.
video		
	x-msvideo	A Microsoft AVI Video for Windows.
	x-sgi-movie	A Silicon Graphics movie.

Server-Side Programs

These days many web pages are not served from static files on the hard drive. Instead, the server generates them dynamically to meet user requests. The content may be pulled from a database or generated algorithmically by a program. Indeed, the actual page delivered to the client may contain data combined from several different sources. In Java, such server-side programs are often written using servlets or Java Server Pages (JSP). They can also be written with other languages, such as C and Perl, or other frameworks, such as ASP and PHP. The concern in this book is not so much with how these programs are written as with how your programs communicate with them. One advantage to HTTP is that it really doesn't matter how the other side of the connection is written, as long as it speaks the same basic HTTP protocol.

The simplest server-side programs run without any input from the user. From the viewpoint of the client, these programs are accessed like any other web page and aren't of much concern to this book. The difference between a web page produced by a program that takes no input and a web page written in static HTML is all on the server side. When writing clients, you don't need to know or care whether the web server is feeding you a file or the output of some program it ran. Your interface to the server is the same in either case.

A slightly more complex server-side program processes user input from HTML forms. A web form is essentially just a way of collecting input from the user, dividing it into neat pieces, and passing those pieces to some program on the server. A client written in Java can perform the same function, either by asking the user for input in its own GUI or by providing its own unique information.

HTTP provides a standard, well understood and well supported means for Java applets and applications to talk to remote systems; therefore, I will cover how to use Java to both receive and send data to the server. There are other ways for Java programs to talk to servers, including Remote Method Invocation (RMI) and SOAP. However, RMI is slow and SOAP is quite complex. By way of contrast, HTTP is mature, robust, better supported across multiple platforms and web servers, and better understood in the web development community.

Example 3-1 and Figure 3-3 show a simple form with two fields that collects a name and an email address. The values the user enters in the form are sent back to the server when the user presses the "Submit Query" button. The program to run when the form data is received is */cgi/reg.pl*; the program is specified in the ACTION attribute of the FORM element. The URL in this parameter is usually a relative URL, as it is in this example.

Example 3-1. A simple form with input fields for a name and an email address

```
<HTML>
<HEAD>
<TITLE>Sample Form</TITLE>
</HEAD>
<BODY>

<FORM METHOD=GET ACTION="/cgi/reg.pl">
<PRE>
Please enter your name:        <INPUT NAME="username" SIZE=40>
Please enter your email address: <INPUT NAME="email" SIZE=40>
</PRE>
<INPUT TYPE="SUBMIT">
</FORM>
</BODY>
</HTML>
```

The web browser reads the data the user types and encodes it in a simple fashion. The name of each field is separated from its value by the equals sign (=). Different

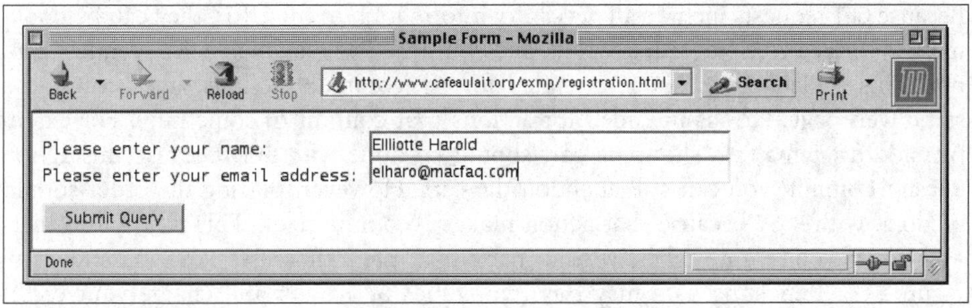

Figure 3-3. A simple form

fields are separated from each other by an ampersand (&). Each field name and value is x-www-form-url-encoded; that is, any non-ASCII or reserved characters are replaced by a percent sign followed by hexadecimal digits giving the value for that character in some character set. Spaces are a special case because they're so common. Instead of being encoded as %20, they become the + sign. The plus sign itself is encoded as %2b. For example, the data from the form in Figure 3-3 is encoded as:

```
username=Elliotte+Harold&email=elharo%40macfaq.com
```

This is called the *query string*.

There are two methods by which the query string can be sent to the server: GET and POST. If the form specifies the GET method, the browser attaches the query string to the URL it sends to the server. Forms that specify POST send the query string on an output stream. The form in Example 3-1 uses GET to communicate with the server, so it connects to the server and sends the following command:

```
GET /cgi/reg.pl?username=Elliotte+Harold&email=elharo%40macfaq.com HTTP/1.0
```

The server uses the path component of the URL to determine which program should handle this request. It passes the query string's set of name-value pairs to that program, which normally takes responsibility for replying to the client.

With the POST method, the web browser sends the usual headers and follows them with a blank line (two successive carriage return/linefeed pairs) and then sends the query string. If the form in Example 3-1 used POST, it would send this to the server:

```
POST /cgi-bin/register.pl HTTP 1.0
Content-type: application/x-www-form-urlencoded
Content-length: 65

username=Elliotte+Harold&email=elharo%40metalab.unc.edu
```

There are many different form tags in HTML that produce pop-up menus, radio buttons, and more. However, although these input widgets appear different to the user, the format of data they send to the server is the same. Each form element provides a name and an encoded string value.

Because GET requests include all necessary information in the URL, they can be book-marked, linked to, spidered, googled, and so forth. The results of a POST request cannot. This is deliberate. GET is intended for noncommital actions, like browsing a static web page. POST is intended for actions that commit to something. For example, adding items to a shopping cart should be done with GET, because this action doesn't commit; you can still abandon the cart. However, placing the order should be done with POST because that action makes a commitment. This is why browsers ask you if you're sure when you go back to a page that uses POST (as shown in Figure 3-4). Reposting data may buy two copies of a book and charge your credit card twice.

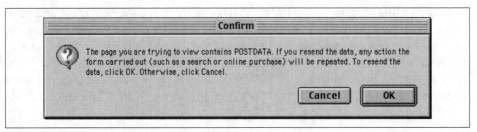

Figure 3-4. Repost confirmation

In practice, POST is vastly overused on the web today. Any safe operation that does not commit the user to anything should use GET rather than POST. Only operations that commit the user should use POST.

CHAPTER 4

Streams

A large part of what network programs do is simple input and output: moving bytes from one system to another. Bytes are bytes; to a large extent, reading data a server sends you is not all that different from reading a file. Sending text to a client is not that different from writing a file. However, input and output (I/O) in Java is organized differently than it is in most other languages, such as Fortran, C, and C++. Consequently, we'll take a few pages to summarize Java's unique approach to I/O.

I/O in Java is built on *streams*. Input streams read data; output streams write data. Different stream classes, like java.io.FileInputStream and sun.net.TelnetOutputStream, read and write particular sources of data. However, all output streams have the same basic methods to write data and all input streams use the same basic methods to read data. After a stream is created, you can often ignore the details of exactly what it is you're reading or writing.

Filter streams can be chained to either an input stream or an output stream. Filters can modify the data as it's read or written—for instance, by encrypting or compressing it—or they can simply provide additional methods for converting the data that's read or written into other formats. For instance, the java.io.DataOutputStream class provides a method that converts an int to four bytes and writes those bytes onto its underlying output stream.

Readers and writers can be chained to input and output streams to allow programs to read and write text (that is, characters) rather than bytes. Used properly, readers and writers can handle a wide variety of character encodings, including multibyte character sets such as SJIS and UTF-8.

Streams are synchronous; that is, when a program (really, a thread) asks a stream to read or write a piece of data, it waits for the data to be read or written before it does anything else. Java 1.4 and later also support non-blocking I/O using channels and buffers. Non-blocking I/O is a little more complicated, but much faster in some high-volume applications, such as web servers. Normally, the basic stream model is all you need and all you should use for clients. Since channels and buffers depend on streams, we'll start with streams and clients and later discuss non-blocking I/O for use with servers in Chapter 12.

Output Streams

Java's basic output class is java.io.OutputStream:

```
public abstract class OutputStream
```

This class provides the fundamental methods needed to write data. These are:

```
public abstract void write(int b) throws IOException
public void write(byte[] data) throws IOException
public void write(byte[] data, int offset, int length)
 throws IOException
public void flush() throws IOException
public void close() throws IOException
```

Subclasses of OutputStream use these methods to write data onto particular media. For instance, a FileOutputStream uses these methods to write data into a file. A TelnetOutputStream uses these methods to write data onto a network connection. A ByteArrayOutputStream uses these methods to write data into an expandable byte array. But whichever medium you're writing to, you mostly use only these same five methods. Sometimes you may not even know exactly what kind of stream you're writing onto. For instance, you won't find TelnetOutputStream in the Java class library documentation. It's deliberately hidden inside the sun packages. It's returned by various methods in various classes in java.net, like the getOutputStream() method of java.net.Socket. However, these methods are declared to return only OutputStream, not the more specific subclass TelnetOutputStream. That's the power of polymorphism. If you know how to use the superclass, you know how to use all the subclasses, too.

OutputStream's fundamental method is write(int b). This method takes an integer from 0 to 255 as an argument and writes the corresponding byte to the output stream. This method is declared abstract because subclasses need to change it to handle their particular medium. For instance, a ByteArrayOutputStream can implement this method with pure Java code that copies the byte into its array. However, a FileOutputStream will need to use native code that understands how to write data in files on the host platform.

Take note that although this method takes an int as an argument, it actually writes an unsigned byte. Java doesn't have an unsigned byte data type, so an int has to be used here instead. The only real difference between an unsigned byte and a signed byte is the interpretation. They're both made up of eight bits, and when you write an int onto a network connection using write(int b), only eight bits are placed on the wire. If an int outside the range 0–255 is passed to write(int b), the least significant byte of the number is written and the remaining three bytes are ignored. (This is the effect of casting an int to a byte.) On rare occasions, however, you may find a buggy third-party class that does something different, such as throwing an `IllegalArgumentException` or always writing 255, so it's best not to rely on this behavior, if possible.

For example, the character generator protocol defines a server that sends out ASCII text. The most popular variation of this protocol sends 72-character lines containing printable ASCII characters. (The printable ASCII characters are those between 33 and 126 inclusive that exclude the various whitespace and control characters.) The first line contains characters 33 through 104, sorted. The second line contains characters 34 through 105. The third line contains characters 35 through 106. This continues through line 29, which contains characters 55 through 126. At that point, the characters wrap around so that line 30 contains characters 56 through 126 followed by character 33 again. Lines are terminated with a carriage return (ASCII 13) and a linefeed (ASCII 10). The output looks like this:

```
!"#$%&'()*+,-./0123456789:;<=>?@ABCDEFGHIJKLMNOPQRSTUVWXYZ[\]^_`abcdefgh
"#$%&'()*+,-./0123456789:;<=>?@ABCDEFGHIJKLMNOPQRSTUVWXYZ[\]^_`abcdefghi
#$%&'()*+,-./0123456789:;<=>?@ABCDEFGHIJKLMNOPQRSTUVWXYZ[\]^_`abcdefghij
$%&'()*+,-./0123456789:;<=>?@ABCDEFGHIJKLMNOPQRSTUVWXYZ[\]^_`abcdefghijk
%&'()*+,-./0123456789:;<=>?@ABCDEFGHIJKLMNOPQRSTUVWXYZ[\]^_`abcdefghijkl
&'()*+,-./0123456789:;<=>?@ABCDEFGHIJKLMNOPQRSTUVWXYZ[\]^_`abcdefghijklm
'()*+,-./0123456789:;<=>?@ABCDEFGHIJKLMNOPQRSTUVWXYZ[\]^_`abcdefghijklmn
```

Since ASCII is a 7-bit character set, each character is sent as a single byte. Consequently, this protocol is straightforward to implement using the basic `write( )` methods, as the next code fragment demonstrates:

```
public static void generateCharacters(OutputStream out)
   throws IOException {

    int firstPrintableCharacter    = 33;
    int numberOfPrintableCharacters = 94;
    int numberOfCharactersPerLine   = 72;

    int start = firstPrintableCharacter;
    while (true) { /* infinite loop */
      for (int i = start; i < start+numberOfCharactersPerLine; i++) {
        out.write((
        (i-firstPrintableCharacter) % numberOfPrintableCharacters)
          + firstPrintableCharacter);
      }
      out.write('\r'); // carriage return
      out.write('\n'); // linefeed
      start = ((start+1) - firstPrintableCharacter)
        % numberOfPrintableCharacters + firstPrintableCharacter;
    }
```

The character generator server class (the exact details of which will have to wait until we discuss server sockets in Chapter 10) passes an `OutputStream` named out to the `generateCharacters( )` method. Bytes are written onto out one at a time. These bytes are given as integers in a rotating sequence from 33 to 126. Most of the arithmetic here is to make the loop rotate in that range. After each 72 character chunk is written, a carriage return and a linefeed are written onto the output stream. The next start character is calculated and the loop repeats. The entire method is declared to throw IOException. That's important because the character generator server will terminate only when the client closes the connection. The Java code will see this as an IOException.

Writing a single byte at a time is often inefficient. For example, every TCP segment that goes out your Ethernet card contains at least 40 bytes of overhead for routing and error correction. If each byte is sent by itself, you may be stuffing the network with 41 times more data than you think you are! Consequently, most TCP/IP implementations buffer data to some extent. That is, they accumulate bytes in memory and send them to their eventual destination only when a certain number have accumulated or a certain amount of time has passed. However, if you have more than one byte ready to go, it's not a bad idea to send them all at once. Using write(byte[] data) or write(byte[] data, int offset, int length) is normally much faster than writing all the components of the data array one at a time. For instance, here's an implementation of the generateCharacters( ) method that sends a line at a time by packing a complete line into a byte array:

```
public static void generateCharacters(OutputStream out)
  throws IOException {

    int firstPrintableCharacter = 33;
    int numberOfPrintableCharacters = 94;
    int numberOfCharactersPerLine = 72;
    int start = firstPrintableCharacter;
    byte[] line = new byte[numberOfCharactersPerLine+2];
    // the +2 is for the carriage return and linefeed

    while (true) { /* infinite loop */
      for (int i = start; i < start+numberOfCharactersPerLine; i++) {
        line[i-start] = (byte) ((i-firstPrintableCharacter)
          % numberOfPrintableCharacters + firstPrintableCharacter);
      }
      line[72] = (byte) '\r'; // carriage return
      line[73] = (byte) '\n'; // line feed
      out.write(line);
      start = ((start+1)-firstPrintableCharacter)
        % numberOfPrintableCharacters + firstPrintableCharacter;
    }

  }
```

The algorithm for calculating which bytes to write when is the same as for the previous implementation. The crucial difference is that the bytes are packed into a byte array before being written onto the network. Also, notice that the int result of the calculation must be cast to a byte before being stored in the array. This wasn't necessary in the previous implementation because the single byte write( ) method is declared to take an int as an argument.

Streams can also be buffered in software, directly in the Java code as well as in the network hardware. Typically, this is accomplished by chaining a BufferedOutputStream or a BufferedWriter to the underlying stream, a technique we'll explore shortly. Consequently, if you are done writing data, it's important to flush the output stream. For example, suppose you've written a 300-byte request to an HTTP 1.1 server that uses HTTP Keep-Alive. You generally want to wait for a response before sending any more data. However, if the output stream has a 1,024-byte buffer, the stream may be waiting for more data to arrive before it sends the data out of its buffer. No more data will be written onto the stream until the server response arrives, but the response is never going to arrive because the request hasn't been sent yet! The buffered stream won't send the data to the server until it gets more data from the underlying stream, but the underlying stream won't send more data until it gets data from the server, which won't send data until it gets the data that's stuck in the buffer! Figure 4-1 illustrates this Catch-22. The flush( ) method breaks the deadlock by forcing the buffered stream to send its data even if the buffer isn't yet full.

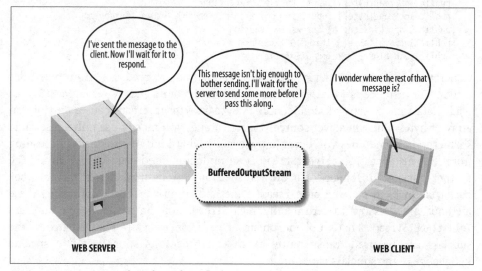

Figure 4-1. Data can get lost if you don't flush your streams

It's important to flush your streams whether you think you need to or not. Depending on how you got hold of a reference to the stream, you may or may not know whether it's buffered. (For instance, System.out is buffered whether you want it to be or not.) If flushing isn't necessary for a particular stream, it's a very low cost operation. However, if it is necessary, it's very necessary. Failing to flush when you need to can lead to unpredictable, unrepeatable program hangs that are extremely hard to diagnose if you don't have a good idea of what the problem is in the first place. As a corollary to all this, you should flush all streams immediately before you close them. Otherwise, data left in the buffer when the stream is closed may get lost.

Finally, when you're done with a stream, close it by invoking its close( ) method. This releases any resources associated with the stream, such as file handles or ports. Once an output stream has been closed, further writes to it throw IOExceptions. However, some kinds of streams may still allow you to do things with the object. For instance, a closed ByteArrayOutputStream can still be converted to an actual byte array and a closed DigestOutputStream can still return its digest.

Input Streams

Java's basic input class is java.io.InputStream:

```
public abstract class InputStream
```

This class provides the fundamental methods needed to read data as raw bytes. These are:

```
public abstract int read( ) throws IOException
public int read(byte[] input) throws IOException
public int read(byte[] input, int offset, int length) throws IOException
public long skip(long n) throws IOException
public int available( ) throws IOException
public void close( ) throws IOException
```

Concrete subclasses of InputStream use these methods to read data from particular media. For instance, a FileInputStream reads data from a file. A TelnetInputStream reads data from a network connection. A ByteArrayInputStream reads data from an array of bytes. But whichever source you're reading, you mostly use only these same six methods. Sometimes you don't know exactly what kind of stream you're reading from. For instance, TelnetInputStream is an undocumented class hidden inside the sun.net package. Instances of it are returned by various methods in the java.net package: for example, the openStream( ) method of java.net.URL. However, these methods are declared to return only InputStream, not the more specific subclass TelnetInputStream. That's polymorphism at work once again. The instance of the subclass can be used transparently as an instance of its superclass. No specific knowledge of the subclass is required.

The basic method of InputStream is the noargs read( ) method. This method reads a single byte of data from the input stream's source and returns it as an int from 0 to 255. End of stream is signified by returning –1. The read( ) method waits and blocks execution of any code that follows it until a byte of data is available and ready to be read. Input and output can be slow, so if your program is doing anything else of importance, try to put I/O in its own thread.

The read( ) method is declared abstract because subclasses need to change it to handle their particular medium. For instance, a ByteArrayInputStream can implement this method with pure Java code that copies the byte from its array. However, a TelnetInputStream needs to use a native library that understands how to read data from the network interface on the host platform.

The following code fragment reads 10 bytes from the InputStream in and stores them in the byte array input. However, if end of stream is detected, the loop is terminated early:

```
byte[] input = new byte[10];
for (int i = 0; i < input.length; i++) {
  int b = in.read();
  if (b  == -1) break;
  input[i] = (byte) b;
}
```

Although read( ) only reads a byte, it returns an int. Thus, a cast is necessary before storing the result in the byte array. Of course, this produces a signed byte from –128 to 127 instead of the unsigned byte from 0 to 255 returned by the read( ) method. However, as long as you're clear about which one you're working with, this is not a major problem. You can convert a signed byte to an unsigned byte like this:

```
int i = b >= 0 ? b : 256 + b;
```

Reading a byte at a time is as inefficient as writing data one byte at a time. Consequently, there are two overloaded read( ) methods that fill a specified array with multiple bytes of data read from the stream, read(byte[] input) and read(byte[] input, int offset, int length). The first method attempts to fill the specified array input. The second attempts to fill the specified subarray of input, starting at offset and continuing for length bytes.

Notice I said these methods *attempt* to fill the array, not that they necessarily succeed. An attempt may fail in several ways. For instance, it's not unheard of that while your program is reading data from a remote web server over a PPP dialup link, a bug in a switch at a phone company central office will disconnect you and several thousand of your neighbors from the rest of the world. This would cause an IOException. More commonly, however, a read attempt won't completely fail but won't completely succeed, either. Some of the requested bytes may be read, but not all of them. For example, you may try to read 1,024 bytes from a network connection, when only 512 have actually arrived from the server; the rest are still in transit. They'll arrive eventually, but they aren't available at this moment. To account for this, the multibyte read methods return the number of bytes actually read. For example, consider this code fragment:

```
byte[] input  = new byte[1024];
int bytesRead = in.read(input);
```

It attempts to read 1,024 bytes from the InputStream in into the array input. However, if only 512 bytes are available, that's all that will be read, and bytesRead will be set to 512. To guarantee that all the bytes you want are actually read, place the read in a loop that reads repeatedly until the array is filled. For example:

```
int bytesRead   = 0;
int bytesToRead = 1024;
byte[] input    = new byte[bytesToRead];
while (bytesRead < bytesToRead) {
  bytesRead += in.read(input, bytesRead, bytesToRead - bytesRead);
}
```

This technique is especially crucial for network streams. Chances are that if a file is available at all, all the bytes of a file are also available. However, since networks move much more slowly than CPUs, it is very easy for a program to empty a network buffer before all the data has arrived. In fact, if one of these two methods tries to read from a temporarily empty but open network buffer, it will generally return 0, indicating that no data is available but the stream is not yet closed. This is often preferable to the behavior of the single-byte read( ) method, which blocks the running thread in the same circumstances.

All three read( ) methods return –1 to signal the end of the stream. If the stream ends while there's still data that hasn't been read, the multibyte read( ) methods return the data until the buffer has been emptied. The next call to any of the read( ) methods will return –1. The –1 is never placed in the array. The array only contains actual data. The previous code fragment had a bug because it didn't consider the possibility that all 1,024 bytes might never arrive (as opposed to not being immediately available). Fixing that bug requires testing the return value of read( ) before adding it to bytesRead. For example:

```
int bytesRead=0;
int bytesToRead=1024;
byte[] input = new byte[bytesToRead];
while (bytesRead < bytesToRead) {
  int result = in.read(input, bytesRead, bytesToRead - bytesRead);
  if (result == -1) break;
  bytesRead += result;
}
```

If you do not want to wait until all the bytes you need are immediately available, you can use the available( ) method to determine how many bytes can be read without blocking. This returns the minimum number of bytes you can read. You may in fact be able to read more, but you will be able to read at least as many bytes as available( ) suggests. For example:

```
int bytesAvailable = in.available( );
byte[] input = new byte[bytesAvailable];
int bytesRead = in.read(input, 0, bytesAvailable);
// continue with rest of program immediately...
```

In this case, you can assert that bytesRead is exactly equal to bytesAvailable. You cannot, however, assert that bytesRead is greater than zero. It is possible that no bytes were available. On end of stream, available( ) returns 0. Generally, read(byte[] input, int offset, int length) returns –1 on end of stream; but if length is 0, then it does not notice the end of stream and returns 0 instead.

On rare occasions, you may want to skip over data without reading it. The skip( ) method accomplishes this task. It's less useful on network connections than when reading from files. Network connections are sequential and normally quite slow, so it's not significantly more time-consuming to read data than to skip over it. Files are random access so that skipping can be implemented simply by repositioning a file pointer rather than processing each byte to be skipped.

As with output streams, once your program has finished with an input stream, it should close it by invoking its close( ) method. This releases any resources associated with the stream, such as file handles or ports. Once an input stream has been closed, further reads from it throw IOExceptions. However, some kinds of streams may still allow you to do things with the object. For instance, you generally won't want to get the message digest from a java.security.DigestInputStream until after the data has been read and the stream closed.

Marking and Resetting

The InputStream class also has three less commonly used methods that allow programs to back up and reread data they've already read. These are:

```
public void mark(int readAheadLimit)
public void reset( ) throws IOException
public boolean markSupported( )
```

In order to reread data, mark the current position in the stream with the mark( ) method. At a later point, you can reset the stream to the marked position using the reset( ) method. Subsequent reads then return data starting from the marked position. However, you may not be able to reset as far back as you like. The number of bytes you can read from the mark and still reset is determined by the readAheadLimit argument to mark( ). If you try to reset too far back, an IOException is thrown. Furthermore, there can be only one mark in a stream at any given time. Marking a second location erases the first mark.

Marking and resetting are usually implemented by storing every byte read from the marked position on in an internal buffer. However, not all input streams support this. Before trying to use marking and resetting, check to see whether the markSupported( ) method returns true. If it does, the stream supports marking and resetting. Otherwise, mark( ) will do nothing and reset( ) will throw an IOException.

In my opinion, this demonstrates very poor design. In practice, more streams *don't* support marking and resetting than *do*. Attaching functionality to an abstract superclass that is not available to many, probably most, subclasses is a very poor idea. It would be better to place these three methods in a separate interface that could be implemented by those classes that provided this functionality. The disadvantage of this approach is that you couldn't then invoke these methods on an arbitrary input stream of unknown type, but in practice, you can't do that anyway because not all streams support marking and resetting. Providing a method such as markSupported( ) to check for functionality at runtime is a more traditional, non-object–oriented solution to the problem. An object-oriented approach would embed this in the type system through interfaces and classes so that it could all be checked at compile time.

The only two input stream classes in java.io that always support marking are BufferedInputStream and ByteArrayInputStream. However, other input streams such as TelnetInputStream may support marking if they're chained to a buffered input stream first.

Filter Streams

InputStream and OutputStream are fairly raw classes. They read and write bytes singly or in groups, but that's all. Deciding what those bytes mean—whether they're integers or IEEE 754 floating point numbers or Unicode text—is completely up to the programmer and the code. However, there are certain extremely common data formats that can benefit from a solid implementation in the class library. For example, many integers passed as parts of network protocols are 32-bit big-endian integers. Much text sent over the Web is either 7-bit ASCII, 8-bit Latin–1, or multi-byte UTF-8. Many files transferred by FTP are stored in the zip format. Java provides a number of filter classes you can attach to raw streams to translate the raw bytes to and from these and other formats.

The filters come in two versions: the filter streams and the readers and writers. The filter streams still work primarily with raw data as bytes: for instance, by compressing the data or interpreting it as binary numbers. The readers and writers handle the special case of text in a variety of encodings such as UTF-8 and ISO 8859-1. Filter streams are placed on top of raw streams such as a TelnetInputStream or a FileOutputStream or other filter streams. Readers and writers can be layered on top of raw streams, filter streams, or other readers and writers. However, filter streams cannot be placed on top of a reader or a writer, so we'll start with filter streams and address readers and writers in the next section.

Filters are organized in a chain, as shown in Figure 4-2. Each link in the chain receives data from the previous filter or stream and passes the data along to the next link in the chain. In this example, a compressed, encrypted text file arrives from the local network interface, where native code presents it to the undocumented TelnetInputStream. A BufferedInputStream buffers the data to speed up the entire process. A CipherInputStream decrypts the data. A GZIPInputStream decompresses the deciphered data. An InputStreamReader converts the decompressed data to Unicode text. Finally, the text is read into the application and processed.

Every filter output stream has the same write( ), close( ), and flush( ) methods as java.io.OutputStream. Every filter input stream has the same read( ), close( ), and available( ) methods as java.io.InputStream. In some cases, such as BufferedInputStream and BufferedOutputStream, these may be the only methods they have. The filtering is purely internal and does not expose any new public interface. However, in most cases, the filter stream adds public methods with additional purposes. Sometimes these are intended to be used in addition to the usual read( ) and

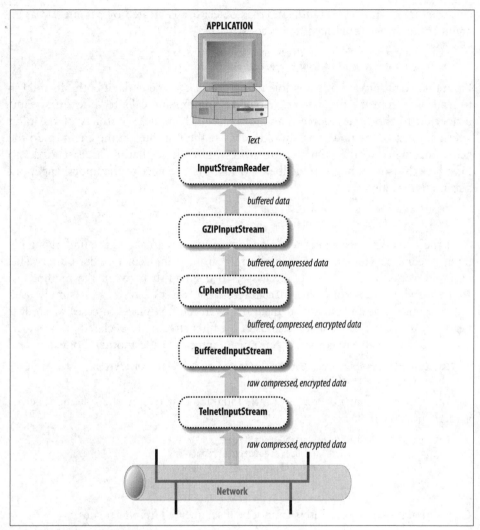

APPLICATION

Text

InputStreamReader

buffered data

GZIPInputStream

buffered, compressed data

CipherInputStream

buffered, compressed, encrypted data

BufferedInputStream

raw compressed, encrypted data

TelnetInputStream

raw compressed, encrypted data

Network

Figure 4-2. The flow of data through a chain of filters

write( ) methods, like the unread( ) method of PushbackInputStream. At other times, they almost completely replace the original interface. For example, it's relatively rare to use the write( ) method of PrintStream instead of one of its print( ) and println( ) methods.

Chaining Filters Together

Filters are connected to streams by their constructors. For example, the following code fragment buffers input from the file *data.txt*. First, a FileInputStream object fin is created by passing the name of the file as an argument to the FileInputStream constructor. Then, a BufferedInputStream object bin is created by passing fin as an argument to the BufferedInputStream constructor:

```
FileInputStream     fin = new FileInputStream("data.txt");
BufferedInputStream bin = new BufferedInputStream(fin);
```

From this point forward, it's possible to use the read( ) methods of both fin and bin to read data from the file *data.txt*. However, intermixing calls to different streams connected to the same source may violate several implicit contracts of the filter streams. Most of the time, you should only use the last filter in the chain to do the actual reading or writing. One way to write your code so that it's at least harder to introduce this sort of bug is to deliberately lose the reference to the underlying input stream. For example:

```
InputStream in = new FileInputStream("data.txt");
in = new BufferedInputStream(in);
```

After these two lines execute, there's no longer any way to access the underlying file input stream, so you can't accidentally read from it and corrupt the buffer. This example works because it's not necessary to distinguish between the methods of InputStream and those of BufferedInputStream. BufferedInputStream is simply used polymorphically as an instance of InputStream in the first place. In cases where it is necessary to use the additional methods of the filter stream not declared in the super-class, you may be able to construct one stream directly inside another. For example:

```
DataOutputStream dout = new DataOutputStream(new BufferedOutputStream(
  new FileOutputStream("data.txt")));
```

Although these statements can get a little long, it's easy to split the statement across several lines, like this:

```
DataOutputStream dout = new DataOutputStream(
                        new BufferedOutputStream(
                         new FileOutputStream("data.txt")
                        )
                       );
```

Connection is permanent. Filters cannot be disconnected from a stream.

There are times when you may need to use the methods of multiple filters in a chain. For instance, if you're reading a Unicode text file, you may want to read the byte order mark in the first three bytes to determine whether the file is encoded as big-endian UCS-2, little-endian UCS-2, or UTF-8, and then select the matching Reader filter for the encoding. Or, if you're connecting to a web server, you may want to read the header the server sends to find the Content-encoding and then use that content encoding to pick the right Reader filter to read the body of the response. Or perhaps you want to send floating point numbers across a network connection using a DataOutputStream and then retrieve a MessageDigest from the DigestOutputStream that the DataOutputStream is chained to. In all these cases, you need to save and use references to each of the underlying streams. However, under no circumstances should you ever read from or write to anything other than the last filter in the chain.

Buffered Streams

The `BufferedOutputStream` class stores written data in a buffer (a protected byte array field named `buf`) until the buffer is full or the stream is flushed. Then it writes the data onto the underlying output stream all at once. A single write of many bytes is almost always much faster than many small writes that add up to the same thing. This is especially true of network connections because each TCP segment or UDP packet carries a finite amount of overhead, generally about 40 bytes' worth. This means that sending 1 kilobyte of data 1 byte at a time actually requires sending 40 kilobytes over the wire, whereas sending it all at once only requires sending a little more than 1K of data. Most network cards and TCP implementations provide some level of buffering themselves, so the real numbers aren't quite this dramatic. Nonetheless, buffering network output is generally a huge performance win.

The `BufferedInputStream` class also has a protected byte array named `buf` that serves as a buffer. When one of the stream's `read( )` methods is called, it first tries to get the requested data from the buffer. Only when the buffer runs out of data does the stream read from the underlying source. At this point, it reads as much data as it can from the source into the buffer, whether it needs all the data immediately or not. Data that isn't used immediately will be available for later invocations of `read( )`. When reading files from a local disk, it's almost as fast to read several hundred bytes of data from the underlying stream as it is to read one byte of data. Therefore, buffering can substantially improve performance. The gain is less obvious on network connections where the bottleneck is often the speed at which the network can deliver data rather than the speed at which the network interface delivers data to the program or the speed at which the program runs. Nonetheless, buffering input rarely hurts and will become more important over time as network speeds increase.

`BufferedInputStream` has two constructors, as does `BufferedOutputStream`:

```
public BufferedInputStream(InputStream in)
public BufferedInputStream(InputStream in, int bufferSize)
public BufferedOutputStream(OutputStream out)
public BufferedOutputStream(OutputStream out, int bufferSize)
```

The first argument is the underlying stream from which unbuffered data will be read or to which buffered data will be written. The second argument, if present, specifies the number of bytes in the buffer. Otherwise, the buffer size is set to 2,048 bytes for an input stream and 512 bytes for an output stream. The ideal size for a buffer depends on what sort of stream you're buffering. For network connections, you want something a little larger than the typical packet size. However, this can be hard to predict and varies depending on local network connections and protocols. Faster, higher-bandwidth networks tend to use larger packets, although eight kilobytes is an effective maximum packet size for UDP on most networks today, and TCP segments are often no larger than a kilobyte.

BufferedInputStream does not declare any new methods of its own. It only overrides methods from InputStream. It does support marking and resetting.

```
public int read( ) throws IOException
public int read(byte[] input, int offset, int length)
 throws IOException
public long skip(long n) throws IOException
public int available( ) throws IOException
public void mark(int readLimit)
public void reset( ) throws IOException
public boolean markSupported( )
```

The two multibyte read( ) methods attempt to completely fill the specified array or subarray of data by reading from the underlying input stream as many times as necessary. They return only when the array or subarray has been completely filled, the end of stream is reached, or the underlying stream would block on further reads. Most input streams (including buffered input streams in Java 1.1 and 1.0) do not behave like this. They read from the underlying stream or data source only once before returning.

BufferedOutputStream also does not declare any new methods of its own. It overrides three methods from OutputStream:

```
public void write(int b) throws IOException
public void write(byte[] data, int offset, int length) throws IOException
public void flush( ) throws IOException
```

You call these methods exactly as you would in any output stream. The difference is that each write places data in the buffer rather than directly on the underlying output stream. Consequently, it is essential to flush the stream when you reach a point at which the data needs to be sent.

PrintStream

The PrintStream class is the first filter output stream most programmers encounter because System.out is a PrintStream. However, other output streams can also be chained to print streams, using these two constructors:

```
public PrintStream(OutputStream out)
public PrintStream(OutputStream out, boolean autoFlush)
```

By default, print streams should be explicitly flushed. However, if the autoFlush argument is true, the stream will be flushed every time a byte array or linefeed is written or a println( ) method is invoked.

As well as the usual write( ), flush( ), and close( ) methods, PrintStream has 9 overloaded print( ) methods and 10 overloaded println( ) methods:

```
public void print(boolean b)
public void print(char c)
```

```
public void print(int i)
public void print(long l)
public void print(float f)
public void print(double d)
public void print(char[] text)
public void print(String s)
public void print(Object o)
public void println()
public void println(boolean b)
public void println(char c)
public void println(int i)
public void println(long l)
public void println(float f)
public void println(double d)
public void println(char[] text)
public void println(String s)
public void println(Object o)
```

Each print( ) method converts its argument to a string in a predictable fashion and writes the string onto the underlying output stream using the default encoding. The println( ) methods do the same thing, but they also append a platform-dependent line separator character to the end of the line they write. This is a linefeed (\n) on Unix (including Mac OS X), a carriage return (\r) on Mac OS 9, and a carriage return/linefeed pair (\r\n) on Windows.

 PrintStream is evil and network programmers should avoid it like the plague!

The first problem is that the output from println( ) is platform-dependent. Depending on what system runs your code, lines may sometimes be broken with a linefeed, a carriage return, or a carriage return/linefeed pair. This doesn't cause problems when writing to the console, but it's a disaster for writing network clients and servers that must follow a precise protocol. Most network protocols such as HTTP and Gnutela specify that lines should be terminated with a carriage return/linefeed pair. Using println( ) makes it easy to write a program that works on Windows but fails on Unix and the Mac. While many servers and clients are liberal in what they accept and can handle incorrect line terminators, there are occasional exceptions. In particular, in conjunction with the bug in readLine( ) discussed shortly, a client running on Mac OS 9 that uses println( ) may hang both the server and the client. To some extent, this could be fixed by using only print( ) and ignoring println( ). However, PrintStream has other problems.

The second problem is that PrintStream assumes the default encoding of the platform on which it's running. However, this encoding may not be what the server or client expects. For example, a web browser receiving XML files will expect them to be encoded in UTF-8 or UTF-16 unless the server tells it otherwise. However, a web server that uses `PrintStream` may well send the files encoded in CP1252 from a U.S.-localized Windows system or SJIS from a Japanese-localized system, whether the client expects or understands those encodings or not. `PrintStream` doesn't provide any mechanism for changing the default encoding. This problem can be patched over by using the related `PrintWriter` class instead. But the problems continue.

The third problem is that `PrintStream` eats all exceptions. This makes `PrintStream` suitable for textbook programs such as HelloWorld, since simple console output can be taught without burdening students with first learning about exception handling and all that implies. However, network connections are much less reliable than the console. Connections routinely fail because of network congestion, phone company misfeasance, remote systems crashing, and many other reasons. Network programs must be prepared to deal with unexpected interruptions in the flow of data. The way to do this is by handling exceptions. However, `PrintStream` catches any exceptions thrown by the underlying output stream. Notice that the declaration of the standard five `OutputStream` methods in `PrintStream` does not have the usual `throws IOException` declaration:

```
public abstract void write(int b)
public void write(byte[] data)
public void write(byte[] data, int offset, int length)
public void flush( )
public void close( )
```

Instead, `PrintStream` relies on an outdated and inadequate error flag. If the underlying stream throws an exception, this internal error flag is set. The programmer is relied upon to check the value of the flag using the `checkError( )` method:

```
public boolean checkError( )
```

If programmers are to do any error checking at all on a `PrintStream`, they must explicitly check every call. Furthermore, once an error has occurred, there is no way to unset the flag so further errors can be detected. Nor is any additional information available about the error. In short, the error notification provided by `PrintStream` is wholly inadequate for unreliable network connections. At the end of this chapter, we'll introduce a class that fixes all these shortcomings.

PushbackInputStream

`PushbackInputStream` is a subclass of `FilterInputStream` that provides a pushback stack so that a program can "unread" bytes onto the input stream. This lets programs add data to a running stream. For example, you could prefix a stream with a header before passing it to another process that needed that header.

The `read( )` and `available( )` methods of `PushbackInputStream` are invoked exactly as with normal input streams. However, they first attempt to read from the pushback buffer before reading from the underlying input stream. What this class adds is `unread( )` methods that push bytes into the buffer:

```
public void unread(int b) throws IOException
```

This method pushes an unsigned byte given as an `int` between 0 and 255 onto the stream. Integers outside this range are truncated to this range as by a cast to byte. Assuming nothing else is pushed back onto this stream, the next read from the stream will return that byte. As multiple bytes are pushed onto the stream by repeated invocations of `unread( )`, they are stored in a stack and returned in a last-in, first-out order. In essence, the buffer is a stack sitting on top of an input stream. Only when the stack is empty will the underlying stream be read.

There are two more `unread( )` methods that push a specified array or subarray onto the stream:

```
public void unread(byte[] input) throws IOException
public void unread(byte[] input, int offset, int length) throws IOException
```

The arrays are stacked in last-in, first-out order. However, bytes popped from the same array will be returned in the order they appeared in the array. That is, the zeroth component of the array will be read before the first component of the array.

By default, the buffer is only one byte long, and trying to unread more than one byte throws an `IOException`. However, the buffer size can be changed by passing a second argument to the constructor:

```
public PushbackInputStream(InputStream in)
public PushbackInputStream(InputStream in, int size)
```

Although `PushbackInputStream` and `BufferedInputStream` both use buffers, `BufferedInputStream` uses them for data read from the underlying input stream, while `PushbackInputStream` uses them for arbitrary data, which may or may not have been read from the stream originally. Furthermore, `PushbackInputStream` does not allow marking and resetting. The `markSupported( )` method of `PushbackInputStream` returns false.

Data Streams

The `DataInputStream` and `DataOutputStream` classes provide methods for reading and writing Java's primitive data types and strings in a binary format. The binary formats used are primarily intended for exchanging data between two different Java programs whether through a network connection, a datafile, a pipe, or some other intermediary. What a data output stream writes, a data input stream can read. However, it happens that the formats are the same ones used for most Internet protocols that exchange binary numbers. For instance, the time protocol uses 32-bit big-endian integers, just like Java's `int` data type. The controlled-load network element service uses 32-bit IEEE 754 floating point numbers, just like Java's `float` data type. (This is probably correlation rather than causation. Both Java and most network protocols were designed by Unix programmers, and consequently both tend to use the formats common to most Unix systems.) However, this isn't true for all network protocols, so check the details of any protocol you use. For instance, the Network Time

Protocol (NTP) represents times as 64-bit unsigned fixed point numbers with the integer part in the first 32 bits and the fraction part in the last 32 bits. This doesn't match any primitive data type in any common programming language, although it is fairly straightforward to work with—at least as far as is necessary for NTP.

The DataOutputStream class offers these 11 methods for writing particular Java data types:

```
public final void writeBoolean(boolean b) throws IOException
public final void writeByte(int b) throws IOException
public final void writeShort(int s) throws IOException
public final void writeChar(int c) throws IOException
public final void writeInt(int i) throws IOException
public final void writeLong(long l) throws IOException
public final void writeFloat(float f) throws IOException
public final void writeDouble(double d) throws IOException
public final void writeChars(String s) throws IOException
public final void writeBytes(String s) throws IOException
public final void writeUTF(String s) throws IOException
```

All data is written in big-endian format. Integers are written in two's complement in the minimum number of bytes possible. Thus, a byte is written as one two's-complement byte, a short as two two's-complement bytes, an int as four two's-complement bytes, and a long as eight two's-complement bytes. Floats and doubles are written in IEEE 754 form in 4 and 8 bytes, respectively. Booleans are written as a single byte with the value 0 for false and 1 for true. Chars are written as two unsigned bytes.

The last three methods are a little trickier. The writeChars( ) method simply iterates through the String argument, writing each character in turn as a 2-byte, big-endian Unicode character (a UTF-16 code point, to be absolutely precise). The writeBytes( ) method iterates through the String argument but writes only the least significant byte of each character. Thus, information will be lost for any string with characters from outside the Latin–1 character set. This method may be useful on some network protocols that specify the ASCII encoding, but it should be avoided most of the time.

Neither writeChars( ) nor writeBytes( ) encodes the length of the string in the output stream. As a result, you can't really distinguish between raw characters and characters that make up part of a string. The writeUTF( ) method does include the length of the string. It encodes the string itself in a *variant* of the UTF-8 encoding of Unicode. Since this variant is subtly incompatible with most non-Java software, it should be used only for exchanging data with other Java programs that use a DataInputStream to read strings. For exchanging UTF-8 text with all other software, you should use an InputStreamReader with the appropriate encoding. (There wouldn't be any confusion if Sun had just called this method and its partner writeString( ) and readString( ) rather than writeUTF( ) and readUTF( ).)

Along with these methods for writing binary numbers and strings, DataOutputStream of course has the usual write( ), flush( ), and close( ) methods any OutputStream class has.

DataInputStream is the complementary class to DataOutputStream. Every format that DataOutputStream writes, DataInputStream can read. In addition, DataInputStream has the usual read( ), available( ), skip( ), and close( ) methods, as well as methods for reading complete arrays of bytes and lines of text.

There are 9 methods to read binary data that match the 11 methods in DataOutputStream (there's no exact complement for writeBytes( ) or writeChars( ); these are handled by reading the bytes and chars one at a time):

```
public final boolean readBoolean( ) throws IOException
public final byte readByte( ) throws IOException
public final char readChar( ) throws IOException
public final short readShort( ) throws IOException
public final int readInt( ) throws IOException
public final long readLong( ) throws IOException
public final float readFloat( ) throws IOException
public final double readDouble( ) throws IOException
public final String readUTF( ) throws IOException
```

In addition, DataInputStream provides two methods to read unsigned bytes and unsigned shorts and return the equivalent int. Java doesn't have either of these data types, but you may encounter them when reading binary data written by a C program:

```
public final int readUnsignedByte( ) throws IOException
public final int readUnsignedShort( ) throws IOException
```

DataInputStream has the usual two multibyte read( ) methods that read data into an array or subarray and return the number of bytes read. It also has two readFully( ) methods that repeatedly read data from the underlying input stream into an array until the requested number of bytes have been read. If enough data cannot be read, an IOException is thrown. These methods are especially useful when you know in advance exactly how many bytes you have to read. This might be the case when you've read the Content-length field out of an HTTP header and thus know how many bytes of data there are:

```
public final int read(byte[] input) throws IOException
public final int read(byte[] input, int offset, int length)
  throws IOException
public final void readFully(byte[] input) throws IOException
public final void readFully(byte[] input, int offset, int length)
  throws IOException
```

Finally, DataInputStream provides the popular readLine( ) method that reads a line of text as delimited by a line terminator and returns a string:

```
public final String readLine( ) throws IOException
```

However, this method should not be used under any circumstances, both because it is deprecated and because it is buggy. It's deprecated because it doesn't properly convert non-ASCII characters to bytes in most circumstances. That task is now handled by the readLine( ) method of the BufferedReader class. However, that method and this one share the same insidious bug: they do not always recognize a single carriage return as ending a line. Rather, readLine( ) recognizes only a linefeed or a carriage return/linefeed pair. When a carriage return is detected in the stream, readLine( ) waits to see whether the next character is a linefeed before continuing. If it is a linefeed, the carriage return and the linefeed are thrown away and the line is returned as a String. If it isn't a linefeed, the carriage return is thrown away, the line is returned as a String, and the extra character that was read becomes part of the next line. However, if the carriage return is the last character in the stream (a very likely occurrence if the stream originates from a Macintosh or a file created on a Macintosh), then readLine( ) hangs, waiting for the last character, which isn't forthcoming.

This problem isn't obvious when reading files because there will almost certainly be a next character: −1 for end of stream, if nothing else. However, on persistent network connections such as those used for FTP and late-model HTTP, a server or client may simply stop sending data after the last character and wait for a response without actually closing the connection. If you're lucky, the connection may eventually time out on one end or the other and you'll get an IOException, although this will probably take at least a couple of minutes. If you're not lucky, the program will hang indefinitely.

Note that it is not enough for your program to merely be running on Windows or Unix to avoid this bug. It must also ensure that it does not send or receive text files created on a Macintosh and that it never talks to Macintosh clients or servers. These are very strong conditions in the heterogeneous world of the Internet. It's much simpler to avoid readLine( ) completely.

Compressing Streams

The java.util.zip package contains filter streams that compress and decompress streams in zip, gzip, and deflate formats. Along with its better-known uses with files, this package allows Java applications to easily exchange compressed data across the network. HTTP 1.1 includes support for compressed file transfer in which the server compresses and the browser decompresses files, in effect trading increasingly cheap CPU power for still-expensive network bandwidth. This process is completely transparent to the user. Of course, it's not transparent to the programmer who has to write the compression and decompression code. However, the java.util.zip filter streams make it a lot more transparent than it otherwise would be.

There are six stream classes that perform compression and decompression; the input streams decompress data and the output streams compress it:

```
public class DeflaterOutputStream extends FilterOutputStream
public class InflaterInputStream extends FilterInputStream
```

```
public class GZIPOutputStream extends FilterOutputStream
public class GZIPInputStream extends FilterInputStream
public class ZipOutputStream extends FilterOutputStream
public class ZipInputStream extends FilterInputStream
```

All of these classes use essentially the same compression algorithm. They differ only in various constants and meta-information included with the compressed data. In addition, a zip stream may contain more than one compressed file.

Compressing and decompressing data with these classes is almost trivially easy. You simply chain the filter to the underlying stream and read or write it like normal. For example, suppose you want to read the compressed file *allnames.gz*. Simply open a FileInputStream to the file and chain a GZIPInputStream to it, like this:

```
FileInputStream fin = new FileInputStream("allnames.gz");
GZIPInputStream gzin = new GZIPInputStream(fin);
```

From this point forward, you can read uncompressed data from gzin using the usual read( ), skip( ), and available( ) methods. For instance, this code fragment reads and decompresses a file named *allnames.gz* in the current working directory:

```
FileInputStream fin   = new FileInputStream("allnames.gz");
GZIPInputStream gzin  = new GZIPInputStream(fin);
FileOutputStream fout = new FileOutputStream("allnames");
int b = 0;
while ((b = gzin.read( )) != -1) fout.write(b);
gzin.close( );
out.flush( );
out.close( );
```

In fact, it isn't even necessary to know that gzin is a GZIPInputStream for this to work. A simple InputStream type works equally well. For example:

```
InputStream in = new GZIPInputStream(new FileInputStream("allnames.gz"));
```

DeflaterOutputStream and InflaterInputStream are equally straightforward. ZipInputStream and ZipOutputStream are a little more complicated because a zip file is actually an archive that may contain multiple entries, each of which must be read separately. Each file in a zip archive is represented as a ZipEntry object whose getName( ) method returns the original name of the file. For example, this code fragment decompresses the archive *shareware.zip* in the current working directory:

```
FileInputStream fin = new FileInputStream("shareware.zip");
ZipInputStream zin = new ZipInputStream(fin);
ZipEntry ze = null;
int b = 0;
while ((ze = zin.getNextEntry( )) != null) {
  FileOutputStream fout = new FileOutputStream(ze.getName( ));
  while ((b = zin.read( )) != -1) fout.write(b);
  zin.closeEntry( );
  fout.flush( );
  fout.close( );
}
zin.close( );
```

Digest Streams

The java.util.security package contains two filter streams that can calculate a message digest for a stream. They are DigestInputStream and DigestOutputStream. A message digest, represented in Java by the java.util.security.MessageDigest class, is a strong hash code for the stream; that is, it is a large integer (typically 20 bytes long in binary format) that can easily be calculated from a stream of any length in such a fashion that no information about the stream is available from the message digest. Message digests can be used for digital signatures and for detecting data that has been corrupted in transit across the network.

In practice, the use of message digests in digital signatures is more important. Mere data corruption can be detected with much simpler, less computationally expensive algorithms. However, the digest filter streams are so easy to use that at times it may be worth paying the computational price for the corresponding increase in programmer productivity. To calculate a digest for an output stream, you first construct a MessageDigest object that uses a particular algorithm, such as the Secure Hash Algorithm (SHA). Pass both the MessageDigest object and the stream you want to digest to the DigestOutputStream constructor. This chains the digest stream to the underlying output stream. Then write data onto the stream as normal, flush it, close it, and invoke the getMessageDigest() method to retrieve the MessageDigest object. Finally, invoke the digest() method on the MessageDigest object to finish calculating the actual digest. Here's an example:

```
MessageDigest sha = MessageDigest.getInstance("SHA");
DigestOutputStream dout = new DigestOutputStream(out, sha);
byte[] buffer = new byte[128];
while (true) {
  int bytesRead = in.read(buffer);
  if (bytesRead < 0) break;
  dout.write(buffer, 0, bytesRead);
}
dout.flush();
dout.close();
byte[] result = dout.getMessageDigest().digest();
```

Calculating the digest of an input stream you read is equally simple. It still isn't quite as transparent as some of the other filter streams because you do need to be at least marginally conversant with the methods of the MessageDigest class. Nonetheless, it's still far easier than writing your own secure hash function and manually feeding it each byte you write.

Of course, you also need a way of associating a particular message digest with a particular stream. In some circumstances, the digest may be sent over the same channel used to send the digested data. The sender calculates the digest as it sends data, while the receiver calculates the digest as it receives the data. When the sender is done, it sends a signal that the receiver recognizes as indicating the end of the stream and then sends the digest. The receiver receives the digest, checks that the digest received is the same as the one calculated locally, and closes the connection. If the digests don't match, the receiver may instead ask the sender to send the message again. Alternatively, both the digest and the files it digests may be stored in the same zip archive. And there are many other possibilities. Situations like this generally call for the design of a relatively formal custom protocol. However, while the protocol may be complicated, the calculation of the digest is straightforward, thanks to the `DigestInputStream` and `DigestOutputStream` filter classes.

Encrypting Streams

The `CipherInputStream` and `CipherOutputStream` classes in the `javax.crypto` package provide encryption and decryption services. They are both powered by a `Cipher` engine object that encapsulates the algorithm used to perform encryption and decryption. By changing the `Cipher` engine object, you change the algorithm that the streams use to encrypt and decrypt. Most ciphers also require a *key* to encrypt and decrypt the data. Symmetric or secret key ciphers use the same key for both encryption and decryption. Asymmetric or public key ciphers use different keys for encryption and decryption. The encryption key can be distributed as long as the decryption key is kept secret. Keys are specific to the algorithm and are represented in Java by instances of the `java.security.Key` interface. The `Cipher` object is set in the constructor. Like all filter stream constructors, these constructors also take another input stream as an argument:

```
public CipherInputStream(InputStream in, Cipher c)
public CipherOutputStream(OutputStream out, Cipher c)
```

 For legal reasons `CipherInputStream` and `CipherOutputStream` are not bundled with the core API in Java 1.3 and earlier. Instead, they are part of a standard extension to Java called the Java Cryptography Extension, JCE for short. This is in the `javax.crypto` package. Sun provides an implementation of this API (available from *http://java.sun.com/ products/jce/*) and various third parties have written independent implementations. Of particular note is the Legion of the Bouncy Castle's open source implementation, which can be downloaded from *http://www.bouncycastle.org/*.

To get a properly initialized `Cipher` object, use the static `Cipher.getInstance()` factory method. This `Cipher` object must be initialized for either encryption or decryption with `init()` before being passed into one of the previous constructors. For example, this code fragment prepares a `CipherInputStream` for decryption using the password "two and not a fnord" and the Data Encryption Standard (DES) algorithm:

```
byte[] desKeyData = "two and not a fnord".getBytes();
DESKeySpec desKeySpec = new DESKeySpec(desKeyData);
SecretKeyFactory keyFactory = SecretKeyFactory.getInstance("DES");
SecretKey desKey = keyFactory.generateSecret(desKeySpec);
```

```
Cipher des = Cipher.getInstance("DES");
des.init(Cipher.DECRYPT_MODE, desKey);
CipherInputStream cin = new CipherInputStream(fin, des);
```

This fragment uses classes from the java.security, java.security.spec, javax.
crypto, and javax.crypto.spec packages. Different implementations of the JCE support different groups of encryption algorithms. Common algorithms include DES,
RSA, and Blowfish. The construction of a key is generally algorithm-specific. Consult the documentation for your JCE implementation for more details.

CipherInputStream overrides most of the normal InputStream methods like read( ) and
available( ). CipherOutputStream overrides most of the usual OutputStream methods
like write( ) and flush( ). These methods are all invoked much as they would be for
any other stream. However, as the data is read or written, the stream's Cipher object
either decrypts or encrypts the data. (Assuming your program wants to work with
unencrypted data—as is commonly the case—a cipher input stream will decrypt the
data and a cipher output stream will encrypt the data.) For example, this code fragment encrypts the file *secrets.txt* using the password "Mary had a little spider":

```
String infile   = "secrets.txt";
String outfile  = "secrets.des";
String password = "Mary had a little spider";

try {

    FileInputStream fin = new FileInputStream(infile);
    FileOutputStream fout = new FileOutputStream(outfile);

    // register the provider that implements the algorithm
    Provider sunJce = new com.sun.crypto.provider.SunJCE( );
    Security.addProvider(sunJce);

    // create a key
    char[] pbeKeyData = password.toCharArray( );
    PBEKeySpec pbeKeySpec = new PBEKeySpec(pbeKeyData);
    SecretKeyFactory keyFactory =
    SecretKeyFactory.getInstance("PBEWithMD5AndDES");
    SecretKey pbeKey = keyFactory.generateSecret(pbeKeySpec);

    // use Data Encryption Standard
    Cipher pbe = Cipher.getInstance("PBEWithMD5AndDES");
    pbe.init(Cipher.ENCRYPT_MODE, pbeKey);
    CipherOutputStream cout = new CipherOutputStream(fout, pbe);

    byte[] input = new byte[64];
    while (true) {
      int bytesRead = fin.read(input);
      if (bytesRead == -1) break;
      cout.write(input, 0, bytesRead);
    }
```

```
        cout.flush( );
        cout.close( );
        fin.close( );

    }
    catch (Exception ex) {
        System.err.println(ex);
    }
```

I admit that this is more complicated than it needs to be. There's a lot of setup work involved in creating the Cipher object that actually performs the encryption. Partly, that's because key generation involves quite a bit more than a simple password. However, a large part of the complication is due to inane U.S. export laws that prevent Sun from fully integrating the JCE with the JDK and JRE. To a large extent, the complex architecture used here is driven by a need to separate the actual encrypting and decrypting code from the cipher stream classes.

Readers and Writers

Many programmers have a bad habit of writing code as if all text were ASCII or at least in the native encoding of the platform. While some older, simpler network protocols, such as daytime, quote of the day, and chargen, do specify ASCII encoding for text, this is not true of HTTP and many other more modern protocols, which allow a wide variety of localized encodings, such as KOI8-R Cyrillic, Big-5 Chinese, and ISO 8859-2 for most Central European languages. Java's native character set is the UTF-16 encoding of Unicode. When the encoding is no longer ASCII, the assumption that bytes and chars are essentially the same things also breaks down. Consequently, Java provides an almost complete mirror of the input and output stream class hierarchy designed for working with characters instead of bytes.

In this mirror image hierarchy, two abstract superclasses define the basic API for reading and writing characters. The java.io.Reader class specifies the API by which characters are read. The java.io.Writer class specifies the API by which characters are written. Wherever input and output streams use bytes, readers and writers use Unicode characters. Concrete subclasses of Reader and Writer allow particular sources to be read and targets to be written. Filter readers and writers can be attached to other readers and writers to provide additional services or interfaces.

The most important concrete subclasses of Reader and Writer are the Input-StreamReader and the OutputStreamWriter classes. An InputStreamReader contains an underlying input stream from which it reads raw bytes. It translates these bytes into Unicode characters according to a specified encoding. An OutputStreamWriter receives Unicode characters from a running program. It then translates those characters into bytes using a specified encoding and writes the bytes onto an underlying output stream.

In addition to these two classes, the `java.io` package provides several raw reader and writer classes that read characters without directly requiring an underlying input stream, including:

- `FileReader`
- `FileWriter`
- `StringReader`
- `StringWriter`
- `CharArrayReader`
- `CharArrayWriter`

The first two classes in this list work with files and the last four work inside Java, so they aren't of great use for network programming. However, aside from different constructors, these classes have pretty much the same public interface as all other reader and writer classes.

Writers

The `Writer` class mirrors the `java.io.OutputStream` class. It's abstract and has two protected constructors. Like `OutputStream`, the `Writer` class is never used directly; instead, it is used polymorphically, through one of its subclasses. It has five `write( )` methods as well as a `flush( )` and a `close( )` method:

```
protected Writer( )
protected Writer(Object lock)
public abstract void write(char[] text, int offset, int length)
  throws IOException
public void write(int c) throws IOException
public void write(char[] text) throws IOException
public void write(String s) throws IOException
public void write(String s, int offset, int length) throws IOException
public abstract void flush( ) throws IOException
public abstract void close( ) throws IOException
```

The `write(char[] text, int offset, int length)` method is the base method in terms of which the other four `write( )` methods are implemented. A subclass must override at least this method as well as `flush( )` and `close( )`, although most override some of the other `write( )` methods as well in order to provide more efficient implementations. For example, given a `Writer` object w, you can write the string "Network" like this:

```
char[] network = {'N', 'e', 't', 'w', 'o', 'r', 'k'};
w.write(network, 0, network.length);
```

The same task can be accomplished with these other methods, as well:

```
w.write(network);
for (int i = 0;  i < network.length;  i++) w.write(network[i]);
w.write("Network");
w.write("Network", 0, 7);
```

All of these examples are different ways of expressing the same thing. Which you use in any given situation is mostly a matter of convenience and taste. However, how many and which bytes are written by these lines depends on the encoding w uses. If it's using big-endian UTF-16, it will write these 14 bytes (shown here in hexadecimal) in this order:

```
00 4E 00 65 00 74 00 77 00 6F 00 72 00 6B
```

On the other hand, if w uses little-endian UTF-16, this sequence of 14 bytes is written:

```
4E 00 65 00 74 00 77 00 6F 00 72 00 6B 00
```

If w uses Latin–1, UTF-8, or MacRoman, this sequence of seven bytes is written:

```
4E 65 74 77 6F 72 6B
```

Other encodings may write still different sequences of bytes. The exact output depends on the encoding.

Writers may be buffered, either directly by being chained to a BufferedWriter or indirectly because their underlying output stream is buffered. To force a write to be committed to the output medium, invoke the flush( ) method:

```
w.flush();
```

The close( ) method behaves similarly to the close( ) method of OutputStream. close( ) flushes the writer, then closes the underlying output stream and releases any resources associated with it:

```
public abstract void close() throws IOException
```

After a writer has been closed, further writes throw IOExceptions.

OutputStreamWriter

OutputStreamWriter is the most important concrete subclass of Writer. An OutputStreamWriter receives characters from a Java program. It converts these into bytes according to a specified encoding and writes them onto an underlying output stream. Its constructor specifies the output stream to write to and the encoding to use:

```
public OutputStreamWriter(OutputStream out, String encoding)
  throws UnsupportedEncodingException
public OutputStreamWriter(OutputStream out)
```

Valid encodings are listed in the documentation for Sun's native2ascii tool included with the JDK and available from *http://java.sun.com/j2se/1.4.2/docs/guide/intl/ encoding.doc.html*. If no encoding is specified, the default encoding for the platform is used. (In the United States, the default encoding is ISO Latin–1 on Solaris and Windows, MacRoman on the Mac.) For example, this code fragment writes the string ἦμος δ'ἠριγένεια φάνη ῥοδοδάκτυλος Ἠώς in the Cp1253 Windows Greek encoding:

```
OutputStreamWriter w = new OutputStreamWriter(
  new FileOutputStream("OdysseyB.txt"), "Cp1253");
w.write("ἦμος δ'ἠριγένεια φάνη ῥοδοδάκτυλος Ἠώς");
```

Other than the constructors, OutputStreamWriter has only the usual Writer methods (which are used exactly as they are for any Writer class) and one method to return the encoding of the object:

```
public String getEncoding( )
```

Readers

The Reader class mirrors the java.io.InputStream class. It's abstract with two protected constructors. Like InputStream and Writer, the Reader class is never used directly, only through one of its subclasses. It has three read( ) methods, as well as skip( ), close( ), ready( ), mark( ), reset( ), and markSupported( ) methods:

```
protected Reader( )
protected Reader(Object lock)
public abstract int read(char[] text, int offset, int length)
 throws IOException
public int read( ) throws IOException
public int read(char[] text) throws IOException
public long skip(long n) throws IOException
public boolean ready( )
public boolean markSupported( )
public void mark(int readAheadLimit) throws IOException
public void reset( ) throws IOException
public abstract void close( ) throws IOException
```

The read(char[] text, int offset, int length) method is the fundamental method through which the other two read( ) methods are implemented. A subclass must override at least this method as well as close( ), although most will override some of the other read( ) methods as well in order to provide more efficient implementations.

Most of these methods are easily understood by analogy with their InputStream counterparts. The read( ) method returns a single Unicode character as an int with a value from 0 to 65,535 or –1 on end of stream. The read(char[] text) method tries to fill the array text with characters and returns the actual number of characters read or –1 on end of stream. The read(char[] text, int offset, int length) method attempts to read length characters into the subarray of text beginning at offset and continuing for length characters. It also returns the actual number of characters read or –1 on end of stream. The skip(long n) method skips n characters. The mark( ) and reset( ) methods allow some readers to reset back to a marked position in the character sequence. The markSupported( ) method tells you whether the reader supports marking and resetting. The close( ) method closes the reader and any underlying input stream so that further attempts to read from it throw IOExceptions.

The exception to the rule of similarity is ready( ), which has the same general purpose as available( ) but not quite the same semantics, even modulo the byte-to-char conversion. Whereas available( ) returns an int specifying a minimum number of bytes that may be read without blocking, ready( ) only returns a boolean indicating whether the reader may be read without blocking. The problem is that some character encodings, such as UTF-8, use different numbers of bytes for different characters. Thus, it's hard to tell how many characters are waiting in the network or filesystem buffer without actually reading them out of the buffer.

InputStreamReader is the most important concrete subclass of Reader. An InputStreamReader reads bytes from an underlying input stream such as a FileInputStream or TelnetInputStream. It converts these into characters according to a specified encoding and returns them. The constructor specifies the input stream to read from and the encoding to use:

```
public InputStreamReader(InputStream in)
public InputStreamReader(InputStream in, String encoding)
 throws UnsupportedEncodingException
```

If no encoding is specified, the default encoding for the platform is used. If an unknown encoding is specified, then an UnsupportedEncodingException is thrown.

For example, this method reads an input stream and converts it all to one Unicode string using the MacCyrillic encoding:

```
public static String getMacCyrillicString(InputStream in)
 throws IOException {

  InputStreamReader r = new InputStreamReader(in, "MacCyrillic");
  StringBuffer sb = new StringBuffer( );
  int c;
  while ((c = r.read( )) != -1) sb.append((char) c);
  r.close( );
  return sb.toString( );

}
```

Filter Readers and Writers

The InputStreamReader and OutputStreamWriter classes act as decorators on top of input and output streams that change the interface from a byte-oriented interface to a character-oriented interface. Once this is done, additional character-oriented filters can be layered on top of the reader or writer using the java.io.FilterReader and java.io.FilterWriter classes. As with filter streams, there are a variety of subclasses that perform specific filtering, including:

- BufferedReader
- BufferedWriter
- LineNumberReader

- PushbackReader
- PrintWriter

Buffered readers and writers

The BufferedReader and BufferedWriter classes are the character-based equivalents of the byte-oriented BufferedInputStream and BufferedOutputStream classes. Where BufferedInputStream and BufferedOutputStream use an internal array of bytes as a buffer, BufferedReader and BufferedWriter use an internal array of chars.

When a program reads from a BufferedReader, text is taken from the buffer rather than directly from the underlying input stream or other text source. When the buffer empties, it is filled again with as much text as possible, even if not all of it is immediately needed, making future reads much faster. When a program writes to a BufferedWriter, the text is placed in the buffer. The text is moved to the underlying output stream or other target only when the buffer fills up or when the writer is explicitly flushed, which can make writes much faster than would otherwise be the case.

BufferedReader and BufferedWriter have the usual methods associated with readers and writers, like read( ), ready( ), write( ), and close( ). They each have two constructors that chain the BufferedReader or BufferedWriter to an underlying reader or writer and set the size of the buffer. If the size is not set, the default size of 8,192 characters is used:

```
public BufferedReader(Reader in, int bufferSize)
public BufferedReader(Reader in)
public BufferedWriter(Writer out)
public BufferedWriter(Writer out, int bufferSize)
```

For example, the earlier getMacCyrillicString( ) example was less than efficient because it read characters one at a time. Since MacCyrillic is a 1-byte character set, it also read bytes one at a time. However, it's straightforward to make it run faster by chaining a BufferedReader to the InputStreamReader, like this:

```
public static String getMacCyrillicString(InputStream in)
 throws IOException {

  Reader r = new InputStreamReader(in, "MacCyrillic");
  r = new BufferedReader(r, 1024);
  StringBuffer sb = new StringBuffer( );
  int c;
  while ((c = r.read( )) != -1) sb.append((char) c);
  r.close( );
  return sb.toString( );

}
```

All that was needed to buffer this method was one additional line of code. None of the rest of the algorithm had to change, since the only InputStreamReader methods used were the read( ) and close( ) methods declared in the Reader superclass and shared by all Reader subclasses, including BufferedReader.

The BufferedReader class also has a readLine( ) method that reads a single line of text and returns it as a string:

```
public String readLine( ) throws IOException
```

This method is supposed to replace the deprecated readLine( ) method in DataInputStream, and it has mostly the same behavior as that method. The big difference is that by chaining a BufferedReader to an InputStreamReader, you can correctly read lines in character sets other than the default encoding for the platform. Unfortunately, this method shares the same bugs as the readLine( ) method in DataInputStream, discussed earlier in this chapter. That is, readline( ) tends to hang its thread when reading streams where lines end in carriage returns, as is commonly the case when the streams derive from a Macintosh or a Macintosh text file. Consequently, you should scrupulously avoid this method in network programs.

It's not all that difficult, however, to write a safe version of this class that correctly implements the readLine( ) method. Example 4-1 is such a SafeBufferedReader class. It has exactly the same public interface as BufferedReader; it just has a slightly different private implementation. I'll use this class in future chapters in situations where it's extremely convenient to have a readLine( ) method.

Example 4-1. The SafeBufferedReader class

```java
package com.macfaq.io;

import java.io.*;

public class SafeBufferedReader extends BufferedReader {

  public SafeBufferedReader(Reader in) {
    this(in, 1024);
  }

  public SafeBufferedReader(Reader in, int bufferSize) {
    super(in, bufferSize);
  }

  private boolean lookingForLineFeed = false;

  public String readLine( ) throws IOException {
    StringBuffer sb = new StringBuffer("");
    while (true) {
      int c = this.read( );
      if (c == -1) { // end of stream
        if (sb.equals("")) return null;
        return sb.toString( );
      }
      else if (c == '\n') {
        if (lookingForLineFeed) {
          lookingForLineFeed = false;
          continue;
```

Example 4-1. The SafeBufferedReader class (continued)

```
      }
      else {
        return sb.toString( );
      }
    }
    else if (c == '\r') {
      lookingForLineFeed = true;
      return sb.toString( );
    }
    else {
      lookingForLineFeed = false;
      sb.append((char) c);
    }
  }
}

}
```

The BufferedWriter( ) class adds one new method not included in its superclass, called newLine( ), also geared toward writing lines:

```
public void newLine( ) throws IOException
```

This method inserts a platform-dependent line-separator string into the output. The line.separator system property determines exactly what the string is: probably a linefeed on Unix and Mac OS X, a carriage return on Mac OS 9, and a carriage return/linefeed pair on Windows. Since network protocols generally specify the required line-terminator, you should not use this method for network programming. Instead, explicitly write the line-terminator the protocol requires.

LineNumberReader

LineNumberReader is a subclass of BufferedReader that keeps track of the current line number. This can be retrieved at any time with the getLineNumber( ) method:

```
public int getLineNumber( )
```

By default, the first line number is 0. However, the number of the current line and all subsequent lines can be changed with the setLineNumber( ) method:

```
public void setLineNumber(int lineNumber)
```

This method adjusts only the line numbers that getLineNumber( ) reports. It does not change the point at which the stream is read.

The LineNumberReader's readLine( ) method shares the same bug as BufferedReader and DataInputStream's, and is not suitable for network programming. However, the line numbers are also tracked if you use only the regular read( ) methods, and these do not share that bug. Besides these methods and the usual Reader methods, LineNumberReader has only these two constructors:

```
public LineNumberReader(Reader in)
public LineNumberReader(Reader in, int bufferSize)
```

Since LineNumberReader is a subclass of BufferedReader, it has an internal character buffer whose size can be set with the second constructor. The default size is 8,192 characters.

PushbackReader

The PushbackReader class is the mirror image of the PushbackInputStream class. As usual, the main difference is that it pushes back chars rather than bytes. It provides three unread( ) methods that push characters onto the reader's input buffer:

```
public void unread(int c) throws IOException
public void unread(char[] text) throws IOException
public void unread(char[] text, int offset, int length)
  throws IOException
```

The first unread( ) method pushes a single character onto the reader. The second pushes an array of characters. The third pushes the specified subarray of characters, starting with text[offset] and continuing through text[offset+length-1].

By default, the size of the pushback buffer is only one character. However, the size can be adjusted in the second constructor:

```
public PushbackReader(Reader in)
public PushbackReader(Reader in, int bufferSize)
```

Trying to unread more characters than the buffer will hold throws an IOException.

PrintWriter

The PrintWriter class is a replacement for Java 1.0's PrintStream class that properly handles multibyte character sets and international text. Sun originally planned to deprecate PrintStream in favor of PrintWriter but backed off when it realized this step would invalidate too much existing code, especially code that depended on System.out. Nonetheless, new code should use PrintWriter instead of PrintStream.

Aside from the constructors, the PrintWriter class has an almost identical collection of methods to PrintStream. These include:

```
public PrintWriter(Writer out)
public PrintWriter(Writer out, boolean autoFlush)
public PrintWriter(OutputStream out)
public PrintWriter(OutputStream out, boolean autoFlush)
public void flush( )
public void close( )
public boolean checkError( )
protected void setError( )
public void write(int c)
public void write(char[] text, int offset, int length)
public void write(char[] text)
public void write(String s, int offset, int length)
public void write(String s)
public void print(boolean b)
```

```
public void print(char c)
public void print(int i)
public void print(long l)
public void print(float f)
public void print(double d)
public void print(char[] text)
public void print(String s)
public void print(Object o)
public void println()
public void println(boolean b)
public void println(char c)
public void println(int i)
public void println(long l)
public void println(float f)
public void println(double d)
public void println(char[] text)
public void println(String s)
public void println(Object o)
```

Most of these methods behave the same for `PrintWriter` as they do for `PrintStream`. The exceptions are the four `write()` methods, which write characters rather than bytes; also, if the underlying writer properly handles character set conversion, so do all the methods of the `PrintWriter`. This is an improvement over the noninternationalizable `PrintStream` class, but it's still not good enough for network programming. `PrintWriter` still has the problems of platform dependency and minimal error reporting that plague `PrintStream`.

It isn't hard to write a `PrintWriter` class that does work for network programming. You simply have to require the programmer to specify a line separator and let the `IOExceptions` fall where they may. Example 4-2 demonstrates. Notice that all the constructors require an explicit line-separator string to be provided.

Example 4-2. SafePrintWriter

```
/*
 * @(#)SafePrintWriter.java 1.0 04/06/28
 *
 * Placed in the public domain
 * No rights reserved.
 */
package com.macfaq.io;

import java.io.*;

/**
 * @version   1.1, 2004-06-28
 * @author   Elliotte Rusty Harold
 * @since Java Network Programming, 2nd edition
 */
public class SafePrintWriter extends Writer {

  protected Writer out;
```

Example 4-2. SafePrintWriter (continued)

```java
  private boolean autoFlush = false;
  private String lineSeparator;
  private boolean closed = false;

  public SafePrintWriter(Writer out, String lineSeparator) {
    this(out, false, lineSeparator);
  }

  public SafePrintWriter(Writer out, char lineSeparator) {
    this(out, false, String.valueOf(lineSeparator));
  }

  public SafePrintWriter(Writer out, boolean autoFlush, String lineSeparator) {
    super(out);
    this.out = out;
    this.autoFlush = autoFlush;
    if (lineSeparator == null) {
      throw new NullPointerException("Null line separator");
    }
    this.lineSeparator = lineSeparator;
  }

  public SafePrintWriter(OutputStream out, boolean autoFlush,
   String encoding, String lineSeparator)
   throws UnsupportedEncodingException {
    this(new OutputStreamWriter(out, encoding), autoFlush, lineSeparator);
  }

  public void flush() throws IOException {

    synchronized (lock) {
      if (closed) throw new IOException("Stream closed");
      out.flush();
    }

  }

  public void close() throws IOException {

    try {
      this.flush();
    }
    catch (IOException ex) {
    }

    synchronized (lock) {
      out.close();
      this.closed = true;
    }

  }
```

Example 4-2. SafePrintWriter (continued)

```java
  public void write(int c) throws IOException {

    synchronized (lock) {
      if (closed) throw new IOException("Stream closed");
      out.write(c);
    }

  }

  public void write(char[] text, int offset, int length) throws IOException {
    synchronized (lock) {
      if (closed) throw new IOException("Stream closed");
      out.write(text, offset, length);
    }
  }

  public void write(char[] text) throws IOException {

    synchronized (lock) {
      if (closed) throw new IOException("Stream closed");
      out.write(text, 0, text.length);
    }

  }

  public void write(String s, int offset, int length) throws IOException {

    synchronized (lock) {
      if (closed) throw new IOException("Stream closed");
      out.write(s, offset, length);
    }

  }

  public void print(boolean b) throws IOException {
    if (b) this.write("true");
    else this.write("false");
  }

  public void println(boolean b) throws IOException {
    if (b) this.write("true");
    else this.write("false");
    this.write(lineSeparator);
    if (autoFlush) out.flush();
  }

  public void print(char c) throws IOException {
    this.write(String.valueOf(c));
  }

  public void println(char c) throws IOException {
    this.write(String.valueOf(c));
```

Example 4-2. SafePrintWriter (continued)

```
      this.write(lineSeparator);
      if (autoFlush) out.flush();
    }

    public void print(int i) throws IOException {
      this.write(String.valueOf(i));
    }

    public void println(int i) throws IOException {
      this.write(String.valueOf(i));
      this.write(lineSeparator);
      if (autoFlush) out.flush();
    }

    public void print(long l) throws IOException {
      this.write(String.valueOf(l));
    }

    public void println(long l) throws IOException {
      this.write(String.valueOf(l));
      this.write(lineSeparator);
      if (autoFlush) out.flush();
    }

    public void print(float f) throws IOException {
      this.write(String.valueOf(f));
    }

    public void println(float f) throws IOException {
      this.write(String.valueOf(f));
      this.write(lineSeparator);
      if (autoFlush) out.flush();
    }

    public void print(double d) throws IOException {
      this.write(String.valueOf(d));
    }

    public void println(double d) throws IOException {
      this.write(String.valueOf(d));
      this.write(lineSeparator);
      if (autoFlush) out.flush();
    }

    public void print(char[] text) throws IOException {
      this.write(text);
    }

    public void println(char[] text) throws IOException {
      this.write(text);
      this.write(lineSeparator);
      if (autoFlush) out.flush();
    }
```

Example 4-2. SafePrintWriter (continued)

```java
  public void print(String s) throws IOException {
    if (s == null) this.write("null");
    else this.write(s);
  }

  public void println(String s) throws IOException {
    if (s == null) this.write("null");
    else this.write(s);
    this.write(lineSeparator);
    if (autoFlush) out.flush();
  }

  public void print(Object o) throws IOException {
    if (o == null) this.write("null");
    else this.write(o.toString());
  }

  public void println(Object o) throws IOException {
    if (o == null) this.write("null");
    else this.write(o.toString());
    this.write(lineSeparator);
    if (autoFlush) out.flush();
  }

  public void println() throws IOException {
    this.write(lineSeparator);
    if (autoFlush) out.flush();
  }

}
```

This class actually extends `Writer` rather than `FilterWriter`, unlike `PrintWriter`. It could extend `FilterWriter` instead; however, this would save only one field and one line of code, since this class needs to override every single method in `FilterWriter` (close( ), flush( ), and all three write( ) methods). The reason for this is twofold. First, the `PrintWriter` class has to be much more careful about synchronization than the `FilterWriter` class. Second, some of the classes that may be used as an underlying `Writer` for this class, notably `CharArrayWriter`, do not implement the proper semantics for close( ) and allow further writes to take place even after the writer is closed. Consequently, programmers have to handle the checks for whether the stream is closed in this class rather than relying on the underlying `Writer` out to do it for them.

This chapter has been a whirlwind tour of the java.io package, covering the bare minimum you need to know to write network programs. For a more detailed and comprehensive look with many more examples, check out my other book in this series, *Java I/O* (O'Reilly).

CHAPTER 5

Threads

Back in the good old days of the Net, circa the early 1990s, we didn't have the Web and HTTP and graphical browsers. Instead, we had Usenet news and FTP and command-line interfaces, and we liked it that way! But as good as the good old days were, there were some problems. For instance, when we were downloading kilobytes of free software from a popular FTP site over our 2,400 bps modems using Kermit, we would often encounter error messages like this one:

```
% ftp eunl.java.sun.com
Connected to eunl.javasoft.com.
220 softwarenl FTP server (wu-2.4.2-academ[BETA- 16]+opie-2.32(1) 981105) ready.
Name (eunl.java.sun.com:elharo): anonymous
530-
530-    Server is busy.  Please try again later or try one of our other
530-    ftp servers at ftp.java.sun.com.  Thank you.
530-
530 User anonymous access denied.
Login failed.
```

In fact, in the days when the Internet had only a few million users instead of a few hundred million, we were far more likely to come across an overloaded and congested site than we are today. The problem was that both the FTP servers bundled with most Unixes and the third-party FTP servers, such as *wu-ftpd*, forked a new process for each connection. 100 simultaneous users meant 100 additional processes to handle. Since processes are fairly heavyweight items, too many could rapidly bring a server to its knees. The problem wasn't that the machines weren't powerful enough or the network fast enough; it was that the FTP servers were (and many still are) poorly implemented. Many more simultaneous users could be served if a new process wasn't needed for each connection.

Early web servers suffered from this problem as well, although the problem was masked a little by the transitory nature of HTTP connections. Since web pages and their embedded images tend to be small (at least compared to the software archives commonly retrieved by FTP) and since web browsers "hang up" the connection after each file is retrieved instead of staying connected for minutes or hours at a time, web users don't put nearly as much load on a server as FTP users do. However, web server performance still degrades as usage grows. The fundamental problem is that while it's easy to write code that handles each incoming connection and each new task as a separate process (at least on Unix), this solution doesn't scale. By the time a server is attempting to handle a thousand or more simultaneous connections, performance slows to a crawl.

There are at least two solutions to this problem. The first is to reuse processes rather than spawning new ones. When the server starts up, a fixed number of processes (say, 300) are spawned to handle requests. Incoming requests are placed in a queue. Each process removes one request from the queue, services the request, then returns to the queue to get the next request. There are still 300 separate processes running, but because all the overhead of building up and tearing down the processes is avoided, these 300 processes can now do the work of 1,000. These numbers are rough estimates. Your exact mileage may vary, especially if your server hasn't yet reached the volume where scalability issues come into play. Still, whatever mileage you get out of spawning new processes, you should be able to do much better by reusing old processes.

The second solution to this problem is to use lightweight threads to handle connections instead of heavyweight processes. Whereas each separate process has its own block of memory, threads are easier on resources because they share memory. Using threads instead of processes can buy you another factor of three in server performance. By combining this with a pool of reusable threads (as opposed to a pool of reusable processes), your server can run nine times faster, all on the same hardware and network connection! While it's still the case that most Java virtual machines keel over somewhere between 700 and 2,000 simultaneous threads, the impact of running many different threads on the server hardware is relatively minimal since they all run within one process. Furthermore, by using a thread pool instead of spawning new threads for each connection, a server can use fewer than a hundred threads to handle thousands of connections per minute.

Unfortunately, this increased performance doesn't come for free. There's a cost in program complexity. In particular, multithreaded servers (and other multithreaded programs) require programmers to address concerns that aren't issues for single-threaded programs, particularly issues of safety and liveness. Because different threads share the same memory, it's entirely possible for one thread to stomp all over the variables and data structures used by another thread. This is similar to the way one program running on a non-memory–protected operating system such as Mac OS 9 or Windows 95 can crash the entire system. Consequently, different threads have to be extremely careful about which resources they use when. Generally, each thread must agree to use certain resources only when it's sure those resources can't change or that it has exclusive access to them. However, it's also possible for two threads to be too careful, each waiting for exclusive access to resources it will never get. This can lead to deadlock, in which two threads are each waiting for resources the other possesses. Neither thread can proceed without the resources that the other thread has reserved, but neither is willing to give up the resources it has already.

 There is a third solution to the problem, which in many cases is the most efficient of all, although it's only available in Java 1.4 and later. Selectors enable one thread to query a group of sockets to find out which ones are ready to be read from or written to, and then process the ready sockets sequentially. In this case, the I/O has to be designed around channels and buffers rather than streams. We'll discuss this in Chapter 12, which demonstrates selector-based solutions to the problems solved in this chapter with threads.

Running Threads

A *thread* with a little *t* is a separate, independent path of execution in the virtual machine. A Thread with a capital *T* is an instance of the java.lang.Thread class. There is a one-to-one relationship between threads executing in the virtual machine and Thread objects constructed by the virtual machine. Most of the time it's obvious from the context which one is meant if the difference is really important. To start a new thread running in the virtual machine, you construct an instance of the Thread class and invoke its start( ) method, like this:

```
Thread t = new Thread( );
t.start( );
```

Of course, this thread isn't very interesting because it doesn't have anything to do. To give a thread something to do, you either subclass the Thread class and override its run( ) method, or implement the Runnable interface and pass the Runnable object to the Thread constructor. I generally prefer the second option since it separates the task that the thread performs from the thread itself more cleanly, but you will see both techniques used in this book and elsewhere. In both cases, the key is the run( ) method, which has this signature:

```
public void run( )
```

You're going to put all the work the thread does in this one method. This method may invoke other methods; it may construct other objects; it may even spawn other threads. However, the thread starts here and it stops here. When the run( ) method completes, the thread dies. In essence, the run( ) method is to a thread what the main( ) method is to a traditional nonthreaded program. A single-threaded program exits when the main( ) method returns. A multithreaded program exits when both the main( ) method and the run( ) methods of all nondaemon threads return. (Daemon threads perform background tasks such as garbage collection and don't prevent the virtual machine from exiting.)

Subclassing Thread

For example, suppose you want to write a program that calculates the Secure Hash Algorithm (SHA) digest for many files. To a large extent, this program is I/O-bound; that is, its speed is limited by the amount of time it takes to read the files from the disk. If you write it as a standard program that processes the files in series, the program's going to spend a lot of time waiting for the hard drive to return the data. This is characteristic of a lot of network programs: they have a tendency to execute faster than the network can supply input. Consequently, they spend a lot of time blocked. This is time that other threads could use, either to process other input sources or to do something that doesn't rely on slow input. (Not all threaded programs share this characteristic. Sometimes, even if none of the threads have a lot of spare time to allot to other threads, it's simply easier to design a program by breaking it into multiple threads that perform independent operations.) Example 5-1 is a subclass of Thread whose run( ) method calculates an SHA message digest for a specified file.

Example 5-1. FileDigestThread

```
import java.io.*;
import java.security.*;

public class DigestThread extends Thread {

  private File input;

  public DigestThread(File input) {
   this.input = input;
  }

  public void run( ) {
    try {
      FileInputStream in = new FileInputStream(input);
      MessageDigest sha = MessageDigest.getInstance("SHA");
      DigestInputStream din = new DigestInputStream(in, sha);
      int b;
      while ((b = din.read( )) != -1) ;
      din.close( );
      byte[] digest = sha.digest( );
      StringBuffer result = new StringBuffer(input.toString( ));
      result.append(": ");
      for (int i = 0; i < digest.length; i++) {
        result.append(digest[i] + " ");
      }
      System.out.println(result);
    }
    catch (IOException ex) {
      System.err.println(ex);
    }
    catch (NoSuchAlgorithmException ex) {
      System.err.println(ex);
    }
```

Example 5-1. FileDigestThread (continued)

```
  }

  public static void main(String[] args) {

    for (int i = 0; i < args.length; i++) {
      File f = new File(args[i]);
      Thread t = new DigestThread(f);
      t.start();
    }

  }

}
```

The main() method reads filenames from the command-line and starts a new DigestThread for each one. The work of the thread is actually performed in the run() method. Here, a DigestInputStream reads the file. Then the resulting digest is printed on System.out. Notice that the entire output from this thread is first built in a local StringBuffer variable result. This is then printed on the console with one method invocation. The more obvious path of printing the pieces one at a time using System.out.print() is not taken. There's a reason for that, which we'll discuss soon.

Since the signature of the run() method is fixed, you can't pass arguments to it or return values from it. Consequently, you need different ways to pass information into the thread and get information out of it. The simplest way to pass information in is to pass arguments to the constructor, which set fields in the Thread subclass, as done here.

Getting information out of a thread back into the original calling thread is trickier because of the asynchronous nature of threads. Example 5-1 sidesteps that problem by never passing any information back to the calling thread and simply printing the results on System.out. Most of the time, however, you'll want to pass the information to other parts of the program. You can store the result of the calculation in a field and provide a getter method to return the value of that field. However, how do you know when the calculation of that value is complete? What do you return if somebody calls the getter method before the value has been calculated? This is quite tricky, and we'll discuss it more later in this chapter.

If you subclass Thread, you should override run() *and nothing else!* The various other methods of the Thread class, start(), stop(), interrupt(), join(), sleep(), and so on, all have very specific semantics and interactions with the virtual machine that are difficult to reproduce in your own code. You should override run() and provide additional constructors and other methods as necessary, but you should not replace any of the other standard Thread methods.

Implementing the Runnable Interface

One way to avoid overriding the standard Thread methods is not to subclass Thread. Instead, write the task you want the thread to perform as an instance of the Runnable interface. This interface declares the run( ) method, exactly the same as the Thread class:

```
public void run( )
```

Other than this method, which any class implementing this interface must provide, you are completely free to create any other methods with any other names you choose, all without any possibility of unintentionally interfering with the behavior of the thread. This also allows you to place the thread's task in a subclass of some other class, such as Applet or HTTPServlet. To start a thread that performs the Runnable's task, pass the Runnable object to the Thread constructor. For example:

```
Thread t = new Thread(myRunnableObject);
t.start( );
```

It's easy to recast most problems that subclass Thread into Runnable forms. Example 5-2 demonstrates by rewriting Example 5-1 to use the Runnable interface rather than subclassing Thread. Aside from the name change, the only modifications that are necessary are changing extends Thread to implements Runnable and passing a DigestRunnable object to the Thread constructor in the main( ) method. The essential logic of the program is unchanged.

Example 5-2. DigestRunnable

```java
import java.io.*;
import java.security.*;

public class DigestRunnable implements Runnable {

  private File input;

  public DigestRunnable(File input) {
   this.input = input;
  }

  public void run( ) {
    try {
      FileInputStream in = new FileInputStream(input);
      MessageDigest sha = MessageDigest.getInstance("SHA");
      DigestInputStream din = new DigestInputStream(in, sha);
      int b;
      while ((b = din.read( )) != -1) ;
      din.close( );
      byte[] digest = sha.digest( );
      StringBuffer result = new StringBuffer(input.toString( ));
      result.append(": ");
      for (int i = 0; i < digest.length; i++) {
        result.append(digest[i] + " ");
```

Example 5-2. DigestRunnable (continued)

```
      }
      System.out.println(result);
    }
    catch (IOException ex) {
      System.err.println(ex);
    }
    catch (NoSuchAlgorithmException ex) {
      System.err.println(ex);
    }

  }

  public static void main(String[] args) {

    for (int i = 0; i < args.length; i++) {
      File f = new File(args[i]);
      DigestRunnable dr = new DigestRunnable(f);
      Thread t = new Thread(dr);
      t.start();
    }

  }

}
```

There's no strong reason to prefer implementing Runnable to extending Thread or vice versa in the general case. In a few special cases, such as Example 5-14 later in this chapter, it may be useful to invoke some instance methods of the Thread class from within the constructor for each Thread object. This requires using a subclass. In some specific cases, it may be necessary to place the run( ) method in a class that extends another class, such as Applet, in which case the Runnable interface is essential. Finally, some object-oriented purists argue that the task that a thread undertakes is not really a kind of Thread, and therefore should be placed in a separate class or interface such as Runnable rather than in a subclass of Thread. I half agree with them, although I don't think the argument is as strong as it's sometimes made out to be. Consequently, I'll mostly use the Runnable interface in this book, but you should feel free to do whatever seems most convenient.

Returning Information from a Thread

One of the hardest things for programmers accustomed to traditional, single-threaded procedural models to grasp when moving to a multithreaded environment is how to return information from a thread. Getting information out of a finished thread is one of the most commonly misunderstood aspects of multithreaded programming. The run( ) method and the start( ) method don't return any values. For example, suppose that instead of simply printing out the SHA digest, as in

Example 5-1 and Example 5-2, the digest thread needs to return the digest to the main thread of execution. Most people's first reaction is to store the result in a field and provide a getter method, as shown in Example 5-3 and Example 5-4. Example 5-3 is a Thread subclass that calculates a digest for a specified file. Example 5-4 is a simple command-line user interface that receives filenames and spawns threads to calculate digests for them.

Example 5-3. A thread that uses an accessor method to return the result

```java
import java.io.*;
import java.security.*;

public class ReturnDigest extends Thread {

  private File input;
  private byte[] digest;

  public ReturnDigest(File input) {
   this.input = input;
  }

  public void run( ) {
    try {
      FileInputStream in = new FileInputStream(input);
      MessageDigest sha = MessageDigest.getInstance("SHA");
      DigestInputStream din = new DigestInputStream(in, sha);
      int b;
      while ((b = din.read( )) != -1) ;
      din.close( );
      digest = sha.digest( );
    }
    catch (IOException ex) {
      System.err.println(ex);
    }
    catch (NoSuchAlgorithmException ex) {
      System.err.println(ex);
    }

  }

  public byte[] getDigest( ) {
    return digest;
  }

}
```

Example 5-4. A main program that uses the accessor method to get the output of the thread

```java
import java.io.*;

public class ReturnDigestUserInterface {

  public static void main(String[] args) {
```

```
    for (int i = 0; i < args.length; i++) {

        // Calculate the digest
        File f = new File(args[i]);
        ReturnDigest dr = new ReturnDigest(f);
        dr.start();

        // Now print the result
        StringBuffer result = new StringBuffer(f.toString());
        result.append(": ");
        byte[] digest = dr.getDigest();
        for (int j = 0; j < digest.length; j++) {
          result.append(digest[j] + " ");
        }
        System.out.println(result);

    }

  }

}
```

The ReturnDigest class stores the result of the calculation in the private field digest, which is accessed via getDigest( ). The main( ) method in ReturnDigestUserInterface loops through a list of files from the command line. It starts a new ReturnDigest thread for each file and then tries to retrieve the result using getDigest( ). However, when you run this program, the result may not be what you expect:

```
D:\JAVA\JNP3\examples\05>java ReturnDigestUserInterface *.java
Exception in thread "main" java.lang.NullPointerException
     at ReturnDigestUserInterface.main(ReturnDigestUserInterface.java,
     Compiled Code)
```

The problem is that the main program gets the digest and uses it before the thread has had a chance to initialize it. Although this flow of control would work in a single-threaded program in which dr.start( ) simply invoked the run( ) method in the same thread, that's not what happens here. The calculations that dr.start( ) kicks off may or may not finish before the main( ) method reaches the call to dr.getDigest( ). If they haven't finished, dr.getDigest( ) returns null, and the first attempt to access digest throws a NullPointerException.

Race Conditions

One possibility is to move the call to dr.getDigest( ) later in the main( ) method, like this:

```
public static void main(String[] args) {

    ReturnDigest[] digests = new ReturnDigest[args.length];
```

```
    for (int i = 0; i < args.length; i++) {

        // Calculate the digest
        File f = new File(args[i]);
        digests[i] = new ReturnDigest(f);
        digests[i].start();

    }

    for (int i = 0; i < args.length; i++) {

        // Now print the result
        StringBuffer result = new StringBuffer(args[i]);
        result.append(": ");
        byte[] digest = digests[i].getDigest();
        for (int j = 0; j < digest.length; j++) {
            result.append(digest[j] + " ");
        }
        System.out.println(result);

    }

}
```

If you're lucky, this will work and you'll get the expected output, like this:

```
D:\JAVA\JNP3\examples\05>java ReturnDigest2 *.java
BadDigestRunnable.java: 73 -77 -74 111 -75 -14 70 13 -27 -28 32 68 -126
43 -27 55 -119 26 -77 6
BadDigestThread.java: 69 101 80 -94 -98 -113 29 -52 -124 -121 -38 -82 39
-4 8 -38 119 96 -37 -99
DigestRunnable.java: 61 116 -102 -120 97 90 53 37 -14 111 -60 -86 -112
124 -54 111 114 -42 -36 -111
DigestThread.java: 69 101 80 -94 -98 -113 29 -52 -124 -121 -38 -82 39
-4 8 -38 119 96 -37 -99
```

But let me emphasize that point about being lucky. You may not get this output. In fact, you may still get a NullPointerException. Whether this code works is completely dependent on whether every one of the ReturnDigest threads finishes before its getDigest() method is called. If the first for loop is too fast and the second for loop is entered before the threads spawned by the first loop start finishing, we're back where we started:

```
D:\JAVA\JNP3\examples\05>java ReturnDigest2 ReturnDigest.java
Exception in thread "main" java.lang.NullPointerException
        at ReturnDigest2.main(ReturnDigest2.java, Compiled Code)
```

Whether you get the correct results or this exception depends on many factors, including how many threads the program spawns, the relative speeds of the CPU and disk on the system where this is run, and the algorithm the Java virtual machine uses to allot time to different threads. This is called a *race condition*. Getting the correct result depends on the relative speeds of different threads, and you can't control those! We need a better way to guarantee that the getDigest( ) method isn't called until the digest is ready.

Polling

The solution most novices adopt is to make the getter method return a flag value (or perhaps throw an exception) until the result field is set. Then the main thread periodically polls the getter method to see whether it's returning something other than the flag value. In this example, that would mean repeatedly testing whether the digest is null and using it only if it isn't. For example:

```
public static void main(String[] args) {

  ReturnDigest[] digests = new ReturnDigest[args.length];

  for (int i = 0; i < args.length; i++) {

    // Calculate the digest
    File f = new File(args[i]);
    digests[i] = new ReturnDigest(f);
    digests[i].start( );

  }

  for (int i = 0; i < args.length; i++) {
    while (true) {
      // Now print the result
      byte[] digest = digests[i].getDigest( );
      if (digest != null) {
        StringBuffer result = new StringBuffer(args[i]);
        result.append(": ");
        for (int j = 0; j < digest.length; j++) {
          result.append(digest[j] + " ");
        }
        System.out.println(result);
        break;
      }
    }
  }

}
```

This solution works. It gives the correct answers in the correct order and it works irrespective of how fast the individual threads run relative to each other. However, it's doing a lot more work than it needs to.

Callbacks

In fact, there's a much simpler, more efficient way to handle the problem. The infinite loop that repeatedly polls each ReturnDigest object to see whether it's finished can be eliminated. The trick is that rather than having the main program repeatedly ask each ReturnDigest thread whether it's finished (like a five-year-old repeatedly asking, "Are we there yet?" on a long car trip, and almost as annoying), we let the thread tell the main program when it's finished. It does this by invoking a method in the main class that started it. This is called a *callback* because the thread calls its creator back when it's done. This way, the main program can go to sleep while waiting for the threads to finish and not steal time from the running threads.

When the thread's run( ) method is nearly done, the last thing it does is invoke a known method in the main program with the result. Rather than the main program asking each thread for the answer, each thread tells the main program the answer. For instance, Example 5-5 shows a CallbackDigest class that is much the same as before. However, at the end of the run( ) method, it passes off the digest to the static CallbackDigestUserInterface.receiveDigest( ) method in the class that originally started the thread.

Example 5-5. CallbackDigest

```
import java.io.*;
import java.security.*;

public class CallbackDigest implements Runnable {

  private File input;

  public CallbackDigest(File input) {
   this.input = input;
  }

  public void run( ) {

    try {
      FileInputStream in = new FileInputStream(input);
      MessageDigest sha = MessageDigest.getInstance("SHA");
      DigestInputStream din = new DigestInputStream(in, sha);
      int b;
      while ((b = din.read( )) != -1) ;
      din.close( );
      byte[] digest = sha.digest( );
      CallbackDigestUserInterface.receiveDigest(digest,
        input.getName( ));
    }
    catch (IOException ex) {
      System.err.println(ex);
    }
    catch (NoSuchAlgorithmException ex) {
      System.err.println(ex);
    }

  }

}
```

The `CallbackDigestUserInterface` class shown in Example 5-6 provides the `main( )` method. However, unlike the `main( )` methods in the other variations of this program in this chapter, this one only starts the threads for the files named on the command line. It does not attempt to actually read, print out, or in any other way work with the results of the calculation. Those functions are handled by a separate method, `receiveDigest( )`. `receiveDigest( )` is not invoked by the `main( )` method or by any method that can be reached by following the flow of control from the `main( )` method. Instead, it is invoked by each thread separately. In effect, `receiveDigest( )` runs inside the digesting threads rather than inside the main thread of execution.

Example 5-6. CallbackDigestUserInterface

```java
import java.io.*;

public class CallbackDigestUserInterface {

  public static void receiveDigest(byte[] digest, String name) {

    StringBuffer result = new StringBuffer(name);
    result.append(": ");
    for (int j = 0; j < digest.length; j++) {
      result.append(digest[j] + " ");
    }
    System.out.println(result);

  }

  public static void main(String[] args) {

    for (int i = 0; i < args.length; i++) {
      // Calculate the digest
      File f = new File(args[i]);
      CallbackDigest cb = new CallbackDigest(f);
      Thread t = new Thread(cb);
      t.start();
    }

  }

}
```

Example 5-5 and Example 5-6 use static methods for the callback so that `CallbackDigest` only needs to know the name of the method in `CallbackDigestUserInterface` to call. However, it's not much harder (and it's considerably more common) to call back to an instance method. In this case, the class making the callback must have a reference to the object it's calling back. Generally, this reference is provided as an argument to the thread's constructor. When the `run( )` method is nearly done, the last thing it does is invoke the instance method on the callback object to pass along the result. For instance, Example 5-7 shows a `CallbackDigest` class that is much the same as before. However, it now has

one additional field, a CallbackDigestUserInterface object called callback. At the
end of the run( ) method, the digest is passed to callback's receiveDigest( )
method. The CallbackDigestUserInterface object itself is set in the constructor.

Example 5-7. InstanceCallbackDigest

```java
import java.io.*;
import java.security.*;


public class InstanceCallbackDigest implements Runnable {

  private File input;
  private InstanceCallbackDigestUserInterface callback;

  public InstanceCallbackDigest(File input,
   InstanceCallbackDigestUserInterface callback) {
    this.input = input;
    this.callback = callback;
  }

  public void run( ) {

    try {
      FileInputStream in = new FileInputStream(input);
      MessageDigest sha = MessageDigest.getInstance("SHA");
      DigestInputStream din = new DigestInputStream(in, sha);
      int b;
      while ((b = din.read( )) != -1) ;
      din.close( );
      byte[] digest = sha.digest( );
      callback.receiveDigest(digest);
    }
    catch (IOException ex) {
      System.err.println(ex);
    }
    catch (NoSuchAlgorithmException ex) {
      System.err.println(ex);
    }

  }

}
```

The CallbackDigestUserInterface class shown in Example 5-8 holds the main( )
method as well as the receiveDigest( ) method used to handle an incoming digest.
Example 5-8 just prints out the digest, but a more expansive class could do other
things as well, such as storing the digest in a field, using it to start another thread, or
performing further calculations on it.

Example 5-8. InstanceCallbackDigestUserInterface

```java
import java.io.*;

public class InstanceCallbackDigestUserInterface {

  private File input;
  private byte[] digest;

  public InstanceCallbackDigestUserInterface(File input) {
    this.input = input;
  }

  public void calculateDigest() {
    InstanceCallbackDigest cb = new InstanceCallbackDigest(input, this);
    Thread t = new Thread(cb);
    t.start();
  }

  void receiveDigest(byte[] digest) {
    this.digest = digest;
    System.out.println(this);
  }

  public String toString() {
    String result = input.getName() + ": ";
    if (digest != null) {
      for (int i = 0; i < digest.length; i++) {
        result += digest[i] + " ";
      }
    }
    else {
      result += "digest not available";
    }
    return result;
  }

  public static void main(String[] args) {

    for (int i = 0; i < args.length; i++) {
      // Calculate the digest
      File f = new File(args[i]);
      InstanceCallbackDigestUserInterface d
       = new InstanceCallbackDigestUserInterface(f);
      d.calculateDigest();
    }

  }

}
```

Using instance methods instead of static methods for callbacks is a little more complicated but has a number of advantages. First, each instance of the main class (InstanceCallbackDigestUserInterface, in this example) maps to exactly one file and can keep track of information about that file in a natural way without needing extra data structures. Furthermore, the instance can easily recalculate the digest for a particular file, if necessary. In practice, this scheme proves a lot more flexible. However, there is one caveat. Notice the addition of the calculateDigest( ) method to start the thread. You might logically think that this belongs in a constructor. However, starting threads in a constructor is dangerous, especially threads that will call back to the originating object. There's a race condition here that may allow the new thread to call back before the constructor is finished and the object is fully initialized. It's unlikely in this case, because starting the new thread is the last thing this constructor does. Nonetheless, it's at least theoretically possible. Therefore, it's good form to avoid launching threads from constructors.

The first advantage of the callback scheme over the polling scheme is that it doesn't waste so many CPU cycles. But a much more important advantage is that callbacks are more flexible and can handle more complicated situations involving many more threads, objects, and classes. For instance, if more than one object is interested in the result of the thread's calculation, the thread can keep a list of objects to call back. Particular objects can register their interest by invoking a method in the Thread or Runnable class to add themselves to the list. If instances of more than one class are interested in the result, a new interface can be defined that all these classes implement. The interface would declare the callback methods. If you're experiencing déjà vu right now, that's probably because you have seen this scheme before. This is *exactly* how events are handled in Swing, the AWT, and JavaBeans. The AWT runs in a separate thread from the rest of the program; components and beans inform you of events by calling back to methods declared in particular interfaces, such as ActionListener and PropertyChangeListener. Your listener objects register their interests in events fired by particular components using methods in the Component class, such as addActionListener( ) and addPropertyChangeListener( ). Inside the component, the registered listeners are stored in a linked list built out of java.awt. AWTEventMulticaster objects. It's easy to duplicate this pattern in your own classes. Example 5-9 shows one very simple possible interface class called DigestListener that declares the digestCalculated( ) method.

Example 5-9. DigestListener interface
```
public interface DigestListener {

  public void digestCalculated(byte[] digest);

}
```

Example 5-10 shows the Runnable class that calculates the digest. Several new methods and fields are added for registering and deregistering listeners. For convenience and simplicity, a java.util.Vector manages the list. The run( ) method no longer directly calls back the object that created it. Instead, it communicates with the private sendDigest( ) method, which sends the digest to all registered listeners. The run( ) method neither knows nor cares who's listening to it. This class no longer knows anything about the user interface class. It has been completely decoupled from the classes that may invoke it. This is one of the strengths of this approach.

Example 5-10. The ListCallbackDigest class

```java
import java.io.*;
import java.security.*;
import java.util.*;

public class ListCallbackDigest implements Runnable {

  private File input;
  List listenerList = new Vector( );

  public ListCallbackDigest(File input) {
   this.input = input;
  }

  public synchronized void addDigestListener(DigestListener l) {
    listenerList.add(l);
  }

  public synchronized void removeDigestListener(DigestListener l) {
    listenerList.remove(l);
  }

  private synchronized  void sendDigest(byte[] digest) {

    ListIterator iterator = listenerList.listIterator( );
    while (iterator.hasNext( )) {
      DigestListener dl = (DigestListener) iterator.next( );
      dl.digestCalculated(digest);
    }

  }

  public void run( ) {

    try {
      FileInputStream in = new FileInputStream(input);
      MessageDigest sha = MessageDigest.getInstance("SHA");
      DigestInputStream din = new DigestInputStream(in, sha);
      int b;
      while ((b = din.read( )) != -1) ;
      din.close( );
      byte[] digest = sha.digest( );
      this.sendDigest(digest);
    }
    catch (IOException ex) {
      System.err.println(ex);
    }
    catch (NoSuchAlgorithmException ex) {
```

Example 5-10. The ListCallbackDigest class (continued)

```
    System.err.println(ex);
  }


 }


}
```

Finally, Example 5-11 is a main program that implements the `DigestListener` interface and exercises the `ListCallbackDigest` class by calculating digests for all the files named on the command line. However, this is no longer the only possible main program. There are now many more possible ways the digest thread could be used.

Example 5-11. ListCallbackDigestUserInterface interface

```java
import java.io.*;

public class ListCallbackDigestUserInterface implements DigestListener {

  private File input;
  private byte[] digest;

  public ListCallbackDigestUserInterface(File input) {
    this.input = input;
  }

  public void calculateDigest( ) {
    ListCallbackDigest cb = new ListCallbackDigest(input);
    cb.addDigestListener(this);
    Thread t = new Thread(cb);
    t.start( );
  }

  public void digestCalculated(byte[] digest) {
    this.digest = digest;
    System.out.println(this);
  }

  public String toString( ) {
    String result = input.getName( ) + ": ";
    if (digest != null) {
      for (int i = 0; i < digest.length; i++) {
        result += digest[i] + " ";
      }
    }
    else {
      result += "digest not available";
    }
    return result;
  }

  public static void main(String[] args) {
```

Example 5-11. ListCallbackDigestUserInterface interface (continued)

```
  for (int i = 0; i < args.length; i++) {
    // Calculate the digest
    File f = new File(args[i]);
    ListCallbackDigestUserInterface d
     = new ListCallbackDigestUserInterface(f);
    d.calculateDigest( );
  }

 }

}
```

Synchronization

My shelves are overflowing with books, including many duplicate books, out-of-date books, and books I haven't looked at for 10 years and probably never will again. Over the years, these books have cost me tens of thousands of dollars, maybe more, to acquire. By contrast, two blocks down the street from my apartment, you'll find the Central Brooklyn Public Library. Its shelves are also overflowing with books; and over its 150 years, it's spent millions on its collection. But the difference is that its books are shared among all the residents of Brooklyn, and consequently the books have very high turnover. Most books in the collection are used several times a year. Although the public library spends a lot more money buying and storing books than I do, the cost per page read is much lower at the library than for my personal shelves. That's the advantage of a shared resource.

Of course, there are disadvantages to shared resources, too. If I need a book from the library, I have to walk over there. I have to find the book I'm looking for on the shelves. I have to stand in line to check the book out, or else I have to use it right there in the library rather than bringing it home with me. Sometimes, somebody else has checked the book out, and I have to fill out a reservation slip requesting that the book be saved for me when it's returned. And I can't write notes in the margins, highlight paragraphs, or tear pages out to paste on my bulletin board. (Well, I can, but if I do, it significantly reduces the usefulness of the book for future borrowers; and if the library catches me, I may lose my borrowing privileges.) There's a significant time and convenience penalty associated with borrowing a book from the library rather than purchasing my own copy, but it does save me money and storage space.

A thread is like a borrower at a library; the thread borrows from a central pool of resources. Threads make programs more efficient by sharing memory, file handles, sockets, and other resources. As long as two threads don't want to use the same resource at the same time, a multithreaded program is much more efficient than the multiprocess alternative, in which each process has to keep its own copy of every resource. The downside of a multithreaded program is that if two threads want the same resource at the same time, one of them will have to wait for the other to finish.

If one of them doesn't wait, the resource may get corrupted. Let's look at a specific example. Consider the run( ) method of Example 5-1 and Example 5-2. As previously mentioned, the method builds the result as a String, and then prints the String on the console using one call to System.out.println( ). The output looks like this:

```
DigestThread.java: 69 101 80 -94 -98 -113 29 -52 -124 -121 -38 -82 39
-4 8 -38 119 96 -37 -99
DigestRunnable.java: 61 116 -102 -120 97 90 53 37 -14 111 -60 -86 -112
124 -54 111 114 -42 -36 -111
DigestThread.class: -62 -99 -39 -19 109 10 -91 25 -54 -128 -101 17 13
-66 119 25 -114 62 -21 121
DigestRunnable.class: 73 15 7 -122 96 66 -107 -45 69 -36 86 -43 103
-104 25 -128 -97 60 14 -76
```

Four threads run in parallel to produce this output. Each writes one line to the console. The order in which the lines are written is unpredictable because thread scheduling is unpredictable, but each line is written as a unified whole. Suppose, however, we used this variation of the run( ) method, which, rather than storing intermediate parts of the result in the String variable result, simply prints them on the console as they become available:

```
public void run( ) {

  try {
    FileInputStream in = new FileInputStream(input);
    MessageDigest sha = MessageDigest.getInstance("SHA");
    DigestInputStream din = new DigestInputStream(in, sha);
    int b;
    while ((b = din.read( )) != -1) ;
    din.close( );
    byte[] digest = sha.digest( );
    System.out.print(input + ": ");
    for (int i = 0; i < digest.length; i++) {
     System.out.print(digest[i] + " ");
    }
    System.out.println( );
  }
  catch (IOException ex) {
    System.err.println(ex);
  }
  catch (NoSuchAlgorithmException ex) {
    System.err.println(ex);
  }

}
```

When you run the program on the same input, the output looks something like this:

```
DigestRunnable.class: 73 15 7 -122 96 66 -107 -45 69 -36 86 -43 103 -104 25
-128 DigestRunnable.java: DigestThread.class: DigestThread.java:
61 -62 69 116 -99 101 -102 -39 80 -120 -19 -94 97 109 -98 90 -97 10 -113 53 60
-91 29 37 14 25 -52 -14 -76 -54 -124 111
-128 -121 -60 -101 -38 -86 17 -82 -112 13 39 124 -66 -4 -54 119 8 111 25 -38 114
-114 119 -42 62 96 -36 -21 -37 -111 121 -99
```

The digests of the different files are all mixed up! There's no telling which number belongs to which digest. Clearly, this is a problem.

The reason this mix-up occurs is that System.out is shared between the four different threads. When one thread starts writing to the console through several System.out. print( ) statements, it may not finish all its writes before another thread breaks in and starts writing its output. The exact order in which one thread preempts the other threads is indeterminate. You'll probably see slightly different output every time you run this program.

We need a way to assign exclusive access to a shared resource to one thread for a specific series of statements. In this example, that shared resource is System.out, and the statements that need exclusive access are:

```
System.out.print(input + ": ");
for (int i = 0; i < digest.length; i++) {
  System.out.print(digest[i] + " ");
}
System.out.println( );
```

Synchronized Blocks

Java's means of assigning exclusive access to an object is the synchronized keyword. To indicate that these five lines of code should be executed together, wrap them in a synchronized block that synchronizes on the System.out object, like this:

```
synchronized (System.out) {
  System.out.print(input + ": ");
  for (int i = 0; i < digest.length; i++) {
    System.out.print(digest[i] + " ");
  }
  System.out.println( );
}
```

Once one thread starts printing out the values, all other threads will have to stop and wait for it to finish before they can print out their values. Synchronization is only a partial lock on an object. Other methods can use the synchronized object if they do so blindly, without attempting to synchronize on the object. For instance, in this case, there's nothing to prevent an unrelated thread from printing on System.out if it doesn't also try to synchronize on System.out. Java provides no means to stop all other threads from using a shared resource. It can only prevent other threads that synchronize on the same object from using the shared resource.

In fact, the PrintStream class internally synchronizes most methods on the PrintStream object, System.out in this example. In other words, every other thread that calls System.out.println( ) will be synchronized on System.out and will have to wait for this code to finish. PrintStream is unique in this respect. Most other OutputStream subclasses do not synchronize themselves.

Synchronization must be considered any time multiple threads share resources. These threads may be instances of the same Thread subclass or use the same Runnable class, or they may be instances of completely different classes. The key is the resources they share, not what classes they are. In Java, all resources are represented by objects that are instances of particular classes. Synchronization becomes an issue only when two threads both possess references to the same object. In the previous example, the problem was that several threads had access to the same PrintStream object, System.out. In this case, it was a static class variable that led to the conflict. However, instance variables can also have problems.

For example, suppose your web server keeps a log file. The log file may be represented by a class like the one shown in Example 5-12. This class itself doesn't use multiple threads. However, if the web server uses multiple threads to handle incoming connections, then each of those threads will need access to the same log file and consequently to the same LogFile object.

Example 5-12. LogFile

```
import java.io.*;
import java.util.*;

public class LogFile {

  private Writer out;

  public LogFile(File f) throws IOException {
    FileWriter fw = new FileWriter(f);
    this.out = new BufferedWriter(fw);
  }

  public void writeEntry(String message) throws IOException {
    Date d = new Date( );
    out.write(d.toString( ));
    out.write('\t');
    out.write(message);
    out.write("\r\n");
  }

  public void close( ) throws IOException {
    out.flush( );
    out.close( );
  }

  protected void finalize( ) {
    try {
      this.close( );
    }
    catch (IOException ex) {
    }
  }

}
```

In this class, the writeEntry( ) method finds the current date and time, then writes into the underlying file using four separate invocations of out.write( ). A problem occurs if two or more threads each have a reference to the same LogFile object and one of those threads interrupts another in the process of writing the data. One thread may write the date and a tab, then the next thread might write three complete entries; then, the first thread could write the message, a carriage return, and a line-feed. The solution, once again, is synchronization. However, here there are two good choices for which object to synchronize on. The first choice is to synchronize on the Writer object out. For example:

```
public void writeEntry(String message) throws IOException {

  synchronized (out) {
    Date d = new Date();
    out.write(d.toString());
    out.write('\t');
    out.write(message);
    out.write("\r\n");
  }

}
```

This works because all the threads that use this LogFile object also use the same out object that's part of that LogFile. It doesn't matter that out is private. Although it is used by the other threads and objects, it's referenced only within the LogFile class. Furthermore, although we're synchronizing here on the out object, it's the writeEntry( ) method that needs to be protected from interruption. The Writer classes all have their own internal synchronization, which protects one thread from interfering with a write( ) method in another thread. (This is not true of input and output streams, with the exception of PrintStream. It is possible for a write to an output stream to be interrupted by another thread.) Each Writer class has a lock field that specifies the object on which writes to that writer synchronize.

The second possibility is to synchronize on the LogFile object itself. This is simple enough to arrange with the this keyword. For example:

```
public void writeEntry(String message) throws IOException {

  synchronized (this) {
    Date d = new Date();
    out.write(d.toString());
    out.write('\t');
    out.write(message);
    out.write("\r\n");
  }

}
```

Synchronized Methods

Since synchronizing the entire method body on the object itself is such a common thing to do, Java provides a shortcut. You can synchronize an entire method on the current object (the this reference) by adding the synchronized modifier to the method declaration. For example:

```
public synchronized void writeEntry(String message)
 throws IOException {

  Date d = new Date();
  out.write(d.toString());
  out.write('\t');
  out.write(message);
  out.write("\r\n");

}
```

Simply adding the synchronized modifier to all methods is not a catchall solution for synchronization problems. For one thing, it exacts a severe performance penalty in many VMs (though more recent VMs have improved greatly in this respect), potentially slowing down your code by a factor of three or more. Second, it dramatically increases the chances of deadlock. Third, and most importantly, it's not always the object itself you need to protect from simultaneous modification or access, and synchronizing on the instance of the method's class may not protect the object you really need to protect. For instance, in this example, what we're really trying to prevent is two threads simultaneously writing onto out. If some other class had a reference to out completely unrelated to the LogFile, this attempt would fail. However, in this example, synchronizing on the LogFile object is sufficient because out is a private instance variable. Since we never expose a reference to this object, there's no way for any other object to invoke its methods except through the LogFile class. Therefore, synchronizing on the LogFile object has the same effect as synchronizing on out.

Alternatives to Synchronization

Synchronization is not always the best solution to the problem of inconsistent behavior caused by thread scheduling. There are a number of techniques that avoid the need for synchronization entirely. The first is to use local variables instead of fields wherever possible. Local variables do not have synchronization problems. Every time a method is entered, the virtual machine creates a completely new set of local variables for the method. These variables are invisible from outside the method and are destroyed when the method exits. As a result, it's impossible for one local variable to be used in two different threads. Every thread has its own separate set of local variables.

Method arguments of primitive types are also safe from modification in separate threads because Java passes arguments by value rather than by reference. A corollary of this is that methods such as `Math.sqrt( )` that simply take zero or more primitive data type arguments, perform some calculation, and return a value without ever interacting with the fields of any class are inherently thread-safe. These methods often either are or should be declared static.

Method arguments of object types are a little trickier because the actual argument passed by value is a reference to the object. Suppose, for example, you pass a reference to an array into a `sort( )` method. While the method is sorting the array, there's nothing to stop some other thread that also has a reference to the array from changing the values in the array.

`String` arguments are safe because they're *immutable*; that is, once a `String` object has been created, it cannot be changed by any thread. An immutable object never changes state. The values of its fields are set once when the constructor runs and never altered thereafter. `StringBuffer` arguments are not safe because they're not immutable; they can be changed after they're created.

A constructor normally does not have to worry about issues of thread safety. Until the constructor returns, no thread has a reference to the object, so it's impossible for two threads to have a reference to the object. (The most likely issue is if a constructor depends on another object in another thread that may change while the constructor runs, but that's uncommon. There's also a potential problem if a constructor somehow passes a reference to the object it's creating into a different thread, but this is also uncommon.)

You can take advantage of immutability in your own classes. It's often the easiest way to make a class thread-safe, often much easier than determining exactly which methods or code blocks to synchronize. To make an object immutable, simply declare all its fields private and don't write any methods that can change them. A lot of classes in the core Java library are immutable, for instance, `java.lang.String`, `java.lang.Integer`, `java.lang.Double`, and many more. This makes these classes less useful for some purposes, but it does make them a lot more thread-safe.

A third technique is to use a thread-unsafe class but only as a private field of a class that is thread-safe. As long as the containing class accesses the unsafe class only in a thread-safe fashion and as long as it never lets a reference to the private field leak out into another object, the class is safe. An example of this technique might be a web server that uses an unsynchronized `LogFile` class but gives each separate thread its own separate log so no resources are shared between the individual threads.

Deadlock

Synchronization can lead to another possible problem: *deadlock*. Deadlock occurs when two threads need exclusive access to the same set of resources and each thread holds the lock on a different subset of those resources. If neither thread is willing to give up the resources it has, both threads come to an indefinite halt. This isn't quite a hang in the classical sense because the program is still active and behaving normally from the perspective of the OS, but to a user the difference is insignificant.

To return to the library example, deadlock is what occurs when Jack and Jill are each writing a term paper on Thomas Jefferson and they both need the two books *Thomas Jefferson and Sally Hemings: An American Controversy* and *Sally Hemings and Thomas Jefferson: History, Memory and Civic Culture*. If Jill has checked out the first book and Jack has checked out the second, and neither is willing to give up the book they have, neither can finish the paper. Eventually the deadline expires and they both get an F. That's the problem of deadlock.

Worse yet, deadlock can be a sporadic, hard-to-detect bug. Deadlock usually depends on unpredictable issues of timing. Most of the time, either Jack or Jill will get to the library first and get both books. In this case, the one who gets the books writes a paper and returns the books; then the other one gets the books and writes their paper. Only rarely will they arrive at the same time and each get one of the two books. 99 times out of 100 or 999 times out of 1,000, a program will run to completion perfectly normally. Only rarely will it hang for no apparent reason. Of course, if a multithreaded server is handling hundreds or thousands of connections a minute, even a problem that occurs only once every million requests can hang the server in short order.

The most important technique for preventing deadlock is to avoid unnecessary synchronization. If there's an alternative approach for ensuring thread safety, such as making objects immutable or keeping a local copy of an object, use it. Synchronization should be a last resort for ensuring thread safety. If you do need to synchronize, keep the synchronized blocks small and try not to synchronize on more than one object at a time. This can be tricky, though, because many of the methods from the Java class library that your code may invoke synchronize on objects you aren't aware of. Consequently, you may in fact be synchronizing on many more objects than you expect.

The best you can do in the general case is carefully consider whether deadlock is likely to be a problem and design your code around it. If multiple objects need the same set of shared resources to operate, make sure they request them in the same order. For instance, if Class A and Class B need exclusive access to Object X and Object Y, make sure that both classes request X first and Y second. If neither requests Y unless it already possesses X, deadlock is not a problem.

Thread Scheduling

When multiple threads are running at the same time (more properly, when multiple threads are available to be run at the same time), you have to consider issues of thread scheduling. You need to make sure that all important threads get at least some time to run and that the more important threads get more time. Furthermore, you want to ensure that the threads execute in a reasonable order. If your web server has 10 queued requests, each of which requires 5 seconds to process, you don't want to process them in series. If you do, the first request will finish in 5 seconds but the second will take 10, the third 15, and so on until the last request, which will have to wait almost a minute to be serviced. By that point, the user has likely gone to another page. By running threads in parallel, you might be able to process all 10 requests in only 10 seconds total. The reason this strategy works is that there's a lot of dead time in servicing a typical web request, time in which the thread is simply waiting for the network to catch up with the CPU—time the VM's thread scheduler can put to good use by other threads. However, CPU-bound threads (as opposed to the I/O-bound threads more common in network programs) may never reach a point where they have to wait for more input. It is possible for such a thread to starve all other threads by taking all the available CPU resources. With a little thought, you can avoid this problem. In fact, starvation is a considerably easier problem to avoid than either mis-synchronization or deadlock.

Priorities

Not all threads are created equal. Each thread has a priority, specified as an integer from 1 to 10. When multiple threads are able to run, the VM will generally run only the highest-priority thread, although that's not a hard-and-fast rule. In Java, 10 is the highest priority and 1 is the lowest. The default priority is 5, and this is the priority that your threads will have unless you deliberately set them otherwise.

 This is exact opposite of the normal Unix way of prioritizing processes, in which the higher the priority number of a process, the less CPU time the process gets.

These three priorities (1, 5, and 10) are often specified as the three named constants Thread.MIN_PRIORITY, Thread.NORM_PRIORITY, and Thread.MAX_PRIORITY:

```
public static final int MIN_PRIORITY  = 1;
public static final int NORM_PRIORITY = 5;
public static final int MAX_PRIORITY  = 10;
```

Sometimes you want to give one thread more time than another. Threads that interact with the user should get very high priorities so that perceived responsiveness will be very quick. On the other hand, threads that calculate in the background should get low priorities. Tasks that will complete quickly should have high priorities. Tasks that take a long time should have low priorities so that they won't get in the way of other tasks. The priority of a thread can be changed using the setPriority() method:

```
public final void setPriority(int newPriority)
```

Attempting to exceed the maximum priority or set a nonpositive priority throws an IllegalArgumentException.

The getPriority() method returns the current priority of the thread:

```
public final int getPriority()
```

For instance, in Example 5-11, you might want to give higher priorities to the threads that do the calculating than the main program that spawns the threads. This is easily achieved by changing the calculateDigest() method to set the priority of each spawned thread to 8:

```
public void calculateDigest() {

    ListCallbackDigest cb = new ListCallbackDigest(input);
    cb.addDigestListener(this);
    Thread t = new Thread(cb);
    t.setPriority(8);
    t.start();

}
```

In general, though, try to avoid using too high a priority for threads, since you run the risk of starving other, lower-priority threads.

Preemption

Every virtual machine has a thread scheduler that determines which thread to run at any given time. There are two kinds of thread scheduling: *preemptive* and *cooperative*. A preemptive thread scheduler determines when a thread has had its fair share of CPU time, pauses that thread, and then hands off control of the CPU to a different thread. A cooperative thread scheduler waits for the running thread to pause itself before handing off control of the CPU to a different thread. A virtual machine that uses cooperative thread scheduling is much more susceptible to thread starvation than a virtual machine that uses preemptive thread scheduling, since one high-priority, uncooperative thread can hog an entire CPU.

All Java virtual machines are guaranteed to use preemptive thread scheduling between priorities. That is, if a lower-priority thread is running when a higher-priority thread becomes able to run, the virtual machine will sooner or later (and probably sooner) pause the lower-priority thread to allow the higher-priority thread to run. The higher-priority thread *preempts* the lower-priority thread.

The situation when multiple threads of the same priority are able to run is trickier. A preemptive thread scheduler will occasionally pause one of the threads to allow the next one in line to get some CPU time. However, a cooperative thread scheduler will not. It will wait for the running thread to explicitly give up control or come to a stopping point. If the running thread never gives up control and never comes to a stopping point and if no higher-priority threads preempt the running thread, all other threads will starve. This is a bad thing. It's important to make sure all your threads periodically pause themselves so that other threads have an opportunity to run.

 A starvation problem can be hard to spot if you're developing on a VM that uses preemptive thread scheduling. Just because the problem doesn't arise on your machine doesn't mean it won't arise on your customers' machines if their VMs use cooperative thread scheduling. Most current virtual machines use preemptive thread scheduling, but some older virtual machines are cooperatively scheduled.

There are 10 ways a thread can pause in favor of other threads or indicate that it is ready to pause. These are:

- It can block on I/O.
- It can block on a synchronized object.
- It can yield.
- It can go to sleep.
- It can join another thread.
- It can wait on an object.
- It can finish.
- It can be preempted by a higher-priority thread.
- It can be suspended.
- It can stop.

You should inspect every run( ) method you write to make sure that one of these conditions will occur with reasonable frequency. The last two possibilities are deprecated because they have the potential to leave objects in inconsistent states, so let's look at the other eight ways a thread can be a cooperative citizen of the virtual machine.

Blocking

Blocking occurs any time a thread has to stop and wait for a resource it doesn't have. The most common way a thread in a network program will voluntarily give up control of the CPU is by blocking on I/O. Since CPUs are much faster than networks and disks, a network program will often block while waiting for data to arrive from the network or be sent out to the network. Even though it may block for only a few milliseconds, this is enough time for other threads to do significant work.

Threads can also block when they enter a synchronized method or block. If the thread does not already possess the lock for the object being synchronized on and some other thread does possess that lock, the thread will pause until the lock is released. If the lock is never released, the thread is permanently stopped.

Neither blocking on I/O nor blocking on a lock will release any locks the thread already possesses. For I/O blocks, this is not such a big deal, since eventually the I/O will either unblock and the thread will continue or an IOException will be thrown and the thread will then exit the synchronized block or method and release its locks. However, a thread blocking on a lock that it doesn't possess will never give up its own locks. If one thread is waiting for a lock that a second thread owns and the second thread is waiting for a lock that the first thread owns, deadlock results.

Yielding

The second way for a thread to give up control is to explicitly yield. A thread does this by invoking the static Thread.yield( ) method:

```
public static void yield( )
```

This signals the virtual machine that it can run another thread if one is ready to run. Some virtual machines, particularly on real-time operating systems, may ignore this hint.

Before yielding, a thread should make sure that it or its associated Runnable object is in a consistent state that can be used by other objects. Yielding does not release any locks the thread holds. Therefore, ideally, a thread should not be synchronized on anything when it yields. If the only other threads waiting to run when a thread yields are blocked because they need the synchronized resources that the yielding thread possesses, then the other threads won't be able to run. Instead, control will return to the only thread that can run, the one that just yielded, which pretty much defeats the purpose of yielding.

Making a thread yield is quite simple in practice. If the thread's run( ) method simply consists of an infinite loop, just put a call to Thread.yield( ) at the end of the loop. For example:

```
public void run( ) {

  while (true) {
    // Do the thread's work...
    Thread.yield( );
  }

}
```

This gives other threads of the same priority the opportunity to run.

If each iteration of the loop takes a significant amount of time, you may want to intersperse more calls to Thread.yield( ) in the rest of the code. This precaution should have minimal effect in the event that yielding isn't necessary.

Sleeping

Sleeping is a more powerful form of yielding. Whereas yielding indicates only that a thread is willing to pause and let other equal-priority threads have a turn, a thread that goes to sleep will pause whether any other thread is ready to run or not. This gives an opportunity to run not only to other threads of the same priority but also to threads of lower priorities . However, a thread that goes to sleep does hold onto all the locks it's grabbed. Consequently, other threads that need the same locks will be blocked even if the CPU is available. Therefore, try to avoid having threads sleeping inside a synchronized method or block.

Sometimes sleeping is useful even if you don't need to yield to other threads. Putting a thread to sleep for a specified period of time lets you write code that executes once every second, every minute, every 10 minutes, and so forth. For instance, if you wrote a network monitor program that retrieved a page from a web server every five minutes and emailed the webmaster if the server had crashed, you could implement it as a thread that slept for five minutes between retrievals.

A thread goes to sleep by invoking one of two overloaded static `Thread.sleep()` methods. The first takes the number of milliseconds to sleep as an argument. The second takes both the number of milliseconds and the number of nanoseconds:

```
public static void sleep(long milliseconds) throws InterruptedException
public static void sleep(long milliseconds, int nanoseconds)
  throws  InterruptedException
```

While most modern computer clocks have at least close-to-millisecond accuracy, nanosecond accuracy is rarer. There's no guarantee that you can actually time the sleep to within a nanosecond or even within a millisecond on any particular virtual machine. If the local hardware can't support that level of accuracy, the sleep time is simply rounded to the nearest value that can be measured. For example:

```
public void run( ) {

  while (true) {
    if (!getPage("http://www.cafeaulait.org/")) {
      mailError("elharo@metalab.unc.edu");
    }
    try {
      Thread.sleep(300000); // 300,000 milliseconds == 5 minutes
    }
    catch (InterruptedException ex) {
      break;
    }
  }

}
```

The thread is not absolutely guaranteed to sleep as long as it wants to. On occasion, the thread may not be woken up until some time after its requested wake-up call, simply because the VM is busy doing other things. It is also possible that some other thread will do something to wake up the sleeping thread before its time. Generally, this is accomplished by invoking the sleeping thread's interrupt( ) method.

```
public void interrupt( )
```

This is one of those cases where the distinction between the thread and the Thread object is important. Just because the thread is sleeping doesn't mean that other threads that are awake can't work with the corresponding Thread object through its methods and fields. In particular, another thread can invoke the sleeping Thread object's interrupt( ) method, which the sleeping thread experiences as an InterruptedException. From that point forward, the thread is awake and executes as normal, at least until it goes to sleep again. In the previous example, an InterruptedException is used to terminate a thread that would otherwise run forever. When the InterruptedException is thrown, the infinite loop is broken, the run( ) method finishes, and the thread dies. The user interface thread can invoke this thread's interrupt( ) method when the user selects Exit from a menu or otherwise indicates that he wants the program to quit.

Joining threads

It's not uncommon for one thread to need the result of another thread. For example, a web browser loading an HTML page in one thread might spawn a separate thread to retrieve every image embedded in the page. If the IMG elements don't have HEIGHT and WIDTH attributes, the main thread might have to wait for all the images to load before it can finish by displaying the page. Java provides three join( ) methods to allow one thread to wait for another thread to finish before continuing. These are:

```
public final void join( ) throws InterruptedException
public final void join(long milliseconds) throws InterruptedException
public final void join(long milliseconds, int nanoseconds)
  throws InterruptedException
```

The first variant waits indefinitely for the *joined* thread to finish. The second two variants wait for the specified amount of time, after which they continue even if the joined thread has not finished. As with the sleep( ) method, nanosecond accuracy is not guaranteed.

The joining thread (that is, the one that invokes the join( ) method) waits for the joined thread (that is, the one whose join( ) method is invoked) to finish. For instance, consider this code fragment. We want to find the minimum, maximum, and median of a random array of doubles. It's quicker to do this with a sorted array. We spawn a new thread to sort the array, then join to that thread to await its results. Only when it's done do we read out the desired values.

```
double[] array = new double[10000];          // 1
for (int i = 0; i < array.length; i++) {     // 2
  array[i] = Math.random( );                 // 3
}                                            // 4
SortThread t = new SortThread(array);        // 5
```

```
    t.start();                                              // 6
    try {                                                   // 7
      t.join();                                             // 8
      System.out.println("Minimum: " + array[0]);           // 9
      System.out.println("Median: " + array[array.length/2]); // 10
      System.out.println("Maximum: " + array[array.length-1]); // 11
    }                                                       // 12
    catch (InterruptedException ex) {                       // 13
    }                                                       // 14
```

First lines 1 through 4 execute, filling the array with random numbers. Then line 5 creates a new SortThread. Line 6 starts the thread that will sort the array. Before we can find the minimum, median, and maximum of the array, we need to wait for the sorting thread to finish. Therefore, line 8 joins the current thread to the sorting thread. At this point, the thread executing these lines of code stops in its tracks. It waits for the sorting thread to finish running. The minimum, median, and maximum are not retrieved in lines 9 through 10 until the sorting thread has finished running and died. Notice that at no point is there a reference to the thread that pauses. It's not the Thread object on which the join( ) method is invoked; it's not passed as an argument to that method. It exists implicitly only as the current thread. If this is within the normal flow of control of the main( ) method of the program, there may not be any Thread variable anywhere that points to this thread.

A thread that's joined to another thread can be interrupted just like a sleeping thread if some other thread invokes its interrupt( ) method. The thread experiences this invocation as an InterruptedException. From that point forward, it executes as normal, starting from the catch block that caught the exception. In the preceding example, if the thread is interrupted, it skips over the calculation of the minimum, median, and maximum because they won't be available if the sorting thread was interrupted before it could finish.

We can use join( ) to fix up Example 5-4. Example 5-4's problem was that the main( ) method tended to outpace the threads whose results the main( ) method was using. It's straightforward to fix this by joining to each thread before trying to use its result. Example 5-13 demonstrates.

Example 5-13. Avoid a race condition by joining to the thread that has a result you need

```java
import java.io.*;

public class JoinDigestUserInterface {

  public static void main(String[] args) {

    ReturnDigest[] digestThreads = new ReturnDigest[args.length];

    for (int i = 0; i < args.length; i++) {

      // Calculate the digest
      File f = new File(args[i]);
```

```
      digestThreads[i] = new ReturnDigest(f);
      digestThreads[i].start( );

  }

  for (int i = 0; i < args.length; i++) {

    try {
      digestThreads[i].join( );
      // Now print the result
      StringBuffer result = new StringBuffer(args[i]);
      result.append(": ");
      byte[] digest = digestThreads[i].getDigest( );
      for (int j = 0; j < digest.length; j++) {
        result.append(digest[j] + " ");
      }
      System.out.println(result);
    }
    catch (InterruptedException ex) {
      System.err.println("Thread Interrupted before completion");
    }

  }

  }

}
```

Since Example 5-13 joins to threads in the same order as the threads are started, this fix also has the side effect of printing the output in the same order as the arguments used to construct the threads, rather than in the order the threads finish. This modification doesn't make the program any slower, but it may occasionally be an issue if you want to get the output of a thread as soon as it's done, without waiting for other unrelated threads to finish first.

Waiting on an object

A thread can *wait* on an object it has locked. While waiting, it releases the lock on the object and pauses until it is notified by some other thread. Another thread changes the object in some way, notifies the thread waiting on that object, and then continues. This differs from joining in that neither the waiting nor the notifying thread has to finish before the other thread can continue. Waiting is used to pause execution until an object or resource reaches a certain state. Joining is used to pause execution until a thread finishes.

Waiting on an object is one of the lesser-known ways a thread can pause. That's because it doesn't involve any methods in the Thread class. Instead, to wait on a particular object, the thread that wants to pause must first obtain the lock on the object

---

using synchronized and then invoke one of the object's three overloaded wait( ) methods:

```
public final void wait( ) throws InterruptedException
public final void wait(long milliseconds) throws InterruptedException
public final void wait(long milliseconds, int nanoseconds)
 throws InterruptedException
```

These methods are not in the Thread class; rather, they are in the java.lang.Object class. Consequently, they can be invoked on any object of any class. When one of these methods is invoked, the thread that invoked it releases the lock on the object it's waiting on (though not any locks it possesses on other objects) and goes to sleep. It remains asleep until one of three things happens:

- The timeout expires.
- The thread is interrupted.
- The object is notified.

The *timeout* is the same as for the sleep( ) and join( ) methods; that is, the thread wakes up after the specified amount of time has passed (within the limits of the local hardware clock accuracy). When the timeout expires, execution of the thread resumes with the statement immediately following the invocation of wait( ). However, if the thread can't immediately regain the lock on the object it was waiting on, it may still be blocked for some time.

Interruption works the same way as sleep( ) and join( ): some other thread invokes the thread's interrupt( ) method. This causes an InterruptedException, and execution resumes in the catch block that catches the exception. The thread regains the lock on the object it was waiting on before the exception is thrown, however, so the thread may still be blocked for some time after the interrupt( ) method is invoked.

The third possibility, *notification*, is new. Notification occurs when some other thread invokes the notify( ) or notifyAll( ) method on the object on which the thread is waiting. Both of these methods are in the java.lang.Object class:

```
public final void notify( )
public final void notifyAll( )
```

These must be invoked on the object the thread was waiting on, not generally on the Thread itself. Before notifying an object, a thread must first obtain the lock on the object using a synchronized method or block. The notify( ) method selects one thread more or less at random from the list of threads waiting on the object and wakes it up. The notifyAll( ) method wakes up every thread waiting on the given object.

Once a waiting thread is notified, it attempts to regain the lock of the object it was waiting on. If it succeeds, execution resumes with the statement immediately following the invocation of wait( ). If it fails, it blocks on the object until its lock becomes available; then execution resumes with the statement immediately following the invocation of wait( ).

For example, suppose one thread is reading a JAR archive from a network connection. The first entry in the archive is the manifest file. Another thread might be interested in the contents of the manifest file even before the rest of the archive is available. The interested thread could create a custom `ManifestFile` object, pass a reference to this object to the thread that would read the JAR archive, and wait on it. The thread reading the archive would first fill the `ManifestFile` with entries from the stream, then notify the `ManifestFile`, then continue reading the rest of the JAR archive. When the reader thread notified the `ManifestFile`, the original thread would wake up and do whatever it planned to do with the now fully prepared `ManifestFile` object. The first thread works something like this:

```
ManifestFile m = new ManifestFile( );
JarThread    t = new JarThread(m, in);
synchronized (m) {
  t.start( );
  try {
    m.wait( );
    // work with the manifest file...
  }
  catch (InterruptedException ex) {
    // handle exception...
  }
}
```

The `JarThread` class works like this:

```
ManifestFile theManifest;
InputStream in;

public JarThread(Manifest m, InputStream in) {
  theManifest = m;
  this.in= in;
}

public void run( ) {

  synchronized (theManifest) {
    // read the manifest from the stream in...
    theManifest.notify( );
  }
  // read the rest of the stream...

}
```

Waiting and notification are more commonly used when multiple threads want to wait on the same object. For example, one thread may be reading a web server log file in which each line contains one entry to be processed. Each line is placed in a java. util.List as it's read. Several threads wait on the List to process entries as they're added. Every time an entry is added, the waiting threads are notified using the notifyAll( ) method. If more than one thread is waiting on an object, notifyAll( ) is preferred, since there's no way to select which thread to notify. When all threads waiting on one object are notified, all will wake up and try to get the lock on the object. However, only one can succeed immediately. That one continues; the rest are blocked until the first one releases the lock. If several threads are all waiting on the same object, a significant amount of time may pass before the last one gets its turn at the lock on the object and continues. It's entirely possible that the object on which the thread was waiting will once again have been placed in an unacceptable state during this time. Thus, you'll generally put the call to wait( ) in a loop that checks the current state of the object. Do not assume that just because the thread was notified, the object is now in the correct state. Check it explicitly if you can't guarantee that once the object reaches a correct state it will never again reach an incorrect state. For example, this is how the client threads waiting on the log file entries might look:

```
private List entries;

public void processEntry( ) {

    synchronized (entries) { // must synchronize on the object we wait on
      while (entries.size( ) == 0) {
        try {
          entries.wait( );
          // We stopped waiting because entries.size( ) became non-zero
          // However we don't know that it's still non-zero so we
          // pass through the loop again to test its state now.
        }
        catch (InterruptedException ex) {
          // If interrupted, the last entry has been processed so
          return;
        }
      }
      String entry = (String) entries.remove(entries.size( )-1);
      // process this entry...
    }

}
```

The code reading the log file and adding entries to the vector might look something like this:

```
public void readLogFile( ) {

  String entry;

  while (true) {
    entry = log.getNextEntry( );
    if (entry == null) {
      // There are no more entries to add to the vector so
      // we have to interrupt all threads that are still waiting.
      // Otherwise, they'll wait forever.
      for (int i = 0; i < threads.length; i++) threads[i].interrupt( );
      break;
    }
```

```
      synchronized (entries) {
        entries.add(0, entry);
        entries.notifyAll();
      }
   }

   }
```

Priority-based preemption

Since threads are preemptive between priorities, you do not need to worry about giving up time to higher-priority threads. A high-priority thread will preempt lower-priority threads when it's ready to run. However, when the high-priority thread finishes running or blocks, it generally won't be the same low-priority thread that runs next. Instead, most non-real–time VMs use a round-robin scheduler so that the lower-priority thread that has been waiting longest will run next.

For example, suppose there are three threads with priority 5 named A, B, and C running in a cooperatively scheduled virtual machine. None of them will yield or block. Thread A starts running first. It runs for a while and is then preempted by thread D, which has priority 6. A stops running. Eventually, thread D blocks, and the thread scheduler looks for the next highest-priority thread to run. It finds three: A, B, and C. Thread A has already had some time to run, so the thread scheduler picks B (or perhaps C; this doesn't have to go in alphabetical order). B runs for a while when thread D suddenly unblocks. Thread D still has higher priority so the virtual machine pauses thread B and lets D run for a while. Eventually, D blocks again, and the thread scheduler looks for another thread to run. Again, it finds A, B, and C, but at this point, A has had some time and B has had some time, but C hasn't had any. So the thread scheduler picks thread C to run. Thread C runs until it is once again preempted by thread D. When thread D blocks again, the thread scheduler finds three threads ready to run. Of the three, however, A ran the longest ago, so the scheduler picks thread A. From this point forward, every time D preempts and blocks and the scheduler needs a new thread to run, it will run the threads A, B, and C in that order, circling back around to A after C.

If you'd rather avoid explicit yielding, you can use a higher-priority thread to force the lower-priority threads to give up time to each other. In essence, you can use a high-priority thread scheduler of your own devising to make all threading preemptive. The trick is to run a high-priority thread that does nothing but sleep and wake up periodically, say every 100 milliseconds. This will split the lower-priority threads into 100-millisecond time slices. It isn't necessary for the thread that's doing the splitting to know anything about the threads it's preempting. It's simply enough that it exists and is running. Example 5-14 demonstrates with a TimeSlicer class that allows you to guarantee preemption of threads with priorities less than a fixed value every timeslice milliseconds.

Example 5-14. A thread that forces preemptive scheduling for lower-priority threads

```java
public class TimeSlicer extends Thread {

  private long timeslice;

  public TimeSlicer(long milliseconds, int priority) {

    this.timeslice = milliseconds;
    this.setPriority(priority);
    // If this is the last thread left, it should not
    // stop the VM from exiting
    this.setDaemon(true);

  }

  // Use maximum priority
  public TimeSlicer(long milliseconds) {
    this(milliseconds, 10);
  }

  // Use maximum priority and 100ms timeslices
  public TimeSlicer() {
    this(100, 10);
  }

  public void run() {

    while (true) {
      try {
        Thread.sleep(timeslice);
      }
      catch (InterruptedException ex) {
      }
    }

  }

}
```

Finish

The final way a thread can give up control of the CPU in an orderly fashion is by *finishing*. When the run( ) method returns, the thread dies and other threads can take over. In network applications, this tends to occur with threads that wrap a single blocking operation, such as downloading a file from a server, so that the rest of the application won't be blocked.

Otherwise, if your run( ) method is so simple that it always finishes quickly enough without blocking, there's a very real question of whether you should spawn a thread at all. There's a nontrivial amount of overhead for the virtual machine in setting up and tearing down threads. If a thread is finishing in a small fraction of a second anyway, chances are it would finish even faster if you used a simple method call rather than a separate thread.

Thread Pools

Adding multiple threads to a program dramatically improves performance, especially for I/O-bound programs such as most network programs. However, threads are not without overhead of their own. Starting a thread and cleaning up after a thread that has died takes a noticeable amount of work from the virtual machine, especially if a program spawns hundreds of threads—not an unusual occurrence for even a low- to medium-volume network server. Even if the threads finish quickly, this can overload the garbage collector or other parts of the VM and hurt performance, just like allocating thousands of any other kind of object every minute. Even more importantly, switching between running threads carries overhead. If the threads are blocking naturally—for instance, by waiting for data from the network—there's no real penalty to this, but if the threads are CPU-bound, then the total task may finish more quickly if you can avoid a lot of switching between threads. Finally, and most importantly, although threads help make more efficient use of a computer's limited CPU resources, there are still only a finite amount of resources to go around. Once you've spawned enough threads to use all the computer's available idle time, spawning more threads just wastes MIPS and memory on thread management.

Fortunately, you can get the best of both worlds by reusing threads. You cannot restart a thread once it's died, but you can engineer threads so that they don't die as soon as they've finished one task. Instead, put all the tasks you need to accomplish in a queue or other data structure and have each thread retrieve a new task from the queue when it's completed its previous task. This is called *thread pooling*, and the data structure in which the tasks are kept is called the *pool*.

The simplest way to implement a thread pool is by allotting a fixed number of threads when the pool is first created. When the pool is empty, each thread waits on the pool. When a task is added to the pool, all waiting threads are notified. When a thread finishes its assigned task, it goes back to the pool for a new task. If it doesn't get one, it waits until a new task is added to the pool.

An alternative is to put the threads themselves in the pool and have the main program pull threads out of the pool and assign them tasks. If no thread is in the pool when a task becomes necessary, the main program can spawn a new thread. As each thread finishes a task, it returns to the pool. (Imagine this scheme as a union hall in which new workers join the union only when full employment of current members is achieved.)

There are many data structures you can use for a pool, although a queue is probably the most efficient for ensuring that tasks are performed in a first-in, first-out order. Whichever data structure you use to implement the pool, however, you have to be extremely careful about synchronization, since many threads will interact with it very close together in time. The simplest way to avoid problems is to use either a java. util.Vector (which is fully synchronized) or a synchronized Collection from the Java Collections API.

Let's look at an example. Suppose you want to gzip every file in the current directory using a java.util.zip.GZIPOutputStream. On the one hand, this is an I/O-heavy operation because all the files have to be read and written. On the other hand, data compression is a very CPU-intensive operation, so you don't want too many threads running at once. This is a good opportunity to use a thread pool. Each client thread will compress files while the main program will determine which files to compress. In this example, the main program is likely to significantly outpace the compressing threads since all it has to do is list the files in a directory. Therefore, it's not out of the question to fill the pool first, then start the threads that compress the files in the pool. However, to make this example as general as possible, we'll allow the main program to run in parallel with the zipping threads.

Example 5-15 shows the GZipThread class. It contains a private field called pool containing a reference to the pool. Here that field is declared to have List type, but it's always accessed in a strictly queue-like first-in, first-out order. The run( ) method removes File objects from the pool and gzips each one. If the pool is empty when the thread is ready to get something new from the pool, then the thread waits on the pool object.

Example 5-15. The GZipThread class

```
import java.io.*;
import java.util.*;
import java.util.zip.*;

public class GZipThread extends Thread {

  private List pool;
  private static int filesCompressed = 0;

  public GZipThread(List pool) {
    this.pool = pool;
  }

  private static synchronized void incrementFilesCompressed( ) {
    filesCompressed++;
  }

  public void run( ) {

    while (filesCompressed != GZipAllFiles.getNumberOfFilesToBeCompressed( )) {

      File input = null;

      synchronized (pool) {
```

Example 5-15. The GZipThread class (continued)

```
      while (pool.isEmpty( )) {
        if (filesCompressed == GZipAllFiles.getNumberOfFilesToBeCompressed( )) {
          System.out.println("Thread ending");
          return;
        }
        try {
          pool.wait( );
        }
        catch (InterruptedException ex) {
        }
      }

      input = (File) pool.remove(pool.size( )-1);
      incrementFilesCompressed( );

    }

    // don't compress an already compressed file
    if (!input.getName( ).endsWith(".gz")) {
      try {
        InputStream in = new FileInputStream(input);
        in = new BufferedInputStream(in);

        File output = new File(input.getParent(), input.getName( ) + ".gz");
        if (!output.exists( )) { // Don't overwrite an existing file
          OutputStream out = new FileOutputStream(output);
          out = new GZIPOutputStream(out);
          out = new BufferedOutputStream(out);
          int b;
          while ((b = in.read( )) != -1) out.write(b);
          out.flush( );
          out.close( );
          in.close( );
        }
      }
      catch (IOException ex) {
        System.err.println(ex);
      }

    } // end if

  } // end while

} // end run

} // end ZipThread
```

Example 5-16 is the main program. It constructs the pool as a Vector object, passes this to four newly constructed GZipThread objects, starts all four threads, and iterates through all the files and directories listed on the command line. Those files and files in those directories are added to the pool for eventual processing by the four threads.

Example 5-16. The GZipThread user interface class

```java
import java.io.*;
import java.util.*;

public class GZipAllFiles {

  public final static int THREAD_COUNT = 4;
  private static int filesToBeCompressed = -1;

  public static void main(String[] args) {

    Vector pool = new Vector();
    GZipThread[] threads = new GZipThread[THREAD_COUNT];

    for (int i = 0; i < threads.length; i++) {
      threads[i] = new GZipThread(pool);
      threads[i].start();
    }

    int totalFiles = 0;
    for (int i = 0; i < args.length; i++) {

      File f = new File(args[i]);
      if (f.exists()) {
        if (f.isDirectory()) {
          File[] files = f.listFiles();
          for (int j = 0; j < files.length; j++) {
            if (!files[j].isDirectory()) { // don't recurse directories
              totalFiles++;
              synchronized (pool) {
                pool.add(0, files[j]);
                pool.notifyAll();
              }
            }
          }
        }
        else {
          totalFiles++;
          synchronized (pool) {
            pool.add(0, f);
            pool.notifyAll();
          }
        }

      } // end if

    } // end for

    filesToBeCompressed = totalFiles;

    // make sure that any waiting thread knows that no
    // more files will be added to the pool
    for (int i = 0; i < threads.length; i++) {
```

Example 5-16. The GZipThread user interface class (continued)

```
      threads[i].interrupt();
    }

  }

  public static int getNumberOfFilesToBeCompressed() {
    return filesToBeCompressed;
  }

}
```

The big question here is how to tell the program that it's done and should exit. You can't simply exit when all files have been added to the pool, because at that point most of the files haven't been processed. Neither can you exit when the pool is empty, because that may occur at the start of the program (before any files have been placed in the pool) or at various intermediate times when not all files have yet been put in the pool but all files that have been put there are processed. The latter possibility also prevents the use of a simple counter scheme.

The solution adopted here is to separately track the number of files that need to be processed (GZipAllFiles.filesToBeCompressed) and the number of files actually processed (GZipThread.filesCompressed). When these two values match, all threads' run() methods return. Checks are made at the start of each of the while loops in the run() method to see whether it's necessary to continue. This scheme is preferred to the deprecated stop() method, because it won't suddenly stop the thread while it's halfway through compressing a file. This gives us much more fine-grained control over exactly when and where the thread stops.

Initially, GZipAllFiles.filesToBeCompressed is set to the impossible value –1. Only when the final number is known is it set to its real value. This prevents early coincidental matches between the number of files processed and the number of files to be processed. It's possible that when the final point of the main() method is reached, one or more of the threads will be waiting. Thus, we interrupt each of the threads (an action that has no effect if the thread is merely processing and not waiting or sleeping) to make sure it checks one last time.

And finally, the last element of this program is the private GZipThread. incrementFilesCompressed() method. This method is synchronized to ensure that if two threads try to update the filesCompressed field at the same time, one will wait. Otherwise, the GZipThread.filesCompressed field could end up one short of the true value and the program would never exit. Since the method is static, all threads synchronize on the same Class object. A synchronized instance method wouldn't be sufficient here.

The complexity of determining when to stop this program is mostly atypical of the more heavily threaded programs you'll write because it does have such a definite ending point: the point at which all files are processed. Most network servers continue indefinitely until some part of the user interface shuts them down. The real solution here is to provide some sort of simple user interface—such as typing a period on a line by itself—that ends the program.

This chapter has been a whirlwind tour of threading in Java, covering the bare minimum you need to know to write multithreaded network programs. For a more detailed and comprehensive look with many more examples, check out *Java Threads*, by Scott Oaks and Henry Wong (O'Reilly). Once you've mastered that book, Doug Lea's *Concurrent Programming in Java* (Addison Wesley) provides a comprehensive look at the traps and pitfalls of concurrent programming from a design patterns perspective.

CHAPTER 6
Looking Up Internet Addresses

Devices connected to the Internet are called *nodes*. Nodes that are computers are called *hosts*. Each node or host is identified by at least one unique number called an Internet address or an IP address. Most current IP addresses are four bytes long; these are referred to as IPv4 addresses. However, a small but growing number of IP addresses are 16 bytes long; these are called IPv6 addresses. (4 and 6 refer to the version of the Internet Protocol, not the number of the bytes in the address.) Both IPv4 and IPv6 addresses are ordered sequences of bytes, like an array. They aren't numbers, and they aren't ordered in any predictable or useful sense.

An IPv4 address is normally written as four unsigned bytes, each ranging from 0 to 255, with the most significant byte first. Bytes are separated by periods for the convenience of human eyes. For example, the address for *hermes.oit.unc.edu* is *152.2.21.2*. This is called the *dotted quad* format.

An IPv6 address is normally written as eight blocks of four hexadecimal digits separated by colons. For example, at the time of this writing, the address of *www.ipv6. com.cn* is *2001:0250:02FF:0210:0250:8BFF:FEDE:67C8*. Leading zeros do not need to be written. Thus, the address of *www.ipv6.com.cn* can be written as *2001:250:2FF: 210:250:8BFF:FEDE:67C8*. A double colon, at most one of which may appear in any address, indicates multiple zero blocks. For example, *FEDC:0000:0000:0000:00DC: 0000:7076:0010* could be written more compactly as *FEDC::DC:0:7076:10*. In mixed networks of IPv6 and IPv4, the last four bytes of the IPv6 address are sometimes written as an IPv4 dotted quad address. For example, *FEDC:BA98:7654:3210:FEDC: BA98:7654:3210* could be written as *FEDC:BA98:7654:3210:FEDC:BA98:118.84.50. 16*. IPv6 is only supported in Java 1.4 and later. Java 1.3 and earlier only support four byte addresses.

IP addresses are great for computers, but they are a problem for humans, who have a hard time remembering long numbers. In the 1950s, it was discovered that most people could remember about seven digits per number; some can remember as many as nine, while others remember as few as five. ("The Magic Number Seven, Plus or Minus Two: Some Limits on Our Capacity for Processing Information," by G. A.

Miller, in the *Psychological Review*, Vol. 63, pp. 81-97.) This is why phone numbers are broken into three- and four-digit pieces with three-digit area codes. Obviously, an IP address, which can have as many as 12 decimal digits, is beyond the capacity of most humans to remember. I can remember about two IP addresses, and then only if I use both daily and the second is on the same subnet as the first.

To avoid the need to carry around Rolodexes full of IP addresses, the Internet's designers invented the Domain Name System (DNS). DNS associates hostnames that humans can remember (such as *hermes.oit.unc.edu*) with IP addresses that computers can remember (such as *152.2.21.2*). Most hosts have at least one hostname. An exception is made for computers that don't have a permanent IP address (like many PCs); because these computers don't have a permanent address, they can't be used as servers and therefore don't need a name, since nobody will need to refer to them.

 Colloquially, people often use "Internet address" to mean a hostname (or even an email address). In a book about network programming, it is crucial to be precise about addresses and hostnames. In this book, an address is always a numeric IP address, never a human-readable hostname.

Some machines have multiple names. For instance, *www.ibiblio.org* and *helios.metalab. unc.edu* are really the same Linux box in Chapel Hill. The name *www.ibiblio.org* really refers to a web site rather than a particular machine. In the past, when this web site moved from one machine to another, the name was reassigned to the new machine so it always pointed to the site's current server. This way, URLs around the Web don't need to be updated just because the site has moved to a new host. Some common names like *www* and *news* are often aliases for the machines providing those services. For example, *news.speakeasy.net* is an alias for my ISP's news server. Since the server may change over time, the alias can move with the service.

On occasion, one name maps to multiple IP addresses. It is then the responsibility of the DNS server to randomly choose machines to respond to each request. This feature is most frequently used for very high traffic web sites, where it splits the load across multiple systems. For instance, *www.oreilly.com* is actually two machines, one at *208.201.239.36* and one at *208.201.239.37*.

Every computer connected to the Internet should have access to a machine called a *domain name server*, generally a Unix box running special DNS software that knows the mappings between different hostnames and IP addresses. Most domain name servers only know the addresses of the hosts on their local network, plus the addresses of a few domain name servers at other sites. If a client asks for the address of a machine outside the local domain, the local domain name server asks a domain name server at the remote location and relays the answer to the requester.

Most of the time, you can use hostnames and let DNS handle the translation to IP addresses. As long as you can connect to a domain name server, you don't need to worry about the details of how names and addresses are passed between your machine, the local domain name server, and the rest of the Internet. However, you will need access to at least one domain name server to use the examples in this chapter and most of the rest of this book. These programs will not work on a standalone computer. Your machine must be connected to the Internet.

The InetAddress Class

The `java.net.InetAddress` class is Java's high-level representation of an IP address, both IPv4 and IPv6. It is used by most of the other networking classes, including `Socket`, `ServerSocket`, `URL`, `DatagramSocket`, `DatagramPacket`, and more. Generally, it includes both a hostname and an IP address.

```
public class InetAddress extends Object implements Serializable
```

 In Java 1.3 and earlier, this class is final. In Java 1.4, it has two subclasses. However, you should not subclass it yourself. Indeed, you can't, because all constructors are package protected.

Creating New InetAddress Objects

There are no public constructors in the `InetAddress` class. However, `InetAddress` has three static methods that return suitably initialized `InetAddress` objects given a little information. They are:

```
public static InetAddress getByName(String hostName)
  throws UnknownHostException
public static InetAddress[] getAllByName(String hostName)
  throws UnknownHostException
public static InetAddress getLocalHost()
  throws UnknownHostException
```

All three of these methods may make a connection to the local DNS server to fill out the information in the `InetAddress` object, if necessary. This has a number of possibly unexpected implications, among them that these methods may throw security exceptions if the connection to the DNS server is prohibited. Furthermore, invoking one of these methods may cause a host that uses a PPP connection to dial into its provider if it isn't already connected. The key thing to remember is that these methods do not simply use their arguments to set the internal fields. They actually make network connections to retrieve all the information they need. The other methods in this class, such as `getAddress()` and `getHostName()`, mostly work with the information provided by one of these three methods. They do not make network connections; on the rare occasions that they do, they do not throw any exceptions. Only these three methods have to go outside Java and the local system to get their work done.

Since DNS lookups can be relatively expensive (on the order of several seconds for a request that has to go through several intermediate servers, or one that's trying to resolve an unreachable host) the InetAddress class caches the results of lookups. Once it has the address of a given host, it won't look it up again, even if you create a new InetAddress object for the same host. As long as IP addresses don't change while your program is running, this is not a problem.

Negative results (host not found errors) are slightly more problematic. It's not uncommon for an initial attempt to resolve a host to fail, but the immediately following one to succeed. What has normally happened in this situation is that the first attempt timed out while the information was still in transit from the remote DNS server. Then the address arrived at the local server and was immediately available for the next request. For this reason, Java only caches unsuccessful DNS queries for 10 seconds.

In Java 1.4 and later, these times can be controlled by the networkaddress.cache.ttl and networkaddress.cache.negative.ttl system properties. networkaddress.cache.ttl specifies the number of seconds a successful DNS lookup will remain in Java's cache. networkaddress.cache.negative.ttl is the number of seconds an unsuccessful lookup will be cached. Attempting to look up the same host again within these limits will only return the same value. −1 is interpreted as "never expire".

Besides locale caching inside the InetAddress class, the local host, the local domain name server, and other DNS servers elsewhere on the Internet may also cache the results of various queries. Java provides no way to control this. As a result, it may take several hours for the information about an IP address change to propagate across the Internet. In the meantime, your program may encounter various exceptions, including UnknownHostException, NoRouteToHostException, and ConnectException, depending on the changes made to the DNS.

Java 1.4 adds two more factory methods that do not check their addresses with the local DNS server. The first creates an InetAddress object with an IP address and no hostname. The second creates an InetAddress object with an IP address and a hostname.

```
public static InetAddress getByAddress(byte[] address)
 throws UnknownHostException  // 1.4
public static InetAddress getByAddress(String hostName, byte[] address)
 throws UnknownHostException  // 1.4
```

Unlike the other three factory methods, these two methods make no guarantees that such a host exists or that the hostname is correctly mapped to the IP address. They throw an UnknownHostException only if a byte array of an illegal size (neither 4 nor 16 bytes long) is passed as the address argument.

public static InetAddress getByName(String hostName) throws UnknownHostException

`InetAddress.getByName()` is the most frequently used of these factory methods. It is a static method that takes the hostname you're looking for as its argument. It looks up the host's IP address using DNS. Call `getByName()` like this:

```
java.net.InetAddress address =
 java.net.InetAddress.getByName("www.oreilly.com");
```

If you have already imported the `java.net.InetAddress` class, which will almost always be the case, you can call `getByName()` like this:

```
InetAddress address = InetAddress.getByName("www.oreilly.com");
```

In the rest of this book, I assume that there is an `import java.net.*;` statement at the top of the program containing each code fragment, as well as any other necessary import statements.

The `InetAddress.getByName()` method throws an `UnknownHostException` if the host can't be found, so you need to declare that the method making the call throws `UnknownHostException` (or its superclass, `IOException`) or wrap it in a `try` block, like this:

```
try {
  InetAddress address = InetAddress.getByName("www.oreilly.com");
  System.out.println(address);
}
catch (UnknownHostException ex) {
  System.out.println("Could not find www.oreilly.com");
}
```

Example 6-1 shows a complete program that creates an `InetAddress` object for *www.oreilly.com* and prints it out.

Example 6-1. A program that prints the address of www.oreilly.com

```
import java.net.*;

public class OReillyByName {

  public static void main (String[] args) {

    try {
      InetAddress address = InetAddress.getByName("www.oreilly.com");
      System.out.println(address);
    }
    catch (UnknownHostException ex) {
      System.out.println("Could not find www.oreilly.com");
    }

  }

}
```

Here's the result:

```
% java OReillyByName
www.oreilly.com/208.201.239.36
```

On rare occasions, you will need to connect to a machine that does not have a hostname. In this case, you can pass a String containing the dotted quad or hexadecimal form of the IP address to InetAddress.getByName( ):

```
InetAddress address = InetAddress.getByName("208.201.239.37");
```

Example 6-2 uses the IP address for *www.oreilly.com* instead of the name.

Example 6-2. A program that prints the address of 208.201.239.37

```
import java.net.*;

public class OReillyByAddress {

  public static void main (String[] args) {

    try {
      InetAddress address = InetAddress.getByName("208.201.239.37");
      System.out.println(address);
    }
    catch (UnknownHostException ex) {
      System.out.println("Could not find 208.201.239.37");
    }

  }

}
```

Here's the result in Java 1.3 and earlier:

```
% java OReillyByAddress
www.oreilly.com/208.201.239.37
```

When you call getByName( ) with an IP address string as an argument, it creates an InetAddress object for the requested IP address without checking with DNS. This means it's possible to create InetAddress objects for hosts that don't really exist and that you can't connect to. The hostname of an InetAddress object created from a string containing an IP address is initially set to that string. A DNS lookup for the actual hostname is performed only when the hostname is requested, either explicitly via getHostName( ) or implicitly through toString( ). That's how *www.oreilly.com* was determined from the dotted quad address *208.201.239.37*. If at the time the hostname is requested and a DNS lookup is finally performed the host with the specified IP address can't be found, then the hostname remains the original dotted quad string. However, no UnknownHostException is thrown.

The toString( ) method in Java 1.4 behaves a little differently than in earlier versions. It does not do a reverse name lookup; thus, the host is not printed unless it is already known, either because it was provided as an argument to the factory method or because getHostName( ) was invoked. In Java 1.4, Example 6-2 produces this output:

```
/208.201.239.37
```

Hostnames are much more stable than IP addresses. Some services have lived at the same hostname for years but have switched IP addresses several times. If you have a choice between using a hostname like *www.oreilly.com* or an IP address like *208.201.239.37*, always choose the hostname. Use an IP address only when a hostname is not available.

public static InetAddress[] getAllByName(String hostName) throws UnknownHostException

Some computers have more than one Internet address. Given a hostname, InetAddress.getAllByName( ) returns an array that contains all the addresses corresponding to that name. Its use is straightforward:

```
InetAddress[] addresses = InetAddress.getAllByName("www.apple.com");
```

Like InetAddress.getByName( ), InetAddress.getAllByName( ) can throw an UnknownHostException, so you need to enclose it in a try block or declare that your method throws UnknownHostException. Example 6-3 demonstrates by returning a complete list of the IP addresses for *www.microsoft.com*.

Example 6-3. A program that prints all the addresses of www.microsoft.com

```java
import java.net.*;

public class AllAddressesOfMicrosoft {

  public static void main (String[] args) {

    try {
      InetAddress[] addresses =
       InetAddress.getAllByName("www.microsoft.com");
      for (int i = 0; i < addresses.length; i++) {
        System.out.println(addresses[i]);
      }
    }
    catch (UnknownHostException ex) {
      System.out.println("Could not find www.microsoft.com");
    }

  }

}
```

Here's the result:

```
% java AllAddressesOfMicrosoft
www.microsoft.com/63.211.66.123
www.microsoft.com/63.211.66.124
```

```
www.microsoft.com/63.211.66.131
www.microsoft.com/63.211.66.117
www.microsoft.com/63.211.66.116
www.microsoft.com/63.211.66.107
www.microsoft.com/63.211.66.118
www.microsoft.com/63.211.66.115
www.microsoft.com/63.211.66.110
```

www.microsoft.com appears to have nine IP addresses. Hosts with more than one address are the exception rather than the rule. Most hosts with multiple IP addresses are very high-volume web servers. Even in those cases, you rarely need to know more than one address.

public static InetAddress getByAddress(byte[] address) throws UnknownHostException // Java 1.4
public static InetAddress getByAddress(String hostName, byte[] address) throws UnknownHostException // Java 1.4

In Java 1.4 and later, you can pass a byte array and optionally a hostname to getByAddress( ) to create an InetAddress object with exactly those bytes. Domain name lookup is not performed. However, if byte array is some length other than 4 or 16 bytes—that is, if it can't be an IPv4 or IPv6 address—an UnknownHostException is thrown.

This is useful if a domain name server is not available or might have inaccurate information. For example, none of the computers, printers, or routers in my basement area network are registered with any DNS server. Since I can never remember which addresses I've assigned to which systems, I wrote a simple program that attempts to connect to all 254 possible local addresses in turn to see which ones are active. (This only took me about 10 times as long as writing down all the addresses on a piece of paper.)

getByAddress(byte[] address) really doesn't do anything getByAddress(String address) doesn't do. In a few cases, it might be marginally faster because it doesn't have to convert a string to a byte array, but that's a trivial improvement. getByAddress(String hostName, byte[] address) does let you create InetAddress objects that don't match or even actively conflict with the information in the local DNS. There might occasionally be a call for this, but the use case is pretty obscure.

public static InetAddress getLocalHost( ) throws UnknownHostException

The InetAddress class contains one final means of getting an InetAddress object. The static method InetAddress.getLocalHost( ) returns the InetAddress of the machine on which it's running. Like InetAddress.getByName( ) and InetAddress. getAllByName( ), it throws an UnknownHostException when it can't find the address of the local machine (though this really shouldn't happen). Its use is straightforward:

```
InetAddress me = InetAddress.getLocalHost( );
```

Example 6-4 prints the address of the machine it's run on.

Example 6-4. Find the address of the local machine

```
import java.net.*;

public class MyAddress {

  public static void main (String[] args) {

    try {
      InetAddress address = InetAddress.getLocalHost();
      System.out.println(address);
    }
    catch (UnknownHostException ex) {
      System.out.println("Could not find this computer's address.");
    }

  }

}
```

Here's the output; I ran the program on *titan.oit.unc.edu*:

```
% java MyAddress
titan.oit.unc.edu/152.2.22.14
```

Whether you see a fully qualified name like *titan.oit.unc.edu* or a partial name like *titan* depends on what the local DNS server returns for hosts in the local domain. If you're not connected to the Internet, and the system does not have a fixed IP address or domain name, you'll probably see *localhost* as the domain name and *127.0.0.1* as the IP address.

Security Issues

Creating a new InetAddress object from a hostname is considered a potentially insecure operation because it requires a DNS lookup. An untrusted applet under the control of the default security manager will only be allowed to get the IP address of the host it came from (its *codebase*) and possibly the local host. Untrusted code is not allowed to create an InetAddress object from any other hostname. This is true whether the code uses the InetAddress.getByName() method, the InetAddress.getAllByName() method, the InetAddress.getLocalHost() method, or something else. Untrusted code can construct an InetAddress object from the string form of the IP address, though it will not perform DNS lookups for such addresses.

Untrusted code is not allowed to perform arbitrary DNS lookups for third-party hosts because of the prohibition against making network connections to hosts other than the codebase. Arbitrary DNS lookups would open a covert channel by which a program could talk to third-party hosts. For instance, suppose an applet downloaded from *www.bigisp.com* wants to send the message "macfaq.dialup.cloud9.net is vulnerable" to *crackersinc.com*. All it has to do is request DNS information for *macfaq.dialup.cloud9.net.is.vulnerable.crackersinc.com*. To resolve that hostname, the applet would contact the local DNS server. The local DNS server would contact the DNS server at *crackersinc.com*. Even though these hosts don't exist, the cracker can inspect the DNS error log for *crackersinc.com* to retrieve the message. This scheme could be considerably more sophisticated with compression, error correction, encryption, custom DNS servers that email the messages to a fourth site, and more, but this version is good enough for a proof of concept. Arbitrary DNS lookups are prohibited because arbitrary DNS lookups leak information.

Untrusted code is allowed to call `InetAddress.getLocalHost( )`. However, this method returns a hostname of *localhost* and an IP address of 127.0.0.1. This is a special hostname and IP address called the *loopback address*. No matter which machine you use this hostname or IP address on, it always refers to the current machine. No specific DNS resolution is necessary. The reason for prohibiting the applet from finding out the true hostname and address is that the computer on which the applet is running may be deliberately hidden behind a firewall. In this case, an applet should not be a channel for information the web server doesn't already have. (Some older browsers, including Netscape 4.x, do allow a little more information about the local host to leak out, including its IP address, but only if no DNS lookup is required to get this information.)

Like all security checks, prohibitions against DNS resolutions can be relaxed for trusted code. The specific `SecurityManager` method used to test whether a host can be resolved is `checkConnect( )`:

```
public void checkConnect(String hostname, int port)
```

When the port argument is –1, this method checks whether DNS may be invoked to resolve the specified host. (If the port argument is greater than –1, this method checks whether a connection to the named host on the specified port is allowed.) The host argument may be either a hostname like *www.oreilly.com*, a dotted quad IP address like *208.201.239.37*, or, in Java 1.4 and later, a hexadecimal IPv6 address like *FEDC::DC:0:7076:10*.

You can grant an applet permission to resolve a host by using the Policy Tool to add a `java.net.SocketPermission` with the action connect and the target being the name of the host you want to allow the applet to resolve. You can use the asterisk wildcard (*) to allow all hosts in particular domains to be resolved. For example, setting the target to **.oreilly.com* allows the applet to resolve the hosts *www.oreilly.com*, *java.oreilly.com*, *perl.oreilly.com*, and all others in the *oreilly.com* domain. Although you'll generally use a hostname to set permissions, Java checks it against the actual IP addresses. In this example, that also allows hosts in the *ora.com* domain to be resolved because this is simply an alias for *oreilly.com* with the same range of IP addresses. To allow all hosts in all domains to be resolved, just set the target to *. Figure 6-1 demonstrates.

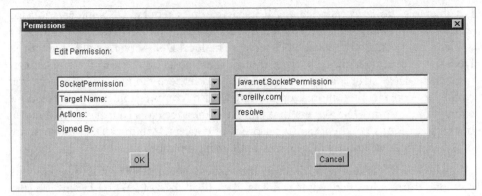

Figure 6-1. Using the Policy Tool to grant DNS resolution permission to all applets

Getter Methods

The InetAddress class contains three getter methods that return the hostname as a string and the IP address as both a string and a byte array:

```
public String getHostName( )
public byte[] getAddress( )
public String getHostAddress( )
```

There are no corresponding setHostName( ) and setAddress( ) methods, which means that packages outside of java.net can't change an InetAddress object's fields behind its back. Therefore, Java can guarantee that the hostname and the IP address match each other. This has the beneficial side effect of making InetAdddress immutable and thus thread-safe.

public String getHostName( )

The getHostName( ) method returns a String that contains the name of the host with the IP address represented by this InetAddress object. If the machine in question doesn't have a hostname or if the security manager prevents the name from being determined, a dotted quad format of the numeric IP address is returned. For example:

```
InetAddress machine = InetAddress.getLocalHost( );
String localhost = machine.getHostName( );
```

In some cases, you may only see a partially qualified name like *titan* instead of the full name like *titan.oit.unc.edu*. The details depend on how the local DNS behaves when resolving local hostnames.

The getHostName( ) method is particularly useful when you're starting with a dotted quad IP address rather than the hostname. Example 6-5 converts the dotted quad address *208.201.239.37* into a hostname by using InetAddress.getByName( ) and then applying getHostName( ) on the resulting object.

Example 6-5. Given the address, find the hostname

```
import java.net.*;

public class ReverseTest {

  public static void main (String[] args) {

    try {
      InetAddress ia = InetAddress.getByName("208.201.239.37");
      System.out.println(ia.getHostName( ));
    }
    catch (Exception ex) {
      System.err.println(ex);
    }

  }

}
```

Here's the result:

```
% java ReverseTest
www.oreillynet.com
```

public String getHostAddress( )

The getHostAddress( ) method returns a string containing the dotted quad format of the IP address. Example 6-6 uses this method to print the IP address of the local machine in the customary format.

Example 6-6. Find the IP address of the local machine

```
import java.net.*;

public class MyAddress {

  public static void main(String[] args) {

    try {
      InetAddress me = InetAddress.getLocalHost( );
      String dottedQuad = me.getHostAddress( );
      System.out.println("My address is " + dottedQuad);
    }
    catch (UnknownHostException ex) {
      System.out.println("I'm sorry. I don't know my own address.");
    }

  }

}
```

Here's the result:

```
% java MyAddress
My address is 152.2.22.14.
```

Of course, the exact output depends on where the program is run.

public byte[] getAddress( )

If you want to know the IP address of a machine (and you rarely do), getAddress( ) returns an IP address as an array of bytes in network byte order. The most significant byte (i.e., the first byte in the address's dotted quad form) is the first byte in the array, or element zero—remember, Java array indices start with zero. To be ready for IPv6 addresses, try not to assume anything about the length of this array. If you need to know the length of the array, use the array's length field:

```
InetAddress me = InetAddress.getLocalHost( );
byte[] address = me.getAddress( ));
```

The bytes returned are unsigned, which poses a problem. Unlike C, Java doesn't have an unsigned byte primitive data type. Bytes with values higher than 127 are treated as negative numbers. Therefore, if you want to do anything with the bytes returned by getAddress( ), you need to promote the bytes to ints and make appropriate adjustments. Here's one way to do it:

```
int unsignedByte = signedByte < 0 ? signedByte + 256 : signedByte;
```

Here, signedByte may be either positive or negative. The conditional operator ? tests whether signedByte is negative. If it is, 256 is added to signedByte to make it positive. Otherwise, it's left alone. signedByte is automatically promoted to an int before the addition is performed so wraparound is not a problem.

One reason to look at the raw bytes of an IP address is to determine the type of the address. Test the number of bytes in the array returned by getAddress( ) to determine whether you're dealing with an IPv4 or IPv6 address. Example 6-7 demonstrates.

Example 6-7. Print the IP address of the local machine

```
import java.net.*;

public class AddressTests {

  public static int getVersion(InetAddress ia) {

    byte[] address = ia.getAddress( );
    if (address.length == 4) return 4;
    else if (address.length == 16) return 6;
    else return -1;

  }

}
```

Address Types

Some IP addresses and some patterns of addresses have special meanings. For instance, I've already mentioned that 127.0.0.1 is the local loopback address. IPv4 addresses in the range 224.0.0.0 to 239.255.255.255 are multicast addresses that send to several subscribed hosts at once. Java 1.4 and later include 10 methods for testing whether an `InetAddress` object meets any of these criteria:

```
public boolean isAnyLocalAddress()
public boolean isLoopbackAddress()
public boolean isLinkLocalAddress()
public boolean isSiteLocalAddress()
public boolean isMulticastAddress()
public boolean isMCGlobal()
public boolean isMCNodeLocal()
public boolean isMCLinkLocal()
public boolean isMCSiteLocal()
public boolean isMCOrgLocal()
```

public boolean isAnyLocalAddress()

This method returns true if the address is a *wildcard address*, false otherwise. A wildcard address matches any address of the local system. This is important if the system has multiple network interfaces, e.g. several Ethernet cards or an Ethernet card and a wireless connection. This is normally important only on servers and gateways. In IPv4, the wildcard address is 0.0.0.0. In IPv6 this address is 0:0:0:0:0:0:0:0 (a.k.a ::).

public boolean isLoopbackAddress()

This method returns true if the address is the loopback address, false otherwise. The loopback address connects to the same computer directly in the IP layer without using any physical hardware. Thus, connecting to the loopback address enables tests to bypass potentially buggy or nonexistent Ethernet, PPP, and other drivers, helping to isolate problems. Connecting to the loopback address is not the same as connecting to the system's normal IP address from the same system. In IPv4, this address is 127.0.0.1. In IPv6, this address is 0:0:0:0:0:0:0:1 (a.k.a. ::1).

public boolean isLinkLocalAddress()

This method returns true if the address is an IPv6 link-local address, false otherwise. This is an address used to help IPv6 networks self-configure, much like DHCP on IPv4 networks but without necessarily using a server. Routers do not forward these packets beyond the local subnet. All link-local addresses begin with the eight bytes FE80:0000.0000:0000. The next eight bytes are filled with a local address, often copied from the Ethernet MAC address assigned by the Ethernet card manufacturer.

public boolean isSiteLocalAddress( )

This method returns true if the address is an IPv6 site-local address, false otherwise. Site-local addresses are similar to link-local addresses except that they may be forwarded by routers within a site or campus but should not be forwarded beyond that site. Site-local addresses begin with the eight bytes FEC0:0000.0000:0000. The next eight bytes are filled with a local address, often copied from the Ethernet MAC address assigned by the Ethernet card manufacturer.

public boolean isMulticastAddress( )

This method returns true if the address is a multicast address, false otherwise. Multicasting broadcasts content to all subscribed computers rather than to one particular computer. In IPv4, multicast addresses all fall in the range 224.0.0.0 to 239.255.255.255. In IPv6, they all begin with byte FF. Multicasting will be discussed in Chapter 14.

public boolean isMCGlobal( )

This method returns true if the address is a global multicast address, false otherwise. A global multicast address may have subscribers around the world. All multicast addresses begin with FF. In IPv6, global multicast addresses begin with FF0E or FF1E depending on whether the multicast address is a well known permanently assigned address or a transient address. In IPv4, all multicast addresses have global scope, at least as far as this method is concerned. As you'll see in Chapter 14, IPv4 uses time-to-live (TTL) values to control scope rather than addressing.

public boolean isMCOrgLocal( )

This method returns true if the address is an organization-wide multicast address, false otherwise. An organization-wide multicast address may have subscribers within all the sites of a company or organization, but not outside that organization. Organization multicast addresses begin with FF08 or FF18, depending on whether the multicast address is a well known permanently assigned address or a transient address.

public boolean isMCSiteLocal( )

This method returns true if the address is a site-wide multicast address, false otherwise. Packets addressed to a site-wide address will only be transmitted within their local site. Organization multicast addresses begin with FF05 or FF15, depending on whether the multicast address is a well known permanently assigned address or a transient address.

public boolean isMCLinkLocal( )

This method returns true if the address is a subnet-wide multicast address, false otherwise. Packets addressed to a link-local address will only be transmitted within their own subnet. Link-local multicast addresses begin with FF02 or FF12, depending on whether the multicast address is a well known permanently assigned address or a transient address.

public boolean isMCNodeLocal( )

This method returns true if the address is an interface-local multicast address, false otherwise. Packets addressed to an interface-local address are not sent beyond the network interface from which they originate, not even to a different network interface on the same node. This is primarily useful for network debugging and testing. Interface-local multicast addresses begin with the two bytes FF01 or FF11, depending on whether the multicast address is a well known permanently assigned address or a transient address.

 The method name is out of sync with current terminology. Earlier drafts of the IPv6 protocol called this type of address "node-local", hence the name "isMCNodeLocal". The IPNG working group actually changed the name before Java 1.4 was released. Unfortunately, Java 1.4 uses the old terminology.

Example 6-8 is a simple program to test the nature of an address entered from the command line using these 10 methods.

Example 6-8. Testing the characteristics of an IP address (Java 1.4 only)

```
import java.net.*;

public class IPCharacteristics {

  public static void main(String[] args) {

    try {
      InetAddress address = InetAddress.getByName(args[0]);

      if (address.isAnyLocalAddress()) {
        System.out.println(address + " is a wildcard address.");
      }
      if (address.isLoopbackAddress()) {
        System.out.println(address + " is loopback address.");
      }

      if (address.isLinkLocalAddress()) {
        System.out.println(address + " is a link-local address.");
      }
      else if (address.isSiteLocalAddress()) {
        System.out.println(address + " is a site-local address.");
      }
      else {
        System.out.println(address + " is a global address.");
      }
```

Example 6-8. Testing the characteristics of an IP address (Java 1.4 only) (continued)

```
    if (address.isMulticastAddress( )) {
      if (address.isMCGlobal( )) {
        System.out.println(address + " is a global multicast address.");
      }
      else if (address.isMCOrgLocal( )) {
        System.out.println(address
          + " is an organization wide multicast address.");
      }
      else if (address.isMCSiteLocal( )) {
        System.out.println(address + " is a site wide multicast address.");
      }
      else if (address.isMCLinkLocal( )) {
        System.out.println(address + " is a subnet wide multicast address.");
      }
      else if (address.isMCNodeLocal( )) {
        System.out.println(address
          + " is an interface-local multicast address.");
      }
      else {
        System.out.println(address + " is an unknown multicast address type.");
      }

    }
    else {
      System.out.println(address + " is a unicast address.");
    }

  }
  catch (UnknownHostException ex) {
    System.err.println("Could not resolve " + args[0]);
  }

 }

}
```

Here's the output from an IPv4 and IPv6 address:

```
$ java  IPCharacteristics 127.0.0.1
/127.0.0.1 is loopback address.
/127.0.0.1 is a global address.
/127.0.0.1 is a unicast address.
$ java  IPCharacteristics 192.168.254.32
/192.168.254.32 is a site-local address.
/192.168.254.32 is a unicast address.
$ java  IPCharacteristics www.oreilly.com
www.oreilly.com/208.201.239.37 is a global address.
www.oreilly.com/208.201.239.37 is a unicast address.
$ java  IPCharacteristics 224.0.2.1
/224.0.2.1 is a global address.
/224.0.2.1 is a global multicast address.
```

```
$ java  IPCharacteristics FF01:0:0:0:0:0:0:1
/ff01:0:0:0:0:0:0:1 is a global address.
/ff01:0:0:0:0:0:0:1 is an interface-local multicast address.
$ java  IPCharacteristics FF05:0:0:0:0:0:0:101
/ff05:0:0:0:0:0:0:101 is a global address.
/ff05:0:0:0:0:0:0:101 is a site wide multicast address.
$ java  IPCharacteristics 0::1
/0:0:0:0:0:0:0:1 is loopback address.
/0:0:0:0:0:0:0:1 is a global address.
/0:0:0:0:0:0:0:1 is a unicast address.
```

Testing Reachability // Java 1.5

Java 1.5 adds two new methods to the InetAddress class that enable applications to test whether a particular node is reachable from the current host; that is, whether a network connection can be made. Connections can be blocked for many reasons, including firewalls, proxy servers, misbehaving routers, and broken cables, or simply because the remote host is not turned on when you try to connect. The isReachable( ) methods allow you to test the connection:

```
public boolean isReachable(int timeout) throws IOException
public boolean isReachable(NetworkInterface interface, int ttl, int timeout)
  throws IOException
```

These methods attempt to connect to the echo port on the remote host site to find out if it's reachable. If the host responds within timeout milliseconds, the methods return true; otherwise, they return false. An IOException will be thrown if there's a network error. The second variant also lets you specify the local network interface the connection is made from and the "time-to-live" (the maximum number of network hops the connection will attempt before being discarded).

In practice, these methods aren't very reliable across the global Internet. Firewalls tend to get in the way of the network protocols Java uses to figure out if a host is reachable or not. However, you may be able to use these methods on the local intranet.

Object Methods

Like every other class, java.net.InetAddress inherits from java.lang.Object. Thus, it has access to all the methods of that class. It overrides three methods to provide more specialized behavior:

```
public boolean equals(Object o)
public int hashCode( )
public String toString( )
```

public boolean equals(Object o)

An object is equal to an InetAddress object only if it is itself an instance of the InetAddress class and it has the same IP address. It does not need to have the same hostname. Thus, an InetAddress object for *www.ibiblio.org* is equal to an InetAddress object for *www.cafeaulait.org* since both names refer to the same IP address. Example 6-9 creates InetAddress objects for *www.ibiblio.org* and *helios.metalab.unc.edu* and then tells you whether they're the same machine.

Example 6-9. Are www.ibiblio.org and helios.metalab.unc.edu the same?

```
import java.net.*;

public class IBiblioAliases {

  public static void main (String args[]) {

    try {
      InetAddress ibiblio = InetAddress.getByName("www.ibiblio.org");
      InetAddress helios = InetAddress.getByName("helios.metalab.unc.edu");
      if (ibiblio.equals(helios)) {
        System.out.println
          ("www.ibiblio.org is the same as helios.metalab.unc.edu");
      }
      else {
        System.out.println
          ("www.ibiblio.org is not the same as helios.metalab.unc.edu");
      }
    }
    catch (UnknownHostException ex) {
      System.out.println("Host lookup failed.");
    }

  }

}
```

When you run this program, you discover:

```
% java IBiblioAliases
www.ibiblio.org is the same as helios.metalab.unc.edu
```

public int hashCode( )

The hashCode( ) method returns an int that is needed when InetAddress objects are used as keys in hash tables. This is called by the various methods of java.util. Hashtable. You will almost certainly not need to call this method directly.

Consistent with the equals( ) method, the int that hashCode( ) returns is calculated solely from the IP address. It does not take the hostname into account. If two InetAddress objects have the same address, then they have the same hash code, even if their hostnames are different. Therefore, if you try to store two objects in a

Hashtable using equivalent InetAddress objects as a key (for example, the InetAddress objects for *helios.metalab.unc.edu* and *www.ibiblio.org*), the second will overwrite the first. If this is a problem, use the String returned by getHostName( ) as the key instead of the InetAddress itself.

public String toString( )

Like all good classes, java.net.InetAddress has a toString( ) method that returns a short text representation of the object. Example 6-1 through Example 6-4 all implicitly called this method when passing InetAddress objects to System.out.println( ). As you saw, the string produced by toString( ) has the form:

```
hostname/dotted quad address
```

Not all InetAddress objects have hostnames. If one doesn't, the dotted quad address is substituted in Java 1.3 and earlier. In Java 1.4, the hostname is set to the empty string. This format isn't particularly useful, so you'll probably never call toString( ) explicitly. If you do, the syntax is simple:

```
InetAddress thisComputer = InetAddress.getLocalHost( );
String address = thisComputer.toString( );
```

Inet4Address and Inet6Address

Java 1.4 introduces two new classes, Inet4Address and Inet6Address, in order to distinguish IPv4 addresses from IPv6 addresses:

```
public final class Inet4Address extends InetAddress
public final class Inet6Address extends InetAddress
```

(In Java 1.3 and earlier, all InetAddress objects represent IPv4 addresses.)

Most of the time, you really shouldn't be concerned with whether an address is an IPv4 or IPv6 address. In the application layer where Java programs reside, you simply don't need to know this (and even if you do need to know, it's quicker to check the size of the byte array returned by getAddress( ) than to use instanceof to test which subclass you have). Mostly these two classes are just implementation details you do not need to concern yourself with. Inet4Address overrides several of the methods in InetAddress but doesn't change their behavior in any public way. Inet6Address is similar, but it does add one new method not present in the superclass, isIPv4CompatibleAddress( ):

```
public boolean isIPv4CompatibleAddress( )
```

This method returns true if and only if the address is essentially an IPv4 address stuffed into an IPv6 container—which means only the last four bytes are non-zero. That is, the address has the form *0:0:0:0:0:0:xxxx*. If this is the case, you can pull off the last four bytes from the array returned by getBytes( ) and use this data to create an Inet4Address instead. However, you rarely need to do this.

The NetworkInterface Class

Java 1.4 adds a `NetworkInterface` class that represents a local IP address. This can either be a physical interface such as an additional Ethernet card (common on firewalls and routers) or it can be a virtual interface bound to the same physical hardware as the machine's other IP addresses. The `NetworkInterface` class provides methods to enumerate all the local addresses, regardless of interface, and to create `InetAddress` objects from them. These `InetAddress` objects can then be used to create sockets, server sockets, and so forth.

Factory Methods

Since `NetworkInterface` objects represent physical hardware and virtual addresses, they cannot be constructed arbitrarily. As with the `InetAddress` class, there are static factory methods that return the `NetworkInterface` object associated with a particular network interface. You can ask for a `NetworkInterface` by IP address, by name, or by enumeration.

public static NetworkInterface getByName(String name) throws SocketException

The getByName( ) method returns a `NetworkInterface` object representing the network interface with the particular name. If there's no interface with that name, it returns null. If the underlying network stack encounters a problem while locating the relevant network interface, a `SocketException` is thrown, but this isn't too likely to happen.

The format of the names is platform-dependent. On a typical Unix system, the Ethernet interface names have the form eth0, eth1, and so forth. The local loopback address is probably named something like "lo". On Windows, the names are strings like "CE31" and "ELX100" that are derived from the name of the vendor and model of hardware on that particular network interface. For example, this code fragment attempts to find the primary Ethernet interface on a Unix system:

```
try {
  NetworkInterface ni = NetworkInterface.getByName("eth0");
  if (ni == null) {
    System.err.println("No such interface:  eth0" );
  }
}
catch (SocketException ex) {
  System.err.println("Could not list sockets." );
}
```

public static NetworkInterface getByInetAddress(InetAddress address) throws SocketException

The getByInetAddress( ) method returns a NetworkInterface object representing the network interface bound to the specified IP address. If no network interface is bound to that IP address on the local host, then it returns null. If anything goes wrong, it throws a SocketException. For example, this code fragment finds the network interface for the local loopback address:

```
try {
  InetAddress local = InetAddress.getByName("127.0.0.1");
  NetworkInterface ni = NetworkInterface.getByName(local);
  if (ni == null) {
    System.err.println("That's weird. No local loopback address.");
  }
}
catch (SocketException ex) {
  System.err.println("Could not list sockets." );
}
catch (UnknownHostException ex) {
  System.err.println("That's weird. No local loopback address.");
}
```

public static Enumeration getNetworkInterfaces( ) throws SocketException

The getNetworkInterfaces( ) method returns a java.util.Enumeration listing all the network interfaces on the local host. Example 6-10 is a simple program to list all network interfaces on the local host:

Example 6-10. A program that lists all the network interfaces

```
import java.net.*;
import java.util.*;

public class InterfaceLister {

    public static void main(String[] args) throws Exception {

        Enumeration interfaces = NetworkInterface.getNetworkInterfaces();
        while (interfaces.hasMoreElements()) {
            NetworkInterface ni = (NetworkInterface) interfaces.nextElement();
            System.out.println(ni);
        }

    }

}
```

Here's the result of running this on the IBiblio login server:

```
% java InterfaceLister
name:eth1 (eth1) index: 3 addresses:
/192.168.210.122;
```

```
name:eth0 (eth0) index: 2 addresses:
/152.2.210.122;

name:lo (lo) index: 1 addresses:
/127.0.0.1;
```

You can see that this host has two separate Ethernet cards plus the local loopback address. Ignore the number of addresses (3, 2, and 1). It's a meaningless number, not the actual number of IP addresses bound to each interface.

Getter Methods

Once you have a NetworkInterface object, you can inquire about its IP address and name. This is pretty much the only thing you can do with these objects.

public Enumeration getInetAddresses( )

A single network interface may be bound to more than one IP address. This situation isn't common these days, but it does happen. The getInetAddresses( ) method returns a java.util.Enumeration containing an InetAddress object for each IP address the interface is bound to. For example, this code fragment lists all the IP addresses for the eth0 interface:

```
NetworkInterface eth0 = NetworkInterrface.getByName("eth0");
Enumeration addresses = eth0.getInetAddresses( );
while (addresses.hasMoreElements( )) {
  System.out.println(addresses.nextElement( ));
}
```

public String getName( )

The getName( ) method returns the name of a particular NetworkInterface object, such as eth0 or lo.

public String getDisplayName( )

The getDisplayName( ) method allegedly returns a more human-friendly name for the particular NetworkInterface—something like "Ethernet Card 0". However, in my tests on Unix, it always returned the same string as getName( ). On Windows, you may see slightly friendlier names such as "Local Area Connection" or "Local Area Connection 2".

Object Methods

The NetworkInterface class defines the equals( ), hashCode( ), and toString( ) methods with the usual semantics:

```
public boolean equals( )
public int hashCode( )
public String toString( )
```

Two NetworkInterface objects are equal if they represent the same physical network interface (e.g., both point to the same Ethernet port, modem, or wireless card) and they have the same IP address. Otherwise, they are not equal.

NetworkInterface does not implement Cloneable, Serializable, or Comparable. NetworkInterface objects cannot be cloned, compared, or serialized.

Some Useful Programs

You now know everything there is to know about the java.net.InetAddress class. The tools in this class alone let you write some genuinely useful programs. Here we'll look at two examples: one that queries your domain name server interactively and another that can improve the performance of your web server by processing log files offline.

HostLookup

nslookup is an old Unix utility that converts hostnames to IP addresses and IP addresses to hostnames. It has two modes: interactive and command-line. If you enter a hostname on the command line, *nslookup* prints the IP address of that host. If you enter an IP address on the command line, *nslookup* prints the hostname. If no hostname or IP address is entered on the command line, *nslookup* enters interactive mode, in which it reads hostnames and IP addresses from standard input and echoes back the corresponding IP addresses and hostnames until you type "exit". Example 6-11 is a simple character mode application called HostLookup, which emulates *nslookup*. It doesn't implement any of *nslookup*'s more complex features, but it does enough to be useful.

Example 6-11. An nslookup clone

```
import java.net.*;
import java.io.*;

public class HostLookup {

  public static void main (String[] args) {

    if (args.length > 0) { // use command line
      for (int i = 0; i < args.length; i++) {
        System.out.println(lookup(args[i]));
      }
    }
    else {
      BufferedReader in = new BufferedReader(new InputStreamReader(System.in));
      System.out.println("Enter names and IP addresses. Enter \"exit\" to quit.");
      try {
        while (true) {
```

Example 6-11. An nslookup clone (continued)

```java
        String host = in.readLine( );
        if (host.equalsIgnoreCase("exit") || host.equalsIgnoreCase("quit")) {
          break;
        }
        System.out.println(lookup(host));
      }
    }
    catch (IOException ex) {
      System.err.println(ex);
    }

  }

} /* end main */


private static String lookup(String host) {

  InetAddress node;

  // get the bytes of the IP address
  try {
    node = InetAddress.getByName(host);
  }
  catch (UnknownHostException ex) {
    return "Cannot find host " + host;
  }

  if (isHostname(host)) {
    return node.getHostAddress( );
  }
  else {  // this is an IP address
    return node.getHostName( );
  }

}  // end lookup

private static boolean isHostname(String host) {

  // Is this an IPv6 address?
  if (host.indexOf(':') != -1) return false;

  char[] ca = host.toCharArray( );
  // if we see a character that is neither a digit nor a period
  // then host is probably a hostname
  for (int i = 0; i < ca.length; i++) {
    if (!Character.isDigit(ca[i])) {
      if (ca[i] != '.') return true;
    }
  }
```

Example 6-11. An nslookup clone (continued)

```
    // Everything was either a digit or a period
    // so host looks like an IPv4 address in dotted quad format
    return false;

  } // end isHostName

} // end HostLookup
```

Here's some sample output; the input typed by the user is in bold:

```
$ java HostLookup utopia.poly.edu
128.238.3.21
$ java HostLookup 128.238.3.21
utopia.poly.edu
$ java HostLookup
Enter names and IP addresses. Enter "exit" to quit.
cs.nyu.edu
128.122.80.78
199.1.32.90
star.blackstar.com
localhost
127.0.0.1
stallio.elharo.com
Cannot find host stallio.elharo.com
stallion.elharo.com
127.0.0.1
127.0.0.1
stallion.elharo.com
java.oreilly.com
208.201.239.37
208.201.239.37
www.oreillynet.com
exit
$
```

There are three methods in the HostLookup program: main( ), lookup( ), and isHostName( ). The main( ) method determines whether there are command-line arguments. If there are command-line arguments, main( ) calls lookup( ) to process each one. If there are no command-line arguments, main( ) chains a BufferedReader to an InputStreamReader chained to System.in and reads input from the user with the readLine( ) method. (The warning about this method in Chapter 4 doesn't apply here because the program is reading from the console, not a network connection.) If the line is "exit", then the program exits. Otherwise, the line is assumed to be a hostname or IP address and is passed to the lookup( ) method.

The lookup( ) method uses InetAddress.getByName( ) to find the requested host, regardless of the input's format; remember that getByName( ) doesn't care if its argument is a name or a dotted quad address. If getByName( ) fails, lookup( ) returns a failure message. Otherwise, it gets the address of the requested system. Then lookup( ) calls isHostName( ) to determine whether the input string host is a hostname such as *cs.nyu.edu*, a dotted quad IPv4 address such as *128.122.153.70*, or a hexadecimal IPv6 address such as *FEDC::DC:0:7076:10*. isHostName( ) first looks for colons, which any IPv6 hexadecimal address will have and no hostname will have. If it finds any, it returns false. Checking for IPv4 addresses is a little trickier because dotted quad addresses don't contain any character that can't appear in a hostname. Instead, isHostName( ) looks at each character of the string; if all the characters are digits or periods, isHostName( ) guesses that the string is a numeric IP address and returns false. Otherwise, isHostName( ) guesses that the string is a hostname and returns true. What if the string is neither? Such an eventuality is very unlikely: if the string is neither a hostname nor an address, getByName( ) won't be able to do a lookup and will throw an exception. However, it would not be difficult to add a test making sure that the string looks valid; this is left as an exercise for the reader. If the user types a hostname, lookup( ) returns the corresponding dotted quad or hexadecimal address using getHostAddress( ). If the user types an IP address, then we use the getHostName( ) method to look up the hostname corresponding to the address, and return it.

Processing Web Server Log Files

Web server logs track the hosts that access a web site. By default, the log reports the IP addresses of the sites that connect to the server. However, you can often get more information from the names of those sites than from their IP addresses. Most web servers have an option to store hostnames instead of IP addresses, but this can hurt performance because the server needs to make a DNS request for each hit. It is much more efficient to log the IP addresses and convert them to hostnames at a later time, when the server isn't busy or even on another machine completely. Example 6-12 is a program called Weblog that reads a web server log file and prints each line with IP addresses converted to hostnames.

Most web servers have standardized on the common log file format, although there are exceptions; if your web server is one of those exceptions, you'll have to modify this program. A typical line in the common log file format looks like this:

```
205.160.186.76 unknown - [17/Jun/2003:22:53:58 -0500] "GET /bgs/greenbg.gif HTTP 1.
0" 200 50
```

This line indicates that a web browser at IP address 205.160.186.76 requested the file */bgs/greenbg.gif* from this web server at 11:53 p.m. (and 58 seconds) on June 17, 2003. The file was found (response code 200) and 50 bytes of data were successfully transferred to the browser.

The first field is the IP address or, if DNS resolution is turned on, the hostname from which the connection was made. This is followed by a space. Therefore, for our purposes, parsing the log file is easy: everything before the first space is the IP address, and everything after it does not need to be changed.

The Common Log File Format

If you want to expand Weblog into a more general web server log processor, you need a little more information about the common log file format. A line in the file has the format:

```
remotehost rfc931 authuser [date] "request" status bytes
```

remotehost
> remotehost is either the hostname or IP address from which the browser connected.

rfc931
> rfc931 is the username of the user on the remote system, as specified by Internet protocol RFC 931. Very few browsers send this information, so it's almost always either unknown or a dash. This is followed by a space.

authuser
> authuser is the authenticated username as specified by RFC 931. Once again, most popular browsers or client systems do not support this; this field usually is filled in with a dash, followed by a space.

[date]
> The date and time of the request are given in brackets. This is the local system time when the request was made. Days are a two-digit number ranging from 01 to 31. The month is Jan, Feb, Mar, Apr, May, Jun, Jul, Aug, Sep, Oct, Nov, or Dec. The year is indicated by four digits. The year is followed by a colon, the hour (from 00 to 23), another colon, two digits signifying the minute (00 to 59), a colon, and two digits signifying the seconds (00 to 59). Then comes the closing bracket and another space.

"request"
> The request line exactly as it came from the client. It is enclosed in quotation marks because it may contain embedded spaces. It is not guaranteed to be a valid HTTP request since client software may misbehave.

status
> A numeric HTTP status code returned to the client. A list of HTTP 1.0 status codes is given in Chapter 3. The most common response is 200, which means the request was successfully processed.

bytes
> The number of bytes of data that was sent to the client as a result of this request.

The dotted quad format IP address is converted into a hostname using the usual methods of java.net.InetAddress. Example 6-12 shows the code.

Example 6-12. Process web server log files

```
import java.net.*;
import java.io.*;
```

Example 6-12. Process web server log files (continued)

```java
import java.util.*;
import com.macfaq.io.SafeBufferedReader;

public class Weblog {

  public static void main(String[] args) {

    Date start = new Date();
    try {
      FileInputStream fin =  new FileInputStream(args[0]);
      Reader in = new InputStreamReader(fin);
      SafeBufferedReader bin = new SafeBufferedReader(in);

      String entry = null;
      while ((entry = bin.readLine()) != null) {

        // separate out the IP address
        int index = entry.indexOf(' ', 0);
        String ip = entry.substring(0, index);
        String theRest = entry.substring(index, entry.length());

        // find the hostname and print it out
        try {
          InetAddress address = InetAddress.getByName(ip);
          System.out.println(address.getHostName() + theRest);
        }
        catch (UnknownHostException ex) {
          System.out.println(entry);
        }

      } // end while
    }
    catch (IOException ex) {
      System.out.println("Exception: " + ex);
    }

    Date end = new Date();
    long elapsedTime = (end.getTime()-start.getTime())/1000;
    System.out.println("Elapsed time: " + elapsedTime + " seconds");

  } // end main

}
```

The name of the file to be processed is passed to `Weblog` as the first argument on the command line. A `FileInputStream` `fin` is opened from this file and an `InputStreamReader` is chained to `fin`. This `InputStreamReader` is buffered by chaining it to an instance of the `SafeBufferedReader` class developed in Chapter 4. The file is processed line by line in a `while` loop.

Each pass through the loop places one line in the String variable entry. entry is then split into two substrings: ip, which contains everything before the first space, and theRest, which is everything after the first space. The position of the first space is determined by entry.indexOf(" ", 0). ip is converted to an InetAddress object using getByName(). getHostName() then looks up the hostname. Finally, the hostname, a space, and everything else on the line (theRest) are printed on System.out. Output can be sent to a new file through the standard means for redirecting output.

Weblog is more efficient than you might expect. Most web browsers generate multiple log file entries per page served, since there's an entry in the log not just for the page itself but for each graphic on the page. And many visitors request multiple pages while visiting a site. DNS lookups are expensive and it simply doesn't make sense to look up each site every time it appears in the log file. The InetAddress class caches requested addresses. If the same address is requested again, it can be retrieved from the cache much more quickly than from DNS.

Nonetheless, this program could certainly be faster. In my initial tests, it took more than a second per log entry. (Exact numbers depend on the speed of your network connection, the speed of the local and remote DNS servers, and network congestion when the program is run.) The program spends a huge amount of time sitting and waiting for DNS requests to return. Of course, this is exactly the problem multithreading is designed to solve. One main thread can read the log file and pass off individual entries to other threads for processing.

A thread pool is absolutely necessary here. Over the space of a few days, even low-volume web servers can easily generate a log file with hundreds of thousands of lines. Trying to process such a log file by spawning a new thread for each entry would rapidly bring even the strongest virtual machine to its knees, especially since the main thread can read log file entries much faster than individual threads can resolve domain names and die. Consequently, reusing threads is essential. The number of threads is stored in a tunable parameter, numberOfThreads, so that it can be adjusted to fit the VM and network stack. (Launching too many simultaneous DNS requests can also cause problems.)

This program is now divided into two classes. The first class, PooledWeblog, shown in Example 6-13, contains the main() method and the processLogFile() method. It also holds the resources that need to be shared among the threads. These are the pool, implemented as a synchronized LinkedList from the Java Collections API, and the output log, implemented as a BufferedWriter named out. Individual threads have direct access to the pool but have to pass through PooledWeblog's log() method to write output.

The key method is processLogFile(). As before, this method reads from the underlying log file. However, each entry is placed in the entries pool rather than being immediately processed. Because this method is likely to run much more quickly than the threads that have to access DNS, it yields after reading each entry. Furthermore, it goes to sleep if there are more entries in the pool than threads available to process them. The amount of time it sleeps depends on the number of threads. This setup avoids using excessive amounts of memory for very large log files. When the last entry is read, the finished flag is set to true to tell the threads that they can die once they've completed their work.

Example 6-13. PooledWebLog

```java
import java.io.*;
import java.util.*;
import com.macfaq.io.SafeBufferedReader;

public class PooledWeblog {

  private BufferedReader in;
  private BufferedWriter out;
  private int numberOfThreads;
  private List entries = Collections.synchronizedList(new LinkedList( ));
  private boolean finished = false;
  private int test = 0;


  public PooledWeblog(InputStream in, OutputStream out,
   int numberOfThreads) {
    this.in = new BufferedReader(new InputStreamReader(in));
    this.out = new BufferedWriter(new OutputStreamWriter(out));
    this.numberOfThreads = numberOfThreads;
  }

  public boolean isFinished( ) {
    return this.finished;
  }

  public int getNumberOfThreads( ) {
    return numberOfThreads;
  }

  public void processLogFile( ) {

    for (int i = 0; i < numberOfThreads; i++) {
      Thread t = new LookupThread(entries, this);
      t.start( );
    }

    try {

      String entry = in.readLine( );
      while (entry != null) {

        if (entries.size( ) > numberOfThreads) {
          try {
            Thread.sleep((long) (1000.0/numberOfThreads));
          }
```

Example 6-13. PooledWebLog (continued)

```
          catch (InterruptedException ex) {}
          continue;
        }

        synchronized (entries) {
          entries.add(0, entry);
          entries.notifyAll( );
        }

        entry = in.readLine( );
        Thread.yield( );

    } // end while
  }

  public void log(String entry) throws IOException {
    out.write(entry + System.getProperty("line.separator", "\r\n"));
    out.flush( );
  }

  public static void main(String[] args) {

    try {
      PooledWeblog tw = new PooledWeblog(new FileInputStream(args[0]),
        System.out, 100);
      tw.processLogFile( );
    }
    catch (FileNotFoundException ex) {
      System.err.println("Usage: java PooledWeblog logfile_name");
    }
    catch (ArrayIndexOutOfBoundsException ex) {
      System.err.println("Usage: java PooledWeblog logfile_name");
    }
    catch (Exception ex) {
      System.err.println(ex);
      e.printStackTrace( );
    }

  } // end main

}
```

The LookupThread class, shown in Example 6-14, handles the detailed work of converting IP addresses to hostnames in the log entries. The constructor provides each thread with a reference to the entries pool it will retrieve work from and a reference to the PooledWeblog object it's working for. The latter reference allows callbacks to the PooledWeblog so that the thread can log converted entries and check to see when the last entry has been processed. It does so by calling the isFinished( ) method in PooledWeblog when the entries pool is empty (i.e., has size 0). Neither an empty pool nor isFinished( ) returning true is sufficient by itself. isFinished( ) returns true after the last entry is placed in the pool, which occurs, at least for a small amount of time, before the last entry is removed from the pool. And entries may be empty while there are still many entries remaining to be read if the lookup threads outrun the main thread reading the log file.

Example 6-14. LookupThread

```java
import java.net.*;
import java.io.*;
import java.util.*;

public class LookupThread extends Thread {

  private List entries;
  PooledWeblog log;    // used for callbacks

  public LookupThread(List entries, PooledWeblog log) {
    this.entries = entries;
    this.log = log;
  }

  public void run( ) {

    String entry;

    while (true) {

      synchronized (entries) {
        while (entries.size( ) == 0) {
          if (log.isFinished( )) return;
          try {
            entries.wait( );
          }
          catch (InterruptedException ex) {
          }
        }
        entry = (String) entries.remove(entries.size( )-1);
      }

      int index = entry.indexOf(' ', 0);
      String remoteHost = entry.substring(0, index);
      String theRest = entry.substring(index, entry.length( ));

      try {
        remoteHost = InetAddress.getByName(remoteHost).getHostName( );
      }
      catch (Exception ex) {
        // remoteHost remains in dotted quad format
      }

      try {
        log.log(remoteHost + theRest);
      }
```

Example 6-14. LookupThread (continued)

```
    catch (IOException ex) {
    }
    this.yield( );

  }

 }

}
```

Using threads like this lets the same log files be processed in parallel—a huge time-savings. In my unscientific tests, the threaded version is 10 to 50 times faster than the sequential version.

The biggest disadvantage to the multithreaded approach is that it reorders the log file. The output statistics aren't necessarily in the same order as the input statistics. For simple hit counting, this doesn't matter. However, there are some log analysis tools that can mine a log file to determine paths users followed through a site. These tools could get confused if the log is out of sequence. If the log sequence is an issue, attach a sequence number to each log entry. As the individual threads return log entries to the main program, the log( ) method in the main program stores any that arrive out of order until their predecessors appear. This is in some ways reminiscent of how network software reorders TCP packets that arrive out of order.

CHAPTER 7

URLs and URIs

The URL class is the simplest way for a Java program to locate and retrieve data from the network. You do not need to worry about the details of the protocol being used, the format of the data being retrieved, or how to communicate with the server; you simply tell Java the URL and it gets the data for you. Although Java can only handle a few protocols and content types out of the box, in later chapters you'll learn how to write and install new content and protocol handlers that extend Java's capabilities to include new protocols and new kinds of data. You'll also learn how to open sockets and communicate directly with different kinds of servers. But that's later; for now, let's see how much can be done with a minimum of work.

The URL Class

The java.net.URL class is an abstraction of a Uniform Resource Locator such as *http:// www.hamsterdance.com/* or *ftp://ftp.redhat.com/pub/*. It extends java.lang.Object, and it is a final class that cannot be subclassed. Rather than relying on inheritance to configure instances for different kinds of URLs, it uses the strategy design pattern. Protocol handlers are the strategies, and the URL class itself forms the context through which the different strategies are selected:

    public final class URL extends Object implements Serializable

Although storing a URL as a string would be trivial, it is helpful to think of URLs as objects with fields that include the scheme (a.k.a. the protocol), hostname, port, path, query string, and fragment identifier (a.k.a. the ref), each of which may be set independently. Indeed, this is almost exactly how the java.net.URL class is organized, though the details vary a little between different versions of Java.

The fields of java.net.URL are only visible to other members of the java.net package; classes that aren't in java.net can't access a URL's fields directly. However, you can set these fields using the URL constructors and retrieve their values using the various getter methods (getHost( ), getPort( ), and so on). URLs are effectively immutable. After a URL object has been constructed, its fields do not change. This has the side effect of making them thread-safe.

Creating New URLs

Unlike the InetAddress objects in Chapter 6, you can construct instances of java. net.URL. There are six constructors, differing in the information they require. Which constructor you use depends on the information you have and the form it's in. All these constructors throw a MalformedURLException if you try to create a URL for an unsupported protocol and may throw a MalformedURLException if the URL is syntactically incorrect.

Exactly which protocols are supported is implementation-dependent. The only protocols that have been available in all major virtual machines are http and file, and the latter is notoriously flaky. Java 1.5 also requires virtual machines to support https, jar, and ftp; many virtual machines prior to Java 1.5 support these three as well. Most virtual machines also support ftp, mailto, and gopher as well as some custom protocols like doc, netdoc, systemresource, and verbatim used internally by Java. The Netscape virtual machine supports the http, file, ftp, mailto, telnet, ldap, and gopher protocols. The Microsoft virtual machine supports http, file, ftp, https, mailto, gopher, doc, and systemresource, but not telnet, netdoc, jar, or verbatim. Of course, support for all these protocols is limited in applets by the security policy. For example, just because an untrusted applet can construct a URL object from a file URL does not mean that the applet can actually read the file the URL refers to. Just because an untrusted applet can construct a URL object from an HTTP URL that points to a third-party web site does not mean that the applet can connect to that site.

If the protocol you need isn't supported by a particular VM, you may be able to install a protocol handler for that scheme. This is subject to a number of security checks in applets and is really practical only for applications. Other than verifying that it recognizes the URL scheme, Java does not make any checks about the correctness of the URLs it constructs. The programmer is responsible for making sure that URLs created are valid. For instance, Java does not check that the hostname in an HTTP URL does not contain spaces or that the query string is x-www-form-URL-encoded. It does not check that a mailto URL actually contains an email address. Java does not check the URL to make sure that it points at an existing host or that it meets any other requirements for URLs. You can create URLs for hosts that don't exist and for hosts that do exist but that you won't be allowed to connect to.

Constructing a URL from a string

The simplest URL constructor just takes an absolute URL in string form as its single argument:

```
public URL(String url) throws MalformedURLException
```

Like all constructors, this may only be called after the new operator, and like all URL constructors, it can throw a MalformedURLException. The following code constructs a URL object from a String, catching the exception that might be thrown:

```
try {
  URL u = new URL("http://www.audubon.org/");
}
catch (MalformedURLException ex)  {
  System.err.println(ex);
}
```

Example 7-1 is a simple program for determining which protocols a virtual machine supports. It attempts to construct a URL object for each of 14 protocols (8 standard protocols, 3 custom protocols for various Java APIs, and 4 undocumented protocols used internally by HotJava). If the constructor succeeds, you know the protocol is supported. Otherwise, a MalformedURLException is thrown and you know the protocol is not supported.

Example 7-1. ProtocolTester

```
/* Which protocols does a virtual machine support? */
import java.net.*;

public class ProtocolTester {

  public static void main(String[] args) {

    // hypertext transfer protocol
    testProtocol("http://www.adc.org");

    // secure http
    testProtocol("https://www.amazon.com/exec/obidos/order2/");

    // file transfer protocol
    testProtocol("ftp://metalab.unc.edu/pub/languages/java/javafaq/");

    // Simple Mail Transfer Protocol
    testProtocol("mailto:elharo@metalab.unc.edu");

    // telnet
    testProtocol("telnet://dibner.poly.edu/");

    // local file access
    testProtocol("file:///etc/passwd");

    // gopher
    testProtocol("gopher://gopher.anc.org.za/");

    // Lightweight Directory Access Protocol
    testProtocol(
      "ldap://ldap.itd.umich.edu/o=University%20of%20Michigan,c=US?postalAddress");
```

Example 7-1. ProtocolTester (continued)

```
   // JAR
   testProtocol(
    "jar:http://cafeaulait.org/books/javaio/ioexamples/javaio.jar!"
       +"/com/macfaq/io/StreamCopier.class");

   // NFS, Network File System
   testProtocol("nfs://utopia.poly.edu/usr/tmp/");

   // a custom protocol for JDBC
   testProtocol("jdbc:mysql://luna.metalab.unc.edu:3306/NEWS");

   // rmi, a custom protocol for remote method invocation
   testProtocol("rmi://metalab.unc.edu/RenderEngine");

   // custom protocols for HotJava
   testProtocol("doc:/UsersGuide/release.html");
   testProtocol("netdoc:/UsersGuide/release.html");
   testProtocol("systemresource://www.adc.org/+/index.html");
   testProtocol("verbatim:http://www.adc.org/");

 }

 private static void testProtocol(String url) {

   try {
     URL u = new URL(url);
     System.out.println(u.getProtocol( ) + " is supported");
   }
   catch (MalformedURLException ex) {
     String protocol = url.substring(0, url.indexOf(':'));
     System.out.println(protocol + " is not supported");
   }

 }

}
```

The results of this program depend on which virtual machine runs it. Here are the
results from Java 1.4.1 on Mac OS X 10.2, which turns out to support all the protocols except Telnet, LDAP, RMI, NFS, and JDBC:

```
% java ProtocolTester
http is supported
https is supported
ftp is supported
mailto is supported
telnet is not supported
file is supported
gopher is supported
ldap is not supported
jar is supported
nfs is not supported
```

```
jdbc is not supported
rmi is not supported
doc is supported
netdoc is supported
systemresource is supported
verbatim is supported
```

Results using Sun's Linux 1.4.2 virtual machine were identical. Other 1.4 virtual machines derived from the Sun code will show similar results. Java 1.2 and later are likely to be the same except for maybe HTTPS, which was only recently added to the standard distribution. VMs that are not derived from the Sun codebase may vary somewhat in which protocols they support. For example, here are the results of running ProtocolTester with the open source Kaffe VM 1.1.1:

```
% java ProtocolTester
http is supported
https is not supported
ftp is supported
mailto is not supported
telnet is not supported
file is supported
gopher is not supported
ldap is not supported
jar is supported
nfs is not supported
jdbc is not supported
rmi is not supported
doc is not supported
netdoc is not supported
systemresource is not supported
verbatim is not supported
```

The nonsupport of RMI and JDBC is actually a little deceptive; in fact, the JDK does support these protocols. However, that support is through various parts of the java.rmi and java.sql packages, respectively. These protocols are not accessible through the URL class like the other supported protocols (although I have no idea why Sun chose to wrap up RMI and JDBC parameters in URL clothing if it wasn't intending to interface with these via Java's quite sophisticated mechanism for handling URLs).

Constructing a URL from its component parts

The second constructor builds a URL from three strings specifying the protocol, the hostname, and the file:

```
public URL(String protocol, String hostname, String file)
  throws MalformedURLException
```

This constructor sets the port to −1 so the default port for the protocol will be used. The file argument should begin with a slash and include a path, a filename, and optionally a fragment identifier. Forgetting the initial slash is a common mistake, and

one that is not easy to spot. Like all URL constructors, it can throw a
MalformedURLException. For example:

```
try {
  URL u = new URL("http", "www.eff.org", "/blueribbon.html#intro");
}
catch (MalformedURLException ex)  {
  // All VMs should recognize http
}
```

This creates a URL object that points to *http://www.eff.org/blueribbon.html#intro*,
using the default port for the HTTP protocol (port 80). The file specification includes
a reference to a named anchor. The code catches the exception that would be thrown
if the virtual machine did not support the HTTP protocol. However, this shouldn't
happen in practice.

For the rare occasions when the default port isn't correct, the next constructor lets
you specify the port explicitly as an int:

```
public URL(String protocol, String host, int port, String file)
  throws MalformedURLException
```

The other arguments are the same as for the URL(String protocol, String host,
String file) constructor and carry the same caveats. For example:

```
try {
  URL u = new URL("http", "fourier.dur.ac.uk", 8000, "/~dma3mjh/jsci/");
}
catch (MalformedURLException ex)  {
  System.err.println(ex);
}
```

This code creates a URL object that points to *http://fourier.dur.ac.uk:8000/~dma3mjh/
jsci/*, specifying port 8000 explicitly.

Example 7-2 is an alternative protocol tester that can run as an applet, making it useful for testing support of browser virtual machines. It uses the three-argument constructor rather than the one-argument constructor in Example 7-1. It also stores the
schemes to be tested in an array and uses the same host and file for each scheme.
This produces seriously malformed URLs like *mailto://www.peacefire.org/bypass/
SurfWatch/*, once again demonstrating that all Java checks for at object construction
is whether it recognizes the scheme, not whether the URL is appropriate.

Example 7-2. A protocol tester applet

```
import java.net.*;
import java.applet.*;
import java.awt.*;

public class ProtocolTesterApplet extends Applet {

  TextArea results = new TextArea( );
```

Example 7-2. A protocol tester applet (continued)

```
public void init( ) {
  this.setLayout(new BorderLayout( ));
  this.add("Center", results);
}

public void start( ) {

  String host = "www.peacefire.org";
  String file = "/bypass/SurfWatch/";

  String[] schemes = {"http",   "https",   "ftp",   "mailto",
                      "telnet", "file",    "ldap",  "gopher",
                      "jdbc",   "rmi",     "jndi",  "jar",
                      "doc",    "netdoc",  "nfs",   "verbatim",
                      "finger", "daytime", "systemresource"};

  for (int i = 0; i < schemes.length; i++) {
    try {
      URL u = new URL(schemes[i], host, file);
      results.append(schemes[i] + " is supported\r\n");
    }
    catch (MalformedURLException ex) {
      results.append(schemes[i] + " is not supported\r\n");
    }
  }

}

}
```

Figure 7-1 shows the results of Example 7-2 in Mozilla 1.4 with Java 1.4 installed. This browser supports HTTP, HTTPS, FTP, mailto, file, gopher, doc, netdoc, verbatim, systemresource, and jar but not HTTPS, ldap, Telnet, jdbc, rmi, jndi, finger or daytime.

Constructing relative URLs

This constructor builds an absolute URL from a relative URL and a base URL:

```
public URL(URL base, String relative) throws MalformedURLException
```

For instance, you may be parsing an HTML document at *http://www.ibiblio.org/javafaq/index.html* and encounter a link to a file called *mailinglists.html* with no further qualifying information. In this case, you use the URL to the document that contains the link to provide the missing information. The constructor computes the new URL as *http://www.ibiblio.org/javafaq/mailinglists.html*. For example:

```
try {
  URL u1 = new URL("http://www.ibiblio.org/javafaq/index.html");
  URL u2 = new URL (u1, "mailinglists.html");
}
catch (MalformedURLException ex) {
    System.err.println(ex);
}
```

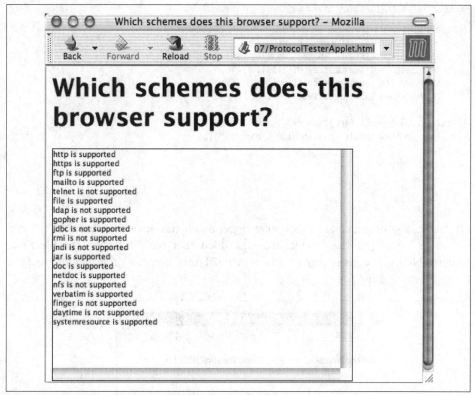

Figure 7-1. The ProtocolTesterApplet running in Mozilla 1.4

The filename is removed from the path of u1 and the new filename *mailinglists.html* is appended to make u2. This constructor is particularly useful when you want to loop through a list of files that are all in the same directory. You can create a URL for the first file and then use this initial URL to create URL objects for the other files by substituting their filenames. You also use this constructor when you want to create a URL relative to the applet's document base or code base, which you retrieve using the getDocumentBase( ) or getCodeBase( ) methods of the java.applet.Applet class. Example 7-3 is a very simple applet that uses getDocumentBase( ) to create a new URL object:

Example 7-3. A URL relative to the web page

```
import java.net.*;
import java.applet.*;
import java.awt.*;

public class RelativeURLTest extends Applet {

  public void init () {
```

Example 7-3. A URL relative to the web page (continued)

```
  try {
    URL base = this.getDocumentBase( );
    URL relative = new URL(base, "mailinglists.html");
    this.setLayout(new GridLayout(2,1));
    this.add(new Label(base.toString( )));
    this.add(new Label(relative.toString( )));
  }
  catch (MalformedURLException ex) {
    this.add(new Label("This shouldn't happen!"));
  }

 }

}
```

Of course, the output from this applet depends on the document base. In the run shown in Figure 7-2, the original URL (the document base) refers to the file *RelativeURL.html*; the constructor creates a new URL that points to the *mailinglists.html* file in the same directory.

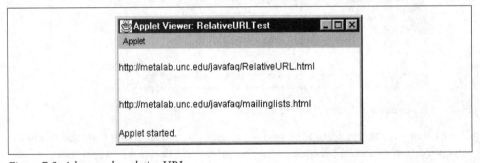

Figure 7-2. A base and a relative URL

When using this constructor with getDocumentBase( ), you frequently put the call to getDocumentBase( ) inside the constructor, like this:

```
    URL relative = new URL(this.getDocumentBase( ), "mailinglists.html");
```

Specifying a URLStreamHandler // Java 1.2

Two constructors allow you to specify the protocol handler used for the URL. The first constructor builds a relative URL from a base URL and a relative part. The second builds the URL from its component pieces:

```
    public URL(URL base, String relative, URLStreamHandler handler) // 1.2
      throws MalformedURLException
    public URL(String protocol, String host, int port, String file, // 1.2
      URLStreamHandler handler) throws MalformedURLException
```

All URL objects have URLStreamHandler objects to do their work for them. These two constructors change from the default URLStreamHandler subclass for a particular protocol to one of your own choosing. This is useful for working with URLs whose schemes aren't supported in a particular virtual machine as well as for adding functionality that the default stream handler doesn't provide, such as asking the user for a username and password. For example:

```
URL u = new URL("finger", "utopia.poly.edu", 79, "/marcus",
  new com.macfaq.net.www.protocol.finger.Handler());
```

The com.macfaq.net.www.protocol.finger.Handler class used here will be developed in Chapter 16.

While the other four constructors raise no security issues in and of themselves, these two do because class loader security is closely tied to the various URLStreamHandler classes. Consequently, untrusted applets are not allowed to specify a URLSreamHandler. Trusted applets can do so if they have the NetPermission specifyStreamHandler. However, for reasons that will become apparent in Chapter 16, this is a security hole big enough to drive the Microsoft money train through. Consequently, you should not request this permission or expect it to be granted if you do request it.

Other sources of URL objects

Besides the constructors discussed here, a number of other methods in the Java class library return URL objects. You've already seen getDocumentBase() from java.applet. Applet. The other common source is getCodeBase(), also from java.applet.Applet. This works just like getDocumentBase(), except it returns the URL of the applet itself instead of the URL of the page that contains the applet. Both getDocumentBase() and getCodeBase() come from the java.applet.AppletStub interface, which java.applet. Applet implements. You're unlikely to implement this interface yourself unless you're building a web browser or applet viewer.

In Java 1.2 and later, the java.io.File class has a toURL() method that returns a *file* URL matching the given file. The exact format of the URL returned by this method is platform-dependent. For example, on Windows it may return something like *file:/D:/ JAVA/JNP3/07/ToURLTest.java*. On Linux and other Unixes, you're likely to see *file: /home/elharo/books/JNP3/07/ToURLTest.java*. In practice, *file* URLs are heavily platform- and program-dependent. Java file URLs often cannot be interchanged with the URLs used by web browsers and other programs, or even with Java programs running on different platforms.

Class loaders are used not only to load classes but also to load resources such as images and audio files. The static ClassLoader.getSystemResource(String name) method returns a URL from which a single resource can be read. The ClassLoader. getSystemResources(String name) method returns an Enumeration containing a list of URLs from which the named resource can be read. Finally, the instance method getResource(String name) searches the path used by the referenced class loader for a URL to the named resource. The URLs returned by these methods may be file URLs,

HTTP URLs, or some other scheme. The name of the resource is a slash-separated list of Java identifiers, such as */com/macfaq/sounds/swale.au* or *com/macfaq/images/ headshot.jpg*. The Java virtual machine will attempt to find the requested resource in the class path—potentially including parts of the class path on the web server that an applet was loaded from—or inside a JAR archive.

Java 1.4 adds the URI class, which we'll discuss soon. URIs can be converted into URLs using the toURL( ) method, provided Java has the relevant protocol handler installed.

There are a few other methods that return URL objects here and there throughout the class library, but most are simple getter methods that return only a URL you probably already know because you used it to construct the object in the first place; for instance, the getPage( ) method of java.swing.JEditorPane and the getURL( ) method of java.net.URLConnection.

Splitting a URL into Pieces

URLs are composed of five pieces:

- The scheme, also known as the protocol
- The authority
- The path
- The fragment identifier, also known as the section or ref
- The query string

For example, given the URL *http://www.ibiblio.org/javafaq/books/jnp/index. html?isbn=1565922069#toc*, the scheme is *http*, the authority is *www.ibiblio.org*, the path is */javafaq/books/jnp/index.html*, the fragment identifier is *toc*, and the query string is *isbn=1565922069*. However, not all URLs have all these pieces. For instance, the URL *http://www.faqs.org/rfcs/rfc2396.html* has a scheme, an authority, and a path, but no fragment identifier or query string.

The authority may further be divided into the user info, the host, and the port. For example, in the URL *http://admin@www.blackstar.com:8080/*, the authority is *admin@www.blackstar.com:8080*. This has the user info *admin*, the host *www.blackstar.com*, and the port *8080*.

Read-only access to these parts of a URL is provided by five public methods: getFile( ), getHost( ), getPort( ), getProtocol( ), and getRef( ). Java 1.3 adds four more methods: getQuery( ), getPath( ), getUserInfo( ), and getAuthority( ).

public String getProtocol( )

The getProtocol( ) method returns a String containing the scheme of the URL, e.g., "http", "https", or "file". For example:

```
URL page = this.getCodeBase( );
System.out.println("This applet was downloaded via "
  + page.getProtocol( ));
```

public String getHost( )

The getHost( ) method returns a String containing the hostname of the URL. For example:

```
URL page = this.getCodeBase( );
System.out.println("This applet was downloaded from " + page.getHost( ));
```

The most recent virtual machines get this method right but some older ones, including Sun's JDK 1.3.0, may return a host string that is not necessarily a valid hostname or address. In particular, URLs that incorporate usernames, like *ftp://anonymous: anonymous@wuarchive.wustl.edu/*, sometimes include the user info in the host. For example, consider this code fragment:

```
URL u = new URL("ftp://anonymous:anonymous@wuarchive.wustl.edu/");
String host = u.getHost( );
```

Java 1.3 sets host to anonymous:anonymous@wuarchive.wustl.edu, not simply wuarchive.wustl.edu. Java 1.4 would return wuarchive.wustl.edu instead.

public int getPort( )

The getPort( ) method returns the port number specified in the URL as an int. If no port was specified in the URL, getPort( ) returns −1 to signify that the URL does not specify the port explicitly, and will use the default port for the protocol. For example, if the URL is *http://www.userfriendly.org/*, getPort( ) returns −1; if the URL is *http://www.userfriendly.org:80/*, getPort( ) returns 80. The following code prints −1 for the port number because it isn't specified in the URL:

```
URL u = new URL("http://www.ncsa.uiuc.edu/demoweb/html-primer.html");
System.out.println("The port part of " + u + " is " + u.getPort( ));
```

public int getDefaultPort( )

The getDefaultPort( ) method returns the default port used for this URL's protocol when none is specified in the URL. If no default port is defined for the protocol, getDefaultPort( ) returns −1. For example, if the URL is *http://www.userfriendly.org/*, getDefaultPort( ) returns 80; if the URL is *ftp://ftp.userfriendly.org:8000/*, getDefaultPort( ) returns 21.

public String getFile( )

The getFile( ) method returns a String that contains the path portion of a URL; remember that Java does not break a URL into separate path and file parts. Everything from the first slash (/) after the hostname until the character preceding the # sign that begins a fragment identifier is considered to be part of the file. For example:

```
URL page = this.getDocumentBase( );
System.out.println("This page's path is " + page.getFile( ));
```

If the URL does not have a file part, Java 1.2 and earlier append a slash to the URL and return the slash as the filename. For example, if the URL is *http://www.slashdot.org* (rather than something like *http://www.slashdot.org/*, getFile() returns /. Java 1.3 and later simply set the file to the empty string.

public String getPath( ) // Java 1.3

The getPath() method, available only in Java 1.3 and later, is a near synonym for getFile(); that is, it returns a String containing the path and file portion of a URL. However, unlike getFile(), it does not include the query string in the String it returns, just the path.

 Note that the getPath() method does not return only the directory path and getFile() does not return only the filename, as you might expect. Both getPath() and getFile() return the full path and filename. The only difference is that getFile() also returns the query string and getPath() does not.

public String getRef( )

The getRef() method returns the fragment identifier part of the URL. If the URL doesn't have a fragment identifier, the method returns null. In the following code, getRef() returns the string xtocid1902914:

```
URL u = new URL(
  "http://www.ibiblio.org/javafaq/javafaq.html#xtocid1902914");
System.out.println("The fragment ID of " + u + " is " + u.getRef());
```

public String getQuery( ) // Java 1.3

The getQuery() method returns the query string of the URL. If the URL doesn't have a query string, the method returns null. In the following code, getQuery() returns the string category=Piano:

```
URL u = new URL(
  "http://www.ibiblio.org/nywc/compositions.phtml?category=Piano");
System.out.println("The query string of " + u + " is " + u.getQuery());
```

In Java 1.2 and earlier, you need to extract the query string from the value returned by getFile() instead.

public String getUserInfo( ) // Java 1.3

Some URLs include usernames and occasionally even password information. This information comes after the scheme and before the host; an @ symbol delimits it. For instance, in the URL *http://elharo@java.oreilly.com/*, the user info is *elharo*. Some URLs also include passwords in the user info. For instance, in the URL *ftp:// mp3:secret@ftp.example.com/c%3a/stuff/mp3/*, the user info is *mp3:secret*. However, most of the time including a password in a URL is a security risk. If the URL doesn't have any user info, getUserInfo( ) returns null. Mailto URLs may not behave like you expect. In a URL like *mailto:elharo@metalab.unc.edu*, *elharo@metalab.unc.edu* is the path, not the user info and the host. That's because the URL specifies the remote recipient of the message rather than the username and host that's sending the message.

public String getAuthority( ) // Java 1.3

Between the scheme and the path of a URL, you'll find the authority. The term *authority* is taken from the Uniform Resource Identifier specification (RFC 2396), where this part of the URI indicates the authority that resolves the resource. In the most general case, the authority includes the user info, the host, and the port. For example, in the URL *ftp://mp3:mp3@138.247.121.61:21000/c%3a/*, the authority is *mp3:mp3@138.247.121.61:21000*. However, not all URLs have all parts. For instance, in the URL *http://conferences.oreilly.com/java/speakers/*, the authority is simply the hostname *conferences.oreilly.com*. The getAuthority( ) method returns the authority as it exists in the URL, with or without the user info and port.

Example 7-4 uses all eight methods to split URLs entered on the command line into their component parts. This program requires Java 1.3 or later.

Example 7-4. The parts of a URL

```
import java.net.*;

public class URLSplitter {

  public static void main(String args[]) {

    for (int i = 0; i < args.length; i++) {
      try {
        URL u = new URL(args[i]);
        System.out.println("The URL is " + u);
        System.out.println("The scheme is " + u.getProtocol( ));
        System.out.println("The user info is " + u.getUserInfo( ));

        String host = u.getHost( );
        if (host != null) {
          int atSign = host.indexOf('@');
          if (atSign != -1) host = host.substring(atSign+1);
          System.out.println("The host is " + host);
        }
        else {
          System.out.println("The host is null.");
        }

        System.out.println("The port is " + u.getPort( ));
        System.out.println("The path is " + u.getPath( ));
        System.out.println("The ref is " + u.getRef( ));
        System.out.println("The query string is " + u.getQuery( ));
      } // end try
```

Example 7-4. The parts of a URL (continued)

```
      catch (MalformedURLException ex) {
        System.err.println(args[i] + " is not a URL I understand.");
      }
      System.out.println( );
    }  // end for

  }  // end main

}  // end URLSplitter
```

Here's the result of running this against several of the URL examples in this chapter:

```
% java URLSplitter     \
 http://www.ncsa.uiuc.edu/demoweb/html-primer.html#A1.3.3.3 \
 ftp://mp3:mp3@138.247.121.61:21000/c%3a/                   \
 http://www.oreilly.com                                     \
 http://www.ibiblio.org/nywc/compositions.phtml?category=Piano \
 http://admin@www.blackstar.com:8080/                       \
The URL is http://www.ncsa.uiuc.edu/demoweb/html-primer.html#A1.3.3.3
The scheme is http
The user info is null
The host is www.ncsa.uiuc.edu
The port is -1
The path is /demoweb/html-primer.html
The ref is A1.3.3.3
The query string is null

The URL is ftp://mp3:mp3@138.247.121.61:21000/c%3a/
The scheme is ftp
The user info is mp3:mp3
The host is 138.247.121.61
The port is 21000
The path is /c%3a/
The ref is null
The query string is null

The URL is http://www.oreilly.com
The scheme is http
The user info is null
The host is www.oreilly.com
The port is -1
The path is
The ref is null
The query string is null

The URL is http://www.ibiblio.org/nywc/compositions.phtml?category=Piano
The scheme is http
The user info is null
The host is www.ibiblio.org
The port is -1
The path is /nywc/compositions.phtml
The ref is null
The query string is category=Piano
```

```
The URL is http://admin@www.blackstar.com:8080/
The scheme is http
The user info is admin
The host is www.blackstar.com
The port is 8080
The path is /
The ref is null
The query string is null
```

Retrieving Data from a URL

Naked URLs aren't very exciting. What's interesting is the data contained in the documents they point to. The URL class has several methods that retrieve data from a URL:

```
public InputStream openStream( ) throws IOException
public URLConnection openConnection( ) throws IOException
public URLConnection openConnection(Proxy proxy) throws IOException // 1.5
public Object getContent( ) throws IOException
public Object getContent(Class[] classes)  throws IOException // 1.3
```

These methods differ in that they return the data at the URL as an instance of different classes.

public final InputStream openStream( ) throws IOException

The openStream( ) method connects to the resource referenced by the URL, performs any necessary handshaking between the client and the server, and returns an InputStream from which data can be read. The data you get from this InputStream is the raw (i.e., uninterpreted) contents of the file the URL references: ASCII if you're reading an ASCII text file, raw HTML if you're reading an HTML file, binary image data if you're reading an image file, and so forth. It does not include any of the HTTP headers or any other protocol-related information. You can read from this InputStream as you would read from any other InputStream. For example:

```
try {
  URL u  = new URL("http://www.hamsterdance.com");
  InputStream in = u.openStream( );
  int c;
  while ((c = in.read( )) != -1) System.out.write(c);
}
catch (IOException ex) {
  System.err.println(ex);
}
```

This code fragment catches an IOException, which also catches the MalformedURLException that the URL constructor can throw, since MalformedURLException subclasses IOException.

Example 7-5 reads a URL from the command line, opens an InputStream from that URL, chains the resulting InputStream to an InputStreamReader using the default encoding, and then uses InputStreamReader's read( ) method to read successive characters from the file, each of which is printed on System.out. That is, it prints the raw data located at the URL: if the URL references an HTML file, the program's output is raw HTML.

Example 7-5. Download a web page

```java
import java.net.*;
import java.io.*;

public class SourceViewer {

  public static void main (String[] args) {

    if  (args.length > 0) {
      try {
        //Open the URL for reading
        URL u = new URL(args[0]);
        InputStream in = u.openStream( );
        // buffer the input to increase performance
        in = new BufferedInputStream(in);
        // chain the InputStream to a Reader
        Reader r = new InputStreamReader(in);
        int c;
        while ((c = r.read( )) != -1) {
          System.out.print((char) c);
        }
      }
      catch (MalformedURLException ex) {
        System.err.println(args[0] + " is not a parseable URL");
      }
      catch (IOException ex) {
        System.err.println(ex);
      }

    } //  end if

  } // end main

} // end SourceViewer
```

And here are the first few lines of output when SourceViewer downloads *http://www.oreilly.com*:

```
% java SourceViewer http://www.oreilly.com
<!DOCTYPE HTML PUBLIC "-//W3C//DTD HTML 4.01 Transitional//EN">
<html xmlns="http://www.w3.org/1999/xhtml" lang="en-US" xml:lang="en-US">
<head>
<title>oreilly.com -- Welcome to O'Reilly Media, Inc. -- computer books, software
conferences, online publishing</title>
<meta name="keywords" content="O'Reilly, oreilly, computer books,
technical books, UNIX, unix, Perl, Java, Linux, Internet, Web, C, C++, Windows,
Windows NT, Security, Sys Admin, System Administration, Oracle, PL/SQL, online books,
books online, computer book online, e-books, ebooks, Perl Conference, Open Source
```

```
Conference, Java Conference, open source, free software, XML, Mac OS X, .Net, dot
net, C#, PHP, CGI, VB, VB Script, Java Script, javascript, Windows 2000, XP,
bioinformatics, web services, p2p" />
<meta name="description" content="O'Reilly is a leader in technical andcomputer book
documentation, online content, and conferences for UNIX, Perl, Java, Linux, Internet,
Mac OS X, C, C++, Windows, Windows NT, Security, Sys Admin, System Administration,
Oracle, Design and Graphics, Online Books, e-books, ebooks, Perl Conference, Java
Conference, P2P Conference" />
```

There are quite a few more lines in that web page; if you want to see them, you can
fire up your web browser.

The shakiest part of this program is that it blithely assumes that the remote URL is
text, which is not necessarily true. It could well be a GIF or JPEG image, an MP3
sound file, or something else entirely. Even if it is text, the document encoding may
not be the same as the default encoding of the client system. The remote host and
local client may not have the same default character set. As a general rule, for pages
that use a character set radically different from ASCII, the HTML will include a META
tag in the header specifying the character set in use. For instance, this META tag specifies the Big-5 encoding for Chinese:

```
<meta http-equiv="Content-Type" content="text/html; charset=big5">
```

An XML document will likely have an XML declaration instead:

```
<?xml version="1.0" encoding="Big5"?>
```

In practice, there's no easy way to get at this information other than by parsing the
file and looking for a header like this one, and even that approach is limited. Many
HTML files hand-coded in Latin alphabets don't have such a META tag. Since Windows, the Mac, and most Unixes have somewhat different interpretations of the
characters from 128 to 255, the extended characters in these documents do not
translate correctly on platforms other than the one on which they were created.

And as if this isn't confusing enough, the HTTP header that precedes the actual document is likely to have its own encoding information, which may completely contradict
what the document itself says. You can't read this header using the URL class, but you
can with the URLConnection object returned by the openConnection( ) method. Encoding
detection and declaration is one of the thornier parts of the architecture of the Web.

public URLConnection openConnection( ) throws IOException

The openConnection( ) method opens a socket to the specified URL and returns a
URLConnection object. A URLConnection represents an open connection to a network
resource. If the call fails, openConnection( ) throws an IOException. For example:

```
try {
  URL u = new URL("http://www.jennicam.org/");
  try {
    URLConnection uc = u.openConnection( );
    InputStream in = uc.getInputStream( );
```

```
    // read from the connection...
  } // end try
  catch (IOException ex) {
    System.err.println(ex);
  }
} // end try
catch (MalformedURLException ex) {
  System.err.println(ex);
}
```

Use this method when you want to communicate directly with the server. The URLConnection gives you access to everything sent by the server: in addition to the document itself in its raw form (e.g., HTML, plain text, binary image data), you can access all the metadata specified by the protocol. For example, if the scheme is HTTP, the URLConnection lets you access the HTTP headers as well as the raw HTML. The URLConnection class also lets you write data to as well as read from a URL—for instance, in order to send email to a mailto URL or post form data. The URLConnection class will be the primary subject of Chapter 15.

Java 1.5 adds one overloaded variant of this method that specifies the proxy server to pass the connection through:

```
public URLConnection openConnection(Proxy proxy) throws IOException
```

This overrides any proxy server set with the usual socksProxyHost, socksProxyPort, http.proxyHost, http.proxyPort, http.nonProxyHosts, and similar system properties. If the protocol handler does not support proxies, the argument is ignored and the connection is made directly if possible.

public final Object getContent( ) throws IOException

The getContent( ) method is the third way to download data referenced by a URL. The getContent( ) method retrieves the data referenced by the URL and tries to make it into some type of object. If the URL refers to some kind of text object such as an ASCII or HTML file, the object returned is usually some sort of InputStream. If the URL refers to an image such as a GIF or a JPEG file, getContent( ) usually returns a java.awt.ImageProducer (more specifically, an instance of a class that implements the ImageProducer interface). What unifies these two disparate classes is that they are not the thing itself but a means by which a program can construct the thing:

```
try {
  URL u = new URL("http://mesola.obspm.fr/");
  Object o = u.getContent( );
  // cast the Object to the appropriate type
  // work with the Object...
}
catch (Exception ex) {
  System.err.println(ex);
}
```

getContent( ) operates by looking at the Content-type field in the MIME header of the data it gets from the server. If the server does not use MIME headers or sends an unfamiliar Content-type, getContent( ) returns some sort of InputStream with which the data can be read. An IOException is thrown if the object can't be retrieved. Example 7-6 demonstrates this.

Example 7-6. Download an object

```java
import java.net.*;
import java.io.*;

public class ContentGetter {

  public static void main (String[] args) {

    if (args.length > 0) {

      //Open the URL for reading
      try {
        URL u = new URL(args[0]);
        try {
          Object o = u.getContent( );
          System.out.println("I got a " + o.getClass().getName( ));
        } // end try
        catch (IOException ex) {
          System.err.println(ex);
        }
      } // end try
      catch (MalformedURLException ex) {
        System.err.println(args[0] + " is not a parseable URL");
      }
    } //  end if

  } // end main

} // end ContentGetter
```

Here's the result of trying to get the content of *http://www.oreilly.com*:

```
% java ContentGetter http://www.oreilly.com/
I got a sun.net.www.protocol.http.HttpURLConnection$HttpInputStream
```

The exact class may vary from one version of Java to the next (in earlier versions, it's been java.io.PushbackInputStream or sun.net.www.http.KeepAliveStream) but it should be some form of InputStream.

Here's what you get when you try to load a header image from that page:

```
% java ContentGetter http://www.oreilly.com/graphics_new/animation.gif
I got a sun.awt.image.URLImageSource
```

Here's what happens when you try to load a Java applet using getContent( ):

```
% java ContentGetter http://www.cafeaulait.org/RelativeURLTest.class
I got a sun.net.www.protocol.http.HttpURLConnection$HttpInputStream
```

Here's what happens when you try to load an audio file using getContent():

```
% java ContentGetter http://www.cafeaulait.org/course/week9/spacemusic.au
I got a sun.applet.AppletAudioClip
```

The last result is the most unusual because it is as close as the Java core API gets to a class that represents a sound file. It's not just an interface through which you can load the sound data.

This example demonstrates the biggest problems with using getContent(): it's hard to predict what kind of object you'll get. You could get some kind of InputStream or an ImageProducer or perhaps an AudioClip; it's easy to check using the instanceof operator. This information should be enough to let you read a text file or display an image.

public final Object getContent(Class[] classes) throws IOException // Java 1.3

Starting in Java 1.3, it is possible for a content handler to provide different views of an object. This overloaded variant of the getContent() method lets you choose what class you'd like the content to be returned as. The method attempts to return the URL's content in the order used in the array. For instance, if you prefer an HTML file to be returned as a String, but your second choice is a Reader and your third choice is an InputStream, write:

```
URL u = new URL("http://www.nwu.org");
Class[] types = new Class[3];
types[0] = String.class;
types[1] = Reader.class;
types[2] = InputStream.class;
Object o = u.getContent(types);
```

You then have to test for the type of the returned object using instanceof. For example:

```
if (o instanceof String) {
  System.out.println(o);
}
else if (o instanceof Reader) {
  int c;
  Reader r = (Reader) o;
  while ((c = r.read()) != -1) System.out.print((char) c);
}
else if (o instanceof InputStream) {
  int c;
  InputStream in = (InputStream) o;
  while ((c = in.read()) != -1) System.out.write(c);
}
else {
  System.out.println("Error: unexpected type " + o.getClass());
}
```

Utility Methods

The URL class contains a couple of utility methods that perform common operations on URLs. The sameFile( ) method determines whether two URLs point to the same document. The toExternalForm( ) method converts a URL object to a string that can be used in an HTML link or a web browser's Open URL dialog.

public boolean sameFile(URL other)

The sameFile( ) method tests whether two URL objects point to the same file. If they do, sameFile( ) returns true; otherwise, it returns false. The test that sameFile( ) performs is quite shallow; all it does is compare the corresponding fields for equality. It detects whether the two hostnames are really just aliases for each other. For instance, it can tell that *http://www.ibiblio.org/* and *http://metalab.unc.edu/* are the same file. However, it cannot tell that *http://www.ibiblio.org:80/* and *http:// metalab.unc.edu/* are the same file or that *http://www.cafeconleche.org/* and *http:// www.cafeconleche.org/index.html* are the same file. sameFile( ) is smart enough to ignore the fragment identifier part of a URL, however. Here's a fragment of code that uses sameFile( ) to compare two URLs:

```
try {
  URL u1 = new URL("http://www.ncsa.uiuc.edu/HTMLPrimer.html#GS");
  URL u2 = new URL("http://www.ncsa.uiuc.edu/HTMLPrimer.html#HD");
  if (u1.sameFile(u2)) {
    System.out.println(u1 + " is the same file as \n" + u2);
  }
  else {
    System.out.println(u1 + " is not the same file as \n" + u2);
  }
}
catch (MalformedURLException ex) {
  System.err.println(ex);
}
```

The output is:

```
http://www.ncsa.uiuc.edu/HTMLPrimer.html#GS is the same file as
http://www.ncsa.uiuc.edu/HTMLPrimer.html#HD
```

The sameFile( ) method is similar to the equals( ) method of the URL class. The main difference between sameFile( ) and equals( ) is that equals( ) considers the fragment identifier (if any), whereas sameFile( ) does not. The two URLs shown here do not compare equal although they are the same file. Also, any object may be passed to equals( ); only URL objects can be passed to sameFile( ).

public String toExternalForm( )

The toExternalForm( ) method returns a human-readable String representing the URL. It is identical to the toString( ) method. In fact, all the toString( ) method does is return `toExternalForm( )`. Therefore, this method is currently redundant and rarely used.

public URI toURI( ) throws URISyntaxException // Java 1.5

Java 1.5 adds a `toURI( )` method that converts a URL object to an equivalent URI object. We'll take up the URI class shortly. In the meantime, the main thing you need to know is that the URI class provides much more accurate, specification-conformant behavior than the URL class. For operations like absolutization and encoding, you should prefer the URI class where you have the option. In Java 1.4 and later, the URL class should be used primarily for the actual downloading of content from the remote server.

The Object Methods

URL inherits from `java.lang.Object`, so it has access to all the methods of the Object class. It overrides three to provide more specialized behavior: `equals( )`, `hashCode( )`, and `toString( )`.

public String toString( )

Like all good classes, `java.net.URL` has a `toString( )` method. Example 7-1 through Example 7-5 implicitly called this method when URLs were passed to `System.out.println( )`. As those examples demonstrated, the String produced by `toString( )` is always an absolute URL, such as *http://www.cafeaulait.org/javatutorial.html*.

It's uncommon to call `toString( )` explicitly. Print statements call `toString( )` implicitly. Outside of print statements, it's more proper to use `toExternalForm( )` instead. If you do call `toString( )`, the syntax is simple:

```
URL codeBase = this.getCodeBase( );
String appletURL = codeBase.toString( );
```

public boolean equals(Object o)

An object is equal to a URL only if it is also a URL, both URLs point to the same file as determined by the `sameFile( )` method, and both URLs have the same fragment identifier (or both URLs don't have fragment identifiers). Since `equals( )` depends on `sameFile( )`, `equals( )` has the same limitations as `sameFile( )`. For example, *http://www.oreilly.com/* is not equal to *http://www.oreilly.com/index.html*, and *http://www.oreilly.com:80/* is not equal to *http://www.oreilly.com/*. Whether this makes sense depends on whether you think of a URL as a string or as a reference to a particular Internet resource.

Example 7-7 creates URL objects for *http://www.ibiblio.org/* and *http://metalab.unc.edu/* and tells you if they're the same using the `equals( )` method.

Example 7-7. Are http://www.ibiblio.org and http://www.metalab.unc.edu the same?

```java
import java.net.*;

public class URLEquality {

  public static void main (String[] args) {

    try {
      URL ibiblio = new URL ("http://www.ibiblio.org/");
      URL metalab = new URL("http://metalab.unc.edu/");
      if (ibiblio.equals(metalab)) {
        System.out.println(ibiblio + " is the same as " + metalab);
      }
      else {
        System.out.println(ibiblio + " is not the same as " + metalab);
      }
    }
    catch (MalformedURLException ex) {
      System.err.println(ex);
    }

  }

}
```

When you run this program, you discover:

```
% java URLEquality
http://www.ibiblio.org/ is the same as http://metalab.unc.edu/
```

public int hashCode( )

The hashCode( ) method returns an int that is used when URL objects are used as keys in hash tables. Thus, it is called by the various methods of java.util.Hashtable. You rarely need to call this method directly, if ever. Hash codes for two different URL objects are unlikely to be the same, but it is certainly possible; there are far more conceivable URLs than there are four-byte integers.

Methods for Protocol Handlers

The last method in the URL class I'll just mention briefly here for the sake of completeness: setURLStreamHandlerFactory( ). It's primarily used by protocol handlers that are responsible for new schemes, not by programmers who just want to retrieve data from a URL. We'll discuss it in more detail in Chapter 16.

public static synchronized void setURLStreamHandlerFactory(URLStreamHandlerFactory factory)

This method sets the URLStreamHandlerFactory for the application and throws a generic Error if the factory has already been set. A URLStreamHandler is responsible for parsing the URL and then constructing the appropriate `URLConnection` object to handle the connection to the server. Most of the time this happens behind the scenes.

The URLEncoder and URLDecoder Classes

One of the challenges faced by the designers of the Web was dealing with the differences between operating systems. These differences can cause problems with URLs: for example, some operating systems allow spaces in filenames; some don't. Most operating systems won't complain about a # sign in a filename; but in a URL, a # sign indicates that the filename has ended, and a fragment identifier follows. Other special characters, nonalphanumeric characters, and so on, all of which may have a special meaning inside a URL or on another operating system, present similar problems. To solve these problems, characters used in URLs must come from a fixed subset of ASCII, specifically:

- The capital letters A–Z
- The lowercase letters a–z
- The digits 0–9
- The punctuation characters - _ . ! ~ * ' (and ,)

The characters : / & ? @ # ; $ + = and % may also be used, but only for their specified purposes. If these characters occur as part of a filename, they and all other characters should be encoded.

The encoding is very simple. Any characters that are not ASCII numerals, letters, or the punctuation marks specified earlier are converted into bytes and each byte is written as a percent sign followed by two hexadecimal digits. Spaces are a special case because they're so common. Besides being encoded as %20, they can be encoded as a plus sign (+). The plus sign itself is encoded as %2B. The / # = & and ? characters should be encoded when they are used as part of a name, and not as a separator between parts of the URL.

 This scheme doesn't work well in heterogeneous environments with multiple character sets. For example, on a U.S. Windows system, é is encoded as %E9. On a U.S. Mac, it's encoded as %8E. The existence of variations is a distinct shortcoming of the current URI specification that should be addressed in the future through Internationalized Resource Identifiers (IRIs).

The URL class does not perform encoding or decoding automatically. You can construct URL objects that use illegal ASCII and non-ASCII characters and/or percent escapes. Such characters and escapes are not automatically encoded or decoded when output by methods such as getPath( ) and toExternalForm( ). You are responsible for making sure all such characters are properly encoded in the strings used to construct a URL object.

Luckily, Java provides a URLEncoder class to encode strings in this format. Java 1.2 adds a URLDecoder class that can decode strings in this format. Neither of these classes will be instantiated.

```
public class URLDecoder extends Object
public class URLEncoder extends Object
```

URLEncoder

In Java 1.3 and earlier, the java.net.URLEncoder class contains a single static method called encode( ) that encodes a String according to these rules:

```
public static String encode(String s)
```

This method always uses the default encoding of the platform on which it runs, so it will produce different results on different systems. As a result, Java 1.4 deprecates this method and replaces it with a method that requires you to specify the encoding:

```
public static String encode(String s, String encoding)
  throws UnsupportedEncodingException
```

Both variants change any nonalphanumeric characters into % sequences (except the space, underscore, hyphen, period, and asterisk characters). Both also encode all non-ASCII characters. The space is converted into a plus sign. These methods are a little over-aggressive; they also convert tildes, single quotes, exclamation points, and parentheses to percent escapes, even though they don't absolutely have to. However, this change isn't forbidden by the URL specification, so web browsers deal reasonably with these excessively encoded URLs.

Both variants return a new String, suitably encoded. The Java 1.3 encode( ) method uses the platform's default encoding to calculate percent escapes. This encoding is typically ISO-8859-1 on U.S. Unix systems, Cp1252 on U.S. Windows systems, MacRoman on U.S. Macs, and so on in other locales. Because both encoding and decoding are platform- and locale-specific, this method is annoyingly non-interoperable, which is precisely why it has been deprecated in Java 1.4 in favor of the variant that requires you to specify an encoding. However, if you just pick the platform default encoding, your program will be as platform- and locale-locked as the Java 1.3 version. Instead, you should always pick UTF-8, never anything else. UTF-8 is compatible with the new IRI specification, the URI class, modern web browsers, and more other software than any other encoding you could choose.

Example 7-8 is a program that uses URLEncoder.encode( ) to print various encoded strings. Java 1.4 or later is required to compile and run it.

Example 7-8. x-www-form-urlencoded strings

```java
import java.net.URLEncoder;
import java.io.UnsupportedEncodingException;


public class EncoderTest {

  public static void main(String[] args) {

    try {
      System.out.println(URLEncoder.encode("This string has spaces",  "UTF-8"));
      System.out.println(URLEncoder.encode("This*string*has*asterisks",  "UTF-8"));
      System.out.println(URLEncoder.encode("This%string%has%percent%signs",
                                           "UTF-8"));
      System.out.println(URLEncoder.encode("This+string+has+pluses",  "UTF-8"));
      System.out.println(URLEncoder.encode("This/string/has/slashes",  "UTF-8"));
      System.out.println(URLEncoder.encode("This\"string\"has\"quote\"marks",
                                           "UTF-8"));
      System.out.println(URLEncoder.encode("This:string:has:colons",  "UTF-8"));
      System.out.println(URLEncoder.encode("This~string~has~tildes",  "UTF-8"));
      System.out.println(URLEncoder.encode("This(string)has(parentheses)",
                                           "UTF-8"));
      System.out.println(URLEncoder.encode("This.string.has.periods",
                                           "UTF-8"));
      System.out.println(URLEncoder.encode("This=string=has=equals=signs",
                                           "UTF-8"));
      System.out.println(URLEncoder.encode("This&string&has&ampersands", "UTF-8"));
      System.out.println(URLEncoder.encode("Thiséstringéhasénon-ASCII characters",
                                           "UTF-8"));
    }
    catch (UnsupportedEncodingException ex) {
      throw new RuntimeException("Broken VM does not support UTF-8");
    }

  }

}
```

Here is the output. Note that the code needs to be saved in something other than ASCII, and the encoding chosen should be passed as an argument to the compiler to account for the non-ASCII characters in the source code.

```
% javac -encoding UTF8 EncoderTest
% java EncoderTest
This+string+has+spaces
This*string*has*asterisks
This%25string%25has%25percent%25signs
This%2Bstring%2Bhas%2Bpluses
This%2Fstring%2Fhas%2Fslashes
This%22string%22has%22quote%22marks
This%3Astring%3Ahas%3Acolons
This%7Estring%7Ehas%7Etildes
This%28string%29has%28parentheses%29
```

```
This.string.has.periods
This%3Dstring%3Dhas%3Dequals%3Dsigns
This%26string%26has%26ampersands
This%C3%A9string%C3%A9has%C3%A9non-ASCII+characters
```

Notice in particular that this method encodes the forward slash, the ampersand, the equals sign, and the colon. It does not attempt to determine how these characters are being used in a URL. Consequently, you have to encode URLs piece by piece rather than encoding an entire URL in one method call. This is an important point, because the most common use of URLEncoder is in preparing query strings for communicating with server-side programs that use GET. For example, suppose you want to encode this query string used for an AltaVista search:

```
pg=q&kl=XX&stype=stext&q=+"Java+I/O"&search.x=38&search.y=3
```

This code fragment encodes it:

```
String query = URLEncoder.encode(
  "pg=q&kl=XX&stype=stext&q=+\"Java+I/O\"&search.x=38&search.y=3");
System.out.println(query);
```

Unfortunately, the output is:

```
pg%3Dq%26kl%3DXX%26stype%3Dstext%26q%3D%2B%22Java%2BI%2FO%22%26search
.x%3D38%26search.y%3D3
```

The problem is that URLEncoder.encode( ) encodes blindly. It can't distinguish between special characters used as part of the URL or query string, like & and = in the previous string, and characters that need to be encoded. Consequently, URLs need to be encoded a piece at a time like this:

```
String query = URLEncoder.encode("pg");
query += "=";
query += URLEncoder.encode("q");
query += "&";
query += URLEncoder.encode("kl");
query += "=";
query += URLEncoder.encode("XX");
query += "&";
query += URLEncoder.encode("stype");
query += "=";
query += URLEncoder.encode("stext");
query += "&";
query += URLEncoder.encode("q");
query += "=";
query += URLEncoder.encode("\"Java I/O\"");
query += "&";
query += URLEncoder.encode("search.x");
query += "=";
query += URLEncoder.encode("38");
query += "&";
query += URLEncoder.encode("search.y");
query += "=";
query += URLEncoder.encode("3");
System.out.println(query);
```

The output of this is what you actually want:

```
pg=q&kl=XX&stype=stext&q=%2B%22Java+I%2FO%22&search.x=38&search.y=3
```

Example 7-9 is a QueryString class that uses the URLEncoder to encode successive name and value pairs in a Java object, which will be used for sending data to server-side programs. When you create a QueryString, you can supply the first name-value pair to the constructor as individual strings. To add further pairs, call the add( ) method, which also takes two strings as arguments and encodes them. The getQuery( ) method returns the accumulated list of encoded name-value pairs.

Example 7-9. -The QueryString class

```java
package com.macfaq.net;

import java.net.URLEncoder;
import java.io.UnsupportedEncodingException;

public class QueryString {

  private StringBuffer query = new StringBuffer( );

  public QueryString(String name, String value) {
    encode(name, value);
  }

  public synchronized void add(String name, String value) {
    query.append('&');
    encode(name, value);
  }

  private synchronized void encode(String name, String value) {
    try {
      query.append(URLEncoder.encode(name, "UTF-8"));
      query.append('=');
      query.append(URLEncoder.encode(value, "UTF-8"));
    }
    catch (UnsupportedEncodingException ex) {
      throw new RuntimeException("Broken VM does not support UTF-8");
    }
  }

  public String getQuery( ) {
    return query.toString( );
  }

  public String toString( ) {
    return getQuery( );
  }

}
```

Using this class, we can now encode the previous example:

```
QueryString qs = new QueryString("pg", "q");
qs.add("kl", "XX");
qs.add("stype", "stext");
qs.add("q", "+\"Java I/O\"");
qs.add("search.x", "38");
qs.add("search.y", "3");
String url = "http://www.altavista.com/cgi-bin/query?" + qs;
System.out.println(url);
```

URLDecoder

The corresponding URLDecoder class has two static methods that decode strings
encoded in x-www-form-url-encoded format. That is, they convert all plus signs to
spaces and all percent escapes to their corresponding character:

```
public static String decode(String s) throws Exception
public static String decode(String s, String encoding)  // Java 1.4
   throws UnsupportedEncodingException
```

The first variant is used in Java 1.3 and 1.2. The second variant is used in Java 1.4
and later. If you have any doubt about which encoding to use, pick UTF-8. It's more
likely to be correct than anything else.

An IllegalArgumentException may be thrown if the string contains a percent sign
that isn't followed by two hexadecimal digits or decodes into an illegal sequence.
Then again it may not be. This is implementation-dependent, and what happens
when an illegal sequence is detected and does not throw an
IllegalArgumentException is undefined. In Sun's JDK 1.4, no exception is thrown
and extra bytes with no apparent meaning are added to the undecodable string. This
is truly brain-damaged, and possibly a security hole.

Since this method does not touch non-escaped characters, you can pass an entire
URL to it rather than splitting it into pieces first. For example:

```
String input = "http://www.altavista.com/cgi-bin/" +
"query?pg=q&kl=XX&stype=stext&q=%2B%22Java+I%2FO%22&search.x=38&search.y=3";
 try {
  String output = URLDecoder.decode(input, "UTF-8");
  System.out.println(output);
 }
```

The URI Class

A URI is an abstraction of a URL that includes not only Uniform Resource Locators
but also Uniform Resource Names (URNs). Most URIs used in practice are URLs,
but most specifications and standards such as XML are defined in terms of URIs. In

Java 1.4 and later, URIs are represented by the java.net.URI class. This class differs from the java.net.URL class in three important ways:

- The URI class is purely about identification of resources and parsing of URIs. It provides no methods to retrieve a representation of the resource identified by its URI.

- The URI class is more conformant to the relevant specifications than the URL class.

- A URI object can represent a relative URI. The URL class absolutizes all URIs before storing them.

In brief, a URL object is a representation of an application layer protocol for network retrieval, whereas a URI object is purely for string parsing and manipulation. The URI class has no network retrieval capabilities. The URL class has some string parsing methods, such as getFile( ) and getRef( ), but many of these are broken and don't always behave exactly as the relevant specifications say they should. Assuming you're using Java 1.4 or later and therefore have a choice, you should use the URL class when you want to download the content of a URL and the URI class when you want to use the URI for identification rather than retrieval, for instance, to represent an XML namespace URI. In some cases when you need to do both, you may convert from a URI to a URL with the toURL( ) method, and in Java 1.5 you can also convert from a URL to a URI using the toURI( ) method of the URL class.

Constructing a URI

URIs are built from strings. Unlike the URL class, the URI class does not depend on an underlying protocol handler. As long as the URI is syntactically correct, Java does not need to understand its protocol in order to create a representative URI object. Thus, unlike the URL class, the URI class can be used for new and experimental URI schemes.

public URI(String uri) throws URISyntaxException

This is the basic constructor that creates a new URI object from any convenient string. For example,

```
URI voice = new URI("tel:+1-800-9988-9938");
URI web   = new URI("http://www.xml.com/pub/a/2003/09/17/stax.html#id=_hbc");
URI book  = new URI("urn:isbn:1-565-92870-9");
```

If the string argument does not follow URI syntax rules—for example, if the URI begins with a colon—this constructor throws a URISyntaxException. This is a checked exception, so you need to either catch it or declare that the method where the constructor is invoked can throw it. However, one syntactic rule is not checked. In contradiction to the URI specification, the characters used in the URI are not limited to ASCII. They can include other Unicode characters, such as ø and é.

Syntactically, there are very few restrictions on URIs, especially once the need to encode non-ASCII characters is removed and relative URIs are allowed. Almost any string can be interpreted as a URI.

public URI(String scheme, String schemeSpecificPart, String fragment) throws URISyntaxException

This constructor is mostly used for nonhierarchical URIs. The scheme is the URI's protocol, such as http, urn, tel, and so forth. It must be composed exclusively of ASCII letters and digits and the three punctuation characters +, -, and .. It must begin with a letter. Passing null for this argument omits the scheme, thus creating a relative URI. For example:

```
URI absolute = new URI("http", "//www.ibiblio.org" , null);
URI relative = new URI(null, "/javafaq/index.shtml", "today");
```

The scheme-specific part depends on the syntax of the URI scheme; it's one thing for an http URL, another for a mailto URL, and something else again for a tel URI. Because the URI class encodes illegal characters with percent escapes, there's effectively no syntax error you can make in this part.

Finally, the third argument contains the fragment identifier, if any. Again, characters that are forbidden in a fragment identifier are escaped automatically. Passing null for this argument simply omits the fragment identifier.

public URI(String scheme, String host, String path, String fragment) throws URISyntaxException

This constructor is used for hierarchical URIs such as http and ftp URLs. The host and path together (separated by a /) form the scheme-specific part for this URI. For example:

```
URI today= new URI("http", "www.ibiblio.org", "/javafaq/index.html", "today");
```

produces the URI *http://www.ibiblio.org/javafaq/index.html#today*.

If the constructor cannot form a legal hierarchical URI from the supplied pieces—for instance, if there is a scheme so the URI has to be absolute but the path doesn't start with /—then it throws a URISyntaxException.

public URI(String scheme, String authority, String path, String query, String fragment) throws URISyntaxException

This constructor is basically the same as the previous one, with the addition of a query string component. For example:

```
URI today= new URI("http", "www.ibiblio.org", "/javafaq/index.html",
                    "referrer=cnet&date=2004-08-23", "today");
```

As usual, any unescapable syntax errors cause a URISyntaxException to be thrown and null can be passed to omit any of the arguments.

public URI(String scheme, String userInfo, String host, int port, String path, String query, String fragment) throws URISyntaxException

This is the master hierarchical URI constructor that the previous two invoke. It divides the authority into separate user info, host, and port parts, each of which has its own syntax rules. For example:

```
URI styles = new URI("ftp", "anonymous:elharo@metalab.unc.edu",
    "ftp.oreilly.com", 21, "/pub/stylesheet", null, null);
```

However, the resulting URI still has to follow all the usual rules for URIs and again, null can be passed for any argument to omit it from the result.

public static URI create(String uri)

This is not a constructor, but rather a static factory method. Unlike the constructors, it does not throw a URISyntaxException. If you're sure your URIs are legal and do not violate any of the rules, you can use this method. For example, this invocation creates a URI for anonymous FTP access using an email address as password:

```
URI styles = URI.create(
    "ftp://anonymous:elharo%40metalab.unc.edu@ftp.oreilly.com:21/pub/stylesheet");
```

If the URI does prove to be malformed, this method throws an IllegalArgumentException. This is a runtime exception, so you don't have to explicitly declare it or catch it.

The Parts of the URI

A URI reference has up to three parts: a scheme, a scheme-specific part, and a fragment identifier. The general format is:

scheme:scheme-specific-part:fragment

If the scheme is omitted, the URI reference is relative. If the fragment identifier is omitted, the URI reference is a pure URI. The URI class has getter methods that return these three parts of each URI object. The getRaw*Foo*( ) methods return the encoded forms of the parts of the URI, while the equivalent get*Foo*( ) methods first decode any percent-escaped characters and then return the decoded part:

```
public String getScheme( )
public String getSchemeSpecificPart( )
public String getRawSchemeSpecificPart( )
public String getFragment( )
public String getRawFragment( )
```

 There's no getRawScheme( ) method because the URI specification requires that all scheme names be composed exclusively of URI-legal ASCII characters and does not allow percent escapes in scheme names.

These methods all return null if the particular URI object does not have the relevant component: for example, a relative URI without a scheme or an http URI without a fragment identifier.

A URI that has a scheme is an *absolute* URI. A URI without a scheme is *relative*. The isAbsolute( ) method returns true if the URI is absolute, false if it's relative:

```
public boolean isAbsolute()
```

The details of the scheme-specific part vary depending on the type of the scheme. For example, in a *tel* URL, the scheme-specific part has the syntax of a telephone number. However, in many useful URIs, including the very common *file* and *http* URLs, the scheme-specific part has a particular hierarchical format divided into an authority, a path, and a query string. The authority is further divided into user info, host, and port. The isOpaque( ) method returns false if the URI is hierarchical, true if it's not hierarchical—that is, if it's opaque:

```
public boolean isOpaque()
```

If the URI is opaque, all you can get is the scheme, scheme-specific part, and fragment identifier. However, if the URI is hierarchical, there are getter methods for all the different parts of a hierarchical URI:

```
public String getAuthority()
public String getFragment()
public String getHost()
public String getPath()
public String getPort()
public String getQuery()
public String getUserInfo()
```

These methods all return the decoded parts; in other words, percent escapes, such as %3C, are changed into the characters they represent, such as <. If you want the raw, encoded parts of the URI, there are five parallel getRaw*Foo*( ) methods:

```
public String getRawAuthority()
public String getRawFragment()
public String getRawPath()
public String getRawQuery()
public String getRawUserInfo()
```

Remember the URI class differs from the URI specification in that non-ASCII characters such as é and ü are never percent-escaped in the first place, and thus will still be present in the strings returned by the getRaw*Foo*( ) methods unless the strings originally used to construct the URI object were encoded.

 There are no getRawPort( ) and getRawHost( ) methods because these components are always guaranteed to be made up of ASCII characters, at least for now. Internationalized domain names are coming, and may require this decision to be rethought in future versions of Java.

In the event that the specific URI does not contain this information—for instance, the URI *http://www.example.com* has no user info, path, port, or query string—the relevant methods return null. getPort() is the single exception. Since it's declared to return an int, it can't return null. Instead, it returns –1 to indicate an omitted port.

For various technical reasons that don't have a lot of practical impact, Java can't always initially detect syntax errors in the authority component. The immediate symptom of this failing is normally an inability to return the individual parts of the authority: port, host, and user info. In this event, you can call parseServerAuthority() to force the authority to be reparsed:

```
public URI parseServerAuthority( ) throws URISyntaxException
```

The original URI does not change (URI objects are immutable), but the URI returned will have separate authority parts for user info, host, and port. If the authority cannot be parsed, a URISyntaxException is thrown.

Example 7-10 uses these methods to split URIs entered on the command line into their component parts. It's similar to Example 7-4 but works with any syntactically correct URI, not just the ones Java has a protocol handler for.

Example 7-10. The parts of a URI

```
import java.net.*;

public class URISplitter {

  public static void main(String args[]) {

    for (int i = 0; i < args.length; i++) {
      try {
        URI u = new URI(args[i]);
        System.out.println("The URI is " + u);
        if (u.isOpaque( )) {
          System.out.println("This is an opaque URI.");
          System.out.println("The scheme is " + u.getScheme( ));
          System.out.println("The scheme specific part is "
           + u.getSchemeSpecificPart( ));
          System.out.println("The fragment ID is " + u.getFragment( ));
        }
        else {
          System.out.println("This is a hierarchical URI.");
          System.out.println("The scheme is " + u.getScheme( ));
          try {
            u = u.parseServerAuthority( );
            System.out.println("The host is " + u.getUserInfo( ));
            System.out.println("The user info is " + u.getUserInfo( ));
            System.out.println("The port is " + u.getPort( ));
          }
          catch (URISyntaxException ex) {
            // Must be a registry based authority
            System.out.println("The authority is " + u.getAuthority( ));
```

Example 7-10. The parts of a URI (continued)

```
        }
        System.out.println("The path is " + u.getPath());
        System.out.println("The query string is " + u.getQuery());
        System.out.println("The fragment ID is " + u.getFragment());
      } // end else
    } // end try
    catch (URISyntaxException ex) {
      System.err.println(args[i] + " does not seem to be a URI.");
    }
    System.out.println();
  } // end for

} // end main

} // end URISplitter
```

Here's the result of running this against three of the URI examples in this section:

```
% java URISplitter tel:+1-800-9988-9938 \
http://www.xml.com/pub/a/2003/09/17/stax.html#id=_hbc \
urn:isbn:1-565-92870-9
The URI is tel:+1-800-9988-9938
This is an opaque URI.
The scheme is tel
The scheme specific part is +1-800-9988-9938
The fragment ID is null

The URI is http://www.xml.com/pub/a/2003/09/17/stax.html#id=_hbc
This is a hierarchical URI.
The scheme is http
The host is null
The user info is null
The port is -1
The path is /pub/a/2003/09/17/stax.html
The query string is null
The fragment ID is id=_hbc

The URI is urn:isbn:1-565-92870-9
This is an opaque URI.
The scheme is urn
The scheme specific part is isbn:1-565-92870-9
The fragment ID is null
```

Resolving Relative URIs

The URI class has three methods for converting back and forth between relative and absolute URIs.

public URI resolve(URI uri)

This method compares the uri argument to this URI and uses it to construct a new URI object that wraps an absolute URI. For example, consider these three lines of code:

```
URI absolute = new URI("http://www.example.com/");
URI relative = new URI("images/logo.png");
URI resolved = absolute.resolve(relative);
```

After they've executed, resolved contains the absolute URI *http://www.example.com/ images/logo.png.*

If the invoking URI does not contain an absolute URI itself, the resolve( ) method resolves as much of the URI as it can and returns a new relative URI object as a result. For example, take these three statements:

```
URI top = new URI("javafaq/books/");
URI relative = new URI("jnp3/examples/07/index.html");
URI resolved = top.resolve(relative);
```

After they've executed, resolved now contains the relative URI *javafaq/books/jnp3/ examples/07/index.html* with no scheme or authority.

public URI resolve(String uri)

This is a convenience method that simply converts the string argument to a URI and then resolves it against the invoking URI, returning a new URI object as the result. That is, it's equivalent to resolve(new URI(str)). Using this method, the previous two samples can be rewritten as:

```
URI absolute = new URI("http://www.example.com/");
URI resolved = absolute.resolve("images/logo.png");
URI top = new URI("javafaq/books/");
resolved = top.resolve("jnp3/examples/07/index.html");
```

public URI relativize(URI uri)

It's also possible to reverse this procedure; that is, to go from an absolute URI to a relative one. The relativize( ) method creates a new URI object from the uri argument that is relative to the invoking URI. The argument is not changed. For example:

```
URI absolute = new URI("http://www.example.com/images/logo.png");
URI top = new URI("http://www.example.com/");
URI relative = top.relativize(absolute);
```

The URI object relative now contains the relative URI *images/logo.png.*

Utility Methods

The URI class has the usual batch of utility methods: equals( ), hashCode( ), toString( ), and compareTo( ).

public boolean equals(Object o)

URIs are tested for equality pretty much as you'd expect. It's not a direct string comparison. Equal URIs must both either be hierarchical or opaque. The scheme and authority parts are compared without considering case. That is, *http* and *HTTP* are the same scheme, and *www.example.com* is the same authority as *www.EXAMPLE.com*. The rest of the URI is case-sensitive, except for hexadecimal digits used to escape illegal characters. Escapes are *not* decoded before comparing. *http://www.example.com/A* and *http://www.example.com/%41* are unequal URIs.

public int hashCode( )

The hashCode( ) method is a usual hashCode( ) method, nothing special. Equal URIs do have the same hash code and unequal URIs are fairly unlikely to share the same hash code.

public int compareTo(Object o)

URIs can be ordered. The ordering is based on string comparison of the individual parts, in this sequence:

- If the schemes are different, the schemes are compared, without considering case.
- Otherwise, if the schemes are the same, a hierarchical URI is considered to be less than an opaque URI with the same scheme.
- If both URIs are opaque URIs, they're ordered according to their scheme-specific parts.
- If both the scheme and the opaque scheme-specific parts are equal, the URIs are compared by their fragments.
- If both URIs are hierarchical, they're ordered according to their authority components, which are themselves ordered according to user info, host, and port, in that order.
- If the schemes and the authorities are equal, the path is used to distinguish them.
- If the paths are also equal, the query strings are compared.
- If the query strings are equal, the fragments are compared.

URIs are not comparable to any type except themselves. Comparing a URI to anything except another URI causes a ClassCastException.

public String toString( )

The toString( ) method returns an *unencoded* string form of the URI. That is, characters like é and \ are not percent-escaped unless they were percent-escaped in the strings used to construct this URI. Therefore, the result of calling this method is not guaranteed to be a syntactically correct URI. This form is sometimes useful for display to human beings, but not for retrieval.

public String toASCIIString( )

The toASCIIString( ) method returns an *encoded* string form of the URI. Characters like é and \ are always percent-escaped whether or not they were originally escaped. This is the string form of the URI you should use most of the time. Even if the form returned by toString( ) is more legible for humans, they may still copy and paste it into areas that are not expecting an illegal URI. toASCIIString( ) always returns a syntactically correct URI.

Proxies

Many systems access the Web and sometimes other non-HTTP parts of the Internet through *proxy servers*. A proxy server receives a request for a remote server from a local client. The proxy server makes the request to the remote server and forwards the result back to the local client. Sometimes this is done for security reasons, such as to prevent remote hosts from learning private details about the local network configuration. Other times it's done to prevent users from accessing forbidden sites by filtering outgoing requests and limiting which sites can be viewed. For instance, an elementary school might want to block access to *http://www.playboy.com*. And still other times it's done purely for performance, to allow multiple users to retrieve the same popular documents from a local cache rather than making repeated downloads from the remote server.

Java programs based on the URL class can work through most common proxy servers and protocols. Indeed, this is one reason you might want to choose to use the URL class rather than rolling your own HTTP or other client on top of raw sockets.

System Properties

For basic operations, all you have to do is set a few system properties to point to the addresses of your local proxy servers. If you are using a pure HTTP proxy, set http.proxyHost to the domain name or the IP address of your proxy server and http.proxyPort to the port of the proxy server (the default is 80). There are several ways to do this, including calling System.setProperty( ) from within your Java code or using the –D options when launching the program. This example sets the proxy server to 192.168.254.254 and the port to 9000:

```
% java -Dhttp.proxyHost=192.168.254.254  -Dhttp.proxyPort=9000  com.domain.Program
```

If you want to exclude a host from being proxied and connect directly instead, set the http.nonProxyHosts system property to its hostname or IP address. To exclude multiple hosts, separate their names by vertical bars. For example, this code fragment proxies everything except *java.oreilly.com* and *xml.oreilly.com*:

```
System.setProperty("http.proxyHost", "192.168.254.254");
System.setProperty("http.proxyPort", "9000");
System.setProperty("http.nonProxyHosts", "java.oreilly.com|xml.oreilly.com");
```

You can also use an asterisk as a wildcard to indicate that all the hosts within a particular domain or subdomain should not be proxied. For example, to proxy everything except hosts in the *oreilly.com* domain:

```
% java -Dhttp.proxyHost=192.168.254.254  -Dhttp.nonProxyHosts=*.oreilly.com  com.
domain.Program
```

If you are using an FTP proxy server, set the `ftp.proxyHost`, `ftp.proxyPort`, and `ftp.nonProxyHosts` properties in the same way.

Java does not support any other application layer proxies, but if you're using a transport layer SOCKS proxy for all TCP connections, you can identify it with the `socksProxyHost` and `socksProxyPort` system properties. Java does not provide an option for nonproxying with SOCKS. It's an all-or-nothing decision.

The Proxy Class

Java 1.5 allows more fine-grained control of proxy servers from within a Java program. Specifically, this allows you to choose different proxy servers for different remote hosts. The proxies themselves are represented by instances of the `java.net.Proxy` class. There are still only three kinds of proxies, HTTP, SOCKS, and direct connections (no proxy at all), represented by three constants in the `Proxy.Type` enum:

- `Proxy.Type.DIRECT`
- `Proxy.Type.HTTP`
- `Proxy.Type.SOCKS`

Besides its type, the other important piece of information about a proxy is its address and port, given as a `SocketAddress` object. For example, this code fragment creates a Proxy object representing an HTTP proxy server on port 80 of *proxy.example.com*:

```
SocketAddress address = new InetSocketAddress("proxy.example.com", 80);
Proxy proxy = new Proxy(Proxy.Type.HTTP, address);
```

Although there are only three kinds of proxy objects, there can be many proxies of the same type for different proxy servers on different hosts.

The ProxySelector Class

Each running Java 1.5 virtual machine has a single `java.net.ProxySelector` object it uses to locate the proxy server for different connections. The default `ProxySelector` merely inspects the various system properties and the URL's protocol to decide how to connect to different hosts. However, you can install your own subclass of ProxySelector in place of the default selector and use it to choose different proxies based on protocol, host, path, time of day, or other criteria.

The key to this class is the abstract select( ) method:

```
public abstract List<Proxy> select(URI uri)
```

Java passes this method a URI object (not a URL object) representing the host to which a connection is needed. For a connection made with the URL class, this object typically has the form *http://www.example.com/* or *ftp://ftp.example.com/pub/files/*, or some such. For a pure TCP connection made with the Socket class, this URI will have the form *socket://host:port:*, for instance, *socket://www.example.com:80*. The ProxySelector object then chooses the right proxies for this type of object and returns them in a List<Proxy>.

The second abstract method in this class you must implement is connectFailed( ):

```
public void connectFailed(URI uri, SocketAddress address, IOException ex)
```

This is a callback method used to warn a program that the proxy server isn't actually making the connection. Example 7-11 demonstrates with a ProxySelector that attempts to use the proxy server at *proxy.example.com* for all HTTP connections unless the proxy server has previously failed to resolve a connection to a particular URL. In that case, it suggests a direct connection instead.

Example 7-11. A ProxySelector that remembers what it can connect to

```
import java.net.*;
import java.util.*;
import java.io.*;

public class LocalProxySelector extends ProxySelector {

  private List failed = new ArrayList();

  public List<Proxy> select(URI uri) {

    List<Proxy> result = new ArrayList<Proxy>();
    if (failed.contains(uri)
      || "http".equalsIgnoreCase(uri.getScheme())) {
        result.add(Proxy.NO_PROXY);
    }
    else {
        SocketAddress proxyAddress
          = new InetSocketAddress( "proxy.example.com", 8000);
        Proxy proxy = new Proxy(Proxy.Type.HTTP, proxyAddress);
        result.add(proxy);
    }

    return result;
```

Example 7-11. A ProxySelector that remembers what it can connect to (continued)

```
  }

  public void connectFailed(URI uri, SocketAddress address, IOException ex) {
    failed.add(uri);
  }

}
```

As I already said, each running virtual machine has exactly one ProxySelector. To change the ProxySelector, pass the new selector to the static ProxySelector. setDefault( ) method, like so:

```
    ProxySelector selector = new LocalProxySelector():
    ProxySelector.setDefault(selector);
```

From this point forward, all connections opened by that virtual machine will ask the ProxySelector for the right proxy to use. You normally shouldn't use this in code running in a shared environment. For instance, you wouldn't change the ProxySelector in a servlet because that would change the ProxySelector for all servlets running in the same container.

Communicating with Server-Side Programs Through GET

The URL class makes it easy for Java applets and applications to communicate with server-side programs such as CGIs, servlets, PHP pages, and others that use the GET method. (Server-side programs that use the POST method require the URLConnection class and are discussed in Chapter 15.) All you need to know is what combination of names and values the program expects to receive, and cook up a URL with a query string that provides the requisite names and values. All names and values must be x-www-form-url-encoded—as by the URLEncoder.encode( ) method, discussed earlier in this chapter.

There are a number of ways to determine the exact syntax for a query string that talks to a particular program. If you've written the server-side program yourself, you already know the name-value pairs it expects. If you've installed a third-party program on your own server, the documentation for that program should tell you what it expects.

On the other hand, if you're talking to a program on a third-party server, matters are a little trickier. You can always ask people at the remote server to provide you with the specifications for talking to their site. However, even if they don't mind doing this, there's probably no single person whose job description includes "telling third-party hackers with whom we have no business relationship exactly how to access our servers." Thus, unless you happen upon a particularly friendly or bored individual who has nothing better to do with their time except write long emails detailing exactly how to access their server, you're going to have to do a little reverse engineering.

 This is beginning to change. A number of web sites have realized the value of opening up their systems to third party developers and have begin publishing developers' kits that provide detailed information on how to construct URLs to access their services. Sites like Safari and Amazon that offer RESTful, URL-based interfaces are easily accessed through the URL class. SOAP-based services like eBay's and Google's are much more difficult to work with.

Many programs are designed to process form input. If this is the case, it's straightforward to figure out what input the program expects. The method the form uses should be the value of the METHOD attribute of the FORM element. This value should be either GET, in which case you use the process described here, or POST, in which case you use the process described in Chapter 15. The part of the URL that precedes the query string is given by the value of the ACTION attribute of the FORM element. Note that this may be a relative URL, in which case you'll need to determine the corresponding absolute URL. Finally, the name-value pairs are simply the NAME attributes of the INPUT elements, except for any INPUT elements whose TYPE attribute has the value submit.

For example, consider this HTML form for the local search engine on my Cafe con Leche site. You can see that it uses the GET method. The program that processes the form is accessed via the URL *http://www.google.com/search*. It has four separate name-value pairs, three of which have default values:

```
<form name="search" action="http://www.google.com/search" method="get">
  <input name="q" />
  <input type="hidden" value="cafeconleche.org" name="domains" />
  <input type="hidden" name="sitesearch" value="cafeconleche.org" />
  <input type="hidden" name="sitesearch2" value="cafeconleche.org" />
   <br />
   <input type="image" height="22" width="55"
      src="images/search_blue.gif" alt="search" border="0"
      name="search-image" />
</form>
```

The type of the INPUT field doesn't matter—for instance, it doesn't matter if it's a set of checkboxes, a pop-up list, or a text field—only the name of each INPUT field and the value you give it is significant. The single exception is a submit input that tells the web browser when to send the data but does not give the server any extra information. In some cases, you may find hidden INPUT fields that must have particular required default values. This form has three hidden INPUT fields.

In some cases, the program you're talking to may not be able to handle arbitrary text strings for values of particular inputs. However, since the form is meant to be read and filled in by human beings, it should provide sufficient clues to figure out what input is expected; for instance, that a particular field is supposed to be a two-letter state abbreviation or a phone number.

A program that doesn't respond to a form is much harder to reverse engineer. For example, at *http://www.ibiblio.org/nywc/bios.phtml*, you'll find a lot of links to PHP pages that talk to a database to retrieve a list of musical works by a particular composer. However, there's no form anywhere that corresponds to this program. It's all done by hardcoded URLs. In this case, the best you can do is look at as many of those URLs as possible and see whether you can guess what the server expects. If the designer hasn't tried to be too devious, this information isn't hard to figure out. For example, these URLs are all found on that page:

```
http://www.ibiblio.org/nywc/compositionsbycomposer.phtml?last=Anderson
    &first=Beth&middle=
http://www.ibiblio.org/nywc/compositionsbycomposer.phtml?last=Austin
    &first=Dorothea&middle=
http://www.ibiblio.org/nywc/compositionsbycomposer.phtml?last=Bliss
    &first=Marilyn&middle=
http://www.ibiblio.org/nywc/compositionsbycomposer.phtml?last=Hart
    &first=Jane&middle=Smith
```

Looking at these, you can guess that this particular program expects three inputs named first, middle, and last, with values that consist of the first, middle, and last names of a composer, respectively. Sometimes the inputs may not have such obvious names. In this case, you have to do some experimenting, first copying some existing values and then tweaking them to see what values are and aren't accepted. You don't need to do this in a Java program. You can simply edit the URL in the Address or Location bar of your web browser window.

 The likelihood that other hackers may experiment with your own server-side programs in such a fashion is a good reason to make them extremely robust against unexpected input.

Regardless of how you determine the set of name-value pairs the server expects, communicating with it once you know them is simple. All you have to do is create a query string that includes the necessary name-value pairs, then form a URL that includes that query string. Send the query string to the server and read its response using the same methods you use to connect to a server and retrieve a static HTML page. There's no special protocol to follow once the URL is constructed. (There is a special protocol to follow for the POST method, however, which is why discussion of that method will have to wait until Chapter 15.)

To demonstrate this procedure, let's write a very simple command-line program to look up topics in the Netscape Open Directory (*http://dmoz.org/*). This site is shown in Figure 7-3 and it has the advantage of being really simple.

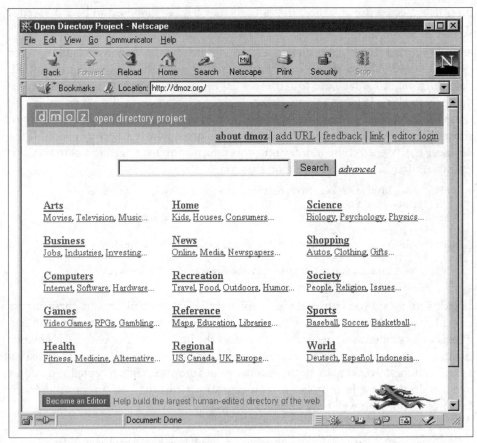

Figure 7-3. The basic user interface for the Open Directory

The basic Open Directory interface is a simple form with one input field named search; input typed in this field is sent to a CGI program at *http://search.dmoz.org/cgi-bin/search*, which does the actual search. The HTML for the form looks like this:

```
<form accept-charset="UTF-8"
      action="http://search.dmoz.org/cgi-bin/search" method="GET">
          <input size=30 name=search>

<input type=submit value="Search">
<a href="http://search.dmoz.org/cgi-bin/search?a.x=0">
<small><i>advanced</i></small></a>
</form>
```

There are only two input fields in this form: the Submit button and a text field named Search. Thus, to submit a search request to the Open Directory, you just need to collect the search string, encode it in a query string, and send it to *http://search.dmoz.org/cgi-bin/search*. For example, to search for "java", you would open a connection to the URL *http://search.dmoz.org/cgi-bin/search?search=java* and read the resulting input stream. Example 7-12 does exactly this.

Example 7-12. Do an Open Directory search

```java
import com.macfaq.net.*;

import java.net.*;
import java.io.*;

public class DMoz {

  public static void main(String[] args) {

    String target = "";

    for (int i = 0; i < args.length; i++) {
      target += args[i] + " ";
    }
    target = target.trim();
    QueryString query = new QueryString("search", target);
    try {
      URL u = new URL("http://search.dmoz.org/cgi-bin/search?" + query);
      InputStream in = new BufferedInputStream(u.openStream());
      InputStreamReader theHTML = new InputStreamReader(in);
      int c;
      while ((c = theHTML.read()) != -1) {
        System.out.print((char) c);
      }
    }
    catch (MalformedURLException ex) {
      System.err.println(ex);
    }
    catch (IOException ex) {
      System.err.println(ex);
    }

  }

}
```

Of course, a lot more effort could be expended on parsing and displaying the results. But notice how simple the code was to talk to this server. Aside from the funky-looking URL and the slightly greater likelihood that some pieces of it need to be x-www-form-url-encoded, talking to a server-side program that uses GET is no harder than retrieving any other HTML page.

Accessing Password-Protected Sites

Many popular sites, such as *The Wall Street Journal*, require a username and password for access. Some sites, such as the W3C member pages, implement this correctly through HTTP authentication. Others, such as the Java Developer Connection, implement it incorrectly through cookies and HTML forms. Java's URL class can access sites that use HTTP authentication, although you'll of course need to tell it what username and password to use. Java does not provide support for sites that use nonstandard, cookie-based authentication, in part because Java doesn't really support cookies in Java 1.4 and earlier, in part because this requires parsing and submitting HTML forms, and, lastly, because cookies are completely contrary to the architecture of the Web. (Java 1.5 does add some cookie support, which we'll discuss in the next chapter. However, it does not treat authentication cookies differently than any other cookies.) You can provide this support yourself using the URLConnection class to read and write the HTTP headers where cookies are set and returned. However, doing so is decidedly nontrivial and often requires custom code for each site you want to connect to. It's really hard to do short of implementing a complete web browser with full HTML forms and cookie support. Accessing sites protected by standard, HTTP authentication is much easier.

The Authenticator Class

The java.net package includes an Authenticator class you can use to provide a username and password for sites that protect themselves using HTTP authentication:

```
public abstract class Authenticator extends Object // Java 1.2
```

Since Authenticator is an abstract class, you must subclass it. Different subclasses may retrieve the information in different ways. For example, a character mode program might just ask the user to type the username and password on System.in. A GUI program would likely put up a dialog box like the one shown in Figure 7-4. An automated robot might read the username out of an encrypted file.

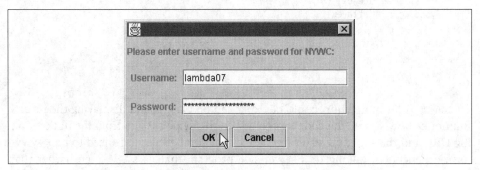

Figure 7-4. An authentication dialog

To make the URL class use the subclass, install it as the default authenticator by passing it to the static Authenticator.setDefault( ) method:

```
public static void setDefault(Authenticator a)
```

For example, if you've written an Authenticator subclass named DialogAuthenticator, you'd install it like this:

```
Authenticator.setDefault(new DialogAuthenticator());
```

You only need to do this once. From this point forward, when the URL class needs a username and password, it will ask the DialogAuthenticator using the static Authenticator.requestPasswordAuthentication() method:

```
public static PasswordAuthentication requestPasswordAuthentication(
    InetAddress address, int port, String protocol, String prompt, String scheme)
    throws SecurityException
```

The address argument is the host for which authentication is required. The port argument is the port on that host, and the protocol argument is the application layer protocol by which the site is being accessed. The HTTP server provides the prompt. It's typically the name of the realm for which authentication is required. (Some large web servers such as *www.ibiblio.org* have multiple realms, each of which requires different usernames and passwords.) The scheme is the authentication scheme being used. (Here the word *scheme* is not being used as a synonym for *protocol*. Rather it is an HTTP authentication scheme, typically basic.)

Untrusted applets are not allowed to ask the user for a name and password. Trusted applets can do so, but only if they possess the requestPasswordAuthentication NetPermission. Otherwise, Authenticator.requestPasswordAuthentication() throws a SecurityException.

The Authenticator subclass must override the getPasswordAuthentication() method. Inside this method, you collect the username and password from the user or some other source and return it as an instance of the java.net.PasswordAuthentication class:

```
protected PasswordAuthentication getPasswordAuthentication()
```

If you don't want to authenticate this request, return null, and Java will tell the server it doesn't know how to authenticate the connection. If you submit an incorrect username or password, Java will call getPasswordAuthentication() again to give you another chance to provide the right data. You normally have five tries to get the username and password correct; after that, openStream() throws a ProtocolException.

Usernames and passwords are cached within the same virtual machine session. Once you set the correct password for a realm, you shouldn't be asked for it again unless you've explicitly deleted the password by zeroing out the char array that contains it.

You can get more details about the request by invoking any of these methods inherited from the Authenticator superclass:

```
protected final InetAddress getRequestingSite()
protected final int        getRequestingPort()
protected final String     getRequestingProtocol()
```

```
protected final String    getRequestingPrompt()
protected final String    getRequestingScheme()
protected final String    getRequestingHost()  // Java 1.4
```

These methods either return the information as given in the last call to
requestPasswordAuthentication() or return null if that information is not available.
(getRequestingPort() returns –1 if the port isn't available.) The last method,
getRequestingHost(), is only available in Java 1.4 and later; in earlier releases you
can call getRequestingSite().getHostName() instead.

Java 1.5 adds two more methods to this class:

```
protected final String getRequestingURL()  // Java 1.5
protected Authenticator.RequestorType getRequestorType()
```

The getRequestingURL() method returns the complete URL for which authentication has been requested—an important detail if a site uses different names and passwords for different files. The getRequestorType() method returns one of the two
named   constants   Authenticator.RequestorType.PROXY   or   Authenticator.
RequestorType.SERVER to indicate whether the server or the proxy server is requesting
the authentication.

The PasswordAuthentication Class

PasswordAuthentication is a very simple final class that supports two read-only properties: username and password. The username is a String. The password is a char
array so that the password can be erased when it's no longer needed. A String would
have to wait to be garbage collected before it could be erased, and even then it might
still exist somewhere in memory on the local system, possibly even on disk if the
block of memory that contained it had been swapped out to virtual memory at one
point. Both username and password are set in the constructor:

```
public PasswordAuthentication(String userName, char[] password)
```

Each is accessed via a getter method:

```
public String getUserName()
public char[] getPassword()
```

The JPasswordField Class

One useful tool for asking users for their passwords in a more or less secure fashion
is the JPasswordField component from Swing:

```
public class JPasswordField extends JTextField
```

This lightweight component behaves almost exactly like a text field. However, anything the user types into it is echoed as an asterisk. This way, the password is safe
from anyone looking over the user's shoulder at what's being typed on the screen.

`JPasswordField` also stores the passwords as a `char` array so that when you're done with the password you can overwrite it with zeros. It provides the `getPassword()` method to return this:

```
public char[] getPassword()
```

Otherwise, you mostly use the methods it inherits from the `JTextField` superclass. Example 7-13 demonstrates a Swing-based `Authenticator` subclass that brings up a dialog to ask the user for his username and password. Most of this code handles the GUI. A `JPasswordField` collects the password and a simple `JTextField` retrieves the username. Figure 7-4 showed the rather simple dialog box this produces.

Example 7-13. A GUI authenticator

```java
package com.macfaq.net;

import java.net.*;
import javax.swing.*;
import java.awt.*;
import java.awt.event.*;

public class DialogAuthenticator extends Authenticator {

  private JDialog passwordDialog;
  private JLabel mainLabel
   = new JLabel("Please enter username and password: ");
  private JLabel userLabel = new JLabel("Username: ");
  private JLabel passwordLabel = new JLabel("Password: ");
  private JTextField usernameField = new JTextField(20);
  private JPasswordField passwordField = new JPasswordField(20);
  private JButton okButton = new JButton("OK");
  private JButton cancelButton = new JButton("Cancel");

  public DialogAuthenticator() {
    this("", new JFrame());
  }

  public DialogAuthenticator(String username) {
    this(username, new JFrame());
  }

  public DialogAuthenticator(JFrame parent) {
    this("", parent);
  }

  public DialogAuthenticator(String username, JFrame parent) {

    this.passwordDialog = new JDialog(parent, true);
    Container pane = passwordDialog.getContentPane();
    pane.setLayout(new GridLayout(4, 1));
    pane.add(mainLabel);
    JPanel p2 = new JPanel();
    p2.add(userLabel);
```

Example 7-13. A GUI authenticator (continued)

```
    p2.add(usernameField);
    usernameField.setText(username);
    pane.add(p2);
    JPanel p3 = new JPanel( );
    p3.add(passwordLabel);
    p3.add(passwordField);
    pane.add(p3);
    JPanel p4 = new JPanel( );
    p4.add(okButton);
    p4.add(cancelButton);
    pane.add(p4);
    passwordDialog.pack( );

    ActionListener al = new OKResponse( );
    okButton.addActionListener(al);
    usernameField.addActionListener(al);
    passwordField.addActionListener(al);
    cancelButton.addActionListener(new CancelResponse( ));

  }

  private void show( ) {

    String prompt = this.getRequestingPrompt( );
    if (prompt == null) {
      String site     = this.getRequestingSite().getHostName( );
      String protocol = this.getRequestingProtocol( );
      int    port     = this.getRequestingPort( );
      if (site != null & protocol != null) {
        prompt = protocol + "://" + site;
        if (port > 0) prompt += ":" + port;
      }
      else {
        prompt = "";
      }

    }

    mainLabel.setText("Please enter username and password for "
      + prompt + ": ");
    passwordDialog.pack( );
    passwordDialog.show( );

  }

  PasswordAuthentication response = null;

  class OKResponse implements ActionListener {

    public void actionPerformed(ActionEvent e) {
```

Example 7-13. A GUI authenticator (continued)

```
      passwordDialog.hide( );
      // The password is returned as an array of
      // chars for security reasons.
      char[] password = passwordField.getPassword( );
      String username = usernameField.getText( );
      // Erase the password in case this is used again.
      passwordField.setText("");
      response = new PasswordAuthentication(username, password);

    }

  }

  class CancelResponse implements ActionListener {

    public void actionPerformed(ActionEvent e) {

      passwordDialog.hide( );
      // Erase the password in case this is used again.
      passwordField.setText("");
      response = null;

    }

  }

  public PasswordAuthentication getPasswordAuthentication( ) {

    this.show( );
    return this.response;

  }

}
```

Example 7-14 is a revised SourceViewer program that asks the user for a name and password using the DialogAuthenticator class.

Example 7-14. A program to download password-protected web pages

```
import java.net.*;
import java.io.*;
import com.macfaq.net.DialogAuthenticator;

public class SecureSourceViewer {

  public static void main (String args[]) {

    Authenticator.setDefault(new DialogAuthenticator( ));

    for (int i = 0; i < args.length; i++) {
```

Example 7-14. A program to download password-protected web pages (continued)

```java
      try {
        //Open the URL for reading
        URL u = new URL(args[i]);
        InputStream in = u.openStream( );
        // buffer the input to increase performance
        in = new BufferedInputStream(in);
        // chain the InputStream to a Reader
        Reader r = new InputStreamReader(in);
        int c;
        while ((c = r.read( )) != -1) {
          System.out.print((char) c);
        }
      }
      catch (MalformedURLException ex) {
        System.err.println(args[0] + " is not a parseable URL");
      }
      catch (IOException ex) {
        System.err.println(ex);
      }

      // print a blank line to separate pages
      System.out.println( );

    } //  end for

    // Since we used the AWT, we have to explicitly exit.
    System.exit(0);

  } // end main

} // end SecureSourceViewer
```

CHAPTER 8

HTML in Swing

As anyone who has ever tried to write code to read HTML can tell you, it's a painful experience. The problem is that although there is an HTML specification, no web designer or browser vendor actually follows it. And the specification itself is extremely loose. Element names may be uppercase, lowercase, or mixed case. Attribute values may or may not be quoted. If they are quoted, either single or double quotes may be used. The < sign may be escaped as < or it may just be left raw in the file. The <P> tag may be used to begin or end a paragraph. Closing </P>, </LI>, and </TD> tags may or may not be used. Tags may or may not overlap. There are just too many different ways of doing the same thing to make parsing HTML an easy task. In fact, the difficulties encountered in parsing real-world HTML were one of the prime motivators for the invention of the much stricter XML, in which what is and is not allowed is precisely specified and all browsers are strictly prohibited from accepting documents that don't measure up to the standard (as opposed to HTML, where most browsers try to fix up bad HTML, thereby leading to the proliferation of nonconformant HTML on the Web, which all browsers must then try to parse).

Fortunately, as of JFC 1.1.1 (included in Java 1.2.2 and later), Sun provides classes for basic HTML parsing and display that shield Java programmers from most of the tribulations of working with raw HTML. The javax.swing.text.html.parser package can read HTML documents in more or less their full, nonstandard atrocity, while the javax.swing.text.html package can render basic HTML in JFC-based applications.

HTML on Components

Most text-based Swing components, such as labels, buttons, menu items, tabbed panes, and tool tips, can have their text specified as HTML. The component will display it appropriately. If you want the label on a JButton to include bold, italic, and plain text, the simplest way is to write the label in HTML directly in the source code like this:

```
JButton jb = new JButton("<html><b><i>Hello World!</i></b></html>");
```

The same technique works for JFC-based labels, menu items, tabbed panes, and tool tips. Example 8-1 and Figure 8-1 show an applet with a multiline JLabel that uses HTML.

Example 8-1. Including HTML in a JLabel

```java
import javax.swing.*;

public class HTMLLabelApplet extends JApplet {

  public void init( ) {

    JLabel theText = new JLabel(
    "<html>Hello! This is a multiline label with <b>bold</b> "
    + "and <i>italic</i> text. <P> "
    + "It can use paragraphs, horizontal lines, <hr> "
    + "<font color=red>colors</font> "
    + "and most of the other basic features of HTML 3.2</html>");

    this.getContentPane( ).add(theText);

  }

}
```

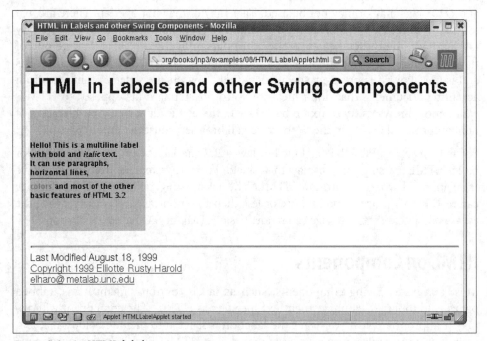

Figure 8-1. An HTML label

You can actually go pretty far with this. Almost all HTML tags are supported, at least partially, including IMG and the various table tags. The only completely unsupported HTML 3.2 tags are <APPLET>, <PARAM>, <MAP>, <AREA>, <LINK>, <SCRIPT>, and <STYLE>. The various frame tags (technically not part of HTML 3.2, though widely used and implemented) are also unsupported. In addition, the various new tags introduced in HTML 4.0 such as BDO, BUTTON, LEGEND, and TFOOT, are unsupported.

Furthermore, there are some limitations on other common tags. First of all, relative URLs in attribute values are not resolved because there's no page for them to be relative to. This most commonly affects the SRC attribute of the IMG element. The simplest way around this is to store the images in the same JAR archive as the applet or application and load them from an absolute *jar* URL. Links will appear as blue underlined text as most users are accustomed to, but nothing happens when you click on one. Forms are rendered, but users can't type input or submit them. Some CSS Level 1 properties such as font-size are supported through the style attribute, but STYLE tags and external stylesheets are not. In brief, the HTML support is limited to static text and images. After all, we're only talking about labels, menu items, and other simple components.

JEditorPane

If you need a more interactive, complete implementation of HTML 3.2, you can use a javax.swing.JEditorPane. This class provides an even more complete HTML 3.2 renderer that can handle frames, forms, hyperlinks, and parts of CSS Level 1. The JEditorPane class also supports plain text and basic RTF, though the emphasis in this book will be on using it to display HTML.

JEditorPane supports HTML in a fairly intuitive way. You simply feed its constructor a URL or a large string containing HTML, then display it like any other component. There are four constructors in this class:

```
public JEditorPane( )
public JEditorPane(URL initialPage) throws IOException
public JEditorPane(String url)  throws IOException
public JEditorPane(String mimeType, String text)
```

The noargs constructor simply creates a JEditorPane with no initial data. You can change this later with the setPage() or setText( ) methods:

```
public void setPage(URL page) throws IOException
public void setPage(String url) throws IOException
public void setText(String html)
```

Example 8-2 shows how to use this constructor to display a web page. JEditorPane is placed inside a JScrollPane to add scrollbars; JFrame provides a home for the JScrollPane. Figure 8-2 shows this program displaying the O'Reilly home page.

Example 8-2. Using a JEditorPane to display a web page

```java
import javax.swing.text.*;
import javax.swing.*;
import java.io.*;
import java.awt.*;

public class OReillyHomePage {

  public static void main(String[] args) {

      JEditorPane jep = new JEditorPane( );
      jep.setEditable(false);

      try {
        jep.setPage("http://www.oreilly.com");
      }
      catch (IOException ex) {
        jep.setContentType("text/html");
        jep.setText("<html>Could not load http://www.oreilly.com </html>");
      }

      JScrollPane scrollPane = new JScrollPane(jep);
      JFrame f = new JFrame("O'Reilly & Associates");
      f.setDefaultCloseOperation(WindowConstants.DISPOSE_ON_CLOSE);
      f.setContentPane(scrollPane);
      f.setSize(512, 342);
      f.show( );

  }

}
```

Figure 8-2 shows how good (or bad) Swing really is at displaying HTML. On the whole, it correctly renders this page containing tables, images, links, colors, fonts, and more with almost no effort from the programmer. However, it has some trouble with table widths, and there are a number of artifacts I can't explain. Generally, the simpler and more basic the page, the better Swing renders it.

What is missing, though, is precisely what's not obvious from this static image: the activity. The links are blue and underlined, but clicking on one won't change the page that's displayed. JavaScript and applets will not run. Shockwave animations and QuickTime movies won't play. Password-protected web pages will be off-limits because there's no way to provide a username and password. You can add all this yourself, but it will require extra code to recognize the relevant parts of the HTML and behave accordingly. Different active content requires different levels of support. Supporting hypertext linking, for example, is fairly straightforward, as we'll explore later. Applets aren't that hard to add either, mostly requiring you to simply parse the HTML to find the tags and parameters and provide an instance of the AppletContext interface. Adding JavaScript is only a little harder, provided that someone has already written a JavaScript interpreter you can use. Fortunately, the Mozilla Project has

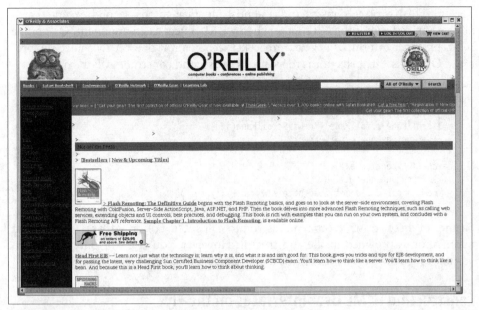

Figure 8-2. The O'Reilly home page shown in a JEditorPane

written the Open Source Rhino (*http://www.mozilla.org/rhino/*) JavaScript interpreter, which you can use in your own work. Apple's QuickTime for Java (*http://www.apple.com/quicktime/qtjava/*) makes QuickTime support almost a no-brainer on Mac and Windows. (A Unix version is sorely lacking, though.) I'm not going to discuss all (or even most) of these in this chapter or this book. Nonetheless, they're available if you need them.

The second JEditorPane constructor accepts a URL object as an argument. It connects to the specified URL, downloads the page it finds, and attempts to display it. If this attempt fails, an IOException is thrown. For example:

```
JFrame f = new JFrame("O'Reilly & Associates");

try {
  URL u = new URL("http://www.oreilly.com");
  JEditorPane jep = new JEditorPane(u);
  jep.setEditable(false);
  JScrollPane scrollPane = new JScrollPane(jep);
  f.setContentPane(scrollPane);
}
catch (IOException ex) {
  f.getContentPane( ).add(
    new Label("Could not load http://www.oreilly.com"));
}

f.setSize(512, 342);
f.show();
```

The third `JEditorPane` constructor is almost identical to the second except that it takes a `String` form of the URL rather than a URL object as an argument. One of the `IOExceptions` it can throw is a `MalformedURLException` if it doesn't recognize the protocol. Otherwise, its behavior is the same as the second constructor. For example:

```
try {
  JEditorPane jep = new JEditorPane("http://www.oreilly.com");
  jep.setEditable(false);
  JScrollPane scrollPane = new JScrollPane(jep);
  f.setContentPane(scrollPane);
}
catch (IOException ex) {
  f.getContentPane( ).add(
   new Label("Could not load http://www.oreilly.com"));
}
```

Neither of these constructors requires you to call setText() or setPage(), since that information is provided in the constructor. However, you can still call these methods to change the page or text that's displayed.

Constructing HTML User Interfaces on the Fly

The fourth `JEditorPane` constructor does not connect to a URL. Rather, it gets its data directly from the second argument. The MIME type of the data is determined by the first argument. For example:

```
JEditorPane jep = new JEditorPane("text/html",
 "<html><h1>Hello World!</h1> <h2>Goodbye World!</h2></html>");
```

This may be useful when you want to display HTML created programmatically or read from somewhere other than a URL. Example 8-3 shows a program that calculates the first 50 Fibonacci numbers and then displays them in an HTML ordered list. Figure 8-3 shows the output.

Example 8-3. Fibonacci sequence displayed in HTML

```
import javax.swing.text.*;
import javax.swing.*;
import java.net.*;
import java.io.*;
import java.awt.*;

public class Fibonacci {

 public static void main(String[] args) {

     StringBuffer result =
      new StringBuffer("<html><body><h1>Fibonacci Sequence</h1><ol>");

     long f1 = 0;
     long f2 = 1;
```

Example 8-3. Fibonacci sequence displayed in HTML (continued)

```java
    for (int i = 0; i < 50; i++) {
      result.append("<li>");
      result.append(f1);
      long temp = f2;
      f2 = f1 + f2;
      f1 = temp;
    }

    result.append("</ol></body></html>");

    JEditorPane jep = new JEditorPane("text/html", result.toString());
    jep.setEditable(false);

    JScrollPane scrollPane = new JScrollPane(jep);
    JFrame f = new JFrame("Fibonacci Sequence");
    f.setDefaultCloseOperation(WindowConstants.DISPOSE_ON_CLOSE);
    f.setContentPane(scrollPane);
    f.setSize(512, 342);
    EventQueue.invokeLater(new FrameShower(f));

  }

  // This inner class avoids a really obscure race condition.
  // See http://java.sun.com/developer/JDCTechTips/2003/tt1208.html#1
  private static class FrameShower implements Runnable {

    private final Frame frame;

    FrameShower(Frame frame) {
      this.frame = frame;
    }

    public void run() {
      frame.setVisible(true);
    }

  }

}
```

The significance of this should be apparent. Your programs now have access to a very powerful styled text engine. That the format used on the backend is HTML is a nice fringe benefit. It means you can use a familiar, easy-to-write format to create a user interface that uses styled text. You don't have quite all the power of QuarkXPress here (nor should you, since HTML doesn't have it), but this is more than adequate for 99% of text display needs, whether those needs are simple program output, help files, database reports, or something more complex.

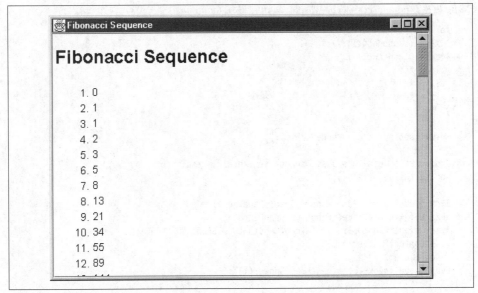

Figure 8-3. The Fibonacci sequence displayed as HTML using a JEditorPane

Handling Hyperlinks

When the user clicks on a link in a noneditable JEditorPane, the pane fires a HyperlinkEvent. As you might guess, this is responded to by any registered HyperlinkListener objects. This follows the same variation of the Observer design pattern used for AWT events and JavaBeans. The javax.swing.event. HyperlinkListener interface defines a single method, hyperlinkUpdate( ):

```
public void hyperlinkUpdate(HyperlinkEvent evt)
```

Inside this method, you'll place the code that responds to the HyperlinkEvent. The HyperlinkEvent object passed to this method contains the URL of the event, which is returned by its getURL( ) method:

```
public URL getURL( )
```

HyperlinkEvents are fired not just when the user clicks the link, but also when the mouse enters or exits the link area. Thus, you'll want to check the type of the event before changing the page with the getEventType( ) method:

```
public HyperlinkEvent.EventType getEventType( )
```

This will return one of the three mnemonic constants HyperlinkEvent.EventType. EXITED, HyperlinkEvent.EventTypeENTERED, or HyperlinkEvent.EventType.ACTIVATED. These are not numbers but static instances of the EventType inner class in the HyperlinkEvent class. Using these instead of integer constants allows for more careful compile-time type checking.

Example 8-4 is an implementation of the HyperLinkListener interface that checks the event fired and, if it's an activated event, switches to the page in the link. A reference to the JEditorPane is stored in a private field in the class so that a callback to make the switch can be made.

Example 8-4. A basic HyperlinkListener class

```java
import javax.swing.*;
import javax.swing.event.*;

public class LinkFollower implements HyperlinkListener {

  private JEditorPane pane;

  public LinkFollower(JEditorPane pane) {
    this.pane = pane;
  }

  public void hyperlinkUpdate(HyperlinkEvent evt) {

    if (evt.getEventType() == HyperlinkEvent.EventType.ACTIVATED) {
      try {
        pane.setPage(evt.getURL());
      }
      catch (Exception ex) {
        pane.setText("<html>Could not load " + evt.getURL() + "</html>");
      }
    }

  }

}
```

Example 8-5 is a very simple web browser. It registers an instance of the Link-Follower class of Example 8-4 to handle any HyperlinkEvents. It doesn't have a Back button, a Location bar, bookmarks, or any frills at all. But it does let you surf the Web by following links. The remaining aspects of the user interface you'd want in a real browser are mostly just exercises in GUI programming, so I'll omit them. But it really is amazing just how easy Swing makes it to write a web browser.

Example 8-5. SimpleWebBrowser

```java
import javax.swing.text.*;
import javax.swing.*;
import java.net.*;
import java.io.*;
import java.awt.*;

public class SimpleWebBrowser {

  public static void main(String[] args) {
```

Example 8-5. SimpleWebBrowser (continued)

```java
    // get the first URL
    String initialPage = "http://www.cafeaulait.org/";
    if (args.length > 0) initialPage = args[0];

    // set up the editor pane
    JEditorPane jep = new JEditorPane();
    jep.setEditable(false);
    jep.addHyperlinkListener(new LinkFollower(jep));

    try {
      jep.setPage(initialPage);
    }
    catch (IOException ex) {
      System.err.println("Usage: java SimpleWebBrowser url");
      System.err.println(ex);
      System.exit(-1);
    }

    // set up the window
    JScrollPane scrollPane = new JScrollPane(jep);
    JFrame f = new JFrame("Simple Web Browser");
    f.setDefaultCloseOperation(WindowConstants.DISPOSE_ON_CLOSE);
    f.setContentPane(scrollPane);
    f.setSize(512, 342);
    EventQueue.invokeLater(new FrameShower(f));

  }

  // Helps avoid a really obscure deadlock condition.
  // See http://java.sun.com/developer/JDCTechTips/2003/tt1208.html#1
  private static class FrameShower implements Runnable {

    private final Frame frame;

    FrameShower(Frame frame) {
      this.frame = frame;
    }

    public void run() {
      frame.setVisible(true);
    }

  }

}
```

The one thing this browser doesn't do is follow links to named anchors inside the body of a particular HTML page. There is a protected scrollToReference() method in JEditorPane that can find the specified named anchor in the currently displayed HTML document and reposition the pane at that point; you can use this method to add this functionality if you so desire:

```java
    protected void scrollToReference(String reference)
```

Reading HTML Directly

The JEditorPane class mostly assumes that you're going to provide either a URL or the string form of a URL and let it handle all the details of retrieving the data from the network. However, it contains one method that allows you to read HTML directly from an input stream. That method is read( ):

```
public void read(InputStream in, Object document) throws IOException
```

This method may be useful if you need to read HTML from a chain of filter streams; for instance, unzipping it before you read it. It could also be used when you need to perform some custom handshaking with the server, such as providing a username and password, rather than simply letting the default connection take place.

The first argument is the stream from which the HTML will be read. The second argument should be an instance of javax.swing.text.html.HTMLDocument. (You can use another type, but if you do, the JEditorPane will treat the stream as plain text rather than HTML.) Although you could use the HTMLDocument( ) noargs constructor to create the HTMLDocument object, the document it creates is missing a lot of style details. You're better off letting a javax.swing.text.html.HTMLEditorKit create the document for you. You get an HTMLEditorKit by passing the MIME type you want to edit (text/html in this case) to the JEditorPane getEditorKitForContentType( ) method like this:

```
EditorKit htmlKit = jep.getEditorKitForContentType("text/html");
```

Finally, before reading from the stream, you have to use the JEditorPane's setEditorKit( ) method to install a javax.swing.text.html.HTMLEditorKit. For example:

```
jep.setEditorKit(htmlKit);
```

This code fragment uses these techniques to load the web page at *http://www.elharo. com*. Here the stream comes from a URL anyway, so this is really more trouble than it's worth compared to the alternative. However, this approach would also allow you to read from a gzipped file, a file on the local drive, data written by another thread, a byte array, or anything else you can hook a stream to:

```
JEditorPane jep = new JEditorPane( );
jep.setEditable(false);
EditorKit htmlKit = jep.getEditorKitForContentType("text/html");
HTMLDocument doc = (HTMLDocument) htmlKit.createDefaultDocument( );
jep.setEditorKit(htmlKit);

try {
  URL u = new URL("http://www.elharo.com");
  InputStream in = u.openStream( );
  jep.read(in, doc);
}
catch (IOException ex) {
  System.err.println(ex);
}
```

```
JScrollPane scrollPane = new JScrollPane(jep);
JFrame f = new JFrame("Macfaq");
f.setContentPane(scrollPane);
f.setSize(512, 342);
EventQueue.invokeLater(new FrameShower(f));
```

This would also be useful if you need to interpose your program in the stream to perform some sort of filtering. For example, you might want to remove IMG tags from the file before displaying it. The methods of the next section can help you do this.

Parsing HTML

Sometimes you want to read HTML, looking for information without actually displaying it on the screen. For instance, more than one author I know has written a "book ticker" program to track the hour-by-hour progress of their books in the Amazon.com bestseller list. The hardest part of this program isn't retrieving the HTML. It's reading through the HTML to find the one line that contains the book's ranking. As another example, consider a Web Whacker–style program that downloads a web site or part thereof to a local PC with all links intact. Downloading the files once you have the URLs is easy. But reading through the document to find the URLs of the linked pages is considerably more complex.

Both of these examples are parsing problems. While parsing a clearly defined language that doesn't allow syntax errors, such as Java or XML, is relatively straightforward, parsing a flexible language that attempts to recover from errors, like HTML, is extremely difficult. It's easier to write in HTML than it is to write in a strict language like XML, but it's much harder to read such a language. Ease of use for the page author has been favored at the cost of ease of development for the programmer.

Fortunately, the javax.swing.text.html and javax.swing.text.html.parser packages include classes that do most of the hard work for you. They're primarily intended for the internal use of the JEditorPane class discussed in the last section. Consequently, they can be a little tricky to get at. The constructors are often not public or hidden inside inner classes, and the classes themselves aren't very well documented. But once you've seen a few examples, they aren't hard to use.

HTMLEditorKit.Parser

The main HTML parsing class is the inner class javax.swing.html.HTMLEditorKit. Parser:

```
public abstract static class HTMLEditorKit.Parser extends Object
```

Since this is an abstract class, the actual parsing work is performed by an instance of its concrete subclass javax.swing.text.html.parser.ParserDelegator:

```
public class ParserDelegator extends HTMLEditorKit.Parser
```

An instance of this class reads an HTML document from a Reader. It looks for five things in the document: start-tags, end-tags, empty-element tags, text, and comments. That covers all the important parts of a common HTML file. (Document type declarations and processing instructions are omitted, but they're rare and not very important in most HTML files, even when they are included.) Every time the parser sees one of these five items, it invokes the corresponding callback method in a particular instance of the javax.swing.text.html.HTMLEditorKit.ParserCallback class. To parse an HTML file, you write a subclass of HTMLEditorKit.ParserCallback that responds to text and tags as you desire. Then you pass an instance of your subclass to the HTMLEditorKit.Parser's parse( ) method, along with the Reader from which the HTML will be read:

```
public void parse(Reader in, HTMLEditorKit.ParserCallback callback,
  boolean ignoreCharacterSet) throws IOException
```

The third argument indicates whether you want to be notified of the character set of the document, assuming one is found in a META tag in the HTML header. This will normally be true. If it's false, then the parser will throw a javax.swing.text. ChangedCharSetException when a META tag in the HTML header is used to change the character set. This would give you an opportunity to switch to a different Reader that understands that character set and reparse the document (this time, setting ignoreCharSet to true since you already know the character set).

parse( ) is the only public method in the HTMLEditorKit.Parser class. All the work is handled inside the callback methods in the HTMLEditorKit.ParserCallback subclass. The parse( ) method simply reads from the Reader in until it's read the entire document. Every time it sees a tag, comment, or block of text, it invokes the corresponding callback method in the HTMLEditorKit.ParserCallback instance. If the Reader throws an IOException, that exception is passed along. Since neither the HTMLEditorKit.Parser nor the HTMLEditorKit.ParserCallback instance is specific to one reader, it can be used to parse multiple files simply by invoking parse( ) multiple times. If you do this, your HTMLEditorKit.ParserCallback class must be fully thread-safe, because parsing takes place in a separate thread and the parse( ) method normally returns before parsing is complete.

Before you can do any of this, however, you have to get your hands on an instance of the HTMLEditorKit.Parser class, and that's harder than it should be. HTMLEditorKit. Parser is an abstract class, so it can't be instantiated directly. Its subclass, javax. swing.text.html.parser.ParserDelegator, is concrete. However, before you can use it, you have to configure it with a DTD, using the protected static methods ParserDelegator.setDefaultDTD( ) and ParserDelegator.createDTD( ):

```
protected static void setDefaultDTD( )
protected static DTD createDTD(DTD dtd, String name)
```

So to create a ParserDelegator, you first need to have an instance of javax.swing. text.html.parser.DTD. This class represents a Standardized General Markup

Language (SGML) document type definition. The DTD class has a protected constructor and many protected methods that subclasses can use to build a DTD from scratch, but this is an API that only an SGML expert could be expected to use. The normal way DTDs are created is by reading the text form of a standard DTD published by someone like the W3C. You should be able to get a DTD for HTML by using the DTDParser class to parse the W3C's published HTML DTD. Unfortunately, the DTDParser class isn't included in the published Swing API, so you can't. Thus, you're going to need to go through the back door to create an HTMLEditorKit.Parser instance. What we'll do is use the HTMLEditorKit.Parser.getParser() method instead, which ultimately returns a ParserDelegator after properly initializing the DTD for HTML 3.2:

```
protected HTMLEditorKit.Parser getParser( )
```

Since this method is protected, we'll simply subclass HTMLEditorKit and override it with a public version, as Example 8-6 demonstrates.

Example 8-6. This subclass just makes the getParser() method public

```
import javax.swing.text.html.*;

public class ParserGetter extends HTMLEditorKit {

  // purely to make this method public
  public HTMLEditorKit.Parser getParser( ){
    return super.getParser( );
  }

}
```

Now that you've got a way to get a parser, you're ready to parse some documents. This is accomplished through the parse( ) method of HTMLEditorKit.Parser:

```
public abstract void parse(Reader input, HTMLEditorKit.ParserCallback
  callback, boolean ignoreCharSet) throws IOException
```

The Reader is straightforward. Simply chain an InputStreamReader to the stream reading the HTML document, probably one returned by the openStream( ) method of java.net.URL. For the third argument, you can pass true to ignore encoding issues (this generally works only if you're pretty sure you're dealing with ASCII text) or false if you want to receive a ChangedCharSetException when the document has a META tag indicating the character set. The second argument is where the action is. You're going to write a subclass of HTMLEditorKit.ParserCallback that is notified of every start-tag, end-tag, empty-element tag, text, comment, and error that the parser encounters.

HTMLEditorKit.ParserCallback

The ParserCallback class is a public inner class inside javax.swing.text.html. HTMLEditorKit:

```
public static class HTMLEditorKit.ParserCallback extends Object
```

It has a single, public noargs constructor:

```
public HTMLEditorKit.ParserCallback( )
```

However, you probably won't use this directly because the standard implementation of this class does nothing. It exists to be subclassed. It has six callback methods that do nothing. You will override these methods to respond to specific items seen in the input stream as the document is parsed:

```
public void handleText(char[] text, int position)
public void handleComment(char[] text, int position)
public void handleStartTag(HTML.Tag tag,
 MutableAttributeSet attributes, int position)
public void handleEndTag(HTML.Tag tag, int position)
public void handleSimpleTag(HTML.Tag tag,
 MutableAttributeSet attributes, int position)
public void handleError(String errorMessage, int position)
```

There's also a flush( ) method you use to perform any final cleanup. The parser invokes this method once after it's finished parsing the document:

```
public void flush( ) throws BadLocationException
```

Let's begin with a simple example. Suppose you want to write a program that strips out all the tags and comments from an HTML document and leaves only the text. You would write a subclass of HTMLEditorKit.ParserCallback that overrides the handleText( ) method to write the text on a Writer. You would leave the other methods alone. Example 8-7 demonstrates.

Example 8-7. TagStripper

```
import javax.swing.text.html.*;
import java.io.*;


public class TagStripper extends HTMLEditorKit.ParserCallback {

  private Writer out;

  public TagStripper(Writer out) {
    this.out = out;
  }

  public void handleText(char[] text, int position) {
    try {
      out.write(text);
      out.flush( );
```

Example 8-7. TagStripper (continued)

```
  }
  catch (IOException ex) {
    System.err.println(ex);
  }
 }

}
```

Now let's suppose you want to use this class to actually strip the tags from a URL. You begin by retrieving a parser using Example 8-5's ParserGetter class:

```
ParserGetter kit = new ParserGetter();
HTMLEditorKit.Parser parser = kit.getParser();
```

Next, construct an instance of your callback class like this:

```
HTMLEditorKit.ParserCallback callback
  = new TagStripper(new OutputStreamWriter(System.out));
```

Then you get a stream you can read the HTML document from. For example:

```
try {
  URL u = new URL("http://www.oreilly.com");
  InputStream in = new BufferedInputStream(u.openStream());
  InputStreamReader r = new InputStreamReader(in);
```

Finally, you pass the Reader and the HTMLEditorKit.ParserCallback to the HTMLEditorKit.Parser's parse() method, like this:

```
    parser.parse(r, callback, false);
  }
  catch (IOException ex) {
    System.err.println(ex);
  }
```

There are a couple of details about the parsing process that are not obvious. First, the parser parses in a separate thread. Therefore, you should not assume that the document has been parsed when the parse() method returns. If you're using the same HTMLEditorKit.ParserCallback object for two separate parses, you need to make all your callback methods thread-safe.

Second, the parser actually skips some of the data in the input. In particular, it normalizes and strips whitespace. If the input document contains seven spaces in a row, the parser will convert that to a single space. Carriage returns, linefeeds, and tabs are all converted to a single space, so you lose line breaks. Furthermore, most text elements are stripped of *all* leading and trailing whitespace. Elements that contain nothing but space are eliminated completely. Thus, suppose the input document contains this content:

```
<H1> Here's    the    Title </H1>

<P> Here's the text </P>
```

What actually comes out of the tag stripper is:

```
Here's the TitleHere's the text
```

The single exception is the PRE element, which maintains all whitespace in its contents unedited. Short of implementing your own parser, I don't know of any way to retain all the stripped space. But you can include the minimum necessary line breaks and whitespace by looking at the tags as well as the text. Generally, you expect a single break in HTML when you see one of these tags:

```
<BR>
<LI>
<TR>
```

You expect a double break (paragraph break) when you see one of these tags:

```
<P>
</H1> </H2> </H3> </H4> </H5> </H6>
<HR>
<DIV>
</UL> </OL> </DL>
```

To include line breaks in the output, you have to look at each tag as it's processed and determine whether it falls in one of these sets. This is straightforward because the first argument passed to each of the tag callback methods is an HTML.Tag object.

HTML.Tag

Tag is a public inner class in the javax.swing.text.html.HTML class.

```
public static class HTML.Tag extends Object
```

It has these four methods:

```
public boolean isBlock( )
public boolean breaksFlow( )
public boolean isPreformatted( )
public String  toString( )
```

The breaksFlow( ) method returns true if the tag should cause a single line break. The isBlock( ) method returns true if the tag should cause a double line break. The isPreformatted( ) method returns true if the tag indicates that whitespace should be preserved. This makes it easy to provide the necessary breaks in the output.

Chances are you'll see more tags than you'd expect when you parse a file. The parser inserts missing closing tags. In other words, if a document contains only a <P> tag, then the parser will report both the <P> start-tag and the implied </P> end-tag at the appropriate points in the document. Example 8-8 is a program that does the best job yet of converting HTML to pure text. It looks for the empty and end-tags, explicit or implied, and, if the tag indicates that line breaks are called for, inserts the necessary number of line breaks.

Example 8-8. LineBreakingTagStripper

```java
import javax.swing.text.*;
import javax.swing.text.html.*;
import javax.swing.text.html.parser.*;
import java.io.*;
import java.net.*;

public class LineBreakingTagStripper
 extends HTMLEditorKit.ParserCallback {

  private Writer out;
  private String lineSeparator;

  public LineBreakingTagStripper(Writer out) {
    this(out, System.getProperty("line.separator", "\r\n"));
  }

  public LineBreakingTagStripper(Writer out, String lineSeparator) {
    this.out = out;
    this.lineSeparator = lineSeparator;
  }

  public void handleText(char[] text, int position) {
    try {
      out.write(text);
      out.flush();
    }
    catch (IOException ex) {
      System.err.println(ex);
    }
  }

  public void handleEndTag(HTML.Tag tag, int position) {

    try {
      if (tag.isBlock()) {
        out.write(lineSeparator);
        out.write(lineSeparator);
      }
      else if (tag.breaksFlow()) {
        out.write(lineSeparator);
      }
    }
    catch (IOException ex) {
      System.err.println(ex);
    }

  }
  public void handleSimpleTag(HTML.Tag tag,
   MutableAttributeSet attributes, int position) {

    try {
      if (tag.isBlock()) {
```

Example 8-8. LineBreakingTagStripper (continued)

```
      out.write(lineSeparator);
      out.write(lineSeparator);
    }
    else if (tag.breaksFlow( )) {
      out.write(lineSeparator);
    }
    else {
      out.write(' ');
    }
  }
  catch (IOException ex) {
    System.err.println(ex);
  }


}

}
```

Most of the time, of course, you want to know considerably more than whether a tag breaks a line. You want to know what tag it is, and behave accordingly. For instance, if you were writing a full-blown HTML-to-TeX or HTML-to-RTF converter, you'd want to handle each tag differently. You test the type of tag by comparing it against these 73 mnemonic constants from the HTML.Tag class:

HTML.Tag.A	HTML.Tag.FRAMESET	HTML.Tag.PARAM
HTML.Tag.ADDRESS	HTML.Tag.H1	HTML.Tag.PRE
HTML.Tag.APPLET	HTML.Tag.H2	HTML.Tag.SAMP
HTML.Tag.AREA	HTML.Tag.H3	HTML.Tag.SCRIPT
HTML.Tag.B	HTML.Tag.H4	HTML.Tag.SELECT
HTML.Tag.BASE	HTML.Tag.H5	HTML.Tag.SMALL
HTML.Tag.BASEFONT	HTML.Tag.H6	HTML.Tag.STRIKE
HTML.Tag.BIG	HTML.Tag.HEAD	HTML.Tag.S
HTML.Tag.BLOCKQUOTE	HTML.Tag.HR	HTML.Tag.STRONG
HTML.Tag.BODY	HTML.Tag.HTML	HTML.Tag.STYLE
HTML.Tag.BR	HTML.Tag.I	HTML.Tag.SUB
HTML.Tag.CAPTION	HTML.Tag.IMG	HTML.Tag.SUP
HTML.Tag.CENTER	HTML.Tag.INPUT	HTML.Tag.TABLE
HTML.Tag.CITE	HTML.Tag.ISINDEX	HTML.Tag.TD
HTML.Tag.CODE	HTML.Tag.KBD	HTML.Tag.TEXTAREA
HTML.Tag.DD	HTML.Tag.LI	HTML.Tag.TH
HTML.Tag.DFN	HTML.Tag.LINK	HTML.Tag.TR
HTML.Tag.DIR	HTML.Tag.MAP	HTML.Tag.TT
HTML.Tag.DIV	HTML.Tag.MENU	HTML.Tag.U
HTML.Tag.DL	HTML.Tag.META	HTML.Tag.UL
HTML.Tag.DT	HTML.Tag.NOFRAMES	HTML.Tag.VAR
HTML.Tag.EM	HTML.Tag.OBJECT	HTML.Tag.IMPLIED

```
HTML.Tag.FONT              HTML.Tag.OL              HTML.Tag.COMMENT
HTML.Tag.FORM              HTML.Tag.OPTION
HTML.Tag.FRAME             HTML.Tag.P
```

These are not int constants. They are object constants to allow compile-time type checking. You saw this trick once before in the javax.swing.event.HyperlinkEvent class. All HTML.Tag elements passed to your callback methods by the HTMLEditorKit. Parser will be one of these 73 constants. They are not just the *same as* these 73 objects; they *are* these 73 objects. There are exactly 73 objects in this class; no more, no less. You can test against them with == rather than equals( ).

For example, let's suppose you need a program that outlines HTML pages by extracting their H1 through H6 headings while ignoring the rest of the document. It organizes the outline as nested lists in which each H1 heading is at the top level, each H2 heading is one level deep, and so on. You would write an HTMLEditorKit. ParserCallback subclass that extracted the contents of all H1, H2, H3, H4, H5, and H6 elements while ignoring all others, as Example 8-9 demonstrates.

Example 8-9. Outliner

```java
import javax.swing.text.*;
import javax.swing.text.html.*;
import javax.swing.text.html.parser.*;
import java.io.*;
import java.net.*;
import java.util.*;

public class Outliner extends HTMLEditorKit.ParserCallback {

  private Writer out;
  private int level = 0;
  private boolean inHeader=false;
  private static String lineSeparator
    = System.getProperty("line.separator", "\r\n");

  public Outliner(Writer out) {
    this.out = out;
  }

  public void handleStartTag(HTML.Tag tag,
    MutableAttributeSet attributes, int position) {

    int newLevel = 0;
    if (tag == HTML.Tag.H1) newLevel = 1;
    else if (tag == HTML.Tag.H2) newLevel = 2;
    else if (tag == HTML.Tag.H3) newLevel = 3;
    else if (tag == HTML.Tag.H4) newLevel = 4;
    else if (tag == HTML.Tag.H5) newLevel = 5;
    else if (tag == HTML.Tag.H6) newLevel = 6;
    else return;
```

Example 8-9. Outliner (continued)

```java
      this.inHeader = true;
      try {
        if (newLevel > this.level) {
          for (int i =0; i < newLevel-this.level; i++) {
            out.write("<ul>" + lineSeparator + "<li>");
          }
        }
        else if (newLevel < this.level) {
          for (int i =0; i < this.level-newLevel; i++) {
            out.write(lineSeparator + "</ul>" + lineSeparator);
          }
          out.write(lineSeparator + "<li>");
        }
        else {
          out.write(lineSeparator + "<li>");
        }
        this.level = newLevel;
        out.flush();
      }
      catch (IOException ex) {
        System.err.println(ex);
      }

    }

    public void handleEndTag(HTML.Tag tag, int position) {

      if (tag == HTML.Tag.H1 || tag == HTML.Tag.H2
       || tag == HTML.Tag.H3 || tag == HTML.Tag.H4
       || tag == HTML.Tag.H5 || tag == HTML.Tag.H6) {
        inHeader = false;
      }

      // work around bug in the parser that fails to call flush
      if (tag == HTML.Tag.HTML) this.flush();

    }


    public void handleText(char[] text, int position) {

      if (inHeader) {
        try {
          out.write(text);
          out.flush();
        }
        catch (IOException ex) {
          System.err.println(ex);
        }
      }
    }


    }
```

Example 8-9. Outliner (continued)

```java
public void flush( ) {
  try {
    while (this.level-- > 0) {
      out.write(lineSeparator + "</ul>");
    }
    out.flush( );
  }
  catch (IOException e) {
    System.err.println(e);
  }
}

private static void parse(URL url, String encoding) throws IOException {
    ParserGetter kit = new ParserGetter( );
    HTMLEditorKit.Parser parser = kit.getParser( );
    InputStream in = url.openStream( );
    InputStreamReader r = new InputStreamReader(in, encoding);
    HTMLEditorKit.ParserCallback callback = new Outliner
      (new OutputStreamWriter(System.out));
    parser.parse(r, callback, true);
}

public static void main(String[] args) {

  ParserGetter kit = new ParserGetter( );
  HTMLEditorKit.Parser parser = kit.getParser( );

  String encoding = "ISO-8859-1";
  URL url = null;
  try {
    url = new URL(args[0]);
    InputStream in = url.openStream( );
    InputStreamReader r = new InputStreamReader(in, encoding);
    // parse once just to detect the encoding
    HTMLEditorKit.ParserCallback doNothing
      = new HTMLEditorKit.ParserCallback( );
    parser.parse(r, doNothing, false);
  }
  catch (MalformedURLException ex) {
    System.out.println("Usage: java Outliner url");
    return;
  }
  catch (ChangedCharSetException ex) {
    String mimeType = ex.getCharSetSpec( );
    encoding = mimeType.substring(mimeType.indexOf("=") + 1).trim( );
  }
  catch (IOException ex) {
    System.err.println(ex);
  }
  catch (ArrayIndexOutOfBoundsException ex) {
    System.out.println("Usage: java Outliner url");
```

Example 8-9. Outliner (continued)

```
      return;
    }

    try {
      parse(url, encoding);
    }
    catch(IOException ex) {
      System.err.println(ex);
    }

  }

}
```

When a heading start-tag is encountered by the handleStartTag( ) method, the necessary number of <ul>, </ul>, and <li> tags are emitted. Furthermore, the inHeading flag is set to true so that the handleText( ) method will know to output the contents of the heading. All start-tags except the six levels of headers are simply ignored. The handleEndTag( ) method likewise considers heading tags only by comparing the tag it receives with the seven tags it's interested in. If it sees a heading tag, it sets the inHeading flag to false again so that body text won't be emitted by the handleText( ) method. If it sees the end of the document via an </html> tag, it flushes out the document. Otherwise, it does nothing. The end result is a nicely formatted group of nested, unordered lists that outlines the document. For example, here's the output of running it against *http://www.cafeconleche.org*:

```
% java Outliner http://www.cafeconleche.org/
<ul>
<li> Cafe con Leche XML News and Resources<ul>
<li>Quote of the Day
<li>Today's News
<li>Recommended Reading
<li>Recent News<ul>
<li>XML Overview
<li>Tutorials
<li>Projects
<li>Seminar Notes
<li>Random Notes
<li>Specifications
<li>Books
<li>XML Resources
<li>Development Tools<ul>
<li>Validating Parsers
<li>Non-validating Parsers
<li>Online Validators and Syntax Checkers
<li>Formatting Engines
<li>Browsers
<li>Class Libraries
<li>Editors
<li>XML Applications
```

```
    <li>External Sites
    </ul>
    </ul>
    </ul>
    </ul>
```

Attributes

When processing an HTML file, you often need to look at the attributes as well as
the tags. The second argument to the handleStartTag() and handleSimpleTag() callback methods is an instance of the javax.swing.text.MutableAttributeSet class. This
object allows you to see what attributes are attached to a particular tag.
MutableAttributeSet is a subinterface of the javax.swing.text.AttributeSet interface:

```
public abstract interface MutableAttributeSet extends AttributeSet
```

Both AttributeSet and MutableAttributeSet represent a collection of attributes on an
HTML tag. The difference is that the MutableAttributeSet interface declares methods to add attributes to, remove attributes from, and inspect the attributes in the set.
The attributes themselves are represented as pairs of java.lang.Object objects, one
for the name of the attribute and one for the value. The AttributeSet interface
declares these methods:

```
public int        getAttributeCount()
public boolean    isDefined(Object name)
public boolean    containsAttribute(Object name, Object value)
public boolean    containsAttributes(AttributeSet attributes)
public boolean    isEqual(AttributeSet attributes)
public AttributeSet copyAttributes()
public Enumeration getAttributeNames()
public Object     getAttribute(Object name)
public AttributeSet getResolveParent()
```

Most of these methods are self-explanatory. The getAttributeCount() method
returns the number of attributes in the set. The isDefined() method returns true if
an attribute with the specified name is in the set, false otherwise. The
containsAttribute(Object name, Object value) method returns true if an attribute
with the given name and value is in the set. The containsAttributes(AttributeSet
attributes) method returns true if all the attributes in the specified set are in this set
with the same values; in other words, if the argument is a subset of the set on which
this method is invoked. The isEqual() method returns true if the invoking
AttributeSet is the same as the argument. The copyAttributes() method returns a
clone of the current AttributeSet. The getAttributeNames() method returns a java.
util.Enumeration of all the names of the attributes in the set. Once you know the
name of one of the elements of the set, the getAttribute() method returns its value.
Finally, the getResolveParent() method returns the parent AttributeSet, which will
be searched for attributes that are not found in the current set. For example, given an
AttributeSet, this method prints the attributes in name=value format:

```
private void listAttributes(AttributeSet attributes) {
  Enumeration e = attributes.getAttributeNames();
  while (e.hasMoreElements()) {
    Object name = e.nextElement();
    Object value = attributes.getAttribute(name);
    System.out.println(name + "=" + value);
  }
}
```

Although the argument and return types of these methods are mostly declared in terms of java.lang.Object, in practice, all values are instances of java.lang.String, while all names are instances of the public inner class javax.swing.text.html.HTML.Attribute. Just as the HTML.Tag class predefines 73 HTML tags and uses a private constructor to prevent the creation of others, so too does the HTML.Attribute class predefine 80 standard HTML attributes (HTML.Attribute.ACTION, HTML.Attribute.ALIGN, HTML.Attribute.ALINK, HTML.Attribute.ALT, etc.) and prohibits the construction of others via a nonpublic constructor. Generally, this isn't an issue, since you mostly use getAttribute(), containsAttribute(), and so forth only with names returned by getAttributeNames(). The 80 predefined attributes are:

HTML.Attribute.ACTION	HTML.Attribute.DUMMY	HTML.Attribute.PROMPT
HTML.Attribute.ALIGN	HTML.Attribute.ENCTYPE	HTML.Attribute.REL
HTML.Attribute.ALINK	HTML.Attribute.ENDTAG	HTML.Attribute.REV
HTML.Attribute.ALT	HTML.Attribute.FACE	HTML.Attribute.ROWS
HTML.Attribute.ARCHIVE	HTML.Attribute.FRAMEBORDER	HTML.Attribute.ROWSPAN
HTML.Attribute.BACKGROUND	HTML.Attribute.HALIGN	HTML.Attribute. SCROLLING
HTML.Attribute.BGCOLOR	HTML.Attribute.HEIGHT	HTML.Attribute.SELECTED
HTML.Attribute.BORDER	HTML.Attribute.HREF	HTML.Attribute.SHAPE
HTML.Attribute. CELLPADDING	HTML.Attribute.HSPACE	HTML.Attribute.SHAPES
HTML.Attribute. CELLSPACING	HTML.Attribute.HTTPEQUIV	HTML.Attribute.SIZE
HTML.Attribute.CHECKED	HTML.Attribute.ID	HTML.Attribute.SRC
HTML.Attribute.CLASS	HTML.Attribute.ISMAP	HTML.Attribute.STANDBY
HTML.Attribute.CLASSID	HTML.Attribute.LANG	HTML.Attribute.START
HTML.Attribute.CLEAR	HTML.Attribute.LANGUAGE	HTML.Attribute.STYLE
HTML.Attribute.CODE	HTML.Attribute.LINK	HTML.Attribute.TARGET
HTML.Attribute.CODEBASE	HTML.Attribute.LOWSRC	HTML.Attribute.TEXT
HTML.Attribute.CODETYPE	HTML.Attribute. MARGINHEIGHT	HTML.Attribute.TITLE
HTML.Attribute.COLOR	HTML.Attribute.MARGINWIDTH	HTML.Attribute.TYPE
HTML.Attribute.COLS	HTML.Attribute.MAXLENGTH	HTML.Attribute.USEMAP
HTML.Attribute.COLSPAN	HTML.Attribute.METHOD	HTML.Attribute.VALIGN
HTML.Attribute.COMMENT	HTML.Attribute.MULTIPLE	HTML.Attribute.VALUE
HTML.Attribute.COMPACT	HTML.Attribute.N	HTML.Attribute. VALUETYPE
HTML.Attribute.CONTENT	HTML.Attribute.NAME	HTML.Attribute.VERSION
HTML.Attribute.COORDS	HTML.Attribute.NOHREF	HTML.Attribute.VLINK
HTML.Attribute.DATA	HTML.Attribute.NORESIZE	HTML.Attribute.VSPACE
HTML.Attribute.DECLARE	HTML.Attribute.NOSHADE	HTML.Attribute.WIDTH
HTML.Attribute.DIR	HTML.Attribute.NOWRAP	

The `MutableAttributeSet` interface adds six methods to add attributes to and remove attributes from the set:

```
public void addAttribute(Object name, Object value)
public void addAttributes(AttributeSet attributes)
public void removeAttribute(Object name)
public void removeAttributes(Enumeration names)
public void removeAttributes(AttributeSet attributes)
public void setResolveParent(AttributeSet parent)
```

Again, the values are strings and the names are `HTML.Attribute` objects.

One possible use for all these methods is to modify documents before saving or displaying them. For example, most web browsers let you save a page on your hard drive as either HTML or text. However, both these formats lose track of images and relative links. The problem is that most pages are full of relative URLs, and these all break when you move the page to your local machine. Example 8-10 is an application called `PageSaver` that downloads a web page to a local hard drive while keeping all links intact by rewriting all relative URLs as absolute URLs.

The `PageSaver` class reads a series of URLs from the command line. It opens each one in turn and parses it. Every tag, text block, comment, and attribute is copied into a local file. However, all link attributes, such as `SRC`, `LOWSRC`, `CODEBASE`, and `HREF`, are remapped to an absolute URL. Note particularly the extensive use to which the `URL` and `javax.swing.text` classes were put; `PageSaver` could be rewritten with string replacements, but that would be considerably more complicated.

Example 8-10. PageSaver

```
import javax.swing.text.*;
import javax.swing.text.html.*;
import javax.swing.text.html.parser.*;
import java.io.*;
import java.net.*;
import java.util.*;

public class PageSaver extends HTMLEditorKit.ParserCallback {

  private Writer out;
  private URL base;

  public PageSaver(Writer out, URL base) {
    this.out = out;
    this.base = base;
  }

  public void handleStartTag(HTML.Tag tag,
   MutableAttributeSet attributes, int position) {
    try {
      out.write("<" + tag);
      this.writeAttributes(attributes);
      // for the <APPLET> tag we may have to add a codebase attribute
```

Example 8-10. PageSaver (continued)

```
     if (tag == HTML.Tag.APPLET
      && attributes.getAttribute(HTML.Attribute.CODEBASE) == null) {
       String codebase = base.toString();
       if (codebase.endsWith(".htm") || codebase.endsWith(".html")) {
         codebase = codebase.substring(0, codebase.lastIndexOf('/'));
       }
       out.write(" codebase=\"" + codebase + "\"");
     }
     out.write(">");
     out.flush();
   }
   catch (IOException ex) {
     System.err.println(ex);
     e.printStackTrace();
   }
 }

 public void handleEndTag(HTML.Tag tag, int position) {
   try {
     out.write("</" + tag + ">");
     out.flush();
   }
   catch (IOException ex) {
     System.err.println(ex);
   }
 }

 private void writeAttributes(AttributeSet attributes)
  throws IOException {

   Enumeration e = attributes.getAttributeNames();
   while (e.hasMoreElements()) {
     Object name = e.nextElement();
     String value = (String) attributes.getAttribute(name);
     try {
       if (name == HTML.Attribute.HREF || name == HTML.Attribute.SRC
        || name == HTML.Attribute.LOWSRC
        || name == HTML.Attribute.CODEBASE ) {
         URL u = new URL(base, value);
         out.write(" " + name + "=\"" + u + "\"");
       }
       else {
         out.write(" " + name + "=\"" + value + "\"");
       }
     }
     catch (MalformedURLException ex) {
       System.err.println(ex);
       System.err.println(base);
       System.err.println(value);
       ex.printStackTrace();
     }
   }
 }
```

Example 8-10. PageSaver (continued)

```java
  public void handleComment(char[] text, int position) {

    try {
      out.write("<!-- ");
      out.write(text);
      out.write(" -->");
      out.flush( );
    }
    catch (IOException ex) {
      System.err.println(ex);
    }

  }

  public void handleText(char[] text, int position) {

    try {
      out.write(text);
      out.flush( );
    }
    catch (IOException ex) {
      System.err.println(ex);
      e.printStackTrace( );
    }

  }

  public void handleSimpleTag(HTML.Tag tag,
   MutableAttributeSet attributes, int position) {
    try {
      out.write("<" + tag);
      this.writeAttributes(attributes);
      out.write(">");
    }
    catch (IOException ex) {
      System.err.println(ex);
      e.printStackTrace( );
    }
  }

  public static void main(String[] args) {

    for (int i = 0; i < args.length; i++) {

      ParserGetter kit = new ParserGetter( );
      HTMLEditorKit.Parser parser = kit.getParser( );

      try {
        URL u = new URL(args[i]);
        InputStream in = u.openStream( );
        InputStreamReader r = new InputStreamReader(in);
        String remoteFileName = u.getFile( );
```

Example 8-10. PageSaver (continued)

```
        if (remoteFileName.endsWith("/")) {
          remoteFileName += "index.html";
        }
        if (remoteFileName.startsWith("/")) {
          remoteFileName = remoteFileName.substring(1);
        }
        File localDirectory = new File(u.getHost());
        while (remoteFileName.indexOf('/') > -1) {
          String part = remoteFileName.substring(0, remoteFileName.indexOf('/'));
          remoteFileName =
              remoteFileName.substring(remoteFileName.indexOf('/')+1);
          localDirectory = new File(localDirectory, part);
        }
        if (localDirectory.mkdirs()) {
          File output = new File(localDirectory, remoteFileName);
          FileWriter out = new FileWriter(output);
          HTMLEditorKit.ParserCallback callback = new PageSaver(out, u);
          parser.parse(r, callback, false);
        }
      }
      catch (IOException ex) {
        System.err.println(ex);
        e.printStackTrace();
      }

    }

  }

}
```

The handleEndTag(), handleText(), and handleComment() methods simply copy their content from the input into the output. The handleStartTag() and handleSimpleTag() methods write their respective tags onto the output but also invoke the private writeAttributes() method. This method loops through the attributes in the set and mostly just copies them onto the output. However, for a few select attributes, such as SRC and HREF, which typically have URL values, it rewrites the values as absolute URLs. Finally, the main() method reads URLs from the command line, calculates reasonable names and directories for corresponding local files, and starts a new PageSaver for each URL.

In the first edition of this book, I included a similar program that downloaded the raw HTML using the URL class and parsed it manually. That program was about a third longer than this one and much less robust. For instance, it did not support frames or the LOWSRC attributes of IMG tags. It went to great effort to handle both quoted and unquoted attribute values and still didn't recognize attribute values enclosed in single quotes. By contrast, this program needs only one extra line of code to support each additional attribute. It is much more robust, much easier to understand (since there's not a lot of detailed string manipulation), and much easier to extend.

This is just one example of the various HTML filters that the javax.swing.text.html package makes easy to write. You could, for example, write a filter that pretty-prints the HTML by indenting the different levels of tags. You could write a program to convert HTML to TeX, XML, RTF, or many other formats. You could write a program that spiders a web site, downloading all linked pages—and this is just the beginning. All of these programs are much easier to write because Swing provides a simple-to-use HTML parser. All you have to do is respond to the individual elements and attributes that the parser discovers in the HTML document. The more difficult problem of parsing the document is removed.

Cookies

Cookies are an atrocious hack perpetrated on the browsing world by Netscape. They are completely contrary to the web architecture. They attempt to graft state onto the deliberately stateless HTTP protocol. Statelessness in HTTP was not a mistake or a design flaw. It was a deliberate design decision that helped the Web scale to the enormous size it's reached today.

On the server side, cookies are never necessary and always a bad idea. There is always a cleaner, simpler, more scalable solution that does not involve cookies. Sadly, a lot of server-side developers don't know this and go blindly forward developing web sites that require client-side developers to support cookies.

Prior to Java 1.5, cookies can be supported only by direct manipulation of the HTTP header. When a server sets a cookie, it includes a Set-Cookie field like this one in the HTTP header:

```
Set-Cookie: user=elharo
```

This sends the browser a cookie with the name "user" and the value "elharo". The value of this field is limited to the printable ASCII characters (because HTTP header fields are limited to the printable ASCII characters). Furthermore, the names may not contain commas, semicolons, or whitespace.

A later version of the spec, RFC 2965, uses a Set-Cookie2 HTTP header instead. The most obvious difference is that this version of the cookie spec requires a version attribute after the name=value pair, like so:

```
Set-Cookie2: user=elharo; Version=1
```

The Version attribute simply indicates the version of the cookie spec in use. Version 1 and the unmarked original version zero are the only ones currently defined. Some servers will send both Set-Cookie and Set-Cookie2 headers. If so, the value in Set-Cookie2 takes precedence if a client understands both. Set-Cookie2 also allows cookie values to be quoted so they can contain internal whitespace. For example, this sets the cookie with the name food and the value "chocolate ice cream".

```
Set-Cookie2: food="chocolate ice cream"; Version=1
```

The quotes are just delimiters. They are not part of the attribute value. However, the attribute values are still limited to printable ASCII characters.

When requesting a document from the same server, the client echoes that cookie back in a Cookie header field in the request it sends to the server:

```
Cookie: user=elharo
```

If the original cookie was set by Set-Cookie2, this begins with a $Version attribute:

```
Cookie: $Version=1;user=elharo
```

The $ sign helps distinguish between cookie attributes and the main cookie name=value pair.

The client's job is simply to keep track of all the cookies it's been sent, and send the right ones back to the original servers at the right time. However, this is a little more complicated because cookies can have attributes identifying the expiration date, path, domain, port, version, and security options.

For example, by default a cookie applies to the server it came from. If a cookie is originally set by *www.foo.example.com*, the browser will only send the cookie back to *www.foo.example.com*. However, a site can also indicate that a cookie applies within an entire subdomain, not just at the original server. For example, this request sets a user cookie for the *entire .foo.example.com* domain:

```
Set-Cookie: user=elharo;Domain=.foo.example.com
```

The browser will echo this cookie back not just to *www.foo.example.com* but also to *lothar.foo.example.com*, *eliza.foo.example.com*, *enoch.foo.example.com*, and any other host somewhere in the *foo.example.com* domain. However, a server can only set cookies for domains it immediately belongs to. *www.foo.example.com* cannot set a cookie for *www.oreilly.com*, *example.com*, or *.com*, no matter how it sets the domain. (In practice, there have been a number of holes and workarounds for this, with severe negative impacts on user privacy.)

If the cookie was set by Set-Cookie2, the client will include the domain that was originally set, like so:

```
Cookie: $Version=1; user=elharo;  $Domain=.foo.example.com
```

However, if it's a version zero cookie, the domain is not echoed back.

Beyond domains, cookies are scoped by path, so they're used for some directories on the server, but not all. The default scope is the original URL and any subdirectories. For instance, if a cookie is set for the URL *http://www.cafeconleche.org/XOM/*, the cookie also applies in *http://www.cafeconleche.org/XOM/apidocs/*, but not in *http://www.cafeconleche.org/slides/* or *http://www.cafeconleche.org/*. However, the default scope can be changed using a Path attribute in the cookie. For example, this next response sends the browser a cookie with the name "user" and the value "elharo" that applies only within the server's */restricted* subtree, not on the rest of the site:

```
Set-Cookie: user=elharo; $Version=1;Path=/restricted
```

When requesting a document in the subtree */restricted* from the same server, the client echoes that cookie back. However, it does not use the cookie in other directories on the site. Again, if and only if the cookie was originally set with Set-Cookie2, the client will include the Path that was originally set, like so:

```
Cookie: user=elharo; $Version=1;$Path=/restricted
```

A cookie can set include both a domain and a path. For instance, this cookie applies in the */restricted* path on any servers within the *example.com* domain:

```
Set-Cookie2: $Version=1;user=elharo; $Path=/restricted;$Domain=.example.com
```

The order of the different cookie attributes doesn't matter, as long as they're all separated by semicolons and the cookie's own name and value come first. However, this isn't true when the client is sending the cookie back to the server. In this case, the path must precede the domain, like so:

```
Cookie: $Version=1;user=elharo; $Path=/restricted;$Domain=.foo.example.com
```

A version zero cookie can be set to expire at a certain point in time by setting the expires attribute to a date in the form Wdy, DD-Mon-YYYY HH:MM:SS GMT. Weekday and month are given as three-letter abbreviations. The rest are numeric, padded with initial zeros if necessary. In the pattern language used by java.text.SimpleDateFormat, this is "E, dd-MMM-yyyy k:m:s 'GMT'". For instance, this cookie expires at 3:23 P.M. on December 21, 2005:

```
Set-Cookie: user=elharo; expires=Wed, 21-Dec-2005 15:23:00 GMT
```

The browser should remove this cookie from its cache after that date has passed.

Set-Cookie2 use a Max-Age attribute that sets the cookie to expire after a certain number of seconds have passed instead of at a specific moment. For instance, this cookie expires one hour (3,600 seconds) after it's first set:

```
Set-Cookie2: user="elharo"; $Version=1;Max-Age=3600
```

The browser should remove this cookie from its cache after this amount of time has elapsed.

Because cookies can contain sensitive information such as passwords and session keys, some cookie transactions should be secure. Exactly what secure means in this context is not specified. Most of the time, it means using HTTPS instead of HTTP, but whatever it means, each cookie can have the secure attribute with no value, like so:

```
Set-Cookie: key=etrogl7*;Domain=.foo.example.com; secure
```

Browsers are supposed to refuse to send such cookies over insecure channels.

Finally, in addition to path, domain, and time, version 1 cookies can be scoped by port. This isn't common, but clients are required to support it. The Port attribute contains a quoted list of whitespace-separated port numbers to which the cookie applies:

```
Set-Cookie2: $Version=1;user=elharo; $Path=/restricted;$Port="8080 8000"
```

For the response, the order is always path, domain, and port, like so:

```
Cookie: $Version=1;user=elharo;  $Path=/restricted; $Domain=.foo.example.com;
$Port="8080 8000"
```

Multiple cookies can be set in one request by separating the name-value pairs with commas. For example, this Set-Cookie header assigns the cookie named user the value "elharo" and the cookie named zip the value "10003":

```
Set-Cookie: user=elharo, zip=10003
```

Each cookie set in this way can also contain attributes. For example, this Set-Cookie header scopes the user cookie to the path /restricted and the zip cookie to the path /weather:

```
Set-Cookie: user=elharo; path=/restricted, zip=10003; path=/weather
```

I've left out a couple of less important details like comments that don't matter much in practice. If you're interested, complete details are available in RFC 2965, *HTTP State Management Mechanism*.

That's how cookies work behind the scenes. In theory, this is all transparent to the user. In practice, the most sophisticated users routinely disable, filter, or inspect cookies to protect their privacy and security so cookies are not guaranteed to work.

Let's wrap this all up in a neat class called Cookie, shown in Example 8-12, with appropriate getter methods for the relevant properties and a factory method that parses HTTP header fields that set cookies. We'll need this in a minute because even as of Java 1.5 there's nothing like this in the standard JDK.

Example 8-11. A cookie class

```
package com.macfaq.http;

import java.net.URI;
import java.text.DateFormat;
import java.text.SimpleDateFormat;
import java.util.Date;

public class Cookie {

  private String  version = "0";
  private String  name;
  private String  value;
  private URI     uri;
  private String  domain;
  private Date  expires;
  private String  path;
  private boolean secure = false;

  private static DateFormat expiresFormat
    = new SimpleDateFormat("E, dd-MMM-yyyy k:m:s 'GMT'");

  // prevent instantiation
  private Cookie( ) {}
```

Example 8-11. A cookie class (continued)

```java
public static Cookie bake(String header, URI uri)
  throws CookieException {

  try {
    String[] attributes = header.split(";");
    String nameValue = attributes[0];
    Cookie cookie = new Cookie( );
    cookie.uri = uri;
    cookie.name = nameValue.substring(0, nameValue.indexOf('='));
    cookie.value = nameValue.substring(nameValue.indexOf('=')+1);
    cookie.path = "/";
    cookie.domain = uri.getHost( );

    if (attributes[attributes.length-1].trim( ).equals("secure")) {
      cookie.secure = true;
    }

    for (int i=1; i < attributes.length; i++) {
      nameValue = attributes[i].trim( );
      int equals = nameValue.indexOf('=');
      if (equals == -1) continue;
      String attributeName = nameValue.substring(0, equals);
      String attributeValue = nameValue.substring(equals+1);
      if (attributeName.equalsIgnoreCase("domain")) {
        String uriDomain = uri.getHost( );
        if (uriDomain.equals(attributeValue)) {
          cookie.domain = attributeValue;
        }
        else {
          if (!attributeValue.startsWith(".")) {
            attributeValue = "." + attributeValue;
          }
          uriDomain = uriDomain.substring(uriDomain.indexOf('.'));
          if (!uriDomain.equals(attributeValue)) {
            throw new CookieException(
              "Server tried to set cookie in another domain");
          }
          cookie.domain = attributeValue;
        }
      }
      else if (attributeName.equalsIgnoreCase("path")) {
        cookie.path = attributeValue;
      }
      else if (attributeName.equalsIgnoreCase("expires")) {
        cookie.expires = expiresFormat.parse(attributeValue);
      }
      else if (attributeName.equalsIgnoreCase("Version")) {
        if (!"1".equals(attributeValue)) {
          throw new CookieException("Unexpected version " + attributeValue);
        }
        cookie.version = attributeValue;
      }
    }
```

Example 8-11. A cookie class (continued)

```
      return cookie;
    }
    catch (Exception ex) {
      // ParseException, StringIndexOutOfBoundsException etc.
      throw new CookieException(ex);
    }

  }

  public boolean isExpired( ) {
    if (expires == null) return false;
    Date now = new Date( );
    return now.after(expires);
  }

  public String getName( ) {
    return name;
  }

  public boolean isSecure( ) {
    return secure;
  }

  public URI getURI( ) {
    return uri;
  }

  public String getVersion( ) {
    return version;
  }

  // should this cookie be sent when retrieving the specified URI?
  public boolean matches(URI u) {

    if (isExpired( )) return false;

    String path = u.getPath( );
    if (path == null) path = "/";

    if (path.startsWith(this.path)) return true;

    return false;
  }

  public String toExternalForm( ) {
    StringBuffer result = new StringBuffer(name);
    result.append("=");
    result.append(value);
    if ("1".equals(version)) {
      result.append(" Version=1");
    }
    return result.toString( );
  }
}
```

Prior to Java 1.5, the only way to support cookies is by direct inspection of the relevant HTTP headers. The URL class does not support this, but the URLConnection class introduced in Chapter 15 does. Java 1.5 adds a new java.net.CookieHandler class that makes this process somewhat easier. You provide a subclass of this abstract class where Java will store all cookies retrieved through the HTTP protocol handler. Once you've done this, when you access an HTTP server through a URL object and the server sends a cookie, Java automatically puts it in the system default cookie handler. When the same VM instance goes back to that server, it sends the cookie.

 I'm writing this section based on betas of Java 1.5. While the information about how cookies are handled in HTTP should be accurate, it's entirely possible a few of the Java details may change by the time Java 1.5 is released. Be sure to compare what you read here with the latest documentation from Sun.

The CookieHandler class is summarized in Example 8-12. As you can see, there are two abstract methods to implement, get() and put(). When Java loads a URL from a server that sets a cookie, it passes the URI it was loading and the complete HTTP headers of the server response to the put() method. The handler can parse the details out of these headers and store them somewhere. When Java tries to load an HTTP URL from a server, it passes the URL and the request HTTP header to the get() method to see if there are any cookies in the store for that URL. Sadly, you have to implement the parsing and storage code yourself. CookieHandler is an abstract class that does not do this for you, even though it's pretty standard stuff.

Example 8-12. CookieHandler

```
package java.net;

public abstract class CookieHandler {

  public CookieHandler()

  public abstract Map<String,List<String>> get(
   URI uri, Map<String,List<String>> requestHeaders)
   throws IOException
  public abstract void put(
   URI uri, Map<String,List<String>> responseHeaders)
   throws IOException

  public static CookieHandler getDefault()
  public static void          setDefault(CookieHandler handler)

}
```

A subclass is most easily implemented by delegating the hard work to the Java Collections API, as Example 8-13 demonstrates. Since CookieHandler is only available in Java 1.5 anyway, I took the opportunity to show off some new features of Java 1.5, including generic types and enhanced for loops. This implementation limits itself to version 0 cookies, which are far and away the most common kind you'll find in practice. If version 1 cookies ever achieve broad adoption, it should be easy to extend these classes to support them.

Example 8-13. A CookieHandler implemented on top of the Java Collections API

```java
package com.macfaq.http;

import java.io.IOException;
import java.net.*;
import java.util.*;

public class CookieStore extends CookieHandler {

  private List<Cookie> store = new ArrayList<Cookie>();

  public Map<String,List<String>> get(URI uri,
   Map<String,List<String>> requestHeaders)
   throws IOException {

      Map<String,List<String>> result = new HashMap<String,List<String>>();
      StringBuffer cookies = new StringBuffer();
      for (Cookie cookie : store) {
        if (cookie.isExpired()) {
          store.remove(cookie);
        }
        else if (cookie.matches(uri)) {
            if (cookies.length() != 0) cookies.append(", ");
            cookies.append(cookie.toExternalForm());
        }
      }

      if (cookies.length() > 0) {
        List<String> temp = new ArrayList<String>(1);
        temp.add(cookies.toString());
        result.put("Cookie", temp);
      }

      return result;

  }

  public void put(URI uri, Map<String,List<String>> responseHeaders)
   throws IOException {

    List<String> setCookies = responseHeaders.get("Set-Cookie");
    for (String next : setCookies) {
      try {
        Cookie cookie = Cookie.bake(next, uri);
        // Is a cookie with this name and URI already in the list?
        // If so, we replace it
        for (Cookie existingCookie : store) {
```

```
        if (cookie.getURI().equals(existingCookie.getURI()) &&
            cookie.getName().equals(existingCookie.getName())) {
          store.remove(existingCookie);
          break;
        }
      }
      store.add(cookie);
    }
    catch (CookieException ex) {
      // Server sent malformed header;
      // log and ignore
      System.err.println(ex);
    }
  }

  }

}
```

When storing a cookie, the responseHeaders argument to the put( ) method contains the complete HTTP response header sent by the server. From this you need to extract any header fields that set cookies (basically, just Set-Cookie and Set-Cookie2). The key to this map is the field name (Set-Cookie or Set-Cookie2). The value of the map entry is a list of cookies set in that field. Each separate cookie is a separate member of the list. That is, Java does divide the header field value along the commas to split up several cookies and pass them in each as a separate entry in the list.

In the other direction, when getting a cookie it's necessary to consider not only the URI but the path for which the cookie is valid. Here, the path is delegated to the Cookie class itself via the matches( ) method. This is hardly the most efficient implementation possible. For each cookie, the store does a linear search through all available cookies. A more intelligent implementation would index the list by URIs and domains, but for simple purposes this solution suffices without being overly complex. A more serious limitation is that this store is not persistent. It lasts only until the driving program exits. Most web browsers would want to store the cookies in a file so they could be reloaded when the browser was relaunched. Nonetheless, this class is sufficient to add basic cookie support to the simple web browser. All that's required is to add this one line at the beginning of the main( ) method in Example 8-5:

```
CookieHandler.setDefault(new com.macfaq.http.CookieStore( ));
```

CHAPTER 9

Sockets for Clients

Data is transmitted across the Internet in packets of finite size called *datagrams*. Each datagram contains a *header* and a *payload*. The header contains the address and port to which the packet is going, the address and port from which the packet came, and various other housekeeping information used to ensure reliable transmission. The payload contains the data itself. However, since datagrams have a finite length, it's often necessary to split the data across multiple packets and reassemble it at the destination. It's also possible that one or more packets may be lost or corrupted in transit and need to be retransmitted or that packets arrive out of order and need to be reordered. Keeping track of this—splitting the data into packets, generating headers, parsing the headers of incoming packets, keeping track of what packets have and haven't been received, and so on—is a lot of work and requires a lot of intricate code.

Fortunately, you don't have to do the work yourself. Sockets allow the programmer to treat a network connection as just another stream onto which bytes can be written and from which bytes can be read. Sockets shield the programmer from low-level details of the network, such as error detection, packet sizes, packet retransmission, network addresses, and more.

Socket Basics

A socket is a connection between two hosts. It can perform seven basic operations:

- Connect to a remote machine
- Send data
- Receive data
- Close a connection
- Bind to a port
- Listen for incoming data
- Accept connections from remote machines on the bound port

Java's Socket class, which is used by both clients and servers, has methods that correspond to the first four of these operations. The last three operations are needed only by servers, which wait for clients to connect to them. They are implemented by the ServerSocket class, which is discussed in the next chapter. Java programs normally use client sockets in the following fashion:

1. The program creates a new socket with a constructor.

2. The socket attempts to connect to the remote host.

3. Once the connection is established, the local and remote hosts get input and output streams from the socket and use those streams to send data to each other. This connection is *full-duplex*; both hosts can send and receive data simultaneously. What the data means depends on the protocol; different commands are sent to an FTP server than to an HTTP server. There will normally be some agreed-upon hand-shaking followed by the transmission of data from one to the other.

4. When the transmission of data is complete, one or both sides close the connection. Some protocols, such as HTTP 1.0, require the connection to be closed after each request is serviced. Others, such as FTP, allow multiple requests to be processed in a single connection.

Investigating Protocols with Telnet

In this chapter, you'll see clients that use sockets to communicate with a number of well-known Internet services such as HTTP, echo, and more. The sockets themselves are simple enough; however, the protocols to communicate with different servers make life complex.

To get a feel for how a protocol operates, you can use Telnet to connect to a server, type different commands to it, and watch its responses. By default, Telnet attempts to connect to port 23. To connect to servers on different ports, specify the port you want to connect to like this:

```
% telnet localhost 25
```

 This example assumes that you're using a Unix system. However, Telnet clients are available for all common operating systems, and they are all pretty similar; for example, on Windows, you might have to type the hostname and the port into a dialog box rather than on the command-line, but otherwise, the clients work the same.

This requests a connection to port 25, the SMTP port, on the local machine; SMTP is the protocol used to transfer email between servers or between a mail client and a server. If you know the commands to interact with an SMTP server, you can send email without going through a mail program. This trick can be used to forge email.

For example, a few years ago, the summer students at the National Solar Observatory in Sunspot, New Mexico, made it appear that the party one of the scientists was throwing after the annual volleyball match between the staff and the students was in fact a victory party for the students. (Of course, the author of this book had absolutely nothing to do with such despicable behavior. ;-)) The interaction with the SMTP server went something like this; input the user types is shown in bold (the names have been changed to protect the gullible):

```
flare% telnet localhost 25
Trying 127.0.0.1 ...
Connected to localhost.sunspot.noao.edu.
Escape character is '^]'.
220 flare.sunspot.noao.edu Sendmail 4.1/SMI-4.1 ready at Fri, 5 Jul 93 13:13:01 MDT
HELO sunspot.noao.edu
250 flare.sunspot.noao.edu Hello localhost [127.0.0.1], pleased to meet you
MAIL FROM: bart
250 bart... Sender ok
RCPT TO: local@sunspot.noao.edu
250 local@sunspot.noao.edu... Recipient ok
DATA
354 Enter mail, end with "." on a line by itself

In a pitiful attempt to reingratiate myself with the students
after their inevitable defeat of the staff on the volleyball
court at 4:00 P.M., July 24, I will be throwing a victory
party for the students at my house that evening at 7:00.
Everyone is invited.

Beer and Ben-Gay will be provided so the staff may drown
their sorrows and assuage their aching muscles after their
public humiliation.

Sincerely,

Bart
.
250 Mail accepted
QUIT
221 flare.sunspot.noao.edu delivering mail
Connection closed by foreign host.
```

Several members of the staff asked Bart why he, a staff member, was throwing a victory party for the students. The moral of this story is that you should never trust email, especially patently ridiculous email like this, without independent verification. The other moral of this story is that you can use Telnet to simulate a client, see how the client and the server interact, and thus learn what your Java program needs to do. Although this session doesn't demonstrate all the features of the SMTP protocol, it's sufficient to enable you to deduce how a simple email client talks to a server.

The Socket Class

The java.net.Socket class is Java's fundamental class for performing client-side TCP operations. Other client-oriented classes that make TCP network connections such as URL, URLConnection, Applet, and JEditorPane all ultimately end up invoking the methods of this class. This class itself uses native code to communicate with the local TCP stack of the host operating system. The methods of the Socket class set up and tear down connections and set various socket options. Because TCP sockets are more or less reliable connections, the interface that the Socket class provides to the programmer is *streams*. The actual reading and writing of data over the socket is accomplished via the familiar stream classes.

The Constructors

The nondeprecated public Socket constructors are simple. Each lets you specify the host and the port you want to connect to. Hosts may be specified as an InetAddress or a String. Ports are always specified as int values from 0 to 65,535. Two of the constructors also specify the local address and local port from which data will be sent. You might need to do this when you want to select one particular network interface from which to send data on a multihomed host.

The Socket class also has two protected constructors (one of which is now public in Java 1.4) that create unconnected sockets. These are useful when you want to set socket options before making the first connection.

public Socket(String host, int port) throws UnknownHostException, IOException

This constructor creates a TCP socket to the specified port on the specified host and attempts to connect to the remote host. For example:

```
try {
  Socket toOReilly = new Socket("www.oreilly.com", 80);
  // send and receive data...
}
catch (UnknownHostException ex) {
  System.err.println(ex);
}
catch (IOException ex) {
  System.err.println(ex);
}
```

In this constructor, the host argument is just a hostname expressed as a String. If the domain name server cannot resolve the hostname or is not functioning, the constructor throws an UnknownHostException. If the socket cannot be opened for some other reason, the constructor throws an IOException. There are many reasons a connection attempt might fail: the host you're trying to reach may not be accepting connections, a dialup Internet connection may be down, or routing problems may be preventing your packets from reaching their destination.

Since this constructor doesn't just create a Socket object but also tries to connect the socket to the remote host, you can use the object to determine whether connections to a particular port are allowed, as in Example 9-1.

Example 9-1. Find out which of the first 1,024 ports seem to be hosting TCP servers on a specified host

```
import java.net.*;
import java.io.*;

public class LowPortScanner {

  public static void main(String[] args) {

    String host = "localhost";

    if (args.length > 0) {
      host = args[0];
    }
    for (int i = 1; i < 1024; i++) {
      try {
        Socket s = new Socket(host, i);
        System.out.println("There is a server on port " + i + " of "
         + host);
      }
      catch (UnknownHostException ex) {
        System.err.println(ex);
        break;
      }
      catch (IOException ex) {
        // must not be a server on this port
      }
    } // end for

  } // end main

} // end PortScanner
```

Here's the output this program produces on my local host. Your results will vary, depending on which ports are occupied. As a rule, more ports will be occupied on a Unix workstation than on a PC or a Mac:

```
% java LowPortScanner
There is a server on port 21 of localhost
There is a server on port 22 of localhost
There is a server on port 23 of localhost
There is a server on port 25 of localhost
There is a server on port 37 of localhost
There is a server on port 111 of localhost
There is a server on port 139 of localhost
There is a server on port 210 of localhost
There is a server on port 515 of localhost
There is a server on port 873 of localhost
```

If you're curious about what servers are running on these ports, try experimenting with Telnet. On a Unix system, you may be able to find out which services reside on which ports by looking in the file */etc/services*. If LowPortScanner finds any ports that are running servers but are not listed in */etc/services*, then that's interesting.

Although this program looks simple, it's not without its uses. The first step to securing a system is understanding it. This program helps you understand what your system is doing so you can find (and close) possible entrance points for attackers. You may also find rogue servers: for example, LowPortScanner might tell you that there's a server on port 800, which, on further investigation, turns out to be an HTTP server somebody is running to serve erotic GIFs, and which is saturating your T1. However, like most security tools, this program can be misused. Don't use LowPortScanner to probe a machine you do not own; most system administrators would consider that a hostile act.

public Socket(InetAddress host, int port) throws IOException

Like the previous constructor, this constructor creates a TCP socket to the specified port on the specified host and tries to connect. It differs by using an InetAddress object (discussed in Chapter 6) to specify the host rather than a hostname. It throws an IOException if it can't connect, but does not throw an UnknownHostException; if the host is unknown, you will find out when you create the InetAddress object. For example:

```
try {
  InetAddress oreilly = InetAddress.getByName("www.oreilly.com");
  Socket oreillySocket = new Socket(oreilly , 80);
  // send and receive data...
}
catch (UnknownHostException ex) {
  System.err.println(ex);
}
catch (IOException ex) {
  System.err.println(ex);
}
```

In the rare case where you open many sockets to the same host, it is more efficient to convert the hostname to an InetAddress and then repeatedly use that InetAddress to create sockets. Example 9-2 uses this technique to improve on the efficiency of Example 9-1.

Example 9-2. Find out which of the ports at or above 1,024 seem to be hosting TCP servers

```
import java.net.*;
import java.io.*;

public class HighPortScanner {

  public static void main(String[] args) {

    String host = "localhost";
```

```
  if (args.length > 0) {
    host = args[0];
  }

  try {
    InetAddress theAddress = InetAddress.getByName(host);
    for (int i = 1024; i < 65536; i++) {
      try {
        Socket theSocket = new Socket(theAddress, i);
        System.out.println("There is a server on port "
         + i + " of " + host);
      }
      catch (IOException ex) {
        // must not be a server on this port
      }
    } // end for
  } // end try
  catch (UnknownHostException ex) {
    System.err.println(ex);
  }

} // end main

} // end HighPortScanner
```

The results of this example are similar to the previous ones, except that HighPortScanner checks ports above 1,023.

public Socket(String host, int port, InetAddress interface, int localPort) throws IOException, UnknownHostException

This constructor creates a socket to the specified port on the specified host and tries to connect. It connects *to* the host and port specified in the first two arguments. It connects *from* the local network interface and port specified by the last two arguments. The network interface may be either physical (e.g., a different Ethernet card) or virtual (a multihomed host). If 0 is passed for the localPort argument, Java chooses a random available port between 1,024 and 65,535.

One situation where you might want to explicitly choose the local address would be on a router/firewall that uses dual Ethernet ports. Incoming connections would be accepted on one interface, processed, and forwarded to the local network from the other interface. Suppose you were writing a program to periodically dump error logs to a printer or send them over an internal mail server. You'd want to make sure you used the inward-facing network interface instead of the outward-facing network interface. For example,

```
  try {
    InetAddress inward = InetAddress.getByName("router");
    Socket socket = new Socket("mail", 25, inward, 0);
```

```
      // work with the sockets...
    }
    catch (UnknownHostException ex) {
      System.err.println(ex);
    }
    catch (IOException ex) {
      System.err.println(ex);
    }
```

By passing 0 for the local port number, I say that I don't care which port is used but I do want to use the network interface bound to the local hostname *router*.

This constructor can throw an IOException for all the usual reasons given in the previous constructors. Furthermore, an UnknownHostException will also be thrown if the remote host cannot be located.

Finally, an IOException (probably a BindException, although again that's just a subclass of IOException and not specifically declared in the throws clause of this method) will be thrown if the socket is unable to bind to the requested local network interface, which tends to limit the portability of applications that use this constructor. You could take deliberate advantage of this to restrict a compiled program to run on only a predetermined host. It would require customizing distributions for each computer and is certainly overkill for cheap products. Furthermore, Java programs are so easy to disassemble, decompile, and reverse engineer that this scheme is far from foolproof. Nonetheless, it might be part of a scheme to enforce a software license.

public Socket(InetAddress host, int port, InetAddress interface, int localPort) throws IOException

This constructor is identical to the previous one except that the host to connect to is passed as an InetAddress, not a String. It creates a TCP socket to the specified port on the specified host from the specified interface and local port, and tries to connect. If it fails, it throws an IOException. For example:

```
    try {
      InetAddress inward = InetAddress.getByName("router");
      InetAddress mail = InetAddress.getByName("mail");
      Socket socket = new Socket(mail, 25, inward, 0);
      // work with the sockets...
    }
    catch (UnknownHostException ex) {
      System.err.println(ex);
    }
    catch (IOException ex) {
      System.err.println(ex);
    }
```

protected Socket( )

The Socket class also has two (three in Java 1.5) constructors that create an object without connecting the socket. You use these if you're subclassing Socket, perhaps to implement a special kind of socket that encrypts transactions or understands your local proxy server. Most of your implementation of a new socket class will be written in a `SocketImpl` object.

The noargs `Socket( )` constructor installs the default `SocketImpl` (from either the factory or a `java.net.PlainSocketImpl`). It creates a new `Socket` without connecting it, and is usually called by subclasses of `java.net.Socket`.

In Java 1.4, this constructor has been made public, and allows you to create a socket that is not yet connected to any host. You can connect later by passing a `SocketAddress` to one of the `connect( )` methods. The most common reason to create a `Socket` object without connecting is to set socket options; many of these cannot be changed after the connection has been made. I'll discuss this soon.

protected Socket(SocketImpl impl)

This constructor installs the `SocketImpl` object `impl` when it creates the new `Socket` object. The `Socket` object is created but is not connected. This constructor is usually called by subclasses of `java.net.Socket`. You can pass `null` to this constructor if you don't need a `SocketImpl`. However, in this case, you must override all the base class methods that depend on the underlying `SocketImpl`. This might be necessary if you were using JNI to talk to something other than the default native TCP stack.

public Socket(Proxy proxy) // Java 1.5

Java 1.5 adds this constructor, which creates an unconnected socket that will use the specified proxy server. Normally, the proxy server a socket uses is controlled by the `socksProxyHost` and `socksProxyPort` system properties, and these properties apply to all sockets in the system. However a socket created by this constructor will use the specified proxy server instead. Most notably, you can pass `Proxy.NO_PROXY` for the argument to bypass all proxy servers completely and connect directly to the remote host. Of course, if a firewall prevents such connections, there's nothing Java can do about it, and the connection will fail.

If you want to use a particular proxy server, you can specify it by its address. For example, this code fragment uses the SOCKS proxy server at *myproxy.example.com* to connect to the host *login.ibiblio.org*:

```
SocetAddress proxyAddress = new InetSocketAddress("myproxy.example.com", 1080);
Proxy proxy = new Proxy(Proxy.Type.SOCKS,  proxyAddress)
Socket s = new Socket(proxy);
SocketAddress remote = new InetSocketAddress("login.ibiblio.org", 25);
s.connect(remote);
```

SOCKS is the only low-level proxy type Java understands. There's also a high-level `Proxy.Type.HTTP` that works in the application layer rather than the transport layer and a `Proxy.Type.DIRECT` that represents proxyless connections.

Getting Information About a Socket

To the programmer, Socket objects appear to have several private fields that are accessible through various getter methods. Actually, sockets have only one field, a SocketImpl; the fields that appear to belong to the Socket actually reflect native code in the SocketImpl. This way, socket implementations can be changed without disturbing the program—for example, to support firewalls and proxy servers. The actual SocketImpl in use is almost completely transparent to the programmer.

public InetAddress getInetAddress( )

Given a Socket object, the getInetAddress( ) method tells you which remote host the Socket is connected to or, if the connection is now closed, which host the Socket was connected to when it was connected. For example:

```
try {
  Socket theSocket = new Socket("java.sun.com", 80);
  InetAddress host = theSocket.getInetAddress( );
  System.out.println("Connected to remote host " + host);
} // end try
catch (UnknownHostException ex) {
  System.err.println(ex);
}
catch (IOException ex) {
  System.err.println(ex);
}
```

public int getPort( )

The getPort( ) method tells you which port the Socket is (or was or will be) connected to on the remote host. For example:

```
try {
  Socket theSocket = new Socket("java.sun.com", 80);
  int port = theSocket.getPort( );
  System.out.println("Connected on remote port " + port);
} // end try
catch (UnknownHostException ex) {
  System.err.println(ex);
}
catch (IOException ex) {
  System.err.println(ex);
}
```

public int getLocalPort( )

There are two ends to a connection: the remote host and the local host. To find the port number for the local end of a connection, call getLocalPort( ). For example:

```
try {
  Socket theSocket = new Socket("java.sun.com", 80, true);
  int localPort = theSocket.getLocalPort( );
```

```
      System.out.println("Connecting from local port " + localPort);
    } // end try
    catch (UnknownHostException ex) {
      System.err.println(ex);
    }
    catch (IOException ex) {
      System.err.println(ex);
    }
```

Unlike the remote port, which (for a client socket) is usually a "well-known port" that has been preassigned by a standards committee, the local port is usually chosen by the system at runtime from the available unused ports. This way, many different clients on a system can access the same service at the same time. The local port is embedded in outbound IP packets along with the local host's IP address, so the server can send data back to the right port on the client.

public InetAddress getLocalAddress( )

The getLocalAddress( ) method tells you which network interface a socket is bound to. You normally use this on a multihomed host, or one with multiple network interfaces. For example:

```
    try {
      Socket theSocket = new Socket(hostname, 80);
      InetAddress localAddress = theSocket.getLocalAddress( );
      System.out.println("Connecting from local address  " + localAddress);
    } // end try
    catch (UnknownHostException ex) {
      System.err.println(ex);
    }
    catch (IOException ex) {
      System.err.println(ex);
    }
```

Example 9-3 reads a list of hostnames from the command-line, attempts to open a socket to each one, and then uses these four methods to print the remote host, the remote port, the local address, and the local port.

Example 9-3. Get a socket's information

```
import java.net.*;
import java.io.*;

public class SocketInfo {

  public static void main(String[] args) {

    for (int i = 0; i < args.length; i++) {
      try {
        Socket theSocket = new Socket(args[i], 80);
        System.out.println("Connected to " + theSocket.getInetAddress( )
         + " on port "  + theSocket.getPort( ) + " from port "
```

Example 9-3. Get a socket's information (continued)

```
                + theSocket.getLocalPort( ) + " of "
                + theSocket.getLocalAddress( ));
      } // end try
    catch (UnknownHostException ex) {
      System.err.println("I can't find " + args[i]);
    }
    catch (SocketException ex) {
      System.err.println("Could not connect to " + args[i]);
    }
    catch (IOException ex) {
      System.err.println(ex);
    }

  } // end for

 } // end main

} // end SocketInfo
```

Here's the result of a sample run. I included *www.oreilly.com* on the command line twice in order to demonstrate that each connection was assigned a different local port, regardless of the remote host; the local port assigned to any connection is unpredictable and depends mostly on what other ports are in use. The connection to *login.ibiblio.org* failed because that machine does not run any servers on port 80:

```
% java SocketInfo www.oreilly.com www.oreilly.com www.macfaq.com login.ibiblio.org
Connected to www.oreilly.com/208.201.239.37 on port 80 from port 49156 of /192.168.
254.25
Connected to www.oreilly.com/208.201.239.37 on port 80 from port 49157 of /192.168.
254.25
Connected to www.macfaq.com/216.254.106.198 on port 80 from port 49158 of /192.168.
254.25
Could not connect to login.ibiblio.org
```

public InputStream getInputStream( ) throws IOException

The getInputStream( ) method returns an input stream that can read data from the socket into a program. You usually chain this InputStream to a filter stream or reader that offers more functionality—DataInputStream or InputStreamReader, for example—before reading input. For performance reasons, it's also a very good idea to buffer the input by chaining it to a BufferedInputStream and/or a BufferedReader.

With an input stream, we can read data from a socket and start experimenting with some actual Internet protocols. One of the simplest protocols is called daytime, and is defined in RFC 867. There's almost nothing to it. The client opens a socket to port 13 on the daytime server. In response, the server sends the time in a human-readable format and closes the connection. You can test the daytime server with Telnet like this:

```
% telnet vision.poly.edu 13
Trying 128.238.42.35...
```

```
Connected to vision.poly.edu.
Escape character is '^]'.
Wed Nov 12 23:39:15 2003
Connection closed by foreign host.
```

The line "Wed Nov 12 23:39:15 2003" is sent by the daytime server. When you read the Socket's InputStream, this is what you will get. The other lines are produced either by the Unix shell or by the Telnet program.

Example 9-4 uses the InputStream returned by getInputStream() to read the time sent by the daytime server.

Example 9-4. A daytime protocol client

```java
import java.net.*;
import java.io.*;

public class DaytimeClient {

  public static void main(String[] args) {

    String hostname;

    if (args.length > 0) {
      hostname = args[0];
    }
    else {
      hostname = "time.nist.gov";
    }

    try {
      Socket theSocket = new Socket(hostname, 13);
      InputStream timeStream = theSocket.getInputStream();
      StringBuffer time = new StringBuffer();
      int c;
      while ((c = timeStream.read()) != -1) time.append((char) c);
      String timeString = time.toString().trim();
      System.out.println("It is " + timeString + " at " + hostname);
    }  // end try
    catch (UnknownHostException ex) {
      System.err.println(ex);
    }
    catch (IOException ex) {
      System.err.println(ex);
    }

  }  // end main

}  // end DaytimeClient
```

DaytimeClient reads the hostname of a daytime server from the command line and uses it to construct a new Socket that connects to port 13 on the server. If the hostname is omitted, the National Institute of Standards and Technology's time server at *time.nist.gov* is used. The client then calls theSocket.getInputStream( ) to get theSocket's input stream, which is stored in the variable timeStream. Since the daytime protocol specifies ASCII, DaytimeClient doesn't bother chaining a reader to the stream. Instead, it just reads the bytes into a StringBuffer one at a time, breaking when the server closes the connection as the protocol requires it to do. Here's what happens:

```
% java DaytimeClient
It is 52956 03-11-13 04:45:28 00 0 0 706.3 UTC(NIST) * at time.nist.gov
% java DaytimeClient vision.poly.edu
It is Wed Nov 12 23:45:29 2003 at vision.poly.edu
```

You can see that the clocks on *time.nist.gov* and *vision.poly.edu* aren't perfectly synchronized. Differences of a few seconds can be caused by the time it takes packets to travel across the Internet. For more details about network timekeeping, see *http://www.boulder.nist.gov/timefreq/service/its.htm*.

On top of that problem, the time servers on these two hosts use different formats. The daytime protocol doesn't specify the format for the time it returns, other than that it be human-readable. Therefore, it is difficult to convert the character data that the server returns to a Java Date in a reliable fashion. If you want to create a Date object based on the time at the server, it's easier to use the time protocol from RFC 868 instead, because it specifies a format for the time.

When reading data from the network, it's important to keep in mind that not all protocols use ASCII or even text. For example, the time protocol specified in RFC 868 specifies that the time be sent as the number of seconds since midnight, January 1, 1900 Greenwich Mean Time. However, this is not sent as an ASCII string like "2,524,521,600" or "–1297728000". Rather, it is sent as a 32-bit, unsigned, big-endian binary number.

 The RFC never actually comes out and says that this is the format used. It specifies 32 bits and assumes you know that all network protocols use big-endian numbers. The fact that the number is unsigned can be determined only by calculating the wraparound date for signed and unsigned integers and comparing it to the date given in the specification (2036). To make matters worse, the specification gives an example of a negative time that can't actually be sent by time servers that follow the protocol. Time is a fairly old protocol, standardized in the early 1980s before the IETF was as careful about such issues as it is today. Nonetheless, if you find yourself implementing a not particularly well-specified protocol, you may have to do a significant amount of testing against existing implementations to figure out what you need to do. In the worst case, different existing implementations may behave differently.

Since this isn't text, you can't easily use Telnet to test such a service, and your program can't read the server response with a Reader or any sort of readLine( ) method.

A Java program that connects to time servers must read the raw bytes and interpret them appropriately. In this example, that job is complicated by Java's lack of a 32-bit unsigned integer type. Consequently, you have to read the bytes one at a time and manually convert them into a long using the bitwise operators << and |. Example 9-5 demonstrates. When speaking other protocols, you may encounter data formats even more alien to Java. For instance, a few network protocols use 64-bit fixed-point numbers. There's no shortcut to handle all possible cases. You simply have to grit your teeth and code the math you need to handle the data in whatever format the server sends.

Example 9-5. A time protocol client

```java
import java.net.*;
import java.io.*;
import java.util.*;

public class TimeClient {

  public final static int    DEFAULT_PORT = 37;
  public final static String DEFAULT_HOST = "time.nist.gov";

  public static void main(String[] args) {

    String hostname = DEFAULT_HOST ;
    int port = DEFAULT_PORT;

    if (args.length > 0) {
      hostname = args[0];
    }

    if (args.length > 1) {
      try {
        port = Integer.parseInt(args[1]);
      }
      catch (NumberFormatException ex) {
        // Stay with the default port
      }
    }

    // The time protocol sets the epoch at 1900,
    // the Java Date class at 1970. This number
    // converts between them.

    long differenceBetweenEpochs = 2208988800L;

    // If you'd rather not use the magic number, uncomment
    // the following section which calculates it directly.

    /*
    TimeZone gmt = TimeZone.getTimeZone("GMT");
    Calendar epoch1900 = Calendar.getInstance(gmt);
    epoch1900.set(1900, 01, 01, 00, 00, 00);
```

Example 9-5. A time protocol client (continued)

```
    long epoch1900ms = epoch1900.getTime().getTime( );
    Calendar epoch1970 = Calendar.getInstance(gmt);
    epoch1970.set(1970, 01, 01, 00, 00, 00);
    long epoch1970ms = epoch1970.getTime().getTime( );

    long differenceInMS = epoch1970ms - epoch1900ms;
    long differenceBetweenEpochs = differenceInMS/1000;
    */

    InputStream raw = null;
    try {
      Socket theSocket = new Socket(hostname, port);
      raw = theSocket.getInputStream( );

      long secondsSince1900 = 0;
      for (int i = 0; i < 4; i++) {
        secondsSince1900 = (secondsSince1900 << 8) | raw.read( );
      }

      long secondsSince1970
       = secondsSince1900 - differenceBetweenEpochs;
      long msSince1970 = secondsSince1970 * 1000;
      Date time = new Date(msSince1970);

      System.out.println("It is " + time + " at " + hostname);

    } // end try
    catch (UnknownHostException ex) {
      System.err.println(ex);
    }
    catch (IOException ex) {
      System.err.println(ex);
    }
    finally {
      try {
        if (raw != null) raw.close( );
      }
      catch (IOException ex) {}
    }

  } // end main

} // end TimeClient
```

Here's the output of this program from a couple of sample runs. Since the time protocol specifies Greenwich Mean Time, the previous differences between time zones are eliminated. Most of the difference that's left simply reflects the clock drift between the two machines:

```
% java TimeClient
It is Wed Nov 12 23:49:15 EST 2003 at time.nist.gov
% java TimeClient vision.poly.edu
It is Wed Nov 12 23:49:20 EST 2003 at vision.poly.edu
```

Like DaytimeClient, TimeClient reads the hostname of the server and an optional port from the command-line and uses it to construct a new Socket that connects to that server. If the user omits the hostname, TimeClient defaults to *time.nist.gov*. The default port is 37. The client then calls theSocket.getInputStream( ) to get an input stream, which is stored in the variable raw. Four bytes are read from this stream and used to construct a long that represents the value of those four bytes interpreted as a 32-bit unsigned integer. This gives the number of seconds that have elapsed since 12:00 A.M., January 1, 1900 GMT (the time protocol's epoch); 2,208,988,800 seconds are subtracted from this number to get the number of seconds since 12:00 A.M., January 1, 1970 GMT (the Java Date class epoch). This number is multiplied by 1,000 to convert it into milliseconds. Finally, that number of milliseconds is converted into a Date object, which can be printed to show the current time and date.

public OutputStream getOutputStream( ) throws IOException

The getOutputStream( ) method returns a raw OutputStream for writing data from your application to the other end of the socket. You usually chain this stream to a more convenient class like DataOutputStream or OutputStreamWriter before using it. For performance reasons, it's a good idea to buffer it as well. For example:

```
Writer out;
try {
  Socket http = new Socket("www.oreilly.com", 80)
  OutputStream raw = http.getOutputStream( );
  OutputStream buffered = new BufferedOutputStream(raw);
  out = new OutputStreamWriter(buffered, "ASCII");
  out.write("GET / HTTP 1.0\r\n\r\n");
  // read the server response...
}
catch (Exception ex) {
  System.err.println(ex);
}
finally {
  try {
    out.close( );
  }
  catch (Exception ex) {}
}
```

The echo protocol, defined in RFC 862, is one of the simplest interactive TCP services. The client opens a socket to port 7 on the echo server and sends data. The server sends the data back. This continues until the client closes the connection. The echo protocol is useful for testing the network to make sure that data is not mangled by a misbehaving router or firewall. You can test echo with Telnet like this:

```
% telnet rama.poly.edu 7
Trying 128.238.10.212...
Connected to rama.poly.edu.
Escape character is '^]'.
This is a test
This is a test
```

```
This is another test
This is another test
9876543210
9876543210
^]
telnet> close
Connection closed.
```

Example 9-6 uses getOutputStream( ) and getInputStream( ) to implement a simple echo client. The user types input on the command line which is then sent to the server. The server echoes it back. The program exits when the user types a period on a line by itself. The echo protocol does not specify a character encoding. Indeed, what it specifies is that the data sent to the server is exactly the data returned by the server. The server echoes the raw bytes, not the characters they represent. Thus, this program uses the default character encoding and line separator of the client system for reading the input from System.in, sending the data to the remote system, and typing the output on System.out. Since an echo server echoes exactly what is sent, it's as if the server dynamically adjusts itself to the client system's conventions for character encoding and line breaks. Consequently, we can use convenient classes and methods such as PrintWriter and readLine( ) that would normally be too unreliable.

Example 9-6. An echo client

```
import java.net.*;
import java.io.*;

public class EchoClient {

  public static void main(String[] args) {

    String hostname = "localhost";

    if (args.length > 0) {
      hostname = args[0];
    }

    PrintWriter out = null;
    BufferedReader networkIn = null;
    try {
      Socket theSocket = new Socket(hostname, 7);
      networkIn = new BufferedReader(
       new InputStreamReader(theSocket.getInputStream( )));
      BufferedReader userIn = new BufferedReader(
       new InputStreamReader(System.in));
      out = new PrintWriter(theSocket.getOutputStream( ));
      System.out.println("Connected to echo server");

      while (true) {
        String theLine = userIn.readLine( );
        if (theLine.equals(".")) break;
        out.println(theLine);
```

Example 9-6. An echo client (continued)

```
      out.flush( );
      System.out.println(networkIn.readLine( ));
    }

  } // end try
  catch (IOException ex) {
    System.err.println(ex);
  }
  finally {
    try {
      if (networkIn != null) networkIn.close( );
      if (out != null) out.close( );
    }
    catch (IOException ex) {}
  }

} // end main

} // end EchoClient
```

As usual, EchoClient reads the name of the host to connect to from the command line. This hostname is used to create a new Socket object on port 7, called theSocket. The socket's InputStream is returned by getInputStream( ) and chained to an InputStreamReader, which is chained to a BufferedReader called networkIn. This reader reads the server responses. Since this client also needs to read input from the user, it creates a second BufferedReader, this one called userIn, which reads from System.in. Next, EchoClient calls theSocket.getOutputStream( ) to get theSocket's output stream, which is used to construct a new PrintWriter called out.

Now that the three streams have been created, it's simply a matter of reading the data from userIn and writing that data back out onto out. Once data has been sent to the echo server, networkIn waits for a response. When networkIn receives a response, it's printed on System.out. In theory, this client could get hung waiting for a response that never comes. However, this is unlikely if the connection can be made in the first place, since the TCP protocol checks for bad packets and automatically asks the server for replacements. When we implement a UDP echo client in Chapter 13, we will need a different approach because UDP does no error checking. Here's a sample run:

```
% java EchoClient rama.poly.edu
Connected to echo server
Hello
Hello
How are you?
How are you?
I'm fine thank you.
I'm fine thank you.
Goodbye
Goodbye
.
```

Example 9-7 is line-oriented. It reads a line of input from the console, sends it to the server, and waits to read a line of output it gets back. However, the echo protocol doesn't require this. It echoes each byte as it receives it. It doesn't really care whether those bytes represent characters in some encoding or are divided into lines. Java does not allow you to put the console into "raw" mode, where each character is read as soon as it's typed instead of waiting for the user to press the Enter key. Consequently, if you want to explore the more immediate echo responses, you must provide a nonconsole interface. You also have to separate the network input from user input and network output. This is because the connection is full duplex but may be subject to some delay. If the Internet is running slow, the user may be able to type and send several characters before the server returns the first one. Then the server may return several bytes all at once. Unlike many protocols, echo does not specify lockstep behavior in which the client sends a request but then waits for the full server response before sending any more data. The simplest way to handle such a protocol in Java is to place network input and output in separate threads.

Closing the Socket

That's almost everything you need to know about client-side sockets. When you're writing a client application, almost all the work goes into handling the streams and interpreting the data. The sockets themselves are very easy to work with; all the hard parts are hidden. That is one reason sockets are such a popular paradigm for network programming. After we cover a couple of remaining methods, you'll know everything you need to know to write TCP clients.

public void close( ) throws IOException

Until now, the examples have assumed that sockets close on their own; they haven't done anything to clean up after themselves. It is true that a socket closes automatically when one of its two streams closes, when the program ends, or when it's garbage collected. However, it is a bad practice to assume that the system will close sockets for you, especially for programs that may run for an indefinite period of time. In a socket-intensive program like a web browser, the system may well hit its maximum number of open sockets before the garbage collector kicks in. The port scanner programs of Example 9-1 and 9-2 are particularly bad offenders in this respect, since it may take a long time for the program to run through all the ports. Shortly, you'll see a new version that doesn't have this problem.

When you're through with a socket, you should call its close( ) method to disconnect. Ideally, you put this in a finally block so that the socket is closed whether an exception is thrown or not. The syntax is straightforward:

```
Socket connection = null;
try {
  connection = new Socket("www.oreilly.com", 13);
  // interact with the socket...
```

```
    } // end try
    catch (UnknownHostException ex) {
      System.err.println(ex);
    }
    catch (IOException ex) {
      System.err.println(ex);
    }
    finally {
      if (connection != null) connection.close();
    }
```

Once a Socket has been closed, its InetAddress, port number, local address, and local port number are still accessible through the getInetAddress( ), getPort( ), getLocalAddress( ), and getLocalPort( ) methods. However, although you can still call getInputStream( ) or getOutputStream( ), attempting to read data from the InputStream or write data to the OutputStream throws an IOException.

Example 9-7 is a revision of the PortScanner program that closes each socket once it's through with it. It does not close sockets that fail to connect. Since these are never opened, they don't need to be closed. In fact, if the constructor failed, connection is actually null.

Example 9-7. Look for ports with socket closing

```
import java.net.*;
import java.io.*;

public class PortScanner {

  public static void main(String[] args) {

    String host = "localhost";

    if (args.length > 0) {
      host = args[0];
    }

    try {
      InetAddress theAddress = InetAddress.getByName(host);
      for (int i = 1; i < 65536; i++) {
        Socket connection = null;
        try {
          connection = new Socket(host, i);
          System.out.println("There is a server on port "
          + i + " of " + host);
        }
        catch (IOException ex) {
          // must not be a server on this port
        }
        finally {
          try {
            if (connection != null) connection.close();
          }
```

Example 9-7. Look for ports with socket closing (continued)

```
        catch (IOException ex) {}
      }
    } // end for
  } // end try
  catch (UnknownHostException ex) {
    System.err.println(ex);
  }

 } // end main

} // end PortScanner
```

Java 1.4 adds an isClosed( ) method that returns true is the socket has been closed, false if it isn't:

```
public boolean isClosed( ) // Java 1.4
```

If you're uncertain about a socket's state, you can check it with this method rather than risking an IOException. For example,

```
if (socket.isClosed( )) {
  // do something...
}
else {
  // do something else...
}
```

However, this is not a perfect test. If the socket has never been connected in the first place, isClosed( ) returns false, even though the socket isn't exactly open.

Java 1.4 also adds an isConnected( ) method:

```
public boolean isConnected( ) // Java 1.4
```

The name is a little misleading. It does not tell you if the socket is currently connected to a remote host (that is, if it is unclosed). Instead it tells you whether the socket has ever been connected to a remote host. If the socket was able to connect to the remote host at all, then this method returns true, even after that socket has been closed. To tell if a socket is currently open, you need to check that isConnected( ) returns true and isClosed( ) returns false. For example:

```
boolean connected = socket.isConnected() && ! socket.isClosed( );
```

Java 1.4 also adds an isBound( ) method:

```
public boolean isBound( ) // Java 1.4
```

Whereas isConnected( ) refers to the remote end of the socket, isBound( ) refers to the local end. It tells you whether the socket successfully bound to the outgoing port on the local system. This isn't very important in practice. It will become more important when we discuss server sockets in the next chapter.

Half-closed sockets // Java 1.3

The close( ) method shuts down both input and output from the socket. On occasion, you may want to shut down only half of the connection, either input or output. Starting in Java 1.3, the shutdownInput( ) and shutdownOutput( ) methods let you close only half of the connection:

```
public void shutdownInput() throws IOException   // Java 1.3
public void shutdownOutput() throws IOException  // Java 1.3
```

This doesn't actually close the socket. However, it does adjust the stream connected to it so that it thinks it's at the end of the stream. Further reads from the input stream will return −1. Further writes to the output stream will throw an IOException.

Many protocols, such as finger, whois, and HTTP begin with the client sending a request to the server, then reading the response. It would be possible to shut down the output after the client has sent the request. For example, this code fragment sends a request to an HTTP server and then shuts down the output, since it won't need to write anything else over this socket:

```
Socket connection = null;
try {
  connection = new Socket("www.oreilly.com", 80);
  Writer out = new OutputStreamWriter(
   connection.getOutputStream( ), "8859_1");
  out.write("GET / HTTP 1.0\r\n\r\n");
  out.flush( );
  connection.shutdownOutput( );
  // read the response...
}
catch (IOException ex) {
}
finally {
  try {
    if (connection != null) connection.close();
  }
    catch (IOException ex) {}
}
```

Notice that even though you shut down half or even both halves of a connection, you still need to close the socket when you're through with it. The shutdown methods simply affect the socket's streams. They don't release the resources associated with the socket such as the port it occupies.

Java 1.4 adds two methods that tell you whether the input and output streams are open or closed:

```
public boolean isInputShutdown( )   // Java 1.4
public boolean isOutputShutdown( )  // Java 1.4
```

You can use these (rather than isConnected( ) and isClosed( )) to more specifically ascertain whether you can read from or write to a socket.

Setting Socket Options

Socket options specify how the native sockets on which the Java Socket class relies send and receive data. You can set four options in Java 1.1, six in Java 1.2, seven in Java 1.3, and eight in Java 1.4:

- TCP_NODELAY
- SO_BINDADDR
- SO_TIMEOUT
- SO_LINGER
- SO_SNDBUF (Java 1.2 and later)
- SO_RCVBUF (Java 1.2 and later)
- SO_KEEPALIVE (Java 1.3 and later)
- OOBINLINE (Java 1.4 and later)

The funny-looking names for these options are taken from the named constants in the C header files used in Berkeley Unix where sockets were invented. Thus they follow classic Unix C naming conventions rather than the more legible Java naming conventions. For instance, SO_SNDBUF really means "Socket Option Send Buffer Size."

TCP_NODELAY

```
public void setTcpNoDelay(boolean on) throws SocketException
public boolean getTcpNoDelay() throws SocketException
```

Setting TCP_NODELAY to true ensures that packets are sent as quickly as possible regardless of their size. Normally, small (one-byte) packets are combined into larger packets before being sent. Before sending another packet, the local host waits to receive acknowledgment of the previous packet from the remote system. This is known as *Nagle's algorithm*. The problem with Nagle's algorithm is that if the remote system doesn't send acknowledgments back to the local system fast enough, applications that depend on the steady transfer of small bits of information may slow down. This issue is especially problematic for GUI programs such as games or network computer applications where the server needs to track client-side mouse movement in real time. On a really slow network, even simple typing can be too slow because of the constant buffering. Setting TCP_NODELAY to true defeats this buffering scheme, so that all packets are sent as soon as they're ready.

setTcpNoDelay(true) turns off buffering for the socket. setTcpNoDelay(false) turns it back on. getTcpNoDelay() returns true if buffering is off and false if buffering is on. For example, the following fragment turns off buffering (that is, it turns on TCP_NODELAY) for the socket s if it isn't already off:

```
if (!s.getTcpNoDelay()) s.setTcpNoDelay(true);
```

These two methods are each declared to throw a SocketException. They will be thrown only if the underlying socket implementation doesn't support the TCP_NODELAY option.

SO_LINGER

```
public void setSoLinger(boolean on, int seconds) throws SocketException
public int getSoLinger() throws SocketException
```

The SO_LINGER option specifies what to do with datagrams that have not yet been sent when a socket is closed. By default, the close() method returns immediately; but the system still tries to send any remaining data. If the linger time is set to zero, any unsent packets are thrown away when the socket is closed. If the linger time is any positive value, the close() method blocks while waiting the specified number of seconds for the data to be sent and the acknowledgments to be received. When that number of seconds has passed, the socket is closed and any remaining data is not sent, acknowledgment or no.

These two methods each throw a SocketException if the underlying socket implementation does not support the SO_LINGER option. The setSoLinger() method can also throw an IllegalArgumentException if you try to set the linger time to a negative value. However, the getSoLinger() method may return –1 to indicate that this option is disabled, and as much time as is needed is taken to deliver the remaining data; for example, to set the linger timeout for the Socket s to four minutes, if it's not already set to some other value:

```
if (s.getTcpSoLinger() == -1) s.setSoLinger(true, 240);
```

The maximum linger time is 65,535 seconds. Times larger than that will be reduced to 65,535 seconds. Frankly, 65,535 seconds (more than 18 hours) is much longer than you actually want to wait. Generally, the platform default value is more appropriate.

SO_TIMEOUT

```
public void setSoTimeout(int milliseconds)
  throws SocketException
publicint getSoTimeout() throws SocketException
```

Normally when you try to read data from a socket, the read() call blocks as long as necessary to get enough bytes. By setting SO_TIMEOUT, you ensure that the call will not block for more than a fixed number of milliseconds. When the timeout expires, an InterruptedIOException is thrown, and you should be prepared to catch it. However, the socket is still connected. Although this read() call failed, you can try to read from the socket again. The next call may succeed.

Timeouts are given in milliseconds. Zero is interpreted as an infinite timeout; it is the default value. For example, to set the timeout value of the Socket object s to 3 minutes if it isn't already set, specify 180,000 milliseconds:

```
if (s.getSoTimeout() == 0) s.setSoTimeout(180000);
```

These two methods each throw a SocketException if the underlying socket implementation does not support the SO_TIMEOUT option. The setSoTimeout() method also throws an IllegalArgumentException if the specified timeout value is negative.

SO_RCVBUF

Most TCP stacks use buffers to improve network performance. Larger buffers tend to improve performance for reasonably fast (say, 10Mbps and up) connections while slower, dialup connections do better with smaller buffers. Generally, transfers of large, continuous blocks of data, which are common in file transfer protocols such as FTP and HTTP, benefit from large buffers, while the smaller transfers of interactive sessions, such as Telnet and many games, do not. Relatively old operating systems designed in the age of small files and slow networks, such as BSD 4.2, use 2-kilobyte buffers. Somewhat newer systems, such as SunOS 4.1.3, use larger 4-kilobyte buffers by default. Still newer systems, such as Solaris, use 8- or even 16-kilobyte buffers. Starting in Java 1.2, there are methods to get and set the suggested receive buffer size used for network input:

```
public void setReceiveBufferSize(int size)// Java 1.2
  throws SocketException, IllegalArgumentException
public int getReceiveBufferSize() throws SocketException  // Java 1.2
```

The getReceiveBufferSize() method returns the number of bytes in the buffer that can be used for input from this socket. It throws a SocketException if the underlying socket implementation does not recognize the SO_RCVBUF option. This might happen on a non-POSIX operating system.

The setReceiveBufferSize() method suggests a number of bytes to use for buffering output on this socket. However, the underlying implementation is free to ignore this suggestion. The setReceiveBufferSize() method throws an IllegalArgument-Exception if its argument is less than or equal to zero. Although it's declared to also throw SocketException, it probably won't in practice since a SocketException is thrown for the same reason as IllegalArgumentException and the check for the IllegalArgument Exception is made first.

SO_SNDBUF

Starting in Java 1.2, there are methods to get and set the suggested send buffer size used for network output:

```
public void setSendBufferSize(int size)              // Java 1.2
  throws SocketException, IllegalArgumentException
public int getSendBufferSize() throws SocketException  // Java 1.2
```

The getSendBufferSize() method returns the number of bytes in the buffer used for output on this socket. It throws a SocketException if the underlying socket implementation doesn't understand the SO_SNDBUF option.

The setSendBufferSize( ) method suggests a number of bytes to use for buffering output on this socket. However, again thegggg client is free to ignore this suggestion. The setSendBufferSize( ) method also throws a SocketException if the underlying socket implementation doesn't understand the SO_SNDBUF option. However, it throws an IllegalArgumentException if its argument is less than or equal to zero.

SO_KEEPALIVE

If SO_KEEPALIVE is turned on, the client will occasionally send a data packet over an idle connection (most commonly once every two hours), just to make sure the server hasn't crashed. If the server fails to respond to this packet, the client keeps trying for a little more than 11 minutes until it receives a response. If it doesn't receive a response within 12 minutes, the client closes the socket. Without SO_KEEPALIVE, an inactive client could live more or less forever without noticing that the server had crashed.

Java 1.3 adds methods to turn SO_KEEPALIVE on and off and to determine its current state:

```
public void setKeepAlive(boolean on) throws SocketException // Java 1.3
public boolean getKeepAlive( ) throws SocketException // Java 1.3
```

The default for SO_KEEPALIVE is false. This code fragment turns SO_KEEPALIVE off, if it's turned on:

```
if (s.getKeepAlive( )) s.setKeepAlive(false);
```

OOBINLINE // Java 1.4

TCP includes a feature that sends a single byte of "urgent" data. This data is sent immediately. Furthermore, the receiver is notified when the urgent data is received and may elect to process the urgent data before it processes any other data that has already been received.

Java 1.4 adds support for both sending and receiving such urgent data. The sending method is named, obviously enough, sendUrgentData( ):

```
public void sendUrgentData(int data) throws IOException  // Java 1.4
```

This method sends the lowest order byte of its argument almost immediately. If necessary, any currently cached data is flushed first.

How the receiving end responds to urgent data is a little confused, and varies from one platform and API to the next. Some systems receive the urgent data separately from the regular data. However, the more common, more modern approach is to place the urgent data in the regular received data queue in its proper order, tell the application that urgent data is available, and let it hunt through the queue to find it.

By default, Java pretty much ignores urgent data received from a socket. However, if you want to receive urgent data inline with regular data, you need to set the OOBIN-LINE option to true using these methods:

```
public void setOOBInline(boolean on) throws SocketException // Java 1.3
public boolean getOOBInline( ) throws SocketException // Java 1.3
```

The default for OOBInline is false. This code fragment turns OOBInline on, if it's turned off:

```
if (s.getOOBInline( )) s.setOOBInline(true);
```

Once OOBInline is turned on, any urgent data that arrives will be placed on the socket's input stream to be read in the usual way. Java does not distinguish it from non-urgent data.

SO_REUSEADDR // Java 1.4

When a socket is closed, it may not immediately release the local address, especially if a connection was open when the socket was closed. It can sometimes wait for a small amount of time to make sure it receives any lingering packets that were addressed to the port that were still crossing the network when the socket was closed. The system won't do anything with any of the late packets it receives. It just wants to make sure they don't accidentally get fed into a new process that has bound to the same port.

This isn't a big problem on a random port, but it can be an issue if the socket has bound to a well-known port because it prevents any other socket from using that port in the meantime. If the SO_REUSEADDR is turned on (it's turned off by default), another socket is allowed to bind to the port even while data may be outstanding for the previous socket.

In Java this option is controlled by these two methods:

```
public void setReuseAddress(boolean on) throws SocketException
public boolean getReuseAddress( ) throws SocketException
```

For this to work, setReuseAddress( ) must be called *before* the new socket binds to the port. This means the socket must be created in an unconnected state using the no-args constructor; then setReuseAddress(true) is called, and the socket is connected using the connect( ) method. Both the socket that was previously connected and the new socket reusing the old address must set SO_REUSEADDR to true for it to take effect.

Class of Service

In the last few years, a lot of thought has gone into deriving different classes of service for different types of data that may be transferred across the Internet. For instance, video needs relatively high bandwidth and low latency for good performance, whereas email can be passed over low-bandwidth connections and even held up for several hours without major harm. It might be wise to price the different classes of service differentially so that people won't ask for the highest class of service automatically. After all, if sending an overnight letter cost the same as sending a package via media mail, we'd all just use Fed Ex overnight, which would quickly become congested and overwhelmed. The Internet is no different.

Currently, four traffic classes have been defined for TCP data, although not all routers and native TCP stacks support them. These classes are low cost, high reliability, maximum throughput, and minimum delay. Furthermore, they can be combined. For instance, you can request the minimum delay available at low cost. These measure are all fuzzy and relative, not hard and fast guarantees of service.

Java lets you inspect and set the class of service for a socket using these two methods:

```
public int getTrafficClass( ) throws SocketException
public void setTrafficClass(int trafficClass) throws SocketException
```

The traffic class is given as an int between 0 and 255. (Values outside this range cause IllegalArgumentExceptions.) This int is a combination of bit-flags. Specifically:

- 0x02: Low cost
- 0x04: High reliability
- 0x08: Maximum throughput
- 0x10: Minimum delay

The lowest order, ones bit must be zero. The other three high order bits are not yet used. For example, this code fragment requests a low cost connection:

```
Socket s = new Socket("www.yahoo.com", 80);
s.setTrafficClass(0x02);
```

This code fragment requests a connection with maximum throughput and minimum delay:

```
Socket s = new Socket("www.yahoo.com", 80);
s.setTrafficClass(0x08 | 0x10);
```

The underlying socket implementation is not required to respect any of these requests. They only provide a hint to the TCP stack about the desired policy. Many implementations ignore these values completely. If the TCP stack is unable to provide the requested class of service, it may but is not required to throw a SocketException.

Java does not provide any means to access pricing information for the different classes of service. Be aware that your ISP may charge you for faster or more reliable connections using these features. (If they make it available at all. This is all still pretty bleeding edge stuff.)

Java 1.5 adds a slightly different method to set preferences, the setPerformancePreferences( ) method:

```
public void setPerformancePreferences(int connectionTime, int latency, int bandwidth)
```

This method expresses the relative preferences given to connection time, latency, and bandwidth. For instance, if connectionTime is 2 and latency is 1 and bandwidth is 3, then maximum bandwidth is the most important characteristic, minimum latency is the least important, and connection time is in the middle. Exactly how any given VM implements this is implementation-dependent. Indeed, it may be a no-op in some implementations. The documentation even suggests using non-TCP/IP sockets, though it's not at all clear what that means.

The Object Methods

The Socket class overrides only one of the standard methods from java.lang.Object, toString( ). Since sockets are transitory objects that typically last only as long as the connection they represent, there's not much need or purpose to storing them in hash tables or comparing them to each other. Therefore, Socket does not override equals( ) or hashCode( ), and the semantics for these methods are those of the Object class. Two Socket objects are equal to each other if and only if they are the same socket.

public String toString( )

The toString( ) method produces a string that looks like this:

```
Socket[addr=www.oreilly.com/198.112.208.11,port=80,localport=50055]
```

This is ugly and useful primarily for debugging. Don't rely on this format; it may change in the future. All parts of this string are accessible directly through other methods (specifically getInetAddress( ), getPort( ), and getLocalPort( )).

Socket Exceptions

Most methods of the Socket class are declared to throw IOException or its subclass, java.net.SocketException:

```
public class SocketException extends IOException
```

However, knowing that a problem occurred is often not sufficient to deal with the problem. Did the remote host refuse the connection because it was busy? Did the remote host refuse the connection because no service was listening on the port? Did the connection attempt timeout because of network congestion or because the host was down? There are several subclasses of SocketException that provide more information about what went wrong and why:

```
public class BindException extends SocketException
public class ConnectException extends SocketException
public class NoRouteToHostException extends SocketException
```

A BindException is thrown if you try to construct a Socket or ServerSocket object on a local port that is in use or that you do not have sufficient privileges to use. A ConnectException is thrown when a connection is refused at the remote host, which usually happens because the host is busy or no process is listening on that port. Finally, a NoRouteToHostException indicates that the connection has timed out.

The java.net package also includes ProtocolException, a direct subclass of IOException:

```
public class ProtocolException extends IOException
```

This is thrown when data is received from the network that somehow violates the TCP/IP specification.

None of these exception classes have any special methods you wouldn't find in any other exception class, but you can take advantage of these subclasses to provide more informative error messages or to decide whether retrying the offending operation is likely to be successful.

Socket Addresses

The SocketAddress class introduced in Java 1.4 represents a connection endpoint. The actual java.net.SocketAddress class is an empty abstract class with no methods aside from a default constructor:

```
package java.net.*;

public abstract class SocketAddress {

  public SocketAddress() {}

}
```

At least theoretically, this class can be used for both TCP and non-TCP sockets. Subclasses of SocketAddress provide more detailed information appropriate for the type of socket. In practice, only TCP/IP sockets are currently supported.

The primary purpose of the SocketAddress class is to provide a convenient store for transient socket connection information such as the IP address and port that can be reused to create new sockets, even after the original socket is disconnected and garbage collected. To this end, the Socket class offers two methods that return SocketAddress objects: getRemoteSocketAddress() returns the address of the system being connected to and getLocalSocketAdddress() returns the address from which the connection is made:

```
public SocketAddress getRemoteSocketAddress()
public SocketAddress getLocalSocketAddress()
```

Both of these methods return null if the socket is not yet connected.

A SocketAddress is necessary to connect an unconnected socket via the connect( ) method:

```
public void connect(SocketAddress endpoint) throws IOException
```

For example, first you might connect to Yahoo, then store its address:

```
Socket socket = new Socket("www.yahoo.com", 80);
SocketAddress yahoo = socket.getRemoteSocketAddress( );
socket.close( );
```

Later, you could reconnect to Yahoo using this address:

```
socket = new Socket( );
socket.connect(yahoo);
```

Not all socket implementations can use the same subclasses of SocketAddress. If an instance of the wrong type is passed to connect( ), it throws an IllegalArgumentException.

You can pass an int as the second argument to specify the number of milliseconds to wait before the connection times out:

```
public void connect(SocketAddress endpoint, int timeout) throws IOException
```

The default, 0, means wait forever.

Examples

HotJava was one of the first large-scale Java programs; it's a web browser that was easily the equal of the early versions of Mosaic. HotJava has been discontinued, but there are numerous network-aware applications written in Java, including the LimeWire Gnutella client, the Eclipse IDE, and the JBoss application server. It is completely possible to write commercial-quality applications in Java; and it is especially possible to write network-aware applications, both clients and servers. This section shows two network clients, finger and whois, to illustrate this point. I stop short of what could be done, but only in the user interface. All the necessary networking code is present. Indeed, once again we find out that network code is easy; it's user interfaces that are hard.

Finger

Finger is a straightforward protocol described in RFC 1288. The client makes a TCP connection to the server on port 79 and sends a one-line query; the server responds to the query and closes the connection. The format of the query is precisely defined, the format of the response somewhat less so. All data transferred should probably be pure printable ASCII text, although unfortunately, the specification contradicts itself repeatedly on this point. The specification also recommends that clients filter out any non-ASCII data they do receive, at least by default. All lines must end with a carriage return/linefeed pair (\r\n in Java parlance).

Failure to filter nonprintable characters allows mischievous users to configure their *.plan* files to reset people's terminals, switch them into graphics mode, or play other tricks accessible to those with intimate knowledge of VT-terminal escape sequences. While amusing to experienced users who recognize what's going on and appreciate the hack value of such *.plan* files, these tricks do confuse and terrify the uninitiated.

The simplest allowable request from the client is a bare carriage return/linefeed pair, which is usually interpreted as a request to show a list of the currently logged-in users. For example:

```
% telnet rama.poly.edu 79
Trying 128.238.10.212...
Connected to rama.poly.edu.
Escape character is '^]'.

Login     Name          TTY      Idle   When      Where
jacola    Jane Colaginae  *pts/7           Tue 08:01  208.34.37.104
marcus    Marcus Tullius   pts/15   13d   Tue 17:33  farm-dialup11.poly.e
matewan   Sepin Matewan   *pts/17  17:    Thu 15:32  128.238.10.177
hengpi    Heng Pin        *pts/10          Tue 10:36  128.238.18.119
nadats    Nabeel Datsun    pts/12   56    Mon 10:38  128.238.213.227
matewan   Sepin Matewan   *pts/8    4     Sun 18:39  128.238.10.177
Connection closed by foreign host.
```

It is also possible to request information about a specific user or username by including that user or username on the query line:

```
% telnet rama.poly.edu 79
Trying 128.238.10.212...
Connected to rama.poly.edu.
Escape character is '^]'.
marcus
Login     Name          TTY      Idle   When      Where
marcus    Marcus Tullius   pts/15   13d   Tue 17:33  farm-dialup11.poly.e
```

The information that finger servers return typically includes the user's full name, where he's connected from, how long he has been connected, and any other information he has chosen to make available in his *.plan* file. A few servers put finger to other uses; for example, several sites give you a list of recent earthquake activity. Vending machines connected to the Internet return a list of items available for purchase. It is possible to request information about users via their first name, last name, or login name. You can also request information about more than one user at a time like this:

```
% telnet rama.poly.edu 79
Trying 128.238.10.212...
Connected to rama.poly.edu.
Escape character is '^]'.
marcus nadats matewan
```

```
Login      Name          TTY     Idle   When     Where
marcus     Marcus Tullius  pts/15  13d Tue 17:33  farm-dialup11.poly.e
nadats     Nabeel Datsun   pts/12   59 Mon 10:38  128.238.213.227
matewan    Sepin Matewan  *pts/17  17: Thu 15:32  128.238.10.177
matewan    Sepin Matewan  *pts/8    8 Sun 18:39  128.238.10.177
Connection closed by foreign host.
```

In this section, we'll develop a Java finger client that allows users to specify a hostname on the command line, followed by zero or more usernames. For example, a typical command line will look like:

```
% java FingerClient hostname user1 user2 ...
```

FingerClient connects to port 79 on the specified host. The socket's OutputStream is chained to an OutputStreamWriter using the ISO 8859-1 encoding, which sends a line consisting of all the names on the command line, followed by a carriage return and a linefeed. Next, the output from the server (which is input to the program) is taken from theSocket.getInputStream( ) and chained first to a BufferedInputStream for performance and then to an InputStreamReader so the server response can be read as text. The server's output is presented to the user on System.out. Example 9-8 shows the code.

Example 9-8. A Java command-line finger client

```java
import java.net.*;
import java.io.*;

public class FingerClient {

  public final static int DEFAULT_PORT = 79;

  public static void main(String[] args) {

    String hostname = "localhost";

    try {
      hostname = args[0];
    }
    catch (ArrayIndexOutOfBoundsException ex) {
      hostname = "localhost";
    }

    Socket connection = null;
    try {
      connection = new Socket(hostname, DEFAULT_PORT);
      Writer out = new OutputStreamWriter(
       connection.getOutputStream( ), "8859_1");
      for (int i = 1; i < args.length; i++) out.write(args[i] + " ");
      out.write("\r\n");
      out.flush( );
      InputStream raw = connection.getInputStream( );
      BufferedInputStream buffer = new BufferedInputStream(raw);
      InputStreamReader in = new InputStreamReader(buffer, "8859_1");
```

Example 9-8. A Java command-line finger client (continued)

```
    int c;
    while ((c = in.read()) != -1) {
     // filter non-printable and non-ASCII as recommended by RFC 1288
      if ((c >= 32 && c < 127) || c == '\t' || c == '\r' || c == '\n')
      {
        System.out.write(c);
      }
    }
  }
  catch (IOException ex) {
    System.err.println(ex);
  }
  finally {
    try {
      if (connection != null) connection.close();
    }
    catch (IOException ex) {}
  }

  }

}
```

Here are some samples of this program running:

```
D:\JAVA\JNP2\examples\10>java FingerClient rama.poly.edu
Login    Name              TTY       Idle   When      Where
jacolag  Jane Colaginae    *pts/7           Tue 08:01  208.34.37.104
hengpi   Heng Pin          pts/9     5      Tue 14:09  128.238.18.119
marcus   Marcus Tullius    pts/15    13d    Tue 17:33  farm-dialup11.poly.e
matewan  Sepin Matewan     *pts/17   17:    Thu 15:32  128.238.10.177
hengpi   Heng Pin          *pts/10          Tue 10:36  128.238.18.119
nadats   Nabeel Datsun     pts/12    1:05   Mon 10:38  128.238.213.227
nadats   Nabeel Datsun     pts/12    1:05   Mon 10:38  128.238.213.227
matewan  Sepin Matewan     *pts/8    14     Sun 18:39  128.238.10.177

D:\JAVA\JNP2\examples\10>java FingerClient rama.poly.edu marcus
Login    Name              TTY       Idle   When      Where
Marcus   Marcus Tullius    pts/15    13d    Tue 17:33  farm-dialup11.poly.e
```

Whois

Whois is a simple directory service protocol defined in RFC 954; it was originally designed to keep track of administrators responsible for Internet hosts and domains. A whois client connects to one of several central servers and requests directory information for a person or persons; it can usually give you a phone number, an email address, and a snail mail address (not necessarily current ones, though). With the explosive growth of the Internet, flaws have become apparent in the whois protocol, most notably its centralized nature. A more complex replacement called whois++ is documented in RFCs 1913 and 1914 but has not been widely implemented.

Let's begin with a simple client to connect to a whois server. The basic structure of the whois protocol is:

1. The client opens a TCP socket to port 43 on the server.

2. The client sends a search string terminated by a carriage return/linefeed pair (\r\n). The search string can be a name, a list of names, or a special command, as discussed below. You can also search for domain names, like *oreilly.com* or *netscape.com*, which give you information about a network.

3. The server sends an unspecified amount of human-readable information in response to the command and closes the connection.

4. The client displays this information to the user.

The search string the client sends has a fairly simple format. At its most basic, it's just the name of the person you're searching for. Here's a simple whois search for "Harold":

```
% telnet whois.internic.net 43
Trying 198.41.0.6...
Connected to whois.internic.net.
Escape character is '^]'.
Harold

Whois Server Version 1.3

Domain names in the .com and .net domains can now be registered
with many different competing registrars. Go to http://www.internic.net
for detailed information.

HAROLD.NET
HAROLD.COM

To single out one record, look it up with "xxx", where xxx is one of the
of the records displayed above. If the records are the same, look them up
with "=xxx" to receive a full display for each record.

>>> Last update of whois database: Tue, 16 Dec 2003 18:36:16 EST <<<

NOTICE: The expiration date displayed in this record is the date the
registrar's sponsorship of the domain name registration in the registry is
currently set to expire. This date does not necessarily reflect the expiration
date of the domain name registrant's agreement with the sponsoring
registrar.  Users may consult the sponsoring registrar's Whois database to
view the registrar's reported date of expiration for this registration.

TERMS OF USE: You are not authorized to access or query our Whois
database through the use of electronic processes that are high-volume and
automated except as reasonably necessary to register domain names or
modify existing registrations; the Data in VeriSign Global Registry
Services' ("VeriSign") Whois database is provided by VeriSign for
information purposes only, and to assist persons in obtaining information
about or related to a domain name registration record. VeriSign does not
```

guarantee its accuracy. By submitting a Whois query, you agree to abide
by the following terms of use: You agree that you may use this Data only
for lawful purposes and that under no circumstances will you use this Data
to: (1) allow, enable, or otherwise support the transmission of mass
unsolicited, commercial advertising or solicitations via e-mail, telephone,
or facsimile; or (2) enable high volume, automated, electronic processes
that apply to VeriSign (or its computer systems). The compilation,
repackaging, dissemination or other use of this Data is expressly
prohibited without the prior written consent of VeriSign. You agree not to
use electronic processes that are automated and high-volume to access or
query the Whois database except as reasonably necessary to register
domain names or modify existing registrations. VeriSign reserves the right
to restrict your access to the Whois database in its sole discretion to ensure
operational stability. VeriSign may restrict or terminate your access to the
Whois database for failure to abide by these terms of use. VeriSign
reserves the right to modify these terms at any time.

The Registry database contains ONLY .COM, .NET, .EDU domains and
Registrars.
Connection closed by foreign host.

Although the previous input has a pretty clear format, that format is regrettably nonstandard. Different whois servers can and do send decidedly different output. For
example, here are the first couple of results from the same search at the main French
whois server, *whois.nic.fr*:

```
% telnet whois.nic.fr 43
telnet whois.nic.fr 43
Trying 192.134.4.18...
Connected to winter.nic.fr.
Escape character is '^]'.
Harold

Tous droits reserves par copyright.
Voir http://www.nic.fr/outils/dbcopyright.html
Rights restricted by copyright.
See http://www.nic.fr/outils/dbcopyright.html

person:        Harold Potier
address:       ARESTE
address:       154 Avenue Du Brezet
address:       63000 Clermont-Ferrand
address:       France
phone:         +33 4 73 42 67 67
fax-no:        +33 4 73 42 67 67
nic-hdl:       HP4305-FRNIC
mnt-by:        OLEANE-NOC
changed:       hostmaster@oleane.net 20000510
changed:       migration-dbm@nic.fr 20001015
source:        FRNIC

person:        Harold Israel
address:       LE PARADIS LATIN
address:       28 rue du Cardinal Lemoine
```

```
address:       Paris, France 75005 FR
phone:         +33 1 43252828
fax-no:        +33 1 43296363
e-mail:        info@cie.fr
nic-hdl:       HI68-FRNIC
notify:        info@cie.fr
changed:       registrar@ns.il 19991011
changed:       migration-dbm@nic.fr 20001015
source:        FRNIC
```

Here each complete record is returned rather than just a list of sites. Other whois servers may use still other formats. This protocol is not at all designed for machine processing. You pretty much have to write new code to handle the output of each different whois server. However, regardless of the output format, each response likely contains a *handle*, which in the Internic output is a domain name, and in the nic.fr output is in the nic-hdl field. Handles are guaranteed to be unique, and are used to get more specific information about a person or a network. If you search for a handle, you will get at most one match. If your search only has one match, either because you're lucky or you're searching for a handle, then the server returns a more detailed record. Here's a search for *oreilly.com*. Because there is only one *oreilly.com* in the database, the server returns all the information it has on this domain:

```
% telnet whois.internic.net 43
Trying 198.41.0.6...
Connected to whois.internic.net.
Escape character is '^]'.
oreilly.com

Whois Server Version 1.3

Domain names in the .com and .net domains can now be registered
with many different competing registrars. Go to http://www.internic.net
for detailed information.

   Domain Name: OREILLY.COM
   Registrar: BULKREGISTER, LLC.
   Whois Server: whois.bulkregister.com
   Referral URL: http://www.bulkregister.com
   Name Server: NS1.SONIC.NET
   Name Server: NS.OREILLY.COM
   Status: ACTIVE
   Updated Date: 17-oct-2002
   Creation Date: 27-may-1997
   Expiration Date: 26-may-2004


>>> Last update of whois database: Tue, 16 Dec 2003 18:36:16 EST <<<
...
Connection closed by foreign host.
```

It's easy to implement a simple whois client that connects to *whois.internic.net* and searches for names entered on the command line. Example 9-9 is just such a client.

The server can be changed using the WHOIS_SERVER system property, which can be set on the command line using the -D option. I won't claim this is an exemplary user interface, but it's simple enough to code and lets the example focus more on the interesting network parts of the problem.

Example 9-9. A command-line whois client

```java
import java.net.*;
import java.io.*;

public class WhoisClient {

  public final static int DEFAULT_PORT = 43;
  public final static String DEFAULT_HOST = "whois.internic.net";

  public static void main(String[] args) {

    String serverName = System.getProperty("WHOIS_SERVER", DEFAULT_HOST);

    InetAddress server = null;
    try {
      server = InetAddress.getByName(serverName);
    }
    catch (UnknownHostException ex) {
      System.err.println("Error: Could not locate whois server "
       + server);
      System.err.println("Usage: java -DWHOIS_SERVER=hostname WhoisClient name");
      return;
    }

    try {
      Socket theSocket = new Socket(server, DEFAULT_PORT);
      Writer out = new OutputStreamWriter(theSocket.getOutputStream( ),
       "8859_1");
      for (int i = 0; i < args.length; i++) out.write(args[i] + " ");
      out.write("\r\n");
      out.flush();
      InputStream raw = theSocket.getInputStream( );
      InputStream in  = new BufferedInputStream(theSocket.getInputStream( ));
      int c;
      while ((c = in.read( )) != -1) System.out.write(c);
    }
    catch (IOException ex) {
      System.err.println(ex);
    }

  }

}
```

The class has two final static fields: the DEFAULT_PORT, 43, and the DEFAULT_HOST, *whois.internic.net*. The host can be changed by setting the WHOISE_SERVER system property. The main( ) method begins by opening a socket to this whois server on port 43. The Socket's OutputStream is chained to an OutputStreamWriter. Then each argument on the command-line is written on this stream and sent out over the socket to the whois server. A carriage return/linefeed is written and the writer is flushed.

Next, the Socket's InputStream is stored in the variable raw, which is buffered using the BufferedInputStream in. Since whois is known to use ASCII, bytes are read from this stream with read( ) and copied onto System.out until read( ) returns –1, signaling the end of the server's response. Each character is simply copied onto System.out.

The whois protocol supports several flags you can use to restrict or expand your search. For example, if you know you want to search for a person named "Elliott" but you aren't sure whether he spells his name "Elliot", "Elliott", or perhaps even something as unlikely as "Elliotte", you would type:

```
% whois Person Partial Elliot
```

This tells the whois server that you want only matches for people (not domains, gateways, groups, or the like) whose names begin with the letters "Elliot". Unfortunately, you need to do a separate search if you want to find someone who spells his name "Eliot". The rules for modifying a search are summarized in Table 9-1. Each prefix should be placed before the search string on the command line.

Table 9-1. Whois prefixes

Prefix	Meaning
Domain	Find only domain records.
Gateway	Find only gateway records.
Group	Find only group records.
Host	Find only host records.
Network	Find only network records.
Organization	Find only organization records.
Person	Find only person records.
ASN	Find only autonomous system number records.
Handle or !	Search only for matching handles.
Mailbox or @	Search only for matching email addresses.
Name or :	Search only for matching names.
Expand or *	Search only for group records and show all individuals in that group.
Full or =	Show complete record for each match.
Partial or suffix	Match records that start with the given string.
Summary or $	Show just the summary, even if there's only one match.
SUBdisplay or %	Show the users of the specified host, the hosts on the specified network, etc.

These keywords are all useful and you could use them with the command-line client of Example 9-9, but they're way too much trouble to remember. In fact, most people don't even know that they exist. They just type "whois Harold" at the command-line and sort through the mess that comes back. A good whois client doesn't rely on users remembering arcane keywords; rather, it shows them the options. Supplying this requires a graphical user interface for end users and a better API for client programmers.

Example 9-10 is a more reusable Whois class. Two fields define the state of each Whois object: host, an InetAddress object, and port, an int. Together, these define the server that this particular Whois object connects to. Five constructors set these fields from various combinations of arguments. Furthermore, the host can be changed using the setHost( ) method.

The main functionality of the class is in one method, lookUpNames( ). The lookUpNames( ) method returns a String containing the whois response to a given query. The arguments specify the string to search for, what kind of record to search for, which database to search in, and whether an exact match is required. We could have used strings or int constants to specify the kind of record to search for and the database to search in, but since there are only a small number of valid values, lookUpNames( ) defines public inner classes with a fixed number of members instead. This solution provides much stricter compile-time type-checking and guarantees the Whois class won't have to handle an unexpected value.

Example 9-10. The Whois class

```
import java.net.*;
import java.io.*;
import com.macfaq.io.SafeBufferedReader;


public class Whois {

  public final static int DEFAULT_PORT = 43;
  public final static String DEFAULT_HOST = "whois.internic.net";

  private int port = DEFAULT_PORT;
  private InetAddress host;

  public Whois(InetAddress host, int port) {
    this.host = host;
    this.port = port;
  }

  public Whois(InetAddress host) {
    this(host, DEFAULT_PORT);
  }

  public Whois(String hostname, int port)
   throws UnknownHostException {
```

Example 9-10. The Whois class (continued)

```
    this(InetAddress.getByName(hostname), port);
  }

  public Whois(String hostname) throws UnknownHostException {
    this(InetAddress.getByName(hostname), DEFAULT_PORT);
  }

  public Whois( ) throws UnknownHostException {
    this(DEFAULT_HOST, DEFAULT_PORT);
  }

  // Items to search for
  public static class SearchFor {

    public static SearchFor ANY = new SearchFor( );
    public static SearchFor NETWORK = new SearchFor( );
    public static SearchFor PERSON = new SearchFor( );
    public static SearchFor HOST = new SearchFor( );
    public static SearchFor DOMAIN = new SearchFor( );
    public static SearchFor ORGANIZATION = new SearchFor( );
    public static SearchFor GROUP = new SearchFor( );
    public static SearchFor GATEWAY = new SearchFor( );
    public static SearchFor ASN = new SearchFor( );

    private SearchFor( ) {};

  }

  // Categories to search in
  public static class SearchIn {

    public static SearchIn ALL = new SearchIn( );
    public static SearchIn NAME = new SearchIn( );
    public static SearchIn MAILBOX = new SearchIn( );
    public static SearchIn HANDLE = new SearchIn( );

    private SearchIn( ) {};

  }

  public String lookUpNames(String target, SearchFor category,
   SearchIn group, boolean exactMatch) throws IOException {

    String suffix = "";
    if (!exactMatch) suffix = ".";

    String searchInLabel  = "";
    String searchForLabel = "";

    if (group == SearchIn.ALL) searchInLabel = "";
    else if (group == SearchIn.NAME) searchInLabel = "Name ";
    else if (group == SearchIn.MAILBOX) searchInLabel = "Mailbox ";
```

Example 9-10. The Whois class (continued)

```
    else if (group == SearchIn.HANDLE) searchInLabel = "!";

    if (category == SearchFor.NETWORK) searchForLabel = "Network ";
    else if (category == SearchFor.PERSON) searchForLabel = "Person ";
    else if (category == SearchFor.HOST) searchForLabel = "Host ";
    else if (category == SearchFor.DOMAIN) searchForLabel = "Domain ";
    else if (category == SearchFor.ORGANIZATION) {
      searchForLabel = "Organization ";
    }
    else if (category == SearchFor.GROUP) searchForLabel = "Group ";
    else if (category == SearchFor.GATEWAY) {
      searchForLabel = "Gateway ";
    }
    else if (category == SearchFor.ASN) searchForLabel = "ASN ";

    String prefix = searchForLabel + searchInLabel;
    String query = prefix + target + suffix;

    Socket theSocket = new Socket(host, port);
    Writer out
     = new OutputStreamWriter(theSocket.getOutputStream( ), "ASCII");
    SafeBufferedReader in = new SafeBufferedReader(new
     InputStreamReader(theSocket.getInputStream( ), "ASCII"));
    out.write(query + "\r\n");
    out.flush( );
    StringBuffer response = new StringBuffer( );
    String theLine = null;
    while ((theLine = in.readLine( )) != null) {
      response.append(theLine);
      response.append("\r\n");
    }
    theSocket.close( );

    return response.toString( );

  }

  public InetAddress getHost( ) {
    return this.host;
  }

  public void setHost(String host)
    throws UnknownHostException {
    this.host = InetAddress.getByName(host);
  }

}
```

Figure 9-1 shows one possible interface for a graphical whois client that depends on Example 9-11 for the actual network connections. This interface has a text field to enter the name to be searched for and a checkbox to determine whether the match should be exact or partial. A group of radio buttons lets users specify which group of records they want to search. Another group of radio buttons chooses the fields that should be searched. By default, this client searches all fields of all records for an exact match.

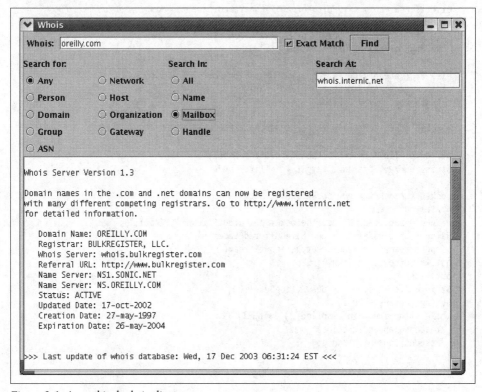

Figure 9-1. A graphical whois client

When a user enters a string in the Whois: text field and presses the Enter or Find button, the program makes a connection to the whois server and retrieves records that match that string. These are placed in the text area in the bottom of the window. Initially, the server is set to *whois.internic.net*, but the user is free to change this setting. Example 9-11 is the program that produces this interface.

Example 9-11. A graphical Whois client interface

```
import javax.swing.*;
import java.awt.*;
import java.awt.event.*;
import java.io.*;
import java.net.*;

public class WhoisGUI extends JFrame {
```

Example 9-11. A graphical Whois client interface (continued)

```
private JTextField searchString = new JTextField(30);
private JTextArea names = new JTextArea(15, 80);
private JButton findButton = new JButton("Find");;
private ButtonGroup searchIn = new ButtonGroup( );
private ButtonGroup searchFor = new ButtonGroup( );
private JCheckBox exactMatch = new JCheckBox("Exact Match", true);
private JTextField chosenServer = new JTextField( );
private Whois server;

public WhoisGUI(Whois whois) {

  super("Whois");
  this.server = whois;
  Container pane = this.getContentPane( );

  Font f = new Font("Monospaced", Font.PLAIN, 12);
  names.setFont(f);
  names.setEditable(false);

  JPanel centerPanel = new JPanel( );
  centerPanel.setLayout(new GridLayout(1, 1, 10, 10));
  JScrollPane jsp = new JScrollPane(names);
  centerPanel.add(jsp);
  pane.add("Center", centerPanel);

  // You don't want the buttons in the south and north
  // to fill the entire sections so add Panels there
  // and use FlowLayouts in the Panel
  JPanel northPanel = new JPanel( );
  JPanel northPanelTop = new JPanel( );
  northPanelTop.setLayout(new FlowLayout(FlowLayout.LEFT));
  northPanelTop.add(new JLabel("Whois: "));
  northPanelTop.add("North", searchString);
  northPanelTop.add(exactMatch);
  northPanelTop.add(findButton);
  northPanel.setLayout(new BorderLayout(2,1));
  northPanel.add("North", northPanelTop);
  JPanel northPanelBottom = new JPanel( );
  northPanelBottom.setLayout(new GridLayout(1,3,5,5));
  northPanelBottom.add(initRecordType( ));
  northPanelBottom.add(initSearchFields( ));
  northPanelBottom.add(initServerChoice( ));
  northPanel.add("Center", northPanelBottom);

  pane.add("North", northPanel);

  ActionListener al = new LookupNames( );
  findButton.addActionListener(al);
  searchString.addActionListener(al);

}
```

Example 9-11. A graphical Whois client interface (continued)

```java
private JPanel initRecordType( ) {

  JPanel p = new JPanel( );
  p.setLayout(new GridLayout(6, 2, 5, 2));
  p.add(new JLabel("Search for:"));
  p.add(new JLabel(""));

  JRadioButton any = new JRadioButton("Any", true);
  any.setActionCommand("Any");
  searchFor.add(any);
  p.add(any);

  p.add(this.makeRadioButton("Network"));
  p.add(this.makeRadioButton("Person"));
  p.add(this.makeRadioButton("Host"));
  p.add(this.makeRadioButton("Domain"));
  p.add(this.makeRadioButton("Organization"));
  p.add(this.makeRadioButton("Group"));
  p.add(this.makeRadioButton("Gateway"));
  p.add(this.makeRadioButton("ASN"));

  return p;

}

private JRadioButton makeRadioButton(String label) {

  JRadioButton button = new JRadioButton(label, false);
  button.setActionCommand(label);
  searchFor.add(button);
  return button;

}

private JRadioButton makeSearchInRadioButton(String label) {

  JRadioButton button = new JRadioButton(label, false);
  button.setActionCommand(label);
  searchIn.add(button);
  return button;

}

private JPanel initSearchFields( ) {

  JPanel p = new JPanel( );
  p.setLayout(new GridLayout(6, 1, 5, 2));
  p.add(new JLabel("Search In: "));

  JRadioButton all = new JRadioButton("All", true);
  all.setActionCommand("All");
  searchIn.add(all);
```

Example 9-11. A graphical Whois client interface (continued)

```
    p.add(all);

    p.add(this.makeSearchInRadioButton("Name"));
    p.add(this.makeSearchInRadioButton("Mailbox"));
    p.add(this.makeSearchInRadioButton("Handle"));

    return p;

}

private JPanel initServerChoice() {

    final JPanel p = new JPanel();
    p.setLayout(new GridLayout(6, 1, 5, 2));
    p.add(new JLabel("Search At: "));

    chosenServer.setText(server.getHost().getHostName());
    p.add(chosenServer);
    chosenServer.addActionListener( new ActionListener() {
        public void actionPerformed(ActionEvent evt) {
            try {
                InetAddress newHost
                  = InetAddress.getByName(chosenServer.getText());
                Whois newServer = new Whois(newHost);
                server = newServer;
            }
            catch (Exception ex) {
                JOptionPane.showMessageDialog(p,
                    ex.getMessage(), "Alert", JOptionPane.ERROR_MESSAGE);
            }
        }
    } );

    return p;

}

class LookupNames implements ActionListener {

    public void actionPerformed(ActionEvent evt) {

        Whois.SearchIn group = Whois.SearchIn.ALL;
        Whois.SearchFor category = Whois.SearchFor.ANY;

        String searchForLabel = searchFor.getSelection().getActionCommand();
        String searchInLabel = searchIn.getSelection().getActionCommand();
        if (searchInLabel.equals("Name")) group = Whois.SearchIn.NAME;
        else if (searchInLabel.equals("Mailbox")) {
            group = Whois.SearchIn.MAILBOX;
        }
        else if (searchInLabel.equals("Handle")) {
            group = Whois.SearchIn.HANDLE;
```

Example 9-11. A graphical Whois client interface (continued)

```
    }

    if (searchForLabel.equals("Network")) {
      category = Whois.SearchFor.NETWORK;
    }
    else if (searchForLabel.equals("Person")) {
      category = Whois.SearchFor.PERSON;
    }
    else if (searchForLabel.equals("Host")) {
      category = Whois.SearchFor.HOST;
    }
    else if (searchForLabel.equals("Domain")) {
      category = Whois.SearchFor.DOMAIN;
    }
    else if (searchForLabel.equals("Organization")) {
      category = Whois.SearchFor.ORGANIZATION;
    }
    else if (searchForLabel.equals("Group")) {
      category = Whois.SearchFor.GROUP;
    }
    else if (searchForLabel.equals("Gateway")) {
      category = Whois.SearchFor.GATEWAY;
    }
    else if (searchForLabel.equals("ASN")) {
      category = Whois.SearchFor.ASN;
    }

    try {
      names.setText("");
      server.setHost(chosenServer.getText());
      String result = server.lookUpNames(searchString.getText(),
       category, group, exactMatch.isSelected());
      names.setText(result);
    }
    catch (IOException ex) {
      JOptionPane.showMessageDialog(WhoisGUI.this,
        ex.getMessage(), "Lookup Failed", JOptionPane.ERROR_MESSAGE);
    }
  }

}

public static void main(String[] args) {

  try {
    Whois server = new Whois();
    WhoisGUI a = new WhoisGUI(server);
    a.setDefaultCloseOperation(WindowConstants.EXIT_ON_CLOSE);
    a.pack();
    EventQueue.invokeLater(new FrameShower(a));

  }
```

Example 9-11. A graphical Whois client interface (continued)

```
      catch (UnknownHostException ex) {
        JOptionPane.showMessageDialog(null, "Could not locate default host "
          + Whois.DEFAULT_HOST, "Error", JOptionPane.ERROR_MESSAGE);
      }

    }

    private static class FrameShower implements Runnable {

      private final Frame frame;

      FrameShower(Frame frame) {
        this.frame = frame;
      }

      public void run() {
       frame.setVisible(true);
      }

    }

}
```

The main( ) method is the usual block of code to start up a standalone application. It constructs a Whois object and, then uses that to construct a WhoisGUI object. Then the WhoisGUI ( ) constructor sets up the graphical user interface. There's a lot of redundant code here, so it's broken out into the private methods initSearchFields( ), initServerChoice( ), makeSearchInRadioButton( ), and makeSearchForRadioButton( ). As usual with LayoutManager-based interfaces, the setup is fairly involved. Since you'd probably use a visual designer to build such an application, I won't describe it in detail here.

When the constructor returns, the main( ) method attaches an anonymous inner class to the window that will close the application when the window is closed. (This isn't in the constructor because other programs that use this class may not want to exit the program when the window closes.) main( ) then packs and shows the window. To avoid an obscure race condition that can lead to deadlock this needs to be done in the event dispatch thread. Hence the FrameShower inner class that implements Runnable and the call to EventQueue.invokeLater( ). From that point on, all activity takes place in the AWT thread.

The first event this program must respond to is the user's typing a name in the Whois: text field and either pressing the Find button or hitting Enter. In this case, the LookupNames inner class passes the information in the text field and the various radio buttons and checkboxes to the server.lookUpNames( ) method. This method returns a String, which is placed in the names text area.

The second event this program must respond to is the user typing a new host in the server text field. In this case, an anonymous inner class tries to construct a new Whois object and store it in the server field. If it fails (e.g., because the user mistyped the hostname), the old server is restored. An alert box informs the user of this event.

This is not a perfect client by any means. The most glaring omission is that it doesn't provide a way to save the data and quit the program. Less obvious until you run the program is that responsiveness suffers because the network connection is made inside the AWT thread. It would be better to place the connections to the server in their own thread and use callbacks to place the data in the GUI as the data is received. However, implementing callbacks would take us too far afield from the topic of network programming, so I leave them as exercises for the reader.

CHAPTER 10

Sockets for Servers

The last chapter discussed sockets from the standpoint of *clients*: programs that open a socket to a server that's listening for connections. However, client sockets themselves aren't enough; clients aren't much use unless they can talk to a server, and the Socket class discussed in the last chapter is not sufficient for writing servers. To create a Socket, you need to know the Internet host to which you want to connect. When you're writing a server, you don't know in advance who will contact you, and even if you did, you wouldn't know when that host wanted to contact you. In other words, servers are like receptionists who sit by the phone and wait for incoming calls. They don't know who will call or when, only that when the phone rings, they have to pick it up and talk to whoever is there. You can't program that behavior with the Socket class alone.

For servers that accept connections, Java provides a ServerSocket class that represents server sockets. In essence, a server socket's job is to sit by the phone and wait for incoming calls. More technically, a server socket runs on the server and listens for incoming TCP connections. Each server socket listens on a particular port on the server machine. When a client on a remote host attempts to connect to that port, the server wakes up, negotiates the connection between the client and the server, and returns a regular Socket object representing the socket between the two hosts. In other words, server sockets wait for connections while client sockets initiate connections. Once a ServerSocket has set up the connection, the server uses a regular Socket object to send data to the client. Data always travels over the regular socket.

The ServerSocket Class

The ServerSocket class contains everything needed to write servers in Java. It has constructors that create new ServerSocket objects, methods that listen for connections on a specified port, methods that configure the various server socket options, and the usual miscellaneous methods such as toString().

In Java, the basic life cycle of a server program is:

1. A new ServerSocket is created on a particular port using a ServerSocket() constructor.

2. The ServerSocket listens for incoming connection attempts on that port using its accept() method. accept() blocks until a client attempts to make a connection, at which point accept() returns a Socket object connecting the client and the server.

3. Depending on the type of server, either the Socket's getInputStream() method, getOutputStream() method, or both are called to get input and output streams that communicate with the client.

4. The server and the client interact according to an agreed-upon protocol until it is time to close the connection.

5. The server, the client, or both close the connection.

6. The server returns to step 2 and waits for the next connection.

If step 4 is likely to take a long or indefinite amount of time, traditional Unix servers such as wu-ftpd create a new process to handle each connection so that multiple clients can be serviced at the same time. Java programs should spawn a thread to interact with the client so that the server can be ready to process the next connection sooner. A thread places a far smaller load on the server than a complete child process. In fact, the overhead of forking too many processes is why the typical Unix FTP server can't handle more than roughly 400 connections without slowing to a crawl. On the other hand, if the protocol is simple and quick and allows the server to close the connection when it's through, then it will be more efficient for the server to process the client request immediately without spawning a thread.

Although threads are lighter-weight than processes on most systems (Linux is the notable exception), too many threads can still be a performance problem. For instance, on most VMs each thread requires about a megabyte of RAM above and beyond what the rest of the program needs. Thus, on a typical modern server with about a gigabyte of RAM, anything close to or beyond a thousand threads is likely to slow down dramatically and eventually crash as the CPU violently and frequently swaps data into and out of RAM. Spawning too many threads is one of the few ways you can reliably crash any Java virtual machine.

Java 1.4 introduces a ServerSocketChannel class that provides non-blocking, multiplexed I/O based on channels rather than streams. With channels, a single thread can process multiple connections, thereby requiring many fewer threads and placing a much smaller load on the VM. This can be highly advantageous for high volume servers on some operating systems. I'll discuss these kinds of servers in Chapter 12. For simple, low-volume servers or any servers that need to run with Java 1.3 or earlier, the techniques discussed in this chapter should be used.

The operating system stores incoming connection requests addressed to a particular port in a first-in, first-out queue. The default length of the queue is normally 50, although it can vary from operating system to operating system. Some operating systems (not Solaris) have a maximum queue length, typically five. On these systems, the queue length will be the largest possible value less than or equal to 50. After the queue fills to capacity with unprocessed connections, the host refuses additional connections on that port until slots in the queue open up. Many (though not all) clients will try to make a connection multiple times if their initial attempt is refused. The operating system manages incoming connections and the queue; your program does not need to worry about it. Several ServerSocket constructors allow you to change the length of the queue if its default length isn't large enough; however, you won't be able to increase the queue beyond the maximum size that the operating system supports.

The Constructors

There are four public ServerSocket constructors:

```
public ServerSocket(int port) throws BindException, IOException
public ServerSocket(int port, int queueLength)
 throws BindException, IOException
public ServerSocket(int port, int queueLength, InetAddress bindAddress)
 throws IOException
public ServerSocket() throws IOException  // Java 1.4
```

These constructors let you specify the port, the length of the queue used to hold incoming connection requests, and the local network interface to bind to. They pretty much all do the same thing, though some use default values for the queue length and the address to bind to. Let's explore these in order.

public ServerSocket(int port) throws BindException, IOException

This constructor creates a server socket on the port specified by the argument. If you pass 0 for the port number, the system selects an available port for you. A port chosen for you by the system is sometimes called an *anonymous port* since you don't know its number. For servers, anonymous ports aren't very useful because clients need to know in advance which port to connect to; however, there are a few situations (which we will discuss later) in which an anonymous port might be useful.

For example, to create a server socket that would be used by an HTTP server on port 80, you would write:

```
try {
  ServerSocket httpd = new ServerSocket(80);
}
catch (IOException ex) {
  System.err.println(ex);
}
```

The constructor throws an IOException (specifically, a BindException) if the socket cannot be created and bound to the requested port. An IOException when creating a ServerSocket almost always means one of two things. Either another server socket, possibly from a completely different program, is already using the requested port, or you're trying to connect to a port from 1 to 1,023 on Unix (including Linux and Mac OS X) without root (superuser) privileges.

You can use this constructor to write a variation on the PortScanner programs of the previous chapter. Example 10-1 checks for ports on the local machine by attempting to create ServerSocket objects on them and seeing on which ports that fails. If you're using Unix and are not running as root, this program works only for ports 1,024 and above.

Example 10-1. Look for local ports

```
import java.net.*;
import java.io.*;

public class LocalPortScanner {

  public static void main(String[] args) {

    for (int port = 1; port <= 65535; port++) {

      try {
        // the next line will fail and drop into the catch block if
        // there is already a server running on the port
        ServerSocket server = new ServerSocket(port);
      }
      catch (IOException ex) {
        System.out.println("There is a server on port " + port + ".");
      } // end catch

    } // end for

  }

}
```

Here's the output I got when running LocalPortScanner on my Windows NT 4.0 workstation:

```
D:\JAVA\JNP2\examples\11>java LocalPortScanner
There is a server on port 135.
There is a server on port 1025.
There is a server on port 1026.
There is a server on port 1027.
There is a server on port 1028.
```

public ServerSocket(int port, int queueLength)
throws IOException, BindException

This constructor opens a server socket on the specified port with a queue length of your choosing. If the machine has multiple network interfaces or IP addresses, then it listens on this port on all those interfaces and IP addresses. The queueLength argument sets the length of the queue for incoming connection requests—that is, how many incoming connections can be stored at one time before the host starts refusing connections. Some operating systems have a maximum queue length, typically five. If you try to expand the queue past that maximum number, the maximum queue length is used instead. If you pass 0 for the port number, the system selects an available port.

For example, to create a server socket on port 5,776 that would hold up to 100 incoming connection requests in the queue, you would write:

```
try {
  ServerSocket httpd = new ServerSocket(5776, 100);
}
catch (IOException ex) {
  System.err.println(ex);
}
```

The constructor throws an IOException (specifically, a BindException) if the socket cannot be created and bound to the requested port. However, no exception is thrown if the queue length is larger than the host OS supports. Instead, the queue length is simply set to the maximum size allowed.

public ServerSocket(int port, int queueLength, InetAddress bindAddress)
throws BindException, IOException

This constructor binds a server socket to the specified port with the specified queue length. It differs from the other two constructors in binding only to the specified local IP address. This constructor is useful for servers that run on systems with several IP addresses because it allows you to choose the address to which you'll listen. That is, the server socket only listens for incoming connections on the specified address; it won't listen for connections that come in through the host's other addresses. The previous two constructors bind to all local IP addresses by default.

For example, *login.ibiblio.org* is a particular Linux box in North Carolina. It's connected to the Internet with the IP address 152.2.210.122. The same box has a second Ethernet card with the local IP address 192.168.210.122 that is not visible from the public Internet, only from the local network. If for some reason I wanted to run a server on this host that only responded to local connections from within the same network, I could create a server socket that listens on port 5,776 of 192.168.210.122 but not on port 5,776 of 152.2.210.122, like so:

```
try {
  ServerSocket httpd = new ServerSocket(5776, 10,
    InetAddress.getByName("192.168.210.122"));
```

```
    }
    catch (IOException ex) {
      System.err.println(ex);
    }
```

The constructor throws an IOException (again, really a BindException) if the socket cannot be created and bound to the requested port or network interface.

public ServerSocket( ) throws IOException // Java 1.4

The public no-args constructor is new in Java 1.4. It creates a ServerSocket object but does not actually bind it to a port so it cannot initially accept any connections. It can be bound later using the bind( ) methods also introduced in Java 1.4:

```
public void bind(SocketAddress endpoint) throws IOException // Java 1.4
public void bind(SocketAddress endpoint, int queueLength) // Java 1.4
  throws IOException
```

The primary use for this feature is to allow programs to set server socket options before binding to a port. Some options are fixed after the server socket has been bound. The general pattern looks like this:

```
ServerSocket ss = new ServerSocket( );
// set socket options...
SocketAddress  http = new InetSocketAddress(80);
ss.bind(http);
```

You can also past null for the SocketAddress to select an arbitrary port. This is like passing 0 for the port number in the other constructors.

Accepting and Closing Connections

A ServerSocket customarily operates in a loop that repeatedly accepts connections. Each pass through the loop invokes the accept( ) method. This returns a Socket object representing the connection between the remote client and the local server. Interaction with the client takes place through this Socket object. When the transaction is finished, the server should invoke the Socket object's close( ) method. If the client closes the connection while the server is still operating, the input and/or output streams that connect the server to the client throw an InterruptedIOException on the next read or write. In either case, the server should then get ready to process the next incoming connection. However, when the server needs to shut down and not process any further incoming connections, you should invoke the ServerSocket object's close( ) method.

public Socket accept( ) throws IOException

When server setup is done and you're ready to accept a connection, call the ServerSocket's accept( ) method. This method "blocks"; that is, it stops the flow of execution and waits until a client connects. When a client does connect, the accept( )

---

method returns a Socket object. You use the streams returned by this Socket's getInputStream( ) and getOutputStream( ) methods to communicate with the client. For example:

```
ServerSocket server = new ServerSocket(5776);
while (true) {
  Socket connection = server.accept( );
  OutputStreamWriter out
   = new OutputStreamWriter(connection.getOutputStream( ));
  out.write("You've connected to this server. Bye-bye now.\r\n");
  connection.close( );
}
```

If you don't want the program to halt while it waits for a connection, put the call to accept( ) in a separate thread.

 If you're using Java 1.4 or later, you have the option to use channels and non-blocking I/O instead of threads. In some (not all) virtual machines, this is much faster than using streams and threads. These techniques will be discussed in Chapter 12.

When exception handling is added, the code becomes somewhat more convoluted. It's important to distinguish between exceptions that should probably shut down the server and log an error message, and exceptions that should just close that active connection. Exceptions thrown by accept( ) or the input and output streams generally should not shut down the server. Most other exceptions probably should. To do this, you'll need to nest your try blocks.

Finally, most servers will want to make sure that all sockets they accept are closed when they're finished. Even if the protocol specifies that clients are responsible for closing connections, clients do not always strictly adhere to the protocol. The call to close( ) also has to be wrapped in a try block that catches an IOException. However, if you do catch an IOException when closing the socket, ignore it. It just means that the client closed the socket before the server could. Here's a slightly more realistic example:

```
try {
  ServerSocket server = new ServerSocket(5776);
  while (true) {
    Socket connection = server.accept( );
    try {
      Writer out
       = new OutputStreamWriter(connection.getOutputStream( ));
      out.write("You've connected to this server. Bye-bye now.\r\n");
      out.flush( );
      connection.close( );
    }
    catch (IOException ex) {
      // This tends to be a transitory error for this one connection;
      // e.g. the client broke the connection early. Consequently,
```

```
      // you don't want to break the loop or print an error message.
      // However, you might choose to log this exception in an error log.
    }
    finally {
      // Guarantee that sockets are closed when complete.
      try {
        if (connection != null) connection.close( );
      }
      catch (IOException ex) {}
    }
  }
  catch (IOException ex) {
    System.err.println(ex);
  }
```

Example 10-2 implements a simple daytime server, as per RFC 867. Since this server just sends a single line of text in response to each connection, it processes each connection immediately. More complex servers should spawn a thread to handle each request. In this case, the overhead of spawning a thread would be greater than the time needed to process the request.

 If you run this program on Unix (including Linux and Mac OS X), you need to run it as root in order to connect to port 13. If you don't want to or can't run it as root, change the port number to something above 1024—say, 1313.

Example 10-2. A daytime server

```java
import java.net.*;
import java.io.*;
import java.util.Date;

public class DaytimeServer {

  public final static int DEFAULT_PORT = 13;

  public static void main(String[] args) {

    int port = DEFAULT_PORT;
    if (args.length > 0) {
      try {
        port = Integer.parseInt(args[0]);
        if (port < 0 || port >= 65536) {
          System.out.println("Port must between 0 and 65535");
          return;
        }
      }
      catch (NumberFormatException ex) {
        // use default port
      }

    }
```

Example 10-2. A daytime server (continued)

```
try {

    ServerSocket server = new ServerSocket(port);

    Socket connection = null;
    while (true) {

        try {
            connection = server.accept();
            Writer out = new OutputStreamWriter(connection.getOutputStream());
            Date now = new Date();
            out.write(now.toString() +"\r\n");
            out.flush();
            connection.close();
        }
        catch (IOException ex) {}
        finally {
            try {
                if (connection != null) connection.close();
            }
            catch (IOException ex) {}
        }

    } // end while

} // end try
catch (IOException ex) {
    System.err.println(ex);
} // end catch

} // end main

} // end DaytimeServer
```

Example 10-2 is straightforward. The first three lines import the usual packages, java.io and java.net, as well as java.util.Date, which provides the time as read by the server's internal clock. There is a single public final static int field (i.e., a constant) in the class DEFAULT_PORT, which is set to the well-known port for a daytime server (port 13). The class has a single method, main( ), which does all the work. If the port is specified on the command line, then it's read from args[0]. Otherwise, the default port is used.

The outer try block traps any IOExceptions that may arise while the ServerSocket object server is constructed on the daytime port or when it accepts connections. The inner try block watches for exceptions thrown while the connections are accepted and processed. The accept( ) method is called within an infinite loop to watch for new connections; like many servers, this program never terminates but continues listening until an exception is thrown or you stop it manually.

The command for stopping a program manually depends on your system; under Unix, NT, and many other systems, CTRL-C will do the job. If you are running the server in the background on a Unix system, stop it by finding the server's process ID and killing it with the kill command (**kill** *pid*).

When a client connects, accept( ) returns a Socket, which is stored in the local variable connection, and the program continues. It calls getOutputStream( ) to get the output stream associated with that Socket and then chains that output stream to a new OutputStreamWriter, out. A new Date object provides the current time. The content is sent to the client by writing its string representation on out with write( ).

Finally, after the data is sent or an exception has been thrown, the finally block closes the connection. Always close a socket when you're finished with it. In the previous chapter, I said that a client shouldn't rely on the other side of a connection to close the socket: that goes triple for servers. Clients time out or crash; users cancel transactions; networks go down in high-traffic periods. For any of these or a dozen more reasons, you cannot rely on clients to close sockets, even when the protocol requires them to, which this one doesn't.

Sending binary, nontext data is not significantly harder. Example 10-3 demonstrates with a time server that follows the time protocol outlined in RFC 868. When a client connects, the server sends a 4-byte, big-endian, unsigned integer specifying the number of seconds that have passed since 12:00 A.M., January 1, 1900 GMT (the epoch). Once again, the current time is found by creating a new Date object. However, since the Date class counts milliseconds since 12:00 A.M., January 1, 1970 GMT rather than seconds since 12:00 A.M., January 1, 1900 GMT, some conversion is necessary.

Example 10-3. A time server

```
import java.net.*;
import java.io.*;
import java.util.Date;

public class TimeServer {

  public final static int DEFAULT_PORT = 37;

  public static void main(String[] args) {

   int port = DEFAULT_PORT;
   if (args.length > 0) {
     try {
       port = Integer.parseInt(args[0]);
       if (port < 0 || port >= 65536) {
         System.out.println("Port must between 0 and 65535");
         return;
       }
```

Example 10-3. A time server (continued)

```
    }
    catch (NumberFormatException ex) {}
}

// The time protocol sets the epoch at 1900,
// the Date class at 1970. This number
// converts between them.

long differenceBetweenEpochs = 2208988800L;

try {
  ServerSocket server = new ServerSocket(port);
    while (true) {
      Socket connection = null;
      try {
        connection = server.accept( );
        OutputStream out = connection.getOutputStream( );
        Date now = new Date( );
        long msSince1970 = now.getTime( );
        long secondsSince1970 = msSince1970/1000;
        long secondsSince1900 = secondsSince1970
         + differenceBetweenEpochs;
        byte[] time = new byte[4];
        time[0]
         = (byte) ((secondsSince1900 & 0x00000000FF000000L) >> 24);
        time[1]
         = (byte) ((secondsSince1900 & 0x0000000000FF0000L) >> 16);
        time[2]
         = (byte) ((secondsSince1900 & 0x000000000000FF00L) >> 8);
        time[3] = (byte) (secondsSince1900 & 0x00000000000000FFL);
        out.write(time);
        out.flush( );
      } // end try
      catch (IOException ex) {
      } // end catch
      finally {
        if (connection != null) connection.close( );
      }
    } // end while
} // end try
catch (IOException ex) {
  System.err.println(ex);
} // end catch

} // end main

} // end TimeServer
```

As with the TimeClient of the previous chapter, most of the effort here goes into working with a data format (32-bit unsigned integers) that Java doesn't natively support.

public void close( ) throws IOException

If you're finished with a server socket, you should close it, especially if the program is going to continue to run for some time. This frees up the port for other programs that may wish to use it. Closing a ServerSocket should not be confused with closing a Socket. Closing a ServerSocket frees a port on the local host, allowing another server to bind to the port; it also breaks all currently open sockets that the ServerSocket has accepted.

Server sockets are closed automatically when a program dies, so it's not absolutely necessary to close them in programs that terminate shortly after the ServerSocket is no longer needed. Nonetheless, it doesn't hurt. For example, the main loop of the LocalPortScanner program might be better written like this so that it doesn't temporarily occupy most of the ports on the system:

```
for (int port = 1; port <= 65535; port++) {

  try {
    // the next line will fail and drop into the catch block if
    // there is already a server running on the port
    ServerSocket server = new ServerSocket(port);
    server.close();
  }
  catch (IOException ex) {
    System.out.println("There is a server on port " + port + ".");
  }

} // end for
```

After the server socket has been closed, it cannot be reconnected, even to the same port.

Java 1.4 adds an isClosed( ) method that returns true if the ServerSocket has been closed, false if it hasn't:

```
public boolean isClosed() // Java 1.4
```

ServerSocket objects that were created with the no-args ServerSocket( ) constructor and not yet bound to a port are not considered to be closed. Invoking isClosed( ) on these objects returns false. Java 1.4 also adds an isBound( ) method that tells you whether the ServerSocket has been bound to a port:

```
public boolean isBound() // Java 1.4
```

As with the isBound( ) method of the Socket class discussed in the last chapter, the name is a little misleading. isBound( ) returns true if the ServerSocket has ever been bound to a port, even if it's currently closed. If you need to test whether a ServerSocket is open, you must check both that isBound( ) returns true and that isClosed( ) returns false. For example:

```
public static boolean isOpen(ServerSocket ss) {
  return ss.isBound() && ! ss.isClosed();
}
```

The get Methods

The ServerSocket class provides two getter methods that tell you the local address and port occupied by the server socket. These are useful if you've opened a server socket on an anonymous port and/or an unspecified network interface. This would be the case, for one example, in the data connection of an FTP session.

public InetAddress getInetAddress( )

This method returns the address being used by the server (the local host). If the local host has a single IP address (as most do), this is the address returned by InetAddress. getLocalHost( ). If the local host has more than one IP address, the specific address returned is one of the host's IP addresses. You can't predict which address you will get. For example:

```
ServerSocket httpd = new ServerSocket(80);
InetAddress ia = httpd.getInetAddress( );
```

If the ServerSocket has not yet bound to a network interface, this method returns null.

public int getLocalPort( )

The ServerSocket constructors allow you to listen on an unspecified port by passing 0 for the port number. This method lets you find out what port you're listening on. You might use this in a peer-to-peer multisocket program where you already have a means to inform other peers of your location. Or a server might spawn several smaller servers to perform particular operations. The well-known server could inform clients what ports they can find the smaller servers on. Of course, you can also use getLocalPort( ) to find a non-anonymous port, but why would you need to? Example 10-4 demonstrates.

Example 10-4. A random port

```
import java.net.*;
import java.io.*;

public class RandomPort {

  public static void main(String[] args) {

    try {
      ServerSocket server = new ServerSocket(0);
      System.out.println("This server runs on port "
        + server.getLocalPort( ));
    }
    catch (IOException ex) {
      System.err.println(ex);
    }

  }

}
```

Here's the output of several runs:

```
D:\JAVA\JNP3\examples\10>java RandomPort
This server runs on port 1154
D:\JAVA\JNP3\examples\10>java RandomPort
This server runs on port 1155
D:\JAVA\JNP3\examples\10>java RandomPort
This server runs on port 1156
```

At least on this VM, the ports aren't really random, but they are at least indeterminate until runtime.

If the ServerSocket has not yet bound to a port, then this method returns –1.

Socket Options

Java 1.3 only supports one socket option for server sockets, SO_TIMEOUT. Java 1.4 adds two more, SO_REUSEADDR and SO_RCVBUF.

SO_TIMEOUT

SO_TIMEOUT is the amount of time, in milliseconds, that accept( ) waits for an incoming connection before throwing a java.io.InterruptedIOException. If SO_TIMEOUT is 0, accept( ) will never time out. The default is to never time out.

Using SO_TIMEOUT is rather rare. You might need it if you were implementing a complicated and secure protocol that required multiple connections between the client and the server where responses needed to occur within a fixed amount of time. However, most servers are designed to run for indefinite periods of time and therefore just use the default timeout value, 0 (never time out). If you want to change this, the setSoTimeout( ) method sets the SO_TIMEOUT field for this server socket object.

```
public void setSoTimeout(int timeout) throws SocketException
public int  getSoTimeout( ) throws IOException
```

The countdown starts when accept( ) is invoked. When the timeout expires, accept( ) throws an InterruptedIOException. (In Java 1.4, it throws SocketTimeoutException, a subclass of InterruptedIOException.) You should set this option before calling accept( ); you cannot change the timeout value while accept( ) is waiting for a connection. The timeout argument must be greater than or equal to zero; if it isn't, the method throws an IllegalArgumentException. For example:

```
try {
  ServerSocket server = new ServerSocket(2048);
  server.setSoTimeout(30000); // block for no more than 30 seconds
  try {
    Socket s = server.accept( );
    // handle the connection
    // ...
  }
```

```
    catch (InterruptedIOException ex) {
      System.err.println("No connection within 30 seconds");
    }
    finally {
      server.close();
    }
  catch (IOException ex) {
    System.err.println("Unexpected IOException: " + e);
  }
```

The getSoTimeout( ) method returns this server socket's current SO_TIMEOUT value. For example:

```
public void printSoTimeout(ServerSocket server) {

  int timeout = server.getSoTimeOut();
  if (timeout > 0) {
    System.out.println(server + " will time out after "
     + timeout + "milliseconds.");
  }
  else if (timeout == 0) {
    System.out.println(server + " will never time out.");
  }
  else {
    System.out.println("Impossible condition occurred in " + server);
    System.out.println("Timeout cannot be less than zero." );
  }

}
```

SO_REUSEADDR // Java 1.4

The SO_REUSEADDR option for server sockets is very similar to the same option for client sockets, discussed in the last chapter. It determines whether a new socket will be allowed to bind to a previously used port while there might still be data traversing the network addressed to the old socket. As you probably expect, there are two methods to get and set this option:

```
public void setReuseAddress(boolean on) throws SocketException
public boolean getReuseAddress() throws SocketException
```

The default value is platform-dependent. This code fragment determines the default value by creating a new ServerSocket and then calling getReuseAddress( ):

```
ServerSocket ss = new ServerSocket(10240);
System.out.println("Reusable: " + ss.getReuseAddress());
```

On the Linux and Mac OS X boxes where I tested this code, server sockets were reusable.

SO_RCVBUF // Java 1.4

The SO_RCVBUF option sets the default receive buffer size for client sockets accepted by the server socket. It's read and written by these two methods:

```
public void setReceiveBufferSize(int size) throws SocketException
public int  getReceiveBufferSize() throws SocketException
```

Setting SO_RCVBUF on a server socket is like calling setReceiveBufferSize() on each individual socket returned by accept() (except that you can't change the receive buffer size after the socket has been accepted). Recall from the last chapter that this option suggests a value for the size of the individual IP packets in the stream. Faster connections will want to use larger packets, although most of the time the default value is fine.

You can set this option before or after the server socket is bound, unless you want to set a receive buffer size larger than 64K. In that case, you must set the option on an unbound ServerSocket before binding it. For example:

```
ServerSocket ss = new ServerSocket();
int receiveBufferSize = ss.getReceiveBufferSize();
if (receiveBufferSize < 131072) {
  ss.setReceiveBufferSize(131072);
}
ss.bind(new InetSocketAddress(8000));
//...
```

public void setPerformancePreferences(int connectionTime, int latency, int bandwidth) // Java 1.5

Java 1.5 adds a slightly different method for setting socket options—the setPerformancePreferences() method:

```
public void setPerformancePreferences(int connectionTime, int latency, int bandwidth)
```

This method expresses the relative preferences given to connection time, latency, and bandwidth. For instance, if connectionTime is 2 and latency is 1 and bandwidth is 3, then maximum bandwidth is the most important characteristic, minimum latency is the least important, and connection time is in the middle. Exactly how any given VM implements this is implementation-dependent. Indeed, it may be a no-op in some implementations. The API documentation for ServerSocket even suggests using non-TCP/IP sockets, although it's not at all clear what that means.

The Object Methods

ServerSocket overrides only one of the standard methods from java.lang.Object, toString(). Thus, equality comparisons test for strict identity and server sockets are problematic in hash tables. Normally, this isn't a large problem.

public String toString( )

A String returned by ServerSocket's toString( ) method looks like this:

```
ServerSocket[addr=0.0.0.0,port=0,localport=5776]
```

addr is the address of the local network interface to which the server socket is bound. This will be 0.0.0.0 if it's bound to all interfaces, as is commonly the case. port is always 0. The localport is the local port on which the server is listening for connections. This method is sometimes useful for debugging, but not much more. Don't rely on it.

Implementation

The ServerSocket class provides two methods for changing the default implementation of server sockets. I'll describe them only briefly here, since they're primarily intended for implementers of Java virtual machines rather than application programmers.

public static void setSocketFactory(SocketImplFactory factory) throws IOException

This method sets the *system's* server SocketImplFactory, which is the factory used to create ServerSocket objects. This is not the same factory that is used to create client Socket objects, though the syntax is similar; you can have one factory for Socket objects and a different factory for ServerSocket objects. You can set this factory only once in a program, however. A second attempt to set the SocketImplFactory throws a SocketException.

protected final void implAccept(Socket s) throws IOException

Subclasses of ServerSocket use this method when they want to override accept( ) so that it returns an instance of their own custom Socket subclass rather than a plain java.net.Socket. The overridden accept( ) method passes its own unconnected Socket object to this method to actually make the connection. You pass an unconnected Socket object to implAccept( ). When implAccept( ) returns, the Socket argument s is connected to a client. For example:

```
public Socket accept( )  throws IOException {
  Socket s = new MySocketSubclass( );
  implAccept(s);
  return s;
}
```

If the server needs to know that the Socket returned by accept( ) has a more specific type than just java.net.Socket, it must cast the return value appropriately. For example:

```
ServerSocket server = new MyServerSocketSubclass(80);
while (true) {
  MySocketSubclass  socket = (MySocketSubclass) server.accept( );;
  // ...
}
```

Some Useful Servers

This section shows several servers you can build with server sockets. It starts with a server you can use to test client responses and requests, much as you use Telnet to test server behavior. Then three different HTTP servers are presented, each with a different special purpose and each slightly more complex than the previous one.

Client Tester

In the previous chapter, you learned how to use Telnet to experiment with servers. There's no equivalent program to test clients, so let's create one. Example 10-5 is a program called ClientTester that runs on a port specified on the command line, shows all data sent by the client, and allows you to send a response to the client by typing it on the command line. For example, you can use this program to see the commands that Internet Explorer sends to a server.

 Clients are rarely as forgiving about unexpected server responses as servers are about unexpected client responses. If at all possible, try to run the clients that connect to this program on a Unix system or some other platform that is moderately crash-proof. Don't run them on Mac OS 9 or Windows ME, which are less stable.

This program uses two threads: one to handle input from the client and the other to send output from the server. Using two threads allows the program to handle input and output simultaneously: it can send a response to the client while receiving a request—or, more to the point, it can send data to the client while waiting for the client to respond. This is convenient because different clients and servers talk in unpredictable ways. With some protocols, the server talks first; with others, the client talks first. Sometimes the server sends a one-line response; often, the response is much larger. Sometimes the client and the server talk at each other simultaneously. Other times, one side of the connection waits for the other to finish before it responds. The program must be flexible enough to handle all these cases. Example 10-5 shows the code.

Example 10-5. A client tester

```
import java.net.*;
import java.io.*;
import com.macfaq.io.SafeBufferedReader; // from Chapter 4

public class ClientTester {

  public static void main(String[] args) {

    int port;
```

Example 10-5. A client tester (continued)

```
    try {
      port = Integer.parseInt(args[0]);
    }
    catch (Exception ex) {
      port = 0;
    }

    try {
      ServerSocket server = new ServerSocket(port, 1);
      System.out.println("Listening for connections on port "
       + server.getLocalPort( ));

      while (true) {
        Socket connection = server.accept( );
        try {
          System.out.println("Connection established with "
           + connection);
          Thread input = new InputThread(connection.getInputStream( ));
          input.start( );
          Thread output
           = new OutputThread(connection.getOutputStream( ));
          output.start( );
          // wait for output and input to finish
          try {
            input.join( );
            output.join( );
          }
          catch (InterruptedException ex) {
          }
        }
        catch (IOException ex) {
          System.err.println(ex);
        }
        finally {
          try {
            if (connection != null) connection.close( );
          }
          catch (IOException ex) {}
        }
      }
    }
    catch (IOException ex) {
      e.printStackTrace( );
    }

  }

}

class InputThread extends Thread {
```

Example 10-5. A client tester (continued)

```
InputStream in;

  public InputThread(InputStream in) {
    this.in = in;
  }

  public void run()  {

    try {
      while (true) {
        int i = in.read( );
        if (i == -1) break;
        System.out.write(i);
      }
    }
    catch (SocketException ex) {
      // output thread closed the socket
    }
    catch (IOException ex) {
      System.err.println(ex);
    }
    try {
      in.close( );
    }
    catch (IOException ex) {
    }

  }

}

class OutputThread extends Thread {

  private Writer out;

  public OutputThread(OutputStream out) {
    this.out = new OutputStreamWriter(out);
  }

  public void run( ) {

    String line;
    BufferedReader in
     = new SafeBufferedReader(new InputStreamReader(System.in));
    try {
      while (true) {
        line = in.readLine( );
        if (line.equals(".")) break;
        out.write(line +"\r\n");
        out.flush( );
      }
    }
```

Example 10-5. A client tester (continued)

```
  catch (IOException ex) {
  }
  try {
    out.close();
  }
  catch (IOException ex) {
  }

}

}
```

The client tester application is split into three classes: ClientTester, InputThread, and OutputThread. The ClientTester class reads the port from the command line, opens a ServerSocket on that port, and listens for incoming connections. Only one connection is allowed at a time, because this program is designed for experimentation, and a slow human being has to provide all responses. Consequently, it sets an unusually short queue length of 1. Further connections will be refused until the first one has been closed.

An infinite while loop waits for connections with the accept( ) method. When a connection is detected, its InputStream is used to construct a new InputThread and its OutputStream is used to construct a new OutputThread. After starting these threads, the program waits for them to finish by calling their join( ) methods.

The InputThread is contained almost entirely in the run( ) method. It has a single field, in, which is the InputStream from which data will be read. Data is read from in one byte at a time. Each byte read is written on System.out. The run( ) method ends when the end of stream is encountered or an IOException is thrown. The most likely exception here is a SocketException thrown because the corresponding OutputThread closed the connection.

The OutputThread reads input from the local user sitting at the terminal and sends that data to the client. Its constructor has a single argument, an output stream for sending data to the client. OutputThread reads input from the user on System.in, which is chained to an instance of the SafeBufferedReader class developed in Chapter 4. The OutputStream that was passed to the constructor is chained to an OutputStreamWriter for convenience. The run( ) method for OutputThread reads lines from the SafeBufferedReader and copies them onto the OutputStreamWriter, which sends them to the client. A period typed on a line by itself signals the end of user input. When this occurs, run( ) exits the loop and out is closed. This has the effect of also closing the socket so that a SocketException is thrown in the input thread, which also exits.

For example, here's the output when Netscape Communicator 4.6 for Windows connected to this server:

```
D:\JAVA\JNP3\examples\10>java ClientTester 80
Listening for connections on port 80
```

```
Connection established with
Socket[addr=localhost/127.0.0.1,port=1033,localport=80]
GET / HTTP/1.0
Connection: Keep-Alive
User-Agent: Mozilla/4.6 [en] (WinNT; I)
Host: localhost
Accept: image/gif, image/x-xbitmap, image/jpeg, image/pjpeg, image/png, */*
Accept-Encoding: gzip
Accept-Language: en
Accept-Charset: iso-8859-1,*,utf-8

<html><body><h1>Hello Client!</h1></body></html>
```

Even minimal exploration of clients can reveal some surprising things. For instance, I didn't know until I wrote this example that Netscape Navigator 4.6 can read .*gz* files just as easily as it can read HTML files. That might be useful for serving large text files full of redundant data.

HTTP Servers

HTTP is a large protocol. As you saw in Chapter 3, a full-featured HTTP server must respond to requests for files, convert URLs into filenames on the local system, respond to POST and GET requests, handle requests for files that don't exist, interpret MIME types, and much, much more. However, many HTTP servers don't need all of these features. For example, many sites simply display an "under construction" message. Clearly, Apache is overkill for a site like this. Such a site is a candidate for a custom server that does only one thing. Java's network class library makes writing simple servers like this almost trivial.

Custom servers aren't useful only for small sites. High-traffic sites like Yahoo! are also candidates for custom servers because a server that does only one thing can often be much faster than a general purpose server such as Apache or Microsoft IIS. It is easy to optimize a special purpose server for a particular task; the result is often much more efficient than a general purpose server that needs to respond to many different kinds of requests. For instance, icons and images that are used repeatedly across many pages or on high-traffic pages might be better handled by a server that read all the image files into memory on startup and then served them straight out of RAM, rather than having to read them off disk for each request. Furthermore, this server could avoid wasting time on logging if you didn't want to track the image requests separately from the requests for the pages they were included in.

Finally, Java isn't a bad language for full-featured web servers meant to compete with the likes of Apache or IIS. Even if you believe CPU-intensive Java programs are slower than CPU-intensive C and C++ programs (something I very much doubt is true in modern VMs), most HTTP servers are limited by bandwidth, not by CPU speed. Consequently, Java's other advantages, such as its half-compiled/half-interpreted nature, dynamic class loading, garbage collection, and memory protection really get a chance to shine. In particular, sites that make heavy use of dynamic content through serv-lets, PHP pages, or other mechanisms can often run much faster when reimplemented on top of a pure or mostly pure Java web server. Indeed, there are several production web servers written in Java, such as the W3C's testbed server Jigsaw (*http://www.w3.org/Jigsaw/*). Many other web servers written in C now include substantial Java components to support the Java Servlet API and Java Server Pages. On many sites, these are replacing the traditional CGIs, ASPs, and server-side includes, mostly because the Java equivalents are faster and less resource-intensive. I'm not going to explore these technologies here since they easily deserve a book of their own. I refer interested readers to Jason Hunter's *Java Servlet Programming* (O'Reilly). However, it is important to note that servers in general and web servers in particular are one area where Java really is competitive with C.

A single-file server

Our investigation of HTTP servers begins with a server that always sends out the same file, no matter what the request. It's called SingleFileHTTPServer and is shown in Example 10-6. The filename, local port, and content encoding are read from the command line. If the port is omitted, port 80 is assumed. If the encoding is omitted, ASCII is assumed.

Example 10-6. An HTTP server that chunks out the same file

```
import java.net.*;
import java.io.*;
import java.util.*;

public class SingleFileHTTPServer extends Thread {

  private byte[] content;
  private byte[] header;
  private int port = 80;

  public SingleFileHTTPServer(String data, String encoding,
   String MIMEType, int port) throws UnsupportedEncodingException {
    this(data.getBytes(encoding), encoding, MIMEType, port);
  }

  public SingleFileHTTPServer(byte[] data, String encoding,
   String MIMEType, int port) throws UnsupportedEncodingException {

    this.content = data;
    this.port = port;
    String header = "HTTP/1.0 200 OK\r\n"
     + "Server: OneFile 1.0\r\n"
     + "Content-length: " + this.content.length + "\r\n"
     + "Content-type: " + MIMEType + "\r\n\r\n";
    this.header = header.getBytes("ASCII");

  }
```

Example 10-6. An HTTP server that chunks out the same file (continued)

```
public void run( ) {

  try {
    ServerSocket server = new ServerSocket(this.port);
    System.out.println("Accepting connections on port "
      + server.getLocalPort( ));
    System.out.println("Data to be sent:");
    System.out.write(this.content);
    while (true) {

      Socket connection = null;
      try {
        connection = server.accept( );
        OutputStream out = new BufferedOutputStream(
                               connection.getOutputStream( )
                             );
        InputStream in  = new BufferedInputStream(
                               connection.getInputStream( )
                             );
        // read the first line only; that's all we need
        StringBuffer request = new StringBuffer(80);
        while (true) {
          int c = in.read( );
          if (c == '\r' || c == '\n' || c == -1) break;
          request.append((char) c);

        }
        // If this is HTTP/1.0 or later send a MIME header
        if (request.toString( ).indexOf("HTTP/") != -1) {
          out.write(this.header);
        }
        out.write(this.content);
        out.flush( );
      }  // end try
      catch (IOException ex) {
      }
      finally {
        if (connection != null) connection.close( );
      }

    } // end while
  } // end try
  catch (IOException ex) {
    System.err.println("Could not start server. Port Occupied");
  }

} // end run


public static void main(String[] args) {

  try {
```

Example 10-6. An HTTP server that chunks out the same file (continued)

```
    String contentType = "text/plain";
    if (args[0].endsWith(".html") || args[0].endsWith(".htm")) {
      contentType = "text/html";
    }

    InputStream in = new FileInputStream(args[0]);
    ByteArrayOutputStream out = new ByteArrayOutputStream( );
    int b;
    while ((b = in.read( )) != -1) out.write(b);
    byte[] data = out.toByteArray( );

    // set the port to listen on
    int port;
    try {
      port = Integer.parseInt(args[1]);
      if (port < 1 || port > 65535) port = 80;
    }
    catch (Exception ex) {
      port = 80;
    }

    String encoding = "ASCII";
    if (args.length >= 2) encoding = args[2];

    Thread t = new SingleFileHTTPServer(data, encoding,
     contentType, port);
    t.start( );

  }
  catch (ArrayIndexOutOfBoundsException ex) {
    System.out.println(
      "Usage: java SingleFileHTTPServer filename port encoding");
  }
  catch (Exception ex) {
    System.err.println(ex);
  }

 }

}
```

The constructors set up the data to be sent along with an HTTP header that includes information about content length and content encoding. The header and the body of the response are stored in byte arrays in the desired encoding so that they can be blasted to clients very quickly.

The SingleFileHTTPServer class itself is a subclass of Thread. Its run( ) method processes incoming connections. Chances are this server will serve only small files and will support only low-volume web sites. Since all the server needs to do for each connection is check whether the client supports HTTP/1.0 and spew one or two relatively small byte arrays over the connection, chances are this will be sufficient. On the other hand, if you find clients are getting refused, you could use multiple threads instead. A lot depends on the size of the file served, the peak number of connections expected per minute, and the thread model of Java on the host machine. Using multiple threads would be a clear win for a server that was even slightly more sophisticated than this one.

The run( ) method creates a ServerSocket on the specified port. Then it enters an infinite loop that continually accepts connections and processes them. When a socket is accepted, an InputStream reads the request from the client. It looks at the first line to see whether it contains the string HTTP. If it sees this string, the server assumes that the client understands HTTP/1.0 or later and therefore sends a MIME header for the file; then it sends the data. If the client request doesn't contain the string HTTP, the server omits the header, sending the data by itself. Finally, the server closes the connection and tries to accept the next connection.

The main( ) method just reads parameters from the command line. The name of the file to be served is read from the first command-line argument. If no file is specified or the file cannot be opened, an error message is printed and the program exits. Assuming the file *can* be read, its contents are read into the byte array data. A reasonable guess is made about the content type of the file, and that guess is stored in the contentType variable. Next, the port number is read from the second command-line argument. If no port is specified or if the second argument is not an integer from 0 to 65,535, port 80 is used. The encoding is read from the third command-line argument, if present. Otherwise, ASCII is assumed. (Surprisingly, some VMs don't support ASCII, so you might want to pick 8859-1 instead.) Then these values are used to construct a SingleFileHTTPServer object and start it running. This is only one possible interface. You could easily use this class as part of some other program. If you added a setter method to change the content, you could easily use it to provide simple status information about a running server or system. However, that would raise some additional issues of thread safety that Example 10-6 doesn't have to address because it's immutable.

Here's what you see when you connect to this server via Telnet; the specifics depend on the exact server and file:

```
% telnet macfaq.dialup.cloud9.net 80
Trying 168.100.203.234...
Connected to macfaq.dialup.cloud9.net.
Escape character is '^]'.
GET / HTTP/1.0
HTTP/1.0 200 OK
Server: OneFile 1.0
Content-length: 959
Content-type: text/html

<!DOCTYPE HTML PUBLIC "-//W3C//DTD HTML 3.2//EN">
<HTML>
<HEAD>
```

```
<TITLE>Under Construction</TITLE>
</HEAD>

<BODY>
...
```

A redirector

Redirection is another simple but useful application for a special-purpose HTTP server. In this section, we develop a server that redirects users from one web site to another—for example, from *cnet.com* to *www.cnet.com*. Example 10-7 reads a URL and a port number from the command line, opens a server socket on the port, and redirects all requests that it receives to the site indicated by the new URL using a 302 FOUND code. Chances are this server is fast enough not to require multiple threads. Nonetheless, threads might be mildly advantageous, especially for a high volume site on a slow network connection. But really for purposes of example more than anything, I've made the server multithreaded. In this example, I chose to use a new thread rather than a thread pool for each connection. This is perhaps a little simpler to code and understand but somewhat less efficient. In Example 10-8, we'll look at an HTTP server that uses a thread pool.

Example 10-7. An HTTP redirector

```java
import java.net.*;
import java.io.*;
import java.util.*;

public class Redirector implements Runnable {

  private int port;
  private String newSite;

  public Redirector(String site, int port) {
    this.port = port;
    this.newSite = site;
  }

  public void run( ) {

    try {

      ServerSocket server = new ServerSocket(this.port);
      System.out.println("Redirecting connections on port "
        + server.getLocalPort( ) + " to " + newSite);

      while (true) {

        try {
          Socket s = server.accept( );
          Thread t = new RedirectThread(s);
          t.start( );
```

Example 10-7. An HTTP redirector (continued)

```
        }  // end try
        catch (IOException ex) {
        }

      } // end while

    } // end try
    catch (BindException ex) {
      System.err.println("Could not start server. Port Occupied");
    }
    catch (IOException ex) {
      System.err.println(ex);
    }

  }  // end run

  class RedirectThread extends Thread {

    private Socket connection;

    RedirectThread(Socket s) {
      this.connection = s;
    }

    public void run( ) {

      try {

        Writer out = new BufferedWriter(
                       new OutputStreamWriter(
                         connection.getOutputStream( ), "ASCII"
                       )
                     );
        Reader in = new InputStreamReader(
                      new BufferedInputStream(
                        connection.getInputStream( )
                      )
                    );

        // read the first line only; that's all we need
        StringBuffer request = new StringBuffer(80);
        while (true) {
          int c = in.read( );
          if (c == '\r' || c == '\n' || c == -1) break;
          request.append((char) c);
        }
        // If this is HTTP/1.0 or later send a MIME header
        String get = request.toString( );
        int firstSpace = get.indexOf(' ');
        int secondSpace = get.indexOf(' ', firstSpace+1);
        String theFile = get.substring(firstSpace+1, secondSpace);
        if (get.indexOf("HTTP") != -1) {
```

Example 10-7. An HTTP redirector (continued)

```
        out.write("HTTP/1.0 302 FOUND\r\n");
        Date now = new Date( );
        out.write("Date: " + now + "\r\n");
        out.write("Server: Redirector 1.0\r\n");
        out.write("Location: " + newSite + theFile + "\r\n");
        out.write("Content-type: text/html\r\n\r\n");
        out.flush( );
      }
      // Not all browsers support redirection so we need to
      // produce HTML that says where the document has moved to.
      out.write("<HTML><HEAD><TITLE>Document moved</TITLE></HEAD>\r\n");
      out.write("<BODY><H1>Document moved</H1>\r\n");
      out.write("The document " + theFile
       + " has moved to\r\n<A HREF=\"" + newSite + theFile + "\">"
       + newSite  + theFile
       + "</A>.\r\n Please update your bookmarks<P>");
      out.write("</BODY></HTML>\r\n");
      out.flush( );

    } // end try
    catch (IOException ex) {
    }
    finally {
      try {
        if (connection != null) connection.close( );
      }
      catch (IOException ex) {}
    }

  }  // end run

}

public static void main(String[] args) {

  int thePort;
  String theSite;

  try {
    theSite = args[0];
    // trim trailing slash
    if (theSite.endsWith("/")) {
      theSite = theSite.substring(0, theSite.length( )-1);
    }
  }
  catch (Exception ex) {
    System.out.println(
     "Usage: java Redirector http://www.newsite.com/ port");
    return;
  }

  try {
```

Example 10-7. An HTTP redirector (continued)

```
      thePort = Integer.parseInt(args[1]);
    }
    catch (Exception ex) {
      thePort = 80;
    }

    Thread t = new Thread(new Redirector(theSite, thePort));
    t.start();

  } // end main

}
```

In order to start the redirector on port 80 and redirect incoming requests to *http://www.ibiblio.org/xml/*, type:

```
D:\JAVA\JNP3\examples\10>java Redirector http://www.ibiblio.org/xml/
Redirecting connections on port 80 to http://www.ibiblio.org/xml/
```

If you connect to this server via Telnet, this is what you'll see:

```
% telnet macfaq.dialup.cloud9.net 80
Trying 168.100.203.234...
Connected to macfaq.dialup.cloud9.net.
Escape character is '^]'.
GET / HTTP/1.0
HTTP/1.0 302 FOUND
Date: Wed Sep 08 11:59:42 PDT 1999
Server: Redirector 1.0
Location: http://www.ibiblio.org/xml/
Content-type: text/html

<HTML><HEAD><TITLE>Document moved</TITLE></HEAD>
<BODY><H1>Document moved</H1>
The document / has moved to
<A HREF="http://www.ibiblio.org/xml/">http://www.ibiblio.org/xml/</A>.
 Please update your bookmarks<P></BODY></HTML>
Connection closed by foreign host.
```

If, however, you connect with a reasonably modern web browser, you should be sent to *http://www.ibiblio.org/xml/* with only a slight delay. You should never see the HTML added after the response code; this is only provided to support older browsers that don't do redirection automatically.

The main( ) method provides a very simple interface that reads the URL of the new site to redirect connections to and the local port to listen on. It uses this information to construct a Redirector object. Then it uses the resulting Runnable object (Redirector implements Runnable) to spawn a new thread and start it. If the port is not specified, Redirector listens on port 80. If the site is omitted, Redirector prints an error message and exits.

The run( ) method of Redirector binds the server socket to the port, prints a brief status message, and then enters an infinite loop in which it listens for connections. Every time a connection is accepted, the resulting Socket object is used to construct a RedirectThread. This RedirectThread is then started. All further interaction with the client takes place in this new thread. The run( ) method of Redirector then simply waits for the next incoming connection.

The run( ) method of RedirectThread does most of the work. It begins by chaining a Writer to the Socket's output stream and a Reader to the Socket's input stream. Both input and output are buffered. Then the run( ) method reads the first line the client sends. Although the client will probably send a whole MIME header, we can ignore that. The first line contains all the information we need. The line looks something like this:

```
GET /directory/filename.html HTTP/1.0
```

It is possible that the first word will be POST or PUT instead or that there will be no HTTP version. The second "word" is the file the client wants to retrieve. This *must* begin with a slash (/). Browsers are responsible for converting relative URLs to absolute URLs that begin with a slash; the server does not do this. The third word is the version of the HTTP protocol the browser understands. Possible values are nothing at all (pre-HTTP/1.0 browsers), HTTP/1.0, or HTTP/1.1.

To handle a request like this, Redirector ignores the first word. The second word is attached to the URL of the target server (stored in the field newSite) to give a full redirected URL. The third word is used to determine whether to send a MIME header; MIME headers are not used for old browsers that do not understand HTTP/1.0. If there is a version, a MIME header is sent; otherwise, it is omitted.

Sending the data is almost trivial. The Writer out is used. Since all the data we send is pure ASCII, the exact encoding isn't too important. The only trick here is that the end-of-line character for HTTP requests is \r\n—a carriage return followed by a linefeed.

The next lines each send one line of text to the client. The first line printed is:

```
HTTP/1.0 302 FOUND
```

This is an HTTP/1.0 response code that tells the client to expect to be redirected. The second line is a Date: header that gives the current time at the server. This line is optional. The third line is the name and version of the server; this line is also optional but is used by spiders that try to keep statistics about the most popular web servers. (It would be very surprising to ever see Redirector break into single digits in lists of the most popular servers.) The next line is the Location: header, which is required for this server. It tells the client where it is being redirected to. Last is the standard Content-type: header. We send the content type text/html to indicate that the client should expect to see HTML. Finally, a blank line is sent to signify the end of the header data.

Everything after this will be HTML, which is processed by the browser and displayed to the user. The next several lines print a message for browsers that do not support redirection, so those users can manually jump to the new site. That message looks like:

```
<HTML><HEAD><TITLE>Document moved</TITLE></HEAD>
<BODY><H1>Document moved</H1>
The document / has moved to
<A HREF="http://www.ibiblio.org/xml/">http://www.ibiblio.org/xml/</A>.
 Please update your bookmarks<P></BODY></HTML>
```

Finally, the connection is closed and the thread dies.

A full-fledged HTTP server

Enough special-purpose HTTP servers. This next section develops a full-blown HTTP server, called JHTTP, that can serve an entire document tree, including images, applets, HTML files, text files, and more. It will be very similar to the SingleFileHTTPServer, except that it pays attention to the GET requests. This server is still fairly lightweight; after looking at the code, we'll discuss other features we might want to add.

Since this server may have to read and serve large files from the filesystem over potentially slow network connections, we'll change its approach. Rather than processing each request as it arrives in the main thread of execution, we'll place incoming connections in a pool. Separate instances of a RequestProcessor class will remove the connections from the pool and process them. Example 10-8 shows the main JHTTP class. As in the previous two examples, the main( ) method of JHTTP handles initialization, but other programs can use this class to run basic web servers.

Example 10-8. The JHTTP web server

```java
import java.net.*;
import java.io.*;
import java.util.*;

public class JHTTP extends Thread {

  private File documentRootDirectory;
  private String indexFileName = "index.html";
  private ServerSocket server;
  private int numThreads = 50;

  public JHTTP(File documentRootDirectory, int port,
   String indexFileName) throws IOException {

    if (!documentRootDirectory.isDirectory()) {
      throw new IOException(documentRootDirectory
        + " does not exist as a directory");
    }
    this.documentRootDirectory = documentRootDirectory;
```

Example 10-8. The JHTTP web server (continued)

```
    this.indexFileName = indexFileName;
    this.server = new ServerSocket(port);
  }

  public JHTTP(File documentRootDirectory, int port)
   throws IOException {
    this(documentRootDirectory, port, "index.html");
  }

  public JHTTP(File documentRootDirectory) throws IOException {
    this(documentRootDirectory, 80, "index.html");
  }

  public void run( ) {

    for (int i = 0; i < numThreads; i++) {
      Thread t = new Thread(
       new RequestProcessor(documentRootDirectory, indexFileName));
      t.start( );
    }
    System.out.println("Accepting connections on port "
     + server.getLocalPort( ));
    System.out.println("Document Root: " + documentRootDirectory);
    while (true) {
      try {
        Socket request = server.accept( );
        RequestProcessor.processRequest(request);
      }
      catch (IOException ex) {
      }
    }

  }

  public static void main(String[] args) {

    // get the Document root
    File docroot;
    try {
      docroot = new File(args[0]);
    }
    catch (ArrayIndexOutOfBoundsException ex) {
      System.out.println("Usage: java JHTTP docroot port indexfile");
      return;
    }

    // set the port to listen on
    int port;
    try {
      port = Integer.parseInt(args[1]);
      if (port < 0 || port > 65535) port = 80;
    }
```

Example 10-8. The JHTTP web server (continued)

```
    catch (Exception ex) {
      port = 80;
    }

    try {
      JHTTP webserver = new JHTTP(docroot, port);
      webserver.start( );
    }
    catch (IOException ex) {
      System.out.println("Server could not start because of an "
       + e.getClass( ));
      System.out.println(e);
    }

  }

}
```

The `main( )` method of the JHTTP class sets the document root directory from `args[0]`. The port is read from `args[1]` or 80 is used for a default. Then a new JHTTP thread is constructed and started. The JHTTP thread spawns 50 RequestProcessor threads to handle requests, each of which retrieves incoming connection requests from the RequestProcessor pool as they become available. The JHTTP thread repeatedly accepts incoming connections and puts them in the RequestProcessor pool.

Each connection is handled by the `run( )` method of the RequestProcessor class shown in Example 10-9. This method waits until it can get a Socket out of the pool. Once it does that, it gets input and output streams from the socket and chains them to a reader and a writer. The reader reads the first line of the client request to determine the version of HTTP that the client supports—we want to send a MIME header only if this is HTTP/1.0 or later—and the requested file. Assuming the method is GET, the file that is requested is converted to a filename on the local filesystem. If the file requested is a directory (i.e., its name ends with a slash), we add the name of an index file. We use the canonical path to make sure that the requested file doesn't come from outside the document root directory. Otherwise, a sneaky client could walk all over the local filesystem by including .. in URLs to walk up the directory hierarchy. This is all we'll need from the client, although a more advanced web server, especially one that logged hits, would read the rest of the MIME header the client sends.

Next, the requested file is opened and its contents are read into a byte array. If the HTTP version is 1.0 or later, we write the appropriate MIME headers on the output stream. To figure out the content type, we call the `guessContentTypeFromName( )` method to map file extensions such as *.html* onto MIME types such as text/html. The byte array containing the file's contents is written onto the output stream and the connection is closed. Exceptions may be thrown at various places if, for example, the file cannot be found or opened. If an exception occurs, we send an appropriate HTTP error message to the client instead of the file's contents.

Example 10-9. The thread pool that handles HTTP requests

```java
import java.net.*;
import java.io.*;
import java.util.*;

public class RequestProcessor implements Runnable {

  private static List pool = new LinkedList();
  private File documentRootDirectory;
  private String indexFileName = "index.html";

  public RequestProcessor(File documentRootDirectory,
   String indexFileName) {

    if (documentRootDirectory.isFile()) {
      throw new IllegalArgumentException(
        "documentRootDirectory must be a directory, not a file");
    }
    this.documentRootDirectory = documentRootDirectory;
    try {
      this.documentRootDirectory
        = documentRootDirectory.getCanonicalFile();
    }
    catch (IOException ex) {
    }
    if (indexFileName != null) this.indexFileName = indexFileName;
  }

  public static void processRequest(Socket request) {

    synchronized (pool) {
      pool.add(pool.size(), request);
      pool.notifyAll();
    }

  }

  public void run() {

    // for security checks
    String root = documentRootDirectory.getPath();

    while (true) {
      Socket connection;
      synchronized (pool) {
        while (pool.isEmpty()) {
          try {
            pool.wait();
          }
          catch (InterruptedException ex) {
          }
        }
        connection = (Socket) pool.remove(0);
      }
```

Example 10-9. The thread pool that handles HTTP requests (continued)

```
try {
  String filename;
  String contentType;
  OutputStream raw = new BufferedOutputStream(
                        connection.getOutputStream( )
                      );
  Writer out = new OutputStreamWriter(raw);
  Reader in = new InputStreamReader(
                new BufferedInputStream(
                  connection.getInputStream( )
                ),"ASCII"
              );
  StringBuffer requestLine = new StringBuffer( );
  int c;
  while (true) {
    c = in.read( );
    if (c == '\r' || c == '\n') break;
    requestLine.append((char) c);
  }

  String get = requestLine.toString( );

  // log the request
  System.out.println(get);

  StringTokenizer st = new StringTokenizer(get);
  String method = st.nextToken( );
  String version = "";
  if (method.equals("GET")) {
    filename = st.nextToken( );
    if (filename.endsWith("/")) filename += indexFileName;
    contentType = guessContentTypeFromName(filename);
    if (st.hasMoreTokens( )) {
      version = st.nextToken( );
    }

    File theFile = new File(documentRootDirectory,
     filename.substring(1,filename.length( )));
    if (theFile.canRead( )
        // Don't let clients outside the document root
      && theFile.getCanonicalPath( ).startsWith(root)) {
      DataInputStream fis = new DataInputStream(
                              new BufferedInputStream(
                                new FileInputStream(theFile)
                              )
                            );
      byte[] theData = new byte[(int) theFile.length( )];
      fis.readFully(theData);
      fis.close( );
      if (version.startsWith("HTTP ")) {  // send a MIME header
        out.write("HTTP/1.0 200 OK\r\n");
        Date now = new Date( );
```

Example 10-9. The thread pool that handles HTTP requests (continued)

```
              out.write("Date: " + now + "\r\n");
              out.write("Server: JHTTP/1.0\r\n");
              out.write("Content-length: " + theData.length + "\r\n");
              out.write("Content-type: " + contentType + "\r\n\r\n");
              out.flush( );
            }  // end if

            // send the file; it may be an image or other binary data
            // so use the underlying output stream
            // instead of the writer
            raw.write(theData);
            raw.flush( );
          }  // end if
          else {  // can't find the file
            if (version.startsWith("HTTP ")) {  // send a MIME header
              out.write("HTTP/1.0 404 File Not Found\r\n");
              Date now = new Date( );
              out.write("Date: " + now + "\r\n");
              out.write("Server: JHTTP/1.0\r\n");
              out.write("Content-type: text/html\r\n\r\n");
            }
            out.write("<HTML>\r\n");
            out.write("<HEAD><TITLE>File Not Found</TITLE>\r\n");
            out.write("</HEAD>\r\n");
            out.write("<BODY>");
            out.write("<H1>HTTP Error 404: File Not Found</H1>\r\n");
            out.write("</BODY></HTML>\r\n");
            out.flush( );
          }
        }
        else {  // method does not equal "GET"
          if (version.startsWith("HTTP ")) {  // send a MIME header
            out.write("HTTP/1.0 501 Not Implemented\r\n");
            Date now = new Date( );
            out.write("Date: " + now + "\r\n");
            out.write("Server: JHTTP 1.0\r\n");
            out.write("Content-type: text/html\r\n\r\n");
          }
          out.write("<HTML>\r\n");
          out.write("<HEAD><TITLE>Not Implemented</TITLE>\r\n");
          out.write("</HEAD>\r\n");
          out.write("<BODY>");
          out.write("<H1>HTTP Error 501: Not Implemented</H1>\r\n");
          out.write("</BODY></HTML>\r\n");
          out.flush( );
        }
      }
      catch (IOException ex) {
      }
      finally {
        try {
          connection.close( );
```

Example 10-9. The thread pool that handles HTTP requests (continued)

```
      }
      catch (IOException ex) {}
    }

  } // end while

} // end run

public static String guessContentTypeFromName(String name) {
  if (name.endsWith(".html") || name.endsWith(".htm")) {
    return "text/html";
  }
  else if (name.endsWith(".txt") || name.endsWith(".java")) {
    return "text/plain";
  }
  else if (name.endsWith(".gif")) {
    return "image/gif";
  }
  else if (name.endsWith(".class")) {
    return "application/octet-stream";
  }
  else if (name.endsWith(".jpg") || name.endsWith(".jpeg")) {
    return "image/jpeg";
  }
  else return "text/plain";
}

} // end RequestProcessor
```

This server is functional but still rather austere. Here are a few features that could be added:

- A server administration interface
- Support for CGI programs and/or the Java Servlet API
- Support for other request methods, such as POST, HEAD, and PUT
- A log file in the common web log file format
- Server-side includes and/or Java Server Pages
- Support for multiple document roots so individual users can have their own sites

Finally, spend a little time thinking about ways to optimize this server. If you really want to use JHTTP to run a high-traffic site, there are a couple of things that can speed this server up. The first and most important is to use a Just-in-Time (JIT) compiler such as HotSpot. JITs can improve program performance by an order of magnitude or more. The second thing to do is implement smart caching. Keep track of the requests you've received and store the data from the most frequently requested files in a Hashtable so that they're kept in memory. Use a low-priority thread to update this cache. Another option for developers using Java 1.4 or later is to use non-blocking I/O and channels instead of threads and streams. We'll explore this possibility in Chapter 12.

CHAPTER 11

Secure Sockets

One of the perennial fears of consumers buying goods over the Internet is that some hacker will steal their credit card number and run up a several-thousand-dollar bill by calling phone sex lines. In reality, it's more likely that a clerk at a department store will read their credit card number from a store receipt than that some hacker will grab it in transit across the Internet. In fact, as of mid-2004, the major online thefts of credit card numbers have been accomplished by stealing the information from poorly secured databases and filesystems *after* the information has been safely transmitted across the Internet. Nonetheless, to make Internet connections more fundamentally secure, sockets can be encrypted. This allows transactions to be confidential, authenticated, and accurate.

However, encryption is a complex subject. Performing it properly requires a detailed understanding not only of the mathematical algorithms used to encrypt data but also of the protocols used to exchange keys and encrypted data. Even a small mistake can open a large hole in your armor and reveal your communications to an eavesdropper. Consequently, writing encryption software is a task best left to experts. Fortunately, nonexperts with only a layperson's understanding of the underlying protocols and algorithms can secure their communications with software designed by experts. Every time you order something from an online store, chances are the transaction is encrypted and authenticated using protocols and algorithms you need to know next to nothing about. As a programmer who wants to write network client software that talks to online stores, you need to know a little more about the protocols and algorithms involved but not a lot more, provided you can use a class library written by experts who do understand the details. If you want to write the server software that runs the online store, then you need to know a little bit more but still not as much as you would if you were designing all this from scratch without reference to other work.

Until recently, such software was subject to the arms control laws of the United States. To some extent it still is. Laws about encryption in other countries range from much stricter than the U.S.'s to nonexistent. This has limited the ability of Sun and other vendors who operate internationally to ship strong encryption software.

Consequently, such capabilities were not built into the standard java.net classes until Java 1.4. Prior to this, they were available as a standard extension called the Java Secure Sockets Extension (JSSE). Although JSSE is now part of the standard distribution of the JDK, it is still hobbled by design decisions made to support earlier, less liberal export control regulations, and it is therefore less simple and easy to use than it could or should be.

Nonetheless, JSSE can secure network communications using the Secure Sockets Layer (SSL) Version 3 and Transport Layer Security (TLS) protocols and their associated algorithms. SSL is a security protocol that enables web browsers to talk to web servers using various levels of confidentiality and authentication.

Secure Communications

Confidential communication through an open channel such as the public Internet absolutely requires that data be encrypted. Most encryption schemes that lend themselves to computer implementation are based on the notion of a key, a slightly more general kind of password that's not limited to text. The clear text message is combined with the bits of the key according to a mathematical algorithm to produce the encrypted cipher text. Using keys with more bits makes messages exponentially more difficult to decrypt by brute-force guessing of the key.

In traditional *secret key* (or *symmetric*) encryption, the same key is used for both encrypting and decrypting the data. Both the sender and the receiver have to possess the single key. Imagine Angela wants to send Gus a secret message. She first sends Gus the key they'll use to exchange the secret. But the key can't be encrypted because Gus doesn't have the key yet, so Angela has to send the key unencrypted. Now suppose Edgar is eavesdropping on the connection between Angela and Gus. He will get the key at the same time that Gus does. From that point forward, he can read anything Angela and Gus say to each other using that key.

In *public key* (or *asymmetric*) encryption, different keys are used to encrypt and decrypt the data. One key, called the public key, is used to encrypt the data. This key can be given to anyone. A different key, called the private key, is used to decrypt the data. This must be kept secret but needs to be possessed by only one of the correspondents. If Angela wants to send a message to Gus, she asks Gus for his public key. Gus sends it to her over an unencrypted connection. Angela uses Gus's public key to encrypt her message and sends it to him. If Edgar is eavesdropping when Gus sends Angela his key, Edgar also gets Gus's public key. However, this doesn't allow Edgar to decrypt the message Angela sends Gus, since decryption requires Gus's private key. The message is safe even if the public key is detected in transit.

Asymmetric encryption can also be used for authentication and message integrity checking. For this use, Angela would encrypt a message with her private key before sending it. When Gus received it, he'd decrypt it with Angela's public key. If the decryption succeeded, Gus would know that the message came from Angela. After all, no one else could have produced a message that would decrypt properly with her public key. Gus would also know that the message wasn't changed en route, either maliciously by Edgar or unintentionally by buggy software or network noise, since any such change would have screwed up the decryption. With a little more effort, Angela can double-encrypt the message, once with her private key, once with Gus's public key, thus getting all three benefits of privacy, authentication, and integrity.

In practice, public key encryption is much more CPU-intensive and much slower than secret key encryption. Therefore, instead of encrypting the entire transmission with Gus's public key, Angela encrypts a traditional secret key and sends it to Gus. Gus decrypts it with his private key. Now Angela and Gus both know the secret key, but Edgar doesn't. Therefore, Gus and Angela can now use faster secret-key encryption to communicate privately without Edgar listening in.

Edgar still has one good attack on this protocol, however. (Very important: the attack is on the protocol used to send and receive messages, *not* on the encryption algorithms used. This attack does not require Edgar to break Gus and Angela's encryption and is completely independent of key length.) Edgar can not only read Gus's public key when he sends it to Angela, but he can also replace it with his own public key! Then when Angela thinks she's encrypting a message with Gus's public key, she's really using Edgar's. When she sends a message to Gus, Edgar intercepts it, decrypts it using his private key, encrypts it using Gus's public key, and sends it on to Gus. This is called a *man-in-the-middle attack*. Working alone on an insecure channel, Gus and Angela have no easy way to protect against this. The solution used in practice is for both Gus and Angela to store and verify their public keys with a trusted third-party certification authority. Rather than sending each other their public keys, Gus and Angela retrieve each other's public key from the certification authority. This scheme still isn't perfect—Edgar may be able to place himself in between Gus and the certification authority, Angela and the certification authority, and Gus and Angela—but it makes life harder for Edgar.

> This discussion has been necessarily brief. Many interesting details have been skimmed over or omitted entirely. If you want to know more, the Crypt Cabal's Cryptography FAQ at *http://www.faqs.org/faqs/cryptography-faq/* is a good place to start. For an in-depth analysis of protocols and algorithms for confidentiality, authentication, and message integrity, Bruce Schneier's *Applied Cryptography* (Wiley & Sons) is the standard introductory text. Finally, Jonathan Knudsen's *Java Cryptography* (O'Reilly) and Scott Oak's *Java Security* (O'Reilly) cover the underlying cryptography and authentication packages on which the JSSE rests.

As this example indicates, the theory and practice of encryption and authentication, both algorithms and protocols, is a challenging field that's fraught with mines and pitfalls to surprise the amateur cryptographer. It is much easier to design a bad encryption algorithm or protocol than a good one. And it's not always obvious which algorithms and protocols are good and which aren't. Fortunately, you don't have to be a cryptography expert to use strong cryptography in Java network programs. JSSE shields you from the low-level details of how algorithms are negotiated, keys are exchanged, correspondents are authenticated, and data is encrypted. JSSE allows you to create sockets and server sockets that transparently handle the negotiations and encryption necessary for secure communication. All you have to do is send your data over the same streams and sockets you're familiar with from previous chapters. The Java Secure Socket Extension is divided into four packages:

`javax.net.ssl`

> The abstract classes that define Java's API for secure network communication.

`javax.net`

> The abstract socket factory classes used instead of constructors to create secure sockets.

`javax.security.cert`

> A minimal set of classes for handling public key certificates that's needed for SSL in Java 1.1. (In Java 1.2 and later, the `java.security.cert` package should be used instead.)

`com.sun.net.ssl`

> The concrete classes that implement the encryption algorithms and protocols in Sun's reference implementation of the JSSE. Technically, these are not part of the JSSE standard. Other implementers may replace this package with one of their own; for instance, one that uses native code to speed up the CPU-intensive key generation and encryption process.

None of these are included as a standard part of the JDK prior to Java 1.4. To use these with Java 1.3 and earlier, you have to download the JSSE from *http://java.sun.com/products/jsse/* and install it. Third parties have also implemented this API, most notably Casey Marshall, who wrote Jessie (*http://www.nongnu.org/jessie/*), an open source implementation of JSSE published under the GPL with library exception.

Sun's reference implementation is distributed as a Zip file, which you can unpack and place anywhere on your system. In the *lib* directory of this Zip file, you'll find three JAR archives: *jcert.jar*, *jnet.jar*, and *jsse.jar*. These need to be placed in your class path or *jre/lib/ext* directory.

Next you need to register the cryptography provider by editing your *jre/lib/ext/security/java.security* file. Open this file in a text editor and look for a line like these:

```
security.provider.1=sun.security.provider.Sun
security.provider.2=com.sun.rsajca.Provider
```

You may have more or fewer providers than this. However many you have, add one more line like this:

```
security.provider.3=com.sun.net.ssl.internal.ssl.Provider
```

You may have to change the "3" to 2 or 4 or 5 or whatever the next number is in the security provider sequence. If you install a third-party JSSE implementation, you'll add another line like this with the class name as specified by your JSSE implementation's documentation.

 If you use multiple copies of the JRE, you'll need to repeat this procedure for each one you use. For reasons that have never been completely clear to me, Sun's JDK installer always places multiple copies of the JRE on my Windows box: one for compiling and one for running. You have to make these changes to both copies to get JSSE programs to run.

If you don't get this right, you'll see exceptions like "java.net.SocketException: SSL implementation not available" when you try to run programs that use the JSSE. Alternatively, instead of editing the *java.policy* file, you can add this line to classes that use Sun's implementation of the JSSE:

```
java.security.Security.addProvider(
  new com.sun.net.ssl.internal.ssl.Provider( ));
```

This may be useful if you're writing software to run on someone else's system and don't want to ask them to modify the *java.policy* file.

Creating Secure Client Sockets

If you don't care very much about the underlying details, using an encrypted SSL socket to talk to an existing secure server is truly straightforward. Rather than constructing a java.net.Socket object with a constructor, you get one from a javax.net. ssl.SSLSocketFactory using its createSocket( ) method. SSLSocketFactory is an abstract class that follows the abstract factory design pattern:

```
public abstract class SSLSocketFactory extends SocketFactory
```

Since the SSLFactorySocket class is itself abstract, you get an instance of it by invoking the static SSLSocketFactory.getDefault( ) method:

```
public static SocketFactory getDefault( ) throws InstantiationException
```

This either returns an instance of SSLSocketFactory or throws an InstantiationException if no concrete subclass can be found. Once you have a reference to the factory, use one of these five overloaded createSocket( ) methods to build an SSLSocket:

```
public abstract Socket createSocket(String host, int port)
 throws IOException, UnknownHostException
public abstract Socket createSocket(InetAddress host, int port)
 throws IOException
public abstract Socket createSocket(String host, int port,
 InetAddress interface, int localPort)
 throws IOException, UnknownHostException
```

```
public abstract Socket createSocket(InetAddress host, int port,
 InetAddress interface, int localPort)
 throws IOException, UnknownHostException
public abstract Socket createSocket(Socket proxy, String host, int port,
 boolean autoClose) throws IOException
```

The first two methods create and return a socket that's connected to the specified host and port or throw an IOException if they can't connect. The third and fourth methods connect and return a socket that's connected to the specified host and port from the specified local network interface and port. The last createSocket( ) method, however, is a little different. It begins with an existing Socket object that's connected to a proxy server. It returns a Socket that tunnels through this proxy server to the specified host and port. The autoClose argument determines whether the underlying proxy socket should be closed when this socket is closed. If autoClose is true, the underlying socket will be closed; if false, it won't be.

The Socket that all these methods return will really be a javax.net.ssl.SSLSocket, a subclass of java.net.Socket. However, you don't need to know that. Once the secure socket has been created, you use it just like any other socket, through its getInputStream( ), getOutputStream( ), and other methods. For example, let's suppose there's a server running on *login.ibiblio.org* on port 7,000 that accepts orders. Each order is sent as an ASCII string using a single TCP connection. The server accepts the order and closes the connection. (I'm leaving out a *lot* of details that would be necessary in a real-world system, such as the server sending a response code telling the client whether the order was accepted.) The orders that clients send look like this:

```
Name: John Smith
Product-ID: 67X-89
Address: 1280 Deniston Blvd, NY NY 10003
Card number: 4000-1234-5678-9017
Expires: 08/05
```

There's enough information in this message to let someone snooping packets use John Smith's credit card number for nefarious purposes. Consequently, before sending this order, you should encrypt it; the simplest way to do that without burdening either the server or the client with a lot of complicated, error-prone encryption code is to use a secure socket. The following code sends the order over a secure socket:

```
try {

  // This statement is only needed if you didn't add
  // security.provider.3=com.sun.net.ssl.internal.ssl.Provider
  // to your java.security file.
  Security.addProvider(new com.sun.net.ssl.internal.ssl.Provider());

  SSLSocketFactory factory
   = (SSLSocketFactory) SSLSocketFactory.getDefault();
  Socket socket = factory.createSocket("login.metalab.unc.edu", 7000);
```

```
    Writer out = new OutputStreamWriter(socket.getOutputStream( ),
      "ASCII");
    out.write("Name: John Smith\r\n");
    out.write("Product-ID: 67X-89\r\n");
    out.write("Address: 1280 Deniston Blvd, NY NY 10003\r\n");
    out.write("Card number: 4000-1234-5678-9017\r\n");
    out.write("Expires: 08/05\r\n");
    out.flush( );
    out.close( );
    socket.close( );

  }
  catch (IOException ex) {
    ex.printStackTrace( );
  }
```

Only the first three statements are noticeably different from what you'd do with an insecure socket. The rest of the code just uses the normal methods of the Socket, OutputStream, and Writer classes.

Reading input is no harder. Example 11-1 is a simple program that connects to a secure HTTP server, sends a simple GET request, and prints out the response.

Example 11-1. HTTPSClient

```java
import java.net.*;
import java.io.*;
import java.security.*;
import javax.net.ssl.*;
import com.macfaq.io.*;

public class HTTPSClient {

  public static void main(String[] args) {

    if (args.length == 0) {
      System.out.println("Usage: java HTTPSClient2 host");
      return;
    }

    int port = 443; // default https port
    String host = args[0];

    try {
      SSLSocketFactory factory
       = (SSLSocketFactory) SSLSocketFactory.getDefault( );

      SSLSocket socket = (SSLSocket) factory.createSocket(host, port);

      // enable all the suites
      String[] supported = socket.getSupportedCipherSuites( );
      socket.setEnabledCipherSuites(supported);
```

Example 11-1. HTTPSClient (continued)

```
    Writer out = new OutputStreamWriter(socket.getOutputStream( ));
    // https requires the full URL in the GET line
    out.write("GET http://" + host + "/ HTTP/1.1\r\n");
    out.write("Host: " + host + "\r\n");
    out.write("\r\n");
    out.flush( );

    // read response
    BufferedReader in = new SafeBufferedReader(
      new InputStreamReader(socket.getInputStream( )));

    // read the header
    String s;
    while (!(s = in.readLine( )).equals("")) {
        System.out.println(s);
    }
    System.out.println( );

    // read the length
    String contentLength = in.readLine( );
    int length = Integer.MAX_VALUE;
    try {
      length = Integer.parseInt(contentLength.trim( ), 16);
    }
    catch (NumberFormatException ex) {
      // This server doesn't send the content-length
      // in the first line of the response body
    }
    System.out.println(contentLength);

    int c;
    int i = 0;
    while ((c = in.read( )) != -1 && i++ < length) {
      System.out.write(c);
    }

    System.out.println( );
    out.close( );
    in.close( );
    socket.close( );

  }
  catch (IOException ex) {
    System.err.println(ex);
  }

 }

}
```

Here are the first few lines of output you get when you connect to the U.S. Postal Service's web site:

```
% java HTTPSClient www.usps.com
HTTP/1.1 200 OK
Server: Netscape-Enterprise/6.0
Date: Wed, 28 Jan 2004 18:13:08 GMT
Content-type: text/html
Set-Cookie: WEBTRENDS_ID=216.254.85.72-1075313584.16566; expires=Fri, 31-Dec-2010 00:
00:00 GMT; path=/
Transfer-Encoding: chunked

b6b
<META HTTP-EQUIV="Content-Type" CONTENT="text/html; charset=UTF-8">
<!DOCTYPE HTML PUBLIC "-//W3C//DTD HTML 4.0 Transitional//EN">
<HTML>
  <HEAD>

    <link rel="stylesheet" href="/common/stylesheets/styles.css" type="text/css">
    <TITLE>USPS - The United States Postal Service (U.S. Postal Service)</TITLE>
```

> When this program was tested for this edition, it initially refused to connect to *www.usps.com* because it couldn't verify the identity of the remote server. The problem was that the root certificates shipped with the version of the JDK I was using (1.4.2_02-b3) had expired. Upgrading to the latest minor version (1.4.2_03-b2) fixed the problem. If you see any exception messages like "No trusted certificate found", try upgrading to the latest minor version of either the JDK (if you're using 1.4 or later) or the JSSE (if you're using Java 1.3 or earlier).

One thing you may notice when you run this program is that it's slower to respond than you might expect. There's a noticeable amount of both CPU and network overhead involved in generating and exchanging the public keys. Even over a fast connection, it can easily take 10 seconds or more for the connection to be established. Consequently, you probably don't want to serve all your content over HTTPS, only the content that really needs to be private.

Methods of the SSLSocket Class

Besides the methods we've already discussed and those it inherits from java.net. Socket, the SSLSocket class has a number of methods for configuring exactly how much and what kind of authentication and encryption is performed. For instance, you can choose weaker or stronger algorithms, require clients to prove their identity, force reauthentication of both sides, and more.

Choosing the Cipher Suites

Different implementations of the JSSE support different combinations of authentication and encryption algorithms. For instance, the implementation Sun bundles with Java 1.4 only supports 128-bit AES encryption, whereas IAIK's iSaSiLk (*http://jce.iaik.tugraz.at/products/02_isasilk/*) supports 256-bit AES encryption. The getSupportedCipherSuites( ) method tells you which combination of algorithms is available on a given socket:

```
public abstract String[] getSupportedCipherSuites( )
```

However, not all cipher suites that are understood are necessarily allowed on the connection. Some may be too weak and consequently disabled. The getEnabledCipherSuites( ) method tells you which suites this socket is willing to use:

```
public abstract String[] getEnabledCipherSuites( )
```

The actual suite used is negotiated between the client and server at connection time. It's possible that the client and the server won't agree on any suite. It's also possible that although a suite is enabled on both client and server, one or the other or both won't have the keys and certificates needed to use the suite. In either case, the createSocket( ) method will throw an SSLException, a subclass of IOException. You can change the suites the client attempts to use via the setEnabledCipherSuites( ) method:

```
public abstract void setEnabledCipherSuites(String[] suites)
```

The argument to this method should be a list of the suites you want to use. Each name must be one of the suites listed by getSupportedCipherSuites( ). Otherwise, an IllegalArgumentException will be thrown. Sun's JDK 1.4 supports these 23 cipher suites:

- SSL_RSA_WITH_RC4_128_MD5
- SSL_RSA_WITH_RC4_128_SHA
- TLS_RSA_WITH_AES_128_CBC_SHA
- TLS_DHE_RSA_WITH_AES_128_CBC_SHA
- TLS_DHE_DSS_WITH_AES_128_CBC_SHA
- SSL_RSA_WITH_3DES_EDE_CBC_SHA
- SSL_DHE_RSA_WITH_3DES_EDE_CBC_SHA
- SSL_DHE_DSS_WITH_3DES_EDE_CBC_SHA
- SSL_RSA_WITH_DES_CBC_SHA
- SSL_DHE_RSA_WITH_DES_CBC_SHA
- SSL_DHE_DSS_WITH_DES_CBC_SHA
- SSL_RSA_EXPORT_WITH_RC4_40_MD5
- SSL_RSA_EXPORT_WITH_DES40_CBC_SHA
- SSL_DHE_RSA_EXPORT_WITH_DES40_CBC_SHA

- SSL_DHE_DSS_EXPORT_WITH_DES40_CBC_SHA

- SSL_RSA_WITH_NULL_MD5

- SSL_RSA_WITH_NULL_SHA

- SSL_DH_anon_WITH_RC4_128_MD5

- TLS_DH_anon_WITH_AES_128_CBC_SHA

- SSL_DH_anon_WITH_3DES_EDE_CBC_SHA

- SSL_DH_anon_WITH_DES_CBC_SHA

- SSL_DH_anon_EXPORT_WITH_RC4_40_MD5

- SSL_DH_anon_EXPORT_WITH_DES40_CBC_SHA

Each name has an algorithm divided into four parts: protocol, key exchange algorithm, encryption algorithm, and checksum. For example, the name SSL_DH_anon_EXPORT_WITH_DES40_CBC_SHA means Secure Sockets Layer Version 3; Diffie-Hellman method for key agreement; no authentication; Data Encryption Standard encryption with 40-bit keys; Cipher Block Chaining, and the Secure Hash Algorithm checksum.

By default, the JDK 1.4 implementation enables all the encrypted authenticated suites (the first 15 members of this list). If you want nonauthenticated transactions or authenticated but unencrypted transactions, you must enable those suites explicitly with the setEnabledCipherSuites( ) method.

Besides key lengths, there's an important difference between DES/AES and RC4-based ciphers. DES and AES are block ciphers; that is, they encrypt a certain number of bits at a time. DES always encrypts 64 bits. If 64 bits aren't available, the encoder has to pad the input with extra bits. AES can encrypt blocks of 128, 192, or 256 bits, but still has to pad the input if it doesn't come out to an even multiple of the block size. This isn't a problem for file transfer applications such as secure HTTP and FTP, where more or less all the data is available at once. However, it's problematic for user-centered protocols such as chat and Telnet. RC4 is a stream cipher that can encrypt one byte at a time and is more appropriate for protocols that may need to send a single byte at a time.

For example, let's suppose that Edgar has some fairly powerful parallel computers at his disposal and can quickly break any encryption that's 64 bits or less and that Gus and Angela know this. Furthermore, they suspect that Edgar can blackmail one of their ISPs or the phone company into letting him tap the line, so they want to avoid anonymous connections that are vulnerable to man-in-the-middle attacks. To be safe, Gus and Angela decide to use at least 111-bit, authenticated encryption. It then behooves them to enable only the strongest available algorithms. This code fragment accomplishes that:

```
String[] strongSuites = {"SSL_DHE_DSS_WITH_3DES_EDE_CBC_SHA",
 "SSL_RSA_WITH_RC4_128_MD5", "SSL_RSA_WITH_RC4_128_SHA",
 "SSL_RSA_WITH_3DES_EDE_CBC_SHA"};
socket.setEnabledCipherSuites(strongSuites);
```

If the other side of the connection doesn't support strong encryption, the socket will throw an exception when they try to read from or write to it, thus ensuring that no confidential information is accidentally transmitted over a weak channel.

Event Handlers

Network communications are slow compared to the speed of most computers. Authenticated network communications are even slower. The necessary key generation and setup for a secure connection can easily take several seconds. Consequently, you may want to deal with the connection asynchronously. JSSE uses the standard event model introduced in Java 1.1 to notify programs when the handshaking between client and server is complete. The pattern is a familiar one. In order to get notifications of handshake-complete events, simply implement the HandshakeCompletedListener interface:

```
public interface HandshakeCompletedListener
  extends java.util.EventListener
```

This interface declares the handshakeCompleted( ) method:

```
public void handshakeCompleted(HandshakeCompletedEvent event)
```

This method receives as an argument a HandshakeCompletedEvent:

```
public class HandshakeCompletedEvent extends java.util.EventObject
```

The HandshakeCompletedEvent class provides four methods for getting information about the event:

```
public SSLSession getSession( )
public String getCipherSuite( )
public X509Certificate[] getPeerCertificateChain( )
 throws SSLPeerUnverifiedException
public SSLSocket getSocket( )
```

Particular HandshakeCompletedListener objects register their interest in handshake-completed events from a particular SSLSocket via its addHandshakeCompletedListener( ) and removeHandshakeCompletedListener( ) methods:

```
public abstract void addHandshakeCompletedListener(
  HandshakeCompletedListener listener)
public abstract void removeHandshakeCompletedListener(
  HandshakeCompletedListener listener) throws IllegalArgumentException
```

Session Management

SSL is commonly used on web servers, and for good reason. Web connections tend to be transitory; every page requires a separate socket. For instance, checking out of Amazon.com on its secure server requires seven separate page loads, more if you have to edit an address or choose gift-wrapping. Imagine if every one of those pages took an extra 10 seconds or more to negotiate a secure connection. Because of the high overhead involved in handshaking between two hosts for secure communications, SSL allows *sessions* to be established that extend over multiple sockets. Different sockets within the same session use the same set of public and private keys. If the secure connection to Amazon.com takes seven sockets, all seven will be established within the same session and use the same keys. Only the first socket within that session will have to endure the overhead of key generation and exchange.

As a programmer using JSSE, you don't need to do anything extra to take advantage of sessions. If you open multiple secure sockets to one host on one port within a reasonably short period of time, JSSE will reuse the session's keys automatically. However, in high-security applications, you may want to disallow session-sharing between sockets or force reauthentication of a session. In the JSSE, sessions are represented by instances of the SSLSession interface; you can use the methods of this interface to check the times the session was created and last accessed, invalidate the session, and get various information about the session:

```
public byte[] getId( )
public SSLSessionContext getSessionContext( )
public long getCreationTime( )
public long getLastAccessedTime( )
public void invalidate( )
public void putValue(String name, Object value)
public Object getValue(String name)
public void removeValue(String name)
public String[] getValueNames( )
public X509Certificate[] getPeerCertificateChain( )
 throws SSLPeerUnverifiedException
public String getCipherSuite( )
public String getPeerHost( )
```

The getSession( ) method of SSLSocket returns the Session this socket belongs to:

```
public abstract SSLSession getSession( )
```

However, sessions are a trade-off between performance and security. It is more secure to renegotiate the key for each and every transaction. If you've got really spectacular hardware and are trying to protect your systems from an equally determined, rich, motivated, and competent adversary, you may want to avoid sessions. To prevent a socket from creating a session that passes false to setEnableSessionCreation( ), use:

```
public abstract void setEnableSessionCreation(boolean allowSessions)
```

The getEnableSessionCreation( ) method returns true if multisocket sessions are allowed, false if they're not:

```
public abstract boolean getEnableSessionCreation( )
```

On rare occasions, you may even want to reauthenticate a connection; that is, throw away all the certificates and keys that have previously been agreed to and start over with a new session. The startHandshake( ) method does this:

```
public abstract void startHandshake( ) throws IOException
```

Client Mode

It's a rule of thumb that in most secure communications, the server is required to authenticate itself using the appropriate certificate. However, the client is not. That is, when I buy a book from Amazon using its secure server, it has to prove to my browser's satisfaction that it is indeed Amazon and not Joe Random Hacker. However, I do not have to prove to Amazon that I am Elliotte Rusty Harold. For the most part, this is as it should be, since purchasing and installing the trusted certificates necessary for authentication is a fairly user-hostile experience that readers shouldn't have to go through just to buy the latest Nutshell handbook. However, this asymmetry can lead to credit card fraud. To avoid problems like this, sockets can be required to authenticate themselves. This strategy wouldn't work for a service open to the general public. However, it might be reasonable in certain internal, high-security applications.

The setUseClientMode( ) method determines whether the socket needs to use authentication in its first handshake. The name of the method is a little misleading. It can be used for both client- and server-side sockets. However, when true is passed in, it means the socket is in client mode (whether it's on the client side or not) and will not offer to authenticate itself. When false is passed, it will try to authenticate itself:

```
public abstract void setUseClientMode(boolean mode)
  throws IllegalArgumentException
```

This property can be set only once for any given socket. Attempting to set it a second time throws an IllegalArgumentException.

The getUseClientMode( ) method simply tells you whether this socket will use authentication in its first handshake:

```
public abstract boolean getUseClientMode( )
```

A secure socket on the server side (that is, one returned by the accept( ) method of an SSLServerSocket) uses the setNeedClientAuth( ) method to require that all clients connecting to it authenticate themselves (or not):

```
public abstract void setNeedClientAuth(boolean needsAuthentication)
  throws IllegalArgumentException
```

This method throws an IllegalArgumentException if the socket is not on the server side.

The getNeedClientAuth( ) method returns true if the socket requires authentication from the client side, false otherwise:

```
public abstract boolean getNeedClientAuth( )
```

Creating Secure Server Sockets

fSecure client sockets are only half of the equation. The other half is SSL-enabled server sockets. These are instances of the javax.net.SSLServerSocket class:

```
public abstract class SSLServerSocket extends ServerSocket
```

Like SSLSocket, all the constructors in this class are protected. Like SSLSocket, instances of SSLServerSocket are created by an abstract factory class, javax.net. SSLServerSocketFactory:

```
public abstract class SSLServerSocketFactory
 extends ServerSocketFactory
```

Also like SSLSocketFactory, an instance of SSLServerSocketFactory is returned by a static SSLServerSocketFactory.getDefault( ) method:

```
public static ServerSocketFactory getDefault( )
```

And like SSLSocketFactory, SSLServerSocketFactory has three overloaded createServerSocket( ) methods that return instances of SSLServerSocket and are easily understood by analogy with the java.net.ServerSocket constructors:

```
public abstract ServerSocket createServerSocket(int port)
 throws IOException
public abstract ServerSocket createServerSocket(int port,
 int queueLength) throws IOException
public abstract ServerSocket createServerSocket(int port,
 int queueLength, InetAddress interface) throws IOException
```

If that were all there was to creating secure server sockets, they would be quite straightforward and simple to use. Unfortunately, that's not all there is to it. The factory that SSLServerSocketFactory.getDefault( ) returns generally only supports server authentication. It does not support encryption. To get encryption as well, server-side secure sockets require more initialization and setup. Exactly how this setup is performed is implementation-dependent. In Sun's reference implementation, a com.sun.net.ssl. SSLContext object is responsible for creating fully configured and initialized secure server sockets. The details vary from JSSE implementation to JSSE implementation, but to create a secure server socket in the reference implementation, you have to:

- Generate public keys and certificates using *keytool*.
- Pay money to have your certificates authenticated by a trusted third party such as Verisign.
- Create an SSLContext for the algorithm you'll use.
- Create a TrustManagerFactory for the source of certificate material you'll be using.
- Create a KeyManagerFactory for the type of key material you'll be using.
- Create a KeyStore object for the key and certificate database. (Sun's default is JKS.)
- Fill the KeyStore object with keys and certificates; for instance, by loading them from the filesystem using the pass phrase they're encrypted with.
- Initialize the KeyManagerFactory with the KeyStore and its pass phrase.
- Initialize the context with the necessary key managers from the KeyManagerFactory, trust managers from the TrustManagerFactory, and a source of randomness. (The last two can be null if you're willing to accept the defaults.)

Example 11-2 demonstrates this procedure with a complete SecureOrderTaker for accepting orders and printing them on System.out. Of course, in a real application, you'd do something more interesting with the orders.

Example 11-2. SecureOrderTaker

```java
import java.net.*;
import java.io.*;
import java.util.*;
import java.security.*;
import javax.net.ssl.*;
import javax.net.*;

public class SecureOrderTaker {

  public final static int DEFAULT_PORT = 7000;
  public final static String algorithm = "SSL";

  public static void main(String[] args) {

    int port = DEFAULT_PORT;
    if (args.length > 0) {
      try {
        port = Integer.parseInt(args[0]);
        if (port < 0 || port >= 65536) {
          System.out.println("Port must between 0 and 65535");
          return;
        }
      }
      catch (NumberFormatException ex) {}
    }

    try {

      SSLContext context = SSLContext.getInstance(algorithm);

      // The reference implementation only supports X.509 keys
      KeyManagerFactory kmf = KeyManagerFactory.getInstance("SunX509");

      // Sun's default kind of key store
      KeyStore ks = KeyStore.getInstance("JKS");

      // For security, every key store is encrypted with a
      // pass phrase that must be provided before we can load
      // it from disk. The pass phrase is stored as a char[] array
      // so it can be wiped from memory quickly rather than
      // waiting for a garbage collector. Of course using a string
      // literal here completely defeats that purpose.
      char[] password = "2andnotafnord".toCharArray( );
      ks.load(new FileInputStream("jnp3e.keys"), password);
      kmf.init(ks, password);

      //
```

Example 11-2. SecureOrderTaker (continued)

```
    context.init(kmf.getKeyManagers( ), null, null);

    SSLServerSocketFactory factory
     = context.getServerSocketFactory( );

    SSLServerSocket server
     = (SSLServerSocket) factory.createServerSocket(port);

    String[] supported = server.getSupportedCipherSuites( );
    String[] anonCipherSuitesSupported = new String[supported.length];
    int numAnonCipherSuitesSupported = 0;
    for (int i = 0; i < supported.length; i++) {
      if (supported[i].indexOf("_anon_") > 0) {
        anonCipherSuitesSupported[numAnonCipherSuitesSupported++] = supported[i];
      }
    }

    String[] oldEnabled = server.getEnabledCipherSuites( );
    String[] newEnabled = new String[oldEnabled.length
     + numAnonCipherSuitesSupported];
    System.arraycopy(oldEnabled, 0, newEnabled, 0, oldEnabled.length);
    System.arraycopy(anonCipherSuitesSupported, 0, newEnabled,
     oldEnabled.length, numAnonCipherSuitesSupported);

    server.setEnabledCipherSuites(newEnabled);
    // Now all the set up is complete and we can focus
    // on the actual communication.
    try {
      while (true) {
        // This socket will be secure,
        // but there's no indication of that in the code!
        Socket theConnection = server.accept( );
        InputStream in = theConnection.getInputStream( );
        int c;
        while ((c = in.read( )) != -1) {
          System.out.write(c);
        }
        theConnection.close( );
      } // end while
    } // end try
    catch (IOException ex) {
      System.err.println(ex);
    } // end catch

} // end try
catch (IOException ex) {
  ex.printStackTrace( );
} // end catch
catch (KeyManagementException ex) {
  ex.printStackTrace( );
} // end catch
catch (KeyStoreException ex) {
```

Example 11-2. SecureOrderTaker (continued)

```
      ex.printStackTrace( );
    } // end catch
    catch (NoSuchAlgorithmException ex) {
      ex.printStackTrace( );
    } // end catch
    catch (java.security.cert.CertificateException ex) {
      ex.printStackTrace( );
    } // end catch
    catch (UnrecoverableKeyException ex) {
      ex.printStackTrace( );
    } // end catch

  } // end main

} // end server
```

This example loads the necessary keys and certificates from a file named *jnp3e.keys* in the current working directory protected with the password "2andnotafnord". What this example doesn't show you is how that file was created. It was built with the *keytool* program that's bundled with the JDK like this:

```
D:\JAVA>keytool -genkey -alias ourstore -keystore jnp3e.keys
Enter keystore password:  2andnotafnord
What is your first and last name?
  [Unknown]:  Elliotte
What is the name of your organizational unit?
  [Unknown]:  Me, Myself, and I
What is the name of your organization?
  [Unknown]:  Cafe au Lait
What is the name of your City or Locality?
  [Unknown]:  Brooklyn
What is the name of your State or Province?
  [Unknown]:  New York
What is the two-letter country code for this unit?
  [Unknown]:  NY
Is <CN=Elliotte, OU="Me, Myself, and I", O=Cafe au Lait, L=Brooklyn,
ST=New York, C=NY> correct?
  [no]:  y

Enter key password for <ourstore>
        (RETURN if same as keystore password):
```

When this is finished, you'll have a file named *jnp3e.keys*, which contains your public keys. However, no one will believe that these are your public keys unless you have them certified by a trusted third party such as Verisign (*http://www.verisign.com/*). Unfortunately, this certification costs money. The cheapest option is $14.95 per year for a Class 1 Digital ID. Verisign hides the sign-up form for this kind of ID deep within its web site, apparently to get you to sign up for the much more expensive options that are prominently featured on its home page. At the time of this writing, the sign-up form is at *https://www.verisign.com/client/*. Verisign has changed this

URL several times in the past, making it much harder to find than its more expensive options. In the more expensive options, Verisign goes to greater lengths to guarantee that you are who you say you are. Before signing up for any kind of digital ID, you should be aware that purchasing one has potentially severe legal consequences. In some jurisdictions, poorly thought-out laws make digital ID owners liable for all purchases made and contracts signed using their digital ID, regardless of whether the ID was stolen or forged. If you just want to explore the JSSE before deciding whether to go through the hassle, expense, and liability of purchasing a verified certificate, Sun includes a verified keystore file called *testkeys*, protected with the password "passphrase", that has some JSSE samples (*http://java.sun.com/products/jsse/*). However, this isn't good enough for real work.

For more information about exactly what's going on and what the various options are, as well as other ways to create key and certificate files, consult the online documentation for the *keytool* utility that came with your JDK, the Java Cryptography Architecture guide at *http://java.sun.com/j2se/1.4.2/docs/guide/security/CryptoSpec. html*, or the previously mentioned books *Java Cryptography*, by Jonathan Knudsen, or *Java Security*, by Scott Oaks (both from O'Reilly).

Another approach is to use cipher suites that don't require authentication. There are six of these in Sun's JDK 1.4: SSL_DH_anon_WITH_RC4_128_MD5, TLS_DH_ anon_WITH_AES_128_CBC_SHA, SSL_DH_anon_WITH_3DES_EDE_CBC_SHA, SSL_DH_anon_WITH_DES_CBC_SHA, SSL_DH_anon_EXPORT_WITH_RC4_ 40_MD5, and SSL_DH_anon_EXPORT_WITH_DES40_CBC_SHA.

These are not enabled by default because they're vulnerable to a man-in-the-middle attack, but at least they allow you to write simple programs without paying Verisign any money.

Methods of the SSLServerSocket Class

Once you've successfully created and initialized an SSLServerSocket, there are a lot of applications you can write using nothing more than the methods inherited from java.net.ServerSocket. However, there are times when you need to adjust its behavior a little. Like SSLSocket, SSLServerSocket provides methods to choose cipher suites, manage sessions, and establish whether clients are required to authenticate themselves. Most of these methods are very similar to the methods of the same name in SSLSocket. The difference is that they work on the server side and set the defaults for sockets accepted by an SSLServerSocket. In some cases, once an SSLSocket has been accepted, you can still use the methods of SSLSocket to configure that one socket rather than all sockets accepted by this SSLServerSocket.

Choosing the Cipher Suites

The SSLServerSocket class has the same three methods for determining which cipher suites are supported and enabled as SSLSocket does:

```
public abstract String[] getSupportedCipherSuites()
public abstract String[] getEnabledCipherSuites()
public abstract void     setEnabledCipherSuites(String[] suites)
```

These methods use the same suite names as the similarly named methods in SSLSocket. The difference is that these methods apply to all sockets accepted by the SSLServerSocket rather than to just one SSLSocket. For example, this code fragment has the effect of enabling anonymous, unauthenticated connections on the SSLServerSocket server. It relies on the names of these suites containing the string "_anon_". This is true for Sun's reference implementations, though there's no guarantee that other implementers will follow this convention:

```
String[] supported = server.getSupportedCipherSuites();
String[] anonCipherSuitesSupported = new String[supported.length];
int numAnonCipherSuitesSupported = 0;
for (int i = 0; i < supported.length; i++) {
  if (supported[i].indexOf("_anon_") > 0) {
    anonCipherSuitesSupported[numAnonCipherSuitesSupported++]
      = supported[i];
  }
}

String[] oldEnabled = server.getEnabledCipherSuites();
String[] newEnabled = new String[oldEnabled.length
 + numAnonCipherSuitesSupported];
System.arraycopy(oldEnabled, 0, newEnabled, 0, oldEnabled.length);
System.arraycopy(anonCipherSuitesSupported, 0, newEnabled,
 oldEnabled.length, numAnonCipherSuitesSupported);

server.setEnabledCipherSuites(newEnabled);
```

This fragment retrieves the list of both supported and enabled cipher suites using getSupportedCipherSuites() and getEnabledCipherSuites(). It looks at the name of every supported suite to see whether it contains the substring "_anon_". If the suite name does contain this substring, the suite is added to a list of anonymous cipher suites. Once the list of anonymous cipher suites is built, it's combined in a new array with the previous list of enabled cipher suites. The new array is then passed to setEnabledCipherSuites() so that both the previously enabled and the anonymous cipher suites can now be used.

Session Management

Both client and server must agree to establish a session. The server side uses the setEnableSessionCreation() method to specify whether this will be allowed and the getEnableSessionCreation() method to determine whether this is currently allowed:

```
public abstract void setEnableSessionCreation(boolean allowSessions)
public abstract boolean getEnableSessionCreation()
```

Session creation is enabled by default. If the server disallows session creation, then a client that wants a session will still be able to connect. It just won't get a session and will have to handshake again for every socket. Similarly, if the client refuses sessions but the server allows them, they'll still be able to talk to each other but without sessions.

Client Mode

The SSLServerSocket class has two methods for determining and specifying whether client sockets are required to authenticate themselves to the server. By passing true to the setNeedClientAuth() method, you specify that only connections in which the client is able to authenticate itself will be accepted. By passing false, you specify that authentication is not required of clients. The default is false. If for some reason you need to know what the current state of this property is, the getNeedClientAuth() method will tell you:

```
public abstract void setNeedClientAuth(boolean flag)
public abstract boolean getNeedClientAuth()
```

The setUseClientMode() method allows a program to indicate that even though it has created an SSLServerSocket, it is and should be treated as a client in the communication with respect to authentication and other negotiations. For example, in an FTP session, the client program opens a server socket to receive data from the server, but that doesn't make it less of a client. The getUseClientMode() method returns true if the SSLServerSocket is in client mode, false otherwise:

```
public abstract void setUseClientMode(boolean flag)
public abstract boolean getUseClientMode()
```

CHAPTER 12
Non-Blocking I/O

Compared to CPUs and memory or even disks, networks are slow. A high-end modern PC is capable of moving data between the CPU and main memory at speeds of around six gigabytes per second. It can move data to and from disk at the much slower but still respectable speed of about 150 megabytes per second.* By contrast, the theoretical maximum on today's fastest local area networks tops out at 120 megabytes per second, though most LANs only support speeds ten to a hundred times slower than that. And the speed across the public Internet is generally at least an order of magnitude smaller than what you see across a LAN. My faster than average SDSL line promises 96 kilobytes per second, but normally delivers only about two-thirds of that. And as I type this, my router has died and I've been reduced to a dialup connection whose bandwidth is less than six kilobytes per second. CPUs, disks, and networks are all speeding up over time. These numbers are all substantially higher than I could have reported in the first couple of editions of this book. Nonetheless, CPUs and disks are likely to remain several orders of magnitude faster than networks for the foreseeable future. The last thing you want to do in these circumstances is make the blazingly fast CPU wait for the (relatively) molasses-slow network.

The traditional Java solution for allowing the CPU to race ahead of the network is a combination of buffering and multithreading. Multiple threads can generate data for several different connections at once and store that data in buffers until the network is actually ready to send it; this approach works well for fairly simple servers and clients without extreme performance needs. However, the overhead of spawning multiple threads and switching between them is nontrivial. For instance, each thread requires about one extra megabyte of RAM. On a large server that may be process-

---

* These are rough, theoretical maximum numbers. Nonetheless, it's worth pointing out that I'm using megabyte to mean 1,024*1,024 bytes and gigabyte to mean 1,024 megabytes. Manufacturers often round the size of a gigabyte down to 1,000 megabytes and the size of a megabyte down to 1,000,000 bytes to make their numbers sound more impressive. Furthermore, networking speeds are often referred to in kilo/mega/giga *bits* per second rather than bytes per second. Here I'm reporting all numbers in bytes so I can compare hard drive, memory, and network bandwidths.

ing thousands of requests a second, it's better not to assign a thread to each connection, even if threads for subsequent requests can be reused, as discussed in Chapter 5. The overhead of thread management severely degrades system performance. It's faster if one thread can take responsibility for multiple connections, pick one that's ready to receive data, fill it with as much data as that connection can manage as quickly as possible, then move on to the next ready connection.

To really work well, this approach needs to be supported by the underlying operating system. Fortunately, pretty much every modern operating system you're likely to be using as a high-volume server supports such non-blocking I/O. However, it might not be well-supported on some client systems of interest, such as PDAs, cell phones, and the like (i.e., J2ME environments). Indeed, the java.nio package that provides this support is not part of any current or planned J2ME profiles. However, the whole new I/O API is designed for and only really matters on servers, which is why I haven't done more than allude to it until we began talking about servers. Client and even peer-to-peer systems rarely need to process so many simultaneous connections that multithreaded, stream-based I/O becomes a noticeable bottleneck. There are some exceptions—a web spider such as Google that downloads millions of pages simultaneously could certainly use the performance boost the new I/O APIs provide—but for most clients the new I/O API is overkill, and not worth the extra complexity it entails.

An Example Client

Although the new I/O APIs aren't specifically designed for clients, they do work for them. I'm going to begin with a client program using the new I/O APIs because it's a little simpler. In particular, many clients can be implemented with one connection at a time, so I can introduce channels and buffers before talking about selectors and non-blocking I/O.

To demonstrate the basics, I'll implement a simple client for the character generator protocol defined in RFC 864. This protocol is designed for testing clients. The server listens for connections on port 19. When a client connects, the server sends a continuous sequence of characters until the client disconnects. Any input from the client is ignored. The RFC does not specify which character sequence to send, but recommends that the server use a recognizable pattern. One common pattern is rotating, 72-character carriage return/linefeed delimited lines of the 95 ASCII printing characters, like this:

```
!"#$%&'( )*+,-./0123456789:;<=>?@ABCDEFGHIJKLMNOPQRSTUVWXYZ[\]^_`abcdefgh
"#$%&'( )*+,-./0123456789:;<=>?@ABCDEFGHIJKLMNOPQRSTUVWXYZ[\]^_`abcdefghi
#$%&'( )*+,-./0123456789:;<=>?@ABCDEFGHIJKLMNOPQRSTUVWXYZ[\]^_`abcdefghij
$%&'( )*+,-./0123456789:;<=>?@ABCDEFGHIJKLMNOPQRSTUVWXYZ[\]^_`abcdefghijk
%&'( )*+,-./0123456789:;<=>?@ABCDEFGHIJKLMNOPQRSTUVWXYZ[\]^_`abcdefghijkl
&'( )*+,-./0123456789:;<=>?@ABCDEFGHIJKLMNOPQRSTUVWXYZ[\]^_`abcdefghijklm
```

I picked this protocol for the examples in this chapter because both the protocol for transmitting the data and the algorithm to generate the data are simple enough that they won't obscure the I/O. However, chargen can transmit a lot of data over a relatively few connections and quickly saturate a network connection. It's thus a good candidate for the new I/O APIs.

When implementing a client that takes advantage of Java 1.4's new I/O APIs, begin by invoking the static factory method SocketChannel.open( ) to create a new java.nio.channels.SocketChannel object. The argument to this method is a java.net.SocketAddress object indicating the host and port to connect to. For example, this fragment connects the channel to *rama.poly.edu* on port 19:

```
SocketAddress rama = new InetSocketAddress("rama.poly.edu", 19);
SocketChannel client = SocketChannel .open(rama);
```

The channel is opened in blocking mode, so the next line of code won't execute until the connection is established. If the connection can't be established, an IOException is thrown.

If this were a traditional client, you'd now ask for the socket's input and/or output streams. However, it's not. With a channel you write directly to the channel itself. Rather than writing byte arrays, you write ByteBuffer objects. We've got a pretty good idea that the lines of text are 74 ASCII characters long (72 printable characters followed by a carriage return/linefeed pair) so we'll create a ByteBuffer that has a 74-byte capacity using the static allocate( ) method:

```
ByteBuffer buffer= ByteBuffer.allocate(74);
```

Pass this ByteBuffer object to the channel's read( ) method. The channel fills this buffer with the data it reads from the socket. It returns the number of bytes it successfully read and stored in the buffer:

```
int bytesRead = client.read(buffer);
```

By default, this will read at least one byte or return –1 to indicate the end of the data, exactly as an InputStream does. It will often read more bytes if more bytes are available to be read. Shortly you'll see how to put this client in non-blocking mode where it will return 0 immediately if no bytes are available, but for the moment this code blocks just like an InputStream. As you could probably guess, this method can also throw an IOException if anything goes wrong with the read.

Assuming there is some data in the buffer—that is, n > 0—this data can be copied to System.out. There are ways to extract a byte array from a ByteBuffer that can then be written on a traditional OutputStream such as System.out. However, it's more informative to stick with a pure, channel-based solution. Such a solution requires wrapping the OutputStream System.out in a channel using the Channels utility class, specifically, its newChannel( ) method:

```
WritableByteChannel output = Channels.newChannel(System.out);
```

You can then write the data that was read onto this output channel connected to System.out. However, before you do that you have to *flip* the buffer so that the output channel starts from the beginning of the data that was read rather than the end:

```
buffer.flip( );
output.write(buffer);
```

You don't have to tell the output channel how many bytes to write. Buffers keep track of how many bytes they contain. However, in general, the output channel is not guaranteed to write all the bytes in the buffer. In this specific case, though, it's a blocking channel and it will either do so or throw an IOException.

You shouldn't create a new buffer for each read and write. That would kill the performance. Instead, reuse the existing buffer. You'll need to clear the buffer before reading into it again:

```
buffer.clear( );
```

This is a little different than flipping. Flipping leaves the data in the buffer intact, but prepares it for writing rather than reading. Clearing resets the buffer to a pristine state.*

Example 12-1 puts this together into a complete client. Because chargen is by design an endless protocol, you'll need to kill the program using Ctrl-C.

Example 12-1. A channel-based chargen client

```
import java.nio.*;
import java.nio.channels.*;
import java.net.*;
import java.io.IOException;

public class ChargenClient {

  public static int DEFAULT_PORT = 19;

  public static void main(String[] args) {

    if (args.length == 0) {
      System.out.println("Usage: java ChargenClient host [port]");
      return;
    }

    int port;
    try {
      port = Integer.parseInt(args[1]);
    }
    catch (Exception ex) {
      port = DEFAULT_PORT;
    }
```

---

* Actually that's a tad simplistic. The old data is still present. It's not overwritten, but it will be overwritten with new data read from the source as soon as possible.

Example 12-1. A channel-based chargen client (continued)

```
try {
  SocketAddress address = new InetSocketAddress(args[0], port);
  SocketChannel client = SocketChannel.open(address);

  ByteBuffer buffer = ByteBuffer.allocate(74);
  WritableByteChannel out = Channels.newChannel(System.out);

  while (client.read(buffer) != -1) {
    buffer.flip( );
    out.write(buffer);
    buffer.clear( );
  }
}
catch (IOException ex) {
    ex.printStackTrace( );
}

  }

}
```

Here's the output from a sample run:

```
$ java ChargenClient rama.poly.edu
 !"#$%&'( )*+,-./0123456789:;<=>?@ABCDEFGHIJKLMNOPQRSTUVWXYZ[\]^_`abcdefg
 !"#$%&'( )*+,-./0123456789:;<=>?@ABCDEFGHIJKLMNOPQRSTUVWXYZ[\]^_`abcdefgh
 "#$%&'( )*+,-./0123456789:;<=>?@ABCDEFGHIJKLMNOPQRSTUVWXYZ[\]^_`abcdefghi
 #$%&'( )*+,-./0123456789:;<=>?@ABCDEFGHIJKLMNOPQRSTUVWXYZ[\]^_`abcdefghij
 $%&'( )*+,-./0123456789:;<=>?@ABCDEFGHIJKLMNOPQRSTUVWXYZ[\]^_`abcdefghijk
 %&'( )*+,-./0123456789:;<=>?@ABCDEFGHIJKLMNOPQRSTUVWXYZ[\]^_`abcdefghijkl
 &'( )*+,-./0123456789:;<=>?@ABCDEFGHIJKLMNOPQRSTUVWXYZ[\]^_`abcdefghijklm
 ...
```

So far, this is just an alternate vision of a program that could have easily been written using streams. The really new feature comes if you want the client to do something besides copying all input to output. You can run this connection in either blocking or non-blocking mode in which read( ) returns immediately even if no data is available. This allows the program to do something else before it attempts to read. It doesn't have to wait for a slow network connection. To change the blocking mode, pass true (block) or false (don't block) to the configureBlocking( ) method. Let's make this connection non-blocking:

```
client.configureBlocking(false);
```

In non-blocking mode, read( ) may return 0 because it doesn't read anything. Therefore the loop needs to be a little different:

```
while (true) {
    // Put whatever code here you want to run every pass through the loop
    // whether anything is read or not
    int n = client.read(buffer);
    if (n > 0) {
```

```
        buffer.flip( );
        out.write(buffer);
        buffer.clear( );
    }
    else if (n == -1) {
        // This shouldn't happen unless the server is misbehaving.
        break;
    }
}
```

There's not a lot of call for this in a one-connection client like this one. Perhaps you could check to see if the user has done something to cancel input, for example. However, as you'll see in the next section, when a program is processing multiple connections, this enables code to run very quickly on the fast connections and more slowly on the slow ones. Each connection gets to run at its own speed without being held up behind the slowest driver on the one-lane road.

An Example Server

Clients are well and good, but channels and buffers are really intended for server systems that need to process many simultaneous connections efficiently. Handling servers requires a third new piece in addition to the buffers and channels used for the client. Specifically, you need selectors that allow the server to find all the connections that are ready to receive output or send input.

To demonstrate the basics, I'll implement a simple server for the character generator protocol. When implementing a server that takes advantage of Java 1.4's new I/O APIs, begin by calling the static factory method ServerSocketChannel.open( ) method to create a new ServerSocketChannel object:

```
ServerSocketChannel serverChannel = ServerSocketChannel .open( );
```

Initially this channel is not actually listening on any port. To bind it to a port, retrieve its ServerSocket peer object with the socket( ) method and then use the bind( ) method on that peer. For example, this code fragment binds the channel to a server socket on port 19:

```
ServerSocket ss = serverChannel.socket( );
ss.bind(new InetSocketAddress(19));
```

As with regular server sockets, binding to port 19 requires you to be root on Unix (including Linux and Mac OS X). Nonroot users can only bind to ports 1024 and higher.

The server socket channel is now listening for incoming connections on port 19. To accept one, call the ServerSocketChannel accept( ) method, which returns a SocketChannel object:

```
SocketChannel clientChannel = serverChannel.accept( );
```

On the server side, you'll definitely want to make the client channel non-blocking to allow the server to process multiple simultaneous connections:

```
clientChannel.configureBlocking(false);
```

You may also want to make the ServerSocketChannel non-blocking. By default, this accept( ) method blocks until there's an incoming connection, like the accept( ) method of ServerSocket. To change this, simply call configureBlocking(false) before calling accept( ):

```
serverChannel.configureBlocking(false);
```

A non-blocking accept( ) returns null almost immediately if there are no incoming connections. Be sure to check for that or you'll get a nasty NullPointerException when trying to use the socket.

There are now two open channels: a server channel and a client channel. Both need to be processed. Both can run indefinitely. Furthermore, processing the server channel will create more open client channels. In the traditional approach, you assign each connection a thread, and the number of threads climbs rapidly as clients connect. Instead, in the new I/O API, you create a Selector that enables the program to iterate over all the connections that are ready to be processed. To construct a new Selector, just call the static Selector.open( ) factory method:

```
Selector selector = Selector.open( );
```

Next you need to register each channel with the selector that monitors it using the channel's register( ) method. When registering, specify the operation you're interested in using a named constant from the SelectionKey class. For the server socket, the only operation of interest is OP_ACCEPT; that is, is the server socket channel ready to accept a new connection?

```
serverChannel.register(selector, SelectionKey.OP_ACCEPT);
```

For the client channels, you want to know something a little different, specifically, whether they're ready to have data written onto them. For this, use the OP_WRITE key:

```
SelectionKey key = clientChannel.register(selector, SelectionKey.OP_WRITE);
```

Both register( ) methods return a SelectionKey object. However, we're only going to need to use that key for the client channels, because there can be more than one of them. Each SelectionKey has an attachment of arbitrary Object type. This is normally used to hold an object that indicates the current state of the connection. In this case, we can store the buffer that the channel writes onto the network. Once the buffer is fully drained, we'll refill it. Fill an array with the data that will be copied into each buffer. Rather than writing to the end of the buffer, then rewinding to the beginning of the buffer and writing again, it's easier just to start with two sequential copies of the data so every line is available as a contiguous sequence in the array:

```
byte[] rotation = new byte[95*2];
for (byte i = ' '; i <= '~'; i++) {
```

```
        rotation[i-' '] = i;
        rotation[i+95-' '] = i;
    }
```

Because this array will only be read from after it's been initialized, you can reuse it for multiple channels. However, each channel will get its own buffer filled with the contents of this array. We'll stuff the buffer with the first 72 bytes of the rotation array, then add a carriage return/linefeed pair to break the line. Then we'll flip the buffer so it's ready for draining, and attach it to the channel's key:

```
ByteBuffer buffer = ByteBuffer.allocate(74);
buffer.put(rotation, 0, 72);
buffer.put((byte) '\r');
buffer.put((byte) '\n');
buffer.flip();
key2.attach(buffer);
```

To check whether anything is ready to be acted on, call the selector's select() method. For a long-running server, this normally goes in an infinite loop:

```
while (true) {
    selector.select ();
    // process selected keys...
}
```

Assuming the selector does find a ready channel, its selectedKeys() method returns a java.util.Set containing one SelectionKey object for each ready channel. Otherwise it returns an empty set. In either case, you can loop through this with a java.util.Iterator:

```
Set readyKeys = selector.selectedKeys();
Iterator iterator = readyKeys.iterator();
while (iterator.hasNext()) {
    SelectionKey key = (SelectionKey) (iterator.next());
    // Remove key from set so we don't process it twice
    iterator.remove();
    // operate on the channel...
}
```

Removing the key from the set tells the selector that we've dealt with it, and the Selector doesn't need to keep giving it back to us every time we call select(). The Selector will add the channel back into the ready set when select() is called again if the channel becomes ready again. It's really important to remove the key from the ready set here, though.

If the ready channel is the server channel, the program accepts a new socket channel and adds it to the selector. If the ready channel is a socket channel, the program writes as much of the buffer as it can onto the channel. If no channels are ready, the selector waits for one. One thread, the main thread, processes multiple simultaneous connections.

In this case, it's easy to tell whether a client or a server channel has been selected because the server channel will only be ready for accepting and the client channels will only be ready for writing. Both of these are I/O operations, and both can throw IOExceptions for a variety of reasons, so you'll want to wrap this all in a try block.

```
try {
  if (key.isAcceptable( )) {
    ServerSocketChannel server = (ServerSocketChannel ) key.channel( );
    SocketChannel  connection = server.accept( );
    connection.configureBlocking(false);
    connection.register(selector, SelectionKey.OP_WRITE);
    // set up the buffer for the client...
  }
  else if (key.isWritable( )) {
    SocketChannel client = (SocketChannel ) key.channel( );
    // write data to client...
  }
}
```

Writing the data onto the channel is easy. Retrieve the key's attachment, cast it to ByteBuffer, and call hasRemaining( ) to check whether there's any unwritten data left in the buffer. If there is, write it. Otherwise, refill the buffer with the next line of data from the rotation array and write that.

```
ByteBuffer buffer = (ByteBuffer) key.attachment( );
if (!buffer.hasRemaining( )) {
  // Refill the buffer with the next line
  // Figure out where the last line started
  buffer.rewind( );
  int first = buffer.get( );
  // Increment to the next character
  buffer.rewind( );
  int position = first - ' ' + 1;
  buffer.put(rotation, position, 72);
  buffer.put((byte) '\r');
  buffer.put((byte) '\n');
  buffer.flip( );
}
client.write(buffer);
```

The algorithm that figures out where to grab the next line of data relies on the characters being stored in the rotation array in ASCII order. It should be familiar to anyone who learned C from Kernighan and Ritchie, but for the rest of us it needs a little explanation. buffer.get( ) reads the first byte of data from the buffer. From this number we subtract the space character (32) because that's the first character in the rotation array. This tells us which index in the array the buffer currently starts at. We add 1 to find the start of the next line and refill the buffer.

In the chargen protocol, the server never closes the connection. It waits for the client to break the socket. When this happens, an exception will be thrown. Cancel the key and close the corresponding channel:

```
      catch (IOException ex) {
        key.cancel( );
        try {
          // You can still get the channel from the key after cancelling the key.
          key.channel().close( );
        }
        catch (IOException cex) {
        }
      }
    }
```

Example 12-2 puts this all together in a complete chargen server that processes multiple connections efficiently in a single thread.

Example 12-2. A non-blocking chargen server

```java
import java.nio.*;
import java.nio.channels.*;
import java.net.*;
import java.util.*;
import java.io.IOException;

public class ChargenServer {

  public static int DEFAULT_PORT = 19;

  public static void main(String[] args) {

    int port;
    try {
      port = Integer.parseInt(args[0]);
    }
    catch (Exception ex) {
      port = DEFAULT_PORT;
    }
    System.out.println("Listening for connections on port " + port);

    byte[] rotation = new byte[95*2];
    for (byte i = ' '; i <= '~'; i++) {
        rotation[i-' '] = i;
        rotation[i+95-' '] = i;
    }

    ServerSocketChannel serverChannel;
    Selector selector;
    try {
      serverChannel = ServerSocketChannel.open( );
      ServerSocket ss = serverChannel.socket( );
      InetSocketAddress address = new InetSocketAddress(port);
      ss.bind(address);
      serverChannel.configureBlocking(false);
      selector = Selector.open( );
      serverChannel.register(selector, SelectionKey.OP_ACCEPT);
    }
    catch (IOException ex) {
```

Example 12-2. A non-blocking chargen server (continued)

```
      ex.printStackTrace( );
      return;
    }

    while (true) {

      try {
        selector.select( );
      }
      catch (IOException ex) {
        ex.printStackTrace( );
        break;
      }

      Set readyKeys = selector.selectedKeys( );
      Iterator iterator = readyKeys.iterator( );
      while (iterator.hasNext( )) {

        SelectionKey key = (SelectionKey) iterator.next( );
        iterator.remove( );
        try {
          if (key.isAcceptable( )) {
            ServerSocketChannel server = (ServerSocketChannel) key.channel( );
            SocketChannel client = server.accept( );
            System.out.println("Accepted connection from " + client);
            client.configureBlocking(false);
            SelectionKey key2 = client.register(selector, SelectionKey.OP_WRITE);
            ByteBuffer buffer = ByteBuffer.allocate(74);
            buffer.put(rotation, 0, 72);
            buffer.put((byte) '\r');
            buffer.put((byte) '\n');
            buffer.flip( );
            key2.attach(buffer);
          }
          else if (key.isWritable( )) {
            SocketChannel client = (SocketChannel) key.channel( );
            ByteBuffer buffer = (ByteBuffer) key.attachment( );
            if (!buffer.hasRemaining( )) {
              // Refill the buffer with the next line
              buffer.rewind( );
              // Get the old first character
              int first = buffer.get( );
              // Get ready to change the data in the buffer
              buffer.rewind( );
              // Find the new first characters position in rotation
              int position = first - ' ' + 1;
              // copy the data from rotation into the buffer
              buffer.put(rotation, position, 72);
              // Store a line break at the end of the buffer
              buffer.put((byte) '\r');
              buffer.put((byte) '\n');
              // Prepare the buffer for writing
```

Example 12-2. A non-blocking chargen server (continued)

```
          buffer.flip( );
        }
        client.write(buffer);
      }
    }
    catch (IOException ex) {
      key.cancel( );
      try {
        key.channel( ).close( );
      }
      catch (IOException cex) {}
    }

  }

 }

 }

}
```

This example only uses one thread. There are situations where you might still want to use multiple threads, especially if different operations have different priorities. For instance, you might want to accept new connections in one high priority thread and service existing connections in a lower priority thread. However, you're no longer required to have a 1:1 ratio between threads and connections, which dramatically improves the scalability of servers written in Java.

It may also be important to use multiple threads for maximum performance. Multiple threads allow the server to take advantage of multiple CPUs. Even with a single CPU, it's often a good idea to separate the accepting thread from the processing threads. The thread pools discussed in Chapter 5 are still relevant even with the new I/O model. The thread that accepts the connections can add the connections it's accepted into the queue for processing by the threads in the pool. This is still faster than doing the same thing without selectors because select( ) ensures you're never wasting any time on connections that aren't ready to receive data. On the other hand, the synchronization issues here are quite tricky, so don't attempt this solution until profiling proves there is a bottleneck.

Buffers

In Chapter 4, I recommended that you always buffer your streams. Almost nothing has a greater impact on the performance of network programs than a big enough buffer. In the new I/O model, however, you're no longer given the choice. All I/O is buffered. Indeed the buffers are fundamental parts of the API. Instead of writing data onto output streams and reading data from input streams, you read and write data from buffers. Buffers may appear to be just an array of bytes as in buffered streams. However, native implementations can connect them directly to hardware or memory or use other, very efficient implementations.

From a programming perspective, the key difference between streams and channels is that streams are byte-based while channels are block-based. A stream is designed to provide one byte after the other, in order. Arrays of bytes can be passed for performance. However, the basic notion is to pass data one byte at a time. By contrast, a channel passes blocks of data around in buffers. Before bytes can be read from or written to a channel, the bytes have to be stored in a buffer, and the data is written or read one buffer at a time.

The second key difference between streams and channels/buffers is that channels and buffers tend to support both reading and writing on the same object. This isn't always true. For instance, a channel that points to a file on a CD-ROM can be read but not written. A channel connected to a socket that has shutdown input could be written but not read. If you try to write to a read-only channel or read from a write-only channel, an UnsupportedOperationException will be thrown. However, more often that not network programs can read from and write to the same channels.

Without worrying too much about the underlying details (which can vary hugely from one implementation to the next, mostly a result of being tuned very closely to the host operating system and hardware), you can think of a buffer as a fixed-size list of elements of a particular, normally primitive data type, like an array. However, it's not necessarily an array behind the scenes. Sometimes it is; sometimes it isn't. There are specific subclasses of Buffer for all of Java's primitive data types except boolean: ByteBuffer, CharBuffer, ShortBuffer, IntBuffer, LongBuffer, FloatBuffer, and DoubleBuffer. The methods in each subclass have appropriately typed return values and argument lists. For example, the DoubleBuffer class has methods to put and get doubles. The IntBuffer class has methods to put and get ints. The common Buffer superclass only provides methods that don't need to know the type of the data the buffer contains. (The lack of primitive-aware generics really hurts here.) Network programs use ByteBuffer almost exclusively, although occasionally one program might use a view that overlays the ByteBuffer with one of the other types.

Besides its list of data, each buffer tracks four key pieces of information. All buffers have the same methods to set and get these values, regardless of the buffer's type:

position
> The next location in the buffer that will be read from or written to. Like most indexes in Java, this starts counting at 0 and has a maximum value one less than the size of the buffer. It can be set or gotten with these two methods:
> ```
> public final int    position( )
> public final Buffer position(int newPosition)
> ```

capacity

The maximum number of elements the buffer can hold. This is set when the buffer is created and cannot be changed thereafter. It can be read with this method:

```
public final int  capacity( )
```

limit

The last location in the buffer that can hold data. You cannot write or read past this point without changing the limit, even if the buffer has more capacity. It is set and gotten with these two methods:

```
public final int    limit( )
public final Buffer limit(int newLimit)
```

mark

A client-specified index in the buffer. It is set at the current position by invoking the mark( ) method. The current position is set to the marked position by invoking reset( ):

```
public final Buffer mark( )
public final Buffer reset( )
```

 No, I can't explain why these methods (and several similar methods in the java.nio packages) don't follow the standard Java getFoo( )/setFoo( ) naming convention. Blame it on the smoke-filled chat rooms in the Java Community Process.

Unlike reading from an InputStream, reading from a buffer does not actually change the buffer's data in any way. It's possible to set the position either forwards or backwards so you can start reading from a particular place in the buffer. Similarly, a program can adjust the limit to control the end of the data that will be read. Only the capacity is fixed.

The common Buffer superclass also provides a few other methods that operate by reference to these common properties.

The clear( ) method "empties" the buffer by setting the position to zero and the limit to the capacity. This allows the buffer to be completely refilled:

```
public final Buffer clear( )
```

However, the clear( ) method does not remove the old data from the buffer. It's still present and could be read using absolute get methods or changing the limit and position again.

The rewind( ) method sets the position to zero, but does not change the limit:

```
public final Buffer rewind( )
```

This allows the buffer to be reread.

The flip( ) method sets the limit to the current position and the position to zero:

```
public final Buffer flip( )
```

It is called when you want to drain a buffer you've just filled.

Finally, there are two methods that return information about the buffer but don't change it. The remaining( ) method returns the number of elements in the buffer between the current position and the limit. The hasRemaining( ) method returns true if the number of remaining elements is greater than zero:

```
public final int     remaining( )
public final boolean hasRemaining( )
```

Creating Buffers

The buffer class hierarchy is based on inheritance but not really on polymorphism, at least not at the top level. You normally need to know whether you're dealing with an IntBuffer or a ByteBuffer or a CharBuffer or something else. You write code to one of these subclasses, not to the common Buffer superclass. However, at the level of IntBuffer/ByteBuffer/CharBuffer, etc., the classes are polymorphic. These classes are abstract too, and you use a factory method to retrieve an implementation-specific subclass such as java.nio.HeapByteBuffer. However, you only treat the actual object as an instance of its superclass, ByteBuffer in this case.

Each typed buffer class has several factory methods that create implementation-specific subclasses of that type in various ways. Empty buffers are normally created by *allocate* methods. Buffers that are prefilled with data are created by *wrap* methods. The allocate methods are often useful for input while the wrap methods are normally used for output.

Allocation

The basic allocate( ) method simply returns a new, empty buffer with a specified fixed capacity. For example, these lines create byte and int buffers, each with a size of 100:

```
ByteBuffer buffer1 = ByteBuffer.allocate(100);
IntBuffer  buffer2 = IntBuffer.allocate(100);
```

The cursor is positioned at the beginning of the buffer; that is, the position is 0. A buffer created by allocate( ) will be implemented on top of a Java array, which can be accessed by the array( ) and arrayOffset( ) methods. For example, you could read a large chunk of data into a buffer using a channel and then retrieve the array from the buffer to pass to other methods:

```
byte[] data1 = buffer1.array( );
int[]  data2 = buffer2.array( );
```

The array( ) method does expose the buffer's private data, so use it with caution. Changes to the backing array are reflected in the buffer and vice versa. The normal pattern here is to fill the buffer with data, retrieve its backing array, and then operate on the array. This isn't a problem as long as you don't write to the buffer after you've started working with the array.

Direct allocation

The ByteBuffer class (but not the other buffer classes) has an additional allocateDirect( ) method that may not create a backing array for the buffer. The VM may implement a directly allocated ByteBuffer using direct memory access to the buffer on an Ethernet card, kernel memory, or something else. It's not required, but it's allowed, and this can improve performance for I/O operations. From an API perspective, the allocateDirect( ) is used exactly like allocate( ):

```
ByteBuffer buffer1 = ByteBuffer.allocateDirect(100);
```

Invoking array( ) and arrayOffset( ) on a direct buffer will throw an UnsupportedOperationException. Direct buffers may be faster on some virtual machines, especially if the buffer is large (roughly a megabyte or more). However, direct buffers are more expensive to create than indirect buffers, so they should only be allocated when the buffer is expected to be around for awhile. The details are highly VM-dependent. As is generally true for most performance advice, you probably shouldn't even consider using direct buffers until measurements prove performance is an issue.

Wrapping

If you already have an array of data that you want to output, you'll normally wrap a buffer around it, rather than allocating a new buffer and copying its components into the buffer one at a time. For example:

```
byte[] data = "Some data".getBytes("UTF-8");
ByteBuffer buffer1 = ByteBuffer.wrap(data);
char[] text = "Some text".toCharArray( );
CharBuffer buffer2 = CharBuffer.wrap(text);
```

Here, the buffer contains a reference to the array, which serves as its backing array. Buffers created by wrapping are never direct. Again, changes to the array are reflected in the buffer and vice versa, so don't wrap the array until you're finished with it.

Filling and Draining

Buffers are designed for sequential access. Besides its list of data, each buffer has a cursor indicating its current position. The cursor is an int that counts from zero to the number of elements in the buffer; the cursor is incremented by one when an element is read from or written to the buffer. It can also be positioned manually. For example, suppose you want to reverse the characters in a string. There are at least a dozen different ways to do this, including using string buffers,* char[] arrays, linked lists, and more. However, if we were to do it with a CharBuffer, we might begin by filling a buffer with the data from the string:

```
String s = "Some text";
CharBuffer buffer = CharBuffer.wrap(s);
```

We can only fill the buffer up to its capacity. If we tried to fill it past its initially set capacity, the put( ) method would throw a BufferOverflowException. Similarly, if we now tried to get( ) from the buffer, there'd be a BufferOverflowException. Before we can read the data out again, we need to flip the buffer:

```
buffer.flip( );
```

This repositions the cursor at the start of the buffer. We can drain it into a new string:

```
String result = "";
while (buffer.hasRemaining( )) {
  result+= buffer.get( );
}
```

Buffer classes also have *absolute* methods that fill and drain at specific positions within the buffer without updating the cursor. For example, ByteBuffer has these two:

```
public abstract byte       get(int index)
public abstract ByteBuffer put(int index, byte b)
```

These both throw IndexOutOfBoundsException if you try to access a position past the limit of the buffer. For example, using absolute methods, you could reverse a string into a buffer like this:

```
String s = "Some text";
CharBuffer buffer = CharBuffer.allocate(s.length( ));
for (int i = 0; i < s.length( ); i++) {
  buffer.put(s.length( ) - i - 1, s.charAt(i));
}
```

Bulk Methods

Even with buffers it's often faster to work with blocks of data rather than filling and draining one element at a time. The different buffer classes have bulk methods that fill and drain an array of their element type.

For example, ByteBuffer has put( ) and get( ) methods that fill and drain a ByteBuffer from a preexisting byte array or subarray:

```
public ByteBuffer get(byte[] dst, int offset, int length)
public ByteBuffer get(byte[] dst)
public ByteBuffer put(byte[] array, int offset, int length)
public ByteBuffer put(byte[] array)
```

---

* By the way, a StringBuffer is not a buffer in the sense of this section. Aside from the very generic notion of buffering, it has nothing in common with the classes being discussed here.

These put methods insert the data from the specified array or subarray, beginning at the current position. The get methods read the data into the argument array or subarray beginning at the current position. Both put and get increment the position by the length of the array or subarray. The put methods throw a `BufferOverflowException` if the buffer does not have sufficient space for the array or subarray. The get methods throw a `BufferUnderflowException` if the buffer does not have enough data remaining to fill the array or subarrray. These are runtime exceptions.

Data Conversion

All data in Java ultimately resolves to bytes. Any primitive data type—int, double, float, etc.—can be written as bytes. Any sequence of bytes of the right length can be interpreted as a primitive datum. For example, any sequence of four bytes corresponds to an `int` or a `float` (actually both, depending on how you want to read it). A sequence of eight bytes corresponds to a `long` or a `double`. The `ByteBuffer` class (and only the `ByteBuffer` class) provides relative and absolute put methods that fill a buffer with the bytes corresponding to an argument of primitive type (except boolean) and relative and absolute get methods that read the appropriate number of bytes to form a new primitive datum:

```
public abstract char       getChar()
public abstract ByteBuffer putChar(char value)
public abstract char       getChar(int index)
public abstract ByteBuffer putChar(int index, char value)
public abstract short      getShort()
public abstract ByteBuffer putShort(short value)
public abstract short      getShort(int index)
public abstract ByteBuffer putShort(int index, short value)
public abstract int        getInt()
public abstract ByteBuffer putInt(int value)
public abstract int        getInt(int index)
public abstract ByteBuffer putInt(int index, int value)
public abstract long       getLong()
public abstract ByteBuffer putLong(long value)
public abstract long       getLong(int index)
public abstract ByteBuffer putLong(int index, long value)
public abstract float      getFloat()
public abstract ByteBuffer putFloat(float value)
public abstract float      getFloat(int index)
public abstract ByteBuffer putFloat(int index, float value)
public abstract double     getDouble()
public abstract ByteBuffer putDouble(double value)
public abstract double     getDouble(int index)
public abstract ByteBuffer putDouble(int index, double value)
```

In the world of new I/O, these methods do the job performed by `DataOutputStream` and `DataInputStream` in traditional I/O. These methods do have an additional ability not present in `DataOutputStream` and `DataInputStream`. You can choose whether to interpret the byte sequences as big-endian or little-endian ints, floats, doubles, etc.

By default, all values are read and written as big-endian; that is, most significant byte first. The two order( ) methods inspect and set the buffer's byte order using the named constants in the ByteOrder class. For example, you can change the buffer to little-endian interpretation like so:

```
if (buffer.order( ).equals(ByteOrder.BIG_ENDIAN)) {
  buffer.order(ByteOrder.LITLLE_ENDIAN);
}
```

Suppose instead of a chargen protocol, you want to test the network by generating binary data. This test can highlight problems that aren't apparent in the ASCII chargen protocol, such as an old gateway configured to strip off the high order bit of every byte, throw away every 2^{30} byte, or put into diagnostic mode by an unexpected sequence of control characters. These are not theoretical problems. I've seen variations on all of these at one time or another.

You could test the network for such problems by sending out every possible int. This would, after about 4.2 billion iterations, test every possible four-byte sequence. On the receiving end, you could easily test whether the data received is expected with a simple numeric comparison. If any problems are found, it is easy to tell exactly where they occurred. In other words, this protocol (call it Intgen) behaves like this:

1. The client connects to the server.

2. The server immediately begins sending four-byte, big-endian integers, starting with 0 and incrementing by 1 each time. The server will eventually wrap around into the negative numbers.

3. The server runs indefinitely. The client closes the connection when it's had enough.

The server would store the current int in a 4-byte long direct ByteBuffer. One buffer would be attached to each channel. When the channel becomes available for writing, the buffer is drained onto the channel. Then the buffer is rewound and the content of the buffer is read with getInt( ). The program then clears the buffer, increments the previous value by one, and fills the buffer with the new value using putInt( ). Finally, it flips the buffer so it will be ready to be drained the next time the channel becomes writable. Example 12-3 demonstrates.

Example 12-3. Intgen server

```
import java.nio.*;
import java.nio.channels.*;
import java.net.*;
import java.util.*;
import java.io.IOException;

public class IntgenServer {

  public static int DEFAULT_PORT = 1919;
```

Example 12-3. Intgen server (continued)

```
public static void main(String[] args) {

  int port;
  try {
    port = Integer.parseInt(args[0]);
  }
  catch (Exception ex) {
    port = DEFAULT_PORT;
  }
  System.out.println("Listening for connections on port " + port);

  ServerSocketChannel serverChannel;
  Selector selector;
  try {
    serverChannel = ServerSocketChannel.open( );
    ServerSocket ss = serverChannel.socket( );
    InetSocketAddress address = new InetSocketAddress(port);
    ss.bind(address);
    serverChannel.configureBlocking(false);
    selector = Selector.open( );
    serverChannel.register(selector, SelectionKey.OP_ACCEPT);
  }
  catch (IOException ex) {
    ex.printStackTrace( );
    return;
  }

  while (true) {

    try {
      selector.select( );
    }
    catch (IOException ex) {
      ex.printStackTrace( );
      break;
    }

    Set readyKeys = selector.selectedKeys( );
    Iterator iterator = readyKeys.iterator( );
    while (iterator.hasNext( )) {

      SelectionKey key = (SelectionKey) iterator.next( );
      iterator.remove( );
      try {
        if (key.isAcceptable( )) {
          ServerSocketChannel server = (ServerSocketChannel ) key.channel( );
          SocketChannel client = server.accept( );
          System.out.println("Accepted connection from " + client);
          client.configureBlocking(false);
          SelectionKey key2 = client.register(selector, SelectionKey.OP_WRITE);
          ByteBuffer output = ByteBuffer.allocate(4);
          output.putInt(0);
```

Example 12-3. Intgen server (continued)

```
            output.flip( );
            key2.attach(output);
        }
        else if (key.isWritable( )) {
          SocketChannel client = (SocketChannel) key.channel( );
          ByteBuffer output = (ByteBuffer) key.attachment( );
          if (! output.hasRemaining( )) {
            output.rewind( );
            int value = output.getInt( );
            output.clear( );
            output.putInt(value+1);
            output.flip( );
          }
          client.write(output);
        }
      }
      catch (IOException ex) {
        key.cancel( );
        try {
          key.channel( ).close( );
        }
        catch (IOException cex) {}
      }

    }

  }

  }

}
```

View Buffers

If you know the ByteBuffer read from a SocketChannel contains nothing but elements of one particular primitive data type, it may be worthwhile to create a *view buffer*. This is a new Buffer object of appropriate type such as DoubleBuffer, IntBuffer, etc., which draws its data from an underlying ByteBuffer beginning with the current position. Changes to the view buffer are reflected in the underlying buffer and vice versa. However, each buffer has its own independent limit, capacity, mark, and position. View buffers are created with one of these six methods in ByteBuffer:

```
public abstract ShortBuffer  asShortBuffer( )
public abstract CharBuffer   asCharBuffer( )
public abstract IntBuffer    asIntBuffer( )
public abstract LongBuffer   asLongBuffer( )
public abstract FloatBuffer  asFloatBuffer( )
public abstract DoubleBuffer asDoubleBuffer( )
```

For example, consider a client for the Intgen protocol. This protocol is only going to read ints, so it may be helpful to use an IntBuffer rather than a ByteBuffer.

Example 12-4 demonstrates. For variety, this client is synchronous and blocking, but it still uses channels and buffers.

Example 12-4. Intgen client

```java
import java.nio.*;
import java.nio.channels.*;
import java.net.*;
import java.io.IOException;

public class IntgenClient {

  public static int DEFAULT_PORT = 1919;

  public static void main(String[] args) {

    if (args.length == 0) {
      System.out.println("Usage: java IntgenClient host [port]");
      return;
    }

    int port;
    try {
      port = Integer.parseInt(args[1]);
    }
    catch (Exception ex) {
      port = DEFAULT_PORT;
    }

    try {
      SocketAddress address = new InetSocketAddress(args[0], port);
      SocketChannel client = SocketChannel.open(address);
      ByteBuffer    buffer = ByteBuffer.allocate(4);
      IntBuffer     view   = buffer.asIntBuffer();

      for (int expected = 0; ; expected++) {
        client.read(buffer);
        int actual = view.get();
        buffer.clear();
        view.rewind();

        if (actual != expected) {
          System.err.println("Expected " + expected + "; was " + actual);
          break;
        }
        System.out.println(actual);
      }
    }
    catch (IOException ex) {
        ex.printStackTrace();
    }

  }

}
```

There's one thing to note here. Although you can fill and drain the buffers using the methods of the IntBuffer class exclusively, data must be read from and written to the channel using the original ByteBuffer of which the IntBuffer is a view. The SocketChannel class only has methods to read and write ByteBuffers. It cannot read or write any other kind of buffer. This also means you need to clear the ByteBuffer on each pass through the loop or the buffer will fill up and the program will halt. The positions and limits of the two buffers are independent and must be considered separately. Finally, if you're working in non-blocking mode, be careful that all the data in the underlying ByteBuffer is drained before reading or writing from the overlaying view buffer. Non-blocking mode provides no guarantee that the buffer will still be aligned on an int/double/char/etc. boundary following a drain. It's completely possible for a non-blocking channel to write half the bytes of an int or a double. When using non-blocking I/O, be sure to check for this problem before putting more data in the view buffer.

Compacting Buffers

Most writable buffers support a compact() method:

```
public abstract ByteBuffer    compact()
public abstract IntBuffer     compact()
public abstract ShortBuffer   compact()
public abstract FloatBuffer   compact()
public abstract CharBuffer    compact()
public abstract DoubleBuffer  compact()
```

(If it weren't for invocation chaining, these six methods could have been replaced by one method in the common Buffer superclass.) Compacting shifts any remaining data in the buffer to the start of the buffer, freeing up more space for elements. Any data that was in those positions will be overwritten. The buffer's position is set to the end of the data so it's ready for writing more data.

Compacting is an especially useful operation when you're *copying*—reading from one channel and writing the data to another using non-blocking I/O. You can read some data into a buffer, write the buffer out again, then compact the data so all the data that wasn't written is at the beginning of the buffer, and the position is at the end of the data remaining in the buffer, ready to receive more data. This allows the reads and writes to be interspersed more or less at random with only one buffer. Several reads can take place in a row, or several writes follow consecutively. If the network is ready for immediate output but not input (or vice versa), the program can take advantage of that. This technique can be used to implement an echo server as shown in Example 12-5. The echo protocol simply responds to the client with whatever data the client sent. Like chargen, it's useful for network testing. Also like chargen, echo relies on the client to close the connection. Unlike chargen, however, an echo server must both read and write from the connection.

Example 12-5. Echo server

```java
import java.nio.*;
import java.nio.channels.*;
import java.net.*;
import java.util.*;
import java.io.IOException;

public class EchoServer {

  public static int DEFAULT_PORT = 7;

  public static void main(String[] args) {

    int port;
    try {
      port = Integer.parseInt(args[0]);
    }
    catch (Exception ex) {
      port = DEFAULT_PORT;
    }
    System.out.println("Listening for connections on port " + port);


    ServerSocketChannel serverChannel;
    Selector selector;
    try {
      serverChannel = ServerSocketChannel.open( );
      ServerSocket ss = serverChannel.socket( );
      InetSocketAddress address = new InetSocketAddress(port);
      ss.bind(address);
      serverChannel.configureBlocking(false);
      selector = Selector.open( );
      serverChannel.register(selector, SelectionKey.OP_ACCEPT);
    }
    catch (IOException ex) {
      ex.printStackTrace( );
      return;
    }

    while (true) {

      try {
        selector.select( );
      }
      catch (IOException ex) {
        ex.printStackTrace( );
        break;
      }

      Set readyKeys = selector.selectedKeys( );
      Iterator iterator = readyKeys.iterator( );
      while (iterator.hasNext()) {
```

Example 12-5. Echo server (continued)

```
      SelectionKey key = (SelectionKey) iterator.next( );
      iterator.remove( );
      try {
        if (key.isAcceptable( )) {
          ServerSocketChannel server = (ServerSocketChannel ) key.channel( );
          SocketChannel client = server.accept( );
          System.out.println("Accepted connection from " + client);
          client.configureBlocking(false);
          SelectionKey clientKey = client.register(
            selector, SelectionKey.OP_WRITE | SelectionKey.OP_READ);
          ByteBuffer buffer = ByteBuffer.allocate(100);
          clientKey.attach(buffer);
        }
        if (key.isReadable( )) {
          SocketChannel client = (SocketChannel) key.channel( );
          ByteBuffer output = (ByteBuffer) key.attachment( );
          client.read(output);
        }
        if (key.isWritable( )) {
          SocketChannel client = (SocketChannel) key.channel( );
          ByteBuffer output = (ByteBuffer) key.attachment( );
          output.flip( );
          client.write(output);
          output.compact( );
        }
      }
      catch (IOException ex) {
        key.cancel( );
        try {
          key.channel().close( );
        }
        catch (IOException cex) {}
      }

    }

  }

  }

}
```

One thing I noticed while writing and debugging this program: the buffer size makes a big difference, although perhaps not in the way you might think. A big buffer can hide a lot of bugs. If the buffer is large enough to hold complete test cases without being flipped or drained, it's very easy to not notice that the buffer isn't being flipped or compacted at the right times because the test cases never actually need to do that. Before releasing your program, try turning the buffer size down to something significantly lower than the input you're expecting. In this case, I tested with a buffer size of 10. This test degrades performance, so you shouldn't ship with such a ridiculously small buffer, but you absolutely should test your code with small buffers to make sure it behaves properly when the buffer fills up.

Duplicating Buffers

It's often desirable to make a copy of a buffer to deliver the same information to two or more channels. The duplicate( ) methods in each of the six typed buffer classes do this:

```
public abstract ByteBuffer    duplicate( )
public abstract IntBuffer     duplicate( )
public abstract ShortBuffer   duplicate( )
public abstract FloatBuffer   duplicate( )
public abstract CharBuffer    duplicate( )
public abstract DoubleBuffer  duplicate( )
```

The return values are not clones. The duplicated buffers share the same data, including the same backing array if the buffer is indirect. Changes to the data in one buffer are reflected in the other buffer. Thus, you should mostly use this method when you're only going to read from the buffers. Otherwise, it can be tricky to keep track of where the data is being modified.

The original and duplicated buffers do have independent marks, limits, and positions even though they share the same data. One buffer can be ahead of or behind the other buffer.

Duplication is useful when you want to transmit the same data over multiple channels, roughly in parallel. You can make duplicates of the main buffer for each channel and allow each channel to run at its own speed. For example, recall the single file HTTP server in Example 10-6. Reimplemented with channels and buffers as shown in Example 12-6, NonblockingSingleFileHTTPServer, the single file to serve is stored in one constant, read-only buffer. Every time a client connects, the program makes a duplicate of this buffer just for that channel, which is stored as the channel's attachment. Without duplicates, one client has to wait till the other finishes so the original buffer can be rewound. Duplicates enable simultaneous buffer reuse.

Example 12-6. A non-blocking HTTP server that chunks out the same file

```
import java.io.*;
import java.nio.*;
import java.nio.channels.*;
import java.util.Iterator;
import java.net.*;

public class NonblockingSingleFileHTTPServer {

  private ByteBuffer contentBuffer;
  private int port = 80;
```

```java
public NonblockingSingleFileHTTPServer(
 ByteBuffer data, String encoding, String MIMEType, int port)
 throws UnsupportedEncodingException {

  this.port = port;
  String header = "HTTP/1.0 200 OK\r\n"
   + "Server: OneFile 2.0\r\n"
   + "Content-length: " + data.limit() + "\r\n"
   + "Content-type: " + MIMEType + "\r\n\r\n";
  byte[] headerData = header.getBytes("ASCII");

  ByteBuffer buffer = ByteBuffer.allocate(
   data.limit() + headerData.length);
  buffer.put(headerData);
  buffer.put(data);
  buffer.flip();
  this.contentBuffer = buffer;

}

public void run() throws IOException {

  ServerSocketChannel serverChannel = ServerSocketChannel.open();
  ServerSocket  serverSocket = serverChannel.socket();
  Selector selector = Selector.open();
  InetSocketAddress localPort = new InetSocketAddress(port);
  serverSocket.bind(localPort);
  serverChannel.configureBlocking(false);
  serverChannel.register(selector, SelectionKey.OP_ACCEPT);

  while (true) {

    selector.select();
    Iterator keys = selector.selectedKeys().iterator();
    while (keys.hasNext()) {
      SelectionKey key = (SelectionKey) keys.next();
      keys.remove();
      try {
        if (key.isAcceptable()) {
          ServerSocketChannel server = (ServerSocketChannel) key.channel();
          SocketChannel channel = server.accept();
          channel.configureBlocking(false);
          SelectionKey newKey = channel.register(selector, SelectionKey.OP_READ);
        }
        else if (key.isWritable()) {
          SocketChannel channel = (SocketChannel) key.channel();
          ByteBuffer buffer = (ByteBuffer) key.attachment();
          if (buffer.hasRemaining()) {
            channel.write(buffer);
          }
          else {  // we're done
            channel.close();
```

```
          }
        }
        else if (key.isReadable( )) {
          // Don't bother trying to parse the HTTP header.
          // Just read something.
          SocketChannel channel = (SocketChannel) key.channel( );
          ByteBuffer buffer = ByteBuffer.allocate(4096);
          channel.read(buffer);
          // switch channel to write-only mode
          key.interestOps(SelectionKey.OP_WRITE);
          key.attach(contentBuffer.duplicate( ));
        }
      }
      catch (IOException ex) {
        key.cancel( );
        try {
          key.channel( ).close( );
        }
        catch (IOException cex) {}
      }
    }
  }
}

public static void main(String[] args) {

  if (args.length == 0) {
    System.out.println(
      "Usage: java NonblockingSingleFileHTTPServer file port encoding");
    return;
  }

  try {
    String contentType = "text/plain";
    if (args[0].endsWith(".html") || args[0].endsWith(".htm")) {
      contentType = "text/html";
    }

    FileInputStream fin = new FileInputStream(args[0]);
    FileChannel in = fin.getChannel( );
    ByteBuffer input = in.map(FileChannel.MapMode.READ_ONLY, 0, in.size( ));

    // set the port to listen on
    int port;
    try {
      port = Integer.parseInt(args[1]);
      if (port < 1 || port > 65535) port = 80;
    }
    catch (Exception ex) {
      port = 80;
    }
```

Example 12-6. A non-blocking HTTP server that chunks out the same file (continued)

```
      String encoding = "ASCII";
      if (args.length > 2) encoding = args[2];

      NonblockingSingleFileHTTPServer server
        = new NonblockingSingleFileHTTPServer(
          input, encoding, contentType, port);
      server.run( );

    }
    catch (Exception ex) {
      ex.printStackTrace( );
      System.err.println(ex);
    }

  }

}
```

The constructors set up the data to be sent along with an HTTP header that includes information about content length and content encoding. The header and the body of the response are stored in a single ByteBuffer so that they can be blasted to clients very quickly. However, although all clients receive the same content, they may not receive it at the same time. Different parallel clients will be at different locations in the file. This is why we duplicate the buffer, so each channel has its own buffer. The overhead is small because all channels do share the same content. They just have different indexes into that content.

All incoming connections are handled by a single Selector in the run( ) method. The initial setup here is very similar to the earlier chargen server. The run( ) method opens a ServerSocketChannel and binds it to the specified port. Then it creates the Selector and registers it with the ServerSocketChannel. When a SocketChannel is accepted, the same Selector object is registered with it. Initially it's registered for reading because the HTTP protocol requires the client to send a request before the server responds.

The response to a read is simplistic. The program reads as many bytes of input as it can up to 4K. Then it resets the interest operations for the channel to writability. (A more complete server would actually attempt to parse the HTTP header request here and choose the file to send based on that information.) Next, the content buffer is duplicated and attached to the channel.

The next time the program passes through the while loop, this channel should be ready to receive data (or if not the next time, the time after that; the asynchronous nature of the connection means we won't see it until it's ready). At this point, we get the buffer out of the attachment, and write as much of the buffer as we can onto the channel. It's no big deal if we don't write it all this time. We'll just pick up where we left off the next pass through the loop. The buffer keeps track of its own position.

Although many incoming clients might result in the creation of many buffer objects, the real overhead is minimal because they'll all share the same underlying data.

The main( ) method just reads parameters from the command line. The name of the file to be served is read from the first command-line argument. If no file is specified or the file cannot be opened, an error message is printed and the program exits. Assuming the file can be read, its contents are mapped into the ByteBuffer array input. (To be perfectly honest, this is complete overkill for the small to medium size files you're most likely to be serving here, and probably would be slower than using an InputStream that reads into a byte array, but I wanted to show you file mapping at least once.) A reasonable guess is made about the content type of the file, and that guess is stored in the contentType variable. Next, the port number is read from the second command-line argument. If no port is specified, or if the second argument is not an integer from 0 to 65,535, port 80 is used. The encoding is read from the third command-line argument if present. Otherwise, ASCII is assumed. Then these values are used to construct a NonblockingSingleFileHTTPServer object and start it running.

Slicing Buffers

Slicing a buffer is a slight variant of duplicating. Slicing also creates a new buffer that shares the same data with the old buffer. However, the slice's initial position is the current position of the original buffer. That is, the slice is like a subsequence of the original buffer that only contains the elements from the current position to the limit. Rewinding the slice only moves it back to the position of the original buffer when the slice was created. The slice can't see anything in the original buffer before that point. Again, there are separate slice( ) methods in each of the six typed buffer classes:

```
public abstract ByteBuffer   slice()
public abstract IntBuffer    slice()
public abstract ShortBuffer  slice()
public abstract FloatBuffer  slice()
public abstract CharBuffer   slice()
public abstract DoubleBuffer slice()
```

This is useful when you have a long buffer of data that is easily divided into multiple parts such as a protocol header followed by the data. You can read out the header then slice the buffer and pass the new buffer containing only the data to a separate method or class.

Marking and Resetting

Like input streams, buffers can be marked and reset if you want to reread some data. Unlike input streams, this can be done to all buffers, not just some of them. For a change, the relevant methods are declared once in the Buffer superclass and inherited by all the various subclasses:

```
public final Buffer mark()
public final Buffer reset()
```

The reset( ) method throws an InvalidMarkException, a runtime exception, if the mark is not set.

The mark is unset if the limit is set to a point below the mark.

Object Methods

The buffer classes all provide the usual equals( ), hashCode( ), and toString( ) methods. They also implement Comparable, and therefore provide compareTo( ) methods. However, buffers are not Serializable or Cloneable.

Two buffers are considered to be equal if:

- They have the same type (e.g., a ByteBuffer is never equal to an IntBuffer but may be equal to another ByteBuffer).
- They have the same number of elements remaining in the buffer.
- The remaining elements at the same relative positions are equal to each other.

Note that equality does not consider the buffers' elements that precede the cursor, the buffers' capacity, limits, or marks. For example, this code fragment would print true even though the first buffer is twice the size of the second:

```
CharBuffer buffer1 = CharBuffer.wrap("12345678");
CharBuffer buffer2 = CharBuffer.wrap("5678");
buffer1.get( );
buffer1.get( );
buffer1.get( );
buffer1.get( );
System.out.println(buffer1.equals(buffer2));
```

The hashCode( ) method is implemented in accordance with the contract for equality. That is, two equal buffers will have equal hash codes and two unequal buffers are very unlikely to have equal hash codes. However, because the buffer's hash code changes every time an element is added to or removed from the buffer, buffers do not make good hash table keys.

Comparison is implemented by comparing the remaining elements in each buffer, one by one. If all the corresponding elements are equal, the buffers are equal. Otherwise, the result is the outcome of comparing the first pair of unequal elements. If one buffer runs out of elements before an unequal element is found and the other buffer still has elements, the shorter buffer is considered to be less than the longer buffer.

The toString( ) method returns strings that look something like this:

```
java.nio.HeapByteBuffer[pos=0 lim=62 cap=62]
```

These are primarily useful for debugging. The notable exception is CharBuffer, which returns a string containing the remaining chars in the buffer.

Channels

Channels move blocks of data into and out of buffers to and from various I/O sources such as files, sockets, datagrams, and so forth. The channel class hierarchy is rather convoluted, with multiple interfaces and many optional operations. However, for purposes of network programming there are only three really important channel classes, SocketChannel, ServerSocketChannel, and DatagramChannel; and for the TCP connections we've talked about so far you only need the first two.

SocketChannel

The SocketChannel class reads from and writes to TCP sockets. The data must be encoded in ByteBuffer objects for reading and writing. Each SocketChannel is associated with a peer Socket object that can be used for advanced configuration, but this requirement can be ignored for applications where the default options are fine.

Connecting

The SocketChannel class does not have any public constructors. Instead, you create a new SocketChannel object using one of the two static open( ) methods:

```
public static SocketChannel open(SocketAddress remote) throws IOException
public static SocketChannel open( ) throws IOException
```

The first variant makes the connection. This method blocks; that is, the method will not return until the connection is made or an exception is thrown. For example:

```
SocketAddress address = new InetSocketAddress("www.cafeaulait.org", 80);
SocketChannel channel = SocketChannel.open(address);
```

The noargs version does not immediately connect. It creates an initially unconnected socket that must be connected later using the connect( ) method. For example:

```
SocketChannel channel = SocketChannel.open( );
SocketAddress address = new InetSocketAddress("www.cafeaulait.org", 80);
channel.connect(address);
```

You might choose this more roundabout approach in order to configure various options on the channel and/or the socket before connecting. Specifically, use this approach if you want to open the channel without blocking:

```
SocketChannel channel = SocketChannel.open( );
SocketAddress address = new InetSocketAddress("www.cafeaulait.org", 80);
channel.configureBlocking(false);
channel.connect( );
```

With a non-blocking channel, the connect( ) method returns immediately, even before the connection is established. The program can do other things while it waits for the operating system to finish the connection. However, before it can actually use the connection, the program must call finishConnect( ):

```
public abstract boolean finishConnect( ) throws IOException
```

(This is only necessary in non-blocking mode. For a blocking channel this method returns true immediately.) If the connection is now ready for use, finishConnect( ) returns true. If the connection has not been established yet, finishConnect( ) returns false. Finally, if the connection could not be established, for instance because the network is down, this method throws an exception.

If the program wants to check whether the connection is complete, it can call these two methods:

```
public abstract boolean isConnected( )
public abstract boolean isConnectionPending( )
```

The isConnected( ) method returns true if the connection is open. The isConnectionPending( ) method returns true if the connection is still being set up but is not yet open.

Reading

To read from a SocketChannel, first create a ByteBuffer the channel can store data in. Then pass it to the read( ) method:

```
public abstract int read(ByteBuffer dst) throws IOException
```

The channel fills the buffer with as much data as it can, then returns the number of bytes it put there. If it encounters the end of stream, it returns –1. If the channel is blocking, this method will read at least one byte or return –1 or throw an exception. If the channel is non-blocking, however, this method may return 0.

Because the data is stored into the buffer at the cursor position, which is updated automatically as more data is added, you can keep passing the same buffer to the read( ) method until the buffer is filled. For example, this loop will read until the buffer is filled or the end of stream is detected:

```
while (buffer.hasRemaining( ) && channel.read(buffer) != -1) ;
```

It is sometimes useful to be able to fill several buffers from one source. This is called a *scatter*. These two methods accept an array of ByteBuffer objects as arguments and fill each one in turn:

```
public final long read(ByteBuffer[] dsts)throws IOException
public final long read(ByteBuffer[] dsts, int offset, int length)throws IOException
```

To fill these, just loop while the last buffer in the list has space remaining. For example:

```
ByteBuffer[] buffers = new ByteBuffer[2];
buffers[0] = ByteBuffer.allocate(1000);
buffers[1] = ByteBuffer.allocate(1000);
while (buffers[1].hasRemaining( ) && channel.read(buffers) != -1) ;
```

Writing

Socket channels have both read and write methods. In general, they are full duplex. In order to write, simply fill a ByteBuffer, flip it, and pass it to one of the write methods, which drains it while copying the data onto the output—pretty much the reverse of the reading process.

The basic write( ) method takes a single buffer as an argument:

```
public abstract int write(ByteBuffer src) throws IOException
```

As with reads (and unlike OutputStreams), this method is not guaranteed to write the complete contents of the buffer if the channel is non-blocking. Again, however, the cursor-based nature of buffers enables you to easily call this method again and again until the buffer is fully drained and the data has been completely written:

```
while (buffer.hasRemaining( ) && channel.write(buffer) != -1) ;
```

It is often useful to be able to write data from several buffers onto one socket. This is called a *gather*. For example, you might want to store the HTTP header in one buffer and the HTTP body in another buffer. The implementation might even fill the two buffers simultaneously using two threads or overlapped I/O. These two methods accept an array of ByteBuffer objects as arguments, and drain each one in turn:

```
public final long write(ByteBuffer[] dsts)throws IOException
public final long write(ByteBuffer[] dsts, int offset, int length)throws IOException
```

The first variant drains all the buffers. The second method drains length buffers, starting with the one at offset.

Closing

Just as with regular sockets, you should close a channel when you're done with it to free up the port and any other resources it may be using:

```
public void close( ) throws IOException
```

Closing an already closed channel has no effect. Attempting to write data to or read data from a closed channel throws an exception. If you're uncertain whether a channel has been closed, check with isOpen( ):

```
public boolean isOpen( )
```

Naturally, this returns false if the channel is closed, true if it's open. (close( ) and isOpen( ) are the only two methods declared in the Channel interface and shared by all channel classes.)

ServerSocketChannel

The ServerSocketChannel class has one purpose: to accept incoming connections. You cannot read from, write to, or connect a ServerSocketChannel. The only operation it supports is accepting a new incoming connection. The class itself only declares four methods, of which accept( ) is the most important. ServerSocketChannel also inherits several methods from its superclasses, mostly related to registering with a Selector for notification of incoming connections. And finally, like all channels it has a close( ) method that's used to shut down the server socket.

Creating server socket channels

The static factory method ServerSocketChannel.open( ) creates a new ServerSocketChannel object. However, the name is a little deceptive. This method does not actually open a new server socket. Instead, it just creates the object. Before you can use it, you need to use the socket( ) method to get the corresponding peer ServerSocket. At this point, you can configure any server options you like, such as the receive buffer size or the socket timeout, using the various setter methods in ServerSocket. Then connect this ServerSocket to a SocketAddress for the port you want to bind to. For example, this code fragment opens a ServerSocketChannel on port 80:

```
try {
  ServerSocketChannel server= ServerSocketChannel.open( );
  ServerSocket socket = serverChannel.socket( );
  SocketAddress address = new InetSocketAddress(80);
  socket.bind(address);
}
catch (IOException ex) {
  System.err.println("Could not bind to port 80 because " + ex.getMessage( ));
}
```

A factory method is used here rather than a constructor so that different virtual machines can provide different implementations of this class, more closely tuned to the local hardware and OS. However, this factory is not user-configurable. The open( ) method always returns an instance of the same class when running in the same virtual machine.

Accepting connections

Once you've opened and bound a ServerSocketChannel object, the accept( ) method can listen for incoming connections:

```
public abstract SocketChannel accept( ) throws IOException
```

accept( ) can operate in either blocking or non-blocking mode. In blocking mode, the accept( ) method waits for an incoming connection. It then accepts that connection and returns a SocketChannel object connected to the remote client. The thread cannot do anything until a connection is made. This strategy might be appropriate for simple servers that can respond to each request immediately. Blocking mode is the default.

A ServerSocketChannel can also operate in non-blocking mode. In this case, the accept( ) method returns null if there are no incoming connections. Non-blocking mode is more appropriate for servers that need to do a lot of work for each connection and thus may want to process multiple requests in parallel. Non-blocking mode is normally used in conjunction with a Selector. To make a ServerSocketChannel non-blocking, pass false to its configureBlocking( ) method.

The accept( ) method is declared to throw an IOException if anything goes wrong. There are several subclasses of IOException that indicate more detailed problems, as well as a couple of runtime exceptions:

ClosedChannelException
> You cannot reopen a ServerSocketChannel after closing it.

AsynchronousCloseException
> Another thread closed this ServerSocketChannel while accept( ) was executing.

ClosedByInterruptException
> Another thread interrupted this thread while a blocking ServerSocketChannel was waiting.

NotYetBoundException
> You called open( ) but did not bind the ServerSocketChannel's peer ServerSocket to an address before calling accept( ). This is a runtime exception, not an IOException.

SecurityException
> The security manager refused to allow this application to bind to the requested port.

The Channels Class

Channels is a simple utility class for wrapping channels around traditional I/O-based streams, readers, and writers, and vice versa. It's useful when you want to use the new I/O model in one part of a program for performance, but still interoperate with legacy APIs that expect streams. It has methods that convert from streams to channels and methods that convert from channels to streams, readers, and writers:

```
public static InputStream newInputStream(ReadableByteChannel ch)
public static OutputStream newOutputStream(WritableByteChannel ch)
public static ReadableByteChannel newChannel(InputStream in)
public static WritableByteChannel newChannel(OutputStream out)
public static Reader newReader (ReadableByteChannel channel,
  CharsetDecoder dec, int minBufferCap)
public static Reader newReader (ReadableByteChannel ch, String encoding)
public static Writer newWriter (WritableByteChannel ch, String encoding)
```

The SocketChannel class discussed in this chapter implements both the ReadableByteChannel and WritableByteChannel interfaces seen in these signatures. ServerSocketChannel implements neither of these because you can't read from or write to it.

For example, all current XML APIs use streams, files, readers, and other traditional I/O APIs to read the XML document. If you're writing an HTTP server designed to process SOAP requests, you may want to read the HTTP request bodies using channels and parse the XML using SAX for performance. In this case, you'd need to convert these channels into streams before passing them to XMLReader's parse( ) method:

```
SocketChannel channel = server.accept( );
processHTTPHeader(channel);
XMLReader parser = XMLReaderFactory.createXMLReader( );
parser.setContentHandler(someContentHandlerObject);
InputStream in = Channels.newInputStream(channel);
parser.parse(in);
```

Readiness Selection

For network programming, the second part of the new I/O APIs is readiness selection, the ability to choose a socket that will not block when read or written. This is primarily of interest to servers, although clients running multiple simultaneous connections with several windows open—such as a web spider or a browser—can take advantage of it as well.

In order to perform readiness selection, different channels are registered with a Selector object. Each channel is assigned a SelectionKey. The program can then ask the Selector object for the set of keys to the channels that are ready to perform the operation you want to perform without blocking.

The Selector Class

The only constructor in Selector is protected. Normally, a new selector is created by invoking the static factory method Selector.open( ):

```
public static Selector open( ) throws IOException
```

The next step is to add channels to the selector. There are no methods in the Selector class to add a channel. The register( ) method is declared in the SelectableChannel class. Not all channels are selectable—in particular, FileChannels aren't selectable—but all network channels are. Thus, the channel is registered with a selector by passing the selector to one of the channel's register methods:

```
public final SelectionKey register(Selector sel, int ops)
   throws ClosedChannelException
public final SelectionKey register(Selector sel, int ops, Object att)
   throws ClosedChannelException
```

This approach feels backwards to me, but it's not hard to use. The first argument is the selector the channel is registering with. The second argument is a named constant from the SelectionKey class identifying the operation the channel is registering for. The SelectionKey class defines four named bit constants used to select the type of the operation:

- `SelectionKey.OP_ACCEPT`
- `SelectionKey.OP_CONNECT`
- `SelectionKey.OP_READ`
- `SelectionKey.OP_WRITE`

These are bit-flag int constants (1, 2, 4, etc.). Therefore, if a channel needs to register for multiple operations in the same selector (e.g., for both reading and writing on a socket), combine the constants with the bitwise or operator (|) when registering:

```
channel.register(selector, SelectionKey.OP_READ | SelectionKey.OP_WRITE);
```

The optional third argument is an attachment for the key. This object is often used to store state for the connection. For example, if you were implementing a web server, you might attach a `FileInputStream` or `FileChannel` connected to the local file the server streams to the client.

After the different channels have been registered with the selector, you can query the selector at any time to find out which channels are ready to be processed. Channels may be ready for some operations and not others. For instance, a channel could be ready for reading but not writing.

There are three methods that select the ready channels. They differ in how long they wait to find a ready channel. The first, `selectNow()`, performs a non-blocking select. It returns immediately if no connections are ready to be processed now:

```
public abstract int selectNow() throws IOException
```

The other two select methods are blocking:

```
public abstract int select() throws IOException
public abstract int select(long timeout) throws IOException
```

The first method waits until at least one registered channel is ready to be processed before returning. The second waits no longer than `timeout` milliseconds for a channel to be ready before returning 0. These methods are useful if your program doesn't have anything to do when no channels are ready to be processed.

When you know the channels are ready to be processed, retrieve the ready channels using `selectedKeys()`:

```
public abstract Set selectedKeys()
```

The return value is just a standard `java.util.Set`. Each item in the set is a `SelectionKey` object. You can iterate through it in the usual way, casting each item to `SelectionKey` in turn. You'll also want to remove the key from the iterator to tell the `Selector` that you've handled it. Otherwise, the `Selector` will keep telling you about it on future passes through the loop.

Finally, when you're ready to shut the server down or when you no longer need the `Selector`, you should close it:

```
public abstract void close() throws IOException
```

This step releases any resources associated with the selector. More importantly, it cancels all keys registered with the selector and interrupts up any threads blocked by one of this selector's select methods.

The SelectionKey Class

SelectionKey objects serve as pointers to channels. They can also hold an object attachment, which is how you normally store the state for the connection on that channel.

SelectionKey objects are returned by the register( ) method when registering a channel with a Selector. However, you don't usually need to retain this reference. The selectedKeys( ) method returns the same objects again inside a Set. A single channel can be registered with multiple selectors.

When retrieving a SelectionKey from the set of selected keys, you often first test what that key is ready to do. There are four possibilities:

```
public final boolean isAcceptable( )
public final boolean isConnectable( )
public final boolean isReadable( )
public final boolean isWritable( )
```

This test isn't always necessary. In some cases, the Selector is only testing for one possibility and will only return keys to do that one thing. But if the Selector does test for multiple readiness states, you'll want to test which one kicked the channel into the ready state before operating on it. It's also possible that a channel is ready to do more than one thing.

Once you know what the channel associated with the key is ready to do, retrieve the channel with the channel( ) method:

```
public abstract SelectableChannel channel( )
```

If you've stored an object in the SelectionKey to hold state information, you can retrieve it with the attachment( ) method:

```
public final Object attachment( )
```

Finally, when you're finished with a connection, deregister its SelectionKey object so the Selector doesn't waste any resources querying it for readiness. I don't know that this is absolutely essential in all cases, but it doesn't hurt. You do this by invoking the key's cancel( ) method:

```
public abstract void cancel( )
```

However, this step is only necessary if you haven't closed the channel. Closing a channel automatically deregisters all keys for that channel in all selectors. Similarly, closing a selector invalidates all keys in that selector.

CHAPTER 13

UDP Datagrams and Sockets

Previous chapters discussed network applications that use the TCP protocol. TCP is designed for reliable transmission of data. If data is lost or damaged in transmission, TCP ensures that the data is resent; if packets of data arrive out of order, TCP puts them back in the correct order; if the data is coming too fast for the connection, TCP throttles the speed back so that packets won't be lost. A program never needs to worry about receiving data that is out of order or incorrect. However, this reliability comes at a price. That price is speed. Establishing and tearing down TCP connections can take a fair amount of time, particularly for protocols such as HTTP, which tend to require many short transmissions.

The User Datagram Protocol (UDP) is an alternative protocol for sending data over IP that is very quick, but not reliable. That is, when you send UDP data, you have no way of knowing whether it arrived, much less whether different pieces of data arrived in the order in which you sent them. However, the pieces that do arrive generally arrive quickly.

The UDP Protocol

The obvious question to ask is why anyone would ever use an unreliable protocol. Surely, if you have data worth sending, you care about whether the data arrives correctly? Clearly, UDP isn't a good match for applications like FTP that require reliable transmission of data over potentially unreliable networks. However, there are many kinds of applications in which raw speed is more important than getting every bit right. For example, in real-time audio or video, lost or swapped packets of data simply appear as static. Static is tolerable, but awkward pauses in the audio stream, when TCP requests a retransmission or waits for a wayward packet to arrive, are unacceptable. In other applications, reliability tests can be implemented in the application layer. For example, if a client sends a short UDP request to a server, it may assume that the packet is lost if no response is returned within an established period of time; this is one way the Domain Name System (DNS) works. (DNS can also operate over TCP.) In fact, you could implement a reliable file transfer protocol using UDP, and many people have: Network File System (NFS), Trivial FTP (TFTP), and FSP, a more distant relative of FTP, all use UDP. (The latest version of NFS can use either UDP or TCP.) In these protocols, the application is responsible for reliability; UDP doesn't take care of it. That is, the application must handle missing or out-of-order packets. This is a lot of work, but there's no reason it can't be done—although if you find yourself writing this code, think carefully about whether you might be better off with TCP.

The difference between TCP and UDP is often explained by analogy with the phone system and the post office. TCP is like the phone system. When you dial a number, the phone is answered and a connection is established between the two parties. As you talk, you know that the other party hears your words in the order in which you say them. If the phone is busy or no one answers, you find out right away. UDP, by contrast, is like the postal system. You send packets of mail to an address. Most of the letters arrive, but some may be lost on the way. The letters probably arrive in the order in which you sent them, but that's not guaranteed. The farther away you are from your recipient, the more likely it is that mail will be lost on the way or arrive out of order. If this is a problem, you can write sequential numbers on the envelopes, then ask the recipients to arrange them in the correct order and send you mail telling you which letters arrived so that you can resend any that didn't get there the first time. However, you and your correspondent need to agree on this protocol in advance. The post office will not do it for you.

Both the phone system and the post office have their uses. Although either one could be used for almost any communication, in some cases one is definitely superior to the other. The same is true of UDP and TCP. The last several chapters have all focused on TCP applications, which are more common than UDP applications. However, UDP also has its place; in this chapter, we'll look at what you can do with UDP in Java. If you want to go further, look at Chapter 14. Multicasting relies on UDP; a multicast socket is a fairly simple variation on a UDP socket.

Java's implementation of UDP is split into two classes: DatagramPacket and DatagramSocket. The DatagramPacket class stuffs bytes of data into UDP packets called *datagrams* and lets you unstuff datagrams that you receive. A DatagramSocket sends as well as receives UDP datagrams. To send data, you put the data in a DatagramPacket and send the packet using a DatagramSocket. To receive data, you receive a DatagramPacket object from a DatagramSocket and then read the contents of the packet. The sockets themselves are very simple creatures. In UDP, everything about a datagram, including the address to which it is directed, is included in the packet itself; the socket only needs to know the local port on which to listen or send.

This division of labor contrasts with the Socket and ServerSocket classes used by TCP. First, UDP doesn't have any notion of a unique connection between two hosts. One socket sends and receives all data directed to or from a port without any concern for whom the remote host is. A single DatagramSocket can send data to and receive data from many independent hosts. The socket isn't dedicated to a single connection, as it is in TCP. In fact, UDP doesn't have any concept of a connection between two hosts; it only knows about individual datagrams. Figuring out who sent what data is the application's responsibility. Second, TCP sockets treat a network connection as a stream: you send and receive data with input and output streams that you get from the socket. UDP doesn't allow this; you always work with individual datagram packets. All the data you stuff into a single datagram is sent as a single packet and is either received or lost as a group. One packet is not necessarily related to the next. Given two packets, there is no way to determine which packet was sent first and which was sent second. Instead of the orderly queue of data that's necessary for a stream, datagrams try to crowd into the recipient as quickly as possible, like a crowd of people pushing their way onto a bus. And occasionally, if the bus is crowded enough, a few packets, like people, may not squeeze on and will be left waiting at the bus stop.

The DatagramPacket Class

UDP datagrams add very little to the IP datagrams they sit on top of. Figure 13-1 shows a typical UDP datagram. The UDP header adds only eight bytes to the IP header. The UDP header includes source and destination port numbers, the length of everything that follows the IP header, and an optional checksum. Since port numbers are given as 2-byte unsigned integers, 65,536 different possible UDP ports are available per host. These are distinct from the 65,536 different TCP ports per host. Since the length is also a 2-byte unsigned integer, the number of bytes in a datagram is limited to 65,536 minus the 8 bytes for the header. However, this is redundant with the datagram length field of the IP header, which limits datagrams to between 65,467 and 65,507 bytes. (The exact number depends on the size of the IP header.) The checksum field is optional and not used in or accessible from application layer programs. If the checksum for the data fails, the native network software silently discards the datagram; neither the sender nor the receiver is notified. UDP is an unreliable protocol, after all.

Although the theoretical maximum amount of data in a UDP datagram is 65,507 bytes, in practice there is almost always much less. On many platforms, the actual limit is more likely to be 8,192 bytes (8K). And implementations are not required to accept datagrams with more than 576 total bytes, including data and headers. Consequently, you should be extremely wary of any program that depends on sending or receiving UDP packets with more than 8K of data. Most of the time, larger packets are simply truncated to 8K of data. For maximum safety, the data portion of a UDP packet should be kept to 512 bytes or less, although this limit can negatively affect performance compared to larger packet sizes. (This is a problem for TCP datagrams

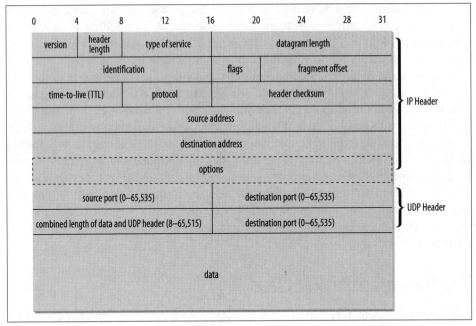

0	4	8	12	16	20	24	28	31	

version	header length	type of service	datagram length	
identification		flags	fragment offset	
time-to-live (TTL)	protocol	header checksum		IP Header
source address				
destination address				
options				
source port (0–65,535)		destination port (0–65,535)		
combined length of data and UDP header (8–65,515)		destination port (0–65,535)		UDP Header
data				

Figure 13-1. The structure of a UDP datagram

too, but the stream-based API provided by Socket and ServerSocket completely shields programmers from these details.)

In Java, a UDP datagram is represented by an instance of the DatagramPacket class:

```
public final class DatagramPacket extends Object
```

This class provides methods to get and set the source or destination address from the IP header, to get and set the source or destination port, to get and set the data, and to get and set the length of the data. The remaining header fields are inaccessible from pure Java code.

The Constructors

DatagramPacket uses different constructors depending on whether the packet will be used to send data or to receive data. This is a little unusual. Normally, constructors are overloaded to let you provide different kinds of information when you create an object, not to create objects of the same class that will be used in different contexts. In this case, all six constructors take as arguments a byte array that holds the datagram's data and the number of bytes in that array to use for the datagram's data. When you want to receive a datagram, these are the only arguments you provide; in addition, the array should be empty. When the socket receives a datagram from the network, it stores the datagram's data in the DatagramPacket object's buffer array, up to the length you specified.

The second set of DatagramPacket constructors is used to create datagrams you will send over the network. Like the first, these constructors require a buffer array and a length, but they also require the InetAddress and port to which the packet is to be sent. In this case, you will pass to the constructor a byte array containing the data you want to send and the destination address and port to which the packet is to be sent. The DatagramSocket reads the destination address and port from the packet; the address and port aren't stored within the socket, as they are in TCP.

Constructors for receiving datagrams

These two constructors create new DatagramPacket objects for receiving data from the network:

```
public DatagramPacket(byte[] buffer, int length)
public DatagramPacket(byte[] buffer, int offset, int length) // Java 1.2
```

When a socket receives a datagram, it stores the datagram's data part in buffer beginning at buffer[0] and continuing until the packet is completely stored or until length bytes have been written into the buffer. If the second constructor is used, storage begins at buffer[offset] instead. Otherwise, these two constructors are identical. length must be less than or equal to buffer.length-offset. If you try to construct a DatagramPacket with a length that will overflow the buffer, the constructor throws an IllegalArgumentException. This is a RuntimeException, so your code is not required to catch it. It is okay to construct a DatagramPacket with a length less than buffer.length-offset. In this case, at most the first length bytes of buffer will be filled when the datagram is received. For example, this code fragment creates a new DatagramPacket for receiving a datagram of up to 8,192 bytes:

```
byte[] buffer = new byte[8192];
DatagramPacket dp = new DatagramPacket(buffer, buffer.length);
```

The constructor doesn't care how large the buffer is and would happily let you create a DatagramPacket with megabytes of data. However, the underlying native network software is less forgiving, and most native UDP implementations don't support more than 8,192 bytes of data per datagram. The theoretical limit for an IPv4 datagram is 65,507 bytes of data, and a DatagramPacket with a 65,507-byte buffer can receive any possible IPv4 datagram without losing data. IPv6 datagrams raise the theoretical limit to 65,536 bytes. In practice, however, many UDP-based protocols such as DNS and TFTP use packets with 512 bytes of data per datagram or fewer. The largest data size in common usage is 8,192 bytes for NFS. Almost all UDP datagrams you're likely to encounter will have 8K of data or fewer. In fact, many operating systems don't support UDP datagrams with more than 8K of data and either truncate, split, or discard larger datagrams. If a large datagram is too big and as a result the network truncates or drops it, your Java program won't be notified of the problem. (UDP is an unreliable protocol, after all.) Consequently, you shouldn't create DatagramPacket objects with more than 8,192 bytes of data.

Constructors for sending datagrams

These four constructors create new `DatagramPacket` objects for sending data across the network:

```
public DatagramPacket(byte[] data, int length,
  InetAddress destination, int port)
public DatagramPacket(byte[] data, int offset, int length,
  InetAddress destination, int port) // Java 1.2
public DatagramPacket(byte[] data, int length,
  SocketAddress destination, int port) // Java 1.4
public DatagramPacket(byte[] data, int offset, int length,
  SocketAddress destination, int port) // Java 1.4
```

Each constructor creates a new `DatagramPacket` to be sent to another host. The packet is filled with `length` bytes of the data array starting at `offset` or 0 if `offset` is not used. If you try to construct a `DatagramPacket` with a length that is greater than `data.length`, the constructor throws an `IllegalArgumentException`. It's okay to construct a `DatagramPacket` object with an `offset` and a `length` that will leave extra, unused space at the end of the data array. In this case, only `length` bytes of data will be sent over the network. The `InetAddress` or `SocketAddress` object `destination` points to the host you want the packet delivered to; the `int` argument `port` is the port on that host.

Choosing a Datagram Size

The correct amount of data to stuff into one packet depends on the situation. Some protocols dictate the size of the packet. For example, *rlogin* transmits each character to the remote system almost as soon as the user types it. Therefore, packets tend to be short: a single byte of data, plus a few bytes of headers. Other applications aren't so picky. For example, file transfer is more efficient with large buffers; the only requirement is that you split files into packets no larger than the maximum allowable packet size.

Several factors are involved in choosing the optimal packet size. If the network is highly unreliable, such as a packet radio network, smaller packets are preferable since they're less likely to be corrupted in transit. On the other hand, very fast and reliable LANs should use the largest packet size possible. Eight kilobytes—that is, 8,192 bytes—is a good compromise for many types of networks.

It's customary to convert the data to a byte array and place it in data *before* creating the `DatagramPacket`, but it's not absolutely necessary. Changing data *after* the datagram has been constructed and *before* it has been sent changes the data in the datagram; the data isn't copied into a private buffer. In some applications, you can take advantage of this. For example, you could store data that changes over time in data and send out the current datagram (with the most recent data) every minute. However, it's more important to make sure that the data doesn't change when you don't want it to. This is especially true if your program is multithreaded, and different threads may write into the data buffer. If this is the case, synchronize the data variable or copy the data into a temporary buffer before you construct the DatagramPacket.

For instance, this code fragment creates a new DatagramPacket filled with the data "This is a test" in ASCII. The packet is directed at port 7 (the echo port) of the host *www.ibiblio.org*:

```
String s = "This is a test";
byte[] data = s.getBytes("ASCII");

try {
  InetAddress ia = InetAddress.getByName("www.ibiblio.org");
  int port = 7;
  DatagramPacket dp = new DatagramPacket(data, data.length, ia, port);
  // send the packet...
}
catch (IOException ex)
}
```

Most of the time, the hardest part of creating a new DatagramPacket is translating the data into a byte array. Since this code fragment wants to send an ASCII string, it uses the getBytes( ) method of java.lang.String. The java.io.ByteArrayOutputStream class can also be very useful for preparing data for inclusion in datagrams.

The get Methods

DatagramPacket has six methods that retrieve different parts of a datagram: the actual data plus several fields from its header. These methods are mostly used for datagrams received from the network.

public InetAddress getAddress( )

The getAddress( ) method returns an InetAddress object containing the address of the remote host. If the datagram was received from the Internet, the address returned is the address of the machine that sent it (the source address). On the other hand, if the datagram was created locally to be sent to a remote machine, this method returns the address of the host to which the datagram is addressed (the destination address). This method is most commonly used to determine the address of the host that sent a UDP datagram, so that the recipient can reply.

public int getPort( )

The getPort( ) method returns an integer specifying the remote port. If this datagram was received from the Internet, this is the port on the host that sent the packet.

If the datagram was created locally to be sent to a remote host, this is the port to which the packet is addressed on the remote machine.

public SocketAddress getSocketAddress( ) // Java 1.4

The getSocketAddress( ) method returns a SocketAddress object containing the IP address and port of the remote host. As is the case for getInetAddress( ), if the datagram was received from the Internet, the address returned is the address of the machine that sent it (the source address). On the other hand, if the datagram was created locally to be sent to a remote machine, this method returns the address of the host to which the datagram is addressed (the destination address). You typically invoke this method to determine the address and port of the host that sent a UDP datagram before you reply. The net effect is not noticeably different than calling getAddress( ) and getPort( ), but if you're using Java 1.4 this saves one method call. Also, if you're using non-blocking I/O, the DatagramChannel class accepts a SocketAddress but not an InetAddress and port.

public byte[] getData( )

The getData( ) method returns a byte array containing the data from the datagram. It's often necessary to convert the bytes into some other form of data before they'll be useful to your program. One way to do this is to change the byte array into a String using the following String constructor:

```
public String(byte[] buffer, String encoding)
```

The first argument, buffer, is the array of bytes that contains the data from the datagram. The second argument contains the name of the encoding used for this string, such as ASCII or ISO-8859-1. Thus, given a DatagramPacket dp received from the network, you can convert it to a String like this:

```
String s = new String(dp.getData( ), "ASCII");
```

If the datagram does not contain text, converting it to Java data is more difficult. One approach is to convert the byte array returned by getData( ) into a ByteArrayInputStream using this constructor:

```
public ByteArrayInputStream(byte[] buffer, int offset, int length)
```

buffer is the byte array to be used as an InputStream. It's important to specify the portion of the buffer that you want to use as an InputStream using the offset and length arguments. When converting datagram data into InputStream objects, offset is either 0 (Java 1.1) or given by the DatagramPacket object's getOffset( ) method (Java 2), and length is given by the DatagramPacket object's getLength( ) method. For example:

```
InputStream in = new ByteArrayInputStream(packet.getData( ),
  packet.getOffset( ), packet.getLength( ));
```

You *must* specify the `offset` and the `length` when constructing the `ByteArrayInputStream`. Do not use the `ByteArrayInputStream( )` constructor that takes only an array as an argument. The array returned by `packet.getData( )` probably has extra space in it that was not filled with data from the network. This space will contain whatever random values those components of the array had when the `DatagramPacket` was constructed.

The `ByteArrayInputStream` can then be chained to a `DataInputStream`:

```
DataInputStream din = new DataInputStream(in);
```

The data can then be read using the `DataInputStream`'s `readInt( )`, `readLong( )`, `readChar( )`, and other methods. Of course, this assumes that the datagram's sender uses the same data formats as Java; it's probably the case when the sender is written in Java, and is often (though not necessarily) the case otherwise. (Most modern computers use the same floating point format as Java, and most network protocols specify two complement integers in network byte order, which also matches Java's formats.)

public int getLength( )

The `getLength( )` method returns the number of bytes of data in the datagram. This is *not* necessarily the same as the length of the array returned by `getData( )`, i.e., `getData( ).length`. The `int` returned by `getLength( )` may be less than the length of the array returned by `getData( )`.

public int getOffset( ) // Java 1.2

This method simply returns the point in the array returned by `getData( )` where the data from the datagram begins.

Example 13-1 uses all the methods covered in this section to print the information in the `DatagramPacket`. This example is a little artificial; because the program creates a `DatagramPacket`, it already knows what's in it. More often, you'll use these methods on a `DatagramPacket` received from the network, but that will have to wait for the introduction of the `DatagramSocket` class in the next section.

Example 13-1. Construct a DatagramPacket to receive data

```
import java.net.*;

public class DatagramExample {

  public static void main(String[] args) {

    String s = "This is a test.";

    byte[] data = s.getBytes( );
    try {
      InetAddress ia = InetAddress.getByName("www.ibiblio.org");
```

Example 13-1. Construct a DatagramPacket to receive data (continued)

```
    int port = 7;
    DatagramPacket dp
     = new DatagramPacket(data, data.length, ia, port);
    System.out.println("This packet is addressed to "
     + dp.getAddress() + " on port " + dp.getPort( ));
    System.out.println("There are " + dp.getLength( )
     + " bytes of data in the packet");
    System.out.println(
       new String(dp.getData(), dp.getOffset(), dp.getLength( )));
  }
  catch (UnknownHostException e) {
    System.err.println(e);
  }

 }

}
```

Here's the output:

```
% java DatagramExample
This packet is addressed to www.ibiblio.org/152.2.254.81 on port 7
There are 15 bytes of data in the packet
This is a test.
```

The set Methods

Most of the time, the six constructors are sufficient for creating datagrams. However, Java also provides several methods for changing the data, remote address, and remote port after the datagram has been created. These methods might be important in a situation where the time to create and garbage collect new DatagramPacket objects is a significant performance hit. In some situations, reusing objects can be significantly faster than constructing new ones: for example, in a networked twitch like Quake that sends a datagram for every bullet fired or every centimeter of movement. However, you would have to use a very speedy connection for the improvement to be noticeable relative to the slowness of the network itself.

public void setData(byte[] data)

The setData( ) method changes the payload of the UDP datagram. You might use this method if you are sending a large file (where large is defined as "bigger than can comfortably fit in one datagram") to a remote host. You could repeatedly send the same DatagramPacket object, just changing the data each time.

public void setData(byte[] data, int offset, int length) // Java 1.2

This overloaded variant of the setData( ) method provides an alternative approach to sending a large quantity of data. Instead of sending lots of new arrays, you can put all the data in one array and send it a piece at a time. For instance, this loop sends a large array in 512-byte chunks:

```
int offset = 0;
DatagramPacket dp = new DatagramPacket(bigarray, offset, 512);
int bytesSent = 0;
while (bytesSent < bigarray.length) {
    socket.send(dp);
    bytesSent += dp.getLength();
    int bytesToSend = bigarray.length - bytesSent;
    int size = (bytesToSend > 512) ? 512 : bytesToSend;
    dp.setData(bigarray, bytesSent, 512);
}
```

On the other hand, this strategy requires either a lot of confidence that the data will in fact arrive or, alternatively, a disregard for the consequences of its not arriving. It's relatively difficult to attach sequence numbers or other reliability tags to individual packets when you take this approach.

public void setAddress(InetAddress remote)

The setAddress( ) method changes the address a datagram packet is sent to. This might allow you to send the same datagram to many different recipients. For example:

```
String s = "Really Important Message";
byte[] data = s.getBytes("ASCII");
DatagramPacket dp = new DatagramPacket(data, data.length);
dp.setPort(2000);
int network = "128.238.5.";
for (int host = 1; host < 255; host++) {
  try {
    InetAddress remote = InetAddress.getByName(network + host);
    dp.setAddress(remote);
    socket.send(dp);
  }
  catch (IOException ex) {
    // slip it; continue with the next host
  }
}
```

Whether this is a sensible choice depends on the application. If you're trying to send to all the stations on a network segment, as in this fragment, you'd probably be better off using the local broadcast address and letting the network do the work. The local broadcast address is determined by setting all bits of the IP address after the network and subnet IDs to 1. For example, Polytechnic University's network address is 128.238.0.0. Consequently, its broadcast address is 128.238.255.255. Sending a datagram to 128.238.255.255 copies it to every host on that network (although some routers and firewalls may block it, depending on its origin).

For more widely separated hosts, you're probably better off using multicasting. Multicasting actually uses the same DatagramPacket class described here. However, it uses different IP addresses and a `MulticastSocket` instead of a `DatagramSocket`. We'll discuss this further in Chapter 14.

public void setPort(int port)

The `setPort()` method changes the port a datagram is addressed to. I honestly can't think of many uses for this method. It could be used in a port scanner application that tried to find open ports running particular UDP-based services such as FSP. Another possibility might be some sort of networked game or conferencing server where the clients that need to receive the same information are all running on different ports as well as different hosts. In this case, `setPort()` could be used in conjunction with `setAddress()` to change destinations before sending the same datagram out again.

public void setAddress(SocketAddress remote) // Java 1.4

The `setSocketAddress()` method changes the address and port a datagram packet is sent to. You can use this when replying. For example, this code fragment receives a datagram packet and responds to the same address with a packet containing the ASCII string "Hello there":

```
DatagramPacket  input = newDatagramPacket(new byte[8192], 8192);
socket.receive(input);
SocketAddress address = input.getSocketAddress();
DatagramPacket output = new DatagramPacket("Hello there".getBytes("ASCII"), 11);
output.setAddress(address);
socket.send(output);
```

You could certainly write the same code using `InetAddress` objects and ports instead of a `SocketAddress`. Indeed, in Java 1.3 and earlier, you have to. The code would be just a few lines longer:

```
DatagramPacket  input = newDatagramPacket(new byte[8192], 8192);
socket.receive(input);
InetAddress address = input.getAddress();
int port = input.getPort();
DatagramPacket output = new DatagramPacket("Hello there".getBytes("ASCII"), 11);
output.setAddress(address);
output.setPort(port);
socket.send(output);
```

public void setLength(int length)

The `setLength()` method changes the number of bytes of data in the internal buffer that are considered to be part of the datagram's data as opposed to merely unfilled space. This method is useful when receiving datagrams, as we'll explore later in this chapter. When a datagram is received, its length is set to the length of the incoming data. This means that if you try to receive another datagram into the same `DatagramPacket`, it's limited to no more than the number of bytes in the first. That is, once you've received a 10-byte datagram, all subsequent datagrams will be truncated to 10 bytes; once you've received a 9-byte datagram, all subsequent datagrams will be truncated to 9 bytes; and so on. This method lets you reset the length of the buffer so that subsequent datagrams aren't truncated.

The DatagramSocket Class

To send or receive a `DatagramPacket`, you must open a datagram socket. In Java, a datagram socket is created and accessed through the `DatagramSocket` class:

```
public class DatagramSocket extends Object
```

All datagram sockets are bound to a local port, on which they listen for incoming data and which they place in the header of outgoing datagrams. If you're writing a client, you don't care what the local port is, so you call a constructor that lets the system assign an unused port (an anonymous port). This port number is placed in any outgoing datagrams and will be used by the server to address any response datagrams. If you're writing a server, clients need to know on which port the server is listening for incoming datagrams; therefore, when a server constructs a `DatagramSocket`, it specifies the local port on which it will listen. However, the sockets used by clients and servers are otherwise identical: they differ only in whether they use an anonymous (system-assigned) or a well-known port. There's no distinction between client sockets and server sockets, as there is with TCP; there's no such thing as a `DatagramServerSocket`.

The Constructors

The `DatagramSocket` constructors are used in different situations, much like the `DatagramPacket` constructors. The first constructor opens a datagram socket on an anonymous local port. The second constructor opens a datagram socket on a well-known local port that listens to all local network interfaces. The third constructor opens a datagram socket on a well-known local port on a specific network interface. Java 1.4 adds a constructor that allows this network interface and port to be specified with a `SocketAddress`. Java 1.4 also adds a protected constructor that allows you to change the implementation class. All five constructors deal only with the local address and port. The remote address and port are stored in the `DatagramPacket`, not the `DatagramSocket`. Indeed, one `DatagramSocket` can send and receive datagrams from multiple remote hosts and ports.

public DatagramSocket( ) throws SocketException

This constructor creates a socket that is bound to an anonymous port. For example:

```
try {
  DatagramSocket client = new DatagramSocket( );
  // send packets...
```

```
    }
    catch (SocketException ex) {
      System.err.println(ex);
    }
```

You would use this constructor in a client that initiates a conversation with a server. In this scenario, you don't care what port the socket is bound to, because the server will send its response to the port from which the datagram originated. Letting the system assign a port means that you don't have to worry about finding an unused port. If for some reason you need to know the local port, you can find out with the `getLocalPort()` method described later in this chapter.

The same socket can receive the datagrams that a server sends back to it. A `SocketException` is thrown if the socket can't be created. It's unusual for this constructor to throw an exception; it's hard to imagine situations in which the socket could not be opened, since the system gets to choose the local port.

public DatagramSocket(int port) throws SocketException

This constructor creates a socket that listens for incoming datagrams on a particular port, specified by the `port` argument. Use this constructor to write a server that listens on a well-known port; if servers listened on anonymous ports, clients would not be able to contact them. A `SocketException` is thrown if the socket can't be created. There are two common reasons for the constructor to fail: the specified port is already occupied, or you are trying to connect to a port below 1,024 and you don't have sufficient privileges (i.e., you are not root on a Unix system; for better or worse, other platforms allow anyone to connect to low-numbered ports).

TCP ports and UDP ports are not related. Two unrelated servers or clients can use the same port number if one uses UDP and the other uses TCP. Example 13-2 is a port scanner that looks for UDP ports in use on the local host. It decides that the port is in use if the `DatagramSocket` constructor throws an exception. As written, it looks at ports from 1,024 and up to avoid Unix's requirement that it run as root to bind to ports below 1,024. You can easily extend it to check ports below 1,024, however, if you have root access or are running it on Windows.

Example 13-2. Look for local UDP ports

```java
import java.net.*;

public class UDPPortScanner {

  public static void main(String[] args) {

    for (int port = 1024; port <= 65535; port++) {
      try {
        // the next line will fail and drop into the catch block if
        // there is already a server running on port i
        DatagramSocket server = new DatagramSocket(port);
```

Example 13-2. Look for local UDP ports (continued)

```
      server.close( );
    }
    catch (SocketException ex) {
      System.out.println("There is a server on port " + port + ".");
    } // end try
  } // end for

  }

}
```

The speed at which `UDPPortScanner` runs depends strongly on the speed of your machine and its UDP implementation. I've clocked Example 13-2 at as little as two minutes on a moderately powered SPARCstation, under 12 seconds on a 1Ghz TiBook, about 7 seconds on a 1.4GHz Athlon system running Linux, and as long as an hour on a PowerBook 5300 running MacOS 8. Here are the results from the Linux workstation on which much of the code in this book was written:

```
% java UDPPortScanner
There is a server on port 2049.
There is a server on port 32768.
There is a server on port 32770.
There is a server on port 32771.
```

The first port, 2049, is an NFS server. The high-numbered ports in the 30,000 range are Remote Procedure Call (RPC) services. Along with RPC, common protocols that use UDP include NFS, TFTP, and FSP.

It's much harder to scan UDP ports on a remote system than to scan for remote TCP ports. Whereas there's always some indication that a listening port, regardless of application layer protocol, has received your TCP packet, UDP provides no such guarantees. To determine that a UDP server is listening, you have to send it a packet it will recognize and respond to.

public DatagramSocket(int port, InetAddress interface) throws SocketException

This constructor is primarily used on multihomed hosts; it creates a socket that listens for incoming datagrams on a specific port and network interface. The `port` argument is the port on which this socket listens for datagrams. As with TCP sockets, you need to be root on a Unix system to create a `DatagramSocket` on a port below 1,024. The `address` argument is an `InetAddress` object matching one of the host's network addresses. A `SocketException` is thrown if the socket can't be created. There are three common reasons for this constructor to fail: the specified port is already occupied, you are trying to connect to a port below 1,024 and you're not root on a Unix system, or address is not the address of one of the system's network interfaces.

public DatagramSocket(SocketAddress interface) throws SocketException // Java 1.4

This constructor is similar to the previous one except that the network interface address and port are read from a SocketAddress. For example, this code fragment creates a socket that only listens on the local loopback address:

```
SocketAddress address = new InetSocketAddress("127.0.0.1", 9999);
DatagramSocket socket = new DatagramSocket(address);
```

protected DatagramSocket(DatagramSocketImpl impl)
throws SocketException // Java 1.4

This constructor enables subclasses to provide their own implementation of the UDP protocol, rather than blindly accepting the default. Unlike sockets created by the other four constructors, this socket is not initially bound to a port. Before using it you have to bind it to a SocketAddress using the bind( ) method, which is also new in Java 1.4:

```
public void bind(SocketAddress addr) throws SocketException
```

You can pass null to this method, binding the socket to any available address and port.

Sending and Receiving Datagrams

The primary task of the DatagramSocket class is to send and receive UDP datagrams. One socket can both send and receive. Indeed, it can send and receive to and from multiple hosts at the same time.

public void send(DatagramPacket dp) throws IOException

Once a DatagramPacket is created and a DatagramSocket is constructed, send the packet by passing it to the socket's send( ) method. For example, if theSocket is a DatagramSocket object and theOutput is a DatagramPacket object, send theOutput using theSocket like this:

```
theSocket.send(theOutput);
```

If there's a problem sending the data, an IOException may be thrown. However, this is less common with DatagramSocket than Socket or ServerSocket, since the unreliable nature of UDP means you won't get an exception just because the packet doesn't arrive at its destination. You may get an IOException if you're trying to send a larger datagram than the host's native networking software supports, but then again you may not. This depends heavily on the native UDP software in the OS and the native code that interfaces between this and Java's DatagramSocketImpl class. This method may also throw a SecurityException if the SecurityManager won't let you communicate with the host to which the packet is addressed. This is primarily a problem for applets and other remotely loaded code.

Example 13-3 is a UDP-based discard client. It reads lines of user input from System.
in and sends them to a discard server, which simply discards all the data. Each line is
stuffed in a DatagramPacket. Many of the simpler Internet protocols, such as discard,
have both TCP and UDP implementations.

Example 13-3. A UDP discard client

```java
import java.net.*;
import java.io.*;

public class UDPDiscardClient {

  public final static int DEFAULT_PORT = 9;

  public static void main(String[] args) {

    String hostname;
    int port = DEFAULT_PORT;

    if (args.length > 0) {
      hostname = args[0];
      try {
      port = Integer.parseInt(args[1]);
      }
      catch (Exception ex) {
        // use default port
      }
    }
    else {
      hostname = "localhost";
    }

    try {
      InetAddress server = InetAddress.getByName(hostname);
      BufferedReader userInput
        = new BufferedReader(new InputStreamReader(System.in));
      DatagramSocket theSocket = new DatagramSocket();
      while (true) {
        String theLine = userInput.readLine();
        if (theLine.equals(".")) break;
        byte[] data = theLine.getBytes();
        DatagramPacket theOutput
          = new DatagramPacket(data, data.length, server, port);
        theSocket.send(theOutput);
      } // end while
    } // end try
    catch (UnknownHostException uhex) {
      System.err.println(uhex);
    }
    catch (SocketException sex) {
      System.err.println(sex);
    }
    catch (IOException ioex) {
```

Example 13-3. A UDP discard client (continued)

```
    System.err.println(ioex);
  }

} // end main

}
```

The `UDPDiscardClient` class should look familiar. It has a single static field, `DEFAULT_PORT`, which is set to the standard port for the discard protocol (port 9), and a single method, `main( )`. The `main( )` method reads a hostname from the command line and converts that hostname to the `InetAddress` object called `server`. A `BufferedReader` is chained to `System.in` to read user input from the keyboard. Next, a `DatagramSocket` object called `theSocket` is constructed. After creating the socket, the program enters an infinite `while` loop that reads user input line by line using `readLine( )`. We are careful, however, to use only `readLine( )` to read data from the console, the one place where it is guaranteed to work as advertised. Since the discard protocol deals only with raw bytes, we can ignore character encoding issues.

In the `while` loop, each line is converted to a byte array using the `getBytes( )` method, and the bytes are stuffed in a new `DatagramPacket`, `theOutput`. Finally, `theOutput` is sent over `theSocket`, and the loop continues. If at any point the user types a period on a line by itself, the program exits. The `DatagramSocket` constructor may throw a `SocketException`, so that needs to be caught. Because this is a discard client, we don't need to worry about data coming back from the server.

public void receive(DatagramPacket dp) throws IOException

This method receives a single UDP datagram from the network and stores it in the pre-existing `DatagramPacket` object dp. Like the `accept( )` method in the `ServerSocket` class, this method blocks the calling thread until a datagram arrives. If your program does anything besides wait for datagrams, you should call `receive( )` in a separate thread.

The datagram's buffer should be large enough to hold the data received. If not, `receive( )` places as much data in the buffer as it can hold; the rest is lost. It may be useful to remember that the maximum size of the data portion of a UDP datagram is 65,507 bytes. (That's the 65,536-byte maximum size of an IP datagram minus the 20-byte size of the IP header and the 8-byte size of the UDP header.) Some application protocols that use UDP further restrict the maximum number of bytes in a packet; for instance, NFS uses a maximum packet size of 8,192 bytes.

If there's a problem receiving the data, an `IOException` may be thrown. In practice, this is rare. Unlike `send( )`, this method does not throw a `SecurityException` if an applet receives a datagram from other than the applet host. However, it will silently discard all such packets. (This behavior prevents a denial-of-service attack against applets that receive UDP datagrams.)

Example 13-4 shows a UDP discard server that receives incoming datagrams. Just for fun, it logs the data in each datagram to System.out so that you can see who's sending what to your discard server.

Example 13-4. The UDPDiscardServer

```java
import java.net.*;
import java.io.*;

public class UDPDiscardServer {

  public final static int DEFAULT_PORT = 9;
  public final static int MAX_PACKET_SIZE = 65507;

  public static void main(String[] args) {

    int port = DEFAULT_PORT;
    byte[] buffer = new byte[MAX_PACKET_SIZE];

    try {
      port = Integer.parseInt(args[0]);
    }
    catch (Exception ex) {
      // use default port
    }

    try {
      DatagramSocket server = new DatagramSocket(port);
      DatagramPacket packet = new DatagramPacket(buffer, buffer.length);
      while (true) {
        try {
          server.receive(packet);
          String s = new String(packet.getData(), 0, packet.getLength( ));
          System.out.println(packet.getAddress() + " at port "
           + packet.getPort() + " says " + s);
          // reset the length for the next packet
          packet.setLength(buffer.length);
        }
        catch (IOException ex) {
          System.err.println(ex);
        }
      } // end while
    } // end try
    catch (SocketException  ex) {
      System.err.println(ex);
    } // end catch

  } // end main

}
```

This is a simple class with a single method, main( ). It reads the port the server listens to from the command line. If the port is not specified on the command line, it listens on port 9. It then opens a DatagramSocket on that port and creates a DatagramPacket with a 65,507-byte buffer—large enough to receive any possible packet. Then the server enters an infinite loop that receives packets and prints the contents and the originating host on the console. A high-performance discard server would skip this step. As each datagram is received, the length of packet is set to the length of the data in that datagram. Consequently, as the last step of the loop, the length of the packet is reset to the maximum possible value. Otherwise, the incoming packets would be limited to the minimum size of all previous packets. You can run the discard client on one machine and connect to the discard server on a second machine to verify that the network is working.

public void close( )

Calling a DatagramSocket object's close( ) method frees the port occupied by that socket. For example:

```
try {
  DatagramSocket server = new DatagramSocket( );
  server.close( );
}
catch (SocketException ex) {
  System.err.println(ex);
}
```

It's never a bad idea to close a DatagramSocket when you're through with it; it's particularly important to close an unneeded socket if the program will continue to run for a significant amount of time. For example, the close( ) method was essential in Example 13-2, UDPPortScanner: if this program did not close the sockets it opened, it would tie up every UDP port on the system for a significant amount of time. On the other hand, if the program ends as soon as you're through with the DatagramSocket, you don't need to close the socket explicitly; the socket is automatically closed upon garbage collection. However, Java won't run the garbage collector just because you've run out of ports or sockets, unless by lucky happenstance you run out of memory at the same time. Closing unneeded sockets never hurts and is good programming practice.

public int getLocalPort( )

A DatagramSocket's getLocalPort( ) method returns an int that represents the local port on which the socket is listening. Use this method if you created a DatagramSocket with an anonymous port and want to find out what port the socket has been assigned. For example:

```
try {
  DatagramSocket ds = new DatagramSocket( );
  System.out.println("The socket is using port " + ds.getLocalPort( ));
}
catch (SocketException ex) {
  ex.printStackTrace( );
}
```

public InetAddress getLocalAddress( )

A DatagramSocket's getLocalAddress( ) method returns an InetAddress object that represents the local address to which the socket is bound. It's rarely needed in practice. Normally, you either know or don't care which address a socket is listening to.

public SocketAddress getLocalSocketAddress( ) // Java 1.4

The getLocalSocketAddress( ) method returns a SocketAddress object that wraps the local interface and port to which the socket is bound. Like getLocalAddress( ), it's a little hard to imagine a realistic use case here. This method probably exists mostly for parallelism with setLocalSocketAddress( ).

Managing Connections

Unlike TCP sockets, datagram sockets aren't very picky about whom they'll talk to. In fact, by default they'll talk to anyone, but this is often not what you want. For instance, applets are only allowed to send datagrams to and receive datagrams from the applet host. An NFS or FSP client should accept packets only from the server it's talking to. A networked game should listen to datagrams only from the people playing the game. In Java 1.1, programs must manually check the source addresses and ports of the hosts sending them data to make sure they're who they should be. However, Java 1.2 adds four methods that let you choose which host you can send datagrams to and receive datagrams from, while rejecting all others' packets.

public void connect(InetAddress host, int port) // Java 1.2

The connect( ) method doesn't really establish a connection in the TCP sense. However, it does specify that the DatagramSocket will send packets to and receive packets from only the specified remote host on the specified remote port. Attempts to send packets to a different host or port will throw an IllegalArgumentException. Packets received from a different host or a different port will be discarded without an exception or other notification.

A security check is made when the connect( ) method is invoked. If the VM is allowed to send data to that host and port, the check passes silently. Otherwise, a SecurityException is thrown. However, once the connection has been made, send( ) and receive( ) on that DatagramSocket no longer make the security checks they'd normally make.

public void disconnect( ) // Java 1.2

The disconnect( ) method breaks the "connection" of a connected DatagramSocket so that it can once again send packets to and receive packets from any host and port.

public int getPort( ) // Java 1.2

If and only if a DatagramSocket is connected, the getPort( ) method returns the remote port to which it is connected. Otherwise, it returns –1.

public InetAddress getInetAddress( ) // Java 1.2

If and only if a DatagramSocket is connected, the getInetAddress( ) method returns the address of the remote host to which it is connected. Otherwise, it returns null.

public InetAddress getRemoteSocketAddress( ) // Java 1.4

If a DatagramSocket is connected, the getRemoteSocketAddress( ) method returns the address of the remote host to which it is connected. Otherwise, it returns null.

Socket Options

The only socket option supported for datagram sockets in Java 1.1 is SO_TIME-OUT. Java 1.2 adds SO_SNDBUF and SO_RCVBUF. Java 1.4 adds SO_REUSE-ADDR and SO_BROADCAST and enables the specification of the traffic class.

SO_TIMEOUT

SO_TIMEOUT is the amount of time, in milliseconds, that receive( ) waits for an incoming datagram before throwing an InterruptedIOException (a subclass of IOException). Its value must be nonnegative. If SO_TIMEOUT is 0, receive( ) never times out. This value can be changed with the setSoTimeout( ) method and inspected with the getSoTimeout( ) method:

```
public synchronized void setSoTimeout(int timeout)
 throws SocketException
public synchronized int getSoTimeout() throws IOException
```

The default is to never time out, and indeed there are few situations in which you would need to set SO_TIMEOUT. You might need it if you were implementing a secure protocol that required responses to occur within a fixed amount of time. You might also decide that the host you're communicating with is dead (unreachable or not responding) if you don't receive a response within a certain amount of time.

The setSoTimeout( ) method sets the SO_TIMEOUT field for a datagram socket. When the timeout expires, an InterruptedIOException is thrown. (In Java 1.4 and later, SocketTimeoutException, a subclass of InterruptedIOException, is thrown instead.) Set this option *before* you call receive( ). You cannot change it while receive( ) is waiting for a datagram. The timeout argument must be greater than or equal to zero; if it is not, setSoTimeout( ) throws a SocketException. For example:

```
try {
  buffer = new byte[2056];
  DatagramPacket dp = new DatagramPacket(buffer, buffer.length);
```

```
       DatagramSocket ds = new DatagramSocket(2048);
       ds.setSoTimeout(30000); // block for no more than 30 seconds
       try {
        ds.receive(dp);
         // process the packet...
       }
       catch (InterruptedIOException ex) {
         ss.close();
         System.err.println("No connection within 30 seconds");
       }
     catch (SocketException ex) {
       System.err.println(ex);
     }
     catch (IOException ex) {
       System.err.println("Unexpected IOException: " + ex);
     }
```

The getSoTimeout( ) method returns the current value of this DatagramSocket object's
SO_TIMEOUT field. For example:

```
     public void printSoTimeout(DatagramSocket ds) {

       int timeout = ds.getSoTimeOut( );
       if (timeout > 0) {
         System.out.println(ds + " will time out after "
          + timeout + "milliseconds.");
       }
       else if (timeout == 0) {
         System.out.println(ds + " will never time out.");
       }
       else {
         System.out.println("Something is seriously wrong with " + ds);
       }

     }
```

SO_RCVBUF

The SO_RCVBUF option of DatagramSocket is closely related to the SO_RCVBUF
option of Socket. It determines the size of the buffer used for network I/O. Larger
buffers tend to improve performance for reasonably fast (say, Ethernet-speed) connections because they can store more incoming datagrams before overflowing. Suffi-
ciently large receive buffers are even more important for UDP than for TCP, since a
UDP datagram that arrives when the buffer is full will be lost, whereas a TCP datagram that arrives at a full buffer will eventually be retransmitted. Furthermore, SO_
RCVBUF sets the maximum size of datagram packets that can be received by the
application. Packets that won't fit in the receive buffer are silently discarded.

DatagramSocket has methods to get and set the suggested receive buffer size used for
network input:

```
     public void setReceiveBufferSize(int size) throws SocketException // Java 1.2
     public int getReceiveBufferSize( ) throws SocketException        // Java 1.2
```

The setReceiveBufferSize( ) method suggests a number of bytes to use for buffering input from this socket. However, the underlying implementation is free to ignore this suggestion. For instance, many 4.3 BSD–derived systems have a maximum receive buffer size of about 52K and won't let you set a limit higher than this. My Linux box was limited to 64K. Other systems raise this to about 240K. The details are highly platform-dependent. Consequently, you may wish to check the actual size of the receive buffer with getReceiveBufferSize( ) after setting it. The getReceiveBufferSize( ) method returns the number of bytes in the buffer used for input from this socket.

Both methods throw a SocketException if the underlying socket implementation does not recognize the SO_RCVBUF option. This might happen on a non-POSIX operating system. The setReceiveBufferSize( ) method throws an IllegalArgumentException if its argument is less than or equal to zero.

SO_SNDBUF

DatagramSocket has methods to get and set the suggested send buffer size used for network output:

```
public void setSendBufferSize(int size)  throws SocketException // Java 1.2
public int getSendBufferSize( ) throws SocketException          // Java 1.2
```

The setSendBufferSize( ) method suggests a number of bytes to use for buffering output on this socket. Once again, however, the operating system is free to ignore this suggestion. Consequently, you'll want to check the result of setSendBufferSize( ) by immediately following it with a call to getSend BufferSize( ) to find out the real the buffer size.

Both methods throw a SocketException if the underlying native network software doesn't understand the SO_SNDBUF option. The setSendBufferSize( ) method also throws an IllegalArgumentException if its argument is less than or equal to zero.

SO_REUSEADDR

The SO_REUSEADDR option does not mean the same thing for UDP sockets as it does for TCP sockets. For UDP, SO_REUSEADDR can control whether multiple datagram sockets can bind to the same port and address *at the same time*. If multiple sockets are bound to the same port, received packets will be copied to all bound sockets. This option is controlled by these two methods:

```
public void setReuseAddress(boolean on) throws SocketException  // Java 1.4
public boolean getReuseAddress( ) throws SocketException        // Java 1.4
```

For this to work reliably, setReuseAddress( ) must be called *before* the new socket binds to the port. This means the socket must be created in an unconnected state using the protected constructor that takes a DatagramImpl as an argument. In other words, it won't work with a plain vanilla DatagramSocket. Reusable ports are most commonly used for multicast sockets, which will be discussed in the next chapter. Datagram channels also create unconnected datagram sockets that can be configured to reuse ports, as you'll see later in this chapter.

SO_BROADCAST

The SO_BROADCAST option controls whether a socket is allowed to send packets to and receive packets from broadcast addresses such as 192.168.254.255, the local network broadcast address for the network with the local address 192.168.254.*. UDP broadcasting is often used for protocols like the JXTA Peer Discovery Protocol and the Service Location Protocol that need to communicate with servers on the local net whose addresses are not known in advance. This option is controlled with these two methods:

```
public void setBroadcast(boolean on) throws SocketException  // Java 1.4
public boolean getBroadcast() throws SocketException          // Java 1.4
```

Routers and gateways do not normally forward broadcast messages, but they can still kick up a lot of traffic on the local network. This option is turned on by default, but if you like you can disable it thusly:

```
socket.setBroadcast(false);
```

This option can be changed after the socket has been bound.

On some implementations, sockets bound to a specific address do not receive broadcast packets. In other words, use the DatagramPacket(int port) constructor, not the DatagramPacket(InetAddress address, int port) constructor to listen to broadcasts. This is necessary in addition to setting the SO_BROADCAST option to true.

Traffic class

Traffic class is essentially the same for UDP as it is for TCP. After all, packets are actually routed and prioritized according to IP, which both TCP and UDP sit on top of. There's really no difference between the setTrafficClass() and getTrafficClass() methods in DatagramSocket and those in Socket. They just have to be repeated here because DatagramSocket and Socket don't have a common superclass. These two methods let you inspect and set the class of service for a socket using these two methods:

```
public int getTrafficClass() throws SocketException // Java 1.4
public void setTrafficClass(int trafficClass) throws SocketException  // Java 1.4
```

The traffic class is given as an int between 0 and 255. (Values outside this range cause IllegalArgumentExceptions.) This int is a combination of bit-flags. Specifically:

- 0x02: Low cost
- 0x04: High reliability
- 0x08: Maximum throughput
- 0x10: Minimum delay

Java always sets the lowest order, ones bit to zero, even if you try to set it to one. The three high-order bits are not yet used. For example, this code fragment requests a low cost connection:

```
DatagramSocket s = new DatagramSocket ();
s.setTrafficClass(0x02);
```

This code fragment requests a connection with maximum throughput and minimum delay:

```
DatagramSocket s = new DatagramSocket ();
s.setTrafficClass(0x08 | 0x10);
```

The underlying socket implementation is not required to respect any of these requests. They hint at the policy that is desired. Probably most current implementations will ignore these values completely. If the local network stack is unable to provide the requested class of service, it may throw a SocketException, but it's not required to and truth be told, it probably won't.

Some Useful Applications

In this section, you'll see several Internet servers and clients that use DatagramPacket and DatagramSocket. Some of these will be familiar from previous chapters because many Internet protocols have both TCP and UDP implementations. When an IP packet is received by a host, the host determines whether the packet is a TCP packet or a UDP datagram by inspecting the IP header. As I said earlier, there's no connection between UDP and TCP ports; TCP and UDP servers can share the same port number without problems. By convention, if a service has both TCP and UDP implementations, it uses the same port for both, although there's no technical reason this has to be the case.

Simple UDP Clients

Several Internet services need to know only the client's address and port; they ignore any data the client sends in its datagrams. Daytime, quote of the day, time, and chargen are four such protocols. Each of these responds the same way, regardless of the data contained in the datagram, or indeed regardless of whether there actually is any data in the datagram. Clients for these protocols simply send a UDP datagram to the server and read the response that comes back. Therefore, let's begin with a simple client called UDPPoke, shown in Example 13-5, which sends an empty UDP packet to a specified host and port and reads a response packet from the same host.

The UDPPoke class has three private fields. The bufferSize field specifies how large a return packet is expected. An 8,192-byte buffer is large enough for most of the protocols that UDPPoke is useful for, but it can be increased by passing a different value to the constructor. The DatagramSocket object socket will be used to both send and receive datagrams. Finally, the DatagramPacket object outgoing is the message sent to the individual servers.

The constructors initialize all three fields using an InetAddress for the host and ints for the port, the buffer length, and the number of milliseconds to wait before timing out. These last three become part of the DatagramSocket field socket. If the buffer length is not specified, 8,192 bytes is used. If the timeout is not given, 30 seconds (30,000 milliseconds) is used. The host, port, and buffer size are also used to construct the outgoing DatagramPacket. Although in theory you should be able to send a datagram with no data at all, bugs in some Java implementations require that you add at least one byte of data to the datagram. The simple servers we're currently considering ignore this data.

Once a UDPPoke object has been constructed, clients will call its poke( ) method to send an empty outgoing datagram to the target and read its response. The response is initially set to null. When the expected datagram appears, its data is copied into the response field. This method returns null if the response doesn't come quickly enough or never comes at all.

The main( ) method merely reads the host and port to connect to from the command line, constructs a UDPPoke object, and pokes it. Most of the simple protocols that this client suits will return ASCII text, so we'll attempt to convert the response to an ASCII string and print it. Not all VMs support the ASCII character encoding, so we'll provide the possibility of using the ASCII superset Latin-1 (8859-1) as a backup.

Example 13-5. The UDPPoke class

```java
import java.net.*;
import java.io.*;

public class UDPPoke {

  private int              bufferSize; // in bytes
  private DatagramSocket socket;
  private DatagramPacket outgoing;

  public UDPPoke(InetAddress host, int port, int bufferSize,
   int timeout) throws SocketException {

    outgoing = new DatagramPacket(new byte[1], 1, host, port);
    this.bufferSize = bufferSize;
    socket = new DatagramSocket(0);
    socket .connect(host, port); // requires Java 2
    socket .setSoTimeout(timeout);

  }

  public UDPPoke(InetAddress host, int port, int bufferSize)
   throws SocketException {
    this(host, port, bufferSize, 30000);
  }

  public UDPPoke(InetAddress host, int port)
   throws SocketException {
```

Example 13-5. The UDPPoke class (continued)

```
    this(host, port, 8192, 30000);
  }

  public byte[] poke( ) throws IOException {

    byte[] response = null;
    try {
      socket .send(outgoing);
      DatagramPacket incoming
        = new DatagramPacket(new byte[bufferSize], bufferSize);
      // next line blocks until the response is received
      socket .receive(incoming);
      int numBytes = incoming.getLength( );
      response = new byte[numBytes];
      System.arraycopy(incoming.getData( ), 0, response, 0, numBytes);
    }
    catch (IOException ex) {
      // response will be null
    }

    // may return null
    return response;
  }

  public static void main(String[] args) {

    InetAddress host;
    int port = 0;

    try {
      host = InetAddress.getByName(args[0]);
      port = Integer.parseInt(args[1]);
      if (port < 1 || port > 65535) throw new Exception( );
    }
    catch (Exception ex) {
      System.out.println("Usage: java UDPPoke host port");
      return;
    }

    try {
      UDPPoke poker = new UDPPoke(host, port);
      byte[] response = poker.poke( );
      if (response == null) {
      System.out.println("No response within allotted time");
      return;
      }
      String result = "";
      try {
        result = new String(response, "ASCII");
      }
      catch (UnsupportedEncodingException e) {
      // try a different encoding
```

Example 13-5. The UDPPoke class (continued)

```
      result = new String(response, "8859_1");
      }
      System.out.println(result);
    }
    catch (Exception ex) {
      System.err.println(ex);
      ex.printStackTrace( );
    }

  } // end main

}
```

For example, this connects to a daytime server over UDP:

```
D:\JAVA\JNP3\examples\13>java UDPPoke rama.poly.edu 13
Sun Oct  3 13:04:22 1999
```

This connects to a chargen server:

```
D:\JAVA\JNP3\examples\13>java UDPPoke rama.poly.edu 19
123456789:;<=>?@ABCDEFGHIJKLMNOPQRSTUVWXYZ[\]^_`abcdefghijklmnopqrstuv
```

Given this class, UDP daytime, time, chargen, and quote of the day clients are almost trivial. Example 13-6 demonstrates a time client. The most complicated part is converting the four raw bytes returned by the server to a java.util.Date object. The same algorithm as in Example 10-5 is used here, so I won't repeat that discussion. The other protocols are left as exercises for the reader.

Example 13-6. A UDP time client

```
import java.net.*;
import java.util.*;

public class UDPTimeClient {

  public final static int DEFAULT_PORT = 37;
  public final static String DEFAULT_HOST = "time-a.nist.gov";

  public static void main(String[] args) {

    InetAddress host;
    int port = DEFAULT_PORT;

    try {
      if (args.length > 0) {
        host = InetAddress.getByName(args[0]);
      }
      else {
        host = InetAddress.getByName(DEFAULT_HOST);
      }
    }
    catch (Exception ex) {
```

Example 13-6. A UDP time client (continued)

```java
      System.out.println("Usage: java UDPTimeClient host port");
      return;
    }

    if (args.length > 1) {
      try {
        port = Integer.parseInt(args[1]);
        if (port <= 0 || port > 65535) port = DEFAULT_PORT;;
      }
      catch (Exception ex){
      }
    }

    try {
      UDPPoke poker = new UDPPoke(host, port);
      byte[] response = poker.poke( );
        if (response == null) {
        System.out.println("No response within allotted time");
        return;
        }
        else if (response.length != 4) {
        System.out.println("Unrecognized response format");
        return;
        }


      // The time protocol sets the epoch at 1900,
      // the Java Date class at 1970. This number
      // converts between them.

      long differenceBetweenEpochs = 2208988800L;

      long secondsSince1900 = 0;
      for (int i = 0; i < 4; i++) {
        secondsSince1900
          = (secondsSince1900 << 8) | (response[i] & 0x000000FF);
      }

      long secondsSince1970
        = secondsSince1900 - differenceBetweenEpochs;
      long msSince1970 = secondsSince1970 * 1000;
      Date time = new Date(msSince1970);

      System.out.println(time);
    }
    catch (Exception ex) {
      System.err.println(ex);
      ex.printStackTrace( );
    }

  }

}
```

UDPServer

Clients aren't the only programs that benefit from a reusable implementation. The servers for these protocols are very similar. They all wait for UDP datagrams on a specified port and reply to each datagram with another datagram. The servers differ only in the content of the datagram that they return. Example 13-7 is a simple UDPServer class that can be subclassed to provide specific servers for different protocols.

The UDPServer class has two fields, the int bufferSize and the DatagramSocket socket, the latter of which is protected so it can be used by subclasses. The constructor opens the DatagramSocket socket on a specified local port to receive datagrams of no more than bufferSize bytes.

UDPServer extends Thread so that multiple instances can run in parallel. Its run( ) method contains an infinite loop that repeatedly receives an incoming datagram and responds by passing it to the abstract respond( ) method. This method will be overridden by particular subclasses in order to implement different kinds of servers.

UDPServer is a very flexible class. Subclasses can send zero, one, or many datagrams in response to each incoming datagram. If a lot of processing is required to respond to a packet, the respond( ) method can spawn a thread to do it. However, UDP servers tend not to have extended interactions with a client. Each incoming packet is treated independently of other packets, so the response can usually be handled directly in the respond( ) method without spawning a thread.

Example 13-7. The UDPServer class

```java
import java.net.*;
import java.io.*;

public abstract class UDPServer extends Thread {

  private    int              bufferSize; // in bytes
  protected DatagramSocket socket;

  public UDPServer(int port, int bufferSize)
   throws SocketException {
    this.bufferSize = bufferSize;
    this.socket = new DatagramSocket(port);
  }

  public UDPServer(int port) throws SocketException {
    this(port, 8192);
  }

  public void run( ) {

    byte[] buffer = new byte[bufferSize];
    while (true) {
      DatagramPacket incoming = new DatagramPacket(buffer, buffer.length);
      try {
```

Example 13-7. The UDPServer class (continued)

```
        socket.receive(incoming);
        this.respond(incoming);
      }
      catch (IOException ex) {
        System.err.println(ex);
      }
    } // end while

  }  // end run

  public abstract void respond(DatagramPacket request);

}
```

The easiest protocol to handle is discard. All we need to do is write a main( ) method that sets the port and start the thread. respond( ) is a do-nothing method. Example 13-8 is a high-performance UDP discard server that does nothing with incoming packets.

Example 13-8. A high-performance UDP discard server

```
import java.net.*;

public class FastUDPDiscardServer extends UDPServer {

  public final static int DEFAULT_PORT = 9;

  public FastUDPDiscardServer( ) throws SocketException {
    super(DEFAULT_PORT);
  }

  public void respond(DatagramPacket packet) {}

  public static void main(String[] args) {

   try {
     UDPServer server = new FastUDPDiscardServer( );
     server.start( );
   }
   catch (SocketException ex) {
     System.err.println(ex);
   }

  }

}
```

Example 13-9 is a slightly more interesting discard server that prints the incoming packets on System.out.

Example 13-9. A UDP discard server

```
import java.net.*;

public class LoggingUDPDiscardServer extends UDPServer {

  public final static int DEFAULT_PORT = 9999;

  public LoggingUDPDiscardServer( ) throws SocketException {
    super(DEFAULT_PORT);
  }

  public void respond(DatagramPacket packet) {

    byte[] data = new byte[packet.getLength( )];
    System.arraycopy(packet.getData( ), 0, data, 0, packet.getLength( ));
    try {
      String s = new String(data, "8859_1");
      System.out.println(packet.getAddress( ) + " at port "
       + packet.getPort( ) + " says " + s);
    }
    catch (java.io.UnsupportedEncodingException ex) {
      // This shouldn't happen
    }

  }

  public static void main(String[] args) {

   try {
     UDPServer erver = new LoggingUDPDiscardServer( );
     server.start( );
   }
   catch (SocketException ex) {
     System.err.println(ex);
   }

  }

}
```

It isn't much harder to implement an echo server, as Example 13-10 shows. Unlike a stream-based TCP echo server, multiple threads are not required to handle multiple clients.

Example 13-10. A UDP echo server

```
import java.net.*;
import java.io.*;

public class UDPEchoServer extends UDPServer {

 public final static int DEFAULT_PORT = 7;
```

Example 13-10. A UDP echo server (continued)

```java
  public UDPEchoServer( ) throws SocketException {
    super(DEFAULT_PORT);
  }

  public void respond(DatagramPacket packet) {

    try {
      DatagramPacket outgoing = new DatagramPacket(packet.getData( ),
        packet.getLength( ), packet.getAddress( ), packet.getPort( ));
      socket.send(outgoing);
    }
    catch (IOException ex) {
      System.err.println(ex);
    }

  }

  public static void main(String[] args) {

   try {
     UDPServer server = new UDPEchoServer( );
     server.start( );
   }
   catch (SocketException ex) {
     System.err.println(ex);
   }

  }

}
```

A daytime server is only slightly more complex. The server listens for incoming UDP datagrams on port 13. When it detects an incoming datagram, it returns the current date and time at the server as a one-line ASCII string. Example 13-11 demonstrates this.

Example 13-11. The UDP daytime server

```java
import java.net.*;
import java.io.*;
import java.util.*;


public class UDPDaytimeServer extends UDPServer {

  public final static int DEFAULT_PORT = 13;

  public UDPDaytimeServer( ) throws SocketException {
    super(DEFAULT_PORT);
  }

  public void respond(DatagramPacket packet) {
```

Example 13-11. The UDP daytime server (continued)

```
  try {
    Date now = new Date();
    String response = now.toString() + "\r\n";
    byte[] data = response.getBytes("ASCII");
    DatagramPacket outgoing = new DatagramPacket(data,
      data.length, packet.getAddress(), packet.getPort());
    socket.send(outgoing);
  }
  catch (IOException ex) {
    System.err.println(ex);
  }

}

  public static void main(String[] args) {

    try {
      UDPServer server = new UDPDaytimeServer();
      server.start();
    }
    catch (SocketException ex) {
      System.err.println(ex);
    }

  }

}
```

A UDP Echo Client

The UDPPoke class implemented earlier isn't suitable for all protocols. In particular, protocols that require multiple datagrams require a different implementation. The echo protocol has both TCP and UDP implementations. Implementing the echo protocol with TCP is simple; it's more complex with UDP because you don't have I/O streams or the concept of a connection to work with. A TCP-based echo client can send a message and wait for a response on the same connection. However, a UDP-based echo client has no guarantee that the message it sent was received. Therefore, it cannot simply wait for the response; it needs to be prepared to send and receive data asynchronously.

This behavior is fairly simple to implement using threads, however. One thread can process user input and send it to the echo server, while a second thread accepts input from the server and displays it to the user. The client is divided into three classes: the main UDPEchoClient class, the SenderThread class, and the ReceiverThread class.

The UDPEchoClient class should look familiar. It reads a hostname from the command line and converts it to an InetAddress object. UDPEchoClient uses this object and the default echo port to construct a SenderThread object. This constructor can throw a SocketException, so the exception must be caught. Then the SenderThread starts. The same DatagramSocket that the SenderThread uses is used to construct a ReceiverThread, which is then started. It's important to use the same DatagramSocket for both sending and receiving data because the echo server will send the response back to the port the data was sent from. Example 13-12 shows the code for the UDPEchoClient.

Example 13-12. The UDPEchoClient class

```java
import java.net.*;
import java.io.*;

public class UDPEchoClient {

  public final static int DEFAULT_PORT = 7;

  public static void main(String[] args) {

    String hostname = "localhost";
    int port = DEFAULT_PORT;

    if (args.length > 0) {
      hostname = args[0];
    }

    try {
      InetAddress ia = InetAddress.getByName(hostname);
      Thread sender = new SenderThread(ia, DEFAULT_PORT);
      sender.start();
      Thread receiver = new ReceiverThread(sender.getSocket());
      receiver.start();
    }
    catch (UnknownHostException ex) {
      System.err.println(ex);
    }
    catch (SocketException ex) {
      System.err.println(ex);
    }

  } // end main

}
```

The SenderThread class reads input from the console a line at a time and sends it to the echo server. It's shown in Example 13-13. The input is provided by System.in, but a different client could include an option to read input from a different stream—perhaps opening a FileInputStream to read from a file. The three fields of this class define the server to which it sends data, the port on that server, and the DatagramSocket that does the sending, all set in the single constructor. The DatagramSocket is connected to the remote server to make sure all datagrams received were in fact sent by the right server. It's rather unlikely that some other server on the

Internet is going to bombard this particular port with extraneous data, so this is not a big flaw. However, it's a good habit to make sure that the packets you receive come from the right place, especially if security is a concern.

The run( ) method processes user input a line at a time. To do this, the BufferedReader userInput is chained to System.in. An infinite loop reads lines of user input. Each line is stored in theLine. A period on a line by itself signals the end of user input and breaks out of the loop. Otherwise, the bytes of data are stored in the data array using the getBytes( ) method from java.lang.String. Next, the data array is placed in the payload part of the DatagramPacket output, along with information about the server, the port, and the data length. This packet is then sent to its destination by socket. This thread then yields to give other threads an opportunity to run.

Example 13-13. The SenderThread class

```
import java.net.*;
import java.io.*;

public class SenderThread extends Thread {

  private InetAddress server;
  private DatagramSocket socket;
  private boolean stopped = false;
  private int port;

  public SenderThread(InetAddress address, int port)
   throws SocketException {
    this.server = address;
    this.port = port;
    this.socket = new DatagramSocket( );
    this.socket.connect(server, port);
  }

  public void halt( ) {
    this.stopped = true;
  }

  public DatagramSocket getSocket( ) {
    return this.socket;
  }

  public void run( ) {

    try {
      BufferedReader userInput
       = new BufferedReader(new InputStreamReader(System.in));
      while (true) {
        if (stopped) return;
        String theLine = userInput.readLine( );
        if (theLine.equals(".")) break;
        byte[] data = theLine.getBytes( );
        DatagramPacket output
```

Example 13-13. The SenderThread class (continued)

```
      = new DatagramPacket(data, data.length, server, port);
      socket.send(output);
      Thread.yield( );
    }
  } // end try
  catch (IOException ex) {
    System.err.println(ex);
  }

 } // end run

}
```

The ReceiverThread class shown in Example 13-14 waits for datagrams to arrive from the network. When a datagram is received, it is converted to a String and printed on System.out for display to the user. A more advanced EchoClient could include an option to send the output elsewhere.

This class has two fields. The more important is the DatagramSocket, theSocket, which must be the same DatagramSocket used by the SenderThread. Data arrives on the port used by that DatagramSocket; any other DatagramSocket would not be allowed to connect to the same port. The second field, stopped, is a boolean used to halt this thread without invoking the deprecated stop( ) method.

The run( ) method is an infinite loop that uses socket's receive( ) method to wait for incoming datagrams. When an incoming datagram appears, it is converted into a String with the same length as the incoming data and printed on System.out. As in the input thread, this thread then yields to give other threads an opportunity to execute.

Example 13-14. The ReceiverThread class

```
import java.net.*;
import java.io.*;

class ReceiverThread extends Thread {

  DatagramSocket socket;
  private boolean stopped = false;

  public ReceiverThread(DatagramSocket ds) throws SocketException {
    this.socket = ds;
  }

  public void halt( ) {
    this.stopped = true;
  }

  public void run( ) {

    byte[] buffer = new byte[65507];
```

Example 13-14. The ReceiverThread class (continued)

```
    while (true) {
      if (stopped) return;
      DatagramPacket dp = new DatagramPacket(buffer, buffer.length);
      try {
        socket.receive(dp);
        String s = new String(dp.getData(), 0, dp.getLength());
        System.out.println(s);
        Thread.yield();
      }
      catch (IOException ex) {
        System.err.println(ex);
      }

    }

  }

}
```

You can run the echo client on one machine and connect to the echo server on a second machine to verify that the network is functioning properly between them.

DatagramChannel

Java 1.4 adds a DatagramChannel class for use in non-blocking UDP applications, just as it adds SocketChannel and ServerSocketChannel for use in non-blocking TCP applications. Like SocketChannel and ServerSocketChannel, DatagramChannel is a subclass of SelectableChannel that can be registered with a Selector. This is useful in servers where one thread can manage communications with multiple different clients. However, UDP is by its nature much more asynchronous than TCP so the net effect is smaller. In UDP it's always been the case that a single datagram socket can process requests from multiple clients for both input and output. What the DatagramChannel class adds is the ability to do this in a non-blocking fashion, so methods return quickly if the network isn't immediately ready to receive or send data.

Using DatagramChannel

DatagramChannel is a near-complete alternate abstraction for UDP I/O. You still need to use the DatagramSocket class to bind a channel to a port. However, you do not have to use it thereafter, nor do you ever use DatagramPacket. Instead, you read and write ByteBuffers, just as you do with a SocketChannel.

Opening a socket

The java.nio.channels.DatagramChannel class does not have any public constructors. Instead, you create a new DatagramChannel object using the static open( ) method:

```
public static DatagramChannel open( ) throws IOException
```

For example:

```
DatagramChannel channel = DatagramChannel .open();
```

This channel is not initially bound to any port. To bind it, you need to access the channel's peer DatagramSocket object using the socket() method:

```
public abstract DatagramSocket socket()
```

For example, this binds a channel to port 3141:

```
SocketAddress address = new InetSocketAddress(3141);
DatagramSocket socket = channel.socket();
socket.bind(address);
```

Connecting

Like DatagramSocket, a DatagramChannel can be connected; that is, it can be configured to only receive datagrams from and send datagrams to one host. This is accomplished with the connect() method:

```
public abstract DatagramChannel connect(SocketAddress remote) throws IOException
```

However, unlike the connect() method of SocketChannel, this method does not actually send or receive any packets across the network because UDP is a connectionless protocol. Thus this method returns fairly quickly, and doesn't block in any meaningful sense. There's no need here for a finishConnect() or isConnectionPending() method. There is an isConnected() method that returns true if and only if the DatagramSocket is connected:

```
public abstract boolean isConnected()
```

This tells you whether the DatagramChannel is limited to one host. Unlike SocketChannel, a DatagramChannel doesn't have to be connected to transmit or receive data.

Finally, there is a disconnect() method that breaks the connection:

```
public abstract DatagramChannel disconnect() throws IOException
```

This doesn't really close anything because nothing was really open in the first place. It just allows the channel to once again send and receive data from multiple hosts.

Connected channels may be marginally faster than unconnected channels in sandbox environments such as applets because the virtual machine only needs to check whether the connection is allowed on the initial call to the connect() method, not every time a packet is sent or received. As always, only concern yourself with this if profiling indicates it is a bottleneck.

Receiving

The receive() method reads one datagram packet from the channel into a ByteBuffer. It returns the address of the host that sent the packet:

```
public abstract SocketAddress receive(ByteBuffer dst) throws IOException
```

If the channel is blocking (the default) this method will not return until a packet has been read. If the channel is non-blocking, this method will immediately return null if no packet is available to read.

If the datagram packet has more data than the buffer can hold, *the extra data is thrown away with no notification of the problem*. You do not receive a BufferOverflowException or anything similar. UDP is unreliable, after all. This behavior introduces an additional layer of unreliability into the system. The data can arrive safely from the network and still be lost inside your own program.

Using this method, we can reimplement the discard server to log the host sending the data as well as the data sent. Example 13-15 demonstrates. It avoids the potential loss of data by using a buffer that's big enough to hold any UDP packet and clearing it before it's used again.

Example 13-15. A UDPDiscardServer based on channels

```java
import java.net.*;
import java.io.*;
import java.nio.*;
import java.nio.channels.*;

public class UDPDiscardServerWithChannels {

  public final static int DEFAULT_PORT = 9;
  public final static int MAX_PACKET_SIZE = 65507;

  public static void main(String[] args) {

    int port = DEFAULT_PORT;
    try {
      port = Integer.parseInt(args[0]);
    }
    catch (Exception ex) {
    }

    try {
      DatagramChannel channel = DatagramChannel.open( );
      DatagramSocket socket = channel.socket( );
      SocketAddress address = new InetSocketAddress(port);
      socket.bind(address);
      ByteBuffer buffer = ByteBuffer.allocateDirect(MAX_PACKET_SIZE);
      while (true) {
        SocketAddress client = channel.receive(buffer);
        buffer.flip( );
        System.out.print(client + " says ");
        while (buffer.hasRemaining()) System.out.write(buffer.get( ));
        System.out.println( );
        buffer.clear( );
      } // end while
    }  // end try
    catch (IOException ex) {
```

Example 13-15. A UDPDiscardServer based on channels (continued)

```
      System.err.println(ex);
    } // end catch

  } // end main

}
```

Sending

The send( ) method writes one datagram packet into the channel from a ByteBuffer to the address specified as the second argument:

```
    public abstract int send(ByteBuffer src, SocketAddress target) throws IOException
```

The source ByteBuffer can be reused if you want to send the same data to multiple clients. Just don't forget to rewind it first.

The send( ) method returns the number of bytes written. This will either be the number of bytes remaining in the output buffer or zero. It is zero if there's not enough room in the network interface's output buffer for the amount of data you're trying to send. Don't overstuff the buffer. If you put more data in the buffer than the network interface can handle, it will never send anything. This method will not fragment the data into multiple packets. It writes everything or nothing.

Example 13-16 demonstrates with a simple echo server based on channels. The receive( ) method reads a packet, much as it did in Example 13-15. However, this time, rather than logging the packet on System.out, it returns the same data to the client that sent it.

Example 13-16. A UDPEchoServer based on channels

```
import java.net.*;
import java.io.*;
import java.nio.*;
import java.nio.channels.*;

public class UDPEchoServerWithChannels {

  public final static int DEFAULT_PORT = 7;
  public final static int MAX_PACKET_SIZE = 65507;

  public static void main(String[] args) {

    int port = DEFAULT_PORT;
    try {
      port = Integer.parseInt(args[0]);
    }
    catch (Exception ex) {
    }

    try {
```

Example 13-16. A UDPEchoServer based on channels (continued)

```
    DatagramChannel channel = DatagramChannel.open( );
    DatagramSocket socket = channel.socket( );
    SocketAddress address = new InetSocketAddress(port);
    socket.bind(address);
    ByteBuffer buffer = ByteBuffer.allocateDirect(MAX_PACKET_SIZE);
    while (true) {
      SocketAddress client = channel.receive(buffer);
      buffer.flip( );
      channel.send(buffer, client);
      buffer.clear( );
    } // end while
  }  // end try
  catch (IOException ex) {
    System.err.println(ex);
  }  // end catch

  }  // end main

}
```

This program is blocking and synchronous. This is much less of a problem for UDP-based protocols than for TCP protocols. The unreliable, packet-based, connection-less nature of UDP means that the server at most has to wait for the local buffer to clear. It does not have to and does not wait for the client to be ready to receive data. There's much less opportunity for one client to get held up behind a slower client.

Reading

Besides the special purpose receive( ) method, DatagramChannel has the usual three read( ) methods:

```
public abstract int read(ByteBuffer dst) throws IOException
public final long read(ByteBuffer[] dsts)throws IOException
public final long read(ByteBuffer[] dsts, int offset, int length)throws IOException
```

However, these methods can only be used on connected channels. That is, before invoking one of these methods, you must invoke connect( ) to glue the channel to a particular remote host. This makes them more suitable for use with clients that know who they'll be talking to than for servers that must accept input from multiple hosts at the same time that are normally not known prior to the arrival of the first packet.

Each of these three methods only reads a single datagram packet from the network. As much data from that datagram as possible is stored in the argument ByteBuffer(s). Each method returns the number of bytes read or –1 if the channel has been closed. This method may return 0 for any of several reasons, including:

- The channel is non-blocking and no packet was ready.
- A datagram packet contained no data.
- The buffer is full.

As with the receive( ) method, if the datagram packet has more data than the ByteBuffer(s) can hold, *the extra data is thrown away with no notification of the problem.* You do not receive a BufferOverflowException or anything similar.

Writing

Naturally, DatagramChannel has the three write methods common to all writable, scattering channels, which can be used instead of the send( ) method:

```
public abstract int write(ByteBuffer src) throws IOException
public final long write(ByteBuffer[] dsts)throws IOException
public final long write(ByteBuffer[] dsts, int offset, int length)throws IOException
```

However, these methods can only be used on connected channels; otherwise they don't know where to send the packet. Each of these methods sends a single datagram packet over the connection. None of these methods are guaranteed to write the complete contents of the buffer(s). However, the cursor-based nature of buffers enables you to easily call this method again and again until the buffer is fully drained and the data has been completely sent, possibly using multiple datagram packets. For example:

```
while (buffer.hasRemaining( ) && channel.write(buffer) != -1) ;
```

We can use the read and write methods to implement a simple UDP echo client. On the client side, it's easy to connect before sending. Because packets may be lost in transit (always remember UDP is unreliable), we don't want to tie up the sending while waiting to receive a packet. Thus, we can take advantage of selectors and nonblocking I/O. These work for UDP pretty much exactly like they worked for TCP in Chapter 12. This time, though, rather than sending text data, let's send one hundred ints from 0 to 99. We'll print out the values returned so it will be easy to figure out if any packets are being lost. Example 13-17 demonstrates.

Example 13-17. A UDP echo client based on channels

```
import java.net.*;
import java.io.*;
import java.nio.*;
import java.nio.channels.*;
import java.util.*;

public class UDPEchoClientWithChannels {

  public  final static int DEFAULT_PORT = 7;
  private final static int LIMIT = 100;

  public static void main(String[] args) {

    int port = DEFAULT_PORT;
    try {
      port = Integer.parseInt(args[1]);
    }
```

Example 13-17. A UDP echo client based on channels (continued)

```
catch (Exception ex) {
}

SocketAddress remote;
try {
  remote = new InetSocketAddress(args[0], port);
}
catch (Exception ex) {
  System.err.println("Usage: java UDPEchoClientWithChannels host [port]");
  return;
}

try {
  DatagramChannel channel = DatagramChannel.open( );
  channel.configureBlocking(false);
  channel.connect(remote);

  Selector selector = Selector.open( );
  channel.register(selector, SelectionKey.OP_READ | SelectionKey.OP_WRITE);

  ByteBuffer buffer = ByteBuffer.allocate(4);
  int n = 0;
  int numbersRead = 0;
  while (true) {
    // wait one minute for a connection
    selector.select(60000);
    Set readyKeys = selector.selectedKeys( );
    if (readyKeys.isEmpty( ) && n == LIMIT) {
      // All packets have been written and it doesn't look like any
      // more are will arrive from the network
      break;
    }
    else {
      Iterator iterator = readyKeys.iterator( );
      while (iterator.hasNext( )) {
        SelectionKey key = (SelectionKey) iterator.next( );
        iterator.remove( );
        if (key.isReadable( )) {
          buffer.clear( );
          channel.read(buffer);
          buffer.flip( );
          int echo = buffer.getInt( );
          System.out.println("Read: " + echo);
          numbersRead++;
        }
        if (key.isWritable( )) {
          buffer.clear( );
          buffer.putInt(n);
          buffer.flip( );
          channel.write(buffer);
          System.out.println("Wrote: " + n);
          n++;
```

Example 13-17. A UDP echo client based on channels (continued)

```
            if (n == LIMIT) {
                // All packets have been written; switch to read-only mode
                key.interestOps(SelectionKey.OP_READ);
            } // end if
        } // end while
    } // end else
} // end while

    } // end while
    System.out.println("Echoed " + numbersRead + " out of " + LIMIT + " sent");
    System.out.println("Success rate: " + 100.0 * numbersRead / LIMIT + "%");

} // end try
catch (IOException ex) {
    System.err.println(ex);
} // end catch

} // end main

}
```

There is one major difference between selecting TCP channels and selecting datagram channels. Because datagram channels are truly connectionless (despite the
connect( ) method), you need to notice when the data transfer is complete and shut
down. In this example, we assume the data is finished when all packets have been
sent and one minute has passed since the last packet was received. Any expected
packets that have not been received by this point are assumed to be lost in the ether.

A typical run produced output like this:

```
Wrote: 0
Read: 0
Wrote: 1
Wrote: 2
Read: 1
Wrote: 3
Read: 2
Wrote: 4
Wrote: 5
Wrote: 6
Wrote: 7
Wrote: 8
Wrote: 9
Wrote: 10
Wrote: 11
Wrote: 12
Wrote: 13
Wrote: 14
Wrote: 15
Wrote: 16
Wrote: 17
Wrote: 18
```

```
Wrote: 19
Wrote: 20
Wrote: 21
Wrote: 22
Read: 3
Wrote: 23
...
Wrote: 97
Read: 72
Wrote: 98
Read: 73
Wrote: 99
Read: 75
Read: 76
...
Read: 97
Read: 98
Read: 99
Echoed 92 out of 100 sent
Success rate: 92.0%
```

Connecting to a remote server a couple of miles and seven hops away (according to traceroute), I saw between 90% and 98% of the packets make the round trip.

Closing

Just as with regular datagram sockets, a channel should be closed when you're done with it to free up the port and any other resources it may be using:

```
public void close( ) throws IOException
```

Closing an already closed channel has no effect. Attempting to write data to or read data from a closed channel throws an exception. If you're uncertain whether a channel has been closed, check with isOpen( ):

```
public boolean isOpen( )
```

This returns false if the channel is closed, true if it's open.

CHAPTER 14

Multicast Sockets

The sockets in the previous chapters are *unicast*: they provide point-to-point communication. Unicast sockets create a connection with two well-defined endpoints; there is one sender and one receiver and, although they may switch roles, at any given time it is easy to tell which is which. However, although point-to-point communications serve many, if not most needs (people have engaged in one-on-one conversations for millennia), many tasks require a different model. For example, a television station broadcasts data from one location to every point within range of its transmitter. The signal reaches every television set, whether or not it's turned on and whether or not it's tuned to that particular station. Indeed, the signal even reaches homes with cable boxes instead of antennas and homes that don't have a television. This is the classic example of broadcasting. It's indiscriminate and quite wasteful of both the electromagnetic spectrum and power.

Videoconferencing, by contrast, sends an audio-video feed to a select group of people. Usenet news is posted at one site and distributed around the world to hundreds of thousands of people. DNS router updates travel from the site, announcing a change to many other routers. However, the sender relies on the intermediate sites to copy and relay the message to downstream sites. The sender does not address its message to every host that will eventually receive it. These are examples of multicasting, although they're implemented with additional application layer protocols on top of TCP or UDP. These protocols require fairly detailed configuration and intervention by human beings. For instance, to join Usenet you have to find a site willing to send news to you and relay your outgoing news to the rest of the world. To add you to the Usenet feed, the news administrator of your news relay has to specifically add your site to their news config files. However, recent developments with the network software in most major operating systems as well as Internet routers have opened up a new possibility—true multicasting, in which the routers decide how to efficiently move a message to individual hosts. In particular, the initial router sends only one copy of the message to a router near the receiving hosts, which then makes multiple copies for different recipients at or closer to the destinations. Internet multicasting is built on top of UDP. Multicasting in Java uses the `DatagramPacket` class introduced in Chapter 13, along with a new `MulticastSocket` class.

What Is a Multicast Socket?

Multicasting is broader than unicast, point-to-point communication but narrower and more targeted than broadcast communication. Multicasting sends data from one host to many different hosts, but not to everyone; the data only goes to clients that have expressed an interest by joining a particular multicast group. In a way, this is like a public meeting. People can come and go as they please, leaving when the discussion no longer interests them. Before they arrive and after they have left, they don't need to process the information at all: it just doesn't reach them. On the Internet, such "public meetings" are best implemented using a multicast socket that sends a copy of the data to a location (or a group of locations) close to the parties that have declared an interest in the data. In the best case, the data is duplicated only when it reaches the local network serving the interested clients: the data crosses the Internet only once. More realistically, several identical copies of the data traverse the Internet; but, by carefully choosing the points at which the streams are duplicated, the load on the network is minimized. The good news is that programmers and network administrators aren't responsible for choosing the points where the data is duplicated or even for sending multiple copies; the Internet's routers handle all that.

IP also supports broadcasting, but the use of broadcasts is strictly limited. Protocols require broadcasts only when there is no alternative, and routers limit broadcasts to the local network or subnet, preventing broadcasts from reaching the Internet at large. Even a few small global broadcasts could bring the Internet to its knees. Broadcasting high-bandwidth data such as audio, video, or even text and still images is out of the question. A single email spam that goes to millions of addresses is bad enough. Imagine what would happen if a real-time video feed were copied to all six hundred million Internet users, whether they wanted to watch it or not.

However, there's a middle ground between point-to-point communications and broadcasts to the whole world. There's no reason to send a video feed to hosts that aren't interested in it; we need a technology that sends data to the hosts that want it, without bothering the rest of the world. One way to do this is to use many unicast streams. If 1,000 clients want to listen to a RealAudio broadcast, the data is sent a thousand times. This is inefficient, since it duplicates data needlessly, but it's orders-of-magnitude more efficient than broadcasting the data to every host on the Internet. Still, if the number of interested clients is large enough, you will eventually run out of bandwidth or CPU power—probably sooner rather than later.

Another approach to the problem is to create static *connection trees*. This is the solution employed by Usenet news and some conferencing systems (notably CUseeMe). Data is fed from the originating site to other servers, which replicate it to still other servers, which eventually replicate it to clients. Each client connects to the nearest server. This is more efficient than sending everything to all interested clients via multiple unicasts, but the scheme is kludgy and beginning to show its age. New sites need to find a place to hook into the tree manually. The tree does not necessarily reflect the best possible topology at any one time, and servers still need to maintain many point-to-point connections to their clients, sending the same data to each one. It would be better to allow the routers in the Internet to dynamically determine the best possible routes for transmitting distributed information and to replicate data only when absolutely necessary. This is where multicasting comes in.

For example, if you're multicasting video from New York and 20 people attached to one LAN are watching the show in Los Angeles, the feed will be sent to that LAN only once. If 50 more people are watching in San Francisco, the data stream will be duplicated somewhere (let's say Fresno) and sent to the two cities. If a hundred more people are watching in Houston, another data stream will be sent there (perhaps from St. Louis); see Figure 14-1. The data has crossed the Internet only three times—not the 170 times that would be required by point-to-point connections, or the millions of times that would be required by a true broadcast. Multicasting is halfway between the point-to-point communication common to the Internet and the broadcast model of television and it's more efficient than either. When a packet is multicast, it is addressed to a multicast group and sent to each host belonging to the group. It does not go to a single host (as in unicasting), nor does it go to every host (as in broadcasting). Either would be too inefficient.

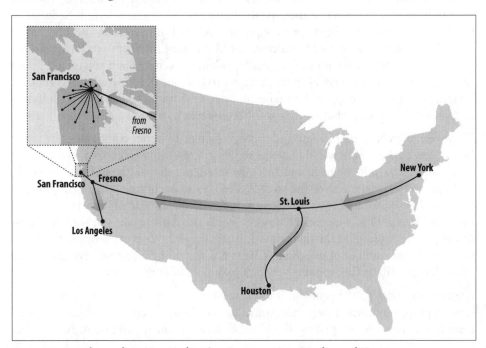

Figure 14-1. Multicast from New York to San Francisco, Los Angeles, and Houston

When people start talking about multicasting, audio and video are the first applications that come to mind; however, they are only the tip of the iceberg. Other possibilities include multiplayer games, distributed filesystems, massively parallel computing, multiperson conferencing, database replication, and more. Multicasting can be used to implement name services and directory services that don't require the client to know a server's address in advance; to look up a name, a host could multicast its request to some well-known address and wait until a response is received from the nearest server. Apple's Rendezvous (a.k.a. Zeroconf) and Sun's Jini both use IP multicasting to dynamically discover services on the local network.

Multicasting should also make it easier to implement various kinds of caching for the Internet, which will be important if the Net's population continues to grow faster than available bandwidth. Martin Hamilton has proposed using multicasting to build a distributed server system for the World Wide Web. ("Evaluating Resource Discovery Applications of IP Multicast", *http://martinh.net/eval/eval.html*, 1995.) For example, a high-traffic web server could be split across multiple machines, all of which share a single hostname, mapped to a multicast address. Suppose one machine chunks out HTML files, another handles images, and a third processes servlets. When a client makes a request to the multicast address, the request is sent to each of the three servers. When a server receives the request, it looks to see whether the client wants an HTML file, an image, or a servlet response. If the server can handle the request, it responds. Otherwise, the server ignores the request and lets the other servers process it. It is easy to imagine more complex divisions of labor between distributed servers.

Multicasting has been designed to fit into the Internet as seamlessly as possible. Most of the work is done by routers and should be transparent to application programmers. An application simply sends datagram packets to a multicast address, which isn't fundamentally different from any other IP address. The routers make sure the packet is delivered to all the hosts in the multicast group. The biggest problem is that multicast routers are not yet ubiquitous; therefore, you need to know enough about them to find out whether multicasting is supported on your network. As far as the application itself, you need to pay attention to an additional header field in the datagrams called the Time-To-Live (TTL) value. The TTL is the maximum number of routers that the datagram is allowed to cross; when it reaches the maximum, it is discarded. Multicasting uses the TTL as an ad hoc way to limit how far a packet can travel. For example, you don't want packets for a friendly on-campus game of Dogfight reaching routers on the other side of the world. Figure 14-2 shows how TTLs limit a packet's spread.

Multicast Addresses and Groups

A *multicast address* is the shared address of a group of hosts called a *multicast group*. We'll talk about the address first. Multicast addresses are IP addresses in the range

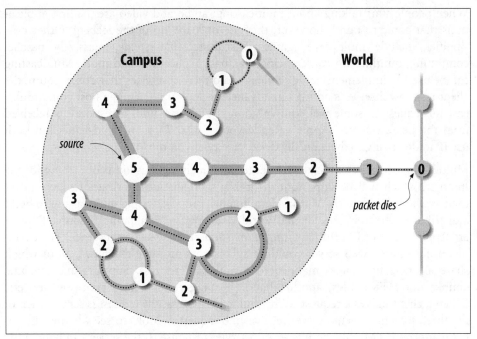

Figure 14-2. Coverage of a packet with a TTL of five

224.0.0.0 to 239.255.255.255. All addresses in this range have the binary digits 1110 as their first four bits. They are called Class D addresses to distinguish them from the more common Class A, B, and C addresses. Like any IP address, a multicast address can have a hostname; for example, the multicast address 224.0.1.1 (the address of the Network Time Protocol distributed service) is assigned the name *ntp.mcast.net*.

A multicast group is a set of Internet hosts that share a multicast address. Any data sent to the multicast address is relayed to all the members of the group. Membership in a multicast group is open; hosts can enter or leave the group at any time. Groups can be either permanent or transient. Permanent groups have assigned addresses that remain constant, whether or not there are any members in the group. However, most multicast groups are transient and exist only as long as they have members. All you have to do to create a new multicast group is pick a random address from 225.0.0.0 to 238.255.255.255, construct an InetAddress object for that address, and start sending it data.

A number of multicast addresses have been set aside for special purposes. *all-systems.mcast.net*, 224.0.0.1, is a multicast group that includes all systems that support multicasting on the local subnet. This group is commonly used for local testing, as is *experiment.mcast.net*, 224.0.1.20. (There is no multicast address that sends data to all hosts on the Internet.) All addresses beginning with 224.0.0 (i.e., addresses from 224.0.0.0 to 224.0.0.255) are reserved for routing protocols and other low-level activities, such as gateway discovery and group membership reporting. Multicast routers never forward datagrams with destinations in this range.

The IANA is responsible for handing out permanent multicast addresses as needed; so far, a few hundred have been specifically assigned. Most of these begin with 224.0., 224.1., 224.2., or 239. Table 14-1 lists a few of these permanent addresses. A few blocks of addresses ranging in size from a few dozen to a few thousand addresses have also been reserved for particular purposes. The complete list is available from *http://www.iana.org/assignments/multicast-addresses*. The remaining 248 million Class D addresses can be used on a temporary basis by anyone who needs them. Multicast routers (*mrouters* for short) are responsible for making sure that two different systems don't try to use the same Class D address at the same time.

Table 14-1. Common permanent multicast addresses

Domain name	IP address	Purpose
BASE-ADDRESS.MCAST.NET	224.0.0.0	The reserved base address. This is never assigned to any multicast group.
ALL-SYSTEMS.MCAST.NET	224.0.0.1	All systems on the local subnet.
ALL-ROUTERS.MCAST.NET	224.0.0.2	All routers on the local subnet.
DVMRP.MCAST.NET	224.0.0.4	All Distance Vector Multicast Routing Protocol (DVMRP) routers on this subnet. An early version of the DVMRP protocol is documented in RFC 1075; the current version has changed substantially.
MOBILE-AGENTS.MCAST. NET	224.0.0.11	Mobile agents on the local subnet.
DHCP-AGENTS.MCAST.NET	224.0.0.12	This multicast group allows a client to locate a Dynamic Host Configuration Protocol (DHCP) server or relay agent on the local subnet.
PIM-ROUTERS.MCAST.NET	224.0.0.13	All Protocol Independent Multicasting (PIM) routers on this subnet.
RSVP-ENCAPSULATION. MCAST.NET	224.0.0.14	RSVP encapsulation on this subnet. RSVP stands for Resource reSerVation setup Protocol, an effort to allow people to reserve a guaranteed amount of Internet bandwidth in advance for an event.
NTP.MCAST.NET	224.0.1.1	The Network Time Protocol.
SGI-DOG.MCAST.NET	224.0.1.2	Silicon Graphics Dogfight game.
NSS.MCAST.NET	224.0.1.6	The Name Service Server.
AUDIONEWS.MCAST.NET	224.0.1.7	Audio news multicast.
SUB-NIS.MCAST.NET	224.0.1.8	Sun's NIS+ Information Service.
MTP.MCAST.NET	224.0.1.9	The Multicast Transport Protocol.
IETF-1-LOW-AUDIO.MCAST. NET	224.0.1.10	Channel 1 of low-quality audio from IETF meetings.
IETF-1- AUDIO.MCAST.NET	224.0.1.11	Channel 1 of high-quality audio from IETF meetings.
IETF-1-VIDEO.MCAST.NET	224.0.1.12	Channel 1 of video from IETF meetings.
IETF-2-LOW-AUDIO.MCAST. NET	224.0.1.13	Channel 2 of low-quality audio from IETF meetings.
IETF-2-AUDIO.MCAST.NET	224.0.1.14	Channel 2 of high-quality audio from IETF meetings.
IETF-2-VIDEO.MCAST.NET	224.0.1.15	Channel 2 of video from IETF meetings.
MUSIC-SERVICE.MCAST.NET	224.0.1.16	Music service.

Table 14-1. Common permanent multicast addresses (continued)

Domain name	IP address	Purpose
SEANET-TELEMETRY. MCAST.NET	224.0.1.17	Telemetry data for the U.S. Navy's SeaNet Project to extend the Internet to vessels at sea. See *http://web.nps.navy.mil/~seanet/Distlearn/cover.htm*.
SEANET-IMAGE.MCAST.NET	224.0.1.18	SeaNet images.
MLOADD.MCAST.NET	224.0.1.19	MLOADD measures the traffic load through one or more network interfaces over a number of seconds. Multicasting is used to communicate between the different interfaces being measured.
EXPERIMENT.MCAST.NET	224.0.1.20	Experiments that do not go beyond the local subnet.
XINGTV.MCAST.NET	224.0.1.23	XING Technology's Streamworks TV multicast.
MICROSOFT.MCAST.NET	224.0.1.24	Used by Windows Internet Name Service (WINS) servers to locate one another.
MTRACE.MCAST.NET	224.0.1.32	A multicast version of traceroute.
JINI-ANNOUNCEMENT.MCAST.NET	224.0.1.84	JINI announcements.
JINI-REQUEST.MCAST.NET	224.0.1.85	JINI requests.
	224.2.0.0– 224.2.255. 255	The Multicast Backbone on the Internet (MBONE) addresses are reserved for multimedia conference calls, i.e., audio, video, whiteboard, and shared web browsing between many people.
	224.2.2.2	Port 9,875 on this address is used to broadcast the currently available MBONE programming. You can look at this with the X Window utility sdr or the Windows/Unix multikit program.
	239.0.0.0– 239.255. 255.255	Administrative scope, in contrast to TTL scope, uses different ranges of multicast addresses to constrain multicast traffic to a particular region or group of routers. For example, the IP addresses from 239.178.0.0 to 239.178.255.255 might be an administrative scope for the state of New York. Data addressed to one of those addresses would not be forwarded outside of New York. The idea is to allow the possible group membership to be established in advance without relying on less-than-reliable TTL values.

The MBONE (or Multicast Backbone on the Internet) is the range of Class D addresses beginning with 224.2. that are used for audio and video broadcasts over the Internet. The word MBONE is sometimes used less restrictively (and less accurately) to mean the portion of the Internet that understands how to route Class D addressed packets.

Clients and Servers

When a host wants to send data to a multicast group, it puts that data in multicast datagrams, which are nothing more than UDP datagrams addressed to a multicast group. Most multicast data is audio or video or both. These sorts of data tend to be relatively large and relatively robust against data loss. If a few pixels or even a whole frame of video is lost in transit, the signal isn't blurred beyond recognition. Therefore, multicast data is sent via UDP, which, though unreliable, can be as much as three times faster than data sent via connection-oriented TCP. (If you think about it, multicast over TCP would be next to impossible. TCP requires hosts to acknowledge that they have received packets; handling acknowledgments in a multicast situation would be a nightmare.) If you're developing a multicast application that can't tolerate data loss, it's your responsibility to determine whether data was damaged in transit and how to handle missing data. For example, if you are building a distributed cache system, you might simply decide to leave any files that don't arrive intact out of the cache.

Earlier, I said that from an application programmer's standpoint, the primary difference between multicasting and using regular UDP sockets is that you have to worry about the TTL value. This is a single byte in the IP header that takes values from 0 to 255; it is interpreted roughly as the number of routers through which a packet can pass before it is discarded. Each time the packet passes through a router, its TTL field is decremented by at least one; some routers may decrement the TTL by two or more. When the TTL reaches zero, the packet is discarded. The TTL field was originally designed to prevent routing loops by guaranteeing that all packets would eventually be discarded; it prevents misconfigured routers from sending packets back and forth to each other indefinitely. In IP multicasting, the TTL limits the multicast geographically. For example, a TTL value of 16 limits the packet to the local area, generally one organization or perhaps an organization and its immediate upstream and downstream neighbors. A TTL of 127, however, sends the packet around the world. Intermediate values are also possible. However, there is no precise way to map TTLs to geographical distance. Generally, the farther away a site is, the more routers a packet has to pass through before reaching it. Packets with small TTL values won't travel as far as packets with large TTL values. Table 14-2 provides some rough estimates relating TTL values to geographical reach. Packets addressed to a multicast group from 224.0.0.0 to 224.0.0.255 are never forwarded beyond the local subnet, regardless of the TTL values used.

Table 14-2. Estimated TTL values for datagrams originating in the continental United States

Destinations	TTL value
The local host	0
The local subnet	1
The local campus—that is, the same side of the nearest Internet router—but on possibly different LANs	16
High-bandwidth sites in the same country, generally those fairly close to the backbone	32
All sites in the same country	48
All sites on the same continent	64
High-bandwidth sites worldwide	128
All sites worldwide	255

Once the data has been stuffed into one or more datagrams, the sending host launches the datagrams onto the Internet. This is just like sending regular (unicast)

UDP data. The sending host begins by transmitting a multicast datagram to the local network. This packet immediately reaches all members of the multicast group in the same subnet. If the Time-To-Live field of the packet is greater than 1, multicast routers on the local network forward the packet to other networks that have members of the destination group. When the packet arrives at one of the final destinations, the multicast router on the foreign network transmits the packet to each host it serves that is a member of the multicast group. If necessary, the multicast router also retransmits the packet to the next routers in the paths between the current router and all its eventual destinations.

When data arrives at a host in a multicast group, the host receives it as it receives any other UDP datagram—even though the packet's destination address doesn't match the receiving host. The host recognizes that the datagram is intended for it because it belongs to the multicast group to which the datagram is addressed, much as most of us accept mail addressed to "Occupant," even though none of us are named Mr. or Ms. Occupant. The receiving host must be listening on the proper port, ready to process the datagram when it arrives.

Routers and Routing

Figure 14-3 shows one of the simplest possible multicast configurations: a single server sending the same data to four clients served by the same router. A multicast socket sends one stream of data over the Internet to the clients' router; the router duplicates the stream and sends it to each of the clients. Without multicast sockets, the server would have to send four separate but identical streams of data to the router, which would route each stream to a client. Using the same stream to send the same data to multiple clients significantly reduces the bandwidth required on the Internet backbone.

Of course, real-world routes can be much more complex, involving multiple hierarchies of redundant routers. However, the goal of multicast sockets is simple: no matter how complex the network, the same data should never be sent more than once over any given network segment. Fortunately, you don't need to worry about routing issues. Just create a MulticastSocket, have the socket join a multicast group, and stuff the address of the multicast group in the DatagramPacket you want to send. The routers and the MulticastSocket class take care of the rest.

The biggest restriction on multicasting is the availability of special multicast routers (mrouters). Mrouters are reconfigured Internet routers or workstations that support the IP multicast extensions. Many consumer-oriented ISPs quite deliberately do not enable multicasting in their routers. In 2004, it is still possible to find hosts between which no multicast route exists (i.e., there is no route between the hosts that travels exclusively over mrouters).

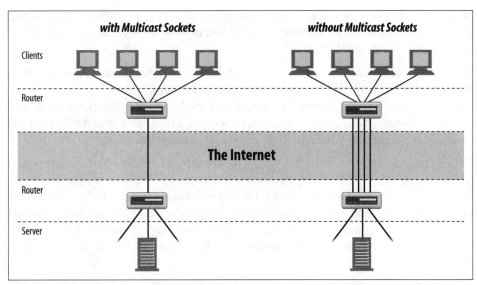

Figure 14-3. With and without multicast sockets

To send and receive multicast data beyond the local subnet, you need a multicast router. Check with your network administrator to see whether your routers support multicasting. You can also try pinging *all-routers.mcast.net*. If any router responds, then your network is hooked up to a multicast router:

```
% ping all-routers.mcast.net
all-routers.mcast.net is alive
```

This still may not allow you to send to or receive from every multicast-capable host on the Internet. For your packets to reach any given host, there must be a path of multicast-capable routers between your host and the remote host. Alternately, some sites may be connected by special multicast tunnel software that transmits multicast data over unicast UDP that all routers understand. If you have trouble getting the examples in this chapter to produce the expected results, check with your local network administrator or ISP to see whether multicasting is actually supported by your routers.

Working with Multicast Sockets

Enough theory. In Java, you multicast data using the java.net.MulticastSocket class, a subclass of java.net.DatagramSocket:

```
public class MulticastSocket extends DatagramSocket
```

As you would expect, MulticastSocket's behavior is very similar to DatagramSocket's: you put your data in DatagramPacket objects that you send and receive with the MulticastSocket. Therefore, I won't repeat the basics; this discussion assumes that you already know how to work with datagrams. If you're jumping around in this book rather than reading it cover to cover, now might be a good time to go back and read Chapter 13 on UDP.

To receive data that is being multicast from a remote site, first create a MulticastSocket with the MulticastSocket( ) constructor. Next, join a multicast group using the MulticastSocket's joinGroup( ) method. This signals the routers in the path between you and the server to start sending data your way and tells the local host that it should pass you IP packets addressed to the multicast group.

Once you've joined the multicast group, you receive UDP data just as you would with a DatagramSocket. That is, you create a DatagramPacket with a byte array that serves as a buffer for data and enter a loop in which you receive the data by calling the receive( ) method inherited from the DatagramSocket class. When you no longer want to receive data, leave the multicast group by invoking the socket's leaveGroup( ) method. You can then close the socket with the close( ) method inherited from DatagramSocket.

Sending data to a multicast address is similar to sending UDP data to a unicast address. You do not need to join a multicast group to send data to it. You create a new DatagramPacket, stuff the data and the address of the multicast group into the packet, and pass it to the send( ) method. The one difference is that you must explicitly specify the packet's TTL value.

There is one caveat to all this: multicast sockets are a security hole big enough to drive a small truck through. Consequently, untrusted code running under the control of a SecurityManager is not allowed to do anything involving multicast sockets. Remotely loaded code is normally allowed to send datagrams to or receive datagrams from the host it was downloaded from. However, multicast sockets don't allow this sort of restriction to be placed on the packets they send or receive. Once you send data to a multicast socket, you have very limited and unreliable control over which hosts receive that data. Consequently, most environments that execute remote code take the conservative approach of disallowing all multicasting.

The Constructors

The constructors are simple. Each one calls the equivalent constructor in the DatagramSocket superclass.

public MulticastSocket( ) throws SocketException

This constructor creates a socket that is bound to an anonymous port (i.e., an unused port assigned by the system). It is useful for clients (i.e., programs that initiate a data transfer) because they don't need to use a well-known port: the recipient replies to the port contained in the packet. If you need to know the port number, look it up with the `getLocalPort( )` method inherited from `DatagramSocket`. This constructor throws a `SocketException` if the `Socket` can't be created. For example:

```
try {
  MulticastSocket ms = new MulticastSocket( );
  // send some datagrams...
}
catch (SocketException se) {
  System.err.println(se);
}
```

public MulticastSocket(int port) throws SocketException

This constructor creates a socket that receives datagrams on a well-known port. The port argument specifies the port on which this socket listens for datagrams. As with regular TCP and UDP unicast sockets, on a Unix system a program needs to be run with root privileges in order to create a `MulticastSocket` on a port numbered from 1 to 1,023.

This constructor throws a `SocketException` if the `Socket` can't be created. A `Socket` can't be created if you don't have sufficient privileges to bind to the port or if the port you're trying to bind to is already in use. Note that since a multicast socket is a datagram socket as far as the operating system is concerned, a `MulticastSocket` cannot occupy a port already occupied by a `DatagramSocket`, and vice versa. For example, this code fragment opens a multicast socket on port 4,000:

```
try {
  MulticastSocket ms = new MulticastSocket(4000);
  // receive incoming datagrams...
}
catch (SocketException ex) {
  System.err.println(ex);
}
```

public MulticastSocket(SocketAddress bindAddress) throws IOException // Java 1.4

Starting in Java 1.4, you can create a `MulticastSocket` using a `SocketAddress` object. If the `SocketAddress` is bound to a port, then this is pretty much the same as the previous constructor. For example, this code fragment also opens a `MulticastSocket` on port 4000 that listens on all network interfaces and addresses:

```
try {
  SocketAddress address = new InetSocketAddress(4000);
  MulticastSocket ms = new MulticastSocket(address);
  // receive incoming datagrams...
}
catch (SocketException ex) {
  System.err.println(ex);
}
```

However, the SocketAddress can also be bound to a specific network interface on the local host, rather than listening on all network interfaces. For example, this code fragment also opens a MulticastSocket on port 4000 that only listens to packets arriving on 192.168.254.32:

```
try {
  SocketAddress address = new InetSocketAddress("192.168.254.32", 4000);
  MulticastSocket ms = new MulticastSocket(address);
  // receive incoming datagrams...
}
catch (SocketException ex) {
  System.err.println(ex);
}
```

Finally, you can pass null to this constructor to create an unbound socket, which would later be connected with the bind( ) method. This is useful when setting socket options that can only be set before the socket is bound. For example, this code fragment creates a multicast socket with SO_REUSEADDR disabled (that option is normally enabled by default for multicast sockets):

```
try {
  MulticastSocket ms = new MulticastSocket(null);
  ms.setReuseAddress(false);
  SocketAddress address = new InetSocketAddress(4000);
  ms.bind(address);
  // receive incoming datagrams...
}
catch (SocketException ex) {
  System.err.println(ex);
}
```

Communicating with a Multicast Group

Once a MulticastSocket has been created, it can perform four key operations:

1. Join a multicast group.
2. Send data to the members of the group.
3. Receive data from the group.
4. Leave the multicast group.

The MulticastSocket class has methods for operations 1, 2, and 4. No new method is required to receive data. The receive( ) method of the superclass, DatagramSocket, suffices for this task. You can perform these operations in any order, with the exception that you must join a group before you can receive data from it (or, for that matter, leave it). You do not need to join a group to send data to it, and the sending and receiving of data may be freely interwoven.

public void joinGroup(InetAddress address) throws IOException

To receive data from a MulticastSocket, you must first join a multicast group. To join a group, pass an InetAddress object for the multicast group to the joinGroup( ) method. If you successfully join the group, you'll receive any datagrams intended for that group. Once you've joined a multicast group, you receive datagrams exactly as you receive unicast datagrams, as shown in the previous chapter. That is, you set up a DatagramPacket as a buffer and pass it into this socket's receive( ) method. For example:

```
try {
  MulticastSocket ms = new MulticastSocket(4000);
  InetAddress ia = InetAddress.getByName("224.2.2.2");
  ms.joinGroup(ia);
  byte[] buffer = new byte[8192];
  while (true) {
    DatagramPacket dp = new DatagramPacket(buffer, buffer.length);
    ms.receive(dp);
    String s = new String(dp.getData( ), "8859_1");
    System.out.println(s);
  }
}
catch (IOException ex) {
  System.err.println(ex);
}
```

If the address that you try to join is not a multicast address (that is, it is not between 224.0.0.0 and 239.255.255.255), the joinGroup( ) method throws an IOException.

A single MulticastSocket can join multiple multicast groups. Information about membership in multicast groups is stored in multicast routers, not in the object. In this case, you'd use the address stored in the incoming datagram to determine which address a packet was intended for.

Multiple multicast sockets on the same machine and even in the same Java program can all join the same group. If so, they'll all receive all data addressed to that group that arrives at the local host.

public void joinGroup(SocketAddress address, NetworkInterface interface) throws IOException // Java 1.4

Java 1.4 adds this overloaded variant of joinGroup( ) that allows you to join a multicast group only on a specified local network interface. A proxy server or firewall might use this to specify that it will accept multicast data from the interface connected to the LAN, but not the interface connected to the global Internet, for instance.

For example, this code fragment attempts to join the group with IP address 224.2.2.2 on the network interface named "eth0", if such an interface exists. If no such interface exists, then it joins on all available network interfaces:

```
MulticastSocket ms = new MulticastSocket(4000);
SocketAddress group = new InetSocketAddress("224.2.2.2", 40);
NetworkInterface ni = NetworkInterface .getByName("eth0");
if (ni != null) {
  ms.joinGroup(group, ni);
}
else {
  ms.joinGroup(group);
}
```

Other than the extra argument specifying the network interface to listen from, this behaves pretty much like the single argument joinGroup( ) method. For instance, passing a SocketAddress object that does not represent a multicast group as the first argument throws an IOException.

public void leaveGroup(InetAddress address) throws IOException

The leaveGroup( ) method signals that you no longer want to receive datagrams from the specified multicast group. A signal is sent to the appropriate multicast router, telling it to stop sending you datagrams. If the address you try to leave is not a multicast address (that is, if it is not between 224.0.0.0 and 239.255.255.255), the method throws an IOException. However, no exception occurs if you leave a multicast group you never joined.

public void leaveGroup(SocketAddress multicastAddress, NetworkInterface interface) throws IOException // Java 1.4

Java 1.4 also allows you to specify that you no longer want to receive datagrams on one particular network interface. Perhaps you do wish to continue receiving datagrams on other network interfaces. For instance, you could join on all interfaces, and then leave just one. To be honest, this is a bit of a stretch. This method was probably included mostly for symmetry with joinGroup( ).

public void send(DatagramPacket packet, byte ttl) throws IOException

Sending data with a MulticastSocket is similar to sending data with a DatagramSocket. Stuff your data into a DatagramPacket object and send it off using the send( ) method inherited from DatagramSocket:

```
public void send(DatagramPacket p) throws IOException
```

The data is sent to every host that belongs to the multicast group to which the packet is addressed. For example:

```
try {
  InetAddress ia = InetAddress.getByName("experiment.mcast.net");
  byte[] data = "Here's some multicast data\r\n".getBytes();
  int port = 4000;
  DatagramPacket dp = new DatagramPacket(data, data.length, ia, port);
```

```
    MulticastSocket ms = new MulticastSocket();
    ms.send(dp);
}
catch (IOException ex) {
    System.err.println(ex);
}
```

However, the MulticastSocket class adds an overloaded variant of the send() method that lets you provide a value for the Time-To-Live field ttl. By default, the send() method uses a TTL of 1; that is, packets don't travel outside the local subnet. However, you can change this setting for an individual packet by passing an integer from 0 to 255 as the second argument to the send() method. For example:

```
DatagramPacket dp = new DatagramPacket(data, data.length, ia, port);
MulticastSocket ms = new MulticastSocket();
ms.send(dp, 64);
```

public void setInterface(InetAddress address) throws SocketException

On a multihomed host, the setInterface() method chooses the network interface used for multicast sending and receiving. setInterface() throws a SocketException if the InetAddress argument is not the address of a network interface on the local machine. It is unclear why the network interface is immutably set in the constructor for unicast Socket and DatagramSocket objects but is variable and set with a separate method for MulticastSocket objects. To be safe, set the interface immediately after constructing a MulticastSocket and don't change it thereafter. Here's how you might use setInterface():

```
MulticastSocket ms;
InetAddress ia;
try {
    ia = InetAddress.getByName("www.ibiblio.org");
    ms = new MulticastSocket(2048);
    ms.setInterface(ia);
    // send and receive data...
}
catch (UnknownHostException ue) {
    System.err.println(ue);
}
catch (SocketException se) {
    System.err.println(se);
}
```

public InetAddress getInterface() throws SocketException

If you need to know the address of the interface the socket is bound to, call getInterface(). It isn't clear why this method would throw an exception; in any case, you must be prepared for it. For example:

```
try {
    MulticastSocket ms = new MulticastSocket(2048);
```

```
      InetAddress ia = ms.getInterface();
    }
    catch (SocketException se) {
      System.err.println(ue);
    }
```

public void setNetworkInterface(NetworkInterface interface) throws SocketException // Java 1.4

The setNetworkInterface( ) method serves the same purpose as the setInterface( ) method; that is, it chooses the network interface used for multicast sending and receiving. However, it does so based on the local name of a network interface such as "eth0" (as encapsulated in a NetworkInterface object) rather than on the IP address bound to that network interface (as encapsulated in an InetAddress object). setNetworkInterface( ) throws a SocketException if the NetworkInterface passed as an argument is not a network interface on the local machine.

public NetworkInterface getNetworkInterface( ) throws SocketException // Java 1.4

The getNetworkInterface( ) method returns a NetworkInterface object representing the network interface on which this MulticastSocket is listening for data. If no network interface has been explicitly set in the constructor or with setNetworkInterface( ), it returns a placeholder object with the address "0.0.0.0" and the index −1. For example, this code fragment prints the network interface used by a socket:

```
NetworkInterface intf = ms.getNetworkInterface();
System.out.println(intf.getName());
```

public void setTimeToLive(int ttl) throws IOException // Java 1.2

The setTimeToLive( ) method sets the default TTL value used for packets sent from the socket using the send(Datagrampacket dp) method inherited from DatagramSocket (as opposed to the send(Datagrampacket dp, byte ttl) method in MulticastSocket). This method is only available in Java 1.2 and later. In Java 1.1, you have to use the setTTL( ) method instead:

```
public void setTTL(byte ttl) throws IOException
```

The setTTL( ) method is deprecated in Java 2 and later because it only allows TTL values from 1 to 127 rather than the full range from 1 to 255.

public int getTimeToLive( ) throws IOException // Java 1.2

The getTimeToLive( ) method returns the default TTL value of the MulticastSocket. It's not needed very much. This method is also available only in Java 1.2 and later. In Java 1.1, you have to use the getTTL( ) method instead:

```
public byte getTTL() throws IOException
```

The getTTL( ) method is deprecated in Java 1.2 and later because it doesn't properly handle TTLs greater than 127—it truncates them to 127. The getTimeToLive( ) method can handle the full range from 1 to 255 without truncation because it returns an int instead of a byte.

public void setLoopbackMode(boolean disable) throws SocketException // Java 1.4

Whether or not a host receives the multicast packets it sends is platform-dependent—that is, whether or not they loop back. Passing true to setLoopback( ) indicates you don't want to receive the packets you send. Passing false indicates you do want to receive the packets you send. However, this is only a hint. Implementations are not required to do as you request.

public boolean getLoopbackMode( ) throws SocketException // Java 1.4

Because loopback mode is only a hint that may not be followed on all systems, it's important to check what the loopback mode is if you're both sending and receiving packets. The getLoopbackMode( ) method returns true if packets are not looped back and false if they are. (This feels backwards to me. I suspect this method was written by a programmer following the ill-advised convention that defaults should always be true.)

If the system is looping packets back and you don't want it to, you'll need to recognize the packets somehow and discard them. If the system is not looping the packets back and you do want it to, store copies of the packets you send and inject them into your internal data structures manually at the same time you send them. You can ask for the behavior you want with setLoopback( ), but you can't count on it.

Two Simple Examples

Most multicast servers are indiscriminate about who they will talk to. Therefore, it's easy to join a group and watch the data that's being sent to it. Example 14-1 is a MulticastSniffer class that reads the name of a multicast group from the command line, constructs an InetAddress from that hostname, and creates a MulticastSocket, which attempts to join the multicast group at that hostname. If the attempt succeeds, MulticastSniffer receives datagrams from the socket and prints their contents on System.out. This program is useful primarily to verify that you are receiving multicast data at a particular host. Most multicast data is binary and won't be intelligible when printed as ASCII.

Example 14-1. Multicast sniffer

```
import java.net.*;
import java.io.*;

public class MulticastSniffer {
```

Example 14-1. Multicast sniffer (continued)

```
public static void main(String[] args) {

    InetAddress group = null;
    int port = 0;

    // read the address from the command line
    try {
      group = InetAddress.getByName(args[0]);
      port = Integer.parseInt(args[1]);
    } // end try
    catch (Exception ex) {
      // ArrayIndexOutOfBoundsException, NumberFormatException,
      // or UnknownHostException
      System.err.println(
        "Usage: java MulticastSniffer multicast_address port");
      System.exit(1);
    }

    MulticastSocket ms = null;

    try {
      ms = new MulticastSocket(port);
      ms.joinGroup(group);

      byte[] buffer = new byte[8192];
      while (true) {
        DatagramPacket dp = new DatagramPacket(buffer, buffer.length);
        ms.receive(dp);
        String s = new String(dp.getData());
        System.out.println(s);
      }
    }
    catch (IOException ex) {
      System.err.println(ex);
    }
    finally {
      if (ms != null) {
        try {
          ms.leaveGroup(group);
          ms.close();
        }
        catch (IOException ex) {}
      }
    }

  }

}
```

The program begins by reading the name and port of the multicast group from the first command-line argument. Next, it creates a new MulticastSocket ms on the specified port. This socket joins the multicast group at the specified InetAddress. Then it enters a loop in which it waits for packets to arrive. As each packet arrives, the program reads its data, converts the data to an ISO Latin-1 String, and prints it on System.out. Finally, when the user interrupts the program or an exception is thrown, the socket leaves the group and closes itself.

MBONE session announcements are broadcast to the multicast group *sap.mcast.net* on port 9,875. You can use this program to listen to those announcements. Generally, if you're connected to the MBONE (not all sites are), you should see a site announcement pop through within the first minute or two. In fact, you'll probably see a lot more. I collected about a megabyte and a half of announcements within the first couple of minutes I had this program running. I show only the first two here:

```
% java MulticastSniffer sap.mcast.net 9875
úv=0
o=ellery 3132060082 3138107776 IN IP4 131.182.10.250
s=NASA TV - Broadcast from NASA HQ
i=NASA TV Multicasting from NASA HQ
u=http://www.nasa.gov/ntv
e=Ellery.Coleman@hq.nasa.gov        (Ellery D. Coleman)
p=+202 651 8512
t=3138107776 3153918976
r=15811200 15811200 0
a=recvonly
a=tool:FVC.COM I-Caster V3.1/3101, Windows95/NT
a=cat:Corporate/Events
m=audio 23748 RTP/AVP 0
c=IN IP4 224.2.203.38/127
m=video 60068 RTP/AVP 31
c=IN IP4 224.2.203.37/127
b=AS:380
a=framerate:9
a=quality:8
a=grayed:0
4 224.2.255.115/15
.77/25
4 RTP wbbesteffort
c=IN IP4 224.2.224.41/25

%Â¡_v=0
o=dax 3137417804 3141052115 IN IP4 horla.enst.fr
s=VREng UDP (Virtual Reality Engine)
i=Virtual Reality Engine: Distributed Interactive 3D Multicast
navigator in Virtual Worlds. For more information and downloading, see
URL: http://www.infres.enst.fr/net/vreng/.
u=http://www.infres.enst.fr/net/vreng/
e=Philippe Dax (ENST) <dax@inf.enst.fr>
p=Philippe Dax (ENST) +33 (0) 145817648
t=0 0
a=tool:sdr v2.9
a=type:test
```

```
m=dis 62239 RTP 99
c=IN IP4 224.2.199.133/127
/3
m=mdesk 64538 RTP/AVP mdesk
c=IN IP4 224.2.160.68/3
e please stop your receiving programs and the stream should stop from
coming to you.
u=http://tv.funet.fi/ohjelmat/index.html
e=Harri Salminen <mice-nsc@nic.funet.fi>
p=Harri Salminen +358 400 358 502
t=3085239600 3299658800
a=tool:CDT mAnnouncer 1.1.2
a=type:broadcast
m=audio 4004 RTP/AVP 0
c=IN IP4 239.239.239.239/40
a=ptime:40
m=video 6006 RTP/AVP 31
c=IN IP4 239.239.239.239/40
m=whiteboard 4206 udp wb
c=IN IP4 224.239.239.245/48
```

MBONE session announcements are not pure ASCII text. In particular, they contain a lot of embedded nulls as well as various characters with their high bit set. Consequently, I've had to take a few liberties with the output to print it in this book. To really handle MBONE session announcements, you'd have to parse the relevant ASCII text out of the binary format and display that. Peter Parnes has written a Java program called mSD that does exactly that. If you're interested, you can find it at *http://www.cdt.luth.se/~peppar/progs/mSD/*. However, since this is a book about network programming and not parsing binary file formats, we'll leave the example here and move on to sending multicast data. Example 14-2 is a `MulticastSender` class that sends data read from the command line to a multicast group. It's fairly simple, overall.

Example 14-2. MulticastSender

```java
import java.net.*;
import java.io.*;

public class MulticastSender {

  public static void main(String[] args) {

    InetAddress ia = null;
    int port = 0;
    byte ttl = (byte) 1;

    // read the address from the command line
    try {
      ia = InetAddress.getByName(args[0]);
      port = Integer.parseInt(args[1]);
      if (args.length > 2) ttl = (byte) Integer.parseInt(args[2]);
    }
```

Example 14-2. MulticastSender (continued)

```
    catch (Exception ex)  {
      System.err.println(ex);
      System.err.println(
       "Usage: java MulticastSender multicast_address port ttl");
      System.exit(1);
    }

    byte[] data = "Here's some multicast data\r\n".getBytes( );
    DatagramPacket dp = new DatagramPacket(data, data.length, ia, port);

    try {
      MulticastSocket ms = new MulticastSocket( );
      ms.joinGroup(ia);
      for (int i = 1; i < 10; i++) {
        ms.send(dp, ttl);
      }
      ms.leaveGroup(ia);
      ms.close( );
    }
    catch (SocketException ex) {
      System.err.println(ex);
    }
    catch (IOException ex) {
      System.err.println(ex);
    }

  }

}
```

Example 14-2 reads the address of a multicast group, a port number, and an optional TTL from the command line. It then stuffs the string "Here's some multicast data\r\n" into the byte array data using the getBytes( ) method of java.lang.String, and places this array in the DatagramPacket dp. Next, it constructs the MulticastSocket ms, which joins the group ia. Once it has joined the group, ms sends the datagram packet dp to the group ia 10 times. The TTL value is set to one to make sure that this data doesn't go beyond the local subnet. Having sent the data, ms leaves the group and closes itself.

Run MulticastSniffer on one machine in your local subnet. Listen to the group *all-systems.mcast.net* on port 4,000, like this:

```
% java MulticastSniffer all-systems.mcast.net 4000
```

Next, send data to that group by running MulticastSender on another machine in your local subnet. You can also run it in a different window on the same machine, although that option is not as exciting. However, you must start running the MulticastSniffer before you start running the MulticastSender. Send to the group *all-systems.mcast.net* on port 4,000, like this:

```
% java MulticastSender all-systems.mcast.net 4000
```

Back on the first machine, you should see this output:

```
Here's some multicast data
Here's some multicast data
Here's some multicast data
Here's some multicast data
Here's some multicast data
Here's some multicast data
Here's some multicast data
Here's some multicast data
Here's some multicast data
```

For this to work beyond the local subnet, the two subnets must each have multicast routers.

CHAPTER 15

URLConnections

URLConnection is an abstract class that represents an active connection to a resource specified by a URL. The URLConnection class has two different but related purposes. First, it provides more control over the interaction with a server (especially an HTTP server) than the URL class. With a URLConnection, you can inspect the header sent by the server and respond accordingly. You can set the header fields used in the client request. You can use a URLConnection to download binary files. Finally, a URLConnection lets you send data back to a web server with POST or PUT and use other HTTP request methods. We will explore all of these techniques in this chapter.

Second, the URLConnection class is part of Java's *protocol handler* mechanism, which also includes the URLStreamHandler class. The idea behind protocol handlers is simple: they separate the details of processing a protocol from processing particular data types, providing user interfaces, and doing the other work that a monolithic web browser performs. The base java.net.URLConnection class is abstract; to implement a specific protocol, you write a subclass. These subclasses can be loaded at runtime by applications. For example, if the browser runs across a URL with a strange scheme, such as *compress*, rather than throwing up its hands and issuing an error message, it can download a protocol handler for this unknown protocol and use it to communicate with the server. Writing protocol handlers is the subject of the next chapter.

Only abstract URLConnection classes are present in the java.net package. The concrete subclasses are hidden inside the sun.net package hierarchy. Many of the methods and fields as well as the single constructor in the URLConnection class are *protected*. In other words, they can only be accessed by instances of the URLConnection class or its subclasses. It is rare to instantiate URLConnection objects directly in your source code; instead, the runtime environment creates these objects as needed, depending on the protocol in use. The class (which is unknown at compile time) is then instantiated using the forName( ) and newInstance( ) methods of the java.lang.Class class.

URLConnection does not have the best-designed API in the Java class library. Since the URLConnection class itself relies on the Socket class for network connectivity, there's little you can do with URLConnection that can't also be done with Socket. The URLConnection class is supposed to provide an easier-to-use, higher-level abstraction for network connections than Socket. In practice, however, most programmers have chosen to ignore it and simply use the Socket class. One of several problems is that the URLConnection class is too closely tied to the HTTP protocol. For instance, it assumes that each file transferred is preceded by a MIME header or something very much like one. However, most classic protocols such as FTP and SMTP don't use MIME headers. Another problem, one I hope to alleviate in this chapter, is that the URLConnection class is extremely poorly documented, so very few programmers understand how it's really supposed to work.

Opening URLConnections

A program that uses the URLConnection class directly follows this basic sequence of steps:

1. Construct a URL object.
2. Invoke the URL object's openConnection( ) method to retrieve a URLConnection object for that URL.
3. Configure the URLConnection.
4. Read the header fields.
5. Get an input stream and read data.
6. Get an output stream and write data.
7. Close the connection.

You don't always perform all these steps. For instance, if the default setup for a particular kind of URL is acceptable, then you're likely to skip step 3. If you only want the data from the server and don't care about any metainformation, or if the protocol doesn't provide any metainformation, you'll skip step 4. If you only want to receive data from the server but not send data to the server, you'll skip step 6. Depending on the protocol, steps 5 and 6 may be reversed or interlaced.

The single constructor for the URLConnection class is protected:

```
protected URLConnection(URL url)
```

Consequently, unless you're subclassing URLConnection to handle a new kind of URL (that is, writing a protocol handler), you can only get a reference to one of these objects through the openConnection( ) methods of the URL and URLStreamHandler classes. For example:

```
try {
  URL u = new URL("http://www.greenpeace.org/");
```

```
    URLConnection uc = u.openConnection( );
}
catch (MalformedURLException ex) {
  System.err.println(ex);
}
catch (IOException ex) {
  System.err.println(ex);
}
```

 In practice, the openConnection( ) method of java.net.URL is the same as the openConnection( ) method of java.net.URLStreamHandler. All a URL object's openConnection( ) method does is call its URLStreamHandler's openConnection( ) method.

The URLConnection class is declared abstract. However, all but one of its methods are implemented. You may find it convenient or necessary to override other methods in the class; but the single method that subclasses must implement is connect( ), which makes a connection to a server and thus depends on the type of service (HTTP, FTP, and so on). For example, a sun.net.www.protocol.file.FileURLConnection's connect( ) method converts the URL to a filename in the appropriate directory, creates MIME information for the file, and then opens a buffered FileInputStream to the file. The connect( ) method of sun.net.www.protocol.http.HttpURLConnection creates a sun.net.www.http.HttpClient object, which is responsible for connecting to the server.

```
public abstract void connect( ) throws IOException
```

When a URLConnection is first constructed, it is unconnected; that is, the local and remote host cannot send and receive data. There is no socket connecting the two hosts. The connect( ) method establishes a connection—normally using TCP sockets but possibly through some other mechanism—between the local and remote host so they can send and receive data. However, getInputStream( ), getContent( ), getHeaderField( ), and other methods that require an open connection will call connect( ) if the connection isn't yet open. Therefore, you rarely need to call connect( ) directly.

Reading Data from a Server

Here is the minimal set of steps needed to retrieve data from a URL using a URLConnection object:

1. Construct a URL object.

2. Invoke the URL object's openConnection( ) method to retrieve a URLConnection object for that URL.

3. Invoke the URLConnection's getInputStream( ) method.

4. Read from the input stream using the usual stream API.

The getInputStream() method returns a generic InputStream that lets you read and parse the data that the server sends.

```
public InputStream getInputStream()
```

Example 15-1 uses the getInputStream() method to download a web page.

Example 15-1. Download a web page with a URLConnection

```java
import java.net.*;
import java.io.*;

public class SourceViewer2 {

  public static void main (String[] args) {

    if  (args.length > 0) {
      try {
        //Open the URLConnection for reading
        URL u = new URL(args[0]);
        URLConnection uc = u.openConnection();
        InputStream raw = uc.getInputStream();
        InputStream buffer = new BufferedInputStream(raw);
        // chain the InputStream to a Reader
        Reader r = new InputStreamReader(buffer);
        int c;
        while ((c = r.read()) != -1) {
          System.out.print((char) c);
        }
      }
      catch (MalformedURLException ex) {
        System.err.println(args[0] + " is not a parseable URL");
      }
      catch (IOException ex) {
        System.err.println(ex);
      }

    } //  end if

  } // end main

} // end SourceViewer2
```

It is no accident that this program is almost the same as Example 7-5. The openStream() method of the URL class just returns an InputStream from its own URLConnection object. The output is identical as well, so I won't repeat it here.

The differences between URL and URLConnection aren't apparent with just a simple input stream as in this example. The biggest differences between the two classes are:

- URLConnection provides access to the HTTP header.
- URLConnection can configure the request parameters sent to the server.
- URLConnection can write data to the server as well as read data from the server.

Reading the Header

HTTP servers provide a substantial amount of information in the header that precedes each response. For example, here's a typical HTTP header returned by an Apache web server:

```
HTTP/1.1 200 OK
Date: Mon, 18 Oct 1999 20:06:48 GMT
Server: Apache/1.3.4 (Unix) PHP/3.0.6 mod_perl/1.17
Last-Modified: Mon, 18 Oct 1999 12:58:21 GMT
ETag: "1e05f2-89bb-380b196d"
Accept-Ranges: bytes
Content-Length: 35259
Connection: close
Content-Type: text/html
```

There's a lot of information there. In general, an HTTP header may include the content type of the requested document, the length of the document in bytes, the character set in which the content is encoded, the date and time, the date the content expires, and the date the content was last modified. However, the information depends on the server; some servers send all this information for each request, others send some information, and a few don't send anything. The methods of this section allow you to query a URLConnection to find out what metadata the server has provided.

Aside from HTTP, very few protocols use MIME headers (and technically speaking, even the HTTP header isn't actually a MIME header; it just looks a lot like one). When writing your own subclass of URLConnection, it is often necessary to override these methods so that they return sensible values. The most important piece of information you may be lacking is the MIME content type. URLConnection provides some utility methods that guess the data's content type based on its filename or the first few bytes of the data itself.

Retrieving Specific Header Fields

The first six methods request specific, particularly common fields from the header. These are:

- Content-type
- Content-length
- Content-encoding
- Date
- Last-modified
- Expires

public String getContentType( )

This method returns the MIME content type of the data. It relies on the web server to send a valid content type. (In a later section, we'll see how recalcitrant servers are handled.) It throws no exceptions and returns null if the content type isn't available. text/html will be the most common content type you'll encounter when connecting to web servers. Other commonly used types include text/plain, image/gif, application/xml, and image/jpeg.

If the content type is some form of text, then this header may also contain a character set part identifying the document's character encoding. For example:

```
Content-type: text/html; charset=UTF-8
```

Or:

```
Content-Type: text/xml; charset=iso-2022-jp
```

In this case, getContentType( ) returns the full value of the Content-type field, including the character encoding. We can use this to improve on Example 15-1 by using the encoding specified in the HTTP header to decode the document, or ISO-8859-1 (the HTTP default) if no such encoding is specified. If a nontext type is encountered, an exception is thrown. Example 15-2 demonstrates:

Example 15-2. Download a web page with the correct character set

```java
import java.net.*;
import java.io.*;

public class EncodingAwareSourceViewer {

  public static void main (String[] args) {

    for (int i = 0; i < args.length; i++) {

      try {
        // set default encoding
        String encoding = "ISO-8859-1";
        URL u = new URL(args[i]);
        URLConnection uc = u.openConnection( );
        String contentType = uc.getContentType( );
        int encodingStart = contentType.indexOf("charset=");
        if (encodingStart != -1) {
            encoding = contentType.substring(encodingStart+8);
        }
        InputStream in = new BufferedInputStream(uc.getInputStream( ));
        Reader r = new InputStreamReader(in, encoding);
        int c;
        while ((c = r.read( )) != -1) {
          System.out.print((char) c);
        }
      }
      catch (MalformedURLException ex) {
```

```
      System.err.println(args[0] + " is not a parseable URL");
    }
    catch (IOException ex) {
      System.err.println(ex);
    }

  } //  end if

 } // end main

} // end EncodingAwareSourceViewer
```

In practice, most servers don't include charset information in their Content-type headers, so this is of limited use.

public int getContentLength( )

The getContentLength( ) method tells you how many bytes there are in the content. Many servers send Content-length headers only when they're transferring a binary file, not when transferring a text file. If there is no Content-length header, getContentLength( ) returns –1. The method throws no exceptions. It is used when you need to know exactly how many bytes to read or when you need to create a buffer large enough to hold the data in advance.

In Chapter 7, we discussed how to use the openStream( ) method of the URL class to download text files from an HTTP server. Although in theory you should be able to use the same method to download a binary file, such as a GIF image or a *.class* byte code file, in practice this procedure presents a problem. HTTP servers don't always close the connection exactly where the data is finished; therefore, you don't know when to stop reading. To download a binary file, it is more reliable to use a URLConnection's getContentLength( ) method to find the file's length, then read exactly the number of bytes indicated. Example 15-3 is a program that uses this technique to save a binary file on a disk.

Example 15-3. Downloading a binary file from a web site and saving it to disk

```
import java.net.*;
import java.io.*;

public class BinarySaver {

  public static void main (String args[]) {

    for (int i = 0; i < args.length; i++) {

      try {
        URL root = new URL(args[i]);
        saveBinaryFile(root);
      }
```

Example 15-3. Downloading a binary file from a web site and saving it to disk (continued)

```
      catch (MalformedURLException ex) {
        System.err.println(args[i] + " is not URL I understand.");
      }
      catch (IOException ex) {
        System.err.println(ex);
      }
    } // end for

  } // end main


  public static void saveBinaryFile(URL u) throws IOException {

    URLConnection uc = u.openConnection( );
    String contentType = uc.getContentType( );
    int contentLength = uc.getContentLength( );
    if (contentType.startsWith("text/") || contentLength == -1 ) {
      throw new IOException("This is not a binary file.");
    }

    InputStream raw = uc.getInputStream( );
    InputStream in  = new BufferedInputStream(raw);
    byte[] data = new byte[contentLength];
    int bytesRead = 0;
    int offset = 0;
    while (offset < contentLength) {
      bytesRead = in.read(data, offset, data.length-offset);
      if (bytesRead == -1) break;
      offset += bytesRead;
    }
    in.close( );

    if (offset != contentLength) {
      throw new IOException("Only read " + offset
        + " bytes; Expected " + contentLength + " bytes");
    }

    String filename = u.getFile( );
    filename = filename.substring(filename.lastIndexOf('/') + 1);
    FileOutputStream fout = new FileOutputStream(filename);
    fout.write(data);
    fout.flush( );
    fout.close( );

  }

} // end BinarySaver
```

As usual, the main( ) method loops over the URLs entered on the command line, passing each URL to the saveBinaryFile( ) method. saveBinaryFile( ) opens a URLConnection uc to the URL. It puts the type into the variable contentType and the content length into the variable contentLength. Next, an if statement checks whether the content type is text or the Content-length field is missing or invalid (contentLength == -1). If either of these is true, an IOException is thrown. If these assertions are both false, we have a binary file of known length: that's what we want.

Now that we have a genuine binary file on our hands, we prepare to read it into an array of bytes called data. data is initialized to the number of bytes required to hold the binary object, contentLength. Ideally, you would like to fill data with a single call to read() but you probably won't get all the bytes at once, so the read is placed in a loop. The number of bytes read up to this point is accumulated into the offset variable, which also keeps track of the location in the data array at which to start placing the data retrieved by the next call to read(). The loop continues until offset equals or exceeds contentLength; that is, the array has been filled with the expected number of bytes. We also break out of the while loop if read() returns –1, indicating an unexpected end of stream. The offset variable now contains the total number of bytes read, which should be equal to the content length. If they are not equal, an error has occurred, so saveBinaryFile() throws an IOException. This is the general procedure for reading binary files from HTTP connections.

Now we are ready to save the data in a file. saveBinaryFile() gets the filename from the URL using the getFile() method and strips any path information by calling filename.substring(theFile.lastIndexOf('/') + 1). A new FileOutputStream fout is opened into this file and the data is written in one large burst with fout.write(b).

public String getContentEncoding( )

This method returns a String that tells you how the content is encoded. If the content is sent unencoded (as is commonly the case with HTTP servers), this method returns null. It throws no exceptions. The most commonly used content encoding on the Web is probably x-gzip, which can be straightforwardly decoded using a java.util.zip.GZipInputStream.

 The content encoding is not the same as the character encoding. The character encoding is determined by the Content-type header or information internal to the document, and specifies how characters are specified in bytes. Content encoding specifies how the bytes are encoded in other bytes.

When subclassing URLConnection, override this method if you expect to be dealing with encoded data, as might be the case for an NNTP or SMTP protocol handler; in these applications, many different encoding schemes, such as BinHex and uuencode, are used to pass eight-bit binary data through a seven-bit ASCII connection.

public long getDate( )

The getDate( ) method returns a long that tells you when the document was sent, in milliseconds since midnight, Greenwich Mean Time (GMT), January 1, 1970. You can convert it to a java.util.Date. For example:

```
Date documentSent = new Date(uc.getDate( ));
```

This is the time the document was sent as seen from the server; it may not agree with the time on your local machine. If the HTTP header does not include a Date field, getDate( ) returns 0.

public long getExpiration( )

Some documents have server-based expiration dates that indicate when the document should be deleted from the cache and reloaded from the server. getExpiration( ) is very similar to getDate( ), differing only in how the return value is interpreted. It returns a long indicating the number of milliseconds after 12:00 A.M., GMT, January 1, 1970, at which point the document expires. If the HTTP header does not include an Expiration field, getExpiration( ) returns 0, which means 12:00 A.M., GMT, January 1, 1970. The only reasonable interpretation of this date is that the document does not expire and can remain in the cache indefinitely.

public long getLastModified( )

The final date method, getLastModified( ), returns the date on which the document was last modified. Again, the date is given as the number of milliseconds since midnight, GMT, January 1, 1970. If the HTTP header does not include a Last-modified field (and many don't), this method returns 0.

Example 15-4 reads URLs from the command line and uses these six methods to print their content type, content length, content encoding, date of last modification, expiration date, and current date.

Example 15-4. Return the header

```
import java.net.*;
import java.io.*;
import java.util.*;

public class HeaderViewer {

  public static void main(String args[]) {

    for (int i=0; i < args.length; i++) {
      try {
        URL u = new URL(args[0]);
        URLConnection uc = u.openConnection( );
        System.out.println("Content-type: " + uc.getContentType( ));
        System.out.println("Content-encoding: "
          + uc.getContentEncoding( ));
```

Example 15-4. Return the header (continued)

```
      System.out.println("Date: " + new Date(uc.getDate( )));
      System.out.println("Last modified: "
        + new Date(uc.getLastModified( )));
      System.out.println("Expiration date: "
        + new Date(uc.getExpiration( )));
      System.out.println("Content-length: " + uc.getContentLength( ));
    }  // end try
    catch (MalformedURLException ex) {
      System.err.println(args[i] + " is not a URL I understand");
    }
    catch (IOException ex) {
      System.err.println(ex);
    }
    System.out.println( );
  }  // end for

 }  // end main

}  // end HeaderViewer
```

Here's the result when used to look at *http://www.oreilly.com*:

```
% java HeaderViewer http://www.oreilly.com
Content-type: text/html
Content-encoding: null
Date: Mon Oct 18 13:54:52 PDT 1999
Last modified: Sat Oct 16 07:54:02 PDT 1999
Expiration date: Wed Dec 31 16:00:00 PST 1969
Content-length: -1
```

The content type of the file at *http://www.oreilly.com* is text/html. No content encoding was used. The file was sent on Monday, October 18, 1999 at 1:54 P.M., Pacific Daylight Time. It was last modified on Saturday, October 16, 1999 at 7:54 A.M. Pacific Daylight Time and it expires on Wednesday, December 31, 1969 at 4:00 P. M., Pacific Standard Time. Did this document really expire 31 years ago? No. Remember that what's being checked here is whether the copy in your cache is more recent than 4:00 P.M. PST, December 31, 1969. If it is, you don't need to reload it. More to the point, after adjusting for time zone differences, this date looks suspiciously like 12:00 A.M., Greenwich Mean Time, January 1, 1970, which happens to be the default if the server doesn't send an expiration date. (Most don't.)

Finally, the content length of –1 means that there was no Content-length header. Many servers don't bother to provide a Content-length header for text files. However, a Content-length header should always be sent for a binary file. Here's the HTTP header you get when you request the GIF image *http://www.oreilly.com/graphics/space.gif*. Now the server sends a Content-length header with a value of 57.

```
% java HeaderViewer http://www.oreilly.com/graphics/space.gif
Content-type: image/gif
```

```
Content-encoding: null
Date: Mon Oct 18 14:00:07 PDT 1999
Last modified: Thu Jan 09 12:05:11 PST 1997
Expiration date: Wed Dec 31 16:00:00 PST 1969
Content-length: 57
```

Retrieving Arbitrary Header Fields

The last six methods requested specific fields from the header, but there's no theoretical limit to the number of header fields a message can contain. The next five methods inspect arbitrary fields in a header. Indeed, the methods of the last section are just thin wrappers over the methods discussed here; you can use these methods to get header fields that Java's designers did not plan for. If the requested header is found, it is returned. Otherwise, the method returns null.

public String getHeaderField(String name)

The getHeaderField( ) method returns the value of a named header field. The name of the header is not case-sensitive and does not include a closing colon. For example, to get the value of the Content-type and Content-encoding header fields of a URLConnection object uc, you could write:

```
String contentType = uc.getHeaderField("content-type");
String contentEncoding = uc.getHeaderField("content-encoding"));
```

To get the Date, Content-length, or Expires headers, you'd do the same:

```
String data = uc.getHeaderField("date");
String expires = uc.getHeaderField("expires");
String contentLength = uc.getHeaderField("Content-length");
```

These methods all return String, not int or long as the getContentLength( ), getExpirationDate( ), getLastModified( ), and getDate( ) methods of the last section did. If you're interested in a numeric value, convert the String to a long or an int.

Do not assume the value returned by getHeaderField( ) is valid. You must check to make sure it is non-null.

public String getHeaderFieldKey(int n)

This method returns the key (that is, the field name: for example, Content-length or Server) of the nth header field. The request method is header zero and has a null key. The first header is one. For example, to get the sixth key of the header of the URLConnection uc, you would write:

```
String header6 = uc.getHeaderFieldKey(6);
```

public String getHeaderField(int n)

This method returns the value of the nth header field. In HTTP, the request method is header field zero and the first actual header is one. Example 15-5 uses this method in conjunction with getHeaderFieldKey( ) to print the entire HTTP header.

Example 15-5. Print the entire HTTP header

```
import java.net.*;
import java.io.*;

public class AllHeaders {

  public static void main(String args[]) {

    for (int i=0; i < args.length; i++) {
      try {
        URL u = new URL(args[i]);
        URLConnection uc = u.openConnection( );
        for (int j = 1; ; j++) {
          String header = uc.getHeaderField(j);
          if (header == null) break;
          System.out.println(uc.getHeaderFieldKey(j) + ": " + header);
        }  // end for
      }  // end try
      catch (MalformedURLException ex) {
        System.err.println(args[i] + " is not a URL I understand.");
      }
      catch (IOException ex) {
        System.err.println(ex);
      }
      System.out.println( );
    }  // end for

  }  // end main

}  // end AllHeaders
```

For example, here's the output when this program is run against *http://www.oreilly.com*:

```
% java AllHeaders http://www.oreilly.com
Server: WN/1.15.1
Date: Mon, 18 Oct 1999 21:20:26 GMT
Last-modified: Sat, 16 Oct 1999 14:54:02 GMT
Content-type: text/html
Title: www.oreilly.com -- Welcome to O'Reilly &amp; Associates!
-- computer  books, software, online publishing
Link: <mailto:webmaster@oreilly.com>; rev="Made"
```

Besides Date, Last-modified, and Content-type headers, this server also provides Server, Title, and Link headers. Other servers may have different sets of headers.

public long getHeaderFieldDate(String name, long default)

This method first retrieves the header field specified by the name argument and tries to convert the string to a long that specifies the milliseconds since midnight, January 1, 1970, GMT. getHeaderFieldDate( ) can be used to retrieve a header field that represents a date: for example, the Expires, Date, or Last-modified headers. To convert the string to an integer, getHeaderFieldDate( ) uses the parseDate( ) method of java.util.Date. The parseDate( ) method does a decent job of understanding and converting most common date formats, but it can be stumped—for instance, if you ask for a header field that contains something other than a date. If parseDate( ) doesn't understand the date or if getHeaderFieldDate( ) is unable to find the requested header field, getHeaderFieldDate( ) returns the default argument. For example:

```
Date expires = new Date(uc.getHeaderFieldDate("expires", 0));
long lastModified = uc.getHeaderFieldDate("last-modified", 0);
Date now = new Date(uc.getHeaderFieldDate("date", 0));
```

You can use the methods of the java.util.Date class to convert the long to a String.

public int getHeaderFieldInt(String name, int default)

This method retrieves the value of the header field name and tries to convert it to an int. If it fails, either because it can't find the requested header field or because that field does not contain a recognizable integer, getHeaderFieldInt( ) returns the default argument. This method is often used to retrieve the Content-length field. For example, to get the content length from a URLConnection uc, you would write:

```
int contentLength = uc.getHeaderFieldInt("content-length", -1);
```

In this code fragment, getHeaderFieldInt( ) returns −1 if the Content-length header isn't present.

Configuring the Connection

The URLConnection class has seven protected instance fields that define exactly how the client makes the request to the server. These are:

```
protected URL     url;
protected boolean doInput = true;
protected boolean doOutput = false;
protected boolean allowUserInteraction = defaultAllowUserInteraction;
protected boolean useCaches = defaultUseCaches;
protected long    ifModifiedSince = 0;
protected boolean connected = false;
```

For instance, if doOutput is true, you'll be able to write data to the server over this URLConnection as well as read data from it. If useCaches is false, the connection bypasses any local caching and downloads the file from the server afresh.

Since these fields are all protected, their values are accessed and modified via obviously named setter and getter methods:

```
public URL     getURL( )
public void    setDoInput(boolean doInput)
public boolean getDoInput( )
public void    setDoOutput(boolean doOutput)
public boolean getDoOutput( )
public void    setAllowUserInteraction(boolean allowUserInteraction)
public boolean getAllowUserInteraction( )
public void    setUseCaches(boolean useCaches)
public boolean getUseCaches( )
```

```
public void      setIfModifiedSince(long ifModifiedSince)
public long      getIfModifiedSince( )
```

You can modify these fields only before the URLConnection is connected (that is, before you try to read content or headers from the connection). Most of the methods that set fields throw an IllegalStateException if they are called while the connection is open. In general, you can set the properties of a URLConnection object only before the connection is opened.

 In Java 1.3 and earlier, the setter methods throw an IllegalAccessError instead of an IllegalStateException. Throwing an *error* instead of an *exception* here is very unusual. An error generally indicates an unpredictable fault in the VM, which usually cannot be handled, whereas an exception indicates a predictable, manageable problem. More specifically, an IllegalAccessError is supposed to indicate that an application is trying to access a nonpublic field it doesn't have access to. According to the class library documentation, "Normally, this error is caught by the compiler; this error can only occur at runtime if the definition of a class has incompatibly changed." Clearly, that's not what's going on here. This was simply a mistake on the part of the programmer who wrote this class, which has been fixed as of Java 1.4.

There are also some getter and setter methods that define the default behavior for all instances of URLConnection. These are:

```
public boolean           getDefaultUseCaches( )
public void              setDefaultUseCaches(boolean defaultUseCaches)
public static void       setDefaultAllowUserInteraction(
    boolean defaultAllowUserInteraction)
public static boolean    getDefaultAllowUserInteraction( )
public static FileNameMap getFileNameMap( )
public static void       setFileNameMap(FileNameMap map)
```

Unlike the instance methods, these methods can be invoked at any time. The new defaults will apply only to URLConnection objects constructed after the new default values are set.

protected URL url

The url field specifies the URL that this URLConnection connects to. The constructor sets it when the URLConnection is created and it should not change thereafter. You can retrieve the value by calling the getURL( ) method. Example 15-6 opens a URLConnection to *http://www.oreilly.com/*, gets the URL of that connection, and prints it.

Example 15-6. Print the URL of a URLConnection to http://www.oreilly.com/

```
import java.net.*;
import java.io.*;
```

```
public class URLPrinter {

  public static void main(String args[]) {

    try {
      URL u = new URL("http://www.oreilly.com/");
      URLConnection uc = u.openConnection( );
      System.out.println(uc.getURL( ));
    }
    catch (IOException ex) {
      System.err.println(ex);
    }

  }

}
```

Here's the result, which should be no great surprise. The URL that is printed is the one used to create the URLConnection.

```
% java URLPrinter
http://www.oreilly.com/
```

protected boolean connected

The boolean field connected is true if the connection is open and false if it's closed. Since the connection has not yet been opened when a new URLConnection object is created, its initial value is false. This variable can be accessed only by instances of java.net.URLConnection and its subclasses.

There are no methods that directly read or change the value of connected. However, any method that causes the URLConnection to connect should set this variable to true, including connect( ), getInputStream( ), and getOutputStream( ). Any method that causes the URLConnection to disconnect should set this field to false. There are no such methods in java.net.URLConnection, but some of its subclasses, such as java. net.HttpURLConnection, have disconnect( ) methods.

If you subclass URLConnection to write a protocol handler, you are responsible for setting connected to true when you are connected and resetting it to false when the connection closes. Many methods in java.net.URLConnection read this variable to determine what they can do. If it's set incorrectly, your program will have severe bugs that are not easy to diagnose.

protected boolean allowUserInteraction

Some URLConnections need to interact with a user. For example, a web browser may need to ask for a username and password. However, many applications cannot assume that a user is present to interact with it. For instance, a search engine robot is probably running in the background without any user to provide a username and password. As its name suggests, the allowUserInteraction field specifies whether user interaction is allowed. It is false by default.

This variable is protected, but the public getAllowUserInteraction( ) method can read its value and the public setAllowUserInteraction( ) method can change it:

```
public void    setAllowUserInteraction(boolean allowUserInteraction)
public boolean getAllowUserInteraction( )
```

The value true indicates that user interaction is allowed; false indicates that there is no user interaction. The value may be read at any time but may be set only before the URLConnection is connected. Calling setAllowUserInteraction( ) when the URLConnection is connected throws an IllegalStateException in Java 1.4 and later, and an IllegalAccessError in Java 1.3 and earlier.

For example, this code fragment opens a connection that could ask the user for authentication if it's required:

```
URL u = new URL("http://www.example.com/passwordProtectedPage.html");
URLConnection uc = u.openConnection( );
uc.setAllowUserInteraction(true);
InputStream in = uc.getInputStream( );
```

Java does not include a default GUI for asking the user for a username and password. If the request is made from an applet, the browser's usual authentication dialog can be relied on. In a standalone application, you first need to install an Authenticator, as discussed in Chapter 7.

Figure 15-1 shows the dialog box that pops up when you try to access a password-protected page. If you cancel this dialog, you'll get a 401 Authorization Required error and whatever text the server sends to unauthorized users. However, if you refuse to send authorization at all—which you can do by pressing OK, then answering No when asked if you want to retry authorization—getInputStream( ) will throw a ProtocolException.

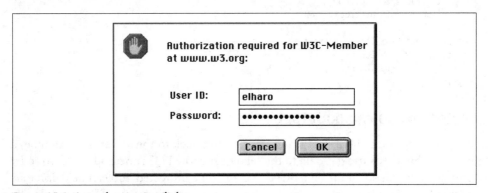

Figure 15-1. An authentication dialog

The static `getDefaultAllowUserInteraction( )` and `setDefaultAllowUserInteraction( )` methods determine the default behavior for `URLConnection` objects that have not set `allowUserInteraction` explicitly. Since the `allowUserInteraction` field is `static` (i.e., a class variable instead of an instance variable), setting it changes the default behavior for all instances of the `URLConnection` class that are created after `setDefaultAllowUserInteraction( )` is called.

For instance, the following code fragment checks to see whether user interaction is allowed by default with `getDefaultAllowUserInteraction( )`. If user interaction is not allowed by default, the code uses `setDefaultAllowUserInteraction( )` to make allowing user interaction the default behavior.

```
if (!URLConnection.getDefaultAllowUserInteraction()) {
  URLConnection.setDefaultAllowUserInteraction(true);
}
```

protected boolean doInput

Most `URLConnection` objects provide input to a client program. For example, a connection to a web server with the GET method would produce input for the client. However, a connection to a web server with the POST method might not. A `URLConnection` can be used for input to the program, output from the program, or both. The protected boolean field `doInput` is `true` if the `URLConnection` can be used for input, `false` if it cannot be. The default is `true`. To access this protected variable, use the public `getDoInput( )` and `setDoInput( )` methods:

```
public void    setDoInput(boolean doInput)
public boolean getDoInput()
```

For example:

```
try {
  URL u = new URL("http://www.oreilly.com");
  URLConnection uc = u.openConnection();
  if (!uc.getDoInput()) {
    uc.setDoInput(true);
  }
  // read from the connection...
catch (IOException ex) {
  System.err.println(ex);
}
```

protected boolean doOutput

Programs can use a `URLConnection` to send output back to the server. For example, a program that needs to send data to the server using the POST method could do so by getting an output stream from a `URLConnection`. The protected boolean field `doOutput` is `true` if the `URLConnection` can be used for output, `false` if it cannot be; it is `false` by default. To access this protected variable, use the getDoOutput( ) and setDoOutput( ) methods:

```
public void    setDoOutput(boolean dooutput)
public boolean getDoOutput( )
```

For example:

```
try {
  URL u = new URL("http://www.oreilly.com");
  URLConnection uc = u.openConnection( );
  if (!uc.getDoOutput( )) {
    uc.setDoOutput(true);
  }
  // write to the connection...
catch (IOException ex) {
  System.err.println(ex);
}
```

When you set doOutput to true for an *http* URL, the request method is changed from GET to POST. In Chapter 7, you saw how to send data to server-side programs with GET. GET is straightforward to work with, but its use should be limited to "safe" operations: operations that don't commit the user or have obvious side effects. For instance, it would be inappropriate to use GET to complete a purchase or add an item to a shopping cart, but you could use GET to search for the items before placing them in the cart. Unsafe operations, which should not be bookmarked or cached, should use POST (or occasionally PUT or DELETE) instead. We'll explore this in more detail later in this chapter when we talk about writing data to a server.

In earlier editions of this book, I suggested using the POST method in preference to GET for long (greater than 255 characters) URLs since some browsers had limits on the maximum length of a URL they could safely handle. In 2004, this is only really an issue with very old browsers no one is likely to be using anymore. I was planning not to even mention this issue in this chapter; but as I worked on an unrelated project during the revision of this chapter, I encountered a *server-side* limitation on URL size while writing a PHP script to process a form. I had over a thousand different fields in a form (a checklist of bird species found in New York City along with observation notes) and over 10K of data in each request. The browser handled the long URL with aplomb. However, faced with such an extreme case, the server refused to process the request until I switched from GET to POST. Thus for *very* long URLs, POST may still be necessary, even for safe operations. Alternately, you could fix the server so it doesn't object to long URLs; but for those of us who don't manage our own servers, this may not always be an option.

protected boolean ifModifiedSince

Many clients, especially web clients, keep caches of previously retrieved documents. If the user asks for the same document again, it can be retrieved from the cache. However, it may have changed on the server since it was last retrieved. The only way to tell is to ask the server. Clients can include an If-Modified-Since in the client request HTTP header. This header includes a date and time. If the document has changed since that time, the server should send it. Otherwise, it should not. Typically, this time is the last time the client fetched the document. For example, this client request says the document should be returned only if it has changed since 7:22:07 A.M., October 31, 2004, Greenwich Mean Time:

```
GET / HTTP/1.1
User-Agent: Java/1.4.2_05
Host: login.metalab.unc.edu:56452
Accept: text/html, image/gif, image/jpeg, *; q=.2, */*; q=.2
Connection: close
If-Modified-Since: Sun, 31 Oct 2004 19:22:07 GMT
```

If the document has changed since that time, the server will send it as usual. Otherwise, it replies with a 304 Not Modified message, like this:

```
HTTP/1.0 304 Not Modified
Server: WN/1.15.1
Date: Tue, 02 Nov 2004 16:26:16 GMT
Last-modified: Fri, 29 Oct 2004 23:40:06 GMT
```

The client then loads the document from its cache. Not all web servers respect the If-Modified-Since field. Some will send the document whether it's changed or not.

The ifModifiedSince field in the URLConnection class specifies the date (in milliseconds since midnight, Greenwich Mean Time, January 1, 1970), which will be placed in the If-Modified-Since header field. Because ifModifiedSince is protected, programs should call the getIfModifiedSince( ) and setIfModifiedSince( ) methods to read or modify it:

```
public long getIfModifiedSince( )
public void setIfModifiedSince(long ifModifiedSince)
```

Example 15-7 prints the default value of ifModifiedSince, sets its value to 24 hours ago, and prints the new value. It then downloads and displays the document—but only if it's been modified in the last 24 hours.

Example 15-7. Set ifModifiedSince to 24 hours prior to now

```
import java.net.*;
import java.io.*;
import java.util.*;

public class Last24 {

  public static void main (String[] args) {
```

Example 15-7. Set ifModifiedSince to 24 hours prior to now (continued)

```
// Initialize a Date object with the current date and time
Date today = new Date( );
long millisecondsPerDay = 24 * 60 * 60 * 1000;

for (int i = 0; i < args.length; i++) {
  try {
    URL u = new URL(args[i]);
    URLConnection uc = u.openConnection( );
    System.out.println("Will retrieve file if it's modified since "
     + new Date(uc.getIfModifiedSince( )));
    uc.setIfModifiedSince((new Date(today.getTime( )
      - millisecondsPerDay)).getTime( ));
    System.out.println("Will retrieve file if it's modified since "
     + new Date(uc.getIfModifiedSince( )));
    InputStream in = new BufferedInputStream(uc.getInputStream( ));
    Reader r = new InputStreamReader(in);
    int c;
    while ((c = r.read( )) != -1) {
      System.out.print((char) c);
    }
    System.out.println( );

  }
  catch (Exception ex) {
    System.err.println(ex);
  }
 }

}

}
```

Here's the result. First, we see the default value: midnight, January 1, 1970, GMT, converted to Pacific Standard Time. Next, we see the new time, which we set to 24 hours prior to the current time:

```
% java Last24 http://www.oreilly.com
Will retrieve file if it's been modified since Wed Dec 31 16:00:00 PST 1969
Will retrieve file if it's been modified since Sun Oct 31 11:17:04 PST 2004
```

Since this document hasn't changed in the last 24 hours, it is not reprinted.

protected boolean useCaches

Some clients, notably web browsers, can retrieve a document from a local cache, rather than retrieving it from a server. Applets may have access to the browser's cache. Starting in Java 1.5, standalone applications can use the java.net. ResponseCache class described later in this chapter. The useCaches variable determines whether a cache will be used if it's available. The default value is true, meaning that the cache will be used; false means the cache won't be used. Because useCaches is protected, programs access it using the getUseCaches( ) and setUseCaches( ) methods:

```
public void    setUseCaches(boolean useCaches)
public boolean getUseCaches( )
```

This code fragment disables caching to ensure that the most recent version of the document is retrieved:

```
try {
  URL u = new URL("http://www.sourcebot.com/");
  URLConnection uc = u.openConnection( );
  if (uc.getUseCaches( )) {
    uc.setUseCaches(false);
  }
}
catch (IOException ex) {
  System.err.println(ex);
}
```

Two methods define the initial value of the useCaches field, getDefaultUseCaches( ) and setDefaultUseCaches( ):

```
public void    setDefaultUseCaches(boolean useCaches)
public boolean getDefaultUseCaches( )
```

Although nonstatic, these methods do set and get a static field that determines the default behavior for all instances of the URLConnection class created after the change. The next code fragment disables caching by default; after this code runs, URLConnections that want caching must enable it explicitly using setUseCaches(true).

```
if (uc.getDefaultUseCaches( )) {
  uc.setDefaultUseCaches(false);
}
```

Timeouts

Java 1.5 adds four methods that allow you to query and modify the timeout values for connections; that is, how long the underlying socket will wait for a response from the remote end before throwing a SocketTimeoutException. These are:

```
public void setConnectTimeout(int timeout)    // Java 1.5
public int  getConnectTimeout( )              // Java 1.5
public void setReadTimeout(int timeout)       // Java 1.5
public int  getReadTimeout( )                 // Java 1.5
```

The setConnectTimeout( )/getConnectTimeout( ) methods control how long the socket waits for the initial connection. The setReadTimeout( )/getReadTimeout( ) methods control how long the input stream waits for data to arrive. All four methods measure timeouts in milliseconds. All four interpret 0 as meaning never time out. Both setter methods throw an IllegalArgumentException if the timeout is negative. For example, this code fragment requests a 30-second connect timeout and a 45-second read timeout:

```
URL u = new URL("http://www.example.org");
URLConnection uc = u.openConnection( );
uc.setConnectTimeout(30000);
uc.setReadTimeout(45000);
```

Configuring the Client Request HTTP Header

In HTTP 1.0 and later, the client sends the server not only a request line, but also a header. For example, here's the HTTP header that Wamcom Mozilla 1.3 for Mac OS uses:

```
Host: stallion.elharo.com:33119
User-Agent: Mozilla/5.0 (Macintosh; U; PPC; en-US; rv:1.3.1) Gecko/20030723 wamcom.
org
Accept: text/xml,application/xml,application/xhtml+xml,text/html;q=0.9,text/
plain;q=0.8,video/x-mng,image/png,image/jpeg,image/gif;q=0.2,*/*;q=0.1
Accept-Language: en-us
Accept-Encoding: gzip,deflate
Accept-Charset: ISO-8859-1,utf-8;q=0.7,*;q=0.7
Connection: close
```

A web server can use this information to serve different pages to different clients, to get and set cookies, to authenticate users through passwords, and more. Placing different fields in the header that the client sends and the server responds with does all of this.

 It's important to understand that this is *not the HTTP header that the server sends to the client* and that it is read by the various getHeaderField( ) and getHeaderFieldKey( ) methods discussed previously. This is the *HTTP header that the client sends to the server*.

Each concrete subclass of URLConnection sets a number of different name-value pairs in the header by default. (Really, only HttpURLConnection does this, since HTTP is the only major protocol that uses headers in this way.) For instance, here's the HTTP header that a connection from the SourceViewer2 program of Example 15-1 sends:

```
User-Agent: Java/1.4.2_05
Host: localhost:33122
Accept: text/html, image/gif, image/jpeg, *; q=.2, */*; q=.2
Connection: keep-alive
```

As you can see, it's a little simpler than the one Mozilla sends, and it has a different user agent and accepts different kinds of files. However, you can modify these and add new fields before connecting.

In Java 1.3 and later, you can add headers to the HTTP header using the setRequestProperty( ) method before you open the connection:

```
public void setRequestProperty(String name, String value)// Java 1.3
```

The setRequestProperty( ) method adds a field to the header of this URLConnection with a specified name and value. This method can be used only before the connection is opened. It throws an IllegalStateException (IllegalAccessError in Java 1.3) if the connection is already open. The getRequestProperty( ) method returns the value of the named field of the HTTP header used by this URLConnection.

HTTP allows one property to have multiple values. In this case, the separate values will be separated by commas. For example, the Accept header sent by Java 1.4.2 shown above has the four values text/html, image/gif, image/jpeg, and *.

 These methods only really have meaning when the URL being connected to is an *http* URL, since only the HTTP protocol makes use of headers like this. While they could possibly have other meanings in other protocols, such as NNTP, this is really just an example of poor API design. These methods should be part of the more specific HttpURLConnection class, not the generic URLConnection class.

For example, web servers and clients store some limited persistent information by using cookies. A cookie is simply a name-value pair. The server sends a cookie to a client using the response HTTP header. From that point forward, whenever the client requests a URL from that server, it includes a Cookie field in the HTTP request header that looks like this:

```
Cookie: username=elharo; password=ACDOX9F23JJJn6G; session=100678945
```

This particular Cookie field sends three name-value pairs to the server. There's no limit to the number of name-value pairs that can be included in any one cookie. Given a URLConnection object uc, you could add this cookie to the connection, like this:

```
uc.setRequestProperty("Cookie",
  "username=elharo; password=ACDOX9F23JJJn6G; session=100678945");
```

The setRequestProperty( ) method does not support this. You can set the same property to a new value, but this changes the existing property value. To add an additional property value, use the addRequestProperty( ) method instead:

```
public void  addRequestProperty(String name, String value)// Java 1.4
```

There's no fixed list of legal headers. Servers will typically ignore any headers they don't recognize. HTTP does put some restrictions on the content of the names and values here. For instance, the names can't contain whitespace and the values can't contain any line breaks. Java enforces the restrictions on fields containing line breaks, but not much else. If a field contains a line break, setRequestProperty( ) and addRequestProperty( ) throw an IllegalArgumentException. Otherwise, it's quite easy to make a URLConnection send malformed headers to the server, so be careful. Some servers will handle the malformed headers gracefully. Some will ignore the bad header and return the requested document anyway, but some will reply with an HTTP 400, Bad Request error.

If for some reason you need to inspect the headers in a URLConnection, there's a standard getter method:

```
public String getRequestProperty(String name)// Java 1.3
```

Java 1.4 also adds a method to get all the request properties for a connection as a Map:

```
public Map getRequestProperties( ) // Java 1.4
```

The keys are the header field names. The values are lists of property values. Both names and values are stored as strings. In other words, using Java 1.5 generic syntax, the signature is:

```
public Map<String,List<String>> getRequestProperties( )
```

Writing Data to a Server

Sometimes you need to write data to a URLConnection—for example, when you submit a form to a web server using POST or upload a file using PUT. The getOutputStream( ) method returns an OutputStream on which you can write data for transmission to a server:

```
public OutputStream getOutputStream( )
```

Since a URLConnection doesn't allow output by default, you have to call setDoOutput(true) before asking for an output stream. When you set doOutput to true for an *http* URL, the request method is changed from GET to POST. In Chapter 7, you saw how to send data to server-side programs with GET. However, GET should be limited to safe operations, such as search requests or page navigation, and not used for unsafe operations that create or modify a resource, such as posting a comment on a web page or ordering a pizza. Safe operations can be bookmarked, cached, spidered, prefetched, and so on. Unsafe operations should not be.

Once you've got the OutputStream, buffer it by chaining it to a BufferedOutputStream or a BufferedWriter. You should generally also chain it to a DataOutputStream, an OutputStreamWriter, or some other class that's more convenient to use than a raw OutputStream. For example:

```
try {

    URL u = new URL("http://www.somehost.com/cgi-bin/acgi");
    // open the connection and prepare it to POST
    URLConnection uc = u.openConnection( );
    uc.setDoOutput(true);

    OutputStream raw = uc.getOutputStream( );
    OutputStream buffered = new BufferedOutputStream(raw);
    OutputStreamWriter out = new OutputStreamWriter(buffered, "8859_1");
    out.write("first=Julie&middle=&last=Harting&work=String+Quartet\r\n");
```

```
        out.flush();
        out.close();

    }
    catch (IOException ex) {
      System.err.println(ex);
    }
```

Sending data with POST is almost as easy as with GET. Invoke setDoOutput(true) and use the URLConnection's getOutputStream( ) method to write the query string rather than attaching it to the URL. Java buffers all the data written onto the output stream until the stream is closed. This is necessary so that it can determine the necessary Content-length header. The query string contains two name-value pairs separated by ampersands. The complete transaction, including client request and server response, looks something like this:

```
% telnet www.ibiblio.org 80
Trying 152.2.210.81...
Connected to www.ibiblio.org.
Escape character is '^]'.
POST /javafaq/books/jnp3/postquery.phtml HTTP/1.0
ACCEPT: text/plain
Content-type: application/x-www-form-urlencoded
Content-length: 65

username=Elliotte+Rusty+Harold&email=elharo%40metalab%2eunc%2eedu
HTTP/1.1 200 OK
Date: Mon, 10 May 2004 21:08:52 GMT
Server: Apache/1.3.29 (Unix) DAV/1.0.3 mod_perl/1.29 PHP/4.3.5
X-Powered-By: PHP/4.3.5
Connection: close
Content-Type: text/html

<html xmlns="http://www.w3.org/1999/xhtml">
<head>
  <title>Query Results</title>
</head>
<body>

<h1>Query Results</h1>

<p>You submitted the following name/value pairs:</p>

<ul>
<li>username = Elliotte Rusty Harold</li>
<li>email = elharo@metalab.unc.edu</li>
</ul>

<hr />
Last Modified May 10, 2004

</body>
</html>
Connection closed by foreign host.
```

For that matter, as long as you control both the client and the server, you can use any other sort of data encoding you like. For instance, SOAP and XML-RPC both POST data to web servers as XML rather than an x-www-form-url-encoded query string. However, if you deviate from the standard, you'll find that your nonconforming client can't talk to most server-side programs or that your nonconforming server-side program can't process requests from most clients. The query string format used here is used by all web browsers and is expected by most server-side APIs and tools.

Example 15-8 is a program called FormPoster that uses the URLConnection class and the QueryString class from Chapter 7 to post form data. The constructor sets the URL. The query string is built using the add( ) method. The post( ) method actually sends the data to the server by opening a URLConnection to the specified URL, setting its doOutput field to true, and writing the query string on the output stream. It then returns the input stream containing the server's response.

The main( ) method is a simple test for this program that sends the name "Elliotte Rusty Harold" and the email address *elharo@metalab.unc.edu* to the resource at *http:// www.cafeaulait.org/books/jnp3/postquery.phtml*. This resource is a simple form tester that accepts any input using either the POST or GET method and returns an HTML page showing the names and values that were submitted. The data returned is HTML; this example simply displays the HTML rather than attempting to parse it. It would be easy to extend this program by adding a user interface that lets you enter the name and email address to be posted—but since doing that triples the size of the program while showing nothing more of network programming, it is left as an exercise for the reader. Once you understand this example, it should be easy to write Java programs that communicate with other server-side scripts.

Example 15-8. Posting a form

```
import java.net.*;
import java.io.*;
import com.macfaq.net.*;

public class FormPoster {

  private URL url;
  // from Chapter 7, Example 7-9
  private QueryString query = new QueryString();

  public FormPoster (URL url) {
    if (!url.getProtocol().toLowerCase().startsWith("http")) {
      throw new IllegalArgumentException(
        "Posting only works for http URLs");
    }
    this.url = url;
  }

  public void add(String name, String value) {
    query.add(name, value);
  }
```

Example 15-8. Posting a form (continued)

```
public URL getURL( ) {
  return this.url;
}

public InputStream post( ) throws IOException {

  // open the connection and prepare it to POST
  URLConnection uc = url.openConnection( );
  uc.setDoOutput(true);
  OutputStreamWriter out
   = new OutputStreamWriter(uc.getOutputStream( ), "ASCII");

  // The POST line, the Content-type header,
  // and the Content-length headers are sent by the URLConnection.
  // We just need to send the data
  out.write(query.toString( ));
  out.write("\r\n");
  out.flush( );
  out.close( );


  // Return the response
  return uc.getInputStream( );

}

public static void main(String args[]) {

  URL url;

  if (args.length > 0) {
    try {
      url = new URL(args[0]);
    }
    catch (MalformedURLException ex) {
      System.err.println("Usage: java FormPoster url");
      return;
    }
  }
  else {
    try {
      url = new URL(
        "http://www.cafeaulait.org/books/jnp3/postquery.phtml");
    }
    catch (MalformedURLException ex) { // shouldn't happen
      System.err.println(ex);
      return;
    }
  }

  FormPoster poster = new FormPoster(url);
  poster.add("name", "Elliotte Rusty Harold");
  poster.add("email", "elharo@metalab.unc.edu");
```

Example 15-8. Posting a form (continued)

```
  try {
    InputStream in = poster.post( );

    // Read the response
    InputStreamReader r = new InputStreamReader(in);
    int c;
    while((c = r.read( )) != -1) {
      System.out.print((char) c);
    }
    System.out.println( );
    in.close( );
  }
  catch (IOException ex) {
    System.err.println(ex);
  }

  }

}
```

Here's the response from the server:

```
% java -classpath .:jnp3e.jar FormPoster
<html xmlns="http://www.w3.org/1999/xhtml">
<head>
        <title>Query Results</title>
</head>
<body>

<h1>Query Results</h1>

<p>You submitted the following name/value pairs:</p>

<ul>
<li>name = Elliotte Rusty Harold</li>
<li>email = elharo@metalab.unc.edu
</li>
</ul>

<hr />
Last Modified May 10, 2004

</body>
</html>
```

The main( ) method tries to read the first command-line argument from args[0]. The argument is optional; if there is an argument, it is assumed to be a URL that can be POSTed to. If there are no arguments, main( ) initializes url with a default URL, *http://www.cafeaulait.org/books/jnp3/postquery.phtml*. main( ) then constructs a FormPoster object. Two name-value pairs are added to this FormPoster object. Next, the post( ) method is invoked and its response read and printed on System.out.

The post( ) method is the heart of the class. It first opens a connection to the URL stored in the url field. It sets the doOutput field of this connection to true since this URLConnection needs to send output and chains the OutputStream for this URL to an ASCII OutputStreamWriter that sends the data; then flushes and closes the stream. *Do not forget to close the stream!* If the stream isn't closed, no data will be sent. Finally, the URLConnection's InputStream is returned.

To summarize, posting data to a form requires these steps:

1. Decide what name-value pairs you'll send to the server-side program.

2. Write the server-side program that will accept and process the request. If it doesn't use any custom data encoding, you can test this program using a regular HTML form and a web browser.

3. Create a query string in your Java program. The string should look like this:

   ```
   name1=value1&name2=value2&name3=value3
   ```

   Pass each name and value in the query string to URLEncoder.encode( ) before adding it to the query string.

4. Open a URLConnection to the URL of the program that will accept the data.

5. Set doOutput to true by invoking setDoOutput(true).

6. Write the query string onto the URLConnection's OutputStream.

7. Close the URLConnection's OutputStream.

8. Read the server response from the URLConnection's InputStream.

Posting forms is considerably more complex than using the GET method described in Chapter 7. However, GET should only be used for safe operations that can be bookmarked and linked to. POST should be used for unsafe operations that should not be bookmarked or linked to.

The getOutputStream( ) method is also used for the PUT request method, a means of storing files on a web server. The data to be stored is written onto the OutputStream that getOutputStream( ) returns. However, this can be done only from within the HttpURLConnection subclass of URLConnection, so discussion of PUT will have to wait a little while.

Content Handlers

The URLConnection class is intimately tied to Java's protocol and content handler mechanism. The protocol handler is responsible for making connections, exchanging headers, requesting particular documents, and so forth. It handles all the overhead of the protocol for requesting files. The content handler deals only with the actual data. It takes the raw input after all headers and so forth are stripped and converts it to the right kind of object for Java to deal with; for instance, an InputStream or an ImageProducer.

Getting Content

The getContent( ) methods of URLConnection use a content handler to turn the raw data of a connection into a Java object.

public Object getContent( ) throws IOException

This method is virtually identical to the getContent( ) method of the URL class. In fact, that method just calls this method. getContent( ) downloads the object selected by the URL of this URLConnection. For getContent( ) to work, the virtual machine needs to recognize and understand the content type. The exact content types supported vary from one VM and version to the next. Sun's JDK 1.5 supports text/plain, image/gif, image/jpeg, image/png, audio/aiff, audio/basic, audio/wav, and a few others. Different VMs and applications may support additional types. For instance, HotJava 3.0 includes a PDF content handler. Furthermore, you can install additional content handlers that understand other content types.

getContent( ) works only for protocols like HTTP, which has a clear understanding of MIME content types. If the content type is unknown or the protocol doesn't understand content types, getContent( ) throws an UnknownServiceException.

public Object getContent(Class[] classes) throws IOException // Java 1.3

This overloaded variant of the getContent( ) method lets you choose what class you'd like the content returned as in order to provide different object representations of data. The method attempts to return the content in the form of one of the classes in the classes array. The order of preference is the order of the array. For instance, if you'd prefer an HTML file to be returned as a String but your second choice is a Reader and your third choice is an InputStream, you would write:

```
URL u = new URL("http://www.thehungersite.com/");
URLConnection uc = u.openConnection()
Class[] types = {String.class, Reader.class, InputStream.class};
Object o = uc.getContent(types);
```

Then test for the type of the returned object using instanceof. For example:

```
if (o instanceof String) {
  System.out.println(o);
}
else if (o instanceof Reader) {
  int c;
  Reader r = (Reader) o;
  while ((c = r.read()) != -1) System.out.print((char) c);
}
else if (o instanceof InputStream) {
  int c;
  InputStream in = (InputStream) o;
  while ((c = in.read()) != -1) System.out.write(c);
}
```

```
    else if (o == null) {
      System.out.println("None of the requested types were available.");
    }
    else {
      System.out.println("Error: unexpected type " + o.getClass());
    }
```

That last else clause shouldn't be reached. If none of the requested types are available, this method is supposed to return null rather than returning an unexpected type.

ContentHandlerFactory

The URLConnection class contains a static Hashtable of ContentHandler objects. Whenever the getContent( ) method of URLConnection is invoked, Java looks in this Hashtable to find the right content handler for the current URL, as indicated by the URL's Content-type. If it doesn't find a ContentHandler object for the MIME type, it tries to create one using a ContentHandlerFactory (which you'll learn more about in Chapter 17). That is, a content handler factory tells the program where it can find a content handler for a text/html file, an image/gif file, or some other kind of file. You can set the ContentHandlerFactory by passing an instance of the java.net. ContentHandlerFactory interface to the setContentHandlerFactory( ) method:

```
    public static void setContentHandlerFactory(ContentHandlerFactory factory)
      throws SecurityException, Error
```

You may set the ContentHandlerFactory only once per application; this method throws a generic Error if it is called a second time. As with most other setFactory( ) methods, untrusted applets will generally not be allowed to set the content handler factory whether one has already been set or not. Attempting to do so throws a SecurityException.

The Object Methods

The URLConnection class overrides only one method from java.lang.Object, toString( ):

```
    public String toString()
```

Even so, there is little reason to print a URLConnection object or to convert one to a String, except perhaps if you are debugging. toString( ) is called the same way as every other toString( ) method.

Security Considerations for URLConnections

URLConnection objects are subject to all the usual security restrictions about making network connections, reading or writing files, and so forth. For instance, a

URLConnection can be created by an untrusted applet only if the URLConnection is pointing to the host that the applet came from. However, the details can be a little tricky because different URL schemes and their corresponding connections can have different security implications. For example, a *jar* URL that points into the applet's own *jar* file should be fine. However, a file URL that points to a local hard drive should not be.

Before attempting to connect a URL, you may want to know whether the connection will be allowed. For this purpose, the URLConnection class has a getPermission() method:

```
public Permission getPermission() throws IOException// Java 1.2
```

This returns a java.security.Permission object that specifies what permission is needed to connect to the URL. It returns null if no permission is needed (e.g., there's no security manager in place). Subclasses of URLConnection return different subclasses of java.security.Permission. For instance, if the underlying URL points to *www.gwbush.com*, getPermission() returns a java.net.SocketPermission for the host *www.gwbush.com* with the connect and resolve actions.

Guessing MIME Content Types

If this were the best of all possible worlds, every protocol and every server would use MIME types to specify the kind of file being transferred. Unfortunately, that's not the case. Not only do we have to deal with older protocols such as FTP that predate MIME, but many HTTP servers that should use MIME don't provide MIME headers at all or lie and provide headers that are incorrect (usually because the server has been misconfigured). The URLConnection class provides two static methods to help programs figure out the MIME type of some data; you can use these if the content type just isn't available or if you have reason to believe that the content type you're given isn't correct. The first of these is URLConnection.guessContentTypeFromName():

```
public static String guessContentTypeFromName(String name)*
```

This method tries to guess the content type of an object based upon the extension in the filename portion of the object's URL. It returns its best guess about the content type as a String. This guess is likely to be correct; people follow some fairly regular conventions when thinking up filenames.

The guesses are determined by the *content-types.properties* file, normally located in the *jre/lib* directory. On Unix, Java may also look at the *mailcap* file to help it guess. Table 15-1 shows the guesses the JDK 1.5 makes. These vary a little from one version of the JDK to the next.

---

* This method is protected in Java 1.3 and earlier, public in Java 1.4 and later.

Table 15-1. Java extension content-type mappings

Extension	MIME content type
No extension, or unrecognized extension	content/unknown
.saveme, .dump, .hqx, .arc, .o, .a, .z, .bin, .exe, .zip, .gz	application/octet-stream
.oda	application/oda
.pdf	application/pdf
.eps, .ai, .ps	application/postscript
.dvi	application/x-dvi
.hdf	application/x-hdf
.latex	application/x-latex
.nc, .cdf	application/x-netcdf
.tex	application/x-tex:
.texinfo, .texi	application/x-texinfo
.t, .tr, .roff	application/x-troff
.man	application/x-troff-man
.me	application/x-troff-me
.ms	application/x-troff-ms
.src, .wsrc	application/x-wais-source
.zip	application/zip
.bcpio	application/x-bcpio
.cpio	application/x-cpio
.gtar	application/x-gtar
.sh, .shar	application/x-shar
.sv4cpio	application/x-sv4cpio:
.sv4crc	application/x-sv4crc
.tar	application/x-tar
.ustar	application/x-ustar
.snd, .au	audio/basic
.aifc, .aif, .aiff	audio/x-aiff
.wav	audio/x-wav
.gif	image/gif
.ief	image/ief
.jfif, .jfif-tbnl, .jpe, .jpg, .jpeg	image/jpeg
.tif, .tiff	image/tiff
.fpx, .fpix	image/vnd.fpx
.ras	image/x-cmu-rast
.pnm	image/x-portable-anymap
.pbm	image/x-portable-bitmap
.pgm	image/x-portable-graymap

Table 15-1. Java extension content-type mappings (continued)

Extension	MIME content type
.ppm	image/x-portable-pixmap
.rgb	image/x-rgb
.xbm, .xpm	image/x-xbitmap
.xwd	image/x-xwindowdump
.png	image/png
.htm, .html	text/html
.text, .c, .cc, .c++, .h, .pl, .txt, .java, .el	text/plain
.tsv	text/tab-separated-values
.etx	text/x-setext
.mpg, .mpe, .mpeg	video/mpeg
.mov, .qt	video/quicktime
.avi	application/x-troff-msvideo
.movie, .mv	video/x-sgi-movie
.mime	message/rfc822
.xml	application/xml

This list is not complete by any means. For instance, it omits various XML applications such as RDF (*.rdf*), XSL (*.xsl*), and so on that should have the MIME type application/xml. It also doesn't provide a MIME type for CSS stylesheets (*.css*). However, it's a good start.

The second MIME type guesser method is URLConnection. guessContentTypeFromStream( ):

```
public static String guessContentTypeFromStream(InputStream in)
```

This method tries to guess the content type by looking at the first few bytes of data in the stream. For this method to work, the InputStream must support marking so that you can return to the beginning of the stream after the first bytes have been read. Java 1.5 inspects the first 11 bytes of the InputStream, although sometimes fewer bytes are needed to make an identification. Table 15-2 shows how Java 1.5 guesses. Note that these guesses are often not as reliable as the guesses made by the previous method. For example, an XML document that begins with a comment rather than an XML declaration would be mislabeled as an HTML file. This method should be used only as a last resort.

Table 15-2. Java first bytes content-type mappings

First bytes in hexadecimal	First bytes in ASCII	MIME content type
0xACED		application/x-java-serialized-object
0xCAFEBABE		application/java-vm
0x47494638	GIF8	image/gif

Table 15-2. Java first bytes content-type mappings (continued)

First bytes in hexadecimal	First bytes in ASCII	MIME content type
0x23646566	#def	image/x-bitmap
0x2158504D32	!XPM2	image/x-pixmap
0x89504E 470D0A1A0A		image/png
0x2E736E64		audio/basic
0x646E732E		audio/basic
0x3C3F786D6C	<?xml	application/xml
0xFEFF003C003F00F7		application/xml
0xFFFE3C003F00F700		application/xml
0x3C21	<!	text/html
0x3C68746D6C	<html	text/html
0x3C626F6479	<body	text/html
0x3C68656164	<head	text/html
0x3C48544D4C	<HTML	text/html
0x3C424F4459	<BODY	text/html
0x3C48454144	<HEAD	text/html
0xFFD8FFE0		image/jpeg
0xFFD8FFEE		image/jpeg
0xFFD8FFE1XXXX4578696600[a]		image/jpeg
0x89504E470D0A1A0A		image/png
0x52494646	RIFF	audio/x-wav
0xD0CF11E0A1B11AE1[b]		image/vnd.fpx

[a] The XX bytes are not checked. They can be anything.

[b] This actually just checks for a Microsoft structured storage document. Several other more complicated checks have to be made before deciding whether this is indeed an image/vnd.fpx document.

ASCII mappings, where they exist, are case-sensitive. For example, guessContentTypeFromStream( ) does not recognize <Html> as the beginning of a text/html file.

HttpURLConnection

The java.net.HttpURLConnection class is an abstract subclass of URLConnection; it provides some additional methods that are helpful when working specifically with *http* URLs:

```
public abstract class HttpURLConnection extends URLConnection
```

In particular, it contains methods to get and set the request method, decide whether to follow redirects, get the response code and message, and figure out whether a proxy server is being used. It also includes several dozen mnemonic constants matching the various HTTP response codes. Finally, it overrides the getPermission() method from the URLConnection superclass, although it doesn't change the semantics of this method at all.

Since this class is abstract and its only constructor is protected, you can't directly create instances of HttpURLConnection. However, if you construct a URL object using an *http* URL and invoke its openConnection() method, the URLConnection object returned will be an instance of HttpURLConnection. Cast that URLConnection to HttpURLConnection like this:

```
URL u = new URL("http://www.amnesty.org/");
URLConnection uc = u.openConnection();
HttpURLConnection http = (HttpURLConnection) uc;
```

Or, skipping a step, like this:

```
URL u = new URL("http://www.amnesty.org/");
HttpURLConnection http = (HttpURLConnection) u.openConnection();
```

 There's another HttpURLConnection class in the undocumented sun. net.www.protocol.http package, a concrete subclass of java.net. HttpURLConnection that actually implements the abstract connect() method:

```
public class HttpURLConnection extends java.net.
HttpURLConnection
```

There's little reason to access this class directly. It doesn't add any important methods that aren't already declared in java.net. HttpURLConnection or java.net.URLConnection. However, any URLConnection you open to an *http* URL will be an instance of this class.

The Request Method

When a web client contacts a web server, the first thing it sends is a request line. Typically, this line begins with GET and is followed by the name of the file that the client wants to retrieve and the version of the HTTP protocol that the client understands. For example:

```
GET /catalog/jfcnut/index.html HTTP/1.0
```

However, web clients can do more than simply GET files from web servers. They can POST responses to forms. They can PUT a file on a web server or DELETE a file from a server. And they can ask for just the HEAD of a document. They can ask the web server for a list of the OPTIONS supported at a given URL. They can even TRACE the request itself. All of these are accomplished by changing the request method from GET to a different keyword. For example, here's how a browser asks for just the header of a document using HEAD:

```
HEAD /catalog/jfcnut/index.html HTTP/1.1
User-Agent: Java/1.4.2_05
```

```
Host: www.oreilly.com
Accept: text/html, image/gif, image/jpeg, *; q=.2, */*; q=.2
Connection: close
```

By default, `HttpURLConnection` uses the GET method. However, you can change this with the `setRequestMethod( )` method:

```
public void setRequestMethod(String method) throws ProtocolException
```

The method argument should be one of these seven case-sensitive strings:

- GET
- POST
- HEAD
- PUT
- OPTIONS
- DELETE
- TRACE

If it's some other method, then a `java.net.ProtocolException`, a subclass of `IOException`, is thrown. However, it's generally not enough to simply set the request method. Depending on what you're trying to do, you may need to adjust the HTTP header and provide a message body as well. For instance, POSTing a form requires you to provide a Content-length header. We've already explored the GET and POST methods. Let's look at the other five possibilities.

 Some web servers support additional, nonstandard request methods. For instance, Apache 1.3 also supports CONNECT, PROPFIND, PROPPATCH, MKCOL, COPY, MOVE, LOCK, and UNLOCK. However, Java doesn't support any of these.

HEAD

The HEAD function is possibly the simplest of all the request methods. It behaves much like GET. However, it tells the server only to return the HTTP header, not to actually send the file. The most common use of this method is to check whether a file has been modified since the last time it was cached. Example 15-9 is a simple program that uses the HEAD request method and prints the last time a file on a server was modified.

Example 15-9. Get the time when a URL was last changed

```
import java.net.*;
import java.io.*;
import java.util.*;

public class LastModified {
```

Example 15-9. Get the time when a URL was last changed (continued)

```
public static void main(String args[]) {

    for (int i=0; i < args.length; i++) {
      try {
        URL u = new URL(args[i]);
        HttpURLConnection http = (HttpURLConnection) u.openConnection( );
        http.setRequestMethod("HEAD");
        System.out.println(u + "was last modified at "
          + new Date(http.getLastModified( )));
      } // end try
      catch (MalformedURLException ex) {
        System.err.println(args[i] + " is not a URL I understand");
      }
      catch (IOException ex) {
        System.err.println(ex);
      }
      System.out.println( );
    } // end for

  } // end main

} // end LastModified
```

Here's the output from one run:

```
D:\JAVA\JNP3\examples\15>java LastModified http://www.ibiblio.org/xml/
http://www.ibiblio.org/xml/was last modified at Thu Aug 19 06:06:57 PDT 2004
```

It wasn't absolutely necessary to use the HEAD method here. We'd have gotten the same results with GET. But if we used GET, the entire file at *http://www.ibiblio.org/xml/* would have been sent across the network, whereas all we cared about was one line in the header. When you can use HEAD, it's much more efficient to do so.

OPTIONS

The OPTIONS request method asks what options are supported for a particular URL. If the request URL is an asterisk (*), the request applies to the server as a whole rather than to one particular URL on the server. For example:

```
OPTIONS /xml/ HTTP/1.1
User-Agent: Java/1.4.2_05
Host: www.ibiblio.org
Accept: text/html, image/gif, image/jpeg, *; q=.2, */*; q=.2
Connection: close
```

The server responds to an OPTIONS request by sending an HTTP header with a list of the commands allowed on that URL. For example, when the previous command was sent, here's what Apache responded:

```
Date: Thu, 21 Oct 2004 18:06:10 GMT
Server: Apache/1.3.4 (Unix) PHP/3.0.6 mod_perl/1.17
Content-Length: 0
```

```
Allow: GET, HEAD, POST, PUT, DELETE, CONNECT, OPTIONS, PATCH, PROPFIND,  PROPPATCH,
MKCOL, COPY, MOVE, LOCK, UNLOCK, TRACE
Connection: close
```

The list of legal commands is found in the Allow field. However, in practice these are just the commands the server understands, not necessarily the ones it will actually perform on that URL. For instance, let's look at what happens when you try the DELETE request method.

DELETE

The DELETE method removes a file at a specified URL from a web server. Since this request is an obvious security risk, not all servers will be configured to support it, and those that are will generally demand some sort of authentication. A typical DELETE request looks like this:

```
DELETE /javafaq/2004march.html HTTP/1.1
User-Agent: Java/1.4.2_05
Host: www.ibiblio.org
Accept: text/html, image/gif, image/jpeg, *; q=.2, */*; q=.2
Connection: close
```

The server is free to refuse this request or ask for identification. For example:

```
Date: Thu, 19 Aug 2004 14:32:15 GMT
Server: Apache/1.3.4 (Unix) PHP/3.0.6 mod_perl/1.17
Allow: GET, HEAD, POST, PUT, DELETE, CONNECT, OPTIONS, PATCH, PROPFIND,
PROPPATCH, MKCOL, COPY, MOVE, LOCK, UNLOCK, TRACE
Connection: close
Transfer-Encoding: chunked
Content-Type: text/html
content-length: 313

<!DOCTYPE HTML PUBLIC "-//IETF//DTD HTML 2.0//EN">
<HTML><HEAD>
<TITLE>405 Method Not Allowed</TITLE>
</HEAD><BODY>
<H1>Method Not Allowed</H1>
The requested method DELETE is not allowed for the
URL /javafaq/2004march.html.<P>
<HR>
<ADDRESS>Apache/1.3.4 Server at www.ibiblio.org Port 80</ADDRESS>
</BODY></HTML>
```

Even if the server accepts this request, its response is implementation-dependent. Some servers may delete the file; others simply move it to a trash directory. Others simply mark it as not readable. Details are left up to the server vendor.

PUT

Many HTML editors and other programs that want to store files on a web server use the PUT method. It allows clients to place documents in the abstract hierarchy of the

---

site without necessarily knowing how the site maps to the actual local filesystem. This contrasts with FTP, where the user has to know the actual directory structure as opposed to the server's virtual directory structure.

Here's a how a browser might PUT a file on a web server:

```
PUT /hello.html HTTP/1.0
Connection: Keep-Alive
User-Agent: Mozilla/4.6 [en] (WinNT; I)
Pragma: no-cache
Host: www.ibiblio.org
Accept: image/gif, image/x-xbitmap, image/jpeg, image/pjpeg, image/png, */*
Accept-Encoding: gzip
Accept-Language: en
Accept-Charset: iso-8859-1,*,utf-8
Content-Length: 364

<!doctype html public "-//w3c//dtd html 4.0 transitional//en">
<html>
<head>
    <meta http-equiv="Content-Type" content="text/html; charset=iso-8859-1">
    <meta name="Author" content="Elliotte Rusty Harold">
    <meta name="GENERATOR" content="Mozilla/4.6 [en] (WinNT; I) [Netscape]">
    <title>Mine</title>
</head>
<body>
<b>Hello</b>
</body>
</html>
```

As with deleting files, allowing arbitrary users to PUT files on your web server is a clear security risk. Generally, some sort of authentication is required and the server must be specially configured to support PUT. The details are likely to vary from server to server. Most web servers do not include full support for PUT out of the box. For instance, Apache requires you to install an additional module just to handle PUT requests.

TRACE

The TRACE request method sends the HTTP header that the server received from the client. The main reason for this information is to see what any proxy servers between the server and client might be changing. For example, suppose this TRACE request is sent:

```
TRACE /xml/ HTTP/1.1
Hello: Push me
User-Agent: Java/1.4.2_05
Host: www.ibiblio.org
Accept: text/html, image/gif, image/jpeg, *; q=.2, */*; q=.2
Connection: close
```

The server should respond like this:

```
Date: Thu, 19 Aug 2004 17:50:02 GMT
Server: Apache/1.3.4 (Unix) PHP/3.0.6 mod_perl/1.17
Connection: close
Transfer-Encoding: chunked
Content-Type: message/http
content-length: 169

TRACE /xml/ HTTP/1.1
Accept: text/html, image/gif, image/jpeg, *; q=.2, */*; q=.2
Connection: close
Hello: Push me
Host: www.ibiblio.org
User-Agent: Java/1.4.2_05
```

The first six lines are the server's normal response HTTP header. The lines from TRACE /xml/ HTTP/1.1 on are the echo of the original client request. In this case, the echo is faithful, although out of order. However, if there were a proxy server between the client and server, it might not be.

Disconnecting from the Server

Recent versions of HTTP support what's known as *Keep-Alive*. Keep-Alive enhances the performance of some web connections by allowing multiple requests and responses to be sent in a series over a single TCP connection. A client indicates that it's willing to use HTTP Keep-Alive by including a Connection field in the HTTP request header with the value Keep-Alive:

```
Connection: Keep-Alive
```

However, when Keep-Alive is used, the server can no longer close the connection simply because it has sent the last byte of data to the client. The client may, after all, send another request. Consequently, it is up to the client to close the connection when it's done.

Java marginally supports HTTP Keep-Alive, mostly by piggybacking on top of browser support. It doesn't provide any convenient API for making multiple requests over the same connection. However, in anticipation of a day when Java will better support Keep-Alive, the HttpURLConnection class adds a disconnect( ) method that allows the client to break the connection:

```
public abstract void disconnect( )
```

In practice, you rarely if ever need to call this.

Handling Server Responses

The first line of an HTTP server's response includes a numeric code and a message indicating what sort of response is made. For instance, the most common response is 200 OK, indicating that the requested document was found. For example:

```
HTTP/1.1 200 OK
Date: Fri, 20 Aug 2004 15:33:40 GMT
Server: Apache/1.3.4 (Unix) PHP/3.0.6 mod_perl/1.17
Last-Modified: Sun, 06 Jun 1999 16:30:33 GMT
ETag: "28d907-657-375aa229"
Accept-Ranges: bytes
Content-Length: 1623
Connection: close
Content-Type: text/html

<HTML>
<HEAD>
rest of document follows...
```

Another response that you're undoubtedly all too familiar with is 404 Not Found, indicating that the URL you requested no longer points to a document. For example:

```
HTTP/1.1 404 Not Found
Date: Fri, 20 Aug 2004 15:39:16 GMT
Server: Apache/1.3.4 (Unix) PHP/3.0.6 mod_perl/1.17
Last-Modified: Mon, 20 Sep 1999 19:25:05 GMT
ETag: "5-14ab-37e68a11"
Accept-Ranges: bytes
Content-Length: 5291
Connection: close
Content-Type: text/html

<html>
<head>
<title>Lost ... and lost</title>
<meta http-equiv="Content-Type" content="text/html; charset=iso-8859-1">
</head>

<body bgcolor="#FFFFFF">
<div align="left">
  <h1>404 FILE NOT FOUND</h1>
Rest of error message follows...
```

There are many other, less common responses. For instance, code 301 indicates that the resource has permanently moved to a new location and the browser should redirect itself to the new location and update any bookmarks that point to the old location. For example:

```
HTTP/1.1 301 Moved Permanently
Date: Fri, 20 Aug 2004 15:36:44 GMT
Server: Apache/1.3.4 (Unix) PHP/3.0.6 mod_perl/1.17
Location: http://www.ibiblio.org/javafaq/books/beans/index.html
Connection: close
Content-Type: text/html
```

```
<!DOCTYPE HTML PUBLIC "-//IETF//DTD HTML 2.0//EN">
<HTML><HEAD>
<TITLE>301 Moved Permanently</TITLE>
</HEAD><BODY>
<H1>Moved Permanently</H1>
The document has moved <A HREF="http://www.ibiblio.org/javafaq/books/beans/index
.html">here</A>.<P>
<HR>
<ADDRESS>Apache/1.3.4 Server at www.ibiblio.org Port 80</ADDRESS>
</BODY></HTML>
```

The first line of this response is called the *response message*. It will not be returned by the various getHeaderField( ) methods in URLConnection. However, HttpURLConnection has a method to read and return just the response message. This is the aptly named getResponseMessage( ):

```
public String getResponseMessage( ) throws IOException
```

Often all you need from the response message is the numeric response code. HttpURLConnection also has a getResponseCode( ) method to return this as an int:

```
public int getResponseCode( ) throws IOException
```

HTTP 1.0 defines 16 response codes. HTTP 1.1 expands this to 40 different codes. While some numbers, notably 404, have become slang almost synonymous with their semantic meaning, most of them are less familiar. The HttpURLConnection class includes 36 named constants representing the most common response codes. These are summarized in Table 15-3.

Table 15-3. The HTTP 1.1 response codes

Code	Meaning	HttpURLConnection constant
1XX	Informational	
100	The server is prepared to accept the request body and the client should send it; a new feature in HTTP 1.1 that allows clients to ask whether the server will accept a request before they send a large amount of data as part of the request.	N/A
101	The server accepts the client's request in the Upgrade header field to change the application protocol; e.g., from HTTP 1.0 to HTTP 1.1.	N/A
2XX	Request succeeded.	
200	The most common response code. If the request method was GET or POST, the requested data is contained in the response along with the usual headers. If the request method was HEAD, only the header information is included.	HTTP_OK
201	The server has created a resource at the URL specified in the body of the response. The client should now attempt to load that URL. This code is sent only in response to POST requests.	HTTP_CREATED
202	This rather uncommon response indicates that a request (generally from POST) is being processed, but the processing is not yet complete, so no response can be returned. However, the server should return an HTML page that explains the situation to the user and provide an estimate of when the request is likely to be completed, and, ideally, a link to a status monitor of some kind.	HTTP_ACCEPTED

Table 15-3. The HTTP 1.1 response codes (continued)

Code	Meaning	HttpURLConnection constant
203	The resource representation was returned from a caching proxy or other local source and is not guaranteed to be up to date.	HTTP_NOT_AUTHORITATIVE
204	The server has successfully processed the request but has no information to send back to the client. This is normally the result of a poorly written form-processing program on the server that accepts data but does not return a response to the user.	HTTP_NO_CONTENT
205	The server has successfully processed the request but has no information to send back to the client. Furthermore, the client should clear the form to which the request is sent.	HTTP_RESET
206	The server has returned the part of the document the client requested using the byte range extension to HTTP, rather than the whole document.	HTTP_PARTIAL
3XX	Relocation and redirection.	
300	The server is providing a list of different representations (e.g., PostScript and PDF) for the requested document.	HTTP_MULT_CHOICE
301	The resource has moved to a new URL. The client should automatically load the resource at this URL and update any bookmarks that point to the old URL.	HTTP_MOVED_PERM
302	The resource is at a new URL temporarily, but its location will change again in the foreseeable future; therefore, bookmarks should not be updated.	HTTP_MOVED_TEMP
303	Generally used in response to a POST form request, this code indicates that the user should retrieve a document other than the one requested (as opposed to a different location for the requested document).	HTTP_SEE_OTHER
304	The If-Modified-Since header indicates that the client wants the document only if it has been recently updated. This status code is returned if the document has not been updated. In this case, the client should load the document from its cache.	HTTP_NOT_MODIFIED
305	The Location header field contains the address of a proxy that will serve the response.	HTTP_USE_PROXY
307	Almost the same as code 303, a 307 response indicates that the resource has moved to a new URL, although it may move again to a different URL in the future. The client should automatically load the page at this URL.	N/A
4XX	Client error.	
400	The client request to the server used improper syntax. This is rather unusual in normal web browsing but more common when debugging custom clients.	HTTP_BAD_REQUEST
401	Authorization, generally a username and password, is required to access this page. Either a username and password have not yet been presented or the username and password are invalid.	HTTP_UNAUTHORIZED
402	Not used today, but may be used in the future to indicate that some sort of digital cash transaction is required to access the resource.	HTTP_PAYMENT_REQUIRED
403	The server understood the request, but is deliberately refusing to process it. Authorization will not help. This might be used when access to a certain page is denied to a certain range of IP addresses.	HTTP_FORBIDDEN

Table 15-3. The HTTP 1.1 response codes (continued)

Code	Meaning	HttpURLConnection constant
404	This most common error response indicates that the server cannot find the requested resource. It may indicate a bad link, a document that has moved with no forwarding address, a mistyped URL, or something similar.	HTTP_NOT_FOUND
405	The request method is not allowed for the specified resource; for instance, you tried to PUT a file on a web server that doesn't support PUT or tried to POST to a URI that only allows GET.	HTTP_BAD_METHOD
406	The requested resource cannot be provided in a format the client is willing to accept, as indicated by the Accept field of the request HTTP header.	HTTP_NOT_ACCEPTABLE
407	An intermediate proxy server requires authentication from the client, probably in the form of a username and password, before it will retrieve the requested resource.	HTTP_PROXY_AUTH
408	The client took too long to send the request, perhaps because of network congestion.	HTTP_CLIENT_TIMEOUT
409	A temporary conflict prevents the request from being fulfilled; for instance, two clients are trying to PUT the same file at the same time.	HTTP_CONFLICT
410	Like a 404, but makes a stronger assertion about the existence of the resource. The resource has been deliberately deleted (not moved) and will not be restored. Links to it should be removed.	HTTP_GONE
411	The client must but did not send a Content-length field in the client request HTTP header.	HTTP_LENGTH_REQUIRED
412	A condition for the request that the client specified in the request HTTP header is not satisfied.	HTTP_PRECON_FAILED
413	The body of the client request is larger than the server is able to process at this time.	HTTP_ENTITY_TOO_LARGE
414	The URI of the request is too long. This is important to prevent certain buffer overflow attacks.	HTTP_REQ_TOO_LONG
415	The server does not understand or accept the MIME content-type of the request body.	HTTP_UNSUPPORTED_TYPE
416	The server cannot send the byte range the client requested.	N/A
417	The server cannot meet the client's expectation given in an Expect-request header field.	N/A
5XX	Server error.	
500	An unexpected condition occurred that the server does not know how to handle.	HTTP_SERVER_ERROR HTTP_INTERNAL_ERROR
501	The server does not have a feature that is needed to fulfill this request. A server that cannot handle POST requests might send this response to a client that tried to POST form data to it.	HTTP_NOT_IMPLEMENTED
502	This code is applicable only to servers that act as proxies or gateways. It indicates that the proxy received an invalid response from a server it was connecting to in an effort to fulfill the request.	HTTP_BAD_GATEWAY
503	The server is temporarily unable to handle the request, perhaps due to overloading or maintenance.	HTTP_UNAVAILABLE

Table 15-3. The HTTP 1.1 response codes (continued)

Code	Meaning	HttpURLConnection constant
504	The proxy server did not receive a response from the upstream server within a reasonable amount of time, so it can't send the desired response to the client.	HTTP_GATEWAY_TIMEOUT
505	The server does not support the version of HTTP the client is using (e.g., the as-yet-nonexistent HTTP 2.0).	HTTP_VERSION

Example 15-10 is a revised source viewer program that now includes the response message. The lines added since SourceViewer2 are in bold.

Example 15-10. A SourceViewer that includes the response code and message

```java
import java.net.*;
import java.io.*;
import javax.swing.*;
import java.awt.*;

public class SourceViewer3 {

  public static void main (String[] args) {

    for (int i = 0; i < args.length; i++) {
      try {

        //Open the URLConnection for reading
        URL u = new URL(args[i]);
        HttpURLConnection uc = (HttpURLConnection) u.openConnection( );
        int code = uc.getResponseCode();
        String response = uc.getResponseMessage();
        System.out.println("HTTP/1.x " + code + " " + response);
        for (int j = 1; ; j++) {
          String header = uc.getHeaderField(j);
          String key = uc.getHeaderFieldKey(j);
          if (header == null || key == null) break;
          System.out.println(uc.getHeaderFieldKey(j) + ": " + header);
        }  // end for
        InputStream in = new BufferedInputStream(uc.getInputStream( ));
        // chain the InputStream to a Reader
        Reader r = new InputStreamReader(in);
        int c;
        while ((c = r.read( )) != -1) {
          System.out.print((char) c);
        }
      }
      catch (MalformedURLException ex) {
        System.err.println(args[0] + " is not a parseable URL");
      }
      catch (IOException ex) {
        System.err.println(ex);
      }
```

```
    } //  end if

  } // end main

} // end SourceViewer3
```

The only thing this program doesn't read that the server sends is the version of HTTP the server is using. There's currently no method to return that. If you need it, you'll just have to use a raw socket instead. Consequently, in this example, we just fake it as "HTTP/1.x", like this:

```
% java SourceViewer3 http://www.oreilly.com
HTTP/1.x 200 OK
Server: WN/1.15.1
Date: Mon, 01 Nov 1999 23:39:19 GMT
Last-modified: Fri, 29 Oct 1999 23:40:06 GMT
Content-type: text/html
Title: www.oreilly.com -- Welcome to O'Reilly &amp; Associates! --
computer  books, software, online publishing
Link: <mailto:webmaster@ora.com>; rev="Made"
<HTML>
<HEAD>
...
```

Error conditions

On occasion, the server encounters an error but returns useful information in the message body nonetheless. For example, when a client requests a nonexistent page from the *www.ibiblio.org* web site, rather than simply returning a 404 error code, the server sends the search page shown in Figure 15-2 to help the user figure out where the missing page might have gone.

The getErrorStream( ) method returns an InputStream containing this data or null if no error was encountered or no data returned:

```
public InputStream getErrorStream( ) // Java 1.2
```

In practice, this isn't necessary. Most implementations will return this data from getInputStream( ) as well.

Redirects

The 300-level response codes all indicate some sort of redirect; that is, the requested resource is no longer available at the expected location but it may be found at some other location. When encountering such a response, most browsers automatically load the document from its new location. However, this can be a security risk, because it has the potential to move the user from a trusted site to an untrusted one, perhaps without the user even noticing.

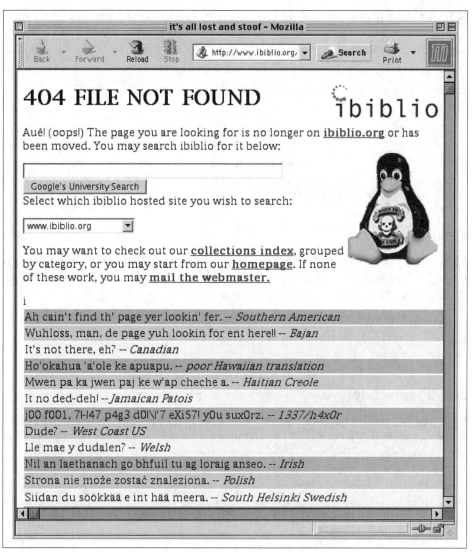

Figure 15-2. IBiblio's 404 page

By default, an HttpURLConnection follows redirects. However, the HttpURLConnection class has two static methods that let you decide whether to follow redirects:

```
public static boolean getFollowRedirects()
public static void    setFollowRedirects(boolean follow)
```

The getFollowRedirects() method returns true if redirects are being followed, false if they aren't. With an argument of true, the setFollowRedirects() method makes HttpURLConnection objects follow redirects. With an argument of false, it prevents them from following redirects. Since these are static methods, they change the behavior of all `HttpURLConnection` objects constructed after the method is invoked. The `setFollowRedirects()` method may throw a `SecurityException` if the security manager disallows the change. Applets especially are not allowed to change this value.

Java has two methods to configure redirection on an instance-by-instance basis. These are:

```
public boolean getInstanceFollowRedirects()   // Java 1.3
public void    setInstanceFollowRedirects(boolean followRedirects)  // Java 1.3
```

If `setInstanceFollowRedirects()` is not invoked on a given `HttpURLConnection`, that `HttpURLConnection` simply follows the default behavior as set by the class method `HttpURLConnection.setFollowRedirects()`.

Proxies

Many users behind firewalls or using AOL or other high-volume ISPs access the web through proxy servers. The `usingProxy()` method tells you whether the particular `HttpURLConnection` is going through a proxy server:

```
public abstract boolean usingProxy() // Java 1.3
```

It returns `true` if a proxy is being used, `false` if not. In some contexts, the use of a proxy server may have security implications.

Streaming Mode

Every request sent to an HTTP server has an HTTP header. One field in this header is the Content-length; that is, the number of bytes in the body of the request. The header comes before the body. However, to write the header you need to know the length of the body, which you may not have yet. Normally the way Java solves this Catch-22 is by caching every thing you write onto the `OutputStream` retrieved from the `HttpURLConnection` until the stream is closed. At that point, it knows how many bytes are in the body so it has enough information to write the Content-length header.

This scheme is fine for small requests sent in response to typical web forms. However, it's burdensome for responses to very long forms or some SOAP messages. It's very wasteful and slow for medium-to-large documents sent with HTTP PUT. It's much more efficient if Java doesn't have to wait for the last byte of data to be written before sending the first byte of data over the network. Java 1.5 offers two solutions to this problem. If you know the size of your data—for instance, you're uploading a file of known size using HTTP PUT—you can tell the `HttpURLConnection` object the size of that data. If you don't know the size of the data in advance, the you can use chunked transfer encoding instead. In chunked transfer encoding, the body of the request is sent in multiple pieces, each with its own separate content length.

To turn on chunked transfer encoding, just pass the size of the chunks you want to the setChunkedStreamingMode( ) method before you connect the URL.

```
public void setChunkedStreamingMode(int chunkLength) // Java 1.5
```

Java will then use a slightly different form of HTTP than the examples in this book. However, to the Java programmer the difference is irrelevant. As long as you're using the URLConnection class instead of raw sockets and as long as the server supports chunked transfer encoding, it should all just work without any further changes to your code. However, not all servers support chunked encoding, though most of the late-model, major ones do. Even more importantly, chunked transfer encoding does get in the way of authentication and redirection. If you're trying to send chunked files to a redirected URL or one that requires password authentication, an HttpRetryException will be thrown. You'll then need to retry the request at the new URL or at the old URL with the appropriate credentials; and this all needs to be done manually without the full support of the HTTP protocol handler you normally have. Therefore, don't use chunked transfer encoding unless you really need it. As with most performance advice, this means you shouldn't implement this optimization until measurements prove the non-streaming default is a bottleneck.

If you do happen to know the size of the request data in advance, Java 1.5 lets you optimize the connection by providing this information to the HttpURLConnection object. If you do this Java can start streaming the data over the network immediately. Otherwise, it has to cache everything you write in order to determine the content length, and only send it over the network after you've closed the stream. If you know exactly how big your data is, pass that number to the setFixedLengthStreamingMode( ) method:

```
public void setFixedLengthStreamingMode(int contentLength)
```

Java will use this number in the HTTP Content-length HTTP header field. However, if you then try to write more or less than the number of bytes given here, Java will throw an IOException. Of course, that will happen later, when you're writing data, not when you first call this method. The setFixedLengthStreamingMode( ) method itself will throw an IllegalArgumentException if you pass in a negative number, or an IllegalStateException if the connection is connected or has already been set to chunked transfer encoding. (You can't use both chunked transfer encoding and fixed-length streaming mode on the same request.)

Fixed-length streaming mode is transparent on the server side. Servers neither know nor care how the Content-length was set as long as it's correct. However, like chunked transfer encoding, streaming mode does interfere authentication and redirection. If either of these is required for a given URL, an HttpRetryException will be thrown; you have to manually retry. Therefore, don't use this mode unless you really need it.

Caches

Web browsers have been caching pages and images for years. If a logo is repeated on every page of a site, the browser normally loads it from the remote server only once, stores it in its cache, and reloads it from the cache whenever it's needed rather than returning to the remote server every time the same page is needed. Several HTTP headers, including Expires and Cache-Control, can control caching.

Java 1.5 finally adds the ability to cache data to the URL and URLConnection classes. By default, Java 1.5 does not cache anything, but you can create your own cache by subclassing the java.net.ResponseCache class and installing it as the system default. Whenever the system tries to load a new URL thorough a protocol handler, it will first look for it in the cache. If the cache returns the desired content, the protocol handler won't need to connect to the remote server. However, if the requested data is not in the cache, the protocol handler will download it. After it's done so, it will put its response into the cache so the content is more quickly available the next time that URL is loaded.

Two abstract methods in the ResponseCache class store and retrieve data from the system's single cache:

```
public abstract CacheResponse get(URI uri, String requestMethod,
  Map<String,List<String>> requestHeaders) throws IOException
public abstract CacheRequest put(URI uri, URLConnection connection)
  throws IOException
```

The put( ) method returns a CacheRequest object that wraps an OutputStream into which the protocol handler will write the data it reads. CacheRequest is an abstract class with two methods, as shown in Example 15-11.

Example 15-11. The CacheRequest class

```
package java.net

public abstract class CacheRequest {

  public abstract OutputStream getBody( ) throws IOException;
  public abstract void abort( );

}
```

The getOutputStream( ) method in the subclass should return an OutputStream that points into the cache's data store for the URI passed to the put( ) method at the same time. For instance, if you're storing the data in a file, then you'd return a FileOutputStream connected to that file. The protocol handler will copy the data it reads onto this OutputStream. If a problem arises while copying (e.g., the server unexpectedly closes the connection), the protocol handler calls the abort( ) method. This method should then remove any data that has been stored from the cache.

Example 15-12 demonstrates a basic `CacheRequest` subclass that passes back a `ByteArrayOutputStream`. Later the data can be retrieved using the getData( ) method, a custom method in this subclass just retrieving the data Java wrote onto the `OutputStream` this class supplied. An obvious alternative strategy would be to store results in files and use a `FileOutputStream` instead.

Example 15-12. A basic CacheRequest subclass

```
import java.net.*;
import java.io.*;
import java.util.*;

public class SimpleCacheRequest extends CacheRequest {

  ByteArrayOutputStream out = new ByteArrayOutputStream( );

  public OutputStream getBody( ) throws IOException {
    return out;
  }

  public void abort( ) {
    out = null;
  }

  public byte[] getData( ) {
    if (out == null) return null;
    else return out.toByteArray( );
  }

}
```

The get( ) method retrieves the data and headers from the cache and returns them wrapped in a `CacheResponse` object. It returns `null` if the desired URI is not in the cache, in which case the protocol handler loads the URI from the remote server as normal. Again, this is an abstract class that you have to implement in a subclass. Example 15-13 summarizes this class. It has two methods, one to return the data of the request and one to return the headers. When caching the original response, you need to store both. The headers should be returned in an unmodifiable map with keys that are the HTTP header field names and values that are lists of values for each named HTTP header.

Example 15-13. The CacheResponse class

```
package java.net;

public abstract class CacheRequest {

  public abstract InputStream getBody( ) ;
  public abstract Map<String,List<String>> getHeaders( );

}
```

Example 15-14 shows a simple `CacheResponse` subclass that is tied to a `SimpleCacheRequest`. In this example, shared references pass data from the request class to the response class. If we were storing responses in files, we'd just need to share the filenames instead. Along with the `SimpleCacheRequest` object from which it will read the data, we must also pass the original `URLConnection` object into the constructor. This is used to read the HTTP header so it can be stored for later retrieval. The object also keeps track of the expiration date (if any) provided by the server for the cached representation of the resource.

Example 15-14. A basic CacheResponse subclass

```java
import java.net.*;
import java.io.*;
import java.util.*;

public class SimpleCacheResponse extends CacheResponse {

  private Map<String,List<String>> headers;
  private SimpleCacheRequest request;
  private Date expires;

  public SimpleCacheResponse(SimpleCacheRequest request, URLConnection uc)
   throws IOException {

    this.request = request;

    // deliberate shadowing; we need to fill the map and
    // then make it unmodifiable
    Map<String,List<String>> headers = new HashMap<String,List<String>>();
    String value = "";
    for (int i = 0;; i++) {
       String name = uc.getHeaderFieldKey(i);
       value = uc.getHeaderField(i);
       if (value == null) break;
       List<String> values = headers.get(name);
       if (values == null) {
         values = new ArrayList<String>(1);
         headers.put(name, values);
       }
       values.add(value);
    }
    long expiration = uc.getExpiration();
    if (expiration != 0) {
      this.expires = new Date(expiration);
    }

    this.headers = Collections.unmodifiableMap(headers);

  }

  public InputStream getBody() {
    return new ByteArrayInputStream(request.getData());
  }
```

Example 15-14. A basic CacheResponse subclass (continued)

```java
  public Map<String,List<String>> getHeaders( )
   throws IOException {
    return headers;
  }

  public boolean isExpired( ) {
    if (expires == null) return false;
    else {
      Date now = new Date( );
      return expires.before(now);
    }
  }
}

}
```

Finally, we need a simple ResponseCache subclass that passes SimpleCacheRequests
and SimpleCacheResponses back to the protocol handler as requested. Example 15-15
demonstrates such a simple class that stores a finite number of responses in memory
in one big HashMap.

Example 15-15. An in-memory ResponseCache

```java
import java.net.*;
import java.io.*;
import java.util.*;
import java.util.concurrent.*;

public class MemoryCache extends ResponseCache {

  private Map<URI, SimpleCacheResponse> responses
   = new ConcurrentHashMap<URI, SimpleCacheResponse>( );
  private int maxEntries = 100;

  public MemoryCache( ) {
    this(100);
  }

  public MemoryCache(int maxEntries) {
    this.maxEntries = maxEntries;
  }

  public CacheRequest put(URI uri, URLConnection uc)
   throws IOException {

    if (responses.size( ) >= maxEntries) return null;

    String cacheControl = uc.getHeaderField("Cache-Control");
    if (cacheControl != null && cacheControl.indexOf("no-cache") >= 0) {
      return null;
    }

    SimpleCacheRequest request = new SimpleCacheRequest( );
    SimpleCacheResponse response = new SimpleCacheResponse(request, uc);
```

Example 15-15. An in-memory ResponseCache (continued)

```
    responses.put(uri, response);
    return request;

}

public CacheResponse get(URI uri, String requestMethod,
  Map<String,List<String>> requestHeaders)
  throws IOException {

    SimpleCacheResponse response = responses.get(uri);
    if (response != null && response.isExpired()) { // check expiration date
      responses.remove(response);
      response = null;
    }
    return response;

  }

}
```

Once a ResponseCache like this one is installed, Java's HTTP protocol handler always uses it, even when it shouldn't. The client code needs to check the expiration dates on anything it's stored and watch out for Cache-Control header fields. The key value of concern is no-cache. If you see this string in a Cache-Control header field, it means any resource representation is valid only momentarily and any cached copy is likely to be out of date almost immediately, so you really shouldn't store it at all.

Each retrieved resource stays in the HashMap until it expires. This example waits for an expired document to be requested again before it deletes it from the cache. A more sophisticated implementation could use a low-priority thread to scan for expired documents and remove them to make way for others. Instead of or in addition to this, an implementation might cache the representations in a queue and remove the oldest documents or those closest to their expiration date as necessary to make room for new ones. An even more sophisticated implementation could track how often each document in the store was accessed and expunge only the oldest and least-used documents.

I've already mentioned that you could implement this on top of the filesystem instead of sitting on top of the Java Collections API. You could also store the cache in a database and you could do a lot of less-common things as well. For instance, you could redirect requests for certain URLs to a local server rather than a remote server halfway around the world, in essence using a local web server as the cache. Or a ResponseCache could load a fixed set of files at launch time and then only serve those out of memory. This might be useful for a server that processes many different SOAP requests, all of which adhere to a few common schemas that can be stored in the cache. The abstract ResponseCache class is flexible enough to support all of these and other usage patterns.

Regrettably, Java only allows one cache at a time. To change the cache object, use the static ResponseCache.setDefault( ) and ResponseCache.getDefault( ) methods:

```
public static ResponseCache getDefault( )
public static void setDefault(ResponseCache responseCache)
```

These set the single cache used by all programs running within the same Java virtual machine. For example, this one line of code installs Example 15-13 in an application:

```
ResponseCache.setDefault(new MemoryCache( ));
```

JarURLConnection

Applets often store their .class files in a JAR archive, which bundles all the classes in one package that still maintains the directory hierarchy needed to resolve fully qualified class names like com.macfaq.net.QueryString. Furthermore, since the entire archive is compressed and can be downloaded in a single HTTP connection, it requires much less time to download the .jar file than to download its contents one file at a time. Some programs store needed resources such as sounds, images, and even text files inside these JAR archives. Java provides several mechanisms for getting the resources out of the JAR archive, but the one that we'll address here is the *jar* URL. The JarURLConnection class supports URLs that point inside JAR archives:

```
public abstract class JarURLConnection extends URLConnection// Java 1.2
```

A *jar* URL starts with a normal URL that points to a JAR archive, such as *http:// www.cafeaulait.org/network.jar* or *file:///D%7C/javafaq/network.jar*. Then the protocol *jar:* is prefixed to this URL. Finally, *!/* and the path to the desired file inside the JAR archive are suffixed to the original URL. For example, to find the file *com/macfaq/ net/QueryString.class* inside the previous *.jar* files, you'd use the URLs *jar:http:// www.cafeaulait.org/network.jar!/com/macfaq/net/QueryString.class* or *jar:file://D%7C/ javafaq/network.jar!/com/macfaq/net/QueryString.class*. Of course, this isn't limited simply to Java *.class* files. You can use *jar* URLs to point to any kind of file that happens to be stored inside a JAR archive, including images, sounds, text, HTML files, and more. If the path is left off, the URL refers to the entire JAR archive, e.g., *jar:http:// www.cafeaulait.org/network.jar!/* or *jar:file:///D%7C/javafaq/network.jar!/*.

Web browsers don't understand *jar* URLs, though. They're used only inside Java programs. To get a JarURLConnection, construct a URL object using a *jar* URL and cast the return value of its openConnection( ) method to JarURLConnection. Java downloads the entire JAR archive to a temporary file, opens it, and positions the file pointer at the beginning of the particular entry you requested. You can then read the contents of the particular file inside the JAR archive using the InputStream returned by getInputStream( ). For example:

```
try {
  //Open the URLConnection for reading
  URL u = new URL(
```

```
    "jar:http://www.cafeaulait.org/course/week1.jar!/week1/05.html");
URLConnection uc = u.openConnection( );

    InputStream in = uc.getInputStream( );
    // chain the InputStream to a Reader
    Reader r = new InputStreamReader(in);
    int c;
    while ((c = r.read( )) != -1) {
      System.out.print((char) c);
    }
  }
  catch (IOException ex) {
    System.err.println(ex);
  }
```

Besides the usual methods of the URLConnection class that JarURLConnection inherits, this class adds eight new methods, mostly to return information about the JAR archive itself. These are:

```
public URL         getJarFileURL( )                         // Java 1.2
public String      getEntryName( )                          // Java 1.2
public JarEntry    getJarEntry( ) throws IOException        // Java 1.2
public Manifest    getManifest( ) throws IOException        // Java 1.2
public Attributes  getAttributes( ) throws IOException      // Java 1.2
public Attributes  getMainAttributes( ) throws IOException  // Java 1.2
public Certificate[] getCertificates( ) throws IOException  // Java 1.2
public abstract JarFile getJarFile( ) throws IOException    // Java 1.2
```

The getJarFileURL( ) method is the simplest. It merely returns the URL of the *jar* file being used by this connection. This generally differs from the URL of the file in the archive being used for this connection. For instance, the *jar* file URL of *jar:http:// www.cafeaulait.org/network.jar!/com/macfaq/net/QueryString.class* is *http://www. cafeaulait.org/network.jar*. The getEntryName( ) returns the other part of the *jar* URL; that is, the path to the file inside the archive. The entry name of *jar:http:// www.cafeaulait.org/network.jar!/com/macfaq/net/QueryString.class* is *com/macfaq/ net/QueryString.class*.

The getJarFile( ) method returns a java.util.jar.JarFile object that you can use to inspect and manipulate the archive contents. The getJarEntry( ) method returns a java.util.jar.JarEntry object for the particular file in the archive that this URLConnection is connected to. It returns null if the URL points to a whole JAR archive rather than a particular entry in the archive.

Much of the functionality of both JarFile and JarEntry is duplicated by other methods in the JarURLConnection class; which to use is mostly a matter of personal preference. For instance, the getManifest( ) method returns a java.util.jar.Manifest object representing the contents of the JAR archive's manifest file. A *manifest file* is included in the archive to supply metainformation about the contents of the archive, such as which file contains the main( ) method and which classes are Java beans. It's called *MANIFEST.MF* and placed in the *META-INF* directory; its contents typically look something like this:

```
Manifest-Version: 1.0
Required-Version: 1.0

Name: com/macfaq/net/FormPoster.class
Java-Bean: true
Last-modified: 10-21-2003
Depends-On: com/macfaq/net/QueryString.class
Digest-Algorithms: MD5
MD5-Digest: XD4578YEEIK9MGX54RFGT7UJUI9810

Name: com/macfaq/net/QueryString.class
Java-Bean: false
Last-modified: 5-17-2003
Digest-Algorithms: MD5
MD5-Digest: YP7659YEEIKOMGJ53RYHG787YI8900
```

The name-value pairs associated with each entry are called the *attributes* of that entry. The name-value pairs not associated with any entry are called the *main attributes* of the archive. The getAttributes( ) method returns a java.util.jar. Attributes object representing the attributes that the manifest file specifies for this *jar* entry, or null if the URL points to a whole JAR archive. The getMainAttributes( ) method returns a java.util.jar.Attributes object representing the attributes that the manifest file specifies for the entire JAR archive as a whole.

Finally, the getCertificates( ) method returns an array of digital signatures (each represented as a java.security.cert.Certificate object) that apply to this *jar* entry, or null if the URL points to a JAR archive instead of a particular entry. These are actually read from separate signature files for each *jar* entry, not from the manifest file. Unlike the other methods of JarURLConnection, getCertificates( ) can be called only after the entire input stream for the *jar* URL has been read. This is because the current hash of the data needs to be calculated, which can be done only when the entire entry is available.

More details about the java.util.jar package, JAR archives, manifest files, entries, attributes, digital signatures, how this all relates to Zip files and Zip and JAR streams, and so forth can be found on Sun's web site at *http://java.sun.com/ j2se/1.4.2/docs/guide/jar/* or in Chapter 9 of my book, *Java I/O* (O'Reilly).

CHAPTER 16

Protocol Handlers

When designing an architecture that would allow them to build a self-extensible browser, the engineers at Sun divided the problem into two parts: handling protocols and handling content. Handling a protocol involves the interaction between a client and a server: generating requests in the correct format, interpreting the headers that come back with the data, acknowledging that the data has been received, etc. Handling the content involves converting the raw data into a format Java understands—for example, an InputStream or an AudioClip. These two problems, handling protocols and handling content, are distinct. The software that displays a GIF image doesn't care whether the image was retrieved via FTP, HTTP, gopher, or some new protocol. Likewise, the protocol handler, which manages the connection and interacts with the server, doesn't care if it's receiving an HTML file or an MPEG movie file; at most, it will extract a content type from the headers to pass along to the content handler.

Java divides the task of handling protocols into a number of pieces. As a result, there is no single class called ProtocolHandler. Instead, four different classes in the java. net package work together to implement the protocol handler mechanism. Those classes are URL, URLStreamHandler, URLConnection, and URLStreamHandlerFactory. URL is the only concrete class in this group; URLStreamHandler and URLConnection are abstract classes and URLStreamHandlerFactory is an interface. Therefore, if you are going to implement a new protocol handler, you have to write concrete subclasses for the URLStreamHandler and the URLConnection. To use these classes, you may also have to write a class that implements the URLStreamHandlerFactory interface.

What Is a Protocol Handler?

The way the URL, URLStreamHandler, URLConnection, and URLStreamHandlerFactory classes work together can be confusing. Everything starts with a URL, which represents a pointer to a particular Internet resource. Each URL specifies the protocol used to access the resource; typical values for the protocol include mailto, http, and ftp. When you construct a URL object from the URL's string representation, the constructor strips the protocol field and passes it to the URLStreamHandlerFactory. The factory's job is to take the protocol, locate the right subclass of URLStreamHandler for the protocol, and create a new instance of that stream handler, which is stored as a field within the URL object. Each application has at most one URLStreamHandlerFactory; once the factory has been installed, attempting to install another will throw an Error.

Now that the URL object has a stream handler, it asks the stream handler to finish parsing the URL string and create a subclass of URLConnection that knows how to talk to servers using this protocol. URLStreamHandler subclasses and URLConnection subclasses always come in pairs; the stream handler for a protocol always knows how to find an appropriate URLConnection for its protocol. It is worth noting that the stream handler does most of the work of parsing the URL. The format of the URL, although standard, depends on the protocol; therefore, it must be parsed by a URLStreamHandler, which knows about a particular protocol, and not by the URL object, which is generic and has no knowledge of specific protocols. This also means that if you are writing a new stream handler, you can define a new URL format that's appropriate to your task.

 New URL schemes should be defined only for genuinely new protocols. They should not be defined for different uses of existing protocols. The iTunes Music Store *itms* scheme and the RSS *feed* scheme are examples of what not to do. Both of these should use *http*.

The URLConnection class, which you learned about in the previous chapter, represents an active connection to an Internet resource. It is responsible for interacting with the server. A URLConnection knows how to generate requests and interpret the headers that the server returns. The output from a URLConnection is the raw data requested with all traces of the protocol (headers, etc.) stripped, ready for processing by a content handler.

In most applications, you don't need to worry about URLConnection objects and stream handlers; they are hidden by the URL class, which provides a simple interface to the functionality you need. When you call the getInputStream( ), getOutputStream( ), and getContent( ) methods of the URL class, you are really calling similarly named methods in the URLConnection class. We have seen that interacting directly with a URLConnection can be convenient when you need a little more control over communication with a server, such as when downloading binary files or posting data to a server-side program.

However, the URLConnection and URLStreamHandler classes are even more important when you need to add new protocols. By writing subclasses of these classes, you can add support for standard protocols such as finger, whois, or NTP that Java doesn't support out of the box. Furthermore, you're not limited to established protocols with well-known services. You can create new protocols that perform database queries, search across multiple Internet search engines, view pictures from binary newsgroups, and more. You can add new kinds of URLs as needed to represent the new types of resources. Furthermore, Java applications can be built so that they load new protocol handlers at runtime. Unlike current browsers such as Mozilla and Internet Explorer, which contain explicit knowledge of all the protocols and content types they can handle, a Java browser can be a relatively lightweight skeleton that loads new handlers as needed. Supporting a new protocol just means adding some new classes in predefined locations, not writing an entirely new release of the browser.

What's involved in adding support for a new protocol? As I said earlier, you need to write two new classes: a subclass of URLConnection and a subclass of URL-StreamHandler. You may also need to write a class that implements the URL-StreamHandlerFactory interface. The URLConnection subclass handles the interaction with the server, converts anything the server sends into an InputStream, and converts anything the client sends into an OutputStream. This subclass must implement the abstract method connect( ); it may also override the concrete methods getInputStream( ), getOutputStream( ), and getContentType( ).

The URLStreamHandler subclass parses the string representation of the URL into its separate parts and creates a new URLConnection object that understands that URL's protocol. This subclass must implement the abstract openConnection( ) method, which returns the new URLConnection to its caller. If the String representation of the URL doesn't look like a standard hierarchical URL, you should also override the parseURL( ) and toExternalForm( ) methods.

Finally, you may need to create a class that implements the URLStreamHandlerFactory interface. The URLStreamHandlerFactory helps the application find the right protocol handler for each type of URL. The URLStreamHandlerFactory interface has a single method, createURLStreamHandler( ), which returns a URLStreamHandler object. This method must find the appropriate subclass of URLStreamHandler given only the protocol (e.g., *ftp*); that is, it must understand the package and class-naming conventions used for stream handlers. Since URLStreamHandlerFactory is an interface, you can place the createURLStreamHandler( ) method in any convenient class, perhaps the main class of your application.

When it first encounters a protocol, Java looks for URLStreamHandler classes in this order:

1. First, Java checks to see whether a URLStreamHandlerFactory is installed. If it is, the factory is asked for a URLStreamHandler for the protocol.

2. If a URLStreamHandlerFactory isn't installed or if Java can't find a URL-StreamHandler for the protocol, Java looks in the packages named in the java. protocol.handler.pkgs system property for a sub-package that shares the protocol name and a class called Handler. The value of this property is a list of package

names separated by a vertical bar (|). Thus, to indicate that Java should seek protocol handlers in the `com.macfaq.net.www` and `org.cafeaulait.protocols` packages, you would add this line to your properties file:

```
java.protocol.handler.pkgs=com.macfaq.net.www|org.cafeaulait.protocols
```

To find an FTP protocol handler (for example), Java first looks for the class `com.macfaq.net.www.ftp.Handler`. If that's not found, Java next tries to instantiate `org.cafeaulait.protocols.ftp.Handler`.

3. Finally, if all else fails, Java looks for a `URLStreamHandler` named `sun.net.www.protocol.`*name*`.Handler`, where *name* is replaced by the name of the protocol; for example, `sun.net.www.protocol.ftp.Handler`.

 In the early days of Java (circa 1995), Sun promised that protocols could be installed at runtime from the server that used them. For instance, in 1996, James Gosling and Henry McGilton wrote: "The HotJava Browser is given a reference to an object (a URL). If the handler for that protocol is already loaded, it will be used. If not, the HotJava Browser will search first the local system and then the system that is the target of the URL." (*The Java Language Environment, A White Paper*, May 1996, *http://java.sun.com/docs/white/langenv/HotJava.doc1.html*) However, the loading of protocol handlers from web sites was never implemented, and Sun doesn't talk much about it anymore.

Most of the time, an end user who wants to permanently install an extra protocol handler in a program such as HotJava will place the necessary classes in the program's class path and add the package prefix to the `java.protocol.handler.pkgs` property. However, a programmer who just wants to add a custom protocol handler to their program at compile time will write and install a `URLStreamHandlerFactory` that knows how to find their custom protocol handlers. The factory can tell an application to look for `URLStreamHandler` classes in any place that's convenient: on a web site, in the same directory as the application, or somewhere in the user's class path.

When each of these classes has been written and compiled, you're ready to write an application that uses the new protocol handler. Assuming that you're using a `URLStreamHandlerFactory`, pass the factory object to the static `URL.setURLStreamHandlerFactory( )` method like this:

```
URL.setURLStreamHandlerFactory(new MyURLStreamHandlerFactory( ));
```

This method can be called only once in the lifetime of an application. If it is called a second time, it will throw an `Error`. Untrusted code will generally not be allowed to install factories or change the `java.protocol.handler.pkgs` property. Consequently, protocol handlers are primarily of use to standalone applications such as HotJava; Netscape and Internet Explorer use their own native C code instead of Java to handle protocols, so they're limited to a fixed set of protocols.

To summarize, here's the sequence of events:

1. The program constructs a URL object.

2. The constructor uses the arguments it's passed to determine the protocol part of the URL, e.g., *http*.

3. The URL( ) constructor tries to find a URLStreamHandler for the given protocol like this:

   a. If the protocol has been used before, the URLStreamHandler object is retrieved from a cache.

   b. Otherwise, if a URLStreamHandlerFactory has been set, the protocol string is passed to the factory's createURLStreamHandler( ) method.

   c. If the protocol hasn't been seen before and there's no URLStreamHandlerFactory, the constructor attempts to instantiate a URLStreamHandler object named *protocol*.Handler in one of the packages listed in the java. protocol.handler.pkgs property.

   d. Failing that, the constructor attempts to instantiate a URLStreamHandler object named *protocol*.Handler in the sun.net.www.protocol package.

   e. If any of these attempts succeed in retrieving a URLStreamHandler object, the URL constructor sets the URL object's handler field. If none of the attempts succeed, the constructor throws a MalformedURLException.

4. The program calls the URL object's openConnection( ) method.

5. The URL object asks the URLStreamHandler to return a URLConnection object appropriate for this URL. If there's any problem, an IOException is thrown. Otherwise, a URLConnection object is returned.

6. The program uses the methods of the URLConnection class to interact with the remote resource.

Instead of calling openConnection( ) in step 4, the program can call getContent( ) or getInputStream( ). In this case, the URLStreamHandler still instantiates a URLConnection object of the appropriate class. However, instead of returning the URLConnection object itself, the URLStreamHandler returns the result of URLConnection's getContent( ) or getInputStream( ) method.

The URLStreamHandler Class

The abstract URLStreamHandler class is a superclass for classes that handle specific protocols—for example, HTTP. You rarely call the methods of the URLStreamHandler class; they are called by other methods in the URL and URLConnection classes. By overriding the URLStreamHandler methods in your own subclass, you teach the URL class how to handle new protocols. Therefore, I'll focus on overriding the methods of URLStreamHandler rather than calling the methods.

The Constructor

You do not create URLStreamHandler objects directly. Instead, when a URL is constructed with a protocol that hasn't been seen before, Java asks the application's URLStreamHandlerFactory to create the appropriate URLStreamHandler subclass for the protocol. If that fails, Java guesses at the fully package-qualified name of the URLStreamHandler class and uses Class.forName( ) to attempt to construct such an object. This means each concrete subclass should have a noargs constructor. The single constructor for URLStreamHandler doesn't take any arguments:

```
public URLStreamHandler( )
```

Because URLStreamHandler is an abstract class, this constructor is never called directly; it is only called from the constructors of subclasses.

Methods for Parsing URLs

The first responsibility of a URLStreamHandler is to split a string representation of a URL into its component parts and use those parts to set the various fields of the URL object. The parseURL( ) method splits the URL into parts, possibly using setURL( ) to assign values to the URL's fields. It is very difficult to imagine a situation in which you would call parseURL( ) directly; instead, you override it to change the behavior of the URL class.

protected void parseURL(URL u, String spec, int start, int limit)

This method parses the String spec into a URL u. All characters in the spec string before start should already have been parsed into the URL u. Characters after limit are ignored. Generally, the protocol will have already been parsed and stored in u before this method is invoked, and start will be adjusted so that it starts with the character after the colon that delimits the protocol.

The task of parseURL( ) is to set u's protocol, host, port, file, and ref fields. It can assume that any parts of the String that are before start and after limit have already been parsed or can be ignored.

The parseURL( ) method that Java supplies assumes that the URL looks more or less like an *http* or other hierarchical URL:

```
protocol://www.host.com:port/directory/another_directory/file#fragmentID
```

This works for *ftp* and *gopher* URLs. It does not work for *mailto* or *news* URLs and may not be appropriate for any new URL schemes you define. If the protocol handler uses URLs that fit this hierarchical form, you don't have to override parseURL( ) at all; the method inherited from URLStreamHandler works just fine. If the URLs are completely different, you must supply a parseURL( ) method that parses the URL completely. However, there's often a middle ground that can make your task easier. If your URL looks somewhat like a standard URL, you can implement a parseURL( )

method that handles the nonstandard portion of the URL and then calls super.parseURL() to do the rest of the work, setting the offset and limit arguments to indicate the portion of the URL that you didn't parse.

For example, a *mailto* URL looks like *mailto:elharo@metalab.unc.edu*. First, you need to figure out how to map this into the URL class's protocol, host, port, file, and ref fields. The protocol is clearly mailto. Everything after the @ can be the host. The hard question is what to do with the username. Since a *mailto* URL really doesn't have a file portion, we will use the URL class's file field to hold the username. The ref can be set to the empty string or null. The parseURL() method that follows implements this scheme:

```
public void parseURL(URL u, String spec, int start, int limit) {

    String protocol = u.getProtocol();
    String host = "";
    int port = u.getPort();
    String file = ""; // really username
    String fragmentID  = null;

    if( start < limit) {
      String address = spec.substring(start, limit);
      int atSign = address.indexOf('@');
      if (atSign >= 0) {
        host = address.substring(atSign+1);
        file = address.substring(0, atSign);
      }
    }
    this.setURL(u, protocol, host, port, file, fragmentID );
  }
```

Rather than borrowing an unused field from the URL object, it's possibly a better idea to store protocol-specific parts of the URL, such as the username, in fields of the URLStreamHandler subclass. The disadvantage of this approach is that such fields can be seen only by your own code; in this example, you couldn't use the getFile() method in the URL class to retrieve the username. Here's a version of parseURL() that stores the username in a field of the Handler subclass. When the connection is opened, the username can be copied into the MailtoURLConnection object that results. That class would provide some sort of getUserName() method:

```
String username = "";

public void parseURL(URL u, String spec, int start, int limit) {

    String protocol = u.getProtocol();
    String host = "";
    int port = u.getPort();
    String file = "";
    String fragmentID  = null;

    if( start < limit) {
```

```
        String address = spec.substring(start, limit);
        int atSign = address.indexOf('@');
        if (atSign >= 0) {
          host = address.substring(atSign+1);
          this.username = address.substring(0, atSign);
        }
      }
      this.setURL(u, protocol, host, port, file, fragmentID );

    }
```

protected String toExternalForm(URL u)

This method puts the pieces of the URL u—that is, its protocol, host, port, file, and ref fields—back together in a String. A class that overrides parseURL( ) should also override toExternalForm( ). Here's a toExternalForm( ) method for a *mailto* URL; it assumes that the username has been stored in the URL's file field:

```
    protected String toExternalForm(URL u) {

      return "mailto:" + u.getFile() + "@" + u.getHost();

    }
```

Since toExternalForm( ) is protected, you probably won't call this method directly. However, it is called by the public toExternalForm( ) and toString( ) methods of the URL class, so any change you make here is reflected when you convert URL objects to strings.

protected void setURL(URL u, String protocol, String host, int port, String authority, String userInfo, String path, String query, String fragmentID) // Java 1.3

This method sets the protocol, host, port, authority, userInfo, path, query, and ref fields of the URL u to the given values. parseURL( ) uses this method to set these fields to the values it has found by parsing the URL. You need to call this method at the end of the parseURL( ) method when you subclass URLStreamHandler.

This method is a little flaky, since the host, port, and user info together make up the authority. In the event of a conflict between them, they're all stored separately, but the host, port, and user info are used in preference to the authority when deciding which site to connect to.

This is actually quite relevant to the *mailto* example, since *mailto* URLs often have query strings that indicate the subject or other header; for example, *mailto: elharo@metalab.unc.edu?subject=JavaReading*. Here the query string is *subject=JavaReading*. Rewriting the parseURL( ) method to support *mailto* URLs in this format, the result looks like this:

```
    public void parseURL(URL u, String spec, int start, int limit) {

      String protocol   = u.getProtocol();
      String host       = "";
```

```
int port        = u.getPort();
String file     = "";
String userInfo = null;
String query    = null;
String fragmentID = null;

if (start < limit) {
  String address = spec.substring(start, limit);
  int atSign = address.indexOf('@');
  int questionMark = address.indexOf('?');
  int hostEnd = questionMark >= 0 ? questionMark : address.length();
  if (atSign >= 0) {
    host = address.substring(atSign+1, hostEnd);
    userInfo = address.substring(0, atSign);
  }
  if (questionMark >= 0 && questionMark > atSign) {
    query = address.substring(questionMark + 1);
  }
}
String authority = "";
if (userInfo != null) authority += userInfo + '@';
authority += host;
if (port >= 0) authority += ":" + port;

this.setURL(u, protocol, host, port, authority, userInfo, file,
  query, fragmentID );

}
```

protected int getDefaultPort( ) // Java 1.3

The getDefaultPort( ) method returns the default port for the protocol, e.g., 80 for HTTP. The default implementation of this method simply returns −1, but each subclass should override that with the appropriate default port for the protocol it handles. For example, here's a getDefaultPort( ) method for the finger protocol that normally operates on port 79:

```
public int getDefaultPort() {
  return 79;
}
```

As well as providing the right port for finger, overriding this method also makes getDefaultPort( ) public. Although there's only a default implementation of this method in Java 1.3, there's no reason you can't provide it in your own subclasses in any version of Java. You simply won't be able to invoke it polymorphically from a reference typed as the superclass.

protected InetAddress getHostAddress(URL u) // Java 1.3

The getHostAddress( ) method returns an InetAddress object pointing to the server in the URL. This requires a DNS lookup, and the method does block while the lookup is made. However, it does not throw any exceptions. If the host can't be located, whether because the URL does not contain host information as a result of a DNS failure or a SecurityException, it simply returns null. The default implementation of this method is sufficient for any reasonable case. It shouldn't be necessary to override it.

protected boolean hostsEqual(URL u1, URL u2) // Java 1.3

The hostsEqual() method determines whether the two URLs refer to the same server. This method does use DNS to look up the hosts. If the DNS lookups succeed, it can tell that, for example, *http://www.ibiblio.org/Dave/this-week.html* and *ftp://metalab.unc.edu/pub/linux/distributions/debian/* are the same host. However, if the DNS lookup fails for any reason, then hostsEqual() falls back to a simple case-insensitive string comparison, in which case it would think these were two different hosts.

The default implementation of this method is sufficient for most cases. You probably won't need to override it. The only case I can imagine where you might want to is if you were trying to make mirror sites on different servers appear equal.

protected boolean sameFile(URL u1, URL u2) // Java 1.3

The sameFile() method determines whether two URLs point to the same file. It does this by comparing the protocol, host, port, and path. The files are considered to be the same only if each of those four pieces is the same. However, it does not consider the query string or the fragment identifier. Furthermore, the hosts are compared by the hostsEqual() method so that *www.ibiblio.org* and *metalab.unc.edu* can be recognized as the same if DNS can resolve them. This is similar to the sameFile() method of the URL class. Indeed, that sameFile() method just calls this sameFile() method.

The default implementation of this method is sufficient for most cases. You probably won't need to override it. You might perhaps want to do so if you need a more sophisticated test that converts paths to canonical paths or follows redirects before determining whether two URLs have the same file part.

protected boolean equals(URL u1, URL u2) // Java 1.3

The final equality method tests almost the entire URL, including protocol, host, file, path, and fragment identifier. Only the query string is ignored. All five of these must be equal for the two URLs to be considered equal. Everything except the fragment identifier is compared by the sameFile() method, so overriding that method changes the behavior of this one. The fragment identifiers are compared by simple string equality. Since the sameFile() method uses hostsEqual() to compare hosts, this method does too. Thus, it performs a DNS lookup if possible and may block. The equals() method of the URL class calls this method to compare two URL objects for equality. Again, you probably won't need to override this method. The default implementation should suffice for most purposes.

protected int hashCode(URL u) // Java 1.3

URLStreamHandlers can change the default hash code calculation by overriding this method. You should do this if you override equals( ), sameFile( ), or hostsEqual( ) to make sure that two equal URL objects will have the same hash code, and two unequal URL objects will not have the same hash code, at least to a very high degree of probability.

A Method for Connecting

The second responsibility of a URLStreamHandler is to create a URLConnection object appropriate to the URL. This is done with the abstract openConnection( ) method.

protected abstract URLConnection openConnection(URL u) throws IOException

This method must be overridden in each subclass of URLConnection. It takes a single argument, u, which is the URL to connect to. It returns an unopened URLConnection, directed at the resource u points to. Each subclass of URLStreamHandler should know how to find the right subclass of URLConnection for the protocol it handles.

The openConnection( ) method is protected, so you usually do not call it directly; it is called by the openConnection( ) method of a URL class. The URL u that is passed as an argument is the URL that needs a connection. Subclasses override this method to handle a specific protocol. The subclass's openConnection( ) method is usually extremely simple; in most cases, it just calls the constructor for the appropriate subclass of URLConnection. For example, a URLStreamHandler for the *mailto* protocol might have an openConnection( ) method that looks like this:

```
protected URLConnection openConnection(URL u) throws IOException {
  return new com.macfaq.net.www.protocol.MailtoURLConnection(u);
}
```

Example 16-1 demonstrates a complete URLStreamHandler for *mailto* URLs. The name of the class is Handler, following Sun's naming conventions. It assumes the existence of a MailtoURLConnection class.

Example 16-1. A mailto URLStreamHandler

```
package com.macfaq.net.www.protocol.mailto;

import java.net.*;
import java.io.*;
import java.util.*;

public class Handler extends URLStreamHandler {

  protected URLConnection openConnection(URL u) throws IOException {
    return new MailtoURLConnection(u);
  }
```

Example 16-1. A mailto URLStreamHandler (continued)

```
public void parseURL(URL u, String spec, int start, int limit) {

    String protocol  = u.getProtocol( );
    String host       = "";
    int    port       = u.getPort( );
    String file       = ""; // really username
    String userInfo   = null;
    String authority  = null;
    String query      = null;
    String fragmentID = null;

    if( start < limit) {
      String address = spec.substring(start, limit);
      int atSign = address.indexOf('@');
      if (atSign >= 0) {
        host = address.substring(atSign+1);
        file = address.substring(0, atSign);
      }
    }

    // For Java 1.2 comment out this next line
    this.setURL(u, protocol, host, port, authority,
                    userInfo, file, query, fragmentID );

    // In Java 1.2 and earlier uncomment the following line:
    // this.setURL(u, protocol, host, port, file, fragmentID );

  }

  protected String toExternalForm(URL u) {

    return "mailto:" + u.getFile() + "@" + u.getHost( );;

  }
}
```

protected URLConnection openConnection(URL u, Proxy p) throws IOException
// Java 1.5

Java 1.5 overloads the openConnection( ) method to allow you to specify a proxy server for the connection. The java.net.Proxy class (also new in Java 1.5) encapsulates the address of a proxy server. Rather than connecting to the host directly, this URLConnection connects to the specified proxy server, which relays data back and forth between the client and the server. Protocols that do not support proxies can simply ignore the second argument.

Normally connections are opened with the usual proxy server settings within that VM. Calling this method is only necessary if you want to use a different proxy server. If you want to bypass the usual proxy server and connect directly instead, pass the constant Proxy.NO_PROXY as the second argument.

Writing a Protocol Handler

To demonstrate a complete protocol handler, let's write one for the finger protocol defined in RFC 1288 and introduced in Chapter 9. Finger is a relatively simple protocol compared to JDK-supported protocols such as HTTP and FTP. The client connects to port 79 on the server and sends a list of usernames followed by a carriage return/linefeed pair. The server responds with ASCII text containing information about each of the named users or, if no names are listed, a list of the currently logged in users. For example:

```
% telnet rama.poly.edu 79
Trying 128.238.10.212...
Connected to rama.poly.edu.
Escape character is '^]'.

Login     Name            TTY      Idle   When    Where
jacola    Jane Colaginae  *pts/7          Tue 08:01  208.34.37.104
marcus    Marcus Tullius   pts/15  13d Tue 17:33  farm-dialup11.poly.e
matewan   Sepin Matewan   *pts/17  17: Thu 15:32  128.238.10.177
hengpi    Heng Pin        *pts/10         Tue 10:36  128.238.18.119
nadats    Nabeel Datsun    pts/12  56 Mon 10:38  128.238.213.227
matewan   Sepin Matewan   *pts/8   4 Sun 18:39  128.238.10.177
Connection closed by foreign host.
```

Or to request information about a specific user:

```
% telnet rama.poly.edu 79
Trying 128.238.10.212...
Connected to rama.poly.edu.
Escape character is '^]'.
marcus
Login     Name            TTY      Idle   When    Where
marcus    Marcus Tullius   pts/15  13d Tue 17:33  farm-dialup11.poly.e
```

Since there's no standard for the format of a finger URL, we will start by creating one. Ideally, this should look as much like an *http* URL as possible. Therefore, we will implement a finger URL like this:

```
finger://hostname:port/usernames
```

Second, we need to determine the content type returned by the finger protocol's getContentType( ) method. New protocols such as HTTP use MIME headers to indicate the content type; in these cases, you do not need to override the default getContentType( ) method provided by the URLConnection class. However, since most protocols precede MIME, you often need to specify the MIME type explicitly or use the static methods URLConnection.guessContentTypeFromName(String name) and URLConnection.guessContentTypeFromStream(InputStream in) to make an educated guess. This example doesn't need anything so complicated, however. A finger server returns ASCII text, so the getContentType( ) method should return the string text/plain. The text/plain MIME type has the advantage that Java already understands it. In the next chapter, you'll learn how to write content handlers that let Java understand additional MIME types.

Example 16-2 is a `FingerURLConnection` class that subclasses `URLConnection`. This class overrides the `getContentType()` and `getInputStream()` methods of `URLConnection` and implements `connect()`. It also has a constructor that builds a new `URLConnection` from a URL.

Example 16-2. The FingerURLConnection class

```
package com.macfaq.net.www.protocol.finger;

import java.net.*;
import java.io.*;

public class FingerURLConnection extends URLConnection {

  private Socket connection = null;

  public final static int DEFAULT_PORT = 79;

  public FingerURLConnection(URL u) {
    super(u);
  }

  public synchronized InputStream getInputStream() throws IOException {

    if (!connected) this.connect();
    InputStream in = this.connection.getInputStream();
    return in;

  }

  public String getContentType() {
    return "text/plain";
  }
  public synchronized void connect() throws IOException {

    if (!connected) {
      int port = url.getPort();
      if ( port < 1 || port > 65535) {
        port = DEFAULT_PORT;
      }
      this.connection = new Socket(url.getHost(), port);
      OutputStream out = this.connection.getOutputStream();
      String names = url.getFile();
      if (names != null && !names.equals("")) {
        // delete initial /
        names = names.substring(1);
        names = URLDecoder.decode(names);
        byte[] result;
        try {
          result = names.getBytes("ASCII");
```

Example 16-2. The FingerURLConnection class (continued)

```
      }
      catch (UnsupportedEncodingException ex) {
        result = names.getBytes( );
      }
      out.write(result);
    }
    out.write('\r');
    out.write('\n');
    out.flush( );
    this.connected = true;
  }
 }
}
```

This class has two fields. connection is a Socket between the client and the server. Both the getInputStream( ) method and the connect( ) method need access to this field, so it can't be a local variable. The second field is DEFAULT_PORT, a final static int, which contains the finger protocol's default port; this port is used if the URL does not specify the port explicitly.

The class's constructor holds no surprises. It just calls the superclass's constructor with the same argument, the URL u. The connect( ) method opens a connection to the specified server on the specified port or, if no port is specified, to the default finger port, 79. It sends the necessary request to the finger server. If any usernames were specified in the file part of the URL, they're sent. Otherwise, a blank line is sent. Assuming the connection is successfully opened (no exception is thrown), it sets the boolean field connected to true. Recall from the previous chapter that connected is a protected field in java.net.URLConnection, which is inherited by this subclass. The Socket that connect( ) opens is stored in the field connection for later use by getInputStream( ). The connect( ) and getInputStream( ) methods are synchronized to avoid a possible race condition on the connected variable.

The getContentType( ) method returns a String containing a MIME type for the data. This is used by the getContent( ) method of java.net.URLConnection to select the appropriate content handler. The data returned by a finger server is almost always ASCII text or some reasonable approximation thereof, so this getContentType( ) method always returns text/plain. The getInputStream( ) method returns an InputStream, which it gets from the Socket that connect created. If the connection has not already been established when getInputStream( ) is called, the method calls connect( ) itself.

Once you have a URLConnection, you need a subclass of URLStreamHandler that knows how to handle a finger server. This class needs an openConnection( ) method that builds a new FingerURLConnection from a URL. Since we defined the *finger* URL as a hierarchical URL, we don't need to implement a parseURL( ) method. Example 16-3 is a stream handler for the finger protocol. For the moment, we're going to use Sun's convention for naming protocol handlers; we call this class Handler and place it in the package com.macfaq.net.www.protocol.finger.

Example 16-3. The finger handler class

```
package com.macfaq.net.www.protocol.finger;

import java.net.*;
import java.io.*;

public class Handler extends URLStreamHandler {

  public int getDefaultPort( ) {
    return 79;
  }

  protected URLConnection openConnection(URL u) throws IOException {
    return new FingerURLConnection(u);
  }

}
```

You can use HotJava to test this protocol handler. Add the following line to your *.hotjava/properties* file or some other place from which HotJava will load it:

```
java.protocol.handler.pkgs=com.macfaq.net.www.protocol
```

Some (but not all) versions of HotJava may also allow you to set the property from the command line:

```
% hotjava -Djava.protocol.handler.pkgs=com.macfaq.net.www.protocol
```

You also need to make sure that your classes are somewhere in HotJava's class path. HotJava does not normally use the CLASSPATH environment variable to look for classes, so just putting them someplace where the JDK or JRE can find them may not be sufficient. Using HotJava 3.0 on Windows with the JDK 1.3, I was able to put my classes in the *jdk1.3/jre/lib/classes* folder. Your mileage may vary depending on the version of HotJava you're using with which version of the JDK on which platform.

Run it and ask for a URL of a site running finger, such as *utopia.poly.edu*. Figure 16-1 shows the result.

More Protocol Handler Examples and Techniques

Now that you've seen how to write one protocol handler, it's not at all difficult to write more. Remember the five basic steps of creating a new protocol handler:

1. Design a URL for the protocol if a standard URL for that protocol doesn't already exist. As of mid-2004, the official list of URL schemes at the IANA (*http://www.iana.org/assignments/uri-schemes*) includes only 43 different URL schemes and reserves three more. For anything else, you need to define your own.

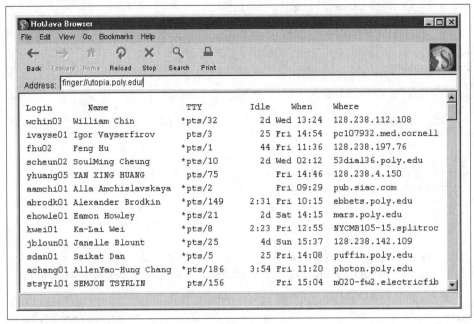

Figure 16-1. HotJava using the finger protocol handler

2. Decide what MIME type should be returned by the protocol handler's getContentType( ) method. The text/plain content type is often appropriate for legacy protocols. Another option is to convert the incoming data to HTML inside getInputStream( ) and return text/html. Binary data often uses one of the many application types. In some cases, you may be able to use the URLConnection. guessContentTypeFromName( ) or URLConnection.guessContentTypeFromStream( ) methods to determine the right MIME type.

3. Write a subclass of URLConnection that understands this protocol. It should implement the connect( ) method and may override the getContentType( ), getOutputStream( ), and getInputStream( ) methods of URLConnection. It also needs a constructor that builds a new URLConnection from a URL.

4. Write a subclass of URLStreamHandler with an openConnection( ) method that knows how to return a new instance of your subclass of URLConnection. Also provide a getDefaultPort( ) method that returns the well-known port for the protocol. If your URL is not hierarchical, override parseURL( ) and toExternalForm( ) as well.

5. Implement the URLStreamHandlerFactory interface and the createStreamHandler( ) method in a convenient class.

Let's look at handlers for two more protocols, daytime and chargen, which will bring up different challenges.

A daytime Protocol Handler

For a daytime protocol handler, let's say that the URL should look like *daytime:///
vision.poly.edu*. We'll allow for nonstandard port assignments in the same way as
with HTTP: follow the hostname with a colon and the port (*daytime:///vision.poly.
edu:2082*). Finally, allow a terminating slash and ignore everything following the
slash. For example, *daytime:///vision.poly.edu/index.html* is equivalent to *daytime:///
vision.poly.edu*. This is similar enough to an *http* URL that the default
toExternalForm( ) and parseURL( ) methods will work.

Although the content returned by the daytime protocol is really text/plain, this protocol handler is going to reformat the data into an HTML page. Then it can return a
content type of text/html and let the web browser display it more dramatically. The
resulting HTML looks like this:

```
<html><head><title>The Time at metalab.unc.edu</title></head><body>
<h1>Fri Oct 29 14:32:07 1999</h1>
</body></html>
```

The trick is that the page can be broken up into three different strings:

- Everything before the time
- The time
- Everything after the time

The first and the third strings can be calculated before the connection is even
opened. We'll formulate these as byte arrays of ASCII text and use them to create
two ByteArrayInputStreams. Then we'll use a SequenceInputStream to combine those
two streams with the data actually returned from the server. Example 16-4 demonstrates. This is a neat trick for protocols such as daytime that return a very limited
amount of data; it can be inserted in a single place in an HTML document. Protocols such as finger that return more complex and less predictable text might need to
use a FilterInputStream that inserts the HTML on the fly instead. And of course, a
third possibility is to simply return a custom content type and use a custom content
handler to display it. This third option is explored in the next chapter.

Example 16-4. The DaytimeURLConnection class

```
package com.macfaq.net.www.protocol.daytime;

import java.net.*;
import java.io.*;

public class DaytimeURLConnection extends URLConnection {

  private Socket connection = null;
  public final static int DEFAULT_PORT = 13;

  public DaytimeURLConnection (URL u) {
    super(u);
  }
```

Example 16-4. The DaytimeURLConnection class (continued)

```java
public synchronized InputStream getInputStream( ) throws IOException {

  if (!connected)  connect( );

  String header = "<html><head><title>The Time at "
   + url.getHost( ) + "</title></head><body><h1>";
  String footer = "</h1></body></html>";
  InputStream in1 = new ByteArrayInputStream(header.getBytes("8859_1"));
  InputStream in2 = this.connection.getInputStream( );
  InputStream in3 = new ByteArrayInputStream(footer.getBytes("8859_1"));

  SequenceInputStream result = new SequenceInputStream(in1, in2);
  result = new SequenceInputStream(result, in3);
  return result;

}

public String getContentType( ) {
  return "text/html";
}

public synchronized void connect( ) throws IOException {

  if (!connected) {
    int port = url.getPort( );
    if ( port <= 0 || port > 65535) {
      port = DEFAULT_PORT;
    }
    this.connection = new Socket(url.getHost( ), port);
    this.connected = true;
  }
}
}
```

This class declares two fields. The first is connection, which is a Socket between the client and the server. The second field is DEFAULT_PORT, a final static int variable that holds the default port for the daytime protocol (port 13) and is used if the URL doesn't specify the port explicitly.

The constructor has no surprises. It just calls the superclass's constructor with the same argument, the URL u. The connect( ) method opens a connection to the specified server on the specified port (or, if no port is specified, to the default port); if the connection opens successfully, connect( ) sets the boolean variable connected to true. Recall from the previous chapter that connected is a protected field in URLConnection that is inherited by this subclass. The Socket that's opened by this method is stored in the connection field for later use by getInputStream( ).

The getContentType( ) method returns a String containing a MIME type for the data. This method is called by the getContent( ) method of URLConnection to select the appropriate content handler. The getInputStream( ) method reformats the text into HTML, so the getContentType( ) method returns text/html.

The getInputStream( ) method builds a SequenceInputStream out of several string literals, the host property of url, and the actual stream provided by the Socket connecting the client to the server. If the socket is not connected when this method is called, the method calls connect( ) to establish the connection.

Next, you need a subclass of URLStreamHandler that knows how to handle a daytime server. This class needs an openConnection( ) method that builds a new DaytimeURLConnection from a URL and a getDefaultPort( ) method that returns the well-known daytime port 13. Since the daytime URL has been made similar to an *http* URL, we don't need to override parseURL( ); once we have written openConnection( ), we're done. Example 16-5 shows the daytime protocol's URLStreamHandler.

Example 16-5. The DaytimeURLStreamHandler class

```
package com.macfaq.net.www.protocol.daytime;

import java.net.*;
import java.io.*;

public class Handler extends URLStreamHandler {

  public int getDefaultPort( ) {
    return 13;
  }

  protected URLConnection openConnection(URL u) throws IOException {
    return new DaytimeURLConnection(u);
  }
}
```

Since we've used the same package-naming convention here as for the previous finger protocol handler, no further changes to HotJava's properties need to be made to let HotJava find this. Just compile the files, put the classes somewhere in HotJava's class path, and load a URL that points to an active daytime server. Figure 16-2 demonstrates.

A chargen Protocol Handler

The chargen protocol, defined in RFC 864, is a very simple protocol designed for testing clients. The server listens for connections on port 19. When a client connects, the server sends an endless stream of characters until the client disconnects. Any input from the client is ignored. The RFC does not specify which character sequence to send but recommends that the server use a recognizable pattern. One

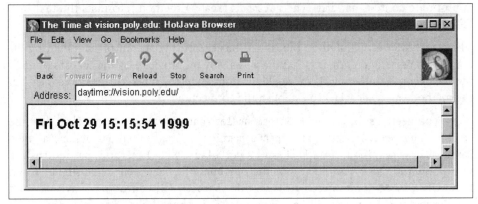

Figure 16-2. HotJava using the daytime protocol handler

common pattern is rotating, 72-character carriage return/linefeed delimited lines of the 95 ASCII printing characters, like this:

```
!"#$%&'( )*+,-./0123456789:;<=>?@ABCDEFGHIJKLMNOPQRSTUVWXYZ[\]^_`abcdefgh
"#$%&'( )*+,-./0123456789:;<=>?@ABCDEFGHIJKLMNOPQRSTUVWXYZ[\]^_`abcdefghi
#$%&'( )*+,-./0123456789:;<=>?@ABCDEFGHIJKLMNOPQRSTUVWXYZ[\]^_`abcdefghij
$%&'( )*+,-./0123456789:;<=>?@ABCDEFGHIJKLMNOPQRSTUVWXYZ[\]^_`abcdefghijk
%&'( )*+,-./0123456789:;<=>?@ABCDEFGHIJKLMNOPQRSTUVWXYZ[\]^_`abcdefghijkl
&'( )*+,-./0123456789:;<=>?@ABCDEFGHIJKLMNOPQRSTUVWXYZ[\]^_`abcdefghijklm
'( )*+,-./0123456789:;<=>?@ABCDEFGHIJKLMNOPQRSTUVWXYZ[\]^_`abcdefghijklmn
( )*+,-./0123456789:;<=>?@ABCDEFGHIJKLMNOPQRSTUVWXYZ[\]^_`abcdefghijklmno
```

The big trick with this protocol is deciding when to stop. A TCP chargen server sends an unlimited amount of data. Most web browsers don't deal well with this. HotJava won't even attempt to display a file until it sees the end of the stream. Consequently, the first thing we'll need is a `FilterInputStream` subclass that cuts off the server (or at least starts ignoring it) after a certain amount of data has been sent. Example 16-6 is such a class.

Example 16-6. FiniteInputStream

```java
package com.macfaq.io;

import java.io.*;

public class FiniteInputStream extends FilterInputStream {

  private int limit = 8192;
  private int bytesRead = 0;

  public FiniteInputStream(InputStream in) {
    this(in, 8192);
  }

  public FiniteInputStream(InputStream in, int limit) {
    super(in);
```

Example 16-6. FiniteInputStream (continued)

```java
    this.limit = limit;
  }

  public int read( ) throws IOException {

    if (bytesRead >= limit) return -1;
    int c = in.read( );
    bytesRead++;
    return c;

  }

  public int read(byte[] data) throws IOException {
    return this.read(data, 0, data.length);
  }

  public int read(byte[] data, int offset, int length)
   throws IOException {

    if (data == null) throw new NullPointerException( );
    else if ((offset < 0) || (offset > data.length) || (length < 0) ||
     ((offset + length) > data.length) || ((offset + length) < 0)) {
       throw new IndexOutOfBoundsException( );
    }
    else if (length == 0) {
      return 0;
    }

    if (bytesRead >= limit) return -1;
    else if (bytesRead + length > limit) {
      int numToRead = bytesRead + length - limit;
      int numRead = in.read(data, offset, numToRead);
      if (numRead == -1) return -1;
      bytesRead += numRead;
      return numRead;
    }
    else { // will not exceed limit
      int numRead = in.read(data, offset, length);
      if (numRead == -1) return -1;
      bytesRead += numRead;
      return numRead;
    }
  }

  public int available( ) throws IOException {
    if (bytesRead >= limit) return 1;
    else return in.available( );
  }
}
```

Next, since there's no standard for the format of a chargen URL, we have to create one. Ideally, this should look as much like an *http* URL as possible. Therefore, we will implement a chargen URL like this:

```
chargen://hostname:port
```

Second, we need to choose the content type to be returned by the chargen protocol handler's getContentType( ) method. A chargen server returns ASCII text, so the getContentType( ) method should return the string text/plain. The advantage of the text/plain MIME type is that Java already understands it.

Example 16-7 is a ChargenURLConnection class that subclasses URLConnection. This class overrides the getContentType( ) and getInputStream( ) methods of URLConnection and implements connect( ). It also has a constructor that builds a new URLConnection from a URL.

Example 16-7. The ChargenURLConnection class

```
package com.macfaq.net.www.protocol.chargen;

import java.net.*;
import java.io.*;
import com.macfaq.io.*;

public class ChargenURLConnection extends URLConnection {

  private Socket connection = null;

  public final static int DEFAULT_PORT = 19;

  public ChargenURLConnection(URL u) {
    super(u);
  }

  public synchronized InputStream getInputStream( ) throws IOException {

    if (!connected) this.connect( );
    return new FiniteInputStream(this.connection.getInputStream( ));

  }

  public String getContentType( ) {
    return "text/plain";
  }

  public synchronized void connect( ) throws IOException {

    if (!connected) {
      int port = url.getPort( );
      if ( port < 1 || port > 65535) {
        port = DEFAULT_PORT;
      }
      this.connection = new Socket(url.getHost( ), port);
```

Example 16-7. The ChargenURLConnection class (continued)

```
      this.connected = true;
    }
  }
}
```

This class has two fields. `connection` is a `Socket` between the client and the server. The second field is `DEFAULT_PORT`, a `final static int` that contains the chargen protocol's default port; this port is used if the URL does not specify the port explicitly.

The class's constructor just passes the URL `u` to the superclass's constructor. The `connect()` method opens a connection to the specified server on the specified port (or, if no port is specified, to the default chargen port, 19) and, assuming the connection is successfully opened, sets the boolean field `connected` to `true`. The `Socket` that `connect()` opens is stored in the field `connection` for later use by `getInputStream()`. The `connect()` method is synchronized to avoid a possible race condition on the `connected` variable.

The `getContentType()` method returns a `String` containing a MIME type for the data. The data returned by a chargen server is always ASCII text, so this `getContentType()` method always returns `text/plain`.

The `getInputStream()` connects if necessary, then gets the `InputStream` from `this. connection`. Rather than returning it immediately, `getInputStream()` first chains it to a `FiniteInputStream`.

Now that we have a `URLConnection`, we need a subclass of `URLStreamHandler` that knows how to handle a chargen server. This class needs an `openConnection()` method that builds a new `ChargenURLConnection` from a URL and a `getDefaultPort()` method that returns the well-known chargen port. Since we defined the *chargen* URL so that it is similar to an *http* URL, we don't need to implement a `parseURL()` method. Example 16-8 is a stream handler for the chargen protocol.

Example 16-8. The chargen Handler class

```
package com.macfaq.net.www.protocol.chargen;

import java.net.*;
import java.io.*;

public class Handler extends URLStreamHandler {

  public int getDefaultPort() {
    return 19;
  }

  protected URLConnection openConnection(URL u) throws IOException {
    return new ChargenURLConnection(u);
  }
}
```

You can use HotJava to test this protocol handler. Run it and ask for a URL of a site running a chargen server, such as *vision.poly.edu*. Figure 16-3 shows the result.

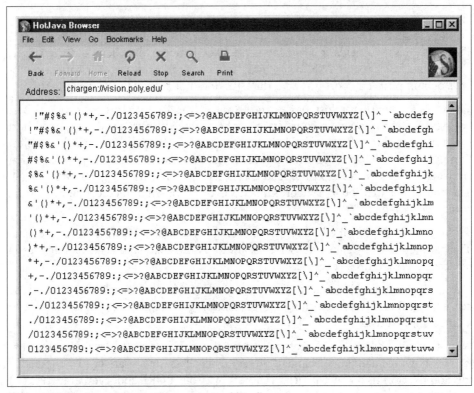

Figure 16-3. HotJava using the chargen protocol handler

The URLStreamHandlerFactory Interface

The last section showed you how to install new protocol handlers that you wrote into HotJava, an application that someone else wrote. However, if you write your own application, you can implement your own scheme for finding and loading protocol handlers. The easiest way is to install a URLStreamHandlerFactory in the application:

```
public abstract interface URLStreamHandlerFactory
```

 Only applications are allowed to install a new URLStreamHandlerFactory. Applets that run in the applet viewer or a web browser must use the URLStreamHandlerFactory that is provided. An attempt to set a different one will fail, either because another factory is already installed or because of a SecurityException.

The URLStreamHandlerFactory interface declares a single method, createURLStreamHandler():

```
public abstract URLStreamHandler createURLStreamHandler(String protocol)
```

This method loads the appropriate protocol handler for the specified protocol. To use this method, write a class that implements the URLStreamHandlerFactory interface and include a createURLStreamHandler() method in that class. The method needs to know how to find the protocol handler for a given protocol. This step is no more complicated than knowing the names and packages of the custom protocols you've implemented.

The createURLStreamHandler() method does not need to know the names of all the installed protocol handlers. If it doesn't recognize a protocol, it should simply return null, which tells Java to follow the default procedure for locating stream handlers; that is, to look for a class named *protocol*.Handler in one of the packages listed in the java.protocol.handler.pkgs system property or in the sun.net.www.protocol package.

To install the stream handler factory, pass an instance of the class that implements the URLStreamHandlerFactory interface to the static method URL. setURLStreamHandlerFactory() at the start of the program. Example 16-9 is a URLStreamHandlerFactory() with a createURLStreamHandler() method that recognizes the finger, daytime, and chargen protocols and returns the appropriate handler from the last several examples. Since these classes are all named Handler, fully package-qualified names are used.

Example 16-9. A URLStreamHandlerFactory for finger, daytime, and chargen

```
package com.macfaq.net.www.protocol;

import java.net.*;

public class NewFactory implements URLStreamHandlerFactory {

  public URLStreamHandler createURLStreamHandler(String protocol) {

    if (protocol.equalsIgnoreCase("finger")) {
      return new com.macfaq.net.www.protocol.finger.Handler();
    }
    else if (protocol.equalsIgnoreCase("chargen")) {
      return new com.macfaq.net.www.protocol.chargen.Handler();
    }
    else if (protocol.equalsIgnoreCase("daytime")) {
      return new com.macfaq.net.www.protocol.daytime.Handler();
    }
    else {
      return null;
    }
  }
}
```

Example 16-9 uses the equalsIgnoreCase( ) method from java.lang.String to test the identity of the protocol; it shouldn't make a difference whether you ask for *finger://rama.poly.edu* or *FINGER://RAMA.POLY.EDU*. If the protocol is recognized, createURLStreamHandler( ) creates an instance of the proper Handler class and returns it; otherwise, the method returns null, which tells the URL class to look for a URLStreamHandler in the standard locations.

Since browsers, HotJava included, generally don't allow you to install your own URLStreamHandlerFactory, this will be of use only in applications. Example 16-10 is a simple character mode program that uses this factory and its associated protocol handlers to print server data on System.out. Notice that it does not import com.macfaq.net.www.protocol.chargen, com.macfaq.net.www.protocol.finger, or com.macfaq.net.www.protocol.daytime. All this program knows is that it has a URL. It does not need to know how that protocol is handled or even how the right URLConnection object is instantiated.

Example 16-10. A SourceViewer program that sets a URLStreamHandlerFactory

```
import java.net.*;
import java.io.*;
import com.macfaq.net.www.protocol.*;

public class SourceViewer4 {
  public static void main (String[] args) {

    URL.setURLStreamHandlerFactory(new NewFactory( ));

    if  (args.length > 0) {
      try {
        //Open the URL for reading
        URL u = new URL(args[0]);
        InputStream in = new BufferedInputStream(u.openStream( ));
        // chain the InputStream to a Reader
        Reader r = new InputStreamReader(in);
        int c;
        while ((c = r.read( )) != -1) {
          System.out.print((char) c);
        }
      }
      catch (MalformedURLException ex) {
        System.err.println(args[0] + " is not a parseable URL");
      }
      catch (IOException ex) {
        System.err.println(ex);
      }
    } //  end if
  } // end main
}  // end SourceViewer3
```

Aside from the one line that sets the URLStreamHandlerFactory, this is almost exactly like the earlier SourceViewer program in Example 7-5 (Chapter 7). For instance, here the program reads from a *finger* URL:

```
D:\JAVA\JNP2\examples\16>java SourceViewer4 finger://rama.poly.edu/
Login        Name            TTY       Idle   When     Where
nadats    Nabeel Datsun      pts/0      55 Fri 16:54   128.238.213.227
marcus    Marcus Tullius    *pts/1      20 Thu 12:12   128.238.10.177
marcus    Marcus Tullius    *pts/5    2:24 Thu 16:42   128.238.10.177
wri       Weber Research Insti pts/10   55 Fri 13:26   rama.poly.edu
jbjovi    John B. Jovien     pts/9     25d Mon 14:54   128.238.213.229
```

Here it reads from a *daytime* URL:

```
% java SourceViewer4 daytime://tock.usno.navy.mil/
<html><head><title>The Time at tock.usno.navy.mil</title></head><body><h1>Fri Oc
t 29 21:22:49 1999
</h1></body></html>
```

However, it still works with all the usual protocol handlers that come bundled with the JDK. For instance here are the first few lines of output when it reads from an *http* URL:

```
% java SourceViewer4 http://www.oreilly.com/oreilly/about.html
<HTML>
<HEAD>
<TITLE>About O'Reilly &amp; Associates</TITLE>
</HEAD>
<BODY LINK="#770000" VLINK="#0000AA" BGCOLOR="#ffffff">

<table border=0 cellspacing=0 cellpadding=0 width=515>
<tr>
<td>
<img src="http://www.oreilly.com/graphics_new/generic_ora_header_wide.gif"
width="515" height="37" ALT="O'Reilly and Associates">
...
```

CHAPTER 17

Content Handlers

Content handlers are one of the ideas that got developers excited about Java in the first place. At the time that Java was first released, Netscape, NCSA, Spyglass, and a few other combatants were fighting a battle over who would control the standards for web browsing. One of the battlegrounds was different browsers' ability to handle various kinds of files. The first browsers understood only HTML. The next generation understood HTML and GIF. JPEG support was soon added. The intensity of this battle meant that new versions of browsers were released every couple of weeks. Netscape made the first attempt to break this infinite loop by introducing plug-ins in Navigator 2.0. Plug-ins are platform-dependent browser extenders written in C that add the ability to view new content types such as Adobe PDF and VRML. However, plug-ins have drawbacks. Each new content type requires the user to download and install a new plug-in, if indeed the right plug-in is even available for the user's platform. To keep up, users had to expend bandwidth and time downloading new browsers and plug-ins, each of which fixed a few bugs and added a few new features.

The Java team saw a way around this dilemma. Their idea was to use Java to download only the parts of the program that had to be updated rather than the entire browser. Furthermore, when the user encountered a web page that used a new content type, the browser could automatically download the code that was needed to view that content type. The user wouldn't have to stop, FTP a plug-in, quit the browser, install the plug-in, restart the browser, and reload the page. The mechanism that the Java team envisioned was the *content handler*. Each new data type that a web site wanted to serve would be associated with a content handler written in Java. The content handler would be responsible for parsing the content and displaying it to the user in the web browser window. The abstract class that content handlers for specific data types such as PNG or RTF would extend was java.net. ContentHandler. James Gosling and Henry McGilton described this scenario in 1996:

> HotJava's dynamic behavior is also used for understanding different types of objects. For example, most Web browsers can understand a small set of image formats (typically GIF, X11 pixmap, and X11 bitmap). If they see some other type, they have no way to deal with it. HotJava, on the other hand, can dynamically link the code from the host that has the image, allowing it to display the new format. So, if someone

invents a new compression algorithm, the inventor just has to make sure that a copy of its Java code is installed on the server that contains the images they want to publish; they don't have to upgrade all the browsers in the world. HotJava essentially upgrades itself on the fly when it sees this new type. (James Gosling and Henry McGilton, *The Java Language Environment, A White Paper*, May 1996, *http://java.sun.com/docs/white/langenv/HotJava.doc1.html*)

Unfortunately, content handlers never really made it out of Sun's white papers into shipping software. The ContentHandler class still exists in the standard library, and it has some uses in custom applications. However, neither HotJava nor any other web browser actually uses it to display content. When HotJava downloads an HTML page or a bitmapped image, it handles it with hardcoded routines that process that particular kind of data. When HotJava encounters an unknown content type, it simply asks the user to locate a helper application that can display the file, almost exactly like a traditional web browser such as Netscape Navigator or Internet Explorer, as Figure 17-1 proves. The promise of dynamically extensible web browsers automatically downloading content handlers for new data types as they encounter them was never realized. Perhaps the biggest problem was that the ContentHandler class was too generic, providing too little information about what kind of object was being downloaded and how it should be displayed.

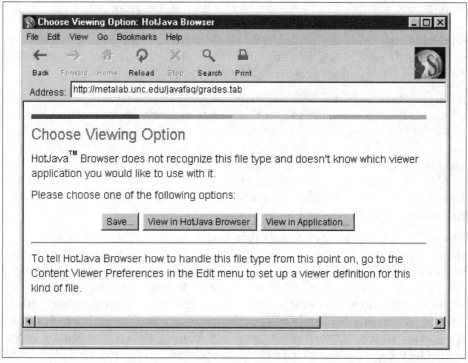

Figure 17-1. HotJava's reaction to an unexpected content type, even though a content handler for this type is installed

A much more robust and better thought-out content handler mechanism is now available under the name JavaBeans Activation Framework. This is a standard extension to Java that provides the necessary API for deciding what to do with arbitrary datatypes at runtime. However, JAF has not yet been used inside web browsers or even widely adopted, although that shouldn't stop you from using it inside your own applications if you find it useful. See *http://java.sun.com/beans/glasgow/jaf.html* for more details.

What Is a Content Handler?

A content handler is an instance of a subclass of `java.net.ContentHandler`:

```
public abstract class ContentHandler extends Object
```

The SAX2 API for XML parsing defines a completely separate interface named `ContentHandler`. This has nothing to do with the content handlers we're discussing in this chapter.

This class knows how to take a `URLConnection` and a MIME type and turn the data coming from the `URLConnection` into a Java object of an appropriate type. Thus, a content handler allows a program to understand new kinds of data. Since Java lowers the bar for writing code below what's needed to write a browser or a Netscape plug-in, the theory is that many different web sites can write custom handlers, rather than having to rely on the overworked browser manufacturers.

Java can already download classes from the Internet. Thus, there isn't much magic to getting it to download a class that can understand a new content type. A content handler is just a *.class* file like any other. The magic is all inside the browser, which knows when and where to request a *.class* file to view a new content type. Of course, some browsers are more magical than others. Currently, the only way to make this work in a browser is in conjunction with an applet that knows how to request the content handler explicitly. It can also be used—in fact, more easily—in a standalone application that ignores browsers completely.

Specifically, a content handler reads data from a `URLConnection` and constructs an object appropriate for the content type from the data. Each subclass of `ContentHandler` handles a specific MIME type and subtype, such as `text/plain` or `image/gif`. Thus, an `image/gif` content handler returns a `URLImageSource` object (a class that implements the `ImageProducer` interface), while a `text/plain` content handler returns a `String`. A database content handler might return a `java.sql.ResultSet` object. An `application/x-macbinhex40` content handler might return a `BinhexDecoder` object written by the same programmer who wrote the `application/x-macbinhex40` content handler.

Content handlers are intimately tied to protocol handlers. In the previous chapter, the getContent( ) method of the URLConnection class returned an InputStream that fed the data from the server to the client. This works for simple protocols that only return ASCII text, such as finger, whois, and daytime. However, returning an input stream doesn't work well for protocols such as FTP, gopher, and HTTP, which can return a lot of different content types, many of which can't be understood as a stream of ASCII text. For protocols like these, getContent( ) needs to check the MIME type and use the createContentHandler( ) method of the application's ContentHandlerFactory to produce a matching content handler. Once a ContentHandler exists, the URLConnection's getContent( ) method calls the ContentHandler's getContent( ) method, which creates the Java object to be returned. Outside of the getContent( ) method of a URLConnection, you rarely, if ever, call any ContentHandler method. Applications should never call the methods of a ContentHandler directly. Instead, they should use the getContent( ) method of URL or URLConnection.

An object that implements the ContentHandlerFactory interface is responsible for choosing the right ContentHandler to go with a MIME type. The static URLConnection.setContentHandlerFactory( ) method installs a ContentHandlerFactory in a program. Only one ContentHandlerFactory may be chosen during the lifetime of an application. When a program starts running, there is no ContentHandlerFactory; that is, the ContentHandlerFactory is null.

When there is no factory, Java looks for content handler classes with the name *type*.*subtype*, where *type* is the MIME type of the content (e.g., text) and *subtype* is the MIME subtype (e.g., html). It looks for these classes first in any packages named by the java.content.handler.pkgs property, then in the sun.net.www.content package. The java.content.handler.pkgs property should contain a list of package prefixes separated from each other by a vertical bar (|). This is similar to how Java finds protocol handlers. For example, if the java.content.handler.pkgs property has the value com.macfaq.net.www.content|org.cafeaulait.content and a program needs a content handler for application/xml files, it first tries to instantiate com.macfaq.net.www.content.application.xml. If that fails, it next tries to instantiate org.cafeaulait.content.application.xml. If that fails, as a last resort, it tries to instantiate sun.net.www.content.application.xml. These conventions are also used to search for a content handler if a ContentHandlerFactory is installed but the createContentHandler( ) method returns null.

To summarize, here's the sequence of events:

1. A URL object is created that points at some Internet resource.

2. The URL's getContent( ) method is invoked.

3. The getContent( ) method of the URL calls the getContent( ) method of its underlying URLConnection.

4. The `URLConnection.getContent()` method calls the nonpublic method `getContentHandler()` to find a content handler for the MIME type and subtype.

5. `getContentHandler()` checks to see whether it already has a handler for this type in its cache. If it does, that handler is returned to `getContent()`. Thus, browsers won't download content handlers for common types such as `text/html` every time the user goes to a new web page.

6. If there wasn't an appropriate `ContentHandler` in the cache and the `ContentHandlerFactory` isn't `null`, `getContentHandler()` calls the `ContentHandlerFactory`'s `createContentHandler()` method to instantiate a new `ContentHandler`. If this is successful, the `ContentHandler` object is returned to `getContent()`.

7. If the `ContentHandlerFactory` is `null` or `createContentHandler()` fails to instantiate a new `ContentHandler`, Java looks for a content handler class named *type.subtype*, where *type* is the MIME type of the content and *subtype* is the MIME subtype in one of the packages named in the `java.content.handler.pkgs` system property. If a content handler is found, it is returned. Otherwise...

8. Java looks for a content handler class named `sun.net.www.content.`*type.subtype*. If it's found, it's returned. Otherwise, `createContentHandler()` returns `null`.

9. If the `ContentHandler` object is not `null`, the `ContentHandler`'s `getContent()` method is called. This method returns an object appropriate for the content type. If the `ContentHandler` is `null`, an `IOException` is thrown.

10. Either the returned object or the exception is passed up the call chain, eventually reaching the method that invoked `getContent()`.

You can affect this chain of events in three ways: first, by constructing a URL and calling its `getContent()` method; second, by creating a new `ContentHandler` subclass that `getContent()` can use; and third, by installing a `ContentHandlerFactory` with `URLConnection.setContentHandlerFactory()`, changing the way the application looks for content handlers.

The ContentHandler Class

A subclass of `ContentHandler` overrides the `getContent()` method to return an object that's the Java equivalent of the content. This method can be quite simple or quite complex, depending almost entirely on the complexity of the content type you're trying to parse. A `text/plain` content handler is quite simple; a `text/rtf` content handler would be very complex.

The `ContentHandler` class has only a simple noargs constructor:

```
public ContentHandler()
```

Since `ContentHandler` is an abstract class, you never call its constructor directly, only from inside the constructors of subclasses.

The primary method of the class, albeit an abstract one, is getContent( ):

```
public abstract Object getContent(URLConnection uc) throws IOException
```

This method is normally called only from inside the getContent( ) method of a URLConnection object. It is overridden in a subclass that is specific to the type of content being handled. getContent( ) should use the URLConnection's InputStream to create an object. There are no rules about what type of object a content handler should return. In general, this depends on what the application requesting the content expects. Content handlers for text-like content bundled with the JDK return some subclass of InputStream. Content handlers for images return ImageProducer objects.

The getContent( ) method of a content handler does not get the full InputStream that the URLConnection has access to. The InputStream that a content handler sees should include only the content's raw data. Any MIME headers or other protocol-specific information that come from the server should be stripped by the URLConnection before it passes the stream to the ContentHandler. A ContentHandler is only responsible for content, not for any protocol overhead that may be present. The URLConnection should have already performed any necessary handshaking with the server and interpreted any headers it sends.

A Content Handler for Tab-Separated Values

To see how content handlers work, let's create a ContentHandler that handles the text/tab-separated-values content type. We aren't concerned with how the tab-separated values get to us. That's for a protocol handler to deal with. All a ContentHandler needs to know is the MIME type and format of the data.

Tab-separated values are produced by many database and spreadsheet programs. A tab-separated file may look something like this (tabs are indicated by arrows).

```
JPE Associates → 341 Lafayette Street, Suite 1025 → New York → NY → 10012
O'Reilly & Associates → 103 Morris Street, Suite A → Sebastopol → CA → 95472
```

In database parlance, each line is a *record*, and the data before each tab is a *field*. It is usually (though not necessarily) true that each field has the same meaning in each record. In the previous example, the first field is the company name.

The first question to ask is: what kind of Java object should we convert the tab-separated values to? The simplest and most general way to store each record is as an array of Strings. Successive records can be collected in a Vector. In many applications, however, you have a great deal more knowledge about the exact format and meaning of the data than we do here. The more you know about the data you're dealing with, the better a ContentHandler you can write. For example, if you know that the data you're downloading represents U.S. addresses, you could define a class like this:

```
public class Address {

    private String name;
    private String street;
```

```
    private String city;
    private String state;
    private String zip;


}
```

This class would also have appropriate constructors and other methods to represent each record. In this example, we don't know anything about the data in advance, or how many records we'll have to store. Therefore, we will take the most general approach and convert each record into an array of strings, using a Vector to store each array until there are no more records. The getContent( ) method can return the Vector of String arrays.

Example 17-1 shows the code for such a ContentHandler. The full package-qualified name is com.macfaq.net.www.content.text.tab_separated_values. This unusual class name follows the naming convention for a content handler for the MIME type text/tab-separated-values. Since MIME types often contain hyphens, as in this example, a convention exists to replace these with the underscore (_). Thus text/tab-separated-values becomes text.tab_separated_values. To install this content handler, all that's needed is to put the compiled *.class* file somewhere the class loader can find it and set the java.content.handler.pkgs property to com.macfaq.net.www.content.

Example 17-1. A ContentHandler for text/tab-separated-values

```java
package com.macfaq.net.www.content.text;

import java.net.*;
import java.io.*;
import java.util.*;
import com.macfaq.io.SafeBufferedReader  // From Chapter 4

public class tab_separated_values extends ContentHandler {

  public Object getContent(URLConnection uc) throws IOException {

    String theLine;
    Vector lines = new Vector( );

    InputStreamReader isr = new InputStreamReader(uc.getInputStream( ));
    SafeBufferedReader in = new SafeBufferedReader(isr);
    while ((theLine = in.readLine( )) != null) {
      String[] linearray = lineToArray(theLine);
      lines.addElement(linearray);
    }

    return lines;

  }

  private String[] lineToArray(String line)  {
```

Example 17-1. A ContentHandler for text/tab-separated-values (continued)

```
    int numFields = 1;
    for (int i = 0; i < line.length(); i++) {
      if (line.charAt(i) == '\t') numFields++;
    }
    String[] fields = new String[numFields];
    int position = 0;
    for (int i = 0; i < numFields; i++) {
      StringBuffer buffer = new StringBuffer();
      while (position < line.length() && line.charAt(position) != '\t') {
        buffer.append(line.charAt(position));
        position++;
      }
      fields[i] = buffer.toString();
      position++;
    }

    return fields;

  }
}
```

Example 17-1 has two methods. The private utility method `lineToArray( )` converts a tab-separated string into an array of strings. This method is for the private use of this subclass and is not required by the `ContentHandler` interface. The more complicated the content you're trying to parse, the more such methods your class will need. The `lineToArray( )` method begins by counting the number of tabs in the string. This sets the `numFields` variable to one more than the number of tabs. An array is created for the fields with the length `numFields`; a `for` loop fills the array with the strings between the tabs; and this array is returned.

> You may have expected a `StringTokenizer` to split the line into parts. However, that class has unusual ideas about what makes up a token. In particular, it interprets multiple tabs in a row as a single delimiter. That is, it never returns an empty string as a token.

The `getContent( )` method starts by instantiating a `Vector`. Then it gets the `InputStream` from the `URLConnection uc` and chains this to an `InputStreamReader`, which is in turn chained to the `SafeBufferedReader` (introduced in Chapter 4) so `getContent( )` can read the array one line at a time in a `while` loop. Each line is fed to the `lineToArray( )` method, which splits it into a `String` array. This array is then added to the `Vector`. When no more lines are left, the loop exits and the `Vector` is returned.

Using Content Handlers

Now that you've written your first `ContentHandler`, let's see how to use it in a program. Files of MIME type `text/tab-separated-values` can be served by gopher servers, HTTP servers, FTP servers, and more. Let's assume you're retrieving a tab-separated-values file from an HTTP server. The filename should end with the *.tsv* or *.tab* extension so that the server knows it's a text/tab-separated-values file.

 Not all servers are configured to support this type out of the box. Consult your server documentation to see how to set up a MIME-type mapping for your server. For instance, to configure my Apache server, I added these lines to my *.htaccess* file:

```
AddType text/tab-separated-values tab

AddType text/tab-separated-values tsv
```

You can test the web server configuration by connecting to port 80 of the web server with Telnet and requesting the file manually:

```
% telnet www.ibiblio.org 80
Trying 127.0.0.1...
Connected to www.ibiblio.org.
Escape character is '^]'.
GET /javafaq/addresses.tab HTTP 1.0

HTTP 1.0 200 OK
Date: Mon, 15 Nov 1999 18:36:51 GMT
Server: Apache/1.3.4 (Unix) PHP/3.0.6 mod_perl/1.17
Last-Modified: Thu, 04 Nov 1999 18:22:51 GMT
Content-type: text/tab-separated-values
Content-length: 163

JPE Associates 341 Lafayette Street, Suite 1025 New York NY 10012
O'Reilly & Associates 103 Morris Street, Suite A Sebastopol CA 95472
Connection closed by foreign host.
```

You're looking for a line that says Content-type: text/tab-separated-values. If you see a Content-type of text/plain, application/octet-stream, or some other value, or you don't see any Content-type at all, the server is misconfigured and must be fixed before you continue.

The application that uses the tab-separated-values content handler does not need to know about it explicitly. It simply has to call the getContent( ) method of URL or URLConnection on a URL with a matching MIME type. Furthermore, the package where the content handler can be found has to be listed in the java.content. handlers.pkg property.

Example 17-2 is a class that downloads and prints a text/tab-separated-values file using the ContentHandler of Example 17-1. However, note that it does not import com.macfaq.net.www.content.text and never references the tab_separated_values class. It does explicitly add com.macfaq.net.www.content to the java.content. handlers.pkgs property because that's the simplest way to make sure this standalone program works. However, the lines that do this could be deleted if the property were set in a property file or from the command line.

Example 17-2. The tab-separated-values ContentTester class

```java
import java.io.*;
import java.net.*;
import java.util.*;

public class TSVContentTester {

  private static void test(URL u) throws IOException {

    Object content = u.getContent();
    Vector v = (Vector) content;
    for (Enumeration e = v.elements() ; e.hasMoreElements() ;) {
      String[] sa = (String[]) e.nextElement();
      for (int i = 0; i < sa.length; i++) {
        System.out.print(sa[i] + "\t");
      }
      System.out.println();
    }

  }

  public static void main (String[] args) {

    // If you uncomment these lines, then you don't have to
    // set the java.content.handler.pkgs property from the
    // command line or your properties files.

/*    String pkgs = System.getProperty("java.content.handler.pkgs", "");
    if (!pkgs.equals("")) {
      pkgs = pkgs + "|";
    }
    pkgs += "com.macfaq.net.www.content";
    System.setProperty("java.content.handler.pkgs", pkgs);  */

    for (int i = 0; i < args.length; i++) {
      try {
        URL u = new URL(args[i]);
        test(u);
      }
      catch (MalformedURLException ex) {
        System.err.println(args[i] + " is not a good URL");
      }
      catch (Exception ex) {
        ex.printStackTrace();
      }
    }
  }
}
```

Here's how you run this program. The arrows indicate tabs:

```
% java -Djava.content.handler.pkgs=com.macfaq.net.www.content\
  TSVContentTester http://www.ibiblio.org/javafaq/addresses.tab
JPE Associates → 341 Lafayette Street, Suite 1025 → New York → NY → 10012
O'Reilly & Associates → 103 Morris Street, Suite A→ Sebastopol → CA → 95472
```

Choosing Return Types

There is one overloaded variant of the getContent( ) method in the ContentHandler class:

```
public Object getContent(URLConnection uc, Class[] classes) // Java 1.3
  throws IOException
```

The difference is the array of java.lang.Class objects passed as the second argument. This allows the caller to request that the content be returned as one of the types in the array and enables content handlers to support multiple types. For example, the text/tab-separated-values content handler could return data as a Vector, an array, a string, or an InputStream. One would be the default used by the single argument getContent( ) method, while the others would be options that a client could request. If the client doesn't request any of the classes this ContentHandler knows how to provide, it returns null.

To call this method, the client invokes the method with the same arguments in a URL or URLConnection object. It passes an array of Class objects in the order it wishes to receive the data. Thus, if it prefers to receive a String but is willing to accept an InputStream and will take a Vector as a last resort, it puts String.class in the zeroth component of the array, InputStream.class in the first component of the array, and Vector.class in the last component of the array. Then it uses instanceof to test what was actually returned and either process it or convert it into the preferred type. For example:

```
Class[] requestedTypes = {String.class, InputStream.class,
 Vector.class};
Object content = url.getContent(requestedTypes);
if (content instanceof String) {
  String s = (String) content;
  System.out.println(s);
}
else if (content instanceof InputStream) {
  InputStream in = (InputStream) content;
  int c;
  while ((c = in.read( )) != -1) System.out.write(c);
}
else if (content instanceof Vector) {
  Vector v = (Vector) content;
  for (Enumeration e = v.elements() ; e.hasMoreElements( ) ;) {
    String[] sa = (String[]) e.nextElement( );
    for (int i = 0; i < sa.length; i++) {
      System.out.print(sa[i] + "\t");
    }
    System.out.println( );
  }
}
else {
  System.out.println("Unrecognized content type " + content.getClass( ));
}
```

To demonstrate this, let's write a content handler that can be used in association with the time protocol. Recall that the time protocol returns the current time at the server as a 4-byte, big-endian, unsigned integer giving the number of seconds since midnight, January 1, 1900, Greenwich Mean Time. There are several obvious candidates for storing this data in a Java content handler, including java.lang.Long (java.lang.Integer won't work since the unsigned value may overflow the bounds of an int), java.util.Date, java.util.Calendar, java.lang.String, and java.io. InputStream, which often works as a last resort. Example 17-3 provides all five options. There's no standard MIME type for the time format. We'll use application for the type to indicate that this is binary data and x-time for the subtype to indicate that this is a nonstandard extension type. It will be up to the time protocol handler to return the right content type.

Example 17-3. A time content handler

```
package com.macfaq.net.www.content.application;

import java.net.*;
import java.io.*;
import java.util.*;

public class x_time extends ContentHandler {

  public Object getContent(URLConnection uc) throws IOException {

    Class[] classes = new Class[1];
    classes[0] = Date.class;
    return this.getContent(uc, classes);

  }

  public Object getContent(URLConnection uc, Class[] classes)
   throws IOException {

    InputStream in = uc.getInputStream( );
    for (int i = 0; i < classes.length; i++) {
      if (classes[i] == InputStream.class) {
        return in;
      }
      else if (classes[i] == Long.class) {
        long secondsSince1900 = readSecondsSince1900(in);
        return new Long(secondsSince1900);
      }
      else if (classes[i] == Date.class) {
        long secondsSince1900 = readSecondsSince1900(in);
        Date time = shiftEpochs(secondsSince1900);
        return time;
      }
      else if (classes[i] == Calendar.class) {
        long secondsSince1900 = readSecondsSince1900(in);
        Date time = shiftEpochs(secondsSince1900);
```

Example 17-3. A time content handler (continued)

```
      Calendar c = Calendar.getInstance( );
      c.setTime(time);
      return c;
    }
    else if (classes[i] == String.class) {
      long secondsSince1900 = readSecondsSince1900(in);
      Date time = shiftEpochs(secondsSince1900);
      return time.toString( );
    }
  }

  return null; // no requested type available

}

private long readSecondsSince1900(InputStream in)
 throws IOException {

  long secondsSince1900 = 0;
  for (int j = 0; j < 4; j++) {
    secondsSince1900 = (secondsSince1900 << 8) | in.read( );
  }
  return secondsSince1900;

}

private Date shiftEpochs(long secondsSince1900) {

  // The time protocol sets the epoch at 1900, the Java Date class
  //   at 1970. This number converts between them.
  long differenceBetweenEpochs = 2208988800L;

  long secondsSince1970 = secondsSince1900 - differenceBetweenEpochs;
  long msSince1970 = secondsSince1970 * 1000;
  Date time = new Date(msSince1970);
  return time;

}
}
```

Most of the work is performed by the second getContent( ) method, which checks to see whether it recognizes any of the classes in the classes array. If so, it attempts to convert the content into an object of that type. The for loop is arranged so that classes earlier in the array take precedence; that is, it first tries to match the first class in the array; next it tries to match the second class in the array; then the third class in the array; and so on. As soon as one class is matched, the method returns so later classes won't be matched even if they're an allowed choice.

Once a type is matched, a simple algorithm converts the four bytes that the time server sends into the right kind of object, either an InputStream, a Long, a Date, a

Calendar, or a String. The InputStream conversion is trivial. The Long conversion is one of those times when it seems a little inconvenient that primitive data types aren't objects. Although you can convert to and return any object type, you can't convert to and return a primitive data type like long, so we return the type wrapper class Long instead. The Date and Calendar conversions require shifting the origin of the time from January 1, 1900 to January 1, 1970 and changing the units from seconds to milliseconds, as discussed in Chapter 9. Finally, the conversion to a String simply converts to a Date and then invokes the Date object's toString() method.

While it would be possible to configure a web server to send data of MIME type application/x-time, this class is really designed to be used by a custom protocol handler. This handler would know not only how to speak the time protocol, but also how to return application/x-time from the getContentType() method. Example 17-4 and Example 17-5 demonstrate such a protocol handler. It assumes that time URLs look like *time://vision.poly.edu:3737/*.

Example 17-4. The URLConnection for the time protocol handler

```
package com.macfaq.net.www.protocol.time;

import java.net.*;
import java.io.*;
import com.macfaq.net.www.content.application.*;

public class TimeURLConnection extends URLConnection {

  private Socket connection = null;
  public final static int DEFAULT_PORT = 37;

  public TimeURLConnection (URL u) {
    super(u);
  }

  public String getContentType( ) {
    return "application/x-time";
  }

  public Object getContent( ) throws IOException {
    ContentHandler ch = new x_time( );
    return ch.getContent(this);
  }

  public Object getContent(Class[] classes) throws IOException {
    ContentHandler ch = new x_time( );
    return ch.getContent(this, classes);
  }

  public InputStream getInputStream( ) throws IOException {
    if (!connected) this.connect( );
      return this.connection.getInputStream( );
  }
```

Example 17-4. The URLConnection for the time protocol handler (continued)

```
    public synchronized void connect( ) throws IOException {

        if (!connected) {
            int port = url.getPort( );
            if ( port < 0 ) {
                port = DEFAULT_PORT;
            }
            this.connection = new Socket(url.getHost( ), port);
            this.connected = true;
        }
    }
}
```

In general, it should be enough for the protocol handler to simply know or be able to deduce the correct MIME content type. However, in a case like this, where both content and protocol handlers must be provided, you can tie them a little more closely together by overriding getContent( ) as well. This allows you to avoid messing with the java.content.handler.pkgs property or installing a ContentHandlerFactory. You will still need to set the java.protocolhandler.pkgs property to point to your package or install a URLStreamHandlerFactory, however. Example 17-5 is a simple URLStreamHandler for the time protocol handler.

Example 17-5. The URLStreamHandler for the time protocol handler

```
package com.macfaq.net.www.protocol.time;

import java.net.*;
import java.io.*;
public class Handler extends URLStreamHandler {

    protected URLConnection openConnection(URL u) throws IOException {
        return new TimeURLConnection(u);
    }
}
```

We could install the time protocol handler into HotJava as we did with protocol handlers in the previous chapter. However, even if we place the time content handler in HotJava's class path, HotJava won't use it. Consequently, I've written a simple standalone application, shown in Example 17-6, that uses these protocol and content handlers to tell the time. Notice that it does not need to import or directly refer to any of the classes involved. It simply lets the URL find the right content handler.

Example 17-6. URLTimeClient

```
import java.net.*;
import java.util.*;
import java.io.*;

public class URLTimeClient {
```

Example 17-6. URLTimeClient (continued)

```
  public static void main(String[] args) {

    System.setProperty("java.protocol.handler.pkgs",
     "com.macfaq.net.www.protocol");

    try {
      // You can replace this with your own time server
      URL u = new URL("time://tock.usno.navy.mil/");
      Class[] types = {String.class, Date.class,
       Calendar.class, Long.class};
      Object o = u.getContent(types);
      System.out.println(o);
    }
    catch (IOException ex) {
     // Let's see what went wrong
     ex.printStackTrace( );
    }
  }
}
```

Here's a sample run:

```
  D:\JAVA\JNP3\examples\17>java URLTimeClient
  Mon Aug 23 21:30:34 EDT 2004
```

In this case, a String object was returned. This was the first choice of URLTimeClient but the last choice of the content handler. The client choice always takes precedence.

The ContentHandlerFactory Interface

A ContentHandlerFactory defines the rules for where ContentHandler classes are stored. Create a class that implements ContentHandlerFactory and give this class a createContentHandler( ) method that knows how to instantiate the right ContentHandler. The createContentHandler( ) method should return null if it can't find a ContentHandler appropriate for a MIME type; null signals Java to look for ContentHandler classes in the default locations. When the application starts, call the URLConnection's setContentHandlerFactory( ) method to set the ContentHandlerFactory. This method may be called only once in the lifetime of an application.

The createContentHandler( ) Method

Just as the createURLStreamHandler( ) method of the URLStreamHandlerFactory interface was responsible for finding and loading the appropriate protocol handler, so too the createContentHandler( ) method of the ContentHandlerFactory interface is responsible for finding and loading the appropriate ContentHandler given a MIME type:

```
  public abstract ContentHandler createContentHandler(String mimeType)
```

This method should be called only by the getContent( ) method of a URLConnection object. For instance, Example 17-7 is a ContentHandlerFactory that knows how to find the right handler for the text/tab-separated-values content handler of Example 17-1.

Example 17-7. TabFactory

```
package com.macfaq.net.www.content;

import java.net.*;

public class TabFactory implements ContentHandlerFactory {

  public ContentHandler createContentHandler(String mimeType)) {

    if (mimeType.equals("text/tab-separated-values") {
      return new com.macfaq.net.www.content.text.tab_separated_values( );
    }
    else {
      return null; // look for the handler in the default locations
    }
  }
}
```

This factory knows how to find only one kind of content handler, but there's no limit to how many a factory can know about. For example, this createContentHandler( ) method also suggests handlers for application/x-time, text/plain, video/mpeg, and model/vrml. Notice that when you're using a ContentHandlerFactory, you don't necessarily have to stick to standard naming conventions for ContentHandler subclasses:

```
    public ContentHandler createContentHandler(String mimeType)) {

      if (mimeType.equals("text/tab-separated-values") {
          return new com.macfaq.net.www.content.text.tab_separated_values( );
      }
      else if (mimeType.equals("application/x-time") {
        return new com.macfaq.net.www.content.application.x_time( );
      }
      else if (mimeType.equals("text/plain") {
        return new sun.net.www.content.text.plain( );
      }
      if (mimeType.equals("video/mpeg") {
        return new com.macfaq.video.MPEGHandler( );
      }
      if (mimeType.equals("model/vrml") {
        return new com.macfaq.threed.VRMLModel( );
      }
      else {
        return null; // look for the handler in the default locations
      }
    }
```

Installing Content Handler Factories

A `ContentHandlerFactory` is installed in an application using the static `URLConnection.setContentHandlerFactory()` method:

```
public static void setContentHandlerFactory(ContentHandlerFactory fac)
```

Note that this method is in the `URLConnection` class, not the `ContentHandler` class. It may be invoked at most once during any run of an application. It throws an `Error` if it is called a second time.

Using a `ContentHandlerFactory` such as the `TabFactory` in Example 17-5, it's possible to write a standalone application that can automatically load the tab-separated-values content handler and that runs without any major hassles with the class path. Example 17-8 is such a program. However, as with most other `setFactory()` methods, untrusted, remotely loaded code such as an applet will generally not be allowed to set the content handler factory. Attempting to do so will throw a `SecurityException`. Consequently, installing new content handlers in applets pretty much requires directly accessing the `getContent()` method of the `ContentHandler` subclass itself. Ideally, this shouldn't be necessary, but until Sun provides better support for downloadable content handlers in browsers, we're stuck with it.

Example 17-8. TabLoader that uses a ContentHandlerFactory

```java
import java.io.*;
import java.net.*;
import java.util.*;
import com.macfaq.net.www.content.*;

public class TabLoader {

  public static void main (String[] args) {

    URLConnection.setContentHandlerFactory(new TabFactory());

    for (int i = 0; i < args.length; i++) {
      try {
        URL u = new URL(args[i]);
        Object content = u.getContent();
        Vector v = (Vector) content;
        for (Enumeration e = v.elements() ; e.hasMoreElements() ;) {
          String[] sa = (String[]) e.nextElement();
          for (int j = 0; j < sa.length; j++) {
            System.out.print(sa[j] + "\t");
          }
          System.out.println();
        }
      }
      catch (MalformedURLException ex) {
        System.err.println(args[i] + " is not a good URL");
      }
      catch (Exception ex) {
```

Example 17-8. TabLoader that uses a ContentHandlerFactory (continued)

```
        ex.printStackTrace( );
      }
    }
  }
}
```

Here's a typical run. As usual, tabs are indicated by arrows:

```
% java TabLoader http://www.ibiblio.org/javafaq/addresses.tab
JPE Associates → 341 Lafayette Street, Suite 1025 → New York → NY → 10012
O'Reilly & Associates → 103 Morris Street, Suite A → Sebastopol → CA → 95472
```

A Content Handler for the FITS Image Format

That's really all there is to content handlers. As one final example, I'll show you how to write a content handler for image files. This kind of handler differs from the text-based content handlers you've already seen in that they generally produce an object that implements the java.awt.ImageProducer interface rather than an InputStream object. The specific example we'll choose is the Flexible Image Transport System (FITS) format in common use among astronomers. FITS files are grayscale, bit-mapped images with headers that determine the bit depth of the picture, the width and the height of the picture, and the number of pictures in the file. Although FITS files often contain several images (typically pictures of the same thing taken at different times), in this example we look at only the first image in a file. For more details about the FITS format and how to handle FITS files, see *The Encyclopedia of Graphics File Formats* by James D. Murray and William vanRyper (O'Reilly).

There are a few key things you need to know to process FITS files. First, FITS files are broken up into blocks of exactly 2,880 bytes. If there isn't enough data to fill a block, it is padded with spaces at the end. Each FITS file has two parts, the header and the primary data unit. The header occupies an integral number of blocks, as does the primary data unit. If the FITS file contains extensions, there may be additional data after the primary data unit, but we ignore that here. Any extensions that are present will not change the image contained in the primary data unit.

The header begins in the first block of the FITS file. It may occupy one or more blocks; the last block may be padded with spaces at the end. The header is ASCII text. Each line of the header is exactly 80 bytes wide; the first eight characters of each header line contain a keyword, which is followed by an equals sign (character 9), followed by a space (10). The keyword is padded on the right with spaces to make it eight characters long. Columns 11 through 30 contain a value; the value may be right-justified and padded on the left with spaces if necessary. The value may be an integer, a floating point number, a T or an F signifying the boolean values true and false, or a string delimited with single quotes. A comment may appear in columns 31 through 80; comments are separated from the value of a field by a slash (/). Here's a simple header taken from a FITS image produced by K. S. Balasubramaniam using the Dunn Solar Telescope at the National Solar Observatory in Sunspot, New Mexico (*http://www.sunspot.noao.edu/*):

```
SIMPLE  =                    T /
BITPIX  =                   16 /
NAXIS   =                    2 /
NAXIS1  =                  242 /
NAXIS2  =                  252 /
DATE    = '19 Aug 1996'        /
TELESC  = 'NSO/SP - VTT'       /
IMAGE   = 'Continuum'          /
COORDS  = 'N29.1W34.2'         /
OBSTIME = '13:59:00 UT'        /
END
```

Every FITS file begins with the keyword SIMPLE. This keyword always has the value T. If this isn't the case, the file is not valid. The second line of a FITS file always has the keyword BITPIX, which tells you how the data is stored. There are five possible values for BITPIX, four of which correspond exactly to Java primitive data types. The most common value of BITPIX is 16, meaning that there are 16 bits per pixel, which is equivalent to a Java short. A BITPIX of 32 is a Java int. A BITPIX of −32 means that each pixel is represented by a 32-bit floating point number (equivalent to a Java float); a BITPIX of −64 is equivalent to a Java double. A BITPIX of 8 means that 8 bits are used to represent each pixel; this is similar to a Java byte, except that FITS uses unsigned bytes ranging from 0 to 255; Java's byte data type is signed, taking values that range from −128 to 127.

The remaining keywords in a FITS file may appear in any order. They are *not* necessarily in the order shown here. In our FITS content handler, we first read all the keywords into a Hashtable and then extract the ones we want by name.

The NAXIS header specifies the number of axes (that is, the dimension) of the primary data array. A NAXIS value of one identifies a one-dimensional image. A NAXIS value of two indicates a normal two-dimensional rectangular image. A NAXIS value of three is called a *data cube* and generally means the file contains a series of pictures of the same object taken at different moments in time. In other words, time is the third dimension. On rare occasions, the third dimension can represent depth: i.e., the file contains a true three-dimensional image. A NAXIS of four means the file contains a sequence of three-dimensional pictures taken at different moments in time. Higher values of NAXIS, while theoretically possible, are rarely seen in practice. Our example is going to look at only the first two-dimensional image in a file.

The NAXIS*n* headers (where *n* is an integer ranging from 1 to NAXIS) give the length of the image in pixels along that dimension. In this example, NAXIS1 is 242, so the image is 242 pixels wide. NAXIS2 is 252, so this image is 252 pixels high. Since FITS images are normally pictures of astronomical bodies like the sun, it doesn't really matter if you reverse width and height. All FITS images contain the SIMPLE, BITPIX, END, and NAXIS keywords, plus a series of NAXIS*n* keywords. These keywords all provide information that is essential for displaying the image.

The next five keywords are specific to this file and may not be present in other FITS files. They give meaning to the image, although they are not needed to display it. The DATE keyword says this image was taken on August 19, 1996. The TELESC keyword says this image was taken by the Vacuum Tower Telescope (VTT) at the National Solar Observatory (NSO) on Sacramento Peak (SP). The IMAGE keyword says that this is a picture of the white light continuum; images taken through spectrographs might look at only a particular wavelength in the spectrum. The COORDS keyword gives the latitude and longitude of the telescope. Finally, the OBSTIME keyword says this image was taken at 1:59 P.M. Universal Time (essentially, Greenwich Mean Time). There are many more optional headers that don't appear in this example. Like the five discussed here, the remaining keywords may help someone interpret an image, but they don't provide the information needed to display it.

The keyword END terminates the header. Following the END keyword, the header is padded with spaces so that it fills a 2,880-byte block. A header may take up more than one 2,880-byte block, but it must always be padded to an integral number of blocks.

The image data follows the header. How the image is stored depends on the value of BITPIX, as explained earlier. Fortunately, these data types are stored in formats (big-endian, two's complement) that can be read directly with a `DataInputStream`. The exact meaning of each number in the image data is completely file-dependent. More often than not, it's the number of electrons that were collected in a specific time interval by a particular pixel in a charge coupled device (CCD); in older FITS files, the numbers could represent the value read from photographic film by a densitometer. However, the unifying theme is that larger numbers represent brighter light. To interpret these numbers as a grayscale image, we map the smallest value in the data to pure black, the largest value in the data to pure white, and scale all intermediate values appropriately. A general-purpose FITS reader cannot interpret the numbers as anything except abstract brightness levels. Without scaling, differences tend to get washed out. For example, a dark spot on the Sun tends to be about 4,000K. That is dark compared to the normal solar surface temperature of 6,000K, but considerably brighter than anything you're likely to see on the surface of the Earth.

Example 17-9 is a FITS content handler. FITS files should be served with the MIME type `image/x-fits`. This is almost certainly not included in your server's default MIME-type mappings, so make sure to add a mapping between files that end in *.fit*, *.fts*, or *.fits* and the MIME type `image/x-fits`.

Example 17-9. An x-fits content handler

```java
package com.macfaq.net.www.content.image;

import java.net.*;
import java.io.*;
import java.awt.image.*;
import java.util.*;

public class x_fits extends ContentHandler {

  public Object getContent(URLConnection uc) throws IOException {

    int width = -1;
    int height = -1;
    int bitpix = 16;
    int[] data = null;
    int naxis = 2;
    Hashtable header = null;

    DataInputStream dis = new DataInputStream(uc.getInputStream( ));
    header = readHeader(dis);

    bitpix = getIntFromHeader("BITPIX  ", -1, header);
    if (bitpix  <= 0) return null;
    naxis = getIntFromHeader("NAXIS  ", -1, header);
    if (naxis  < 1) return null;
    width = getIntFromHeader("NAXIS1  ", -1, header);
    if (width  <= 0) return null;
    if (naxis == 1) height = 1;
    else height = getIntFromHeader("NAXIS2  ", -1, header);
    if (height  <= 0) return null;

    if (bitpix == 16) {
      short[] theInput =  new short[height * width];
      for (int i = 0; i < theInput.length; i++) {
        theInput[i] = dis.readShort( );
      }
      data = scaleArray(theInput);
    }
    else if (bitpix == 32) {
      int[] theInput =  new int[height * width];
      for (int i = 0; i < theInput.length; i++) {
        theInput[i] = dis.readInt( );
      }
      data = scaleArray(theInput);
    }
    else if (bitpix == 64) {
      long[] theInput =  new long[height * width];
      for (int i = 0; i < theInput.length; i++) {
        theInput[i] = dis.readLong( );
      }
      data = scaleArray(theInput);
    }
```

Example 17-9. An x-fits content handler (continued)

```
  else if (bitpix == -32) {
    float[] theInput = new float[height * width];
    for (int i = 0; i < theInput.length; i++) {
      theInput[i] = dis.readFloat( );
    }
    data = scaleArray(theInput);
  }
  else if (bitpix == -64) {
    double[] theInput = new double[height * width];
    for (int i = 0; i < theInput.length; i++) {
      theInput[i] = dis.readDouble( );
    }
    data = scaleArray(theInput);
  }
  else {
    System.err.println("Invalid BITPIX");
    return null;
  } // end if-else-if

  return new MemoryImageSource(width, height, data, 0, width);

} // end getContent

private Hashtable readHeader(DataInputStream dis)
 throws IOException {

  int blocksize = 2880;
  int fieldsize = 80;
  String key, value;
  int linesRead = 0;

  byte[] buffer = new byte[fieldsize];

  Hashtable header = new Hashtable( );
  while (true) {
    dis.readFully(buffer);
    key = new String(buffer, 0, 8, "ASCII");
    linesRead++;
    if (key.substring(0, 3).equals("END")) break;
    if (buffer[8] != '=' || buffer[9] != ' ') continue;
    value = new String(buffer, 10, 20, "ASCII");
    header.put(key, value);
  }
  int linesLeftToRead
   = (blocksize - ((linesRead * fieldsize) % blocksize))/fieldsize;
  for (int i = 0; i < linesLeftToRead; i++) dis.readFully(buffer);

  return header;

}

private int getIntFromHeader(String name, int defaultValue,
```

Example 17-9. An x-fits content handler (continued)

```
  Hashtable header) {

    String s = "";
    int result = defaultValue;

    try {
      s = (String) header.get(name);
    }
    catch (NullPointerException ex) {
      return defaultValue;
    }
    try {
      result = Integer.parseInt(s.trim( ));
    }
    catch (NumberFormatException ex) {
      System.err.println(ex);
      System.err.println(s);
      return defaultValue;
    }

    return result;

  }

  private int[] scaleArray(short[] theInput) {

    int data[] = new int[theInput.length];
    int max = 0;
    int min = 0;
    for (int i = 0; i < theInput.length; i++) {
      if (theInput[i] > max) max = theInput[i];
      if (theInput[i] < min) min = theInput[i];
    }
    long r = max - min;
    double a = 255.0/r;
    double b = -a * min;
    int opaque = 255;
    for (int i = 0; i < data.length; i++) {
      int temp = (int) (theInput[i] * a + b);
      data[i] =  (opaque << 24)  | (temp << 16)  | (temp << 8) | temp;
    }
    return data;

  }

  private int[] scaleArray(int[] theInput) {

    int data[] = new int[theInput.length];
    int max = 0;
    int min = 0;
    for (int i = 0; i < theInput.length; i++) {
      if (theInput[i] > max) max = theInput[i];
```

Example 17-9. An x-fits content handler (continued)

```
      if (theInput[i] < min) min = theInput[i];
  }
  long r = max - min;
  double a = 255.0/r;
  double b = -a * min;
  int opaque = 255;
  for (int i = 0; i < data.length; i++) {
    int temp = (int) (theInput[i] * a + b);
    data[i] =  (opaque << 24)  | (temp << 16)  | (temp << 8) | temp;
  }
  return data;

}

private int[] scaleArray(long[] theInput) {

  int data[] = new int[theInput.length];
  long max = 0;
  long min = 0;
  for (int i = 0; i < theInput.length; i++) {
    if (theInput[i] > max) max = theInput[i];
    if (theInput[i] < min) min = theInput[i];
  }
  long r = max - min;
  double a = 255.0/r;
  double b = -a * min;
  int opaque = 255;
  for (int i = 0; i < data.length; i++) {
    int temp = (int) (theInput[i] * a + b);
    data[i] =  (opaque << 24)  | (temp << 16)  | (temp << 8) | temp;
  }
  return data;

}

private int[] scaleArray(double[] theInput) {

  int data[] = new int[theInput.length];
  double max = 0;
  double min = 0;
  for (int i = 0; i < theInput.length; i++) {
    if (theInput[i] > max) max = theInput[i];
    if (theInput[i] < min) min = theInput[i];
  }
  double r = max - min;
  double a = 255.0/r;
  double b = -a * min;
  int opaque = 255;
  for (int i = 0; i < data.length; i++) {
    int temp = (int) (theInput[i] * a + b);
    data[i] =  (opaque << 24)  | (temp << 16)  | (temp << 8) | temp;
  }
```

Example 17-9. An x-fits content handler (continued)

```
    return data;

  }

  private int[] scaleArray(float[] theInput) {

    int data[] = new int[theInput.length];
    float max = 0;
    float min = 0;
    for (int i = 0; i < theInput.length; i++) {
      if (theInput[i] > max) max = theInput[i];
      if (theInput[i] < min) min = theInput[i];
    }
    double r = max - min;
    double a = 255.0/r;
    double b = -a * min;
    int opaque = 255;
    for (int i = 0; i < data.length; i++) {
      int temp = (int) (theInput[i] * a + b);
      data[i] = (opaque << 24) | (temp << 16) | (temp << 8) | temp;
    }
    return data;
  }
}
```

The key method of the x_fits class is getContent( ); it is the one method that the ContentHandler class requires subclasses to implement. The other methods in this class are all utility methods that help to break up the program into easier-to-digest chunks. getContent( ) is called by a URLConnection, which passes a reference to itself in the argument uc. The getContent( ) method reads data from that URLConnection and uses it to construct an object that implements the ImageProducer interface. To simplify the task of creating an ImageProducer, we create an array of image data and use a MemoryImageSource object, which implements the ImageProducer interface, to convert that array into an image. getContent( ) returns this MemoryImageSource.

MemoryImageSource has several constructors. The one invoked here requires us to provide the width and height of the image, an array of integer values containing the RGB data for each pixel, the offset of the start of that data in the array, and the number of pixels per line in the array:

```
    public MemoryImageSource(int width, int height, int[] pixels,
      int offset, int scanlines);
```

The width, height, and pixel data can be read from the header of the FITS image. Since we are creating a new array to hold the pixel data, the offset is zero and the scanlines are the width of the image.

Our content handler has a utility method called readHeader( ) that reads the image header from uc's InputStream. This method returns a Hashtable containing the keywords and their values as String objects. Comments are thrown away. readHeader( )

reads 80 bytes at a time, since that's the length of each field. The first eight bytes are transformed into the String key. If there is no key, the line is a comment and is ignored. If there is a key, then the eleventh through thirtieth bytes are stored in a String called value. The key-value pair is stored in the Hashtable. This continues until the END keyword is spotted. At this point, we break out of the loop and read as many lines as necessary to finish the block. (Recall that the header is padded with spaces to make an integral multiple of 2,880.) Finally, readHeader( ) returns the Hashtable header.

After the header has been read into the Hashtable, the InputStream is now pointing at the first byte of data. However, before we're ready to read the data, we must extract the height, width, and bits per pixel of the primary data unit from the header. These are all integer values, so to simplify the code we use the getIntFromHeader(String name, int defaultValue, Hashtable header) method. This method takes as arguments the name of the header whose value we want (e.g., BITPIX), a default value for that header, and the Hashtable that contains the header. This method retrieves the value associated with the string name from the Hashtable and casts the result to a String object—we know this cast is safe because we put only String data into the Hashtable. This String is then converted to an int using Integer.parseInt(s.trim( )); we then return the resulting int. If an exception is thrown, getIntFromHeader( ) returns the defaultValue argument instead. In this content handler, we use an impossible flag value (–1) as the default to indicate that getIntFromHeader( ) failed.

getContent( ) uses getIntFromHeader( ) to retrieve four crucial values from the header: NAXIS, NAXIS1, NAXIS2, and BITPIX. NAXIS is the number of dimensions in the primary data array; if it is greater than or equal to two, we read the width and height from NAXIS1 and NAXIS2. If there are more than two dimensions, we still read a single two-dimensional frame from the data. A more advanced FITS content handler might read subsequent frames and include them below the original image or display the sequence of images as an animation. If NAXIS is one, the width is read from NAXIS1 and the height is set to one. (A FITS file with NAXIS as one would typically be produced from observations that used a one-dimensional CCD.) If NAXIS is less than one, there's no image data at all, so we return null.

Now we are ready to read the image data. The data can be stored in one of five formats, depending on the value of BITPIX: unsigned bytes, shorts, ints, floats, or doubles. This is where the lack of generics that can handle primitive types makes coding painful: we need to repeat the algorithm for reading data five times, once for each of the five possible data types. In each case, the data is first read from the stream into an array of the appropriate type called theInput. Then this array is passed to the scaleArray( ) method, which returns a scaled array. scaleArray( ) is an overloaded method that reads the data in theInput and copies the data into the int array theData, while scaling the data to fall from 0 to 255; there is a different version of scaleArray( ) for each of the five data types it might need to handle. Thus, no matter what format the data starts in, it becomes an int array with values from 0 to 255.

This data now needs to be converted into grayscale RGB values. The standard 32-bit RGB color model allows 256 different shades of gray, ranging from pure black to pure white; 8 bits are used to represent opacity, usually called "alpha". To get a particular shade of gray, the red, green, and blue bytes of an RGB triple should all be set to the same value, and the alpha value should be 255 (fully opaque). Thinking of these as four byte values, we need colors like 255.127.127.127 (medium gray) or 255. 255.255.255 (pure white). These colors are produced by the lines:

```
int temp = (int) (theInput[i] * a + b);
theData[i] = (opaque << 24) | (temp << 16) | (temp << 8) | temp;
```

Once it has converted every pixel in theInput[] into a 32-bit color value and stored the result in theData[], scaleArray() returns theData. The only thing left for getContent() to do is feed this array, along with the header values previously retrieved, into the MemoryImageSource constructor and return the result.

This FITS content handler has one glaring problem. The image has to be completely loaded before the method returns. Since FITS images are quite literally astronomical in size, loading the image can take a significant amount of time. It would be better to create a new class for FITS images that implements the ImageProducer interface and into which the data can be streamed asynchronously. The ImageConsumer that eventually displays the image can use the methods of ImageProducer to determine when the height and width are available, when a new scanline has been read, when the image is completely loaded or errored out, and so on. getContent() would spawn a separate thread to feed the data into the ImageProducer and would return almost immediately. However, a FITS ImageProducer would not be able to take significant advantage of progressive loading because the file format doesn't unambiguously define what each data value means; before we can generate RGB pixels, we must read all of the data and find the minimum and maximum values.

Example 17-10 is a simple ContentHandlerFactory that recognizes FITS images. For all types other than image/x-fits, it returns null so that the default locations will be searched for content handlers.

Example 17-10. The FITS ContentHandlerFactory

```
import java.net.*;

public class FitsFactory implements ContentHandlerFactory {

  public ContentHandler createContentHandler(String mimeType) {

    if (mimeType.equalsIgnoreCase("image/x-fits")) {
      return new com.macfaq.net.www.content.image.x_fits();
    }
    return null;

  }
}
```

Example 17-11 is a simple program that tests this content handler by loading and displaying a FITS image from a URL. In fact, it can display any image type for which a content handler is installed. However, it does use the FitsFactory to recognize FITS images.

Example 17-11. The FITS viewer

```java
import java.awt.*;
import javax.swing.*;
import java.awt.image.*;
import java.net.*;
import java.io.*;

public class FitsViewer extends JFrame {

  private URL url;
  private Image theImage;

  public FitsViewer(URL u) {
    super(u.getFile( ));
    this.url = u;
  }

  public void loadImage( ) throws IOException {

    Object content = this.url.getContent( );
    ImageProducer producer;
    try {
      producer = (ImageProducer) content;
    }
    catch (ClassCastException e) {
      throw new IOException("Unexpected type " + content.getClass( ));
    }
    if (producer == null) theImage = null;
    else {
      theImage = this.createImage(producer);
      int width = theImage.getWidth(this);
      int height = theImage.getHeight(this);
      if (width > 0 && height > 0) this.setSize(width, height);
    }

  }

  public void paint(Graphics g) {
    if (theImage != null) g.drawImage(theImage, 0, 0, this);
  }

  public static void main(String[] args) {

    URLConnection.setContentHandlerFactory(new FitsFactory( ));
    for (int i = 0; i < args.length; i++) {
      try {
        FitsViewer f = new FitsViewer(new URL(args[i]));
```

Example 17-11. The FITS viewer (continued)

```
        f.setSize(252, 252);
        f.loadImage( );
        f.show( );
      }
      catch (MalformedURLException ex) {
        System.err.println(args[i] + " is not a URL I recognize.");
      }
      catch (IOException ex) {
        ex.printStackTrace( );
      }
    }
  }
}
```

The FitsViewer program extends JFrame. The main( ) method loops through all the command-line arguments, creating a new window for each one. Then it loads the image into the window and shows it. The loadImage( ) method actually downloads the requested picture by implicitly using the content handler of Example 17-9 to convert the FITS data into a java.awt.Image object stored in the field theImage. If the width and the height of the image are available (as they will be for a FITS image using our content handler but maybe not for some other image types that load the image in a separate thread), then the window is resized to the exact size of the image. The paint( ) method simply draws this image on the screen. Most of the work is done inside the content handler. In fact, this program can actually display images of any type for which a content handler is installed and available. For instance, it works equally well for GIF and JPEG images. Figure 17-2 shows this program displaying a picture of part of solar granulation.

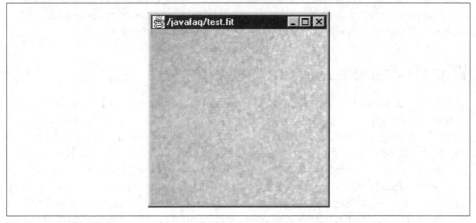

Figure 17-2. The FitsViewer application displaying a FITS image of solar granulation

CHAPTER 18

Remote Method Invocation

Historically, networking has been concerned with two fundamental applications. The first application is moving files and data between hosts and is handled by FTP, SMTP, HTTP, NFS, IMAP, POP, and many other protocols. The second application is allowing one host to run programs on another host. This is the traditional province of Telnet, rlogin, Remote Procedure Call (RPC), and a lot of database middleware. Most of this book has implicitly concerned itself with file and data transfer. Remote Method Invocation (RMI), however, is an example of the second application for networking: running a program on a remote host from a local machine.

RMI is a core Java API and class library that allows Java programs running in one Java virtual machine to call methods in objects running in a different virtual machine, even when the two virtual machines are running on physically separate hosts. In essence, parts of a single Java program run on a local computer while other parts of the same program run on a remote host. RMI creates the illusion that this distributed program is running on one system with one memory space holding all the code and data used on either side of the actual physical connection.

What Is Remote Method Invocation?

RMI lets Java objects on different hosts communicate with each other in a way that's similar to how objects running in the same virtual machine communicate with each other: by calling methods in objects. A remote object lives on a server. Each remote object implements a remote interface that specifies which of its methods can be invoked by clients. Clients invoke the methods of the remote object almost exactly as they invoke local methods. For example, an object running on a local client can pass a database query as a String argument to a method in a database object running on a remote server to ask it to sum up a series of records. The server can return the result to the client as a double. This is more efficient than downloading all the records and summing them up locally. Java-compatible web servers can implement remote methods that allow clients to ask for a complete index of the public files on the site. This could dramatically reduce the time a server spends filling requests from web spiders such as Google. Indeed, Excite already uses a non-Java–based version of this idea.

From the programmer's perspective, remote objects and methods work pretty much like the local objects and methods you're accustomed to. All the implementation details are hidden. You just import one package, look up the remote object in a registry (which takes one line of code), and make sure that you catch `RemoteException` when you call the object's methods. From that point on, you can use the remote object almost as freely and easily as you use an object running on your own system. The abstraction is not perfect. Remote method invocation is much slower and less reliable than regular local method invocation. Things can and do go wrong with remote method invocation that do not affect local method invocations. For instance, a local method invocation is not subject to a Verizon technician disconnecting your DSL line while working on the phone line next door. Network failures of this type are represented as `RemoteExceptions`. However, RMI tries to hide the difference between local and remote method invocation to the maximum extent possible.

More formally, a *remote object* is an object with methods that may be invoked from a different Java virtual machine than the one in which the object itself lives, generally one running on a different computer. Each remote object implements one or more *remote interfaces* that declare which methods of the remote object can be invoked by the foreign system. RMI is the facility by which a Java program running on one machine, say *java.oreilly.com*, can invoke a method in an object on a completely different machine, say *www.ibiblio.org*.

For example, suppose *weather.centralpark.org* is an Internet-connected PC at the Central Park weather station that monitors the temperature, humidity, pressure, wind speed and direction, and similar information through connections to various instruments, and it needs to make this data available to remote users. A Java program running on that PC can offer an interface like Example 18-1 that provides the current values of the weather data.

Example 18-1. The weather interface

```
import java.rmi.*;
import java.util.Date;

public interface Weather extends Remote {

  public double getTemperature( ) throws RemoteException;
  public double getHumidity( ) throws RemoteException;
  public double getPressure( ) throws RemoteException;
  public double getWindSpeed( ) throws RemoteException;
  public double getWindDirection( ) throws RemoteException;
  public double getLatitude( ) throws RemoteException;
  public double getLongitude( ) throws RemoteException;
  public Date   getTime( ) throws RemoteException;

}
```

Normally, this interface is limited to other programs running on that same PC—indeed, in the same virtual machine. However, remote method invocations allow other virtual machines running on other computers in other parts of the world to invoke these methods to retrieve the weather data. For instance, a Java program running on my workstation at *stallion.elharo.com* could look up the current weather object in the RMI registry at *weather.centralpark.org*. The registry would send it a reference to the object running in *weather.centralpark.org*'s virtual machine. My program could then use this reference to invoke the getTemperature( ) method. The getTemperature( ) method would execute on the server in Central Park, not on my local machine. However, it would return the double value back to my local program running in Brooklyn. This is simpler than designing and implementing a new socket-based protocol for communication between the weather station and its clients. The details of making the connections between the hosts and transferring the data are hidden in the RMI classes.

So far we've imagined a public service that's accessible to all. However, clearly there are some methods you don't want just anyone invoking. More RMI applications than not will have a strictly limited set of permitted users. RMI itself does not provide any means of limiting who's allowed to access RMI servers. These capabilities can be added to RMI programs through the Java Authentication and Authorization Service (JAAS). JAAS is an abstract interface that can be configured with different service providers to support a range of different authentication schemes and different stores for the authentication data.

Object Serialization

When an object is passed to or returned from a Java method, what's really transferred is a reference to the object. In most current implementations of Java, references are handles (doubly indirected pointers) to the location of the object in memory. Passing objects between two machines thus raises some problems. The remote machine can't read what's in the memory of the local machine. A reference that's valid on one machine isn't meaningful on the other.

There are two ways around this problem. The first way is to convert the object to a sequence of bytes and send these bytes to the remote machine. The remote machine receives the bytes and reconstructs them into a copy of the object. However, changes to this copy are not automatically reflected in the original object. This is like pass-by-value.

The second way around this problem is to pass a special remote reference to the object. When the remote machine invokes a method on this reference, that invocation travels back across the Internet to the local machine that originally created the object. Changes made on either machine are reflected on both ends of the connection because they share the same object. This is like pass-by-reference.

Converting an object into a sequence of bytes is more difficult than it appears at first glance because object fields can be references to other objects; the objects these fields point to also need to be copied when the object is copied. And these objects may point to still other objects that also need to be copied. Object serialization is a scheme by which objects can be converted into bytes and then passed around to other machines, which rebuild the original object from the bytes. These bytes can also be written to disk and read back from disk at a later time, allowing you to save the state of an entire program or a single object.

For security reasons, Java places some limitations on which objects can be serialized. All Java primitive types can be serialized, but nonremote Java objects can be serialized only if they implement the java.io.Serializable interface. Basic Java types that implement Serializable include String and Component. Container classes such as Vector are serializable if all the objects they contain are serializable. Furthermore, subclasses of a serializable class are also serializable. For example, java.lang.Integer and java.lang.Float are serializable because the class they extend, java.lang.Number, is serializable. Exceptions, errors, and other throwable objects are always serializable. Most AWT and Swing components, containers, and events are serializable. However, event adapters, image filters, and peer classes are not. Streams, readers and writers, and most other I/O classes are not serializable. Type wrapper classes are serializable except for Void. Classes in java.math are serializable. Classes in java.lang. reflect are not serializable. The URL class is serializable. However, Socket, URLConnection, and most other classes in java.net are not. If in doubt, the class library documentation will tell you whether a given class is serializable.

 Object serialization is discussed in much greater detail in Chapter 11 of my previous book, *Java I/O* (O'Reilly).

CORBA

RMI isn't the final word in distributed object systems. Its biggest limitation is that you can call only methods written in Java. What if you already have an application written in some other language, such as C++, and you want to communicate with it? The most general solution for distributed objects is CORBA, the Common Object Request Broker Architecture. CORBA lets objects written in different languages communicate with each other. Java hooks into CORBA through the Java-IDL. This goes beyond the scope of this book; to find out about these topics, see:

- Java-IDL (*http://java.sun.com/products/jdk/idl/*)
- CORBA for Beginners (*http://www.omg.org/gettingstarted/corbafaq.htm*)
- The CORBA FAQ list (*http://www4.informatik.uni-erlangen.de/~geier/corba-faq/*)
- *Client/Server Programming with Java and CORBA* by Dan Harkey and Robert Orfali (Wiley)

Under the Hood

The last two sections skimmed over a lot of details. Fortunately, Java hides most of the details from you. However, it never hurts to understand how things really work.

The fundamental difference between remote objects and local objects is that remote objects reside in a different virtual machine. Normally, object arguments are passed to methods and object values are returned from methods by referring to something in a particular virtual machine. This is called *passing a reference*. However, this method doesn't work when the invoking method and the invoked method aren't in the same virtual machine; for example, object 243 in one virtual machine has nothing to do with object 243 in a different virtual machine. In fact, different virtual machines may implement references in completely different and incompatible ways.

Therefore, three different mechanisms are used to pass arguments to and return results from remote methods, depending on the type of the data being passed. Primitive types (int, boolean, double, and so on) are passed by value, just as in local Java method invocation. References to remote objects (that is, objects that implement the Remote interface) are passed as *remote references* that allow the recipient to invoke methods on the remote objects. This is similar to the way local object references are passed to local Java methods. Objects that do not implement the Remote interface are passed by value; that is, complete copies are passed, using object serialization. Objects that do not allow themselves to be serialized cannot be passed to remote methods. Remote objects run on the server but can be called by objects running on the client. Nonremote, serializable objects run on the client system.

To make the process as transparent to the programmer as possible, communication between a remote object client and a server is implemented in a series of layers, as shown in Figure 18-1.

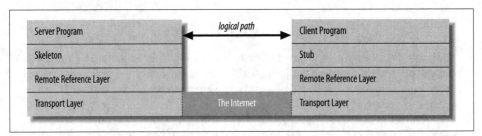

Figure 18-1. The RMI layer model

To the programmer, the client appears to talk directly to the server. In reality, the client program talks only to a stub object that stands in for the real object on the remote system. The stub passes that conversation along to the remote reference layer, which talks to the transport layer. The transport layer on the client passes the data across the Internet to the transport layer on the server. The server's transport layer then communicates with the server's remote reference layer, which talks to a piece of server software called the *skeleton*. The skeleton communicates with the server itself. (Servers written in Java 1.2 and later can omit the skeleton layer.) In the other direction (server-to-client), the flow is simply reversed. Logically, data flows horizontally (client-to-server and back), but the actual flow of data is vertical.

This approach may seem overly complex, but remember that most of the time you don't need to think about it, any more than you need to think about how a telephone translates your voice into a series of electrical impulses that get translated back to sound at the other end of the phone call. The goal of RMI is to allow your program to pass arguments to and return values from methods without worrying about how those arguments and return values will move across the network. At worst, you'll simply need to handle one additional kind of exception a remote method might throw.

Before you can call a method in a remote object, you need a reference to that object. To get this reference, ask a *registry* for it by name. The registry is like a mini-DNS for remote objects. A client connects to the registry and gives it the URL of the remote object that it wants. The registry replies with a reference to the object that the client can use to invoke methods on the server.

In reality, the client is only invoking local methods in a *stub*. The stub is a local object that implements the remote interfaces of the remote object; this means that the stub has methods matching the signatures of all the methods the remote object exports. In effect, the client thinks it is calling a method in the remote object, but it is really calling an equivalent method in the stub. Stubs are used in the client's virtual machine in place of the real objects and methods that live on the server; you may find it helpful to think of the stub as the remote object's surrogate on the client. When the client invokes a method, the stub passes the invocation to the remote reference layer.

The remote reference layer carries out a specific remote reference protocol, which is independent of the specific client stubs and server skeletons. The remote reference layer is responsible for understanding what a particular remote reference means. Sometimes the remote reference may refer to multiple virtual machines on multiple hosts. In other situations, the reference may refer to a single virtual machine on the local host or a virtual machine on a remote host. In essence, the remote reference layer translates the local reference to the stub into a remote reference to the object on the server, whatever the syntax or semantics of the remote reference may be. Then it passes the invocation to the transport layer.

The transport layer sends the invocation across the Internet. On the server side, the transport layer listens for incoming connections. Upon receiving an invocation, the transport layer forwards it to the remote reference layer on the server. The remote reference layer converts the remote references sent by the client into references for the local virtual machine. Then it passes the request to the skeleton. The skeleton reads the arguments and passes the data to the server program, which makes the actual method call. If the method call returns a value, that value is sent down through the skeleton, remote reference, and transport layers on the server side, across the Internet and then up through the transport, remote reference, and stub layers on the client side. In Java 1.2 and later, the skeleton layer is omitted and the server talks directly to the remote reference layer. Otherwise, the protocol is the same.

Implementation

Most of the methods you need for working with remote objects are in three packages: `java.rmi`, `java.rmi.server`, and `java.rmi.registry`. The `java.rmi` package defines the classes, interfaces, and exceptions that will be seen on the client side. You need these when you're writing programs that access remote objects but are not themselves remote objects. The `java.rmi.server` package defines the classes, interfaces, and exceptions that will be visible on the server side. Use these classes when you are writing a remote object that will be called by clients. The `java.rmi.registry` package defines the classes, interfaces, and exceptions that are used to locate and name remote objects.

In this chapter and in Sun's documentation, the server side is always considered to be "remote" and the client is always considered "local". This can be confusing, particularly when you're writing a remote object. When writing a remote object, you're probably thinking from the viewpoint of the server, so that the client appears to be remote.

The Server Side

To create a new remote object, first define an interface that extends the `java.rmi.Remote` interface. `Remote` is a marker interface that does not have any methods of its own; its sole purpose is to tag remote objects so that they can be identified as such. One definition of a remote object is an instance of a class that implements the `Remote` interface, or any interface that extends `Remote`.

Your subinterface of `Remote` determines which methods of the remote object clients may call. A remote object may have many public methods, but only those declared in a remote interface can be invoked remotely. The other public methods may be invoked only from within the virtual machine where the object lives.

Each method in the subinterface must declare that it throws `RemoteException`. `RemoteException` is the superclass for most of the exceptions that can be thrown when RMI is used. Many of these are related to the behavior of external systems and networks and are thus beyond your control.

Example 18-2 is a simple interface for a remote object that calculates Fibonacci numbers of arbitrary size. (Fibonacci numbers are the sequence that begins 1, 1, 2, 3, 5, 8, 13 . . . in which each number is the sum of the previous two.) This remote object can run on a high-powered server to calculate results for low-powered clients. The interface declares two overloaded getFibonacci( ) methods, one of which takes an int as an argument and the other of which takes a BigInteger. Both methods return BigInteger because Fibonacci numbers grow very large very quickly. A more complex remote object could have many more methods.

Example 18-2. The Fibonacci interface

```
import java.rmi.*;
import java.math.BigInteger;

public interface Fibonacci extends Remote {

  public BigInteger getFibonacci(int n) throws RemoteException;
  public BigInteger getFibonacci(BigInteger n) throws RemoteException;

}
```

Nothing in this interface says anything about how the calculation is implemented. For instance, it could be calculated directly, using the methods of the java.math. BigInteger class. It could be done equally easily with the more efficient methods of the com.ibm.BigInteger class from IBM's alphaWorks (*http://www.alphaworks.ibm.com/ tech/bigdecimal*). It could be calculated with ints for small values of n and BigInteger for large values of n. Every calculation could be performed immediately, or a fixed number of threads could be used to limit the load that this remote object places on the server. Calculated values could be cached for faster retrieval on future requests, either internally or in a file or database. Any or all of these are possible. The client neither knows nor cares how the server gets the result as long as it produces the correct one.

The next step is to define a class that implements this remote interface. This class should extend java.rmi.server.UnicastRemoteObject, either directly or indirectly (i.e., by extending another class that extends UnicastRemoteObject):

```
public class UnicastRemoteObject extends RemoteServer
```

Without going into too much detail, the UnicastRemoteObject provides a number of methods that make remote method invocation work. In particular, it marshals and unmarshals remote references to the object. (*Marshalling* is the process by which arguments and return values are converted into a stream of bytes that can be sent over the network. *Unmarshalling* is the reverse: the conversion of a stream of bytes into a group of arguments or a return value.)

If extending UnicastRemoteObject isn't convenient—for instance, because you'd like to extend some other class—you can instead export your object as a remote object by passing it to one of the static UnicastRemoteObject.exportObject( ) methods:

```
public static RemoteStub exportObject(Remote obj)
  throws RemoteException
public static Remote exportObject(Remote obj, int port)  // Java 1.2
```

```
      throws RemoteException
  public static Remote exportObject(Remote obj, int port,   // Java 1.2
    RMIClientSocketFactory csf, RMIServerSocketFactory ssf)
    throws RemoteException
```

These create a remote object that uses your object to do the work. It's similar to how a Runnable object can be used to give a thread something to do when it's inconvenient to subclass Thread. However, this approach has the downside of preventing the use of dynamic proxies in Java 1.5, so you need to manually deploy stubs. (In Java 1.4 and earlier, you always have to use stubs.)

There's one other kind of RemoteServer in the standard Java class library, the java.rmi.activation.Activatable class:

```
  public abstract class Activatable extends RemoteServer // Java 1.2
```

A UnicastRemoteObject exists only as long as the server that created it still runs. When the server dies, the object is gone forever. Activatable objects allow clients to reconnect to servers at different times across server shutdowns and restarts and still access the same remote objects. It also has static Activatable.exportObject() methods to invoke if you don't want to subclass Activatable.

Example 18-3, the FibonacciImpl class, implements the remote interface Fibonacci. This class has a constructor and two getFibonacci() methods. Only the getFibonacci() methods will be available to the client, because they're the only ones defined by the Fibonacci interface. The constructor is used on the server side but is not available to the client.

Example 18-3. The FibonacciImpl class

```
import java.rmi.*;
import java.rmi.server.UnicastRemoteObject;
import java.math.BigInteger;

public class FibonacciImpl extends UnicastRemoteObject implements Fibonacci {

  public FibonacciImpl() throws RemoteException {
    super();
  }

  public BigInteger getFibonacci(int n) throws RemoteException {
    return this.getFibonacci(new BigInteger(Long.toString(n)));
  }

  public BigInteger getFibonacci(BigInteger n) throws RemoteException {

    System.out.println("Calculating the " + n + "th Fibonacci number");
    BigInteger zero = new BigInteger("0");
    BigInteger one  = new BigInteger("1");

    if (n.equals(zero)) return one;
    if (n.equals(one)) return one;
```

Example 18-3. The FibonacciImpl class (continued)

```
    BigInteger i   = one;
    BigInteger low  = one;
    BigInteger high  = one;

    while (i.compareTo(n) == -1) {
      BigInteger temp = high;
      high = high.add(low);
      low = temp;
      i = i.add(one);
    }

    return high;

  }
}
```

The FibonacciImpl( ) constructor just calls the superclass constructor that exports the object; that is, it creates a UnicastRemoteObject on some port and starts it listening for connections. The constructor is declared to throw RemoteException because the UnicastRemoteObject constructor can throw that exception.

The getFibonacci(int n) method is trivial. It simply returns the result of converting its argument to a BigInteger and calling the second getFibonacci( ) method. The second method actually performs the calculation. It uses BigInteger throughout the calculation to allow for arbitrarily large Fibonacci numbers of an arbitrarily large index to be calculated. This can use a lot of CPU power and huge amounts of memory. That's why you might want to move it to a special-purpose calculation server rather than performing the calculation locally.

Although getFibonacci( ) is a remote method, there's nothing different about the method itself. This is a simple case, but even vastly more complex remote methods are not algorithmically different than their local counterparts. The only difference— that a remote method is declared in a remote interface and a local method is not—is completely external to the method itself.

Next, we need to write a server that makes the Fibonacci remote object available to the world. Example 18-4 is such a server. All it has is a main( ) method. It begins by entering a try block that catches RemoteException. Then it constructs a new FibonacciImpl object and binds that object to the name "fibonacci" using the Naming class to talk to the local registry. A registry keeps track of the available objects on an RMI server and the names by which they can be requested. When a new remote object is created, the object adds itself and its name to the registry with the Naming. bind( ) or Naming.rebind( ) method. Clients can then ask for that object by name or get a list of all the remote objects that are available. Note that there's no rule that says the name the object has in the registry has to have any necessary relation to the class name. For instance, we could have called this object "Fred". Indeed, there might be multiple instances of the same class all bound in a registry, each with a different name. After registering itself, the server prints a message on System.out signaling that it is ready to begin accepting remote invocations. If something goes wrong, the catch block prints a simple error message.

Example 18-4. The FibonacciServer class

```
import java.net.*;
import java.rmi.*;

public class FibonacciServer {

  public static void main(String[] args) {

    try {
      FibonacciImpl f = new FibonacciImpl( );
      Naming.rebind("fibonacci", f);
      System.out.println("Fibonacci Server ready.");
    }
     catch (RemoteException rex) {
      System.out.println("Exception in FibonacciImpl.main: " + rex);
    }
    catch (MalformedURLException ex) {
      System.out.println("MalformedURLException " + ex);
    }

  }

}
```

Although the main( ) method finishes fairly quickly here, the server will continue to run because a nondaemon thread is spawned when the FibonacciImpl object is bound to the registry. This completes the server code you need to write.

Compiling the Stubs

RMI uses stub classes to mediate between local objects and the remote objects running on the server. Each remote object on the server is represented by a stub class on the client. The stub contains the information in the Remote interface (in this example, that a Fibonacci object has two getFibonacci( ) methods). Java 1.5 can sometimes generate these stubs automatically as they're needed, but in Java 1.4 and earlier, you must manually compile the stubs for each remote class. Even in Java 1.5, you still have to manually compile stubs for remote objects that are not subclasses of UnicastRemoteObject and are instead exported by calling UnicastRemoteObject. exportObject( ).

Fortunately, you don't have to write stub classes yourself: they can be generated automatically from the remote class's byte code using the *rmic* utility included with the JDK. To generate the stubs for the `FibonacciImpl` remote object, run *rmic* on the remote classes you want to generate stubs for. For example:

```
% rmic FibonacciImpl
% ls Fibonacci*
Fibonacci.class        FibonacciImpl_Stub.class  FibonacciServer.java
FibonacciImpl.class    Fibonacci.java
FibonacciImpl.java     FibonacciServer.class
```

rmic reads the *.class* file of a class that implements `Remote` and produces *.class* files for the stubs needed for the remote object. The command-line argument to *rmic* is the fully package-qualified class name (e.g., `com.macfaq.rmi.examples.Chat`, not just `Chat`) of the remote object class.

rmic supports the same command-line options as the *javac* compiler: for example, `-classpath` and `-d`. For instance, if the class doesn't fall in the class path, you can specify the location with the `-classpath` command-line argument. The following command searches for *FibonacciImpl.class* in the directory *test/classes*:

```
% rmic -classpath test/classes FibonacciImpl
```

Starting the Server

Now you're ready to start the server. There are actually two servers you need to run, the remote object itself (`FibonacciServer` in this example) and the registry that allows local clients to download a reference to the remote object. Since the server expects to talk to the registry, you must start the registry first. Make sure all the stub and server classes are in the server's class path and type:

```
% rmiregistry &
```

On Windows, you start it from a DOS prompt like this:

```
C:> start rmiregistry
```

In both examples, the registry runs in the background. The registry tries to listen to port 1,099 by default. If it fails, especially with a message like "java.net. SocketException: Address already in use", then some other program is using port 1099, possibly (though not necessarily) another registry service. You can run the registry on a different port by appending a port number like this:

```
% rmiregistry 2048 &
```

If you use a different port, you'll need to include that port in URLs that refer to this registry service.

Finally, you're ready to start the server. Run the server program just as you'd run any Java class with a `main( )` method:

```
% java FibonacciServer
Fibonacci Server ready.
```

Now the server and registry are ready to accept remote method calls. Next we'll write a client that connects to these servers to make such remote method calls.

The Client Side

Before a regular Java object can call a method, it needs a reference to the object whose method it's going to call. Before a client object can call a remote method, it needs a remote reference to the object whose method it's going to call. A program retrieves this remote reference from a registry on the server where the remote object runs. It queries the registry by calling the registry's lookup( ) method. The exact naming scheme depends on the registry; the java.rmi.Naming class provides a URL-based scheme for locating objects. As you can see in the following code, these URLs have been designed so that they are similar to *http* URLs. The protocol is *rmi*. The URL's file field specifies the remote object's name. The fields for the hostname and the port number are unchanged:

```
Object o1 = Naming.lookup("rmi://login.ibiblio.org/fibonacci");
Object o2 = Naming.lookup("rmi://login.ibiblio.org:2048/fibonacci");
```

Like objects stored in Hashtables, Vectors, and other data structures that store objects of different classes, the object that is retrieved from a registry loses its type information. Therefore, before using the object, you must cast it to the remote interface that the remote object implements (not to the actual class, which is hidden from clients):

```
Fibonacci calculator = (Fibonacci) Naming.lookup("fibonacci");
```

Once a reference to the object has been retrieved and its type restored, the client can use that reference to invoke the object's remote methods pretty much as it would use a normal reference variable to invoke methods in a local object. The only difference is that you'll need to catch RemoteException for each remote invocation. For example:

```
try {
  BigInteger f56 = calculator.getFibonacci(56);
  System.out.println("The 56th Fibonacci number is " + f56);
  BigInteger f156 = calculator.getFibonacci(new BigInteger(156));
  System.out.println("The 156th Fibonacci number is " + f156);
}
catch (RemoteException ex) {
  System.err.println(ex)
}
```

Example 18-5 is a simple client for the Fibonacci interface of the last section.

Example 18-5. The FibonacciClient

```
import java.rmi.*;
import java.net.*;
import java.math.BigInteger;
```

Example 18-5. The FibonacciClient (continued)

```java
public class FibonacciClient {

  public static void main(String args[]) {

    if (args.length == 0 || !args[0].startsWith("rmi:")) {
      System.err.println(
        "Usage: java FibonacciClient rmi://host.domain:port/fibonacci number");
      return;
    }

    try {
      Object o = Naming.lookup(args[0]);
      Fibonacci calculator = (Fibonacci) o;
      for (int i = 1; i < args.length; i++) {
        try {
          BigInteger index = new BigInteger(args[i]);
          BigInteger f = calculator.getFibonacci(index);
          System.out.println("The " + args[i] + "th Fibonacci number is "
           + f);
        }
        catch (NumberFormatException e) {
          System.err.println(args[i] + "is not an integer.");
        }
      }
    }
    catch (MalformedURLException ex) {
      System.err.println(args[0] + " is not a valid RMI URL");
    }
    catch (RemoteException ex) {
      System.err.println("Remote object threw exception " + ex);
    }
    catch (NotBoundException ex) {
      System.err.println(
        "Could not find the requested remote object on the server");
    }
  }
}
```

Compile the class as usual. Notice that because the object that `Naming.lookup( )` returns is cast to a `Fibonacci`, either the *Fibonacci.java* or *Fibonacci.class* file needs to be available on the local host. A general requirement for compiling a client is to have either the byte or source code for the remote interface you're connecting to. To some extent, you can relax this a little bit by using the reflection API, but you'll still need to know at least something about the remote interface's API. Most of the time, this isn't an issue, since the server and client are written by the same programmer or team. The point of RMI is to allow a VM to invoke methods on remote objects, not to compile against remote objects.

Running the Client

Go back to the client system. Make sure that the client system has *FibonacciClient.class*, *Fibonacci.class*, and *FibonacciImpl_Stub.class* in its class path. (If both the client and the server are running Java 1.5, you don't need the stub class.) On the client system, type:

```
C:\>java FibonacciClient rmi://host.com/fibonacci 0 1 2 3 4 5 55 155
```

You should see:

```
The 0th Fibonacci number is 1
The 1th Fibonacci number is 1
The 2th Fibonacci number is 2
The 3th Fibonacci number is 3
The 4th Fibonacci number is 5
The 5th Fibonacci number is 8
The 55th Fibonacci number is 225851433717
The 155th Fibonacci number is 17889034785183316825745528789179
```

The client converts the command-line arguments to `BigInteger` objects. It sends those objects over the wire to the remote server. The server receives each of those objects, calculates the Fibonacci number for that index, and sends a `BigInteger` object back over the Internet to the client. Here, I'm using a PC for the client and a remote Unix box for the server. You can actually run both server and client on the same machine, although that's not as interesting.

Loading Classes at Runtime

All the client really has to know about the remote object is its remote interface. Everything else it needs—for instance, the stub classes—can be loaded from a web server (though not an RMI server) at runtime using a class loader. Indeed, this ability to load classes from the network is one of the unique features of Java. This is especially useful in applets. The web server can send the browser an applet that communicates back with the server; for instance, to allow the client to read and write files on the server. However, as with any time that classes are loaded from a potentially untrusted host, they must be checked by a `SecurityManager`.

Unfortunately, while remote objects are actually quite easy to work with when you can install the necessary classes in the local client class path, doing so when you have to dynamically load the stubs and other classes is fiendishly difficult. The class path, the security architecture, and the reliance on poorly documented environment variables are all bugbears that torment Java programmers. Getting a local client object to download remote objects from a server requires manipulating all of these in precise detail. Making even a small mistake prevents programs from running, and only the most generic of exceptions is thrown to tell the poor programmers what they did wrong. Exactly how difficult it is to make the programs work depends on the context in which the remote objects are running. In general, applet clients that use RMI are somewhat easier to manage than standalone application clients. Standalone applications are feasible if the client can be relied on to have access to the same *.class* files as the server has. Standalone applications that need to load classes from the server border on impossible.

Example 18-6 is an applet client for the Fibonacci remote object. It has the same basic structure as the FibonacciClient in Example 18-5. However, it uses a TextArea to display the message from the server instead of using System.out.

Example 18-6. An applet client for the Fibonacci object

```java
import java.applet.Applet;
import java.awt.*;
import java.awt.event.*;
import java.rmi.*;
import java.math.BigInteger;

public class FibonacciApplet extends Applet {

  private TextArea   resultArea
   = new TextArea("", 20, 72, TextArea.SCROLLBARS_BOTH);
  private TextField inputArea  = new TextField(24);
  private Button calculate = new Button("Calculate");
  private String server;

  public void init() {

    this.setLayout(new BorderLayout());

    Panel north = new Panel();
    north.add(new Label("Type a non-negative integer"));
    north.add(inputArea);
    north.add(calculate);
    this.add(resultArea, BorderLayout.CENTER);
    this.add(north, BorderLayout.NORTH);
    Calculator c = new Calculator();
    inputArea.addActionListener(c);
    calculate.addActionListener(c);
    resultArea.setEditable(false);

    server = "rmi://" + this.getCodeBase().getHost() + "/fibonacci";

  }

  class Calculator implements ActionListener {

    public void actionPerformed(ActionEvent evt) {

      try {
        String input = inputArea.getText();
        if (input != null) {
          BigInteger index = new BigInteger(input);
          Fibonacci f = (Fibonacci) Naming.lookup(server);
```

Example 18-6. An applet client for the Fibonacci object (continued)

```
      BigInteger result =  f.getFibonacci(index);
      resultArea.setText(result.toString( ));
    }
  }
  catch (Exception ex) {
    resultArea.setText(ex.getMessage( ));
  }
  }
 }
}
```

You'll notice that the *rmi* URL is built from the applet's own codebase. This helps avoid nasty security problems that arise when an applet tries to open a network connection to a host other than the one it came from. RMI-based applets are certainly not exempt from the usual restrictions on network connections.

Example 18-7 is a simple HTML file that can be used to load the applet from the web browser.

Example 18-7. FibonacciApplet.html

```
<html>
<head>
<title>RMI Applet</title>
</head>
<body>
<h1>RMI Applet</h1>

<p>
<applet align="center" code="FibonacciApplet" width="300" height="100">
</applet>
<hr />
</p>
</body>
</html>
```

Place *FibonacciImpl_Stub.class*, *Fibonacci.class*, *FibonacciApplet.html*, and *FibonacciServer.class* in the same directory on your web server. Add this directory to the server's class path and start *rmiregistry* on the server. Then start FibonacciServer on the server. For example:

```
% rmiregistry &
% java FibonacciServer &
```

Make sure that both of these are running on the actual web server machine. Many web server farms use different machines for site maintenance and web serving, even though both mount the same filesystems. To get past the applet security restriction, both *rmiregistry* and FibonacciServer have to be running on the machine that serves the *FibonacciApplet.class* file to web clients.

Now load *FibonacciApplet.html* into a web browser from the client. Figure 18-2 shows the result.

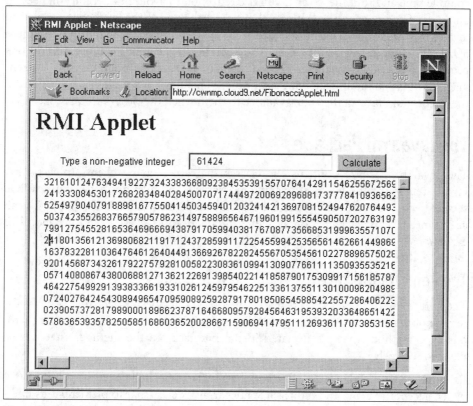

Figure 18-2. The Fibonacci applet

For applications, it's much easier if you can load all the classes you need before running the program. You can load classes from a web server running on the same server the remote object is running on, if necessary. To do this, set the java.rmi.server. codebase Java system property on the server (where the remote object runs) to the URL where the *.class* files are stored on the network. For example, to specify that the classes can be found at *http://www.cafeaulait.org/rmi2/*, you would type:

```
% java -Djava.rmi.server.codebase=http://www.cafeaulait.org/rmi2/ FibonacciServer &
Fibonacci Server ready.
```

If the classes are in packages, the java.rmi.server.codebase property points to the directory containing the top-level *com* or *org* directory rather than the directory containing the *.class* files themselves. Both servers and clients will load the *.class* files from this location if the files are not found in the local class path first.

Loading classes from the remote server makes the coupling between the server and the client a little less tight. However, any client program you write will normally have to know quite a bit about the system it's talking to in order to do something useful. This usually involves having at least the remote interface available on the client at compile time and runtime. Even if you use reflection to avoid that, you'll still need to know the signatures and something about the behavior of the methods you plan to invoke. RMI just doesn't lend itself to truly loose coupling like you might see in a SOAP or, better yet, RESTful server. The RMI design metaphor is more running one program on several machines than it is having several programs on different machines that communicate with each other. Therefore, it's easiest if both sides of the connection have all the code available to them when the program starts up.

The java.rmi Package

The java.rmi package contains the classes that are seen by clients (objects that invoke remote methods). Both clients and servers should import java.rmi. While servers need a lot more infrastructure than is present in this package, java.rmi is all clients need. This package contains one interface, three classes, and a handful of exceptions.

The Remote Interface

The Remote interface tags objects as remote objects. It doesn't declare any methods; remote objects usually implement a subclass of Remote that does declare some methods. The methods that are declared in the interface are the methods that can be invoked remotely.

Example 18-8 is a database interface that declares a single method, SQLQuery( ), which accepts a String and returns a String array. A class that implements this interface would include the code to send an SQL query to a database and return the result as a String array.

Example 18-8. A database interface

```
import java.rmi.*;

public interface SQL extends Remote {

  public String[] SQLQuery(String query) throws RemoteException;

}
```

An SQLImpl class that implemented the SQL interface would probably have more methods, some of which might be public. However, only the SQLQuery( ) method can be invoked by a client. Because the Remote interface is not a class, a single object can implement multiple Remote subinterfaces. In this case, any method declared in any Remote interface can be invoked by a client.

The Naming Class

The java.rmi.Naming class talks to a registry running on the server in order to map URLs like *rmi://login.ibiblio.org/myRemoteObject* to particular remote objects on particular hosts. You can think of a registry as a DNS for remote objects. Each entry in the registry has a name and an object reference. Clients give the name (via a URL) and get back a reference to the remote object.

As you've seen, an *rmi* URL looks exactly like an *http* URL except that the scheme is rmi instead of http. Furthermore, the path part of the URL is an arbitrary name that the server has bound to a particular remote object, not a filename.

The biggest deficiency of Naming is that for security reasons (avoiding man-in-the-middle attacks), it has to run on the same server as the remote objects. It cannot register multiple objects on several different servers. If this is too restrictive, a Java Naming and Directory Interface (JNDI) context can add an additional layer of indirection so that multiple RMI registries can be presented through a single directory. Clients need only know the address of the main JNDI directory. They do not need to know the addresses of all the individual RMI registries the JNDI context is proxying for.

The Naming class has five public methods: list( ), to list all the names bound in the registry; lookup( ), to find a specific remote object given its URL; bind( ), to bind a name to a specific remote object; rebind( ), to bind a name to a different remote object; and unbind( ), to remove a name from the registry. Let's look at these methods in turn.

public static String[] list(String url) throws RemoteException, MalformedURLException

The list( ) method returns an array of strings, one for each URL that is currently bound. The url argument is the URL of the Naming registry to query. Only the protocol, host, and port are used. The path part of the URL is ignored. list( ) throws a MalformedURLException if url is not a valid *rmi* URL. A RemoteException is thrown if anything else goes wrong, such as the registry's not being reachable or refusing to supply the requested information.

Example 18-9 is a simple program that lists all the names currently bound in a particular registry. It's sometimes useful when debugging RMI problems. It allows you to determine whether the names you're using are the names the server expects.

Example 18-9. RegistryLister

```
import java.rmi.*;

public class RegistryLister {

  public static void main(String[] args) {
```

Example 18-9. RegistryLister (continued)

```
    int port = 1099;

    if (args.length == 0) {
      System.err.println("Usage: java RegistryLister host port");
      return;
    }

    String host = args[0];

    if (args.length > 1) {
      try {
        port = Integer.parseInt(args[1]);
        if (port <1 || port > 65535) port = 1099;
      }
      catch (NumberFormatException ex) {}

    }

    String url = "rmi://" + host + ":" + port + "/";
    try {
      String[] remoteObjects = Naming.list(url);
      for (int i = 0; i < remoteObjects.length; i++) {
        System.out.println(remoteObjects[i]);
      }
    }
    catch (RemoteException ex) {
      System.err.println(ex);
    }
    catch (java.net.MalformedURLException ex) {
      System.err.println(ex);
    }
  }
}
```

Here's a result from a run against the RMI server I was using to test the examples in this chapter:

```
% java RegistryLister login.ibiblio.org
rmi://login.ibiblio.org:1099/fibonacci
rmi://login.ibiblio.org:1099/hello
```

You can see that the format for the strings is full *rmi* URLs rather than just names. It turns out this is a bug; in Java 1.4.1 and later, the bug has been fixed. In these versions, the scheme part of the URI is no longer included. In other words, the output looks like this:

```
//login.ibiblio.org:1099/fibonacci
//login.ibiblio.org:1099/hello
```

public static Remote lookup(String url) throws RemoteException, NotBoundException, AccessException, MalformedURLException

A client uses the lookup( ) method to retrieve the remote object associated with the file portion of the name; so, given the URL *rmi://login.ibiblio.org:2001/myRemoteObject*, it would return the object bound to myRemoteObject from *login.ibiblio.org* on port 2,001.

This method throws a NotBoundException if the remote server does not recognize the name. It throws a RemoteException if the remote registry can't be reached; for instance, because the network is down or because no registry service is running on the specified port. An AccessException is thrown if the server refuses to look up the name for the particular host. Finally, if the URL is not a proper *rmi* URL, it throws a MalformedURLException.

public static void bind(String url, Remote object) throws RemoteException, AlreadyBoundException, MalformedURLException, AccessException

A server uses the bind( ) method to link a name like myRemoteObject to a remote object. If the binding is successful, clients will be able to retrieve the remote object stub from the registry using a URL like *rmi://login.ibiblio.org:2001/myRemoteObject*.

Many things can go wrong with the binding process. bind( ) throws a MalformedURLException if url is not a valid *rmi* URL. It throws a RemoteException if the registry cannot be reached. It throws an AccessException, a subclass of RemoteException, if the client is not allowed to bind objects in this registry. If the URL is already bound to a local object, it throws an AlreadyBoundException.

public static void unbind(String url) throws RemoteException, NotBoundException, AlreadyBoundException, MalformedURLException, AccessException // Java 1.2

The unbind( ) method removes the object with the given URL from the registry. It's the opposite of the bind( ) method. What bind( ) has bound, unbind( ) releases. unbind( ) throws a NotBoundException if url was not bound to an object in the first place. Otherwise, this method can throw the same exceptions for the same reasons as bind( ).

public static void rebind(String url, Remote object) throws RemoteException, AccessException, MalformedURLException

The rebind( ) method is just like the bind( ) method, except that it binds the URL to the object, even if the URL is already bound. If the URL is already bound to an object, the old binding is lost. Thus, this method does not throw an Already-BoundException. It can still throw RemoteException, AccessException, or MalformedURLException, which have the same meanings as they do when thrown by bind( ).

The RMISecurityManager Class

A client loads stubs from a potentially untrustworthy server; in this sense, the relationship between a client and a stub is somewhat like the relationship between a browser and an applet. Although a stub is only supposed to marshal arguments and unmarshal return values and send them across the network, from the standpoint of the virtual machine, a stub is just another class with methods that can do just about anything. Stubs produced by *rmic* shouldn't misbehave; but there's no reason someone couldn't handcraft a stub that would do all sorts of nasty things, such as reading files or erasing data. The Java virtual machine does not allow stub classes to be loaded across the network unless there's some SecurityManager object in place. (Like other classes, stub classes can always be loaded from the local class path.) For applets, the standard AppletSecurityManager fills this need. Applications can use the RMISecurityManager class to protect themselves from miscreant stubs:

```
public class RMISecurityManager extends SecurityManager
```

In Java 1.1, this class implements a policy that allows classes to be loaded from the server's codebase (which is not necessarily the same as the server itself) and allows the necessary network communications between the client, the server, and the codebase. In Java 1.2 and later, the RMISecurityManager doesn't allow even that, and this class is so restrictive, it's essentially useless. In the Java 1.5 documentation, Sun finally admitted the problem: "RMISecurityManager implements a policy that is no different than the policy implemented by SecurityManager. Therefore an RMI application should use the SecurityManager class or another application-specific SecurityManager implementation instead of this class."

Remote Exceptions

The java.rmi package defines 16 exceptions, listed in Table 18-1. Most extend java.rmi.RemoteException. java.rmi.RemoteException extends java.io.IOException. AlreadyBoundException and NotBoundException extend java.lang.Exception. Thus, all are checked exceptions that must be enclosed in a try block or declared in a throws clause. There's also one runtime exception, RMISecurityException, a subclass of SecurityException.

Remote methods depend on many things that are not under your control: for example, the state of the network and other necessary services such as DNS. Therefore, any remote method can fail: there's no guarantee that the network won't be down when the method is called. Consequently, all remote methods must be declared to throw the generic RemoteException and all calls to remote methods should be wrapped in a try block. When you just want to get a program working, it's simplest to catch RemoteException:

```
try {
  // call remote methods...
}
```

```
catch (RemoteException ex) {
  System.err.println(ex);
}
```

More robust programs should try to catch more specific exceptions and respond accordingly.

Table 18-1. Remote exceptions

Exception	Meaning
AccessException	A client tried to do something that only local objects are allowed to do.
AlreadyBoundException	The URL is already bound to another object.
ConnectException	The server refused the connection.
ConnectIOException	An I/O error occurred while trying to make the connection between the local and the remote host.
MarshalException	An I/O error occurred while attempting to marshal (serialize) arguments to a remote method. A corrupted I/O stream could cause this exception; making the remote method call again might be successful.
UnmarshalException	An I/O error occurred while attempting to unmarshal (deserialize) the value returned by a remote method. A corrupted I/O stream could cause this exception; making the remote method call again might be successful.
NoSuchObjectException	The object reference is invalid or obsolete. This might occur if the remote host becomes unreachable while the program is running, perhaps because of network congestion, system crash, or other malfunction.
NotBoundException	The URL is not bound to an object. This might be thrown when you try to reference an object whose URL was rebound out from under it.
RemoteException	The generic superclass for all exceptions having to do with remote methods.
ServerError	Despite the name, this is indeed an exception, not an error. It indicates that the server threw an error while executing the remote method.
ServerException	A RemoteException was thrown while the remote method was executing.
StubNotFoundException	The stub for a class could not be found. The stub file may be in the wrong directory on the server, there could be a namespace collision between the class that the stub substitutes for and some other class, or the client could have requested the wrong URL.
UnexpectedException	Something unforeseen happened. This is a catchall that occurs only in bizarre situations.
UnknownHostException	The host cannot be found. This is very similar to java.net.UnknownHostException.

The RemoteException class contains a single public field called detail:

```
public Throwable detail
```

This field may contain the actual exception thrown on the server side, so it gives you further information about what went wrong. For example:

```
try {
  // call remote methods...
}
catch (RemoteException ex) {
  System.err.println(ex.detail);
```

```
      ex.detail.printStackTrace( );
    }
```

In Java 1.4 and later, use the standard getCause( ) method to return the nested exception instead:

```
    try {
      // call remote methods...
    }
    catch (RemoteException ex) {
      System.err.println(ex.getCause( ));
      ex.getCause( ).printStackTrace( );
    }
```

The java.rmi.registry Package

How does a client that needs a remote object locate that object on a distant server? More precisely, how does it get a remote reference to the object? Clients find out what remote objects are available by querying the server's *registry*. A registry advertises the availability of the server's remote objects. Clients query the registry to find out what remote objects are available and to get remote references to those objects. You've already seen one: the java.rmi.Naming class for interfacing with registries.

The Registry interface and the LocateRegistry class allow clients to retrieve remote objects on a server by name. A RegistryImpl is a subclass of RemoteObject, which links names to particular RemoteObject objects. Clients use the methods of the LocateRegistry class to retrieve the RegistryImpl for a specific host and port.

The Registry Interface

The java.rmi.registry.Registry interface has five public methods: bind( ), to bind a name to a specific remote object; list( ), to list all the names bound in the registry; lookup( ), to find a specific remote object given its URL; rebind( ), to bind a name to a different remote object; and unbind( ), to remove a name from the registry. All of these behave exactly as previously described in the java.rmi.Naming class, which implements this interface. Other classes that implement this interface may use a different scheme for mapping names to particular objects, but the methods still have the same meaning and signatures.

Besides these five methods, the Registry interface also has one field, Registry. REGISTRY_PORT, the default port on which the registry listens. Its value is 1099.

The LocateRegistry Class

The java.rmi.registry.LocateRegistry class lets the client find the registry in the first place. This is achieved with five overloaded versions of the static LocateRegistry.getRegistry( ) method:

```
public static Registry getRegistry() throws RemoteException
public static Registry getRegistry(int port) throws RemoteException
public static Registry getRegistry(String host) throws RemoteException
public static Registry getRegistry(String host, int port)
  throws RemoteException
public static Registry getRegistry(String host, int port,   // Java 1.2
  RMIClientSocketFactory factory) throws RemoteException
```

Each of these methods returns a `Registry` object that can be used to get remote objects by name. `LocateRegistry.getRegistry()` returns a stub for the `Registry` running on the local host on the default port, 1,099. `LocateRegistry.getRegistry(int port)` returns a stub for the `Registry` running on the local host on the specified port. `LocateRegistry.getRegistry(String host)` returns a stub for the `Registry` for the specified host on the default port, 1,099. `LocateRegistry.getRegistry(String host, int port)` returns a stub for the `Registry` on the specified host on the specified port. Finally, `LocateRegistry.getRegistry(String host, int port, RMIClientSocketFactory factory)` returns a stub to the registry running on the specified host and port, which will be contacted using sockets created by the provided `java.rmi.server.RMIClientSocketFactory` object. If the host `String` is null, `getRegistry()` uses the local host; if the port argument is negative, it uses the default port. Each of these methods can throw an arbitrary `RemoteException`.

For example, a remote object that wanted to make itself available to clients might do this:

```
Registry r = LocateRegistry.getRegistry();
r.bind("My Name", this);
```

A remote client that wished to invoke this remote object might then say:

```
Registry r = LocateRegistry.getRegistry("thehost.site.com");
RemoteObjectInterface tro = (RemoteObjectInterface) r.lookup("MyName");
tro.invokeRemoteMethod();
```

The final two methods in the `LocateRegistry` class are the overloaded `LocateRegistry.createRegistry()` methods. These create a registry and start it listening on the specified port. As usual, each can throw a `RemoteException`. Their signatures are:

```
public static Registry createRegistry(int port) throws RemoteException
public static Registry createRegistry(int port,
  RMIClientSocketFactory csf, RMIServerSocketFactory ssf) // Java 1.2
  throws RemoteException
```

The java.rmi.server Package

The `java.rmi.server` package is the most complex of all the RMI packages; it contains the scaffolding for building remote objects and thus is used by objects whose methods will be invoked by clients. The package defines 6 exceptions, 9 interfaces, and 10–12 classes (depending on the Java version). Fortunately, you only need to be familiar with a few of these in order to write remote objects. The important classes are the RemoteObject class, which is the basis for all remote objects; the RemoteServer class, which extends RemoteObject; and the UnicastRemoteObject class, which extends RemoteServer. Any remote objects you write will likely either use or extend Unicast-RemoteObject. Clients that call remote methods but are not themselves remote objects don't use these classes and therefore don't need to import java.rmi.server.

The RemoteObject Class

Technically, a remote object is not an instance of the RemoteObject class but an instance of any class that implements a Remote interface. In practice, most remote objects will be instances of a subclass of java.rmi.server.RemoteObject:

```
public abstract class RemoteObject extends Object
  implements Remote, Serializable
```

You can think of this class as a special version of java.lang.Object for remote objects. It provides toString(), hashCode(), clone(), and equals() methods that make sense for remote objects. If you create a remote object that does not extend RemoteObject, you need to override these methods yourself.

The equals() method compares the remote object references of two RemoteObjects and returns true if they point to the same RemoteObject. As with the equals() method in the Object class, you may want to override this method to provide a more meaningful definition of equality.

The toString() method returns a String that describes the RemoteObject. Most of the time, toString() returns the hostname and port from which the remote object came as well as a reference number for the object. You can override this method in your own subclasses to provide more meaningful string representations.

The hashCode() method maps a presumably unique int to each unique object; this integer may be used as a key in a Hashtable. It returns the same value for all remote references that refer to the same remote object. Thus, if a client has several remote references to the same object on the server, or multiple clients have references to that object, they should all have the same hash code.

The final instance method in this class is getRef():

```
public RemoteRef getRef() // Java 1.2
```

This returns a remote reference to the class:

```
public abstract interface RemoteRef extends Externalizable
```

There's also one static method, RemoteObject.toStub():

```
public static Remote toStub(Remote ro) // Java 1.2
  throws NoSuchObjectException
```

`RemoteObject.toStub( )` converts a given remote object into the equivalent stub object for use in the client virtual machine, which can help you dynamically generate stubs from within your server without using *rmic*.

The RemoteServer Class

The `RemoteServer` class extends `RemoteObject`; it is an abstract superclass for server implementations such as `UnicastRemoteObject`. It provides a few simple utility methods needed by most server objects:

```
public abstract class RemoteServer extends RemoteObject
```

`UnicastRemoteObject` is the most commonly used subclass of `RemoteServer` included in the core library. Two others, `Activatable` and `ActivationGroup`, are found in the `java.rmi.activation` package. You can add others (for example, a UDP or multicast remote server) by writing your own subclass of `RemoteServer`.

Constructors

`RemoteServer` has two constructors:

```
protected RemoteServer( )
protected RemoteServer(RemoteRef r)
```

However, you won't instantiate this class yourself. Instead, you will instantiate a subclass like `UnicastRemoteObject`. That class's constructor calls one of these protected constructors from the first line of its constructor.

Getting information about the client

The `RemoteServer` class has one method to locate the client with which you're communicating:

```
public static String getClientHost( ) throws ServerNotActiveException
```

`RemoteServer.getClientHost( )` returns a `String` that contains the hostname of the client that invoked the currently running method. This method throws a `ServerNotActiveException` if the current thread is not running a remote method.

Logging

For debugging purposes, it is sometimes useful to see the calls that are being made to a remote object and the object's responses. You get a log for a `RemoteServer` by passing an `OutputStream` object to the `setLog( )` method:

```
public static void setLog(OutputStream out)
```

Passing `null` turns off logging. For example, to see all the calls on `System.err` (which sends the log to the Java console), you would write:

```
myRemoteServer.setLog(System.err);
```

Here's some log output I collected while debugging the Fibonacci programs in this chapter:

```
Sat Apr 29 12:20:36 EDT 2000:RMI:TCP Accept-1:[titan.oit.unc.edu:
sun.rmi.transport.DGCImpl[0:0:0, 2]: java.rmi.dgc.Lease
dirty(java.rmi.server.ObjID[], long, java.rmi.dgc.Lease)]
Fibonacci Server ready.
Sat Apr 29 12:21:27 EDT 2000:RMI:TCP Accept-2:[macfaq.dialup.cloud9.net:
sun.rmi.transport.DGCImpl[0:0:0, 2]: java.rmi.dgc.Lease
dirty(java.rmi.server.ObjID[], long, java.rmi.dgc.Lease)]
Sat Apr 29 12:22:36 EDT 2000:RMI:TCP Accept-3:[macfaq.dialup.cloud9.net: sun.rmi.
transport.DGCImpl[0:0:0, 2]: java.rmi.dgc.Lease
dirty(java.rmi.server.ObjID[], long, java.rmi.dgc.Lease)]
Sat Apr 29 12:22:39 EDT 2000:RMI:TCP Accept-3:[macfaq.dialup.cloud9.net:
FibonacciImpl[0]: java.math.BigInteger getFibonacci(java.math.BigInteger)]
Sat Apr 29 12:22:39 EDT 2000:RMI:TCP Accept-3:[macfaq.dialup.cloud9.net:
FibonacciImpl[0]: java.math.BigInteger getFibonacci(java.math.BigInteger)]
```

If you want to add extra information to the log along with what's provided by the RemoteServer class, you can retrieve the log's PrintStream with the getLog( ) method:

```
public static PrintStream getLog( )
```

Once you have the print stream, you can write on it to add your own comments to the log. For example:

```
PrintStream p = RemoteServer.getLog( );
p.println("There were " + n + " total calls to the remote object.");
```

The UnicastRemoteObject Class

The UnicastRemoteObject class is a concrete subclass of RemoteServer. To create a remote object, you can extend UnicastRemoteObject and declare that your subclass implements some subinterface of java.rmi.Remote. The methods of the interface provide functionality specific to the class, while the methods of UnicastRemoteObject handle general remote object tasks like marshalling and unmarshalling arguments and return values. All of this happens behind the scenes. As an application programmer, you don't need to worry about it.

A UnicastRemoteObject runs on a single host, uses TCP sockets to communicate, and has remote references that do not remain valid across server restarts. While this is a good general-purpose framework for remote objects, it is worth noting that you can implement other kinds of remote objects. For example, you may want a remote object that uses UDP, or one that remains valid if the server is restarted, or even one that distributes the load across multiple servers. To create remote objects with these properties, extend RemoteServer directly and implement the abstract methods of that class. However, if you don't need anything so esoteric, it's much easier to subclass UnicastRemoteObject.

The UnicastRemoteObject class has three protected constructors:

```
protected UnicastRemoteObject( ) throws RemoteException
protected UnicastRemoteObject(int port)                  // Java 1.2
  throws RemoteException
protected UnicastRemoteObject(int port, RMIClientSocketFactory csf,
  RMIServerSocketFactory ssf) throws RemoteException  // Java 1.2
```

When you write a subclass of UnicastRemoteObject, you call one of these constructors, either explicitly or implicitly, in the first line of each constructor of your subclass. All three constructors can throw a RemoteException if the remote object cannot be created.

The noargs constructor creates a UnicastRemoteObject that listens on an anonymous port chosen at runtime. By the way, this is an example of an obscure situation I mentioned in Chapter 9 and Chapter 10. The server is listening on an anonymous port. Normally, this situation is next to useless because it is impossible for clients to locate the server. In this case, clients locate servers by using a registry that keeps track of the available servers and the ports they are listening to.

The downside to listening on an anonymous port is that it's not uncommon for a firewall to block connections to that port. The next two constructors listen on specified ports so you can ask the network administrators to allow traffic for those ports through the firewall.

If the network administrators are uncooperative, you'll need to use HTTP tunneling or a proxy server or both. The third constructor also allows you to specify the socket factories used by this UnicastRemoteObject. In particular, you can supply a socket factory that returns sockets that know how to get through the firewall.

The UnicastRemoteObject class has several public methods:

```
public Object clone( ) throws CloneNotSupportedException
public static RemoteStub exportObject(Remote r) throws RemoteException
public static Remote exportObject(Remote r, int port)
  throws RemoteException      // Java 1.2
public static Remote exportObject(Remote r, int port,
  RMIClientSocketFactory csf, RMIServerSocketFactory ssf)
  throws RemoteException      // Java 1.2
public static boolean unexportObject(Remote r, boolean force)
  throws NoSuchObjectException // Java 1.2
```

The clone( ) method simply creates a clone of the remote object. You call the UnicastRemoteObject.exportObject( ) to use the infrastructure that UnicastRemoteObject provides for an object that can't subclass UnicastRemoteObject. Similarly, you pass an object UnicastRemoteObject.unexportObject( ) to stop a particular remote object from listening for invocations.

Exceptions

The `java.rmi.server` package defines a few more exceptions. The exceptions and their meanings are listed in Table 18-2. All but `java.rmi.server.Server-NotActiveException` extend, directly or indirectly, `java.rmi.RemoteException`. All are checked exceptions that must be caught or declared in a `throws` clause.

Table 18-2. java.rmi.server exceptions

Exception	Meaning
ExportException	You're trying to export a remote object on a port that's already in use.
ServerNotActiveException	An attempt was made to invoke a method in a remote object that wasn't running.
ServerCloneException	An attempt to clone a remote object on the server failed.
SocketSecurityException	This subclass of `ExportException` is thrown when the `SecurityManager` prevents a remote object from being exported on the requested port.

This chapter has been a fairly quick look at Remote Method Invocation. For a more detailed treatment, see *Java RMI*, by William Grosso (O'Reilly).

The JavaMail API

Email was the Internet's first killer app and still generates more Internet traffic than any protocol except HTTP. One of the most frequently asked questions about Java is how to send email from a Java applet or application. While it's certainly possible to write a Java program that uses sockets to communicate with mail servers, this requires detailed knowledge of some fairly complicated protocols, such as SMTP, POP, and IMAP. Just as the URL class makes interacting with HTTP servers a lot simpler than it would be with raw sockets, so too can a class library dedicated to handling email make writing email clients a lot simpler.

The JavaMail API is a standard extension to Java that provides a class library for email clients. It's a required component of the Java 2 Platform, Enterprise Edition (J2EE). The JavaMail API can be implemented in 100% Pure Java™ using sockets and streams, and indeed Sun's reference implementation is so implemented. Programs use the JavaMail API to communicate with SMTP, POP, and IMAP servers to send and receive email. By taking advantage of this API, you can avoid focusing on the low-level protocol details and focus instead on what you want to say with the message. Additional providers can add support for other mail systems such as Hotmail or MH. You can even install providers that add support for NNTP, the protocol used to transport Usenet news.

There's no limit to the uses Java programs have for the JavaMail API. Most obviously, you can write standard email clients such as Eudora. Or it can be used for email-intensive applications such as mailing list managers, like listproc. But the JavaMail API is also useful as a part of larger applications that simply need to send or receive a little email. For instance, a server-monitoring application such as Whistle Blower can periodically load pages from a web server running on a different host and email the webmaster if the web server has crashed. An applet can use email to send data to any process or person on the Internet that has an email address, in essence using the web server's SMTP server as a simple proxy to bypass the usual security restrictions about whom an applet is allowed to talk to. In reverse, an applet can talk to an IMAP server on the applet host to receive data from many hosts around the

Net. A newsreader could be implemented as a custom service provider that treats NNTP as just one more means of exchanging messages. And that's just the beginning of the sort of programs the JavaMail API makes it very straightforward to write.

What Is the JavaMail API?

The JavaMail API is a fairly high-level representation of the basic components of any email system. The components are represented by abstract classes in the javax.mail package. For instance, the abstract class javax.mail.Message represents an email message. It declares abstract methods to get and set various kinds of envelope information for the message, such as the sender and addressee, the date sent, and the subject of the message. The abstract class javax.mail.Folder represents a message container. It declares abstract methods to get messages from a folder, move messages between folders, and delete messages from a folder.

These classes are all abstract because they don't make many assumptions about how the email is stored or transferred between machines. For instance, they do not assume that messages are sent using SMTP or that they're structured as specified in RFC 822. Concrete subclasses of these classes specialize the abstract classes to particular protocols and mail formats. If you want to work with standard Internet email, you might use javax.mail.MimeMessage instead of javax.mail.Message, javax.mail. InternetAddress instead of javax.mail.Address, and com.sun.mail.imap.IMAPStore instead of javax.mail.Store. If you were writing code for a Lotus Notes–based system, you'd use different concrete implementation classes but the same abstract base classes.

The JavaMail API roughly follows the abstract factory design pattern. This pattern allows you to write your code based on the abstract superclasses without worrying too much about the lower-level details. The protocols and formats used and the associated concrete implementation classes are determined mostly by one line of code early in your program that names the protocol. Changing the protocol name goes 90% of the way to porting your program from one protocol (say, POP) to another (say, IMAP).

Service providers implement particular protocols. A service provider is a group of concrete subclasses of the abstract JavaMail API classes that specialize the general API to a particular protocol and mail format. These subclasses are probably (though not necessarily) organized into one package. Some of these (IMAP, SMTP) are provided by Sun with its reference implementation in the undocumented com.sun.mail package. Others (NNTP, MH) are available from third parties. And some (POP) are available from both Sun and third parties. The purpose of the abstract JavaMail API is to shield you from low-level details like this. You don't write code to access an IMAP server or a POP server. You write your programs to speak to the JavaMail API. Then, the JavaMail API uses the service provider to speak to the server using its native protocol. This is middleware for email. All you need to do to add a new protocol is install the service provider's JAR file. Simple, carefully designed programs that use only the core features of the JavaMail API may be able to use the new provider without even being recompiled. Of course, programs that make use of special features of individual protocols may need to be rewritten.

Since mail arrives from the network at unpredictable times, the JavaMail API relies on an event-based callback mechanism to handle incoming mail. This is exactly the same pattern (even using some of the same classes) found in the AWT and Java-Beans. The `javax.mail.event` package defines about half a dozen different kinds of mail events, as well as the associated listener interfaces and adapter classes for these events.

While many people still fondly recall the early days of ASCII email and even ASCII pictures, modern email messages contain a bewildering array of multilingual text and multimedia data encoded in formats such as Base64, quoted-printable, BinHex, and uuencode. To handle this, the JavaMail API uses the JavaBeans Activation Framework (JAF) to describe and display this content.

This chapter covers Version 1.3.1 of the JavaMail API, which is compatible with Java 1.1.8 and higher. The JavaMail API is a standard extension to Java, not part of the core JDK or JRE class library, even in Java 1.5. (It is a standard part of J2EE.) Consequently, you'll need to download it separately from Sun and install it on your system. It's freely available from *http://java.sun.com/products/javamail*. It comes as a Zip archive containing documentation, sample code, and the all-important *mail.jar* file. This file contains the actual *.class* files that implement the JavaMail API. To compile or run the examples in this chapter, you'll need to add this file to your class path, either by adding its path to the CLASSPATH environment variable or by placing *mail.jar* in your *jre/lib/ext* directory.

The JavaBeans Activation Framework is also a standard extension to Java, not part of the core API. You can download it from *http://java.sun.com/products/javabeans/jaf/*. This download contains the *activation.jar* archive, which you'll also need to place in your class path.

Finally, you may want to add some additional providers. Sun's implementation includes POP3, SMTP, and IMAP providers. However, third parties have written providers for other protocols such as Hotmail, NNTP, Exchange, and more. Table 19-1 lists some of these.

Table 19-1. Mail providers

Product (company)	URL	Protocols	License
JavaMail (Sun)	http://java.sun.com/products/javamail/	SMTP, IMAP, POP3	Free
JavaMail/Exchange Service Provider (JESP): (Intrinsyc Software)	http://support.intrinsyc.com/jesp/	Microsoft Exchange	Payware

Table 19-1. Mail providers (continued)

Product (company)	URL	Protocols	License
ICE MH JavaMail Provider (ICE Engineering, Inc.)	http://www.trustice.com/java/icemh	MH	Public domain
POPpers (Y. Miyadate)	http://www2s.biglobe.ne.jp/~dat/java/project/poppers/index_en.html	POP3	GPL
JDAVMail (Luc Claes)	http://jdavmail.sourceforge.net	Hotmail	LGPL
JHTTPMail (Laurent Michalkovic)	http://jhttpmail.sourceforge.net/	Hotmail	LGPL
GNU JavaMail	http://www.gnu.org/software/classpathx/javamail/	POP3, NNTP, SMTP, IMAP, mbox, maildir	GPL with library exception

Sending Email

Sending messages is the most basic email need of a Java program. While email clients like Eudora and mailing list managers like listproc are the only common programs that receive messages, all sorts of programs send messages. For instance, web browsers can submit HTML forms via email. Security scanning tools like Satan can run in the background and email their results to the administrator when they're done. When the Unix cron program detects a misconfigured *crontab* file, it emails the error to the owner. Books & Writers runs a popular service that tracks the sales rank of authors' books on Amazon.com and notifies them periodically via email. A massively parallel computation like the SETI@home project can submit individual results via email. Some multiplayer games like chess can be played across the network by emailing the moves back and forth (though this scheme wouldn't work for faster-moving games like Quake or even for speed chess). And these are just a few of the different kinds of programs that send email. In today's wired world, by far the simplest way to notify users of an event when they're not sitting in front of the computer that the program is running on is to send them email.

The JavaMail API provides everything programs need to send email. To send a message, a program follows these eight simple steps:

1. Set the `mail.host` property to point to the local mail server.

2. Start a mail session with the `Session.getInstance( )` method.

3. Create a new `Message` object, probably by instantiating one of its concrete subclasses.

4. Set the message's From: address.

5. Set the message's To: address.

6. Set the message's Subject:.

7. Set the content of the message.

8. Send the message with the `Transport.send( )` method.

The order of these steps is not especially rigid. For instance, steps 4 through 7 can be performed in any order. Individually, each of the steps is quite simple.

The first step is to set up the properties for the mail session. The only property you have to set in order to send mail is `mail.host`. This is configured as a `java.util.Properties` object rather than an environment variable. For example, this code fragment sets the `mail.host` property to *mail.cloud9.net*:

```
Properties props = new Properties();
props.put("mail.host", "mail.cloud9.net");
```

Your programs will of course have to set this property to the name of your own mail server. These properties are used to retrieve a `Session` object from the `Session.getInstance()` factory method, like this:

```
Session mailConnection = Session.getInstance(props, null);
```

The `Session` object represents an ongoing communication between a program and one mail server. The second argument to the `getInstance()` method, `null` here, is a `javax.mail.Authenticator` that will ask the user for a password if the server requests one. We'll discuss this more later in the section on password authentication. Most of the time, you do not need to provide a username and password to send email when using the local SMTP server, only to receive it.

The `Session` object is used to construct a new `Message` object:

```
Message msg = new MimeMessage(mailConnection);
```

I specify the `MimeMessage` class in particular since I know I'm sending Internet email. However, this is the one place where I do explicitly choose a format for the email message. In some cases, this may not be necessary if I can copy the incoming message format instead.

Now that I have a `Message` object, I need to set up its fields and contents. The From: address and To: address will each be `javax.mail.internet.InternetAddress` objects. You can provide either an email address alone or an email address and a real name:

```
Address bill = new InternetAddress("god@microsoft.com", "Bill Gates");
Address elliotte = new InternetAddress("elharo@metalab.unc.edu");
```

The `setFrom()` method allows us to say who's sending the message by setting the From: header. There's no protection against forgery. It's quite easy for me to masquerade as Bill Gates at a (presumably) fictitious email address:

```
msg.setFrom(bill);
```

The `setRecipient()` method is slightly more complex. You not only have to specify the address that the message will be sent to, but how that address is used; that is, as a To: field, a Cc: field, or a Bcc: field. These are indicated by three mnemonic constants of the `Message.RecipientType` class:

```
Message.RecipientType.TO
Message.RecipientType.CC
Message.RecipientType.BCC
```

For example:

```
msg.setRecipient(Message.RecipientType.TO, elliotte);
```

The subject is set as a simple string of text. For example:

```
msg.setSubject("You must comply.");
```

The body is also set as a single string of text. However, along with that text, you need to provide the MIME type of the text. The most common type is text/plain. For example:

```
msg.setContent("Resistance is futile. You will be assimilated!",
  "text/plain");
```

Finally, the static Transport.send( ) method connects to the mail server specified by the mail.host property and sends the message on its way:

```
Transport.send(msg);
```

Example 19-1 puts all these steps together into a standalone program that sends the following message:

```
Date: Mon, 29 Nov 1999 15:55:42 -0500 (EST)
From: Bill Gates <god@microsoft.com>
To: elharo@metalab.unc.edu
Subject: You must comply.

Resistance is futile. You will be assimilated!
```

I've shown this message in standard RFC 822 format used for Internet email. However, that isn't necessary. The main point is that you need to know the addressee (*elharo@metalab.unc.edu*), the sender (*god@microsoft.com*), and the subject and body of the message.

Example 19-1. Sending a very simple mail message

```java
import javax.mail.*;
import javax.mail.internet.*;
import java.util.*;

public class Assimilator {

  public static void main(String[] args) {

    try {
      Properties props = new Properties( );
      props.put("mail.host", "mail.cloud9.net");

      Session mailConnection = Session.getInstance(props, null);
      Message msg = new MimeMessage(mailConnection);

      Address bill = new InternetAddress("god@microsoft.com",
        "Bill Gates");
      Address elliotte = new InternetAddress("elharo@metalab.unc.edu");
```

Example 19-1. Sending a very simple mail message (continued)

```
      msg.setContent("Resistance is futile. You will be assimilated!",
       "text/plain");
      msg.setFrom(bill);
      msg.setRecipient(Message.RecipientType.TO, elliotte);
      msg.setSubject("You must comply.");

      Transport.send(msg);

    }
    catch (Exception ex) {
      ex.printStackTrace( );
    }

  }
}
```

Sending Email from an Application

Example 19-1 is a simple application that sends a fixed message to a known address with a specified subject. Once you see how to do this, it's straightforward to replace the strings that give the message address, subject, and body with data read from the command line, a GUI, a database, or some other source. For instance, Example 19-2 is a very simple GUI for sending email. Figure 19-1 shows the program running. The mail code is all tied up in the actionPerformed( ) method and looks very similar to the main( ) method of Example 19-1. The big difference is that now the host, subject, From: address, To: address, and text of the message are all read from the GUI components at runtime rather than being hardcoded as string literals in the source code. The rest of code is related to setting up the GUI and has little to do with the JavaMail API.

Example 19-2. A graphical SMTP client

```
import javax.mail.*;
import javax.mail.internet.*;
import java.util.*;
import javax.swing.*;
import java.awt.event.*;
import java.awt.*;

public class SMTPClient extends JFrame {

  private JButton     sendButton   = new JButton("Send Message");
  private JLabel      fromLabel    = new JLabel("From: ");
  private JLabel      toLabel      = new JLabel("To: ");
  private JLabel      hostLabel    = new JLabel("SMTP Server: ");
  private JLabel      subjectLabel = new JLabel("Subject: ");
  private JTextField  fromField    = new JTextField(40);
  private JTextField  toField      = new JTextField(40);
  private JTextField  hostField    = new JTextField(40);
  private JTextField  subjectField = new JTextField(40);
```

Example 19-2. A graphical SMTP client (continued)

```java
private JTextArea    message        = new JTextArea(40, 72);
private JScrollPane jsp             = new JScrollPane(message);

public SMTPClient() {

  super("SMTP Client");
  Container contentPane = this.getContentPane();
  contentPane.setLayout(new BorderLayout());

  JPanel labels = new JPanel();
  labels.setLayout(new GridLayout(4, 1));
  labels.add(hostLabel);

  JPanel fields = new JPanel();
  fields.setLayout(new GridLayout(4, 1));
  String host = System.getProperty("mail.host", "");
  hostField.setText(host);
  fields.add(hostField);

  labels.add(toLabel);
  fields.add(toField);

  String from = System.getProperty("mail.from", "");
  fromField.setText(from);
  labels.add(fromLabel);
  fields.add(fromField);

  labels.add(subjectLabel);
  fields.add(subjectField);

  Box north = Box.createHorizontalBox();
  north.add(labels);
  north.add(fields);

  contentPane.add(north, BorderLayout.NORTH);

  message.setFont(new Font("Monospaced", Font.PLAIN, 12));
  contentPane.add(jsp, BorderLayout.CENTER);

  JPanel south = new JPanel();
  south.setLayout(new FlowLayout(FlowLayout.CENTER));
  south.add(sendButton);
  sendButton.addActionListener(new SendAction());
  contentPane.add(south, BorderLayout.SOUTH);

  this.pack();

}

class SendAction implements ActionListener {

  public void actionPerformed(ActionEvent evt) {
```

Example 19-2. A graphical SMTP client (continued)

```java
    try {
      Properties props = new Properties( );
      props.put("mail.host", hostField.getText( ));

      Session mailConnection = Session.getInstance(props, null);
      final Message msg = new MimeMessage(mailConnection);

      Address to = new InternetAddress(toField.getText( ));
      Address from = new InternetAddress(fromField.getText( ));

      msg.setContent(message.getText( ), "text/plain");
      msg.setFrom(from);
      msg.setRecipient(Message.RecipientType.TO, to);
      msg.setSubject(subjectField.getText( ));

      // This can take a non-trivial amount of time so
      // spawn a thread to handle it.
      Runnable r = new Runnable( ) {
        public void run( ) {
          try {
            Transport.send(msg);
          }
          catch (Exception ex) {
            ex.printStackTrace( );
          }
        }
      };
      Thread t = new Thread(r);
      t.start( );

      message.setText("");
    }
    catch (Exception ex) {
      // I should really bring up a more specific error dialog here.
      ex.printStackTrace( );
    }

  }

}

public static void main(String[] args) {

  SMTPClient client = new SMTPClient( );
  // Next line requires Java 1.3 or later. I want to set up the
  // exit behavior here rather than in the constructor since
  // other programs that use this class may not want to exit
  // the application when the SMTPClient window closes.
  client.setDefaultCloseOperation(JFrame.EXIT_ON_CLOSE);
  client.show( );

}
}
```

This is far from an ideal program. The GUI could be more cleanly separated from the mailing code. And it would be better to bring up an error dialog if something went wrong rather than just printing a stack trace of the exception on System.err. However, since none of that would teach us anything about the JavaMail API, I leave it all as an exercise for the interested reader.

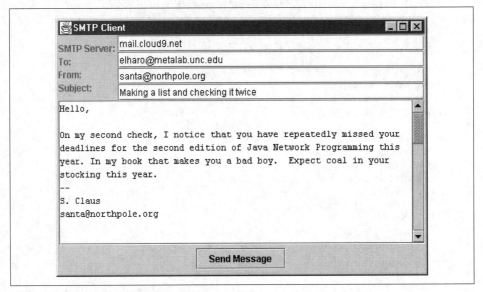

Figure 19-1. A simple GUI mail program

Sending Email from an Applet

In terms of GUIs and the JavaMail API, there's no difference between sending email from an applet and an application. However, the browser's security manager can get in your way. Like everything else in this book, the JavaMail API can't get around the normal restrictions on network connections from applets and other remotely loaded code. An applet that wants to send email can still talk only to the host the applet itself came from.

Fortunately, however, many hosts that run web servers also run SMTP servers. If this is the case, it's quite straightforward for an applet to send email. The JavaMail API and the Java Activation Framework on which it depends aren't included with most browsers, but since they're implemented in pure Java in the javax package, browsers can download the necessary classes from the server. For example, this APPLET element references not only the applet's own code but also the *mail.jar* and *activation.jar* files for the JavaMail API and the Java Activation Framework, respectively:

```
<APPLET CODE=SMTPApplet ARCHIVE="activation.jar,mail.jar"
        WIDTH=600 HEIGHT=400>
    <PARAM NAME="to" VALUE="hamp@sideview.mtsterling.ky.us">
```

```
    <PARAM NAME="subject" VALUE="Hay Orders">
    <PARAM NAME="from" VALUE="noone">
</APPLET>
```

Example 19-3 is a simple applet that sends email. The address to send email to and the subject are read from `PARAM` tags. The address to send email from is also read from a `PARAM` tag, but the user has the option to change it. The text to send is typed into a text area by the user. Finally, the server is determined by looking at the applet's codebase.

Example 19-3. An applet that sends email

```java
import java.applet.*;
import javax.mail.*;
import javax.mail.internet.*;
import java.util.Properties;
import java.awt.event.*;
import java.awt.*;

public class SMTPApplet extends Applet {

  private Button     sendButton   = new Button("Send Message");
  private Label      fromLabel    = new Label("From: ");
  private Label      subjectLabel = new Label("Subject: ");
  private TextField  fromField    = new TextField(40);
  private TextField  subjectField = new TextField(40);
  private TextArea   message      = new TextArea(30, 60);

  private String toAddress = "";

  public SMTPApplet() {

    this.setLayout(new BorderLayout());

    Panel north = new Panel();
    north.setLayout(new GridLayout(3, 1));

    Panel n1 = new Panel();
    n1.add(fromLabel);
    n1.add(fromField);
    north.add(n1);

    Panel n2 = new Panel();
    n2.add(subjectLabel);
    n2.add(subjectField);
    north.add(n2);

    this.add(north, BorderLayout.NORTH);

    message.setFont(new Font("Monospaced", Font.PLAIN, 12));
    this.add(message, BorderLayout.CENTER);

    Panel south = new Panel();
```

Example 19-3. An applet that sends email (continued)

```
    south.setLayout(new FlowLayout(FlowLayout.CENTER));
    south.add(sendButton);
    sendButton.addActionListener(new SendAction());
    this.add(south, BorderLayout.SOUTH);

  }

  public void init() {

    String subject = this.getParameter("subject");
    if (subject == null) subject = "";
    subjectField.setText(subject);

    toAddress = this.getParameter("to");
    if (toAddress == null) toAddress = "";

    String fromAddress = this.getParameter("from");
    if (fromAddress == null) fromAddress = "";
    fromField.setText(fromAddress);

  }

  class SendAction implements ActionListener {

    public void actionPerformed(ActionEvent evt) {

      try {
        Properties props = new Properties();
        props.put("mail.host", getCodeBase().getHost());

        Session mailConnection = Session.getInstance(props, null);
        final Message msg = new MimeMessage(mailConnection);

        Address to = new InternetAddress(toAddress);
        Address from = new InternetAddress(fromField.getText());

        msg.setContent(message.getText(), "text/plain");
        msg.setFrom(from);
        msg.setRecipient(Message.RecipientType.TO, to);
        msg.setSubject(subjectField.getText());

        // This can take a non-trivial amount of time so
        // spawn a thread to handle it.
        Runnable r = new Runnable() {
          public void run() {
            try {
              Transport.send(msg);
            }
            catch (Exception ex) {
              ex.printStackTrace();
            }
          }
        }
```

Example 19-3. An applet that sends email (continued)

```
        };
        Thread t = new Thread(r);
        t.start();

        message.setText("");
      }
      catch (Exception ex) {
        // We should really bring up a more specific error dialog here.
        ex.printStackTrace();
      }
    }
  }
}
```

Figure 19-2 shows this applet running in Internet Explorer 4.0.1 on the Macintosh. I've been careful to only use methods and classes available in Java 1.1 so this applet runs across the most web browsers possible. I also avoided using Swing so that there'd be one less large JAR file to download. As it is, the *mail.jar* and *activation.jar* files that this applet requires take up almost 300K, more than I'm comfortable with, but manageable on a fast connection.

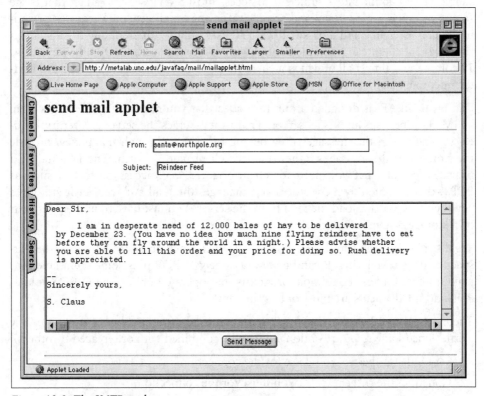

Figure 19-2. The SMTP applet

Proper behavior of this applet depends on several external factors:

- The browser must support at least Java 1.1 with a security model no stricter than the default.
- The *mail.jar* and *activation.jar* files must be available in the applet's codebase.
- The web server that serves the applet must also be an SMTP server willing to relay mail from the client system to the receiver system. These days, most open SMTP relays have been shut down to avoid abuse by spammers, so this can be a sticking point. If it is, you'll get an exception like this:

```
javax.mail.SendFailedException: 550 <hamp@sideview.mtsterling.ky.us>... Relaying
denied
```

However, you should at least be able to send email to addresses in the web server's domain. You may be able to set up one of these addresses to automatically forward the messages to their eventual recipient.

Receiving Mail

Receiving mail is considerably more complex than sending it. For instance, where a simple HELO command is sufficient to access most SMTP servers (a fact that is the source of much forged email and spam), retrieving email generally requires providing both a username and a password. SMTP uses only 14 different commands, and a simple email client can be implemented with just five of them. POP3, however, has 12 commands, almost all of which a client must be able to handle; IMAP4 has 24 different commands.

The JavaMail API is designed around the idea that you're retrieving messages from an IMAP or perhaps an NNTP server. That is, it assumes the server can return headers separate from the messages they belong to, search through mailboxes, provide the storage for the messages rather than the client, and so forth. The JavaMail API provides less of what you need for client-oriented mail access protocols, such as POP3, that assume the client stores and manages the mail archive, but it still gives you the tools to download the mail from the server. You just have to implement your own storage system on the client.

We'll begin with the simpler POP protocol, then move on to IMAP. From the perspective of JavaMail, IMAP can be viewed largely as POP plus some commands for manipulating folders. For simple programs that operate only on the INBOX folder, POP and IMAP clients are more or less the same.

There are about 12 steps to reading a remote mailbox (the number of steps can vary a little, since some steps are optional or can be combined with or replaced by others):

1. Set up the properties you'll use for the connection.
2. Construct the Authenticator you'll use for the connection.
3. Get a Session object with Session.getDefaultInstance( ).

4. Use the session's getStore( ) method to return a Store.

5. Connect to the store.

6. Get the INBOX folder from the store with the getFolder( ) method.

7. Open the INBOX folder.

8. Open the folder you want inside the INBOX folder. Repeat as many times as necessary to reach the folder you're seeking.

9. Get the messages from the folder as an array of Message objects.

10. Iterate through the array of messages, processing each one in turn using the methods of the Message class. For instance, you might print out each message or simply display the sender, subject, and other vital information in a GUI for the user to select from, as in Figure 19-3.

11. Close the folder.

12. Close the store.

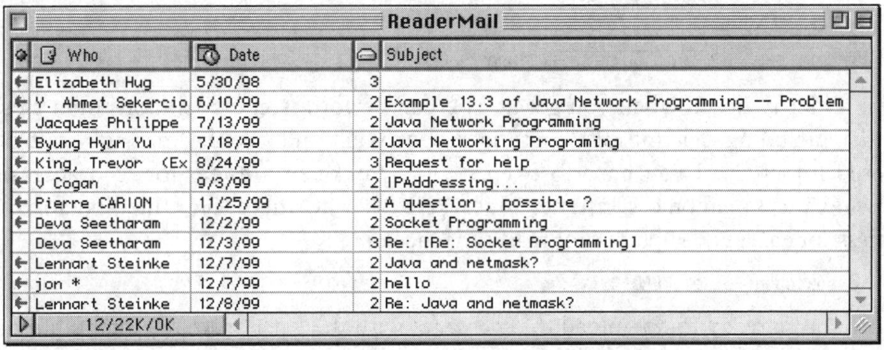

	Who		Date		Subject
←	Elizabeth Hug		5/30/98	3	
←	Y. Ahmet Sekercio		6/10/99	2	Example 13.3 of Java Network Programming -- Problem
←	Jacques Philippe		7/13/99	2	Java Network Programming
←	Byung Hyun Yu		7/18/99	2	Java Networking Programing
←	King, Trevor (Ex		8/24/99	3	Request for help
←	V Cogan		9/3/99	2	IPAddressing...
←	Pierre CARION		11/25/99	2	A question , possible ?
←	Deva Seetharam		12/2/99	2	Socket Programming
	Deva Seetharam		12/3/99	3	Re: [Re: Socket Programming]
←	Lennart Steinke		12/7/99	2	Java and netmask?
←	jon *		12/7/99	2	hello
←	Lennart Steinke		12/8/99	2	Re: Java and netmask?

12/22K/OK

Figure 19-3. A GUI for selecting mail messages

Each of these steps is individually quite simple. The first is to set up the properties for the mail session. Properties you might want to set include mail.host, mail.store. protocol, mail.user, mail.pop3.user, and mail.pop3.host. However, you don't absolutely need to set any of these. If the Session will only be used to retrieve mail, an empty Properties object is enough. For example:

```
Properties props = new Properties( );
```

Next, you'll want to create an instance of the javax.mail.Authenticator class (more properly, an instance of a concrete subclass of the abstract Authenticator class) that can ask the user for a password. For now, we'll simply hardcode those values and pass null instead of an actual Authenticator. We'll fix this later when we discuss authentication:

```
Authenticator a = null;
```

Next, use these `Properties` and `Authenticator` objects to get a `Session` instance, like this:

```
Session session = Session.getDefaultInstance(props, a);
```

Ask the session for a store for the provider. Here, we want a provider for POP3:

```
Store store = session.getStore("POP3");
```

Finally, you're ready to actually connect to the store using the `connect()` method. You'll need to provide the host to connect to and the username and password to use:

```
store.connect("mail.cloud9.net", "elharo", "my_password");
```

You can pass `null` for the password to indicate that the previously specified `Authenticator` should be queried for the password.

Now that the store is connected, you're ready to open a folder in the store. This step is really more oriented to IMAP than POP, since POP servers don't keep track of different folders. They simply provide all of a user's incoming mail as one undifferentiated amalgam. For purposes of the JavaMail API, POP3 providers use the folder name INBOX:

```
Folder inbox = store.getFolder("INBOX");
```

The folder is closed when you get it. You can perform some operations on a closed folder including deleting or renaming it, but you can't get the messages out of a closed folder. First you have to open it. You can open a folder for read access by passing the mnemonic constant `Folder.READ_ONLY` to the `open()` method for read access, or `Folder.READ_WRITE` for read/write access:

```
inbox.open(Folder.READ_ONLY);
```

Now you're ready to download the messages with the `getMessages()` method, which returns an array containing all the messages in the folder:

```
Message[] messages = inbox.getMessages();
```

(If you were using IMAP instead of POP, this step would not actually download the messages. Each one would stay on the server until you accessed it specifically. You'd just get a pointer to the actual message.)

The `Message` class provides many methods for working with individual messages. It has methods to get the various header fields of the message, get the content of the message, reply to the message, and more. We'll discuss these soon, when we talk about the `Message` and `MimeMessage` classes. For now, we'll do just about the simplest thing imaginable—print each message on `System.out` using the message's `writeTo()` method:

```
for (int i = 0; i < messages.length; i++) {
  System.out.println("------------ Message " + (i+1)
  + " ------------");
  messages[i].writeTo(System.out);
}
```

Once you're done with the messages, close the folder and then close the message store with the aptly named close( ) methods:

```
inbox.close(false);
store.close( );
```

The false argument to the folder's close( ) method indicates that we do not want the server to actually expunge any deleted messages in the folder. We simply want to break our connection to this folder.

Example 19-4 puts this all together with a simple program that downloads and prints out the contents of a specified POP mailbox. Messages are simply dumped on System.out in the default encoding. The servers, usernames, and so forth are all hard-coded. However, Example 19-4 quickly demonstrates most of the key points of receiving mail with the JavaMail API. A more advanced program would include an appropriate GUI.

Example 19-4. POP3Client

```java
import javax.mail.*;
import javax.mail.internet.*;
import java.util.*;
import java.io.*;

public class POP3Client {

  public static void main(String[] args) {

    Properties props = new Properties( );

    String host = "utopia.poly.edu";
    String username = "eharold";
    String password = "mypassword";
    String provider = "pop3";

    try {

      // Connect to the POP3 server
      Session session = Session.getDefaultInstance(props, null);
      Store store = session.getStore(provider);
      store.connect(host, username, password);

      // Open the folder
      Folder inbox = store.getFolder("INBOX");
      if (inbox == null) {
        System.out.println("No INBOX");
        System.exit(1);
      }
      inbox.open(Folder.READ_ONLY);

      // Get the messages from the server
      Message[] messages = inbox.getMessages( );
      for (int i = 0; i < messages.length; i++) {
```

Example 19-4. POP3Client (continued)

```
        System.out.println("------------ Message " + (i+1)
         + " ------------");
        messages[i].writeTo(System.out);
      }

      // Close the connection
      // but don't remove the messages from the server
      inbox.close(false);
      store.close();

    }
    catch (Exception ex) {
      ex.printStackTrace();
    }
  }
}
```

Here's some sample output I got when I pointed it at an account I don't use much:

```
D:\JAVA\JNP3\examples\19>java POP3Client
------------ Message 1 ------------
Received: (from eharold@localhost)
        by utopia.poly.edu (8.8.8/8.8.8) id QAA05728
        for eharold; Tue, 30 Nov 1999 16:14:29 -0500 (EST)
Date: Tue, 30 Nov 1999 16:14:29 -0500 (EST)
From: Elliotte Harold <eharold@utopia.poly.edu>
Message-Id: <199911302114.QAA05728@utopia.poly.edu>
To: eharold@utopia.poly.edu
Subject: test
Content-Type: text
X-UIDL: 87e3f1ba71738c8f772b15e3933241f0
Status: RO

hello you

------------ Message 2 ------------
Received: from russian.cloud9.net (russian.cloud9.net [
.4])
        by utopia.poly.edu (8.8.8/8.8.8) with ESMTP id OAA28428
        for <eharold@utopia.poly.edu>; Wed, 1 Dec 1999 14:05:06 -0500 (
Received: from [168.100.203.234] (macfaq.dialup.cloud9.net [168.100.203
        by russian.cloud9.net (Postfix) with ESMTP id 24B93764F
        for <eharold@utopia.poly.edu>; Wed,  1 Dec 1999 14:02:50 -0500
Mime-Version: 1.0
X-Sender: macfaq@mail.cloud9.net
Message-Id: <v04210100b46b1f97969d@[168.100.203.234]>
Date: Wed, 1 Dec 1999 13:55:40 -0500
To: eharold@utopia.poly.edu
From: Elliotte Rusty Harold <elharo@macfaq.com>
Subject: New system
Content-Type: text/plain; charset="us-ascii" ; format="flowed"
X-UIDL: 01fd5cbcf1768fc6c28f9c8f934534b5
```

```
Just thought you'd be happy to know that now that I've got my desk
moved over from my old apartment, I've finally ordered the Windows NT
system I've been promising for months.
--
David
```

About the only change you'd need to make to port this program to IMAP would be
setting the provider variable to imap instead of pop3.

Password Authentication

Hardcoding passwords in source code, as Example 19-4 does, is a very bad idea to
say the least. If a password is required, you should ask the user for it at runtime. Furthermore, when the user types the password, it should not be displayed on the
screen. Ideally, it should not even be transmitted in clear text across the network,
although in fact many current clients and servers do exactly that.

When you open a connection to a message store, the JavaMail API allows you to provide a javax.mail.Authenticator object that it can use to get the username and password. Authenticator is an abstract class:

```
public abstract class Authenticator extends Object
```

When the provider needs to know a username or password, it calls back to the
getPasswordAuthentication( ) method in a user-defined subclass of Authenticator.
This returns a PasswordAuthentication object containing this information:

```
protected PasswordAuthentication getPasswordAuthentication( )
```

 These two classes are almost exactly the same as the java.net.
Authenticator and java.net.PasswordAuthentication classes discussed in
Chapter 7. However, those classes are available only in Java 1.2 and later.
To make the JavaMail API work in Java 1.1, Sun had to duplicate their
functionality in the javax.mail package. Sun could have included java.
net.Authenticator and java.net.PasswordAuthentication in *mail.jar*, but
that would have meant that the JavaMail API could not be certified as
100% Pure Java. However, everything you learned about java.net.
Authenticator and java.net.PasswordAuthentication in Chapter 7 is true
of javax.mail.Authenticator and javax.mail.PasswordAuthentication in
this chapter. The only thing you have to watch out for is that if you
import both java.net.* and javax.mail.* in a class, your source code
will have to use fully qualified names like java.net.Authenticator instead
of short names like Authenticator.

To add runtime password authentication to your programs, subclass Authenticator
and override getPasswordAuthentication( ) with a method that knows how to securely
ask the user for a password. One useful tool for this process is the JPasswordField component from Swing. Example 19-5 demonstrates a Swing-based Authenticator subclass that brings up a dialog to ask the user for their username and password.

Example 19-5. A GUI authenticator

```java
import javax.mail.*;
import javax.swing.*;
import java.awt.*;
import java.awt.event.*;


public class MailAuthenticator extends Authenticator {

  private JDialog passwordDialog = new JDialog(new JFrame( ), true);
  private JLabel mainLabel = new JLabel(
   "Please enter your user name and password: ");
  private JLabel userLabel = new JLabel("User name: ");
  private JLabel passwordLabel = new JLabel("Password: ");
  private JTextField usernameField = new JTextField(20);
  private JPasswordField passwordField = new JPasswordField(20);
  private JButton okButton = new JButton("OK");

  public MailAuthenticator( ) {
    this("");
  }

  public MailAuthenticator(String username) {

    Container pane = passwordDialog.getContentPane( );
    pane.setLayout(new GridLayout(4, 1));
    pane.add(mainLabel);
    JPanel p2 = new JPanel( );
    p2.add(userLabel);
    p2.add(usernameField);
    usernameField.setText(username);
    pane.add(p2);
    JPanel p3 = new JPanel( );
    p3.add(passwordLabel);
    p3.add(passwordField);
    pane.add(p3);
    JPanel p4 = new JPanel( );
    p4.add(okButton);
    pane.add(p4);
    passwordDialog.pack( );

    ActionListener al = new HideDialog( );
    okButton.addActionListener(al);
    usernameField.addActionListener(al);
    passwordField.addActionListener(al);

  }

  class HideDialog implements ActionListener {

    public void actionPerformed(ActionEvent e) {
      passwordDialog.hide( );
    }

  }
```

Example 19-5. A GUI authenticator (continued)

```
public PasswordAuthentication getPasswordAuthentication( ) {

    passwordDialog.show( );

    // getPassword( ) returns an array of chars for security reasons.
    // We need to convert that to a String for
    // the PasswordAuthentication( ) constructor.
    String password = new String(passwordField.getPassword( ));
    String username = usernameField.getText( );
    // Erase the password in case this is used again.
    // The provider should cache the password if necessary.
    passwordField.setText("");
    return new PasswordAuthentication(username, password);

    }
}
```

Most of this code is just for handling the GUI. Figure 19-4 shows the rather simple dialog box this produces.

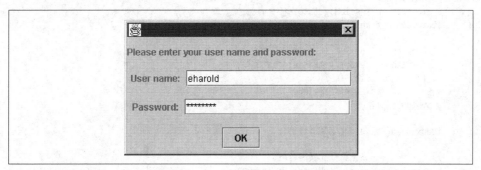

Figure 19-4. An authentication dialog

Interestingly, `JPasswordField` takes more pains to be secure than `PasswordAuthentication` does. `JPasswordField` stores passwords as an array of chars so that when you're done with the password, you can overwrite it with nulls. This means the password exists in memory for less time and the virtual memory system is less likely to swap the program out to disk and leave the password there in clear text. However, `PasswordAuthentication` stores passwords as strings, which are immutable and therefore may be unintentionally stored on the disk.

Modifying the POP client to support this style of authentication is straightforward, as Example 19-6 demonstrates. We replace the hardcoded username and password with nulls and pass an instance of `MailAuthenticator` as the second argument to `connect( )`. The only other change is that we call `System.exit( )` at the end of the `main( )` method, since the program will no longer exit when the `main( )` method returns once the AWT thread has been started.

Example 19-6. A POP client that asks the user for the password as necessary

```java
import javax.mail.*;
import javax.mail.internet.*;
import java.util.*;
import java.io.*;


public class SecurePOP3Client {

  public static void main(String[] args) {

    Properties props = new Properties( );

    String host = "utopia.poly.edu";
    String provider = "pop3";

    try {

      // Connect to the POP3 server
      Session session = Session.getDefaultInstance(props,
       new MailAuthenticator( ));
      Store store = session.getStore(provider);
      store.connect(host, null, null);

      // Open the folder
      Folder inbox = store.getFolder("INBOX");
      if (inbox == null) {
        System.out.println("No INBOX");
        System.exit(1);
      }
      inbox.open(Folder.READ_ONLY);

      // Get the messages from the server
      Message[] messages = inbox.getMessages( );
      for (int i = 0; i < messages.length; i++) {
        System.out.println("------------ Message " + (i+1)
        + " ------------");
        messages[i].writeTo(System.out);
      }

      // Close the connection
      // but don't remove the messages from the server
      inbox.close(false);
      store.close( );

    }
    catch (Exception ex) {
      ex.printStackTrace( );
    }
```

```
    // since we brought up a GUI returning from main( ) won't exit
    System.exit(0);

  }
}
```

Addresses

The `javax.mail.Address` class is very simple. It's an abstract class that exists mainly to be subclassed by other, protocol-specific address classes:

```
    public abstract class Address extends Object
```

There are two of these subclasses in the standard JavaMail API: `InternetAddress` for SMTP email and `NewsAddress` for Usenet newsgroups:

```
    public class InternetAddress extends Address
    public class NewsAddress extends Address
```

Providers of other mail protocols would also subclass `Address` with classes that represented their style of address.

The Address Class

The `Address` class itself is extremely simple. It has only three methods, all abstract, two of which are simple utility methods that override the corresponding methods in `java.lang.Object`:

```
    public abstract String getType( )
    public abstract String toString( )
    public abstract boolean equals(Object o)
```

Since all three of these methods are abstract, there aren't any guarantees about the methods' semantics, since all must be overridden in subclasses. However, this does require that subclasses provide their own implementations of `equals( )` and `toString( )` rather than relying on the rather generic implementations available from `java.lang.Object`. In general, the `getType( )` method returns a string such as "rfc822" or "news" that indicates the kind of `Address` object this is.

The InternetAddress Class

An `InternetAddress` object represents an RFC 822–style email address. This is the standard Internet-style email address that is rapidly supplanting all other proprietary formats. It looks like *elharo@metalab.unc.edu* or *ask_tim@oreilly.com*. However, it can contain a name as well—for instance, *ask_tim@oreilly.com (Tim O'Reilly)*.

The state of an InternetAddress object is maintained by three protected fields:

```
protected String address
protected String personal
protected String encodedPersonal
```

The address field is the actual email address—for example, *ask_tim@oreilly.com*. The personal field is the name—for example, *Tim O'Reilly*. Although Java strings are pure Unicode that can express names like Erwin Schrödinger or 藤沢淳, the strings used in mail headers must be pure ASCII in order to pass through most existing mail software. Consequently, Java's Unicode strings need to be converted to pure ASCII using a sort of hexadecimal escape. The details of this conversion are described in RFC 2047, *MIME (Multipurpose Internet Mail Extensions) Part Three: Message Header Extensions for Non-ASCII Text*. The encoded string is placed in the encodedPersonal field. All of these fields will be initially set in the constructor. There are four overloaded constructors for InternetAddress objects:

```
public InternetAddress( )
public InternetAddress(String address) throws AddressException
public InternetAddress(String address, String personal)
  throws UnsupportedEncodingException
public InternetAddress(String address, String personal, String charset)
  throws UnsupportedEncodingException
```

They are used exactly as you'd expect. For example:

```
Address tim = new InternetAddress("ask_tim@oreilly.com", "Tim O'Reilly");
```

Although two of these methods are declared to throw UnsupportedEncodingException, this should happen only in the last method and then only if the name of the character set is not recognized by the VM. (For example, Java 1.1 does not recognize "ASCII", although in that case, you don't really need to specify a character set.)

There are nine instance methods in this class—three setter methods, three getter methods, and three utility methods:

```
public void setAddress(String address)
public void setPersonal(String name, String charset)
  throws UnsupportedEncodingException
public void setPersonal(String name)
  throws UnsupportedEncodingException
public String getAddress( )
public String getPersonal( )
public String getType( )
public String toString( )
public boolean equals(Object o)
public int hashCode( )
```

The setAddress( ) method sets the address field of the object to the specified value. The setPersonal( ) method sets the personal and encodedPersonal fields to the specified value (after encoding it, as necessary). The getAddress( ) and getPersonal( )

methods return the values of the address and personal or decoded encodedPersonal fields, respectively. Finally, the getType( ) method returns the string "rfc822".

The toString( ) method returns an email address suitable for use in a To: or From: field of an RFC 822 email message. The equals( ) and hashCode( ) methods have their usual semantics.

There are also five static utility methods, four of which convert addresses to and from strings:

```
public static String toString(Address[] addresses)
  throws ClassCastException
public static String toString(Address[] addresses, int used)
  throws ClassCastException
public static InternetAddress[] parse(String addressList)
  throws AddressException
public static InternetAddress[] parse(String s, boolean strict)
  throws AddressException
```

The InternetAddress.toString( ) methods convert an array of Address objects into a comma-separated list of addresses encoded in pure ASCII, possibly folded onto multiple lines. The optional used argument gives the number of characters that will precede this string in the header field, such as To: or Cc:, into which this string will be inserted. This information lets toString( ) decide where it needs to break the lines. A ClassCastException is thrown if any of the Address objects in the array are not more specifically InternetAddress objects.

The two parse( ) methods perform this operation in reverse, converting a comma-separated String of addresses into an array of InternetAddress objects. Setting the optional strict argument to false changes the behavior so that strings that use whitespace instead of commas (or whitespace and commas) to separate email addresses are also understood. All four of these methods are useful for message header fields that contain multiple addresses; for example, a Cc: that's directed to six people.

Finally, the getLocalAddress( ) method checks several system properties (mail.from, mail.user, mail.host, and user.name) as well as InetAddress.getLocalName( ) to determine the email address of the current user:

```
public static InternetAddress getLocalAddress(Session session)
```

For example, this code fragment tries to use the user's own email address rather than one hardcoded into the program as a string:

```
msg.setFrom(InternetAddress.getLocalAddress());
```

However, there's no guarantee that any of these properties will necessarily give the user's true address.

The NewsAddress Class

Perhaps a little surprisingly, with an appropriate service provider, the JavaMail API can also access Usenet news. The API is mostly the same as for reading a POP or IMAP mailbox. However, instead of using an `InternetAddress`, you use a `NewsAddress`:

```
public class NewsAddress extends Address
```

A `NewsAddress` object represents a Usenet newsgroup name, such as *comp.lang.java. machine*. It may include the hostname for the news server as well. The state of a `NewsAddress` object is maintained by two protected fields:

```
protected String newsgroup
protected String host
```

The `newsgroup` field contains the name of the newsgroup—for example, *netscape. devs-java*. The host field is either null or contains the hostname of the news server— for example, *secnews.netscape.com*. Both of these fields are set in the constructor. There are three overloaded constructors for `NewsAddress` objects:

```
public NewsAddress()
public NewsAddress(String newsgroup)
public NewsAddress(String newsgroup, String host)
```

They are used exactly as you'd expect. For example:

```
Address netscape_java = new NewsAddress("netscape.devs-java.",
  "secnews.netscape.com");
```

There are eight instance methods in this class—three getter methods, two setter methods, and three utility methods:

```
public String  getType()
public String  getHost()
public String  getNewsgroup()
public void    setNewsgroup(String newsgroup)
public void    setHost(String host)
public String  toString()
public boolean equals(Object o)
public int     hashCode()
```

The `setNewsgroup()` and `setHost()` methods set the newsgroup and host fields of the object to the specified values. The `getNewsgroup()` and `getHost()` methods return the values of the newsgroup and host fields. Finally, the `getType()` method returns the string "news".

The `toString()` method returns the newsgroup name in a form suitable for the Newsgroups: header field of a Usenet posting. The `equals()` and `hashCode()` methods have their usual semantics.

There are also two static utility methods for converting addresses to and from strings:

```
public static String toString(Address[] addresses)
  throws ClassCastException
```

```
public static NewsAddress[] parse(String newsgroups)
  throws AddressException
```

The toString( ) method converts an array of Address objects into a comma-separated list of newsgroup names. A ClassCastException is thrown if any of the Address objects in the array are not more specifically NewsAddress objects. The parse( ) method reverses this operation, converting a comma-separated String of newsgroup names, such as "comp.lang.java.programmer,comp.lang.java.gui,comp.lang.java.help", into an array of NewsAddress objects. It throws an AddressException if the newsgroups argument is not a comma-separated list of newsgroup names.

Sun's implementation of the JavaMail API does not include a service provider for news, however; so although you can create news addresses, before you can actually read and post news, you'll need to install a service provider that does support it. Table 19-1 lists some possible sources of news providers. Once you've got one, reading news is as straightforward as talking to an IMAP server.

The URLName Class

javax.mail.URLName represents the name of a URL; that is, it treats a URL as a string, but does not attempt to connect to or resolve any of the parts of the string. URL names are mainly used as convenient ways to identify folders and stores with non-standard URLs, such as *pop3://elharo:mypassword@mail.metalab.unc.edu:110/INBOX*, that don't have a matching protocol handler:

```
public class URLName Object
```

The methods of URLName are very similar to those of java.net.URL discussed in Chapter 7, except that all those involving actual connections have been deleted. What's left is a bunch of methods for breaking a URL string into its component parts or building a URL from pieces.

The Constructors

There are three overloaded URLName constructors. One takes the individual pieces of a URL as arguments, another takes a java.net.URL object, and a third takes a String containing a URL:

```
public URLName(String protocol, String host, int port, String file,
  String userName, String password)
public URLName(URL url)
public URLName(String url)
```

Constructing a URLName doesn't require a protocol handler for the scheme be available. All the operations on the URLName take place with simple substring manipulation, allowing the URLName class to support nonstandard URLs like *pop3://eharold:password@utopia.poly.edu/INBOX* or *imap://elharo@metalab.unc.edu/*

Speaking/SD2005West. These URLName objects can be used to refer to particular folders on the server.

Parsing Methods

These seven getter methods are the main purpose for this class. They return individual pieces of the URL:

```
public int    getPort( )
public String getProtocol( )
public String getFile( )
public String getRef( )
public String getHost( )
public String getUsername( )
public String getPassword( )
```

These methods can all be easily understood by analogy with the similarly named methods in java.net.URL. Except for getPort( ), these methods all return null if the piece is missing. getPort( ) returns −1 if the port is not explicitly included in the URL.

There's also a getURL( ) method that converts a URLName to a java.net.URL. Since doing so requires that Java have a protocol handler for the URL's scheme, this method can throw a MalformedURLException:

```
public URL getURL( ) throws MalformedURLException
```

Finally, there are the usual three utility methods with the usual semantics:

```
public boolean equals(Object o)
public int     hashCode( )
public String  toString( )
```

The toString( ) method simply returns the string form of the URL. The equals( ) method is underspecified but in practice any two URLName objects that are character by character identical will compare equal. However, JavaMail does not consider case to be significant in domain names. http://www.example.com and http://WWW.EXAMPLE.COM are equal. Surprisingly, it does consider case to be significant in URL schemes. That is, http://www.example.com is not equal to HTTP://www.example.com. Finally, JavaMail recognizes / as the default path; for example, http://www.example.com is equal to http://www.example.com/. The hashCode( ) method is implemented accordingly.

We can use the URLName class to provide an interface for an email client that is completely protocol-independent. All information about protocol, host, and other details is provided by a URL read from the command line. Example 19-7 demonstrates.

Example 19-7. A protocol-independent mail client

```
import javax.mail.*;
import javax.mail.internet.*;
import java.util.*;
import java.io.*;

public class MailClient {
```

Example 19-7. A protocol-independent mail client (continued)

```
  public static void main(String[] args) {

    if (args.length == 0) {
      System.err.println(
       "Usage: java MailClient protocol://username:password@host/foldername");
      return;
    }

    URLName server = new URLName(args[0]);

    try {

      Session session = Session.getDefaultInstance(new Properties( ),
       null);

      // Connect to the server and open the folder
      Folder folder = session.getFolder(server);
      if (folder == null) {
        System.out.println("Folder " + server.getFile( ) + " not found.");
        System.exit(1);
      }
      folder.open(Folder.READ_ONLY);

      // Get the messages from the server
      Message[] messages = folder.getMessages( );
      for (int i = 0; i < messages.length; i++) {
        System.out.println("------------ Message " + (i+1)
         + " ------------");
        messages[i].writeTo(System.out);
      }

      // Close the connection
      // but don't remove the messages from the server
      folder.close(false);

    }
    catch (Exception ex) {
      ex.printStackTrace( );
    }
  }
}
```

URLName does make the code a little more compact since it moves some information from the source code to the command line. Besides eliminating the obvious variables and string literals for username, host, and so forth, we've managed to eliminate any direct reference to the Store class. A typical run starts like this:

```
% java MailClient pop3://eharold:mypassword@utopia.poly.edu/INBOX
------------ Message 1 ------------
Received: (from eharold@localhost)
        by utopia.poly.edu (8.8.8/8.8.8) id QAA05728
        for eharold; Tue, 30 Nov 1999 16:14:29 -0500 (EST)
```

```
Date: Tue, 30 Nov 1999 16:14:29 -0500 (EST)
From: Elliotte Harold <eharold@utopia.poly.edu>
Message-Id: <199911302114.QAA05728@utopia.poly.edu>
To: eharold@utopia.poly.edu
Subject: test
Content-Type: text
X-UIDL: 87e3f1ba71738c8f772b15e3933241f0
Status: RO

hello you
```

For demonstration purposes, this program includes the password in the URL. In general, however, that's a huge security risk. It would be much better to use a runtime Authenticator, as Example 19-6 did. Of course, ultimately it's very questionable whether this is really a superior interface to Example 19-6 and its ilk.

The Message Class

The javax.mail.Message class is the abstract superclass for all individual emails, news postings, and similar messages:

```
public abstract class Message extends Object implements Part
```

There's one concrete Message subclass in the standard JavaMail API, javax.mail. internet.MimeMessage. This is used for both email and Usenet news messages. Service providers are free to add classes for their own message formats. For instance, IBM might provide a NotesMessage class for Lotus Notes.

The Message class mainly declares abstract getter and setter methods that define the common properties of most messages. These properties include the addressees of the message, the recipients of the message, the subject and content of the message, and various other attributes. You can think of these as properties of the envelope that contains the message.

Furthermore, the Message class implements the Part interface. The Part interface mostly handles the body of an email message. It declares methods for getting and setting the content type of the message body, getting and setting the actual message body content, getting and setting arbitrary headers from the message, and getting input streams that are fed by the message body. The main body part of a message can contain other parts. This is used to handle attachments, message bodies that are available in multiple formats, and other multipart emails. Since the Message class is abstract and needs to be subclassed by concrete classes such as MimeMessage, most of these methods are not actually redeclared in Message but can be invoked by any actual instance of Message. We'll begin by discussing the methods actually declared in Message, then move on to those declared in Part.

Creating Messages

The Message class has three constructors:

```
protected Message( )
protected Message(Folder folder, int messageNumber)
protected Message(Session session)
```

Since all the constructors are protected, they are primarily for the use of subclasses such as MimeMessage. If you're sending a message, you'll use one of the constructors in the subclass instead. If you're reading messages, the Folder or Session you're reading from will create the Message objects and pass them to you.

Replying to messages

If you already have a Message object, one way to create a new Message object is to reply to the existing one using the reply( ) method:

```
public abstract Message reply(boolean replyToAll)
  throws MessagingException
```

This method creates a new Message object with the same subject prefixed with "Re:", and addressed to the sender of the original message. If replyToAll is true, the message is addressed to all known recipients of the original message. The content of the message is empty. If you want to quote the original message, you'll have to do that yourself.

Getting messages from folders

You've already seen that when you're reading email, the JavaMail API creates Message objects to represent the messages it finds on the server. The primary means of doing this are the getMessage( ) and getMessages( ) methods in the Folder class:

```
public abstract Message getMessage(int messageNumber)
  throws MessagingException
public Message[] getMessages(int start, int end)
  throws MessagingException
public Message[] getMessages(int[] messageNumbers)
  throws MessagingException
public Message[] getMessages( ) throws MessagingException
```

The first three methods require the caller to specify which messages it wants. The last simply returns all messages in the folder. What's actually returned are stubs holding the places of the actual messages. The text and headers of the message won't necessarily be retrieved until some method of the Message class is invoked that requires this information.

Basic Header Info

A typical RFC 822 message contains a header that looks something like this:

```
From levi@blazing.sunspot.noao.edu Fri Aug  5 10:57:08 1994
Date: Fri, 27 Aug 2004 10:57:04 +0700
```

```
From: levi@blazing.sunspot.noao.edu (Denise Levi)
To: volleyball@sunspot.noao.edu
Subject: Apologies
Content-Length: 517
Status: RO
X-Lines: 13
```

The exact fields in the header can vary, but most messages contain at least a From: field, a To: field, a Date: field, and a Subject: field. Other common fields include Cc: (carbon copies) and Bcc: (blind carbon copies). In general, these will be accessible through getter and setter methods.

The From address

These four methods get and set the From: field of a message:

```
public abstract Address[] getFrom( ) throws MessagingException
public abstract void setFrom( ) throws MessagingException,
 IllegalWriteException, IllegalStateException
public abstract void setFrom(Address address)
 throws MessagingException, IllegalWriteException, IllegalStateException
public abstract void addFrom(Address[] addresses)
 throws MessagingException, IllegalWriteException, IllegalStateException
```

The getFrom( ) method returns an array of Address objects, one for each address listed in the From: header. (In practice, it's rare for a message to be *from* more than one address. It's quite common for a message to be addressed *to* more than one address.) It returns null if the From: header isn't present in the message. It throws a MessagingException if the From: header is malformed in some way.

The noargs setFrom( ) and addFrom( ) methods set and modify the From: headers of outgoing email messages. The noargs setFrom( ) method sets the header to the current value of the mail.user property or, as a fallback, the user.name property. The setFrom( ) method with arguments sets the value of the From: header to the listed addresses. The addFrom( ) method adds the listed addresses to any addresses that already exist in the header. All three of these methods can throw a MessagingException if one of the addresses they use isn't in the right format. They can also throw an IllegalWriteException if the From: field of the given Message object cannot be changed or an IllegalStateException if the entire Message object is read-only.

The Reply-to address

Some messages contain a Reply-to: header indicating that any replies should be sent to a different address than the one that sent the message. There are two methods to set and get these addresses:

```
public Address[] getReplyTo( ) throws MessagingException
public void setReplyTo(Address[] addresses) throws MessagingException,
 MethodNotSupportedException, IllegalWriteException,
 IllegalStateException
```

The semantics of these methods are the same as for the equivalent getFrom() and setFrom() methods—in fact, the default implementation of getReplyTo() simply returns getFrom()—with the single caveat that an implementation that doesn't support separate Reply-to: addresses may throw a MethodNotSupportedException when setReplyTo() is invoked.

The recipient addresses

Whereas the sender of the message is generally found only in the From: header, the recipients of the message are often split across the To:, Cc:, and Bcc: fields. Rather than providing separate methods for each of these fields, the various getRecipients() and setRecipients() methods rely on a Message.RecipientType argument to determine which field's value is desired. RecipientType is a public inner class in javax.mail.Message whose private constructor limits it to exactly these three static objects:

```
Message.RecipientType.TO
Message.RecipientType.CC
Message.RecipientType.BCC
```

There are two methods to find the addressees of the Message:

```
public abstract Address[] getRecipients(Message.RecipientType type)
  throws MessagingException
public Address[] getAllRecipients() throws MessagingException
```

The getRecipients() method returns an array of Address objects, one for each address listed in the specified header. It returns null if the specified header isn't present in the message. It throws a MessagingException if the specified header is malformed in some way. The getAllRecipients() method does the same thing, except that it combines the contents of the To:, Cc:, and Bcc: headers.

There are two methods to set the recipients of the message while replacing any previous recipients and two methods to add recipients to the message:

```
public abstract void setRecipients(Message.RecipientType type,
  Address[] addresses) throws MessagingException, IllegalWriteException,
  IllegalStateException
public void setRecipient(Message.RecipientType type, Address address)
  throws MessagingException, IllegalWriteException
public abstract void addRecipients(Message.RecipientType type,
  Address[] addresses) throws MessagingException,
  IllegalWriteException, IllegalStateException
public void addRecipient(Message.RecipientType type, Address address)
  throws MessagingException, IllegalWriteException
```

All four of these methods can throw a MessagingException, typically because one of the addresses isn't in the right format. They can also throw an IllegalWriteException if the specified field of the given Message object cannot be changed or an IllegalStateException if the entire Message object is read-only.

The subject of the message

Since the subject is simply a single string of text, it's easy to set and get with these two methods:

```
public abstract String getSubject( ) throws MessagingException
public abstract void    setSubject(String subject) throws
 MessagingException, IllegalWriteException, IllegalStateException
```

As with earlier setter methods, null is returned if the subject field isn't present in the message. An IllegalWriteException is thrown if the program isn't allowed to set the value of the Subject: field and an IllegalStateException is thrown if the program isn't allowed to change the message at all.

The date of the message

Messages also have sent and received dates. Three methods allow programs to access these fields:

```
public abstract Date getSentDate( ) throws MessagingException
public abstract void setSentDate(Date date) throws MessagingException,
 IllegalWriteException, IllegalStateException
public abstract Date getReceivedDate( ) throws MessagingException
```

The underlying implementation is responsible for converting the textual date format found in a message header like "Fri, 20 Aug 2004 10:57:04 +0700" to a java.util. Date object. As usual, a MessagingException indicates some problem with the format of the underlying message, an IllegalWriteException indicates that the field cannot be changed, and an IllegalStateException indicates that the entire message cannot be changed.

Example 19-8 is a simple example program that follows the basic pattern of the last several mail-reading programs. However, this one no longer uses writeTo( ). Instead, it uses the methods in this section to print just the headers. Furthermore, it prints them in a particular order regardless of their order in the actual message on the server. Finally, it ignores the less important headers such as X-UIDL: and Status:. The static InternetAddress.toString( ) method converts the arrays that most of these methods return into simple, comma-separated strings.

Example 19-8. A program to read mail headers

```
import javax.mail.*;
import javax.mail.internet.*;
import java.util.*;

public class HeaderClient {

  public static void main(String[] args) {
    if (args.length == 0) {
      System.err.println(
        "Usage: java HeaderClient protocol://username@host/foldername");
      return;
```

Example 19-8. A program to read mail headers (continued)

```
      }

      URLName server = new URLName(args[0]);

    try {

        Session session = Session.getDefaultInstance(new Properties(),
         new MailAuthenticator(server.getUsername()));

        // Connect to the server and open the folder
        Folder folder = session.getFolder(server);
        if (folder == null) {
          System.out.println("Folder " + server.getFile() + " not found.");
          System.exit(1);
        }
        folder.open(Folder.READ_ONLY);

        // Get the messages from the server
        Message[] messages = folder.getMessages();
        for (int i = 0; i < messages.length; i++) {
          System.out.println("------------ Message " + (i+1)
           + " ------------");
          // Here's the big change...
          String from = InternetAddress.toString(messages[i].getFrom());
          if (from != null) System.out.println("From: " + from);
          String replyTo = InternetAddress.toString(
           messages[i].getReplyTo());
          if (replyTo != null) System.out.println("Reply-to: "
           + replyTo);
          String to = InternetAddress.toString(
           messages[i].getRecipients(Message.RecipientType.TO));
          if (to != null) System.out.println("To: " + to);
          String cc = InternetAddress.toString(
          messages[i].getRecipients(Message.RecipientType.CC));
          if (cc != null) System.out.println("Cc: " + cc);
          String bcc = InternetAddress.toString(
           messages[i].getRecipients(Message.RecipientType.BCC));
          if (bcc != null) System.out.println("Bcc: " + to);
          String subject = messages[i].getSubject();
          if (subject != null) System.out.println("Subject: " + subject);
          Date sent = messages[i].getSentDate();
          if (sent != null) System.out.println("Sent: " + sent);
          Date received = messages[i].getReceivedDate();
          if (received != null) System.out.println("Received: " + received);

          System.out.println();
        }

        // Close the connection
        // but don't remove the messages from the server
        folder.close(false);
```

Example 19-8. A program to read mail headers (continued)

```
    }
    catch (Exception ex) {
      ex.printStackTrace();
    }

    // Since we may have brought up a GUI to authenticate,
    // we can't rely on returning from main() to exit
    System.exit(0);

  }
}
```

Here's some typical output. Several of the requested strings were null because the fields simply weren't present in the messages in the INBOX; for instance, Cc: and Bcc:. HeaderClient checks for the fields and simply omits them if they're not present.

```
% java HeaderClient pop3://eharold@utopia.poly.edu/INBOX
------------ Message 1 ------------
From: Elliotte Harold <eharold@utopia.poly.edu>
Reply-to: Elliotte Harold <eharold@utopia.poly.edu>
To: eharold@utopia.poly.edu
Subject: test
Sent: Tue Nov 30 13:14:29 PST 1999

------------ Message 2 ------------
From: Elliotte Rusty Harold <elharo@macfaq.com>
Reply-to: Elliotte Rusty Harold <elharo@macfaq.com>
To: eharold@utopia.poly.edu
Subject: New system
Sent: Wed Dec 01 10:55:40 PST 1999

------------ Message 3 ------------
From: Dr. Mickel <Greatsmiles@mail.com>
Reply-to: Dr. Mickel <Greatsmiles@mail.com>
To: eharold@utopia.poly.edu
Subject: Breath RX Products now available Online!
Sent: Thu Dec 02 03:45:52 PST 1999
```

Notice that none of these messages have received dates. That's because the receive time is not part of the message envelope itself. It has to be provided by the server, and POP servers don't provide it. An IMAP server would be much more likely to include a received date, as will be shown in Example 19-9.

Saving changes

When you invoke one of the previous set or add methods, some implementations store the changes immediately. Others, however, may not. The saveChanges() method commits the changes made to a Message object:

```
public abstract void saveChanges() throws MessagingException,
    IllegalWriteException, IllegalStateException
```

This is not quite a flush. The actual changes may not be committed to disk until the folder containing the message is closed. However, this method does ensure that the changes are stored in the folder and will be saved when the folder is saved.

Flags

Mail programs can save extra information about the messages that are not part of the messages themselves. For instance, Pine lets me know whether I've replied to or read a message, and so on. As Figure 19-5 shows, this information is indicated by symbols and letters in the lefthand column. D means a message has been deleted; A means it's been answered; N is a new message that hasn't been read yet; and so forth. In the JavaMail API, these are all represented as *flags*. A flag is an instance of the javax.mail.Flags class:

```
public class Flags extends Object implements Cloneable
```

Seven flags are predefined as instances of the public static inner class Flags.Flag. These are:

```
Flags.Flag.ANSWERED
Flags.Flag.DELETED
Flags.Flag.DRAFT
Flags.Flag.FLAGGED
Flags.Flag.RECENT
Flags.Flag.SEEN
Flags.Flag.USER
```

In addition, some implementations may allow arbitrary user-defined flags. If so, the USER flag is set.

Figure 19-5. Pine shows flags as letters in the lefthand column

The getFlags( ) method returns the flags of a particular message:

```
public abstract Flags getFlags() throws MessagingException
```

The isSet( ) method tests whether a specified flag is set for the given message:

```
public boolean isSet(Flags.Flag flag) throws MessagingException
```

Finally, the setFlags( ) and setFlag( ) methods set or unset (depending on the second argument) the flag indicated by the first argument:

```
public abstract void setFlags(Flags flag, boolean set)
  throws MessagingException, IllegalWriteException,
  IllegalStateException
public void setFlag(Flags.Flag flag, boolean set) throws
  MessagingException, IllegalWriteException, IllegalStateException
```

You delete messages by setting their Flags.Flag.DELETED flag to true. For example, to delete message:

```
message.setFlag(Flags.Flag.DELETED, true);
```

This only marks the message as deleted. It does not actually expunge it from the file on the server. Until the message is expunged, it can still be undeleted by setting Flags.Flag.DELETED back to false.

Example 19-9 is a slight modification of Example 19-8, HeaderClient, which prints the flags as well. As a general rule, POP servers won't report flags. Only a protocol that stores messages and forwards them, such as IMAP or mbox, will report flags.

Example 19-9. A program to read mailbox flags

```java
import javax.mail.*;
import javax.mail.internet.*;
import java.util.*;

public class FlagsClient {

  public static void main(String[] args) {

    if (args.length == 0) {
      System.err.println(
      "Usage: java FlagsClient protocol://username@host/foldername");
      return;
    }

    URLName server = new URLName(args[0]);

    try {

      Session session = Session.getDefaultInstance(new Properties(),
        new MailAuthenticator(server.getUsername()));

      // Connect to the server and open the folder
      Folder folder = session.getFolder(server);
```

Example 19-9. A program to read mailbox flags (continued)

```java
if (folder == null) {
  System.out.println("Folder " + server.getFile() + " not found.");
  System.exit(1);
}
folder.open(Folder.READ_ONLY);

// Get the messages from the server
Message[] messages = folder.getMessages();
for (int i = 0; i < messages.length; i++) {
  System.out.println("------------ Message " + (i+1)
   + " ------------");
  // Get the headers
  String from = InternetAddress.toString(messages[i].getFrom());
  if (from != null) System.out.println("From: " + from);
  String replyTo = InternetAddress.toString(
   messages[i].getReplyTo());
  if (replyTo != null) System.out.println("Reply-to: "
   + replyTo);
  String to = InternetAddress.toString(
   messages[i].getRecipients(Message.RecipientType.TO));
  if (to != null) System.out.println("To: " + to);
  String cc = InternetAddress.toString(
  messages[i].getRecipients(Message.RecipientType.CC));
  if (cc != null) System.out.println("Cc: " + cc);
  String bcc = InternetAddress.toString(
   messages[i].getRecipients(Message.RecipientType.BCC));
  if (bcc != null) System.out.println("Bcc: " + to);
  String subject = messages[i].getSubject();
  if (subject != null) System.out.println("Subject: " + subject);
  Date sent = messages[i].getSentDate();
  if (sent != null) System.out.println("Sent: " + sent);
  Date received = messages[i].getReceivedDate();
  if (received != null) System.out.println("Received: " + received);

  // Now test the flags:
  if (messages[i].isSet(Flags.Flag.DELETED)) {
    System.out.println("Deleted");
  }
  if (messages[i].isSet(Flags.Flag.ANSWERED)) {
    System.out.println("Answered");
  }
  if (messages[i].isSet(Flags.Flag.DRAFT)) {
    System.out.println("Draft");
  }
  if (messages[i].isSet(Flags.Flag.FLAGGED)) {
    System.out.println("Marked");
  }
  if (messages[i].isSet(Flags.Flag.RECENT)) {
    System.out.println("Recent");
  }
  if (messages[i].isSet(Flags.Flag.SEEN)) {
    System.out.println("Read");
```

Example 19-9. A program to read mailbox flags (continued)

```
        }
        if (messages[i].isSet(Flags.Flag.USER)) {
          // We don't know what the user flags might be in advance
          // so they're returned as an array of strings
          String[] userFlags = messages[i].getFlags().getUserFlags();
          for (int j = 0; j < userFlags.length; j++) {
            System.out.println("User flag: " + userFlags[j]);
          }
        }

        System.out.println();
      }

      // Close the connection
      // but don't remove the messages from the server
      folder.close(false);

    }
    catch (Exception ex) {
      ex.printStackTrace();
    }

    // Since we may have brought up a GUI to authenticate,
    // we can't rely on returning from main() to exit
    System.exit(0);

  }
}
```

Here's a sample run. The first message has been read and deleted. The second message has no set flags; it hasn't been read, deleted, or answered. The third message has been read and answered but not deleted. Notice that I'm using an IMAP server instead of a POP server:

```
% java FlagsClient imap://elharo@mail.metalab.unc.edu/INBOX
------------ Message 1 ------------
From: Mike Hall <mikehall@spacestar.com>
Reply-to: Mike Hall <mikehall@spacestar.com>
To: mrj-dev@public.lists.apple.com
Subject: Re: dialog box, parents & X-platform
Sent: Mon Dec 13 05:24:38 PST 1999
Received: Mon Dec 13 06:33:00 PST 1999
Deleted
Read

------------ Message 2 ------------
From: Kapil Madan <kapil.madan@MIT-MISYS.COM>
Reply-to: XML-INTEREST@JAVA.SUN.COM
To: XML-INTEREST@JAVA.SUN.COM
Subject: Re: first mail to the list!
Sent: Mon Dec 13 06:19:46 PST 1999
Received: Mon Dec 13 06:40:00 PST 1999
```

```
------------ Message 3 ------------
From: Jim Jackl-Mochel <jmochel@foliage.com>
Reply-to: Jim Jackl-Mochel <jmochel@foliage.com>
To: elharo@metalab.unc.edu
Subject: CPreProcessorStream
Sent: Mon Dec 13 07:14:00 PST 1999
Received: Mon Dec 13 07:08:00 PST 1999
Answered
Read
```

Folders

Messages received from the network (as opposed to sent to the network) generally belong to some Folder. The getFolder( ) method returns a reference to the Folder object that contains this Message:

```
public Folder getFolder( )
```

It returns null if the message isn't contained in a folder.

Within a folder, messages are organized from first (message 1) to last. The getMessageNumber( ) method returns the relative position of this Message in its Folder:

```
public int getMessageNumber( )
```

Messages that aren't in any folder have number 0. Message numbers may change while a program is running if other messages are added to or deleted from a folder.

There's also a protected setMessageNumber( ) method, but it's only for service providers, not for user code:

```
protected void setMessageNumber(int number)
```

We'll talk more about folders and what they can do at the end of this chapter. One of the things you can do with a folder is expunge messages from it. This physically deletes the message if it's already been marked as deleted. (A merely deleted message can be "undeleted", whereas an expunged message cannot be.) If a message is expunged, there may still be a Message object pointing to the message, but almost all methods on the message will throw a MessagingException. Thus, it may be important to check whether a message has been expunged before working with it. The isExpunged( ) method does that:

```
public boolean isExpunged( )
```

There's also a protected setExpunged( ) method, but it's only for service providers, not for user code:

```
protected void setExpunged(boolean expunged)
```

Searching

The final method left in the Message class is match( ). The match( ) method determines whether a Message satisfies particular search criteria. We'll discuss this more in a bit when we talk about searching folders:

```
public boolean match(SearchTerm term) throws MessagingException
```

The Part Interface

Both `Message` and `BodyPart` implement the `Part` interface. Every `Message` is a `Part`. However, some parts may contain other parts. The `Part` interface declares three kinds of methods:

- Methods for getting and setting the attributes of the part
- Methods for getting and setting the headers of the part
- Methods for getting and setting the contents of the part

The attributes of the part are things such as the size of the message or the date it was received, details that aren't explicitly specified in the message's header. The headers, by contrast, are name-value pairs included at the front of the part. Finally, the content of the part is the actual data that the message is trying to transmit.

Attributes

The JavaMail API defines five attributes for parts:

Size
> The approximate number of bytes in the part

Line count
> The number of lines in the part

Disposition
> Whether the part is an attachment or should be displayed inline

Description
> A brief text summary of the part

Filename
> The name of the file that the attachment came from

Not all parts have all attributes. For instance, a part that does not represent an attached file is unlikely to have a filename attribute. Each attribute is mapped to a getter method:

```
public int    getSize() throws MessagingException
public int    getLineCount() throws MessagingException
public String getDisposition() throws MessagingException
public String getDescription() throws MessagingException
public String getFileName() throws MessagingException, ParseException
```

Generally, the getter method returns null or −1 if a part doesn't possess the requested attribute. It throws a `MessagingException` if there's some problem retrieving the message; for instance, if the connection goes down while the message is being retrieved.

The `getSize()` method returns the approximate number of bytes in the part. Depending on the server and protocol, this may or may not account for changes in the size caused by operations such as Base64 encoding the data.

The getLineCount( ) method returns the approximate number of lines in the content of the part or –1 if the number of lines isn't known. Again, the number returned may or may not account for changes in the size of the part caused by the part's encoding.

The getDisposition( ) method returns a string indicating whether the content should be presented inline or as an attachment. The value returned should either be null (the disposition is not known) or one of the two named constants Part.INLINE or Part.ATTACHMENT:

```
public static final String ATTACHMENT = "attachment";
public static final String INLINE    = "inline";
```

If the disposition is Part.ATTACHMENT, getFileName( ) should return the name of the file to save the attachment in. Otherwise, getFileName( ) probably returns null. However, some email clients, including Netscape 4.5 for Windows, do not properly set the Content-disposition header for attachments. Consequently, when receiving messages with attachments that were sent by Navigator, you'll often get a null disposition but a non-null filename. In practice, it seems more reliable to assume that any body part with a non-null filename is an attachment regardless of the Content-disposition header, and any body part with no filename and no Content-disposition header should be displayed inline if possible. If it's not possible—for instance, if you can't handle the MIME type—you can either ask the user for a filename or pick some reasonable default, such as *attachment1.tif*.

Normally, the filename includes only the actual name of the file but not any of the directories the file was in. It's up to the application receiving the message to decide where to put the incoming file. For instance, Eudora generally stores attachments in the Attachments folder inside the Eudora folder. However, the user has an option to pick a different location. Since it's not uncommon to receive multiple attachments with the same name over time, check to see whether a file with the attached file's name already exists before writing out the attachment. If a similarly named file does exist, you'll have to rename the attachment in some reasonable fashion—for instance, by appending a 1 or a 2 to it: e.g., *vcard1.vcf*, *vcard2.vcf*, and so on.

The description, disposition, and filename attributes also have setter methods. However, the size and line count attributes are determined by the content of the part rather than a setter method:

```
public void setDisposition(String disposition) throws
 MessagingException, IllegalWriteException, IllegalStateException
public void setFileName(String filename) throws MessagingException,
 IllegalWriteException, IllegalStateException
public void setDescription(String description) throws
 MessagingException, IllegalWriteException, IllegalStateException
```

The setter methods all throw a MessagingException if there's some problem while changing the message. They can also throw an IllegalWriteException if the relevant attribute of the part cannot be modified or an IllegalStateException if the part belongs to a read-only folder.

The setDisposition( ) method determines whether the part is to be viewed inline or as an attachment. Although it's declared to take a String as an argument, this String should be one of the two named constants, Part.INLINE or Part.ATTACHMENT. Parts that are attachments generally have a filename included in their metainformation. This name can be set with the setFileName( ) method. Finally, the setDescriptionMethod( ) can take any String at all to add a description to the part.

Example 19-10 is a simple program that connects to a mail server and reads the attributes of the messages in the mailbox. Since each message is itself a part (even if it contains other parts), we can invoke these methods on the entire message.

Example 19-10. A program to read mail attributes

```
import javax.mail.*;
import javax.mail.internet.*;
import java.util.*;

public class AttributeClient {

  public static void main(String[] args) {

    if (args.length == 0) {
      System.err.println(
       "Usage: java AttributeClient protocol://username@host/foldername");
      return;
    }

    URLName server = new URLName(args[0]);

    try {

      Session session = Session.getDefaultInstance(new Properties( ),
       new MailAuthenticator(server.getUsername( )));

      // Connect to the server and open the folder
      Folder folder = session.getFolder(server);
      if (folder == null) {
        System.out.println("Folder " + server.getFile( ) + " not found.");
        System.exit(1);
      }
      folder.open(Folder.READ_ONLY);

      // Get the messages from the server
      Message[] messages = folder.getMessages( );
      for (int i = 0; i < messages.length; i++) {
        System.out.println("------------ Message " + (i+1)
         + " ------------");
        String from = InternetAddress.toString(messages[i].getFrom( ));
        if (from != null) System.out.println("From: " + from);
        String to = InternetAddress.toString(
         messages[i].getRecipients(Message.RecipientType.TO));
        if (to != null) System.out.println("To: " + to);
```

Example 19-10. A program to read mail attributes (continued)

```
          String subject = messages[i].getSubject();
          if (subject != null) System.out.println("Subject: " + subject);
          Date sent = messages[i].getSentDate();
          if (sent != null) System.out.println("Sent: " + sent);

          System.out.println();
          // Here's the attributes...
          System.out.println("This message is approximately "
           + messages[i].getSize() + " bytes long.");
          System.out.println("This message has approximately "
           + messages[i].getLineCount() + " lines.");
          String disposition = messages[i].getDisposition();
          if (disposition == null) ; // do nothing
          else if (disposition.equals(Part.INLINE)) {
            System.out.println("This part should be displayed inline");
          }
          else if (disposition.equals(Part.ATTACHMENT)) {
            System.out.println("This part is an attachment");
            String fileName = messages[i].getFileName();
            if (fileName != null) {
              System.out.println("The file name of this attachment is "
              + fileName);
            }
          }
          String description = messages[i].getDescription();
          if (description != null) {
            System.out.println("The description of this message is "
              + description);
          }

        }

        // Close the connection
        // but don't remove the messages from the server
        folder.close(false);

      }
      catch (Exception ex) {
        ex.printStackTrace();
      }

      // Since we may have brought up a GUI to authenticate,
      // we can't rely on returning from main() to exit
      System.exit(0);

  }
}
```

Here's some typical output. I used an IMAP server because most of these methods don't work nearly as well with POP servers. IMAP servers can give you the attributes of a message without making you download the entire message, but POP servers aren't that sophisticated:

```
% java AttributeClient imap://elharo@mail.sunsite.unc.edu/INBOX
------------ Message 1 ------------
From: "Richman, Jeremy" <jrichman@hq.ileaf.com>
To: 'xsl-list' <XSL-List@mulberrytech.com>
Subject: Re: New twist: eliminating nodes with duplicate content
Sent: Mon Dec 06 08:37:51 PST 1999

This message is approximately 3391 bytes long.
This message has approximately 87 lines.
------------ Message 2 ------------
From: schererm@us.ibm.com
To: Unicode List <unicode@unicode.org>
Subject: Re: Number ordering
Sent: Mon Dec 06 11:00:28 PST 1999

This message is approximately 1554 bytes long.
This message has approximately 18 lines.
------------ Message 3 ------------
From: John Posner <jjp@connix.com>
To: 'Nakita Watson' <nakita@oreilly.com>
Subject: RE: Another conference Call
Sent: Mon Dec 06 11:16:38 PST 1999
This message is approximately 1398 bytes long.
This message has approximately 19 lines.
```

Headers

Classes that implement the `Part` interface—for example, `Message`—generally declare methods to return specific headers such as To: or From:. The `Part` interface, by contrast, declares methods to get and set arbitrary headers regardless of name.

The `getHeader()` method gets the values of all the headers with a name that matches the name argument. Some headers such as Received: can have multiple values and can be included in a message multiple times, so this method returns those values as an array of strings. It returns `null` if no header with that name is present in this `Part`:

```
public String[] getHeader(String name) throws MessagingException
```

The `setHeader()` method adds a new header to an outgoing message:

```
public void setHeader(String name, String value) throws
  MessagingException, IllegalWriteException, IllegalStateException
```

If there's already a header with this name, that header is deleted and the new one inserted in its place—unless the folder in which the message resides is read-only, in which case an `IllegalStateException` is thrown.

By contrast, the `addHeader()` method adds a header with the specified name but does not replace any that exist:

```
public void addHeader(String name, String value) throws
  MessagingException, IllegalWriteException, IllegalStateException
```

The removeHeader( ) method deletes all instances of the named header from this Part:

```
public void removeHeader(String name) throws MessagingException,
   IllegalWriteException, IllegalStateException
```

The getAllHeaders( ) method returns a java.util.Enumeration object containing all the headers in this message:

```
public Enumeration getAllHeaders( ) throws MessagingException
```

The Enumeration contains one javax.mail.Header object for each header in the message:

```
public class Header extends Object
```

The Header class is very simple, with just a constructor to set the name and value of the header, and getName( ) and getValue( ) methods to return them:

```
public Header(String name, String value)
public String getName( )
public String getValue( )
```

Finally, the getMatchingHeaders( ) method returns an Enumeration containing all the headers in this message with names that are one of the strings in the argument names array. The getNonMatchingHeaders( ) method returns an Enumeration containing all the headers in this message with names that are *not* one of the strings in the argument names array. Again, the Enumeration contains Header objects:

```
public Enumeration getMatchingHeaders(String[] names)
  throws MessagingException
public Enumeration getNonMatchingHeaders(String[] names)
  throws MessagingException
```

You may recall that Example 19-8, HeaderClient, printed only a few prespecified headers, such as To: and From:. With the methods of the Part interface (that Message implements), it's easy to expand this to cover all headers in the message, whether known in advance or not. Example 19-11 demonstrates. This ability is important because Internet email can contain arbitrary headers; it's not limited to just a few headers mentioned in the relevant RFCs. For instance, some graphical mail clients for X Windows use a completely nonstandard X-Face: header, whose value is a 48-pixel by 48-pixel, black-and-white, uuencoded bitmap of the sender's countenance. Other clients use custom headers for purposes both more serious and sillier.

Example 19-11. A program to read mail headers

```
import javax.mail.*;
import javax.mail.internet.*;
import java.util.*;


public class AllHeaderClient {

  public static void main(String[] args) {
```

Example 19-11. A program to read mail headers (continued)

```
    if (args.length == 0) {
      System.err.println(
       "Usage: java AllHeaderClient protocol://username@host/foldername");
      return;
    }

    URLName server = new URLName(args[0]);

    try {

      Session session = Session.getDefaultInstance(new Properties( ),
       new MailAuthenticator(server.getUsername( )));

      // Connect to the server and open the folder
      Folder folder = session.getFolder(server);
      if (folder == null) {
        System.out.println("Folder " + server.getFile( ) + " not found.");
        System.exit(1);
      }
      folder.open(Folder.READ_ONLY);

      // Get the messages from the server
      Message[] messages = folder.getMessages( );
      for (int i = 0; i < messages.length; i++) {
        System.out.println("------------ Message " + (i+1)
         + " ------------");
        // Here's the difference...
        Enumeration headers = messages[i].getAllHeaders( );
        while (headers.hasMoreElements( )) {
          Header h = (Header) headers.nextElement( );
          System.out.println(h.getName() + ": " + h.getValue( ));
        }
        System.out.println( );
      }

      // Close the connection
      // but don't remove the messages from the server
      folder.close(false);

    }
    catch (Exception ex) {
      ex.printStackTrace( );
    }

    // Since we may have brought up a GUI to authenticate,
    // we can't rely on returning from main( ) to exit
    System.exit(0);

  }
}
```

Here's a typical run:

```
% java AllHeaderClient pop3://eharold@utopia.poly.edu/INBOX
------------ Message 1 ------------
Received: (from eharold@localhost)
        by utopia.poly.edu (8.8.8/8.8.8) id QAA05728
        for eharold; Tue, 30 Nov 1999 16:14:29 -0500 (EST)
Date: Tue, 30 Nov 1999 16:14:29 -0500 (EST)
From: Elliotte Harold <eharold@utopia.poly.edu>
Message-Id: <199911302114.QAA05728@utopia.poly.edu>
To: eharold@utopia.poly.edu
Subject: test
Content-Type: text
X-UIDL: 87e3f1ba71738c8f772b15e3933241f0
Status: RO


------------ Message 2 ------------
Received: from russian.cloud9.net (russian.cloud9.net [168.100.1.4])
        by utopia.poly.edu (8.8.8/8.8.8) with ESMTP id OAA28428
        for <eharold@utopia.poly.edu>; Wed, 1 Dec 1999 14:05:06 -0500 (EST)
Received: from [168.100.203.234] (macfaq.dialup.cloud9.net [168.100.203.234])
        by russian.cloud9.net (Postfix) with ESMTP id 24B93764F8
        for <eharold@utopia.poly.edu>; Wed,  1 Dec 1999 14:02:50 -0500 (EST)
Mime-Version: 1.0
X-Sender: macfaq@mail.cloud9.net
Message-Id: <v04210100b46b1f97969d@[168.100.203.234]>
Date: Wed, 1 Dec 1999 13:55:40 -0500
To: eharold@utopia.poly.edu
From: Elliotte Rusty Harold <elharo@macfaq.com>
Subject: New system
Content-Type: text/plain; charset="us-ascii" ; format="flowed"
X-UIDL: 01fd5cbcf1768fc6c28f9c8f934534b5
Status: RO


------------ Message 3 ------------
Received: from russian.cloud9.net (russian.cloud9.net [168.100.1.4])
        by utopia.poly.edu (8.8.8/8.8.8) with ESMTP id HAA17345
        for <eharold@utopia.poly.edu>; Thu, 2 Dec 1999 07:55:04 -0500 (EST)
Received: from [168.100.203.234] (macfaq.dialup.cloud9.net [168.100.203.234])
        by russian.cloud9.net (Postfix) with ESMTP id C036A7630E
        for <eharold@utopia.poly.edu>; Thu,  2 Dec 1999 07:54:58 -0500 (EST)
Mime-Version: 1.0
X-Sender: elharo@luna.oit.unc.edu
Message-Id: <v04210100b46c0c686ecc@[168.100.203.234]>
Date: Thu, 2 Dec 1999 06:45:52 -0500
To: eharold@utopia.poly.edu
From: "Dr. Mickel" <Greatsmiles@mail.com>(by way of Elliotte Rusty Harold)
Subject: Breath RX Products now available Online!
Sender: elharo@metalab.unc.edu
Content-Type: text/plain; charset="us-ascii" ; format="flowed"
X-UIDL: 40fa8af2aca1a8c11994f4c56b792720
Status: RO
```

Content

Every part has content that can be represented as a sequence of bytes. For instance, in a part that's a simple email message, the content is the body of the message. However, in multipart messages, this content may itself contain other parts. The content of each of these parts can be represented as a sequence of bytes. Furthermore, this sequence of bytes may represent some more specific content type, such as a uuencoded GIF image or a Base64-encoded WAV audio clip.

Reading the contents of the part

The Part interface declares two methods for determining a part's MIME content type. The getContentType( ) method returns the MIME content type of the part as a string; for example: text/plain; charset="us-ascii"; format= "flowed". It returns null if the content type can't be determined:

```
public String getContentType( ) throws MessagingException
```

The isMimeType( ) method returns true if this part has the specified MIME type and subtype. Additional parameters, such as charset, are ignored:

```
public boolean isMimeType(String mimeType) throws MessagingException
```

The Part interface also declares several methods that return the content as a variety of different Java objects, including InputStream, String, DataHandler, and more. The getInputStream( ) method returns an InputStream from which the part's content can be read:

```
public InputStream getInputStream( ) throws IOException,
    MessagingException
```

If the part's content has been encoded in some way—for example, Base64-encoded—then the InputStream reads the decoded content. The JavaMail API supports all common encodings except the BinHex format used for Macintosh files. If it encounters a BinHex-encoded attachment, it strips the MIME headers but otherwise leaves the BinHex data untouched. BinHex documents are tough to deal with on most platforms because of the unusual two-fork nature of a Mac file. Unless you're a real Mac expert, you're probably better off using a third-party utility such as StuffIt Expander (*http://www.stuffit.com/*) to decode the file.

Another possibility is to request a DataHandler for the content with the getDataHandler( ) method. The DataHandler class comes from the Java Activation Framework. It declares methods to help decide what to do with the content—for instance, by finding the right Java bean or helper application to display the content:

```
public javax.activation.DataHandler getDataHandler( )
    throws MessagingException
```

A third possibility is to request the content as an unspecified Java object using the getContent( ) method:

```
public Object getContent( ) throws IOException, MessagingException
```

This is reminiscent of the getContent( ) method of java.net.URL. However, rather than relying on the poorly designed content handler mechanism, this getContent( ) method uses the Java Activation Framework, so the behavior is a little more clearly specified. Most of the time, if the content type is text/plain, a String will be returned. If the content type is multipart, then regardless of the subtype, a javax.mail.Multipart object is returned. If the content type is some other type that is recognized by the underlying DataHandler, an appropriate Java object is returned. Finally, if the type is unrecognized, an InputStream is returned.

You can change which objects are returned for which content types by providing your own DataHandler, installed with the setDataHandler( ) method:

```
public void setDataHandler(javax.activation.DataHandler  handler)
  throws MessagingException, IllegalWriteException, IllegalStateException
```

Although this method is declared to throw the usual group of exceptions, it's perhaps a little less likely to actually do so, since setting the DataHandler only affects the Message object rather than the actual message stored on the server.

Writing the contents of the part

When sending a message, you naturally must set the message's contents. Since email messages are text, the most straightforward way is just to provide the text of the part with setText( ):

```
public void setText(String text) throws MessagingException,
  IllegalWriteException, IllegalStateException
```

The setText( ) method sets the MIME type to text/plain. Other objects can be made into content as well, provided the part has a DataHandler that understands how to convert them to encoded text. This is done with the setContent( ) method:

```
public void setContent(Object o, String type) throws
  MessagingException, IllegalWriteException, IllegalStateException
```

Another way to write the contents of a part is by using an OutputStream. The writeTo( ) method writes the content of the Part onto an OutputStream. If necessary, it will encode the content using Base64, quoted-printable, or some other format as specified by the DataHandler:

```
public void writeTo(OutputStream out) throws IOException,
  MessagingException
```

In fact, this not only writes the content of this Part, it also writes the attributes and headers of the part. Example 19-4 used this to provide a simple way of getting an entire email message in one fell swoop. It's most convenient, though, when you want to send an entire message to an SMTP server in one method call.

Finally, multiple parts can be added to a part by wrapping them in a Multipart object and passing that to setContent( ):

```
public void setContent(Multipart mp) throws MessagingException,
  IllegalWriteException, IllegalStateException
```

In this case, the entire message typically has a content type such as `multipart/mixed`, `multipart/signed`, or `multipart/alternative`. The individual parts of the message are all enclosed in one envelope but each part of the message has its own content type, content encoding, and data. The multiple parts may be used to present different forms of the same document (e.g., HTML and plain-text mail), a document and metainformation about the document (e.g., a message and the MD5 digest of the message), or several different documents (e.g., a message and several attached files). The next section expands on this process.

Multipart Messages and File Attachments

The way all the different text and binary file types are encoded into raw text that can be passed through 7-bit email gateways is fairly ingenious and rather detailed. Fortunately, the JavaMail API shields you from those details, interesting as they are. To send a multipart message using the JavaMail API, all you have to do is add the parts to a `MimeMultipart` object, then pass that object to the Message's `setContent()` method. To receive a multipart message, you simply process each of the parts individually.

Most of the methods for building and deconstructing multipart messages are in the abstract `javax.mail.Multipart` class:

```
public abstract class Multipart extends Object
```

However, since this class is abstract, you'll generally start with a `javax.mail.internet.MimeMultipart` object instead:

```
public class MimeMultipart extends Multipart
```

Each part you add to a `Multipart` is an instance of the abstract `javax.mail.BodyPart` class that implements the `Part` interface of the last section:

```
public abstract class BodyPart extends Object implements Part
```

In Internet email, the concrete subclass of `BodyPart` you'll use is `javax.mail.internet.MimeBodyPart`:

```
public class MimeBodyPart extends BodyPart implements MimePart
```

Most of the methods you need in the `MimeBodyPart` and `BodyPart` classes are the ones you're already familiar with from the `Part` interface, methods such as `setContent()` and `setDataHandler()`. There are also three methods to read the contents of a `Multipart` object:

```
public String    getContentType()
public int        getCount() throws MessagingException
public BodyPart getBodyPart(int index)
   throws IndexOutOfBoundsException, MessagingException
```

The `getContentType()` method returns the MIME media type of the entire `Multipart`, which is typically something like `multipart/mixed` or `multipart/alternative`. This is not the same as the MIME types of the individual parts, which are something like text/plain or image/gif.

The getCount( ) method returns the number of parts in this Multipart. The getBodyPart( ) method returns a particular part. Parts are numbered starting at 0, like the components of an array. Example 19-12 is very similar to Example 19-11, AllHeaderClient. However, Example 19-12 adds the necessary code to handle the body of the message. If the message is a single-part message, it's simply printed on System.out. However, if the message has multiple parts, each part is handled separately. If the part has a multipart content type itself, processMultipart( ) is called recursively. If the part has no filename, does not have the disposition Part. ATTACHMENT, and has MIME type text/plain, it's assumed to be an inline message and is printed on System.out. Otherwise, it's assumed to be an attachment and is saved into an appropriate file. If necessary, the static File.createTempFile( ) method generates a reasonable name for the file.

Example 19-12. A mail client that handles multipart messages with attached files

```
import javax.mail.*;
import javax.mail.internet.*;
import java.util.*;
import java.io.*;

public class AllPartsClient {

  public static void main(String[] args) {

    if (args.length == 0) {
      System.err.println(
       "Usage: java AllPartsClient protocol://username@host:port/foldername");
      return;
    }
    URLName server = new URLName(args[0]);

    try {

      Session session = Session.getDefaultInstance(new Properties( ),
       new MailAuthenticator(server.getUsername( )));

      // Connect to the server and open the folder
      Folder folder = session.getFolder(server);
      if (folder == null) {
        System.out.println("Folder " + server.getFile( ) + " not found.");
        System.exit(1);
      }
      folder.open(Folder.READ_ONLY);

      // Get the messages from the server
      Message[] messages = folder.getMessages( );
      for (int i = 0; i < messages.length; i++) {
        System.out.println("------------ Message " + (i+1)
```

Example 19-12. A mail client that handles multipart messages with attached files (continued)

```
        + " ------------");

      // Print message headers
      Enumeration headers = messages[i].getAllHeaders();
      while (headers.hasMoreElements()) {
        Header h = (Header) headers.nextElement();
        System.out.println(h.getName() + ": " + h.getValue());
      }
      System.out.println();

      // Enumerate parts
      Object body = messages[i].getContent();
      if (body instanceof Multipart) {
        processMultipart((Multipart) body);
      }
      else { // ordinary message
        processPart(messages[i]);
      }

      System.out.println();

    }

    // Close the connection
    // but don't remove the messages from the server
    folder.close(false);

  }
  catch (Exception ex) {
    ex.printStackTrace();
  }

  // Since we may have brought up a GUI to authenticate,
  // we can't rely on returning from main() to exit
  System.exit(0);

}

public static void processMultipart(Multipart mp)
 throws MessagingException {

  for (int i = 0; i < mp.getCount(); i++) {
    processPart(mp.getBodyPart(i));
  }

}

public static void processPart(Part p) {

  try {
    String fileName = p.getFileName();
    String disposition = p.getDisposition();
```

```
        String contentType = p.getContentType( );
        if (contentType.toLowerCase( ).startsWith("multipart/")) {
          processMultipart((Multipart)  p.getContent( ) );
        }
        else if (fileName == null
         && (Part.ATTACHMENT.equalsIgnoreCase(disposition)
         || !contentType.equalsIgnoreCase("text/plain"))) {
          // pick a random file name. This requires Java 1.2 or later.
          fileName = File.createTempFile("attachment", ".txt").getName( );
        }
        if (fileName == null) { // likely inline
          p.writeTo(System.out);
        }
        else {
          File f = new File(fileName);
          // find a file that does not yet exist
          for (int i = 1; f.exists( ); i++) {
            String newName = fileName + " " + i;
            f = new File(newName);
          }
          OutputStream out = new BufferedOutputStream(new FileOutputStream(f));

          // We can't just use p.writeTo( ) here because it doesn't
          // decode the attachment. Instead we copy the input stream
          // onto the output stream which does automatically decode
          // Base-64, quoted printable, and a variety of other formats.
          InputStream in = new BufferedInputStream(p.getInputStream( ));
          int b;
          while ((b = in.read( )) != -1) out.write(b);
          out.flush( );
          out.close( );
          in.close( );
        }
      }
      catch (Exception ex) {
        System.err.println(e);
        ex.printStackTrace( );
      }
    }
  }
}
```

You can also get a part from a multipart message by passing an OutputStream to the part's writeTo( ) method:

```
public abstract void writeTo(OutputStream out)
  throws IOException, MessagingException
```

However, this differs from the approach taken in Example 19-12 in that it does not decode the part before writing it. It leaves whatever Base64, BinHex, or quoted-printable encoding the sender applied to the attachment alone. Instead, it simply writes the raw data.

Attaching files (or other documents) to messages you send is more complicated. To attach a file to a message, you first have to wrap the data in a BodyPart object and add it to the Multipart using one of the two addBodyPart( ) methods:

```
public void addBodyPart(BodyPart part)
  throws IllegalWriteException, MessagingException
public void addBodyPart(BodyPart part, int index)
  throws IllegalWriteException, MessagingException
```

The first variant simply appends the part to the end of the message. The second variant adds the given part at the specified position. If the position is greater than the number of parts in the message, the part is simply added to the end. If it's added somewhere in the middle, this may cause the positions of other parts to change. If the message can't be changed, an IllegalWriteException is thrown.

The tricky part is creating the BodyPart object. You first need to guess a reasonable MIME content type for the file (text/plain and application/octet-stream are the most common types). Next, read the file and convert it into some class of Java object. Then install a javax.activation.DataHandler class that knows how to convert your data class according to your chosen MIME type. Once you've done all this, you can create a new MimeBodyPart object and use the various methods of the Part interface to set attributes such as the filename and the content disposition.

There are also two removeBodyPart( ) methods that delete a specified part from the message, although these aren't as commonly used:

```
public boolean removeBodyPart(BodyPart part)
  throws IllegalWriteException, MessagingException
public void removeBodyPart(int index)
  throws IndexOutOfBoundsException, MessagingException
```

If the message can't be changed, an IllegalWriteException is thrown. If the specified index doesn't identify a part, an IndexOutOfBoundsException is thrown. If the specified part isn't present in the message, a MessagingException is thrown.

MIME Messages

MIME was designed mainly for Internet email and specifically organized to be backward-compatible with existing protocols and software. Therefore, a typical Internet email message is in fact a MIME message. The only concrete subclass of Message in the JavaMail API is javax.mail.internet.MimeMessage:

```
public class MimeMessage extends Message implements MimePart
```

This class declares almost 70 public and protected methods. However, with the natural exception of the constructors, almost all of these either override methods from the Message superclass or implement methods declared by the Part interface. The only new methods are a baker's dozen declared in the MimePart interface, a subinterface of Part:

```
public interface MimePart extends Part
```

Most of these methods are very similar to methods in Part or Message. However, they have features that are unlikely to be found in non-MIME messages. For instance, a MIME part may have an MD5 digest, which would be encoded as an extra header inside the part. Thus, the MimePart interface declares and the MimeMessage class implements two methods to set and get this digest:

```
public String getContentMD5() throws MessagingException
public void    setContentMD5(String md5) throws MessagingException,
  IllegalWriteException, IllegalStateException
```

The addHeaderLine() method adds a string of text to the header of the message. It's up to you to make sure that this string will actually make sense in the header:

```
public void addHeaderLine(String line) throws
  MessagingException, IllegalWriteException, IllegalStateException
```

The getHeader() method returns the value of every header in the message with the given name. If there are multiple headers with this name, the string separates the values of the different headers with the specified delimiter string:

```
public String getHeader(String name, String delimiter)
  throws MessagingException
```

The getAllHeaderLines() method returns a java.util.Enumeration containing every header in the message. The Enumeration contains String objects, one per header. Each String contains the full name and value; for example, "Subject: Re: Java 5 support". It is not divided into a separate name and value:

```
public Enumeration getAllHeaderLines() throws MessagingException
```

The getMatchingHeaderLines() method returns all header lines with names given in the names argument array. The getNonMatchingHeaderLines() method does the reverse; it returns the header lines with a name not mentioned in the names argument:

```
public Enumeration getMatchingHeaderLines(String[] names)
  throws MessagingException
public Enumeration getNonMatchingHeaderLines(String[] names)
  throws MessagingException
```

The getEncoding() method returns the encoding of this MIME part as a String as given by the Content-transfer-encoding: header. The typical encoding for a plain-text email is seven-bit or perhaps eight-bit or quoted-printable. The typical encoding for a file attachment is Base64:

```
public String getEncoding() throws MessagingException
```

The getContentID() method returns a string that uniquely identifies this part as given by the part's Content-ID: field. A typical ID might look like <Pine.LNX.4. 10.9912290930220.8058@akbar.nevex.com>. It returns null if the part doesn't have a content ID:

```
public String getContentID() throws MessagingException
  IllegalWriteException, IllegalStateException
```

The getContentLanguage( ) method returns the value of the Content-language: header. This is a comma-separated list of two (or more) letter abbreviations for languages, as defined by RFC 1766. For example, English is "en" and French is "fr". It returns null if the part doesn't have a Content-language: header.

```
public String[] getContentLanguage( ) throws MessagingException
```

There's also a setContentLanguage( ) method that you might use when sending a message:

```
public void setContentLanguage(String[] languages) throws
  MessagingException, IllegalWriteException, IllegalStateException
```

Finally, the two setText( ) methods set the content of the part with the MIME type text/plain. The second setText( ) method also lets you specify the character set—for example, us-ascii or ISO 8859-1:

```
public void setText(String text) throws MessagingException
public void setText(String text, String charset)
  throws MessagingException
```

Folders

So far, we've worked mostly with the INBOX folder. This is the default folder in which most mail resides until the user filters or saves it into some other folder. On some systems, it may actually reside in a file called INBOX. On other systems, it may be called something different. Nonetheless, you can always access it from the Java-Mail API using the name INBOX.

Most mail programs allow you to organize your messages into different folders. These folders are hierarchical; that is, one folder may contain another folder. In particular, in the IMAP protocol, servers store the messages in different folders from which clients retrieve and manipulate the messages as necessary. POP servers, by contrast, generally send all the messages to the user when the user connects and rely on the client to store and manage them. The primary advantage of the IMAP approach over POP is that it allows users to easily access their entire email archives from multiple client machines.

The JavaMail API represents IMAP-like folders as instances of the abstract Folder class:

```
public abstract class Folder extends Object
```

This class declares methods for requesting named folders from servers, deleting messages from folders, searching for particular messages in folders, listing the messages in a folder, and so forth. Most of these methods are declared abstract. When you ask a session, a store, or a folder to give you one of the folders it contains, it will give you an instance of a concrete subclass appropriate for the protocol in use: IMAP, POP, mbox, or whatever. The reference implementation of the JavaMail API knows how to do these operations only for IMAP servers. However, some third-party implementations provide these operations in local mailbox folders stored on the client's filesystem as well.

Opening Folders

You cannot create folders directly. The only constructor is protected:

```
protected Folder(Store store)
```

Instead, you get a Folder from a Session, a Store, or another Folder like this:

```
Folder outbox = container.getFolder("sent-mail");
```

There are actually three getFolder( ) methods, one each in the Session, Store, and Folder classes. They all have the same signature and behave similarly:

```
public abstract Folder getFolder(String name) throws MessagingException
```

These methods share an annoying idiosyncrasy with the File class. Getting a Folder object doesn't imply that the named Folder actually exists on the server. To tell whether the folder is really present, you have to test for it with the exists( ) method:

```
public boolean exists( ) throws MessagingException
```

When you first get a folder, it's closed. Before you can read the messages it contains, you have to open the folder using the open( ) method:

```
public abstract void open(int mode)
  throws FolderNotFoundException, MessagingException
```

The mode argument should be one of the two named constants Folder.READ_ONLY or Folder.READ_WRITE. Some but not all implementations allow you to open multiple read-only connections to one real folder using multiple Folder objects. However, all implementations allow at most one Folder object to have write access to a folder at one time.

Some operations discussed in this section, such as searching or retrieving messages from a folder, can only be performed on an open folder. Others, such as deleting or changing the name of a folder, can only be done to a closed folder. The isOpen( ) method returns true if the folder is open, false if it's closed:

```
public abstract boolean isOpen( )
```

Generally, trying to do something with a closed folder that requires the folder to be open or vice versa will throw a java.lang.IllegalStateException. This is a runtime exception, so it doesn't need to be explicitly caught or declared.

When you're done with a folder, close it using the close( ) method:

```
public abstract void close(boolean expunge)
  throws FolderNotFoundException, MessagingException
```

If the expunge argument is true, any deleted messages in the folder are deleted from the actual file on the server. Otherwise, they're simply marked as deleted, but the message can still be undeleted.

Basic Folder Info

The Folder class has eight methods that return basic information about a folder:

```
public abstract String getName( )
public abstract String getFullName( )
public URLName        getURLName( ) throws MessagingException
public abstract Folder getParent( ) throws MessagingException
public abstract int    getType( ) throws MessagingException
public int            getMode( ) throws IllegalStateException
public Store          getStore( )
public abstract char  getSeparator( )
  throws FolderNotFoundException, MessagingException
```

The getName( ) method returns the name of the folder, such as "Reader Mail", whereas the getFullName( ) method returns the complete hierarchical name from the root, such as "books/JNP3E/Reader Mail". The getURLName( ) method includes the server; for instance, "imap://elharo@mail.metalab.unc.edu/books/JNP3E/Reader Mail". In this example, the slash character is the separator between nested folders. The separator can vary from implementation to implementation, but the getSeparator( ) method always tells you what it is.

The getParent( ) method returns the name of the folder that contains this folder; e.g., "JNP3E" for the previous Reader Mail example.

The getType( ) method returns an int indicating whether the folder can contain messages and/or other folders. If it can contain messages but not folders, getType( ) returns the named constant Folder.HOLDS_MESSAGES. If it can contain folders but not messages, getType( ) returns the named constant Folder.HOLDS_FOLDERS. If it can contain both folders and messages, getType( ) returns the bitwise union Folder.HOLDS_FOLDERS & Folder.HOLDS _MESSAGES.

The getMode( ) method tells you whether a folder allows writing. It returns one of the two named constants (Folder.READ_ONLY or Folder.READ_WRITE) or −1 if the mode is unknown. Finally, the getStore( ) method returns the Store object from which this folder was retrieved.

Managing Folders

The create( ) method creates a new folder in this folder's Store:

```
public abstract boolean create(int type) throws MessagingException
```

The type of the folder should be one of the named constants `Folder.HOLDS_MESSAGES` or `Folder.HOLDS_FOLDERS`, depending on whether it will hold other folders or messages. It returns `true` if the creation succeeded, `false` if it didn't.

The `delete()` method deletes this folder, but only if the folder is closed. Otherwise, it throws an `IllegalStateException`:

```
public abstract boolean delete(boolean recurse) throws
    IllegalStateException, FolderNotFoundException, MessagingException
```

If there are messages in this folder, they are deleted along with the folder. If the folder contains subfolders, the subfolders are deleted if the recurse argument is true. If the recurse argument is not true, the folder will only be deleted if it does not contain any subfolders. If it does contain subfolders, the delete fails. If the folder does contain subfolders and also contains messages, it's implementation-dependent whether the messages will be deleted even though the folder itself isn't. If the delete succeeds, the method returns true; otherwise, it returns false.

The `renameTo()` method changes the name of this folder. A folder must be closed to be renamed. Otherwise, an `IllegalStateException` is thrown. This method returns true if the folder is successfully renamed, false if it isn't:

```
public abstract boolean renameTo(Folder f) throws
    IllegalStateException, FolderNotFoundException, MessagingException
```

Managing Messages in Folders

On occasion, you may find a need to put a message in a folder. There's only one method to do this, `appendMessages()`:

```
public abstract void appendMessages(Message[] messages)
    throws FolderNotFoundException, MessagingException
```

As the name implies, the messages in the array are placed at the end of this folder.

The `copyMessages()` method copies messages into this folder from a specified folder given as an argument:

```
public void copyMessages(Message[] messages, Folder destination) throws
    IllegalStateException, FolderNotFoundException, MessagingException
```

The copied messages are appended to the destination folder. They are not removed from the source folder. To move a message, you have to copy it from the source to the destination, delete it from the source folder, and finally expunge the source folder.

To delete a message from a folder, set its `Flags.Flag.DELETED` flag to true. To physically remove deleted messages from a folder, you have to call its `expunge()` method:

```
public abstract Message[] expunge() throws MessagingException,
    IllegalStateException, FolderNotFoundException
```

After a message has been expunged, there may still be Message objects that refer to it. In this case, almost any method call on such an object, except isExpunged( ) and getMessageNumber( ), will throw an exception.

Subscriptions

Some implementations (though not the default IMAP implementation) allow you to subscribe to particular folders. This would be most appropriate for an NNTP provider, where a typical server offers thousands of newsgroups, but the typical user will want to retrieve messages from a few dozen of these, at most. Each newsgroup would be represented as a Folder object. A subscription to the newsgroup's Folder indicates that the user wants to retrieve messages from that newsgroup:

```
public boolean isSubscribed( )
public void    setSubscribed(boolean subscribe)
  throws FolderNotFoundException, MethodNotSupportedException,
  MessagingException
```

If a provider doesn't support subscription, setSubscribed( ) throws a MethodNotSupportedException and isSubscribed( ) returns false.

Listing the Contents of a Folder

Folders are hierarchical. That is, a folder can contain other folders. There are four methods to list the folders that a folder contains:

```
public Folder[] list( )
  throws FolderNotFoundException, MessagingException
public Folder[] listSubscribed( )
  throws FolderNotFoundException, MessagingException
public abstract Folder[] list(String pattern)
  throws FolderNotFoundException, MessagingException
public Folder[] listSubscribed(String pattern)
  throws FolderNotFoundException, MessagingException
```

The first method returns an array listing the folders that this folder contains. The second method returns an array listing all the subscribed folders that this folder contains.

The third and fourth methods repeat these first two, except they allow you to specify a pattern. Only folders whose full names match the pattern will be in the returned array. The pattern is a string giving the name of the folders that match. However, the string can contain the % character, which is a wildcard that matches any sequence of characters not including the hierarchy separator, and *, which matches any sequence of characters including the hierarchy separator.

Checking for Mail

The getMessageCount( ) method returns the number of messages in this folder:

```
public abstract int getMessageCount( )
  throws FolderNotFoundException, MessagingException
```

This method can be invoked on an open or closed folder. However, in the case of a closed folder, this method may (or may not) return −1 to indicate that the exact number of messages isn't easily available.

The hasNewMessages( ) method returns true if new messages have been added to the folder since it was last opened (not since the last time you checked!):

```
public abstract boolean hasNewMessages()
   throws FolderNotFoundException, MessagingException
```

The getNewMessageCount( ) method uses a slightly different approach for determining how many new messages there are. It checks the number of messages in the folder whose RECENT flag is set:

```
public int getNewMessageCount()
   throws FolderNotFoundException, MessagingException
```

Unlike hasNewMessages( ), getNewMessageCount( ) can be invoked on either an open or a closed folder. However, in the case of a closed folder, getNewMessageCount( ) may return −1 to indicate that the real answer would be too expensive to obtain.

The getUnreadMessageCount( ) method is similar but returns the number of messages in the folder that do not have a SEEN flag set:

```
public int getUnreadMessageCount()
   throws FolderNotFoundException, MessagingException
```

Like getNewMessageCount( ), getUnreadMessageCount( ) can be invoked on either an open or a closed folder. However, in the case of a closed folder, it may return −1 to indicate that the real answer would be too expensive to obtain.

Getting Messages from Folders

The Folder class provides four methods for retrieving messages from open folders:

```
public abstract Message getMessage(int messageNumber) throws
   IndexOutOfBoundsException, FolderNotFoundException,
   IllegalStateException, MessagingException
public Message[] getMessages() throws FolderNotFoundException,
   IllegalStateException, MessagingException
public Message[] getMessages(int start, int end) throws
   IndexOutOfBoundsException, FolderNotFoundException,
   IllegalStateException, MessagingException
public Message[] getMessages(int[] messageNumbers) throws
   IndexOutOfBoundsException, FolderNotFoundException,
   IllegalStateException, MessagingException
```

The getMessage( ) method returns the nth message in the folder. The first message in the folder is number 1 (not 0). Message numbers may change when messages are expunged from the folder. An IndexOutOfBoundsException is thrown if you ask for message n and there are $n − 1$ or fewer messages in the folder.

The first getMessages( ) method returns an array of Message objects representing all the messages in this folder. The second getMessages( ) method returns an array of Message objects from the folder, beginning with start and finishing with end, inclusive. The third getMessages( ) method returns an array containing only those messages specifically identified by number in the messageNumbers array.

All four of these methods only create the Message objects and fill in the minimal number of fields in those objects. The actual text and other content of the message will only be fetched from the server when the Message's methods that use those things are invoked. This means, for example, that you can't get all the messages from the server, then hang up your PPP connection and work with them offline. There is, however, a fetch( ) method, which fills in certain parts of the Message objects with actual data from the server:

```
public void fetch(Message[] messages, FetchProfile fp)
  throws IllegalStateException, MessagingException
```

The messages argument is an array containing the Message objects to be prefetched. The FetchProfile argument specifies which headers in the messages to prefetch. However, this is still just a suggestion. Implementations are free to ignore this request and fetch the message content only when it's actually needed.

You can request prefetching of individual headers such as Subject: by name. You can also request prefetching of three predefined blocks of information: the envelope (essentially the subject and addressees of the message), the flags of the message, or the content info of the messages. The three groups you can ask for are given as constant FetchProfile.Item objects. They are FetchProfile.Item.ENVELOPE, FetchProfile.Item.FLAGS, and FetchProfile.Item.CONTENT_INFO.

The FetchProfile class has a simple noargs constructor as well as methods for constructing a new profile, adding particular items and headers to the profile, and testing whether a particular item is part of a particular profile:

```
public FetchProfile( )
public void add(FetchProfile.Item item)
public void add(String headerName)
public boolean contains(FetchProfile.Item item)
public boolean contains(String headerName)
public FetchProfile.Item[] getItems( )
public String[] getHeaderNames( )
```

For example, suppose you wanted to download just the subjects, the To: addresses, and the content information of a block of messages. Fetch them like this:

```
Message[] messages = folder.getMessages( );
FetchProfile fp = new FetchProfile( );
fp.add(FetchProfile.Item.CONTENT_INFO);
fp.add("Subject");
fp.add("To");
```

Searching Folders

If the server supports searching (as many IMAP servers do and most POP servers don't), it's easy to search a folder for the messages meeting certain criteria. The criteria are encoded in SearchTerm objects:

```
public abstract class SearchTerm extends Object
```

The SearchTerm class is abstract, but the JavaMail API provides many subclasses for performing common searches:

```
public abstract class   AddressTerm         extends SearchTerm
public abstract class   FlagTerm            extends SearchTerm
public abstract class   StringTerm          extends SearchTerm
public final    class   FromTerm            extends AddressTerm
public final    class   FromStringTerm      extends AddressStringTerm
public final    class   ReceipientTerm      extends AddressTerm
public final    class   AddressStringTerm   extends StringTerm
public final    class   BodyTerm            extends StringTerm
public final    class   HeaderTerm          extends StringTerm
public final    class   MessageIDTerm       extends StringTerm
public final    class   SubjectTerm         extends StringTerm
public abstract class   DateTerm            extends ComparisonTerm
public final    class   ReceivedDateTerm    extends DateTerm
public final    class   SentDateTerm        extends DateTerm
```

It also provides several classes for combining searches:

```
public final    class AndTerm          extends SearchTerm
public abstract class ComparisonTerm   extends SearchTerm
public final    class NotTerm          extends SearchTerm
public final    class OrTerm           extends SearchTerm
```

And of course, you can write your own subclasses that implement your own search logic. To implement a search, write a subclass and override the subclass's match( ) method to describe your search:

```
public abstract boolean match(Message message)
```

This method returns true if the message argument satisfies the search and false if it doesn't.

Set up a SearchTerm matching your desired parameters and pass it to one of these two search( ) methods in the Folder class:

```
public Message[] search(SearchTerm term) throws SearchException,
  FolderNotFoundException, IllegalStateException, MessagingException
public Message[] search(SearchTerm term, Message[] messages)
  throws SearchException, FolderNotFoundException,
  IllegalStateException, MessagingException
```

A SearchException indicates that the search term is more complicated than the implementation can handle. For example, this search term seeks out all messages from *billg@microsoft.com*:

```
Address billg   = new InternetAddress("billg@microsoft.com");
SearchTerm term = new FromTerm(billg);
```

This search term looks for all messages from *billg@microsoft.com* after 2003:

```
Address billg      = new InternetAddress("billg@microsoft.com");
SearchTerm term1 = new FromTerm(billg);
Date millennium  = Calendar.getInstance().set(2004, 0, 1).getTime( );
SearchTerm term2 = new SentDateTerm(ComparisonTerm.GE, millennium);
SearchTerm term  = new AndTerm(term1, term2);
```

Example 19-13 is a simple variation of the `MailClient` program in Example 19-7. It allows the user to list email addresses on the command line after the initial URL, like this:

```
% java SearchClient imap://elharo@mail.metalab.unc.edu/INBOX
willis@nvx.com billg@microsoft.com
```

Only messages from the specified users will be returned. However, if no email addresses are given, all messages will be returned.

Example 19-13. A mail client that searches by From: address

```java
import javax.mail.*;
import javax.mail.search.*;
import javax.mail.internet.*;
import java.util.*;
import java.io.*;

public class SearchClient {
  public static void main(String[] args) {

    if (args.length == 0) {
      System.err.println(
        "Usage: java SearchClient protocol://username@host/foldername");
      return;
    }

    URLName server = new URLName(args[0]);

    try {

      Session session = Session.getDefaultInstance(new Properties( ),
        new MailAuthenticator(server.getUsername( )));

      // Connect to the server and open the folder
      Folder folder = session.getFolder(server);
      if (folder == null) {
        System.out.println("Folder " + server.getFile( ) + " not found.");
        System.exit(1);
      }
      folder.open(Folder.READ_ONLY);

      SearchTerm term = null;
      if (args.length > 1) {
        SearchTerm[] terms = new SearchTerm[args.length-1];
        for (int i = 1; i < args.length; i++) {
```

Example 19-13. A mail client that searches by From: address (continued)

```
        Address a = new InternetAddress(args[i]);
        terms[i-1] = new FromTerm(new InternetAddress(args[i]));
      }
    if (terms.length > 1) term = new OrTerm(terms);
    else term = terms[0];
  }

  // Get the messages from the server
  Message[] messages;
  if (term == null)  {
    messages = folder.getMessages();
  }
  else {
    messages = folder.search(term);
  }
  for (int i = 0; i < messages.length; i++) {
    System.out.println("------------ Message " + (i+1)
      + " ------------");

    // Print message headers
    Enumeration headers = messages[i].getAllHeaders();
    while (headers.hasMoreElements()) {
      Header h = (Header) headers.nextElement();
      System.out.println(h.getName() + ": " + h.getValue());
    }
    System.out.println();

    // Enumerate parts
    Object body = messages[i].getContent();
    if (body instanceof Multipart) {
      processMultipart((Multipart) body);
    }
    else { // ordinary message
      processPart(messages[i]);
    }

    System.out.println();

  }

  // Close the connection
  // but don't remove the messages from the server
  folder.close(false);

}
catch (Exception ex) {
  ex.printStackTrace();
}

// Since we may have brought up a GUI to authenticate,
// we can't rely on returning from main() to exit
```

Example 19-13. A mail client that searches by From: address (continued)

```
    System.exit(0);

  }

  public static void processMultipart(Multipart mp)
   throws MessagingException {

    for (int i = 0; i < mp.getCount(); i++) {
      processPart(mp.getBodyPart(i));
    }

  }

  public static void processPart(Part p) {

    try {
      // I'd prefer to test the Content-Disposition header here.
      // However, too many common email clients don't use it.
      String fileName = p.getFileName();
      if (fileName == null) { // likely inline
        p.writeTo(System.out);
      }
      else if (fileName != null) {
        File f = new File(fileName);
        // find a version that does not yet exist
        for (int i = 1; f.exists(); i++) {
          String newName = fileName + " " + i;
          f = new File(newName);
        }
        FileOutputStream out = new FileOutputStream(f);

        // We can't just use p.writeTo() here because it doesn't
        // decode the attachment. Instead we copy the input stream
        // onto the output stream which does automatically decode
        // Base-64, quoted printable, and a variety of other formats.
        InputStream in = new BufferedInputStream(p.getInputStream());
        int b;
        while ((b = in.read()) != -1) out.write(b);
        out.flush();
        out.close();
        in.close();
      }
    }
    catch (Exception ex) {
      System.err.println(e);
      ex.printStackTrace();
    }
  }
}
```

Flags

It's sometimes useful to be able to change the flags for an entire group of messages at once. The Folder class has two methods for doing this:

```
public void setFlags(Message[] messages, Flags flag, boolean value)
  throws IllegalStateException, MessagingException
public void setFlags(int start, int end, Flags flag, boolean value)
  throws IllegalStateException, MessagingException
public void setFlags(int[] messageNumbers, Flags flag, boolean value)
  throws IndexOutOfBoundsException, IllegalStateException,
  MessagingException
```

Ultimately, these are just conveniences. There's nothing you can do with these methods that you can't do by setting the flags on each message individually with the setFlags( ) method of the Message class. In fact, the default implementation simply invokes that method on each message in the specified block of messages.

The Folder class also has a getPermanentFlags( ) method to return the flags that this folder will supply for all messages. This includes all the flags except the user-defined flags, which are applied only to particular messages that the user has flagged. For instance, not all folder implementations track whether messages have been answered:

```
public abstract Flags getPermanentFlags( )
```

Event Handling

Many email programs can be configured to periodically check for incoming email in the background. One way to structure an email program is as a series of responses to unpredictable events. This is much like programming for a graphical user interface, and indeed the JavaMail API uses the same basic patterns to handle mail events that the AWT and Swing use to handle GUI events.

The JavaMail API defines six different kinds of mail events, all in the javax.mail. event package. They are all subclasses of MailEvent:

```
public abstract class MailEvent extends EventObject
```

The six concrete kinds of mail events, the first four of which involve folders, are:

ConnectionEvent
    A Folder (or Store or Transport) has been opened, closed, or disconnected.

FolderEvent
    A Folder has been created, deleted, or renamed.

MessageChangedEvent
    The message's envelope or flags have changed.

MessageCountEvent
    A message was added to or deleted from a Folder.

StoreEvent

> A notification or alert from a Store.

TransportEvent

> A notification from a Transport that a message was delivered, partially delivered, or failed to be delivered.

There are six listener interfaces corresponding to the six kinds of events:

```
public interface ConnectionListener     extends EventListener
public interface FolderListener         extends EventListener
public interface MessageChangedListener extends EventListener
public interface MessageCountListener   extends EventListener
public interface StoreListener          extends EventListener
public interface TransportListener      extends EventListener
```

Each of these interfaces declares one or more methods that must be provided by implementing classes. For example, the ConnectionListener class declares these three methods:

```
public void opened(ConnectionEvent e)
public void disconnected(ConnectionEvent e)
public void closed(ConnectionEvent e)
```

The FolderListener interface declares these three methods:

```
public void folderCreated(FolderEvent e)
public void folderDeleted(FolderEvent e)
public void folderRenamed(FolderEvent e)
```

Four of these events can be fired by folders. Consequently, there are 14 addXXXListener( ), removeXXXListener( ), and notifyXXXListener( ) methods in the Folder class:

```
public    void addConnectionListener(ConnectionListener l)
public    void removeConnectionListener(ConnectionListener l)
protected void notifyConnectionListeners(int type)
public    void addFolderListener(FolderListener l)
public    void removeFolderListener(FolderListener l)
protected void notifyFolderListeners(int type)
protected void notifyFolderRenamedListeners(Folder folder)
public    void addMessageCountListener(MessageCountListener l)
public    void removeMessageCountListener(MessageCountListener l)
protected void notifyMessageAddedListeners(Message[] messages)
protected void notifyMessageRemovedListeners(boolean removed,
  Message[] messages)
public    void addMessageChangedListener(MessageChangedListener l)
public    void removeMessageChangedListener(MessageChangedListener l)
protected void notifyMessageChangedListeners(int type, Message message)
```

The addXXXListener( ) methods add an implementation of the particular interface to the list of listeners. The removeXXXListener( ) methods remove an implementation from that list. The notifyXXXListener( ) methods are not used directly; instead, they're used by instances of Folder and its subclasses to notify registered listeners of particular events. All of this works exactly as it does in the AWT and Swing, just with different events.

Utility Methods

Finally, for completeness's sake, I'll note that the Folder class overrides two methods from java.lang.Object, finalize( ) and toString( ):

```
protected void finalize( ) throws Throwable
public String toString( )
```

Neither of these is especially important to the client programmer.

Index

We'd like to hear your suggestions for improving our indexes. Send email to *index@oreilly.com*.

IP addresses (*continued*)
    InetAddress class, and, 152
    IPv4 format, 150
    IPv6 format, 150
    multicast addresses, 473
    non-routable addresses, 32
    testing reachability (Java 1.5), 167
IP datagram headers, 24
IP (Internet Protocol), 27
    broadcasting, 471
    IPv4 vs. IPv6, 28
IPv6 link-local addresses, 163
IPv6 site-local addresses, 164
IRIs (Internationalized Resource
        Identifiers), 208
isAbsolute( ) method (URI class), 217
isAnyLocalAddress( ) method, 163
isBlock( ) method (HTML.Tag class), 253
isBound( ) methods
    ServerSocket class, 336
    Socket class, 296
isClosed( ) method (Socket class), 296
isConnected( ) methods
    DatagramChannel class, 462
    Socket class, 296
    SocketChannel class, 416
isHostName( ) method, HostLookup
        program, 175
isInputShutdown( ) and isOutputShutdown
        methods (Socket class), 297
isLinkLocalAddress( ) method, 163
isLoopbackAddress method, 163
isMCGlobal( ) method, 164
isMCLinkLocal( ) method, 164
isMCNodeLocal( ) method, 165
isMCOrgLocal( ) method, 164
isMCSiteLocal( ) method, 164
isMimeType( ) method (Part interface), 690
isMulticastAddress( ) method, 164
isOpaque( ) method (URI class), 217
isOpen( ) methods
    DatagramChannel class, 469
    Folder class, 699
    SocketChannel class, 417
isPreformatted( ) method (HTML.Tag
        class), 253
ISPs (Internet Service Providers), 20
isSet( ) method (Flags class), 678
isSiteLocalAddress( ) method, 164
isSubscribed( ) method (Folder class), 702

J

J2ME (Java 2 Micro Edition), 15
JAR archives, 549
    manifest files, 550
JarURLConnection class, 549–551
    methods, 550
Java, 1
    case sensitivity, xix
    cookie support, lack of, 230
    data transmission, balancing network and
        CPU speed differential, 384
    network-aware applications, 306
    security, 16–17
    supported operating systems, xvi
    Swing (see Swing)
    Version 1.4, xvi
        Inet4Address and Inet6Address
            classes, 169
        NetworkInterface class (see
            NetworkInterface class)
    Version 1.5, xvi
        CookieHandler class, 272
        testing reachability, 167
    versions, xvi
Java 2 Micro Edition (J2ME), 15
Java extension content-type mappings, 526
Java first bytes content-type mappings, 527
Java Runtime Environment, registration of
        security extensions, 367
Java TV API, 16
JavaBeans Activation Framework, 643
java.io package, 67–104
JavaMail API, 641–711
    addresses, 663–667
        Address class, 663
        InternetAddress class, 663–665
        NewsAddress class, 666
    authentication, 659–661
    code examples
        applet that sends email, 651–653
        graphical SMTP clients, 647–649
        GUI authenticator, 660
        mail client for multipart messages with
            attache files, 693–695
        mail client that searches by From:
            address, 706–708
        POP client that requests password as
            necessary, 662
        program to read mail attributes, 684
        program to read mail
            headers, 674–676, 687

R

race conditions, 113

RandomPort, 337

RC4 and DES/AES-based ciphers, comparison, 373

read( ) methods
  DatagramChannel class, 465
  InputStream class, 72–74
  JEditorPane class, 247
  SocketChannel class, 416

Reader class, 94–95
  methods, 94

readers, 67

readiness selection, 420–422

readLine( ) method (DataInputStream class), 85

rebind( ) methods
  Naming class, 631
  Registry interface, 634

receive( ) methods
  DatagramChannel class, 462
  DatagramSocket class, 440

ReceiverThread class, 460

recipient (To:, Cc:, and Bcc:) header information, 673

records, 585

redirection, 351

Redirector, 351–356
  main( ) method, 354
  multi-threading, 351
  RedirectThread object, 355
  run( ) method, 355

register( ) method (SelectableChannel class), 420

registries, 615

Registry interface, 634

REGISTRY_PORT field (Registry interface), 634

relative URIs, 217

relative URLs, 52

relativize( ) method (URI class), 220

reliable protocol vs. unreliable protocols, 26

remaining( ) method (Buffer classes), 398

Remote interface, 616, 628

remote objects, 611

remote references, 614

RemoteException class, 632–634

RemoteExceptions, 611

RemoteObject class, 636

RemoteServer class, 637

removeBodyPart( ) methods (Multipart class), 696

removeHeader( ) method (Part interface), 687

renameTo( ) method (Folder class), 701

Rendezvous, 473

reply( ) method (Message class), 671

Reply-to: header information, 672

requestPasswordAuthentication( ) method (Authenticator class), 231

reset( ) methods
  Buffer classes, 397, 413
  InputStream class, 75

resolve( ) method (URI class), 220

resolveURI( ) method (URI class), 220

response codes, HTTP 1.1, 536–539

response messages, 536

ResponseCache class, 544

ReturnDigest class, 112

rewind( ) method (Buffer classes), 397

RFCs (Requests for Comments), 38, 41–43
  cookies and RFC 2965, 269

RMI (Remote Method Invocation), 610–640
  classes, loading at runtime, 624–628
  client side, 622
    running the client, 624
  code examples
    applet client for the Fibonacci object, 625
    database interface, 628
    FibonacciApplet.html, 626
    FibonacciClient, 622
    FibonacciImpl class, 618
    FibonacciServer class, 620
    RegistryLister, 629
    weather interface, 611
  description, 610–616
  implementation, 616–624
  java.rmi.package, 628–634
    Naming class, 629–631
    remote exceptions, 632–634
    Remote interface, 628
  java.rmi.registry package, 634
    LocateRegistry class, 634
    Registry interface, 634
  java.rmi.server package, 635–640
    exceptions, 640
  necessary packages, 616
  object serialization, 612–613
    limitations, 613
  registries, 615
  remote exceptions, 633
  RemoteObject class, 636
  RemoteServer class, 637

About the Author

Elliotte Rusty Harold is an internationally respected writer, programmer, and educator, both on the Internet and off. He got his start by writing FAQ lists for the Macintosh newsgroups on Usenet and has since branched out into writing books. He lectures about Java and object-oriented programming at Polytechnic University in Brooklyn. His Cafe au Lait web site at *http://metalab.unc.edu/javafaq/* has become one of the most popular independent Java sites on the Internet.

Elliotte is originally from New Orleans, Louisiana, where he returns periodically in search of a decent bowl of gumbo. However, he currently resides in the Prospect Heights neighborhood of Brooklyn with his wife Beth and cats Charm (named after the quark) and Marjorie (named after his mother-in-law). When not writing books, he enjoys working on genealogy, mathematics, and quantum mechanics. His previous books include *The Java Developer's Resource, Java Secrets, JavaBeans, XML in a Nutshell, XML: Extensible Markup Language, The XML Bible,* and *Java I/O.*

Colophon

Our look is the result of reader comments, our own experimentation, and feedback from distribution channels. Distinctive covers complement our distinctive approach to technical topics, breathing personality and life into potentially dry subjects.

The animal on the cover of *Java Network Programming*, Third Edition, is a North American river otter (*Lutra canadensis*). These small carnivores are found in all major waterways of the United States and Canada, and in almost every habitat except the tundra and the hot, dry regions of the southwestern U.S. They weigh about 20 pounds and are approximately two and a half feet long, and females tend to be about a third smaller than males. Their diet consists mainly of aquatic animals like fish and frogs, but since they spend about two-thirds of their time on land, they also eat the occasional bird or rodent. Two layers of fur—a coarse outer coat and a thick, dense inner coat—protect a river otter from the cold, and, in fact, they seem to enjoy playing in snow and ice. When diving, a river otter's pulse rate slows to only 20 beats per minute from its normal 170, conserving oxygen and allowing the otter to stay underwater longer. These animals are sociable and domesticated easily, and in Europe, a related species was once trained to catch fish for people to eat.

Colleen Gorman was the production editor and copyeditor for *Java Network Programming*, Third Edition. Sada Preisch proofread the book. Sarah Sherman and Claire Cloutier provided quality control. Mary Agner provided production assistance. John Bickelhaupt wrote the index.

Emma Colby designed the cover of this book, based on a series design by Edie Freedman. The cover image is a 19th-century engraving from the Dover Pictorial Archive. Clay Fernald produced the cover layout with QuarkXPress 4.1 using Adobe's ITC Garamond font.

David Futato designed the interior layout. This book was converted by Julie Hawks to FrameMaker 5.5.6 with a format conversion tool created by Erik Ray, Jason McIntosh, Neil Walls, and Mike Sierra that uses Perl and XML technologies. The text font is Linotype Birka; the heading font is Adobe Myriad Condensed; and the code font is LucasFont's TheSans Mono Condensed. The illustrations that appear in the book were produced by Robert Romano and Jessamyn Read using Macromedia FreeHand MX and Adobe Photoshop CS. The tip and warning icons were drawn by Christopher Bing. This colophon was written by Leanne Soylemez.

Better than e-books

Search

inside electronic versions of thousands of books

Browse

books by category. With Safari researching any topic is a snap

Find

answers in an instant

Read books from cover to cover. Or, simply click to the page you need.

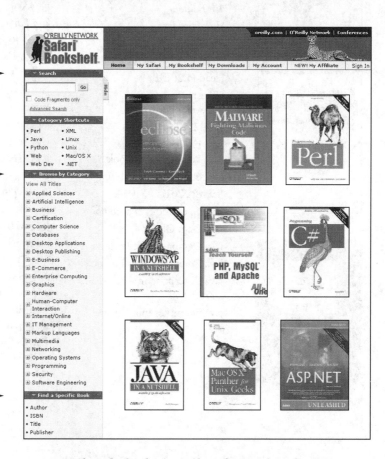

Search Safari! The premier electronic reference library for programmers and IT professionals

Related Titles Available from O'Reilly

Java

Ant: The Definitive Guide

Better, Faster, Lighter Java

Eclipse

Eclipse Cookbook

Enterprise JavaBeans,
4th Edition

Hardcore Java

Head First Java

Head First Servlets & JSP

Head First EJB

Hibernate:
A Developer's Notebook

J2EE Design Patterns

Java 1.5 Tiger:
A Developer's Notebook

Java & XML Data Binding

Java & XML

Java Cookbook, 2nd Edition

Java Data Objects

Java Database Best Practices

Java Enterprise Best Practices

Java Enterprise in a Nutshell,
2nd Edition

Java Examples in a Nutshell,
3rd Edition

Java Extreme Programming
Cookbook

Java in a Nutshell, 4th Edition

Java Management Extensions

Java Message Service

Java Network Programming,
2nd Edition

Java NIO

Java Performance Tuning,
2nd Edition

Java RMI

Java Security, 2nd Edition

JavaServer Faces

Java ServerPages, 2nd Edition

Java Servlet & JSP Cookbook

Java Servlet Programming,
2nd Edition

Java Swing, 2nd Edition

Java Web Services in a Nutshell

Learning Java, 2nd Edition

Mac OS X for Java Geeks

Programming Jakarta Struts
2nd Edition

Tomcat: The Definitive Guide

WebLogic:
The Definitive Guide

O'REILLY®

Our books are available at most retail and online bookstores.
To order direct: 1-800-998-9938 • order@oreilly.com • www.oreilly.com
Online editions of most O'Reilly titles are available by subscription at safari.oreilly.com

Keep in touch with O'Reilly

1. Download examples from our books

To find example files for a book, go to:

www.oreilly.com/catalog

select the book, and follow the "Examples" link.

2. Register your O'Reilly books

Register your book at *register.oreilly.com*

Why register your books?
Once you've registered your O'Reilly books you can:

- Win O'Reilly books, T-shirts or discount coupons in our monthly drawing.
- Get special offers available only to registered O'Reilly customers.
- Get catalogs announcing new books (US and UK only).
- Get email notification of new editions of the O'Reilly books you own.

3. Join our email lists

Sign up to get topic-specific email announcements of new books and conferences, special offers, and O'Reilly Network technology newsletters at:

elists.oreilly.com

It's easy to customize your free elists subscription so you'll get exactly the O'Reilly news you want.

4. Get the latest news, tips, and tools

www.oreilly.com

- "Top 100 Sites on the Web"—PC Magazine
- CIO Magazine's Web Business 50 Awards

Our web site contains a library of comprehensive product information (including book excerpts and tables of contents), downloadable software, background articles, interviews with technology leaders, links to relevant sites, book cover art, and more.

5. Work for O'Reilly

Check out our web site for current employment opportunities:

jobs.oreilly.com

6. Contact us

O'Reilly & Associates
1005 Gravenstein Hwy North
Sebastopol, CA 95472 USA

TEL: 707-827-7000 or 800-998-9938
(6am to 5pm PST)

FAX: 707-829-0104

order@oreilly.com
For answers to problems regarding your order or our products. To place a book order online, visit:

www.oreilly.com/order_new

catalog@oreilly.com
To request a copy of our latest catalog.

booktech@oreilly.com
For book content technical questions or corrections.

corporate@oreilly.com
For educational, library, government, and corporate sales.

proposals@oreilly.com
To submit new book proposals to our editors and product managers.

international@oreilly.com
For information about our international distributors or translation queries. For a list of our distributors outside of North America check out:

international.oreilly.com/distributors.html

adoption@oreilly.com
For information about academic use of O'Reilly books, visit:

academic.oreilly.com

O'REILLY®

Our books are available at most retail and online bookstores.
To order direct: 1-800-998-9938 • order@oreilly.com • www.oreilly.com
Online editions of most O'Reilly titles are available by subscription at *safari.oreilly.com*